To Daniel
September, 1997

Happy Birthday
from Mum & Dad.

PETER COOK

Also by Harry Thompson

Tintin – Hergé and His Creation
Richard Ingrams – Lord of the Gnomes
The Man In The Iron Mask

PETER COOK

A Biography

Harry Thompson

Hodder & Stoughton

To John Wallis
1970–1996

Copyright © 1997 by Harry Thompson

First published in 1997
by Hodder and Stoughton
A division of Hodder Headline PLC

The right of Harry Thompson to be identified as the Author
of the Work has been asserted by him in accordance with
the Copyright, Designs and Patents Act 1988.

10 9 8 7 6 5 4 3 2 1

British Library Cataloguing in Publication Data

A CIP catalogue record for this title
is available from the British Library

ISBN: 0 340 64968 2

Typeset by Hewer Text Composition Services, Edinburgh
Printed and bound in Great Britain by
Mackays of Chatham PLC

Hodder and Stoughton Ltd
A division of Hodder Headline PLC
338 Euston Road
London NW1 3BH

Contents

List of Illustrations   vii
Acknowledgements   ix
Introduction   xi

1 Raised by Goats: Early Life, 1937–51   1
2 I'm Much Bigger Than You Are, Sir:
   Radley and Abroad, 1951–57   16
3 I Could Have Been a Judge,
   But I Never Had the Latin: Cambridge, 1957–60   45
4 So That's the Way You Like It: Beyond the Fringe, 1960–62   89
5 Sorry, Sir, There Is a £5 Waiting List:
   The Establishment Club, 1961–62   120
6 Heaving Thighs Across Manhattan: America, 1962–64   140
7 The Seductive Brethren: *Private Eye*, 1964–70   161
8 We're Always Ready to be Jolted Out of Our Seats,
   Here at the BBC: Pete and Dud, 1964–67   175
9 Nice Though This Be I Seek Yet Further Kicks:
   Family Life, 1964–71   224
10 Learning to Fly Underwater: Pete and Dud, 1968–71   248
11 3-D Lobster: The Humour of Peter Cook   287
12 I Can't Talk Now, 'Cos He's Here:
   Behind the Fridge, 1971–75   306
13 I Don't Want to See Plays About Rape,
   Sodomy and Drug Addiction – I Can Get All That at Home:
   Derek and Clive, 1973–79   335

14 You Are to Be a Stud, Dud:
    Dudley's Hollywood Success, 1979–83   368
15 Whereupon I Immediately Did Nothing:
    The Single Life, 1983–89   394
16 Now That the World Is In My Grasp, It Seems a
    Fitting Time to Go: The Final Years, 1989–95   441
17 Zsa Zsa Man Dies: Death and Aftermath, 1995–97   466

    Notes   483
    Index   499

List of Illustrations

Section I

Peter's parents, Alec and Margaret Cook
Alec Cook in the Nigerian bush
Peter and his sister Sarah in Gibraltar
Peter at St Bede's preparatory school
As Doll Common in *The Alchemist*, March 1954
Peter with his sister Elizabeth in Lyme Regis, summer 1957
As Launcelot Gobbo in *The Merchant of Venice*, June 1958
As Dapper in *The Alchemist*, November 1958
Programme for the Radley College *Black and White Blues*,
    March 1956
Peter's 21st birthday invitation, November 1958
Jonathan Miller, Alan Bennett, Dudley Moore and Peter in
    Beyond the Fringe
With Elizabeth Taylor in America
Wendy, Peter's first wife
Publicity pose for *Not Only . . . But Also*
Pete and Dud
Peter Sellers in *Not Only . . . But Also*, March 1965
Peter and Dudley as the Finsbury Brothers in *The Wrong Box*,
    September 1965
Peter and John Lennon in the *Not Only . . . But Also*
    Christmas Special, 1966
Peter and Dudley as Jeff and Johnny Jupiter in *Not Only . . . But Also*
E. L. Wisty and M'Lud

Section II

As the Mad Hatter in *Alice in Wonderland*, 1966
With Richard Ingrams at Durham University on a *Private Eye* promotional tour, October 1966
Judy Scott-Fox, Wendy, Peter, Daisy and Lucy Cook, circa 1967
Peter as the Devil in *Bedazzled*, 1967
With Dudley as leaping nuns *of the Order of St Beryl* in *Bedazzled*
Peter and Dudley in *The Bedsitting Room*, June 1968
As Greta Garbo in *Not Only . . . But Also*, February 1970
Peter with Judy Huxtable, January 1971
As Elvis Presley on *Where Do I Sit?*, February 1971
Peter and with Judy Huxtable, 1970
A promotional shot for *Behind the Fridge*
Peter, Dudley and Spike Milligan in Australia with *Behind the Fringe*, November 1972
Peter, Lucy and Daisy in New York, summer 1974
Publicity pose for *Revolver*, March 1978
Derek and Clive
Peter, June 1979
With one of Judy's lambs at Mitchell Leys Farm, 1981
With Mimi Kennedy in publicity pose for *The Two of Us*, April 1981
Rainbow George
Peter and Ian Hislop, outside the offices of *Private Eye*
With Lin Chong Cook, his third wife
Peter with daughters Lucy and Daisy at Daisy's wedding
Playing Perudo with Sting, November 1994

Acknowledgements

My profoundest thanks and admiration go to Peter's sister, Sarah Seymour, without whose insight, hard work and kindness this book would have been a waste of time even to attempt. Heartfelt thanks, too, to Peter's first two wives Wendy and Judy Cook, for the time and trouble they took; to Peter's daughters Lucy and Daisy, and Daisy's husband Simon Hardy, for the immense help they gave me; to Peter's third wife, Lin; and also to Peter's sister Elizabeth for her assistance, and to Dudley Moore for kindly racking his brains at such length.

For their colossal exertions in the researching of this book, my heartfelt thanks go to those stalwarts of the Peter Cook Appreciation Society, the late John Wallis (aka Reg Futtock-Armitage) and Paul Hamilton. Many thanks also to my wife Fiona Duff and my father Gordon Thompson, who helped me at great length despite having no choice in the matter; and to Tim Harrold, for his patient and thoughtful work. Thanks too to Neil Trevithick, Louis Heaton, Caroline Wright, Sam Peters, Liz McGrath, Danny Dignan, Peter Rea, David Taylor, Warren Prentice, Alex McLeod, Anna Ransom, Mathew Mellor, Hilary Lowinger, Michael Barfield and Jim Anderson. Peter Cook's comments in this book are taken from interviews with the author carried out between 1990 and 1993, unless otherwise stated. Thanks especially to the following authors, whose interviews with Peter and others I have quoted from: Ronald Bergan (*Beyond the Fringe . . . And Beyond* Virgin Books); John Hind (*Comic Inquisition* Virgin Books); Roger Wilmut (*From Fringe to Flying Circus* Eyre Methuen); Barbra Paskin (*Dudley Moore* Sidgwick and Jackson).

To all those who kindly sat down and contributed their memories of

Peter, or helped in some other way, yet more profound thanks: Douglas Adams; Nigel Agar; Geoffrey Allibone; Clive Anderson; James Ashby; Lientenant Colonel J. A. Aylen; David Baddiel; Humphrey Barclay; Michael Bawtree; Alan Bennett; John Bird; Christopher Booker; Deborah Bosley; Richard Brooks; Gaye Brown; Clive Bull; John Butcher; Paul Butters; David Cash; George Clare; Michael Codron; Tim Coghlan; Jeremy Cotton; Richard Cottrell; John Crabbe; Jeremy Crampton; Stephen Dixon; Willie Donaldson; Stanley Donen; John Dwyer; Christopher Ellis; Harry Enfield; Barry Fantoni; Christopher Fenwick; Peter Fincham; Paul Foot; John Fortune; The Rev. Canon Maurice Friggens; David Frost; Jeffrey Frost; Stephen Fry; Harriet Garland; Anthony Garrett; James Gilbert; Kevin Godley; Sidney Gottlieb; Major General Robin Grist, CB, OBE, DL; Robin Gunn; Anthony Hole; Dr Chris Hall; Alexander Hamilton; Claude Harz; Terry Hathaway; David Hill; Ian Hislop; Barry Humphries; Professor John Hunter; Professor Martin Hunter; Eric Idle; Richard Ingrams; Halfdan Johnson; Neil Johnstone; Griff Rhys Jones; Jay and Fran Landesman; Roger Law; Christopher Leigh; John Lloyd; The Rt. Hon. Sir Peter Lloyd, MP; Roddy Loder-Symonds; James Macdonald; Hugh Macdonald; A. J. Macfarlane; Derek Maltwood; Professor John Mattock; Rory McGrath; Joe McGrath; John McLauchlan; Jonathan Miller; Tom Morkill; Ian Napier; Trevor Nunn; Andrew Osmond; Michael Palmer; Ciara Parkes; Sue Parkin; Michael Parkinson; Anthony Penfold; Peter Raby; Nicholas Rau; Ian Robertson; Tom Rosenthal; Jonathan Ross; Keith Ross; the late Willie Rushton; Nick Salaman; Justin Sbresni; Neil Shand; Robert Carter Shaw; Paul Sharpling; Ned Sherrin; Clive Simeon; Noel Slocock; Mel Smith; Dr Chris Smith; Anthony Macdonald Smith; Michael Stubbs; Martin Tomkinson; Tony Verity; Robin Voelcker; Michael Waite; Bill Wallis; Peter Way; George Weiss; John Wells; Neville Wells; Michael Wild; Michael Winterton.

Introduction

Peter wanted to call his autobiography *3-D Lobster*. The cover design was to feature himself, attired in cloth cap and mac, in bed with Jayne Mansfield and brandishing a huge embossed lobster. Inevitably, he never got round to writing it. He had other titles – *Retired and Emotional*, *Who Are These People?*, *Can I Go Now?* and *I've Forgotten* among them – but *3-D Lobster* was the best, speaking as it did of one of his comic enthusiasms, rather than of weariness or resignation.

I first encountered Peter Cook in 1982, when I was working as a trainee on the BBC's *Children in Need* programme. A few years before, some halfwit at the corporation had authorised the destruction of all the *Not Only . . . But Also* programmes kept on videotape, on the grounds that the tapes themselves represented a reusable resource. Unlike the myriad local news reports from Halifax and Weston-super-Mare, catalogued and stored with the religious fervour that only the great God of News can inspire in the imagination-free TV executive, these marvellous comedy programmes were regarded as trivial by definition, mere ephemera to be discarded without compunction. Besides, union agreements forbade the repeat of programmes more than two years old, so as far as the Corporation was concerned the material was all but useless. Mrs Thatcher, at that time, was no more than a gleam in the Conservative Party's eye.

Peter had pleaded with the BBC, offering to replace each tape with a brand new one, and to pay for the future storage costs of the condemned programmes. Impossible, replied the apparatchiks: generous though his offer was, the system was simply not flexible enough to accommodate it. Failing that, he argued, could he not at least retain a cassette copy of each show, so that the programmes would not be lost to posterity? Out of the question, came the reply. The material was BBC copyright. It could not possibly be allowed off the premises, and that went for the limited amount of filmed material that survived as well. Peter's pleas were in vain, and the tapes were wiped. One shudders to think what was recorded over them.

Not Only . . . But Also had been my favourite TV programme as a child. As part of my *Children in Need* duties, I volunteered for the task of choosing ten 'Classic Comedy Clips', mainly so that I could gain access to the film library, surreptitiously record the surviving material on to VHS and restore it to its authors. It was nerve-janglingly exciting to dust off the bulky 35 mm film cans, prise them open and thread their contents on to the antiquated viewing machine: in some cases, I was the first person to see these programmes for seventeen years. I even managed to damage one film, which snapped in two (it still bears a clumsy repair) when I laced it up wrongly. I didn't dare call expert help, as I didn't really have a convincing explanation for what I was up to. Eventually, the deed was done and two copies were dispatched to *Private Eye*, one for Peter and one for Dudley Moore. Of course, I kept a copy for myself. Dudley, I discovered during the research for this book, never got his cassette. Relations between Peter and Dudley were not at their best in 1982.

I was lucky enough to work with Peter many times in subsequent years, on the Radio 4 *News Quiz*, on *Have I Got News For You* and *The Bore of the Year Awards* for BBC Television. He even suggested, jokingly, that I should write his biography. He knew, by then, that *3-D Lobster* would never see the light of day. I last saw him in the summer of 1994, when we and a few others sat round watching the World Cup Final on television. I thought by then that I had got to know him a little. I now realise that I barely knew him at all.

CHAPTER 1

Raised by Goats
Early Life, 1937–51

There are those who say – and Peter Cook himself was among them – that most of his humour was autobiographical. Others – and Peter Cook himself was among them – contend that this simply isn't the case. The truth, of course, lies somewhere in the middle. Peter's humour was indeed littered with incidents from his own life, but he tended to parody his background, or veer off surreally at a tangent from it, rather than straightforwardly disguise it with a veneer of jokes. Too much significance should not therefore be read into what can nevertheless be an absorbing game, that of tracing back threads of reality through his labyrinthine mental processes. 'Raised by goats . . . nanny-goats . . . raised by nannies. Bingo! I only just got that one the other day,' says Peter's sister Sarah.

Peter Edward Cook was indeed raised by nannies, or by a combination of nannies and grannies at any rate; not as traumatic a father substitute as Sir Arthur Streeb-Greebling's flock of goats, but a father substitute for all that. For successive generations the Cook family put service to the Empire above mere family considerations, representing their monarch dutifully in a variety of distant locations, while the sons they produced were sent home to boarding schools to begin the process anew. Theirs was a line of gentle, witty, dutiful and impeccably-mannered men, with melancholy souls that undoubtedly owed much to their lonely, separated childhoods.

Peter's grandfather, Edward Cook, was Traffic Manager for the Federated Malay States Railway in Kuala Lumpur. It was there, one evening in May, 1914, that he went out into the garden and blew his brains out with a revolver, in a fit of depression brought on by nervousness at a forthcoming promotion to acting General Manager. Tributes in the *Malay Mail* spoke of an immensely popular character, able, energetic, kindly and thoughtful, but whose cheerful and amusing exterior skilfully concealed an easily depressed temperament. It is a description that will be familiar to anyone who knew the young Peter Cook. Like Peter, his grandfather had been known as 'Cookie' to his friends, one of whom wrote: 'His last words were "Don't think unkindly of me, I must have rest." God send you have found it, Cookie'.[1]

His widow Minnie kept the suicide a secret throughout her life; indeed it was not until Peter traced his family history through *Debrett's* that the details came to light. He found it a disturbing revelation, as much for the discovery of his grandmother's lifelong burden as for the unfortunate facts themselves. Often, his own father Alec had sat there examining Edward Cook's photograph for the hundredth time and wishing aloud that he had known him. Alec had been eight at the time and several thousand miles away, enduring the rigours of life at the Imperial Service College, Windsor.

The school was a direct descendant of the United Services College, which had spawned Rudyard Kipling and formed the basis for his brutal 'Stalky & Co.' stories. It was an institution so cold in winter that boys would sneak off to the boiler room and hang like bats from the hot water pipes. Eventually Alec Cook triumphed through the mud and ice, made a place in the First XI, became Captain of School and won a scholarship to Pembroke College, Cambridge in 1924. Money was tight: he and his best friend Bob Church were so poor that they shared the same pair of white gloves, one each in the top pocket, for functions. But the fatherless boy showed ability and determination, and in 1928 won a place as a Cadet in the Colonial Office. He was posted to the Calabar Province of Nigeria, and set sail from Liverpool at once.

The life of an Assistant District Officer, which Alec became when he had completed his training, was a solitary one. It involved acting as a kind of touring King Solomon, with a detachment of native police in tow, arbitrating on everything from land disputes to problems of male impotence. Contact with other Englishmen, which occurred just once a month, ought to have been an occasion for wild celebration, but being Englishmen a quiet pipe and a scratchy gramophone record were generally the order of the day. 'My father used to receive news by boat, six months after it was published,' Peter recalled. 'He'd open *The Times* and say, "Good God, Worcester are 78 for 6."

'He did something extraordinary actually. He was very young, had no knowledge of any of the three main languages spoken, yet was suddenly in charge of a hundred square miles of territory. This was his life – at least as I understood it from reading his diaries. He travelled around from village to village with trunks, and was entirely reliant on a local interpreter, and the trick of it was to hope you'd chosen an honest interpreter because otherwise it was all nonsense. They were tremendously alarming circumstances to live in – to have to reach moral or judicial decisions over a society about which, at least when you arrived, you knew absolutely nothing.'[2]

Perhaps surprisingly, it was a system that worked. The unscrupulous early colonial adventurers had been replaced, by the 1930s, with a cadre of earnest, dedicated, honest young men. According to Peter's youngest sister Elizabeth, 'My father was a product of the age. It would never have occurred to him not to give his life to the Empire in a philanthropic way. But at the same time he was a witty man, and there'd be a quiet little smile about it all, without questioning the overall principle of the thing.' A dry, slightly subversive humour lay behind Alec Cook's scrupulously polite exterior, a characteristic that was to be magnified several times over in his son.

By 1936 Alec had grown into an attractive and charming man, tall and slim, gangly but graceful, with prematurely grey hair and the Cook family's prominent asymmetrical ears. A smoker, he was much given to worrying over problems, and had a taste for P. G. Wodehouse and Stravinsky. Colonial officers were given four months' leave after every eighteen months of continuous duty, so every couple of years he would sail home. On one such break, while staying with Bob Church's family in Eastbourne, he met, fell in love with and utterly charmed Margaret Mayo, the daughter of a local solicitor.

Charles Mayo, her father, cut something of a dash in South Coast society, roaring up at court cases by motorbike, a pipe jutting between his clenched teeth. Something of a ladies' man, he had been rusticated from St John's College, Oxford for antics that he would never divulge. He had served unscathed and with distinction in the Great War as an officer with the Royal Sussex Regiment, and had actually contributed a humorous article or two to *Punch* magazine from the trenches. After the war he represented Sussex at rugby, hockey and badminton, before settling down to provincial respectability as President of the Eastbourne West Country Association, Chairman of the Willingdon Golf Club and a freemason so loyal that his family were forced to eat meat from the worst butcher in town. He practised as a solicitor in a firm he helped found, called Mayo and Perkins ('I want you to lay down your life, Perkins. We need a futile gesture at this stage. It will raise the whole tone of the war' – one of the more memorable passages from *Beyond the Fringe*).

Charles Mayo loved humorous writing of all sorts, and his study was lined with leather-bound copies of *Punch*. His daughters Joan and Margaret (Madge for short) grew up into tremendous gigglers, both of them notably pretty and rather popular with the chaps down at the tennis club. Margaret was academically brilliant – she had cut quite a swathe through St Winifred's School for Girls – and it was a source of eternal regret to her that at the time, her family had not yet amassed enough money to send her to university. For the rest of her life she was assiduously self-taught, immersing herself in everything from the violin to the works of Edward Gibbon. She had left England, instead of pursuing further education, and had become governess to a wealthy Jewish family in Prague. When events in Europe began to deteriorate, she returned home, to divide her time between the trim lawns of the Golf Club and bravely squeamish volunteer work as a Red Cross nurse at the Sailors' and Soldiers' Home in Upperton Road.

Alec Cook's clever mind and exotic lifestyle appealed to Margaret's intellectually frustrated side. They suited each other well. They were both warm, kind, conservative, respectable people with a shared sense of humour. Their differences – she was deeply religious, he less so, she was rather untidy, he precise and meticulous – were of a sort that they would successfully work to overcome. They married on 20 June 1936 at St Mary's, Eastbourne, in a flurry of feather boas and big hats. Colonel and Mrs Church contributed a set of trays, Captain and Mrs Carpendale gave a flower vase, Colonel and Mrs Garwood donated a mirror, while Sir Alexander and Lady Maguire chipped in with some dessert knives and forks. The contribution of Perkins, who also attended, was not recorded. Margaret and Alec bundled the whole lot up into their luggage, and set sail for Nigeria on 1 July.

Margaret was not to spend long in the Nigerian bush. Within a few months of her arrival she fell pregnant, and returned at once to England. It was deemed officially that West Africa was no place to bring up a European child, and so began a long and complicated pattern of separations that were to bedevil Cook family life for the next twenty years. While Alec sadly presided over his miniature kingdom alone, Margaret made the journey not to Eastbourne, where her friends were, but to a new life in Torquay. Her parents had separated while she was in Africa, and by an amazing coincidence her mother's family home in Devon, long since sold, had recently come back on the market. Caroline Mayo had snapped it up using money from an inheritance, and set about sprucing it into a suitable home for her daughter and her imminent grandson.

'Bythorn', standing in Bronshill Road, Torquay, was a large, boxy, substantial and slightly gloomy house, too big to be ordinary, too hemmed-in to be grand, at the end of a dark, mysterious driveway. There were mullioned windows, a verandah, a monkey-puzzle tree in the garden: altogether, a place with recesses and hidden depths for an infant to explore, but a slightly intimidating house perhaps, not the kind you could imagine ringing with the sound of childish laughter. Its new occupant, Peter Edward Cook, was actually born at St Chad's nursing home, on 17 November 1937. He was a striking baby, possessed of memorable, startling, dark eyes, that gazed out and transfixed you from under beautiful thick lashes which would one day send his sisters into agonies of jealousy. Peter had inherited a perfect combination of his father's elegant bone structure and his mother's soft, feminine face, tempered slightly by Alec's somewhat inelegant 1930s ears.

Madge wrote to her husband, who had been promoted to District Officer in her absence: 'Darling, once more I salute you as DO. Even more however I salute you as the father of the most beautiful baby that ever happened. I have entered the ranks of doting mothers, and really speaking without fear or favour, he is rather a nice one. I do so wish you were here to see him. He was an enormous creature – 8¾ lbs, so gave me some unpleasant moments, but one soon forgets all the horrors. He has quantities of mouse coloured hair, lovely deep blue eyes set quite far apart, quite long eyelashes, and the beginnings of eyebrows which he lifts rather cynically at the world. He is long in the body and has lovely dimples on his knees. Aphra said he had a very brainy forehead . . . Take great care of yourself darling and come back soon, love from Margaret. P. S. I cried when I read your letter that came with the flowers, but they were tears of happiness such as you read about in books. Thank you again so much, sweetheart.' With her letter, Madge dispatched a selection of rich Christmas puddings to keep Alec fortified on hot, lonely nights in the bush. Madge's mum wrote to him as well, congratulating him on his beautiful son and sending him a useful selection of Christmas puddings.

Alec was due home on leave in February 1938. Early in January, Margaret wrote to keep him informed of their son's precocious developments. 'Darling, I can think of very little else except your arrival. A refrain jigs in my head to the tune of 'The Campbells are coming' – 'Alec is coming, hurray, hurray.' Our son is still practically perfect. His only fault is that he makes a most fearful din between his 6 p.m. and 10 p.m. feed. He appears to have lungs of brass. I let Nannie go out on Sunday night and he really excelled himself. I was very relieved to see her back again. He grows more and more intelligent. I hope he isn't too forward because he really is rather remarkably so. He now goes out for a walk in his pram every afternoon. Nannie thought the wind rather cold so we dressed him up in a blue bonnet with bows under the chin. He looked very comical and was simply furious!'

At the age of three months, Peter was finally introduced to Alec, who recorded the event in Margaret's baby book: 'First viewed by father. Showed slight apprehension, but soon became gracious and accepted strange phenomenon. Some resemblance to said father now noticeable in shape of head and ears.' Alec's leave was an idyllic four months, but as it drew to a close Margaret had to face the moment she had been secretly dreading since her pregnancy had first been diagnosed. It was time for her, as the dutiful wife of a District Officer, to accompany her husband back to Nigeria to resume his duties, and to leave her baby behind in England. Before the summer had even started, they were gone.

Truth be told, Margaret detested Nigeria, not that Nigeria ever had a chance – for it was Nigeria and the Colonial Service that were responsible for this most agonising of partings. Peter's sister Elizabeth Cook remembers that her mother 'really hated the place – the fact that it separated her from Peter and later on from Sarah was really heartbreaking for her.' There is no doubt that her utter devotion to her son was fortified and intensified by the distance involved, and that despite the baffling and dislocated nature of Peter's early childhood, he returned her affection with fierce intensity as he grew up. She later confessed to her son the lifelong feelings of guilt she had endured as a result of leaving him behind.

Granny Mayo, a quiet, gentle, frail, elegant and occasionally anxious woman with rheumatism, lavished maternal dedication on baby Peter in her daughter's stead, but not having any acquaintances with similar-sized offspring in the area, she found the business of importing friends for him to play with elaborate and difficult. Peter's first birthday party was almost entirely attended by adults: Granny Mayo wrote to Margaret in Nigeria to tell her that Aunt Joan had given him a tambourine and a toy truck, Dorothy and her husband had provided a teddy bear, Mrs Reade had donated some handkerchiefs and Miss Perrett had chipped in with a doll. 'I asked Miss Perrett to bring Mrs Denham's boy but they were engaged,' she offered. A distant relative eventually managed to rustle up a little girl called Mary, and the two children sat there surrounded by a ring of grown-ups. The upside of this lifestyle was a pleasing degree of precocity. 'The baby has gone', wrote Granny Cook to her daughter-in-law. 'In his place an alert, interested small boy. So like his father at this age.' Then, remembering her own separations from the young Alec, she added wistfully, 'The years roll back as I look at his dear little face, and I am a mother again, with a small son to whom I was the world.'

Alec and Margaret's next home leave came round in the summer of 1939. It took Peter a week to accept his mother, a lot longer before he would go near his father. Alec was a keen cine enthusiast, and exorcised the frustrated artist within himself by making his son the star of a series of elegant little films. He would cut dramatically from the ironwork of Peter's stout Victorian pram to the enormous treetrunk legs of the nanny coming down the gloomy stairs. A finger moved the hands of the clock while the levels fell in Peter's milk bottles. The child's tiny hands strayed ineptly across the keys of a Bechstein grand piano.

Viewed sixty years later, the small boy toddling through the grainy celluloid is instantly recognisable: the familiar sweep of floppy hair across the forehead, the elegant features beginning to emerge from the podgy face. He is prodigiously well-wrapped, in one shot trussed and buttoned up in a woollen coat of the Hardy Amies variety favoured by the Queen, elsewhere in a little double-breasted jacket, jodhpurs and a pixie hat, like a Teutonic garden gnome. In fact Peter spends much of the film tottering after the gardener, a tall rigid figure dressed gravely in cloth cap, waistcoat and ankle-length black apron, a spade ever-present by his side. Peter apes his movements using a miniature trowel.

The gardener was Peter's principal friend, not least because of all the other interesting friends that were literally turned up by his work – worms, snails, beetles, ants, newts, lizards and the like. Peter was utterly fascinated by creepy-crawlies of every description. Most fascinating of all were bees, although this was something of a love-hate relationship. He knew that these were little creatures to be feared – 'does not like bees' recorded his father in the baby book – but at the same time their little stripy bodies mesmerised him. As time went on the tiny living creatures of the garden came to supplant the teddy bears and toy trucks and handkerchiefs he had been given to play with.

Alec and Margaret's return to Nigeria was overshadowed by the prospect of war, and the knowledge that even the limited access to their son they had so far enjoyed was about to be curtailed. When hostilities broke out, Alec was ordered to arrest any Germans he found in the neighbourhood. Margaret was appointed as a cypher clerk in a government office in Lagos, on ten shillings a month: the contract pointed out sternly that 'Your appointment does not render you eligible for leave.' Peter would not see his mother for several years.

Once the front railings of 'Bythorn' had been taken away to be melted down and made into Spitfires, the war in Torquay was largely uneventful. Only two bombs fell in the area. One would have killed a child, had its mother not had the foresight to borrow Peter's old pram – the pram met

its end, but its St Pancras-strength ironwork protected its occupant. The
other, a doodlebug, landed on a house down the road and blew the householder, a Mrs Jean Gatty, unharmed into the middle of the street, together
with the bath she was in at the time. The incident turned up, somewhat
adulterated, in a later *Not Only . . . But Also* sketch, when Sir Arthur
Streeve-Greevling (as he was then) was asked how he met his wife:

> I found her during the war. She blew into the sitting room with
> a bit of shrapnel and became embedded in the sofa. One thing
> led to her mother, and we were married within the hour.

For the young Peter, however, the war's most dramatic incident came
when he went to sleep with a jar of tadpoles by his bedside, upset it by
accident during the night, and woke the next morning to find ten dead
ones lying like dried currants on his pillow.

As it turned out, Alec managed one solo trip back to England early on
in the war, and took his son for a fortnight's farm holiday at Chagford,
where he noticed that Peter had become 'very observant, and fond of
making running commentaries when out for a walk'. Alec and Margaret
were also jointly allowed a brief trip home in 1943. But for the most
part, entertainment was in the hands of Aunt Joan, when she wasn't
driving ambulances, her husband Roy, who taught Peter to ride a bike,
and Granny Mayo. She tried taking him to a panto, without much success
– 'I had to be bound and gagged – it was almost as bad as English
folk-dancing, and that was the worst'[3] said Peter many years later. The
housekeeper, Mrs Brimacombe, fared better with a trip to Plainmoor
to see Torquay United play in 1944. 'I became a complete fanatic,'
remembered Peter. 'I used to queue up an hour-and-a-half beforehand
to get in the front row by the halfway line. By the time the players came
out, I had to rush off to the gents, so I always came back to find I'd lost
my place.'[4]

Most of the real entertaining, however, was done by Peter himself.
Like her daughter, Granny Mayo was a great giggler, and her grandson
realised very early on that he possessed the capacity to make her laugh.
This cheered them both up immensely in the absence of his mother and
father, and he found it easy to keep her entertained with a string of silly
voices and jokes. When Granny Cook came to tea, for instance, he would
balance an ink bottle on top of the door, which the grown-ups had to affect
not to notice, to keep the possibility of a spillage alive. He was an avid
reader, and loved A. A. Milne, *Alice in Wonderland* (chunks of which later
turned up wholesale in *Not Only . . . But Also*) and *Babar the Elephant*. His

Babar book, which he was given in 1941, featured a vivid and memorable passage in which Babar falls asleep on a long, dark evening and has a nightmare. 'Tap! Tap! Tap!' goes a hideous old woman at the window, who is surrounded by a crowd of ugly creatures – another passage that found its way into a familiar Pete and Dud sketch.

At the tail end of 1944 Peter was joined by his mother at last. She had become pregnant with her second child, Sarah, who was born in January 1945, and had 'hastened home through U-boat infested seas to prevent her child being an African' (this at least was how Peter recounted the story, while transferring it to himself, in the promotional material for *Beyond the Fringe*). It was now Alec's turn to suffer the misery of separation, and the joys of having to entertain himself. He made a short film – a dramatisation of the song *Frankie and Johnnie* – and also set about writing a book, which was never finished or published, about the District Officer's lot.

'A European can feel pretty lonely in Nigeria', he wrote, 'lonely for his own civilisation, for art, music and the theatre, for gaiety and good talk, for the sight of a beautiful woman conscious of the perfection of her gown, for femininity, mildness and the gentle way of life. For weeks on end the D.O. may not see another European, unless he is fortunate enough to be accompanied by his wife. [This is] the main drawback of life in Nigeria, the tragic division of a wife's time, the portioning of her life between her husband and her children. I do not underestimate the climate and the bugs that breed in it, but the average bout of malaria is no worse than a bad cold or a slight touch of 'flu in England. It is the mind and not the body that is most severely tried [here].'

By this time Alec Cook was in sole charge of a thousand square miles of territory containing almost half a million members of the Ibo tribe, and was about to be promoted further, to Assistant Secretary. One of his principal tasks was to help set up the Native Authority, a forerunner of the Independent post-colonial government. He and his colleagues were in effect being asked to prepare the Colonial Service for dissolution, and to sign the death warrant for their own species. It was not a task that disturbed him unduly – he believed that the British legacy would be a sound one. The democratic councils and law courts going up across the country 'would symbolise a declaration of relentless warfare against fear and darkness, against trickery and juju and the evil and revolting practices connected therewith.' Nigeria, he pointed out, was administered 'not by Huns but by Britons'.

He remained apprehensive, however, that independence would almost certainly arrive prematurely, before a sufficient level of moral integrity had ingrained itself in Nigerian society. He wrote of his fellow District Officers that 'honesty comes naturally to them, they have imbibed it with their mothers' milk . . . to such men the graft and corruption indigenous to West Africa causes great mental distress.' He would, nonetheless, when the time came, don for the last time 'his white uniform with the tight collar, gird his ceremonial sword about him, pull on his black shiny boots with the assistance of the domestic staff, and gingerly descend the iron steps to deliver a suitable address on the privileges and duties of being British.' The hint of amused irony behind the genuine conviction that he was doing something worthwhile is unmistakable.

At the end of the war, Alec Cook returned to England, to be reintroduced to his son for the first time in Peter's living memory. Peter recalled the moment: 'I suppose I first realised who my father was when I was seven, when he came back with some very black bananas from Nigeria. And I thanked him for those. But I didn't quite know who he was and I was told he was my father. So we shook hands and agreed on it. He was a total stranger to me.'[5] Throughout the remainder of their lives Peter utterly adored his parents, and they too ached with affection for their son; but the physical distance between them was matched by a slight distance in emotional understanding, a gap that was bridged by great love but not always by true intimacy. 'I never really knew my father,'[6] Peter admitted, in a sad echo of his father's own complaint.

The reunion between Peter and his parents was to be short-lived. Alec was posted suddenly to Gibraltar, to take up the job of Financial Secretary to the Colony. Margaret went with him, and because the Mediterranean was considered officially suitable for young children, so did baby Sarah. Peter was to be left behind again, but this time he was also to be separated from Granny Mayo, and Aunt Joan and Uncle Roy. With only a few terms' sporadic education at a Torquay day school under his belt, it was time for Peter to go to a proper boarding school. St Bede's was chosen, an Eastbourne prep school in the process of returning home from its wartime exile in Exmoor, that would be close to Grandfather Mayo should any emergency arise. When it was time to say goodbye, Peter sobbed uncontrollably on the platform.

St Bede's School is a cluster of rambling, spacious, mock half-timbered buildings purpose-built in 1895, which stands on a breezy headland near the white cliffs at Beachy Head. Today it is a bustling, friendly and sumptuously well-equipped school for some four hundred boys and girls, most of them from Eastbourne itself. In 1945 it was a freezing, regimented institution, all parquet flooring and rough carbolic soap, where ninety boys were carefully watched for dangerous signs of self-expression. As a small, lonely, asthmatic child, Peter was easy prey for bullies, and suffered badly at the hands of an unpleasant older boy called Ramsbotham. He learned quickly that the techniques used to keep Granny Mayo entertained could be profitably employed to prevent Ramsbotham hitting him. Using a combination of 'wit and sarcasm', as he described it, he was able to deflect his tormentor's attentions on to others.

His teachers would have preferred to see Peter stand up and fight rather than joke his way out of a corner – his first school report dismissed him as 'cynical' – but the authorities were soon won over by his academic brilliance. His brave enthusiasm on the football field, where he graced the inside left position with one or two tricks learned from Torquay United's Don Mills, also stood him in good stead. In time he gained a decent measure of popularity and a reputation as the school wit. On one occasion the annual nativity play ground to a halt, when the next boy due on stage was found collapsed helpless with laughter in the wings after Peter had whispered something in his ear.

Despite having arrived at a modus vivendi, Peter was desperately unhappy at St Bede's, not that he would ever have admitted as much to his parents. Having his appendix removed in 1948 didn't help matters. According to his sister Sarah, 'Peter had the toughest deal as far as being left behind was concerned. When I was sent away to school later, I whinged like anything about it all, I hated it. But Peter never moaned – I never once heard him complain. It's taken me a long time to realise how difficult it was for my parents too – as a child you only see it from a child's point of view. Nobody was being cruel intentionally: that was just the way things were.' His mother wrote to him once a week – Margaret wrote to each of her children once a week for as long as she lived – but it was no substitute for her actual presence. Peter confided the truth of his childhood loneliness only to his wives, in later years. As long as his parents lived, he would breezily tell any inquisitive journalist that as a boy he had 'really loved visiting all those different places.'[7] In fact, he lived for the school holidays in Gibraltar entirely because it meant seeing his family again.

As Sarah grew up, she became Peter's constant holiday companion, on a series of expeditions to investigate Gibraltar's creepy-crawlies. They caught little fish at Rosea Bay using home-made rods and bait, and fed them to the cat. They rescued terrapins from a dried-up river bed in Spain, and made a pond for them among the figs and geraniums of their rambling garden. Peter installed a fearsome-looking pet praying mantis in a shoe box, which terrified the life out of his sister. Anything that crept, or crawled, or buzzed, Peter would try and keep it in a cardboard box. In May 1947 he was apprehended by Spanish customs, trying to smuggle a tortoise across the border in a teapot.

It was the custom for Bob Church to send Alec an annual subscription to the *Reader's Digest* as a present, and Peter was absolutely fascinated to read an article therein about killer bees. This became something of an obsession, and he would lead Sarah on hunts lasting many hours for an elusive flower named the 'Bee Orchid'. In return, Peter would patiently sit through endless dolly's tea parties and beach picnics organised by his little sister. 'Despite the age gap, I never felt bossed, teased, patronised or merely tolerated by him – not then, not ever,' says Sarah. Peter was undoubtedly content. Compared to life at St Bede's, Gibraltar was an absolute idyll. On one occasion Errol Flynn's yacht dropped anchor in the bay, and Peter swam out with his autograph book clamped between his teeth. Flynn's wife went down below, and returned with the scrawled inscription 'Hiya Pete'. 'He had signed. I swam away happily. There has never been a thrill quite like that since.'[8]

At last, Peter got the chance to befriend his father. They played golf and tennis, and went fishing together. On occasion the family would even have a little flutter on the races. In 1951, Alec Cook dreamed that the Derby would be won by a horse called Nickel Penny. He then found out that there was a horse running at 40–1 called Nickel Coin, so – ever cautious – he only placed a small bet on it. A friend of his placed a much larger bet, and won a fortune when it scraped home in first place. Alec also introduced the concept of a national lottery to Gibraltar, and placed his family on strict orders not to purchase a ticket. He was terrified that his wife might actually win something in his own draw. Margaret nicknamed her husband 'the sea green incorruptible' because of his constant scrupulous integrity. This clear moral sense, with its absolute respect for the truth, was passed down to his son wholesale, along with Alec's melancholy core and his sharp sense of humour.

Humour was enjoyed in the Cook household very much on a shared basis. The whole family loved to play around with words, and Peter's predilection for taking a subject and running with it very much came from his father. Favourite family jokes were usually based on word play, often spoonerisms, such as the school report accusing a pupil of tasting the whole worm. Humorous books were an important influence: Wodehouse, Beachcomber, *1066 and All That*, and the savagely accurate Geoffrey Willans–Ronald Searle creation, Nigel Molesworth. Most popular of all were the delightfully bleak *Ruthless Rhymes* and *More Ruthless Rhymes* by

Harry Grahame, illustrated by Ridgewell, short verses redolent of Edward Lear's more macabre moments. Peter's favourite, of course, was the one entitled 'Prebendary Gorm':

> When Mrs Gorm (Aunt Heloise)
> Was stung to death by savage bees,
> Her husband (Prebendary Gorm)
> Put on his veil, and took the swarm
> He's publishing a book, next May,
> On 'How to make Bee Keeping Pay'.

This was accompanied by an illustration of Mrs Gorm, her entire head hidden beneath a cloud of furious killer bees, a few of whom are stinging the dog for good measure, while her husband stands behind her grinning heartily in bee-proof gear. Some of the *Ruthless Rhymes* were quite advanced:

> Weep not for little Leonie
> Abducted by a French Marquis,
> Though loss of honour was a wrench
> Just think how it's improved her French.

Generally speaking, though, the family's humour was dry, witty and very English, and always stopped short of being crude. When Peter drew a picture in Sarah's autograph book of their little sister Elizabeth (who was born in 1952) sitting on her potty, Sarah rubbed it out with much embarrassment before anyone could see it. Few of the family's comic favourites were brash or American or both, although Peter personally enjoyed the Goons, Dean Martin and Jerry Lewis, the Marx Brothers and Abbott and Costello, whom his parents didn't much care for. An exception to this was Frank Crumit, whose comic songs *Abdul Abulbul Amir*, *The Gay Caballero* and *The Song of the Prune* were frequently played. Alec's expansive collection of 78rpm records also took in Stanley Holloway, whose lugubrious monologues usually concerned plain-speaking little Lancastrians failing to bat their eyelids in the presence of kings, lions and other impressive authority figures. Looking back on his career in the mid-1980s, Peter admitted that 'Only in my forties have I realised that a lot of my sense of humour comes from my parents – that's quite humbling, in a way.'[9]

The atmosphere in the Cook household was correspondingly polite and relaxed. Alec and Margaret were gentle and loving parents. They had no need for any formal imposition of discipline: the perfect manners they had instilled in their children kept order for them. 'There were certain things I knew not to do with them present'[10] was how Peter later summed up their disciplinary policy. A key part of the Cook family's code of manners was the stress put on not being boring – never outstaying one's welcome, for instance – while being prepared to suffer it from others. This had a profound effect on Peter, who was careful never to bore anyone throughout his life, and yet whose ability to converse politely when cornered by pub bores was justly famous. The importance of not burdening others with one's own trivial problems was perhaps best expressed by the family nanny, who was trapped with Sarah on a blazing passenger vessel – happily both later escaped unhurt – and yet managed to get a cable off to Margaret Cook. It read: 'SHIP ON FIRE. DO NOT WORRY.' Peter, of course, was beset with problems in his later life, but would never have dreamed of disturbing his family with them.

All of which is not to say that the family stood on ceremony. After all, Alec Cook, a man sufficiently important to have his signature printed on Gibraltar's pound notes, happily skipped down the street to school holding his daughter's hand every morning. When a ship carrying ammunition exploded in the harbour, he told Sarah that everyone at the Secretariat had hidden under the table playing bears. The Cooks' was a happy house, full of laughter and music – Margaret played violin in the Gibraltar Symphony Orchestra – often with a party in full swing. But always there was the underlying sadness, on both sides, of Peter's returns to school. Peter's career plan remained largely unspoken but generally understood: that he would follow his father and his father before him into overseas service on behalf of his country. To achieve that end, sacrifices needed to be made. Peter's smile would evaporate and turn to tears at the airport. Eleanor Hudson, an old school friend of Margaret's, would meet Peter on his arrival in Britain and arrange his transfer to school: she remembers him as a quiet, solemn charge, contemplative of his fate.

Peter had in fact triumphed at St Bede's, as far as the authorities there were concerned. His final term's report, in the summer of 1951, concluded that 'Originality of thought and a command of words give him a maturity of style beyond his years. In speech or essay he is never dull and his work should always be interesting.' His Headmaster added: 'A very excellent term. I think he should have a very promising future at Radley.' For Radley, one of England's great public schools, was where Peter was bound, an even larger and more intimidating institution, promising greater challenges to be faced and bigger bullies to be faced down.

Sir Arthur Streeb-Greebling, in interview many years later, defended his decision to bring up his own son Roger in the traditional English manner:

> 'We had him educated privately.'
> 'But not by governesses.'
> 'No, by goats. Not by governesses, goats.'
> 'Despite your own childhood experiences with goats.'
> 'Well it was either that, or King's School Canterbury. And I'm not entirely heartless you know.'[11]

CHAPTER 2

I'm Much Bigger Than You Are, Sir

Radley and Abroad, 1951–57

For a public school, St Peter's College, Radley is a relatively youthful institution. It was founded in 1847, around a large red-brick Georgian box of a mansion, set in 700 acres of parkland near Abingdon in Oxfordshire. Other buildings appeared over the years, dotted about the park like mushrooms, including the school theatre, which – rather bizarrely – was a prefabricated, corrugated-iron cathedral originally intended for Newfoundland. As befitting an establishment born in a flush of educational modernism, the school's linguistic emphasis was upon French, rather than Latin, as the language of international diplomacy. Radley had strong links with overseas service, which was why Peter had been sent there. In the words of one contemporary, Robin Gunn, 'It was a very insular society, geared to producing characters self-sufficient enough to govern the natives in distant, lonely, steamy parts of the globe.'

Although barely a century old when Peter arrived there, Radley had equipped itself enthusiastically with the idiosyncratic traditions and vocabulary fundamental to any great public school's daily life. Masters were called Dons. The Headmaster was known as the Warden. School boarding houses were called Socials. Every boy wore a gown and carried a ring binder called a Block. The school played rugby in winter – Peter's beloved football was regarded with condescension – while in summer the 'wet-bobs' rowed and the 'dry-bobs' played cricket. First years had to have all their jacket buttons done up, which could then be loosened at the rate of one a year.

The Prefects – one per Social – were cocks of the walk. They alone were allowed to carry their gowns, to stroll past the clock tower (others had to jog past it in single file), and to go to the lavatory with the cubicle door shut. They had their own common room, 'Pup's study', which the senior Prefect had the unique privilege of being allowed to enter via the window, up an external flight of stone steps. The Prefects had complete authority to beat the younger boys in their charge, who in turn had to fag for them. Masters didn't do much beating, although as a contemporary of Peter's, Nick Salaman, recalls: 'There was one master who gave beating talks. "How would you feel if I beat you? Tell me how uncomfortable that would feel" and so on. I don't think he actually ever beat anyone. He just liked to talk about it, that was his pleasure.'

New arrivals at Radley in the autumn of 1951 had to undergo a variety of initiation ceremonies. The contents of the Radley 'Grey Book' (so named because it wasn't grey) had to be learned off by heart, including the names of all the masters, the initials of every boy in the Social and all the school rituals. Then a penny was balanced upon the new boy's forehead and a rolled-up copy of *Country Life* was stuffed into the waistband of his trousers. He was then ordered to tilt his head back at such an angle that the penny would drop into the funnel formed by the magazine; or at least that was what he was told would happen. In reality a gallon jug of iced water was poured down the funnel while he was staring at the ceiling. Failure to pass these tests – undue flinching, in other words – or any other minor transgressions such as farting in chapel, were punished by 'Lacing', in which the victim was forced to complete several circuits of the ping pong table while being whacked with hockey sticks. The rigours of the African bush, the thinking presumably went, would one day be as nothing by comparison.

The Radley day began at 6.45 a.m. with a compulsory and thorough icy shower, as checked off by a Prefect reclining in an adjacent hot tub. There were lessons before breakfast, then bed-making and chapel. Every morning at eleven there were compulsory star-jumps in front of the mansion, followed by more lessons, compulsory games in the afternoon (or military training once a week), prep in the evenings, then bed. Boys dashed headlong, gowns flying, from one place to another. There simply was no time for socialising. Only on Saturday evenings and on Sundays did the conveyor belt slow up; unless you were fagging for your Senior, of course, in which case much of the weekend was spent shoe-cleaning, toast-making and warming outside lavatory seats.

Peter's Social, named like all of them after the master in charge, was Thompson's. J. V. P. Thompson, nicknamed 'Rutch' for reasons that nobody can remember, was an odd, slightly deaf man with a booming voice and a bristling moustache, who had a habit of taking his spectacles off and winding them round and round in his ears in order to extract the wax. He was unmarried, so his Social had to go without the softening presence of a Master's wife and family. Junior boys in Thompson's lived for the first four terms in a huge, cold, barn-like structure, separated by six-foot partitions into a series of cubicles and corridors, 'like holes in an oddly carved up rabbit warren' according to Peter Raby, another of Peter's contemporaries. Only in January of their third year were boys given the use of a study in an adjacent octagonal building.

It goes without saying that Peter's first year or so at Radley was utterly, miserably unhappy. He intensely disliked the authority the school exercised over him and those who applied it. A slight, asthmatic figure, always dressed in the same shabby, ill-fitting gown or blue sports jacket on Sundays – his parents' salary did not run to an extensive wardrobe – he was easy meat for bullies, of whom there were many. Dr Sid Gottlieb, later Peter's great friend, occasional physician and confidant, recalls that 'Peter hated Radley in those days. My God, it was a really terrible, cruel time.' Peter's first wife Wendy remembers that 'He did share with me how sometimes he would bang his head on the wall in despair in the night because he couldn't breathe and I think he felt so abandoned. He really had a very lonely time.' None of his school fellows, of course, were privy to his inner agonies. His best friend at the time, Jonathan Harlow, wrote later that 'Peter seemed to be less affected than most of us either by the miseries or the exaltations of adolescence. Perhaps he merely talked less about himself – even when we knew each other very well, he never mentioned his home or his parents. But if he did not seem particularly unhappy, he was not yet master of that permanent good humour which was to mark him later.'[1] The word 'master' was an apt choice – Peter was indeed gradually refining the use of good humour as a self-defence. 'I hated the first two years,' he explained, 'because of being bullied. And I was as cowardly as the next man. I didn't enjoy getting beaten up, and I disliked being away from home – that part was horrid. But it started a sort of defence mechanism in me, trying to make people laugh so that they wouldn't hit me. I could make fun of other people and therefore make the person who was about to bully me laugh instead.'[2] How many times, over the years, has the British comedy industry had cause to be grateful to generations of public school bullies.

Peter's particular bête noire at Radley was the Senior Prefect, Ted Dexter, later to become England's cricket Captain, whose majestic timing with a cricket ball was matched by his majestic timing with a cane. According to Peter's schoolfriend Michael Bawtree, 'Prefects were dazzling and terrifying. They could punish and harass at whim. But Dexter was even more astral than the rest, as a cricketing, rackets-playing, rugby-playing hero. He was also extremely lordly, elegant, rich, well-dressed and assured, with something of a "sneer of cold command". Can you imagine anyone more likely to get young Peter's goat?' Even in later life, according to Sid Gottlieb, Peter was still 'really angry' at the treatment he had received at the hands of Dexter. 'He referred to him as the equivalent of an SS brute, always lashing out.' Peter himself, his tongue pushed slightly into his cheek for public consumption, concluded that 'That's where I got my sense of injustice about the world, Ted Dexter. I was always envious of him, because he used to drive an Alfa Romeo. And he beat me for drinking cider at the Henley Regatta. Now OK, you weren't allowed to drink cider at the Henley Regatta, so perhaps I deserved to be beaten. What I thought was a little unfair was that I had just seen him coming out of the pub with a bottle of scotch.'[3]

As well as having to endure the disciplinary attentions of Dexter and his sort, Peter found that his pretty features attracted a different kind of unwelcome attention from some of the older boys. Asked later by Michael Parkinson what his chief memory of Radley was, he replied: 'Trying to avoid buggery. I've always wanted to look up one old acquaintance of mine – and I won't mention his name, he'll know perfectly well who he is, the dirty sod. I was a young, quite pretty boy, I was number three in the charts, and he was a prefect, and he came into my cubicle. I was reading a magazine, and he sat on the bed and put his hand up the back of my pyjamas and started stroking my back. And he said, "Do you mind that, Cook?" And I said "Yes . . .". In fact I didn't mind at all, but I felt I ought to say yes, because my master had had me in at the beginning of term and had said, "As a young boy, Cook, you will discover that there are a lot of other boys at this school. And sometimes . . . the older boys . . . do things to the younger boys. And if anybody, er, er . . . you probably know what I mean." And I didn't really know what he meant.'[4] Asked later by *Playboy* magazine how he had lost his virginity at the school, he retorted 'At what end?'

Sarah Cook, meanwhile, was on her way to prep school in Blandford Forum, an experience which, coming after the joys of growing up in Gibraltar, mirrored the miseries of Peter's lifestyle. She found herself pitched into a dark dormitory full of unfamiliar sobbing girls, one of whom used to hug her knees and rock back and forth like a psychiatric inmate. She wrote to her parents, 'I can't find a friend now. Nobody will play with me, and it is jolly lonely. Nobody seems to want to play with me.' Peter had been separated and alone for a lot longer, and so was much better trained than this. His emotions stayed firmly battened down, as was the Radley way. He did miss Sarah though, and wrote to tell her that he had found a mole and put it in a cardboard box.

Peter had learned at St Bede's the value of keeping your head down and not being a cry baby, and in due course he began to flourish as he had done there. His school fellows remember his early years as entirely unremarkable. He was a scrupulously obedient military cadet. He was quietly respectful and diligent in class. He did not act in plays. He was not much good at sport, but he bravely did his best. In fact he absolutely detested rugby: 'I was forced to play it. For some reason I was placed at full back. I spent the whole time avoiding the ball. Often they'd forget what to do and actually come at me. In my rush to get away from the ball once, I fell on it. I was then hacked to bits by the forwards' feet and got a spurious reputation for courage. Had it not been for breaking a shin-bone I might have been forced to play for the Sixth XV.'[5] In such a sports-mad establishment – Radley was named 'Top sports school of the year' by *The Field* in 1952 – this reputation for fearlessness was a vital one to have acquired.

In class, Peter's efforts reflected the unthinking conservatism of every public schoolboy's sheltered lifestyle in the early fifties. 'I wrote this absolutely ghastly essay which won a prize. As far as I can remember it called for the chemical castration of the unintelligent working-classes. I think it was chemical castration, nothing cruel. The idea was to prevent their breeding. I was just pompous, witless and hopeless. People say I've got more reactionary in my old age, when in fact I've moved to the left from my very solid Nazi position at the age of thirteen.'[6] Peter's teachers recognised him as officer material, and at the end of his first year appointed him Head of Thompson's Social Hall, a large scruffy room where juniors gathered and kept their belongings in horse boxes. Paul ('Bill') Butters, who joined the Social as a new boy at the start of the following year, saw a different side of the young Peter Cook from that observed by his teachers: 'Peter was even at the early age of fifteen a boy who inspired respect. But it was his quick wit and ability to see the funny side of authority that was particularly attractive.'

His school reports acknowledged a 'creditable standard of performance', but expressed concern over the 'withdrawn' or 'aloof' side of his nature. Thompson himself wrote that Peter 'continues to show intelligence and an original approach – though he must not overdo the latter. As Head of Social Hall he has set a good example, though I have noticed some of the aloofness mentioned by his Form Master . . . it has rather diminished positive impact. His long period off games through injury has no doubt been a contributory difficulty.' In January 1953 he moved up to a study in the octagon, where his studymate J. A. Aylen found him to be an easy, cheerful companion, who did not suffer fools gladly but who was never rude to them. While life could not be said to be looking up to any great extent, he had at least established a modus vivendi, as at St Bede's.

That very month, however, Peter suffered a shattering blow. His holidays in Gibraltar had remained the shining beacon at the end of every term, making life at Radley that much easier to endure. Now, suddenly, his father was posted back to Nigeria, to become Permanent Secretary of the country's Eastern Region, based at Enugu. It was something of a compliment – the Colonial Service there had missed Alec Cook's abilities in the preceding eight years – but being sent back halfway round the world was the last thing that the Cook family wanted. Swallowing his disappointment, Peter wrote to his father, a Molesworthian masterpiece of noncommittal irrelevance: 'The weather here is very cold and a good deal of snow has fallen. Yesterday the Intersocial Rowing Competition began. We were just beaten by 3½ seconds but we have a very young crew and we should be very good next year. The Hockey 1st XI have been winning all their matches. I watched Joe Davis on TV the other day he was absolutely marvellous and got 2 breaks over 100 against Walter Donaldson.' To his mother, Peter wrote in scarcely more intimate terms: 'Yesterday was Field Day and we had an all day exercise in full corps uniform. Angels One Five is being shown here at College sometime next week. Thompsons are doing very well in the athletics cup. By the way back Little Yid for the National. Lots of love, Peter.' A world of emotional disturbance lay between his polite lines, distressingly devoid of any useful expression of feelings.

Peter's academic performance collapsed. His report that term spoke of dissipation, a lack of energy and 'somnolent lapses'. Thompson concluded that 'There can be no doubt about Peter's ability but I am disappointed that he does not make more positive use of it. I recall literary and artistic talent which he seems content to let sleep, doing in the classroom no more than is required of him and making little effort to find outside avenues of fulfilment. There are faint signs already that it may lead to a most undesirable cynicism of outlook.' The warden added a comment, that 'I want to see him do MUCH better than this – we all know he can and he knows it too.' Peter had already applied, prematurely one would think at the age of fifteen, to Pembroke College, Cambridge, his father's alma mater; but such future academic rewards were undoubtedly beginning to drift out of view.

Salvation came in the shape of his mother, who was finding the demands of the Colonial Service something of a trial. The thought of leaving baby Elizabeth behind as she had left Peter proved too much for her, and she agreed with Alec that she would stay in England for much of his second Nigerian tour of duty. Instead Peter was able to join his mother and sisters at Aunt Joan's that Easter, and spent the holidays happily fishing and playing golf. In June Margaret obtained two £6 tickets for the Coronation, and took Peter out of school to go and see it. For the first time in his life, he found himself living in the same country as most of his immediate family, able to go on outings with his mother like anybody else. Suddenly, all was right with the world. As if to prove it, Ted Dexter left Radley and his childhood asthma began to clear up at the same time.

The effect on Peter's school reports was immediate and electric. Thompson noted the sudden improvement, 'under the stimulus of impending examination', and remarked that 'He begins to see how he may find scope for his talents in our general community life.' Within a term or two his Social tutor was enthusing further: 'Peter's linguistic abilities, allied to a sensitive imagination, are assuring splendid results and arousing high hopes for his academic future.' His form master recognised the change in 'an alert and intelligent young man, very ready to be interested and to take delight in his studies. He works conscientiously, thinks clearly and writes fluently.'

Margaret Cook paid an extended visit to her husband in the latter part of 1953. Then, early in 1954, she set about finding a permanent English home, and settled on Knollside, a spacious cottage with an oversized conservatory in Uplyme, just outside Lyme Regis. Now it was Alec's turn to be lonely and downcast. 'The house in Lyme Regis sounds nice, but £5800 is a lot, and what happens if I retire and get a job in England not in the vicinity? Have you heard of any unfurnished houses to let? I know they are said to be few and far between – I know very little about life in England. I understand your desire to have a house which I share, but there are obvious snags. Anyway, let me know what else you find in your prowlings. I am sorry to be so vague about my future but it is very difficult to forecast what may happen during the next year or 18 months; what I do know is that I find these separations very hard to bear, and I am pretty sure I shall have had enough of this job by September 1955.'

Alec's solitary lifestyle had been enlivened only by the visit of a passing bishop. 'He proved to be quite a live wire – fond of his noggin. It was a pleasant change to have some conversation. Otherwise life is the same all round. I went for a walk to the river this evening, but I didn't see any kingfishers as I had hoped to. I listened in avidly to the Queen's arrival in Gibraltar and was not dry-eyed at the end of it. I'm glad she is back home again safe and sound. I did not imagine there would be any nonsense at Gibraltar and should have felt so ashamed had there been. I had a nice letter from Peter, mainly about fishing, and one from Sarah too. Peter seems to have loved his holidays – you can congratulate yourself on having made a great success of them. I am very much looking forward to meeting Peter again and agree that he is a son to be proud of. I do think we can take credit for having placed both Peter and Sarah in nice schools. Give my love to Sarah and Elizabeth. I am always reminded of the latter when the chuck-chucks mill around at breakfast on my solitary porch. Tons of love darling – I expect things will work out – from Alec.'

Undeterred by her husband's financial misgivings, Margaret went ahead and bought the house, and a Labrador to go with it, and the family spent the summer of 1954 redecorating their new home. Peter's letters to his father brimmed with excitement as never before: 'The curtains are up! The carpets are down! and the chandelier for the sitting room is up too, and the garden is as wild as ever. I like the house very much and am painting the conservatory which is a great suntrap.' Peter also set to work on the garden, and took a keen interest in its upkeep for years to come. He was rewarded for his efforts with a brand new dark grey flannel suit from Austin Reed's in Exeter, 'which looks very well'.

In June 1955 Peter had further cause for excitement. 'Dear Daddy, I read in *The Times* yesterday that you have been decorated with the CMG. Heartiest congratulations! You certainly deserved it and Granny will be thrilled.' He was genuinely bursting with pride at his father's achievement. That summer the whole family holidayed in Nigeria. Margaret and Elizabeth went on ahead, and as Eleanor Hudson was unable to look after Peter and Sarah in London, he and his sister had the unparalleled adventure of staying unsupervised at the Rubens Hotel in Victoria for a night. Peter took her to see the Crazy Gang at the Victoria Palace, where she was hit on the head by a rubber ball hurled from the stage.

The presence of his entire family intensified the pressure that Alec Cook felt to retire from the Colonial Service. His mother, too, perhaps mindful of his father's fate, ventured the opinion that 'You have another big job to do, in England. Making a happy home for your three dear children and Margaret, and giving them a background of wise and loving care. Children miss so much if the father is away.' That autumn Alec Cook sailed to England to collect his CMG at Buckingham Palace, and never returned to Nigeria. A few years later the Colonial Service itself packed up its bags and went home – prematurely, its officers felt – leaving the country to independence and the eventual bloody civil war that Alec and his colleagues had informed Whitehall would inevitably ensue.

At Radley, the return of his mother and in due course his father acted as a catalyst, spurring Peter on not just academically but socially. The sardonic wit he had employed primarily as a defensive tool was now put to use in entertaining his schoolfellows. One of his most popular gifts was an ability to mimic most of the members of staff, with an accuracy, a degree of comic invention and a recklessness that far outstripped that shown by any of his colleagues. First, perhaps unsurprisingly, was 'Rutch' himself, who according to Peter's then studymate Aylen was 'perfect for lampooning. Myopic, pipe-smoking, tatty smelly mackintosh, strutted rather than walked, introspective, devoid of charm. Peter's first target, and he did it well. Peter caricatured him by habit, perhaps by nature, but never maliciously.' Then there were impressions of Warden Milligan's languid Etonian drawl – 'merciless' according to another contemporary – and of Ivor Gilliat, a boisterous gurgling toad of a master who was overfond of young boys, 'a perversion which Peter took great glee in publicising' according to classmate Stephen Dixon. Rather than merely mimic his victims, Peter applied his father's gift of spinning a comic web around a simple original premise. Jonathan Harlow recalls: 'A scrap of speech . . . would become the starting point for a whole persona so wild and wonderful that the original could never again be seen as ordinary mortal. Thus our benign and blameless chaplain was transformed before our very ears into a monster of depravity, ruthlessness and Jesuitical guile: Richelieu, Torquemada, Alexander VI and Pope John rolled into one.'[7]

The most memorable of all Peter's comic creations was without doubt Mr Boylett. Arthur Boylett was Radley's High Table butler, a short, balding gentleman in his fifties, always attired in shabby tails, a grey waistcoat and tie, whose job it was to wait personally on the Warden at mealtimes. Mr Boylett's generally cheerful demeanour contrasted with his nasally monotonous voice and his habit of making unintentionally humorous pronouncements. 'There's plenty more where that came from, if you get my meaning' he would announce conspiratorially, as he served up another helping of potatoes. Boylett first came to the broad attention of the pupils when he accidentally swept the High Table breadcrumbs into the lap of one of the prefects. 'Well, they were your crumbs,' he explained. Peter made it his business to buttonhole the unfortunate butler between meals: 'Boylett used to tell me these terribly boring – which he thought interesting – facts. He said "You know that stone which is lying just outside the left hand side of the gravel driveway as you go out? I sold that yesterday, because I thought I saw it move." And he kept selling things which he thought he saw move. I had long conversations with him about moving stones, and twigs he'd seen which had hovered in a strange way and might be valuable. "I thought I saw it move" became the catchphrase for anything.'[8] Peter was to take the catchphrase and the character on to Cambridge University, and then on to television, where Mr Boylett metamorphosed into E. L. Wisty.

Peter would loudly announce, as Boylett, that he had bought up all the grass at Radley, on the grounds that he had seen it move, only for the bottom to fall out of the market. He even developed a Boylett walk. 'By now Peter was a gangling 17-year-old,' recalls Paul Butters, 'and he would keep his fellows amused in Social by walking up and down the markets miming the luckless Boylett. Once Peter had paraded one way down the markets as Boylett, he would return, often behind the Social Tutor himself, imitating the luckless Rutch. When Boylett and Thompson had been completely dissected, it would be the turn of the Chaplain. This time, Peter's mimicry extended down Covered Passage (the main passage down to the refectory). Peter's face would screw up to imitate the Chaplain and his legs would follow the same upright path, as he chanted the words that we all imagined our Chaplain to be mumbling under his breath – "I hope, I hope, I hope it is the Pope".'

This was a mightily dangerous game to play, yet Peter pulled off the remarkable trick of laughing loudly at the system and yet being wholly accepted by it. All are agreed that his pastiches of Boylett and the masters were largely unmalicious; but that would hardly have been a defence if discovered. The Radley authorities were simply unaware of the three-ring circus being organised, in many cases quite literally, behind their backs; and if they had been made aware, they would have found it difficult to reconcile the nature of the crime with the exquisitely polite, diligent and well-mannered boy who had already been marked down as a future Head of Social. Richard Cottrell, another schoolfellow, explains that 'Peter had a very confident, assured persona and could switch on dependability at the bat of an eyelid. There was a lot of "the speed of the hand deceives the eye" stuff going on.'

Peter spent much of his life on the edge of authority. On military field days he, Michael Bawtree and others would find a hedge away from the proceedings and sit behind it, wetting themselves with laughter at the formalities being enacted on the other side of the privet. As an alternative to the detested rugby, he began to organise illicit football games at the end of a half-mile long forest track. The games multiplied until, by February

1955, the *Radleian* magazine was lamenting that 'Every square mile of waste land is dedicated to the cult of association football.' Any formal occasion, like dinner in hall, was a cue for Peter to send his schoolfellows into fits of laughter. 'The fact that one of his major characters was based on the High Table butler, and that another was Warden Milligan, meant that every meal was an agony of suppressed hysteria' says Bawtree.[9] The Warden, who had arrived at the school soon after Dexter left, had gradually replaced the former Head Boy as Peter's least favourite authority symbol. 'For Peter, Milligan's smoothness, his unctuousness, were pretty hard to bear. He found the man's whole gushing public persona a piece of Old Etonian fakery. By this time, of course, Peter was a senior boy, so Milligan was less of a threat, and more a figure of fun, than Dexter. I don't remember Peter ever mimicking Dexter, but he mimicked Milligan all the time.'

It must be stressed, though, that Peter was not a revolutionary or an anarchist. He was certainly not left-wing. He had simply learned to manipulate the system to his own benefit. He may have disliked it, but he fully intended to succeed within it rather than go about the futile task of trying to replace it. Jonathan Harlow says of his immediate circle: 'We were not rebels. Incidents or individuals we might deplore or scoff at. But I think that throughout our time there we accepted the system. It had, after all, a sort of serial democracy. Each year's intake in turn would succeed by chronological progression to a growing degree of immunity, tolerance and privilege, enhanced opportunities for self-expression and, finally, authority for itself. And the traditionalism, the values which were simply assumed rather than spelt out, with the cloistering from any countervalues, exerted an insidious but powerful pressure to conform.'[10] Much of Radley's cruelty was inflicted on junior boys by senior boys, as part of the school's policy of allowing pupils to govern themselves wherever possible; the upside of this cycle of brutality was an atmosphere in which genuinely talented senior boys had the freedom to flourish, as long as they did not actually try to buck the system.

One of the measures of a good public school is its willingness to promote the artistic or academically-minded boy to positions of power, rather than simply handing over authority wholesale to the First XV. As a famous sporting school, Radley had a tendency to plump for the latter option, but there was always room for the occasional gifted non-sportsman to go all the way to the top. Peter was one such exception, as – despite his famous rugby injury – he could hardly be described as an athlete. Indeed, his only subsequent memorable contribution to the official sporting life of the school came when he was unable to complete a cricket match through being utterly helpless with laughter, after a novice discus thrower on an adjacent field spun round so many times that he lost his sense of direction and hurled his discus into the middle of the cricket pitch by mistake.

Instead, Peter threw himself wholeheartedly into the theatre as an actor, in a series of increasingly extrovert and comic parts. One of Radley's great attractions was its drama department, run by a humane, witty and liberal English master named Peter Way. Rather than content itself with a mere school play each year, Radley could boast an annual drama festival, together with all sorts of lesser productions at different times. In order to get round the fact that Sunday was the only free day for rehearsals, the drama department had negotiated an extension to bedtime for all those involved in a play, which in turn acted as a spur to recruitment.

Peter's first tentative steps on the stage came in 1953, in the wake of his mother's decision to base herself in England, when he volunteered for the role of the Socialist Duchess in *Stuck in a Lift*: a performance so unmemorable that the school magazine ignored it entirely. More convincing was his interpretation of Doll Common in *The Alchemist* in March 1954 (his willowy good looks and big eyelashes usually earned him one of the female parts). This galvanised the *Radleian's* drama critic to credit him with a 'a breadth and gusto which gave a richly authentic atmosphere to the whole production'. Nick Salaman, who played Subtle, remembers Peter's performance as 'Dashing. He made a very fine eccentric prostitute.' It was clear that he was beginning to develop a talent for farce.

In Thompson's entry for the November 1954 drama festival he was cast as the Wicked Fairy in Peter Ustinov's *Love of Four Colonels*. Peter Raby, who played the Good Fairy, remembers his performance as 'Wonderful. He dominated the production quite naturally with his comic energy and timing.' A role in Milton's *Comus* was followed in March 1956 by the part of Don Adriano de Armado in *Love's Labour's Lost*. By now the *Radleian* was going into raptures: 'Peter Cook was the very recipe of a fantastic: a measure of Malvolio, an atom of Aguecheek, and a pinch of Polonius, the whole garnished with sprigs of Shallow, Jacques and Quince. Here was a wonderful display of virtuosity.' Peter filled the role with exaggerated Spanish mannerisms, great swooping bows, contortions and swirls of his hat, and delivered the whole in a comic parody of antique Spanish speech – 'Just on the edge of being totally overdone but not quite', according to one of the audience, Alexander Hamilton. Even his English master was moved to describe the performance on Peter's school report as 'A delightful creation, a model of fluent gesture and comic overstatement.'

By 1955 Peter was sufficiently confident to start mounting his own self-penned revues. A Cook revue became an event not to be missed, particularly as each production contained a number of delicately veiled parodies of members of staff, using jokes and catchphrases that only the boys were privy to. Terry Hathaway, now a London cab driver, whose older sister was on the Radley staff, remembers how she used to urge the whole family to come and see one of the revues, in order to catch sight of this hilarious schoolboy performer. The most original of Peter's creations was his leading role as a dung beetle; the most memorable, though, was the semi-improvised *Gold Mine Revue* of December 1955, which stuck for ever in the minds of all who saw it. In this production, Peter appeared in a double act for the first time ever, with Paul Butters taking the stooge role later filled professionally by Dudley Moore. Explains Butters: 'Our moment really arrived in the autumn term of 1955, when, as usual, the school hired critics from the BBC to come and judge the Social plays. On this occasion that old trooper Geoffrey Keen, together with a colleague, Desmond Llewellyn, came down and, as often happens when there are two commentators, they made somewhat of a hash of judging the eight plays. At the end of that term Peter and I decided to put on a Christmas revue, and we came on at the end as the top billing, as Geoffrey Keen and Desmond Llewellyn, unable to remember which one was which. It was the first time that Peter had really found his niche. He needed no more than an adequate foil to demonstrate his genius.'

At this point in the performance, Peter took over proceedings. A. Hill, who had appeared earlier in the show in a jazz quartet and had by now slipped eagerly into the audience, relates what followed: 'Peter's act was unexpected, brilliant, and apparently totally unscripted and unrehearsed. It left me and the rest of the audience holding our sides and aching all over from convulsions of laughter. The curtains went back to reveal a very complicated and unlikely set, the most prominent feature of which was a vast fishing net draped from the top right to the lower left of the stage. Peter began to present a criticism of an imaginary production. His brilliant observation of the dress and speech of the real adjudicator and his inventive comments on what was clearly an absurd 'play' were priceless, as was the way in which he moved from serious criticism to total farce. Needless to say, at one point he advised the rearrangement of the set and, in illustrating the advantages to be gained, he became hopelessly entangled with the fish net. The curtain fell with Peter scarcely visible inside a tightly wound ball of netting, rocking gently on the stage. The audience screamed for more. It was a truly memorable performance.'

Peter had judged correctly that an open lampoon of the outside BBC adjudicators would not be so close to home as to offend the school authorities. His report concluded that 'Although he is never afraid to be controversial, this has been a very successful term.' Thompson added, 'More and more Peter fulfils our hopes intellectually and imaginatively; he's naturally happy in this achievement and therefore more open-hearted than of old.' Towards the end of 1955 Peter was appointed Head of his Social and School Prefect; but Thompson had a warning for him. As well as his 'sparkle and wit', he would require 'a sympathetic understanding of, and interest in, people of all sorts and conditions, many of them very different from himself'.

The Social Tutor had correctly diagnosed a certain emotional distance in Peter's dealings with the other boys. Despite his increasing popularity and burgeoning confidence, the shy, unsure and vulnerable child who had arrived at Radley remained nervously beneath the surface. According to Noel Slocock, 'He loved talking and he loved to have an audience and he particularly needed other people to spark off. But I think all that sprang in a sense from somebody who inside was quite a shy person.' Christopher Leigh, another contemporary, recalls that Peter 'seemed to be, in a way, a bit of a loner. I don't think you actually ever got to know him really well, although one spent a lot of time with him.' According to Michael Bawtree, behind his many voices 'Peter always seemed vaguely uneasy, and blushing even: when he was not being funny in his brilliant, gothic, extravagant way, he was surprisingly awkward.'[11] Peter's second wife Judy is in no doubt that he 'became a performer to release a part of him that was inhibited.'

Nor, although it was well hidden, had Peter's distaste for brutal authority and the people who delighted in exercising it evaporated upon attaining some power himself. According to Bawtree, 'There's no question, in my view, that even Peter at Radley was disposed to be black about life. He was scornful of people in authority, and particularly despised any kind of lordliness or unctuousness, or indeed any kind of self-importance or fat-cattery. His remedy for this contempt – and it was deeply felt, even violent – was to mimic and mock these people. And because he was good at this he made us laugh. And so he found a way of riding out the contempt, but he didn't lose it – he merely neutralised it, and when the mockery and voices stopped, the disgust returned. The more extreme his laughter and mockery, the more effectively it was able to assuage the nausea.'

Having, as he put it, 'oiled' his way to the top, Peter made an unusually gentle and humane prefect. He abolished all the detailed and ludicrous rules and initiation ceremonies that had made his own early days in

Thompson's so miserable, and put an end to Prefects' Beatings: 'We didn't go to a master and say "This is a ridiculous system", we just didn't enforce the rules.'[12] When ordered by a master to beat a boy, a task he abhorred, Peter would play loud music so as not to have to listen to his handiwork, and always put the minimum possible effort into it. He was approachable: one of the junior boys, Anthony Penfold, had been the victim of bullying. 'I was in a bit of a state, aged fifteen, in tears etc. I went to Peter Cook as Head of the Social for help. Radley was a fairly tough place in those days and most other prefects would have sent me away with a flea in my ear for being wet.' Peter, however, sorted the matter out quietly and kindly. 'He was extremely popular, even though he wasn't in the normal Ted Dexter mould of College Prefects.' Or precisely because he wasn't in the normal mould.

One of the tasks of a prefect was to inspect the junior dormitory of his Social just after lights out, and punish anyone talking or moving about. Robert Carter Shaw, another Thompson's junior, remembers that Peter would flick on a bedside light instead. 'Then he kept us all agog by practising conjuring tricks, particularly one where he made balls disappear from between his fingers. At the end of term he put on a conjuring show for the whole school – the only time I remember a boy doing a special show for the school by himself.' Thompson expressed reservations about the number of stage performances attracting Peter away from the Social, and about the absence of 'an iron hand within the velvet glove'; but he also grudgingly admitted that the Cook method – 'an individual (and on the face of it rather tenuous) course' – had been a success. Peter had been sensible enough to balance this dangerous liberalism by gritting his teeth and leading the Social Rugby XV from the front: 'His spirited Rugger for the Social has been an unexpected and most creditable contribution,' gushed Thompson.

Soon the Prefects' Common Room had fallen sway to the new mood. Two of Peter's friends, Michael Bawtree and Jonathan Harlow, had got in among the sportsmen, and together they argued to extend the abolition of Prefects' Beatings across the whole school. The measure was agreed by all – 'except for one bastard who continued to do it, and we didn't talk to him.'[13] The thick oak door of Pup's Study only partially muffled the constant sound of uproarious laughter as Peter kept his fellow prefects amused with a constant stream of imitations and jokes. He would sprawl his long, gangly frame in a worn and dirty easy chair, one of his legs casually draped over the wooden arm, eating with a spoon directly from a warmed-up tin of baked beans, regaling the room with a near-continuous improvised comic monologue. On the rare occasions when the flow dried up, he would turn to the *Telegraph* or *Times* crossword, which he would polish off in just five minutes.

By his final year Peter was known and generally – although not universally – admired throughout the school. According to one pupil, Jeffrey Frost, 'He was remarkable not least for his humanity, kindness and generosity. He could always be relied upon to listen carefully to an idea or problem, and then respond openly and helpfully, without irony. He was careful, never dismissive.' Always, he managed the remarkable trick of combining absolute truthfulness with immaculate good manners. He usually refrained from using his celebrated wit as a weapon, but there is no doubt that the capacity to do so was there: on bad days he would occasionally be too sarcastic for his own good. 'I was normally pleased to be in his company,' said another contemporary, A. J. MacFarlane, 'but he could make one feel very small if he felt so inclined. Mostly, though, he was good-natured, and he had a ready smile.'

Whatever his inner doubts, the public face of Peter Cook was never downcast. When not writing sketches, he churned out comic articles and cartoons, and succeeded in getting one of his first efforts into the 'Charivari' section of *Punch*. 'I was thrilled to bits, I got four guineas. I worked out I could live by writing two of these items a week. But then after that I couldn't get anything into the magazine at all. Either I lost my sense of humour or they did.' Ever-optimistic, Peter continued to send batch after batch of cartoons to them, which would inevitably be returned in the following week's post. He also wrote a radio script, which was rejected by the BBC, principally because it was a thinly-veiled pastiche of *The Goons*. He received a kind letter from the BBC's Peter Titheridge pointing out that it was actually a very good Goon script, but why didn't he write something of his own? The script then landed on the desk of Spike Milligan, who was so impressed that he invited Peter up to London for lunch. This was a huge thrill, as Milligan and Sellers were probably his all-time comic heroes, although sadly neither Peter nor Spike Milligan could subsequently remember what was discussed. In fact Peter had developed the habit of falling mysteriously ill on Friday evenings, when *The Goon Show* was playing on the sanatorium radio. 'The genial matron seemed quite unaware of this weekly pattern of feeling a bit under the weather,'[14] he explained.

There is no question that whatever reservations Peter may have had about Radley, he was finally beginning to enjoy himself. His school reports now rated his work as 'outstanding', with 'a very lively critical intelligence, a capacity for sustained work, great powers of literary creation and appreciation.' He was 'thoroughly enjoyable to teach'. He won many

of the prizes the school had to offer, including the German prize and the
Birt Prize for Public Speaking. In 1955 he entered the Radley Festival of
Prose with a piece which had already won the Medrington Short Story
Prize the previous year. Entitled 'Bric-a-brac', it was a horror story that
– without delving too deeply into amateur psychology – perhaps carried
a faint hint of disturbed depths on the part of the author. It told of a
baby-sitter who wakes from a nap to find the child dead in her arms,
only for the couple who hired her to be utterly unconcerned.

> The baby was sprawled over her lap limp and white, like a wet
> handkerchief. All the colour was drained from its cheeks and the
> blue eyes were glazed fishily. No breath warmed its blue tinted
> lips. The child was dead. An empty void clutched at her heart. The
> flabby chill of dead flesh seeped through the cloth. She could feel
> the outlines of the dead baby's back pressing down on her knees.
> It was a sickening sensation, like holding a lump of cold carrion.

Then again, most adolescent boys entertain a passion for the gothic.

At the tail end of 1955, Peter received the good news that he had
been accepted by Pembroke College, Cambridge, his father's old college.
Academically, he could afford to ease off the throttle a little. 'I had a life of
complete luxury in my last year. I don't think I've ever laughed as much.
I was already in at Cambridge. I had two fags. I had breakfast in bed. I
used to go to the pictures and fish for trout in the lake. I did a bit of
teaching, a bit of lying in the fields, and I organised bootleg games of
soccer. It was delightful.'[15] Finally, soccer even gained a limited measure
of official recognition, when a Lower Sixth boy, Ian Robertson, persuaded
some members of staff to take part in a masters v. boys match, despite
a little official huffing and puffing. The Naval section of the Cadet Corps
lowered the cross bar on the rugby posts to 8 feet, and the game – in
which Peter played – was watched by the whole school.

Most of Peter's friends look back on their last year or so at Radley with
extreme nostalgic admiration. Noel Slocock, for instance: 'We were very
disciplined early on by both the Dons and the more senior boys, but I
think when we "broke through" and began to fulfil ourselves, Peter with
his drama and all the rest of it, and the Dons became friends, it became a
golden time, which was actually very difficult to recapture in later life as
we took up more serious responsibilities.' Peter's own later reflections on
life at Radley tended to be rather more schizophrenic, alternating between
similar cosy trawls through memorable moments and an aggrieved sardonic
resentment that he had ever been sent there.

One of the memories he preferred to dredge up was the sixth-formers' termly dance against a local girls' school – against, not with. 'We never won,' he said. It was the boys' first and only chance to explore and get to grips with heterosexual sex, and Peter was very much in the Radley vanguard. He purchased a violently snazzy tie and a bottle of Old Spice, and despite the predatory advances of acne about his features, he had enough elegance, urbanity and wit to score heavily with the opposite sex. On one occasion he almost managed to achieve sexual congress in the school organ loft. After each dance the boys would compile a chart of the 'Top Ten Tarts' among their number, selected for their success in getting off with the girls. Peter was repeatedly voted No. 2, to his intense disappointment. 'I was bubbling under for three terms. I'll never forget the boy who was No. 1: T. S. Blower. Terence Blower. It is indelibly planted upon my memory.'[16]

Otherwise, the only woman in the boys' orbit was the matron. Peter recalled that 'On one occasion, weak with laughter after a particularly hilarious episode of *The Goons*, I told her that I felt "strangely feeble". The good lady carried me to the bathroom, took off my pyjamas and gave me a bath. During the course of this she soaped my back with her bare hands. This innocent action caused me severe pleasure and embarrassment which I disguised with a large sponge. Later I exaggerated the incident to my friends, and intimated that rather more had gone on: thus an impeccable matron's name became sullied by the school's rumour-mills.'[17]

Peter's final triumph was saved for his last few weeks at the school. Along with its flourishing drama department and theatre, Radley possessed an entirely separate marionette theatre, created and run by Chris Ellis, the good-natured, enthusiastic and resourceful art master. Every year a traditional but substantial opera or light opera would be mounted with the assistance of the school orchestra, such as *The Magic Flute, The Beggar's Opera* or *The Pirates of Penzance*. In 1956, Ellis decided it was time for the boys to create their own original musical. He already knew Michael Bawtree to be a talented musician and arranger from previous productions, and a natural choice to compose the score; but he had no idea who should write the book. In the cloistered world of the art department, he had not yet come across the celebrated Peter Cook. So he asked the members of the Marionette Society to decide for themselves. The vote was unanimous, and Peter was approached to fulfil Ellis's unusual commission. The result was *The Black and While Blues*, the story of Mr Slump, an evangelical jazz musician who takes his band to Africa to convert the natives away from cannibalism. Peter not only wrote the script, but produced the play, carved many of the puppets' faces and took the lead role himself. About the only thing he couldn't do was sing very well – his voice was frustratingly unequal to the simplest musical task – so whenever Mr Slump burst into song, the head of the choir George Clare had to take over.

Peter spent much of his final term rushing round – 'like a maniac', according to one puppeteer, Ian Napier – organising auditions, holding rehearsals, persuading model-makers and puppeteers to join up, designing posters and selling tickets. He charmed the much-maligned matron and one of the master's wives into running up the costumes on their sewing machines. He persuaded a real girl – Diana Llewellyn Jones, daughter of one of the Social Tutors – to play the role of the Slump band's torch singer, Bertha Kittens. Creative abilities aside, Peter was revealing himself to be an organisational genius. 'He manipulated people in such a way that they were pleased to do it,' explains another of the puppeteers, Christopher Leigh. 'He had such a quick, dry sense of humour that the whole workshop was always in fits of laughter, whether things were going right or going wrong. He could always bring that smile to your face which made for such splendid working conditions, even though the workshop was extremely cramped as you might imagine. And after every show there was always an (illicit) party, which he was very much the ringleader of. He produced a great esprit de corps.'

Interference from the masters was kept to a minimum, although a poster showing an illustration of Bertha Kittens had to be withdrawn after a complaint from the Sub-Warden that she was showing too much leg. Chris Ellis, too, remained a little unsure of precisely what he had set in train: 'To cover possible weaknesses, I suggested that the book should be couched in rhyming couplets – and that is how it was reluctantly written.'[18] In fact this proviso almost certainly hampered rather than helped the scriptwriter. The production proved to be witty only in the *Salad Days* sense, 'educated' English humour in the tradition of Slade and Reynolds or Flanders and Swann, sung for the most part by small boys sounding exactly like Celia Johnson. Take for instance this female plea for a handsome suitor:

> If I could find one
> A handsome and kind one
> To give me a life I'd enjoy,
> Oh I'd be engaged to the boy.
> And then we'd go dancing together
> In cloudy and sunshiney weather
> But dash! I'd forgotten
> That all men are rotten.

Or this, from a number about the man-eating beasts of the African bush:

> Oh Lord deliver us
> From animals carnivorous
> Oh Lord protect us
> Let them not select us!

As befitted the son of an enlightened and humane Colonial Officer brought up in the conservative atmosphere of Radley College, the show's attitude to the African native was extremely well-intentioned, if rather patronising by today's standards:

> We've cocked a snook at the colour bar
> Hurrah for the female darkie!
> Black and white will always mix
> Who cares if the kids are khaki!

Thirty years before Paul McCartney and Stevie Wonder's *Ebony and Ivory* came Peter's equally earnest *Black and White*:

> We're just like two piano keys
> One is black and the other is white
> Both in perfect harmony
> And we keep in tune day and night

Peter later professed himself on a number of occasions to be seriously embarrassed by this 'diabolical' piece of work, which was not at all fair to his youthful self. 'It had a hideously naive premise and really was quite appalling,'[19] he informed Roger Wilmut in 1980. By 1986 he had mellowed in his approach, when he told John Hind that 'It was rather jolly, and pretty good for fourteen or fifteen. I still have people who come up to me and say it's better than anything I've done since.'[20] A guarded reappraisal, given that he had actually been eighteen when he had written it. What is not in doubt, though, is the enormous scale of its success in March 1956. After the first performance, tickets actually changed hands on the black market at several times their face value. The staff were delighted that such an innocuous tale had been so professionally produced, but what they had of course entirely missed was the layer of caricature within the performance that was causing all the excitement. The old Etonian African chief encountered by Slump, a character also played by Peter (who recited rather than sang his part in a kind of strangled Rex Harrison voice), was quite clearly based on the celebrated foibles of Ivor Gilliat. The Warden, too, was satirised at every turn, partly via the Eton connection. One of his catchphrases, an emphatic 'Not a scrap!', was echoed in the chorus line of the Slump Band's marching song, 'Not a jot, not a tittle, NOT A SCRAP!' sung very loud by all concerned. Mild stuff, perhaps, but not at Radley in 1956.

So successful was *The Black and White Blues* that when the third and final show finished, the cast trooped off to the Isis Recording Studios in Oxford to make a 78rpm record of various songs from the show, of which some five hundred copies were successfully offloaded on to boys and staff. Sadly, Michael Waite, a junior who played one of the female parts, was halfway through recording his solo number when his voice suddenly broke. 'I was of that age, unfortunately. The tapes rolled again, and yes, it happened again. After the third attempt Peter and Michael were so frustrated that they left it on the record.' Where it can still be heard today, under a ton of scratches.

There is no doubt that *The Black and White Blues*, along with his other stage triumphs, had ignited a spark within Peter, a tiny little flame of rebellion against his smooth passage towards the Foreign Office. He later confessed to *The Times* that he had secretly 'wanted to be an entertainer since puberty.' In his final report, Thompson spoke of a boy with 'an unruffled temperament who has had considerable influence, especially in his own cultural field. He has qualities – not least a certain elusiveness – which should render him a most useful member of the Foreign Service.' Peter himself, in the space marked 'Plans for the future' on his Leaving Boys Report Form, wrote 'BBC, Films, TV, Sherry.' It was intended as a joke, but like many a joke it concealed the truth.

The Radley generation of 1956 then broke up and went their separate ways, mostly into the army on National Service. From the autumn onwards, Jonathan Harlow would serve in the Mediterranean with the Royal Artillery, Noel Slocock with the Coldstream Guards. Avoiding this chore was Peter's next task, something he accomplished with customary urbanity and style. Drawing on the long-vanished childhood asthma that remained on his medical record, he claimed to have an allergy to feathers, which of course in those days filled every army pillow. It was explained to him with great regret that he would not be able to serve his country. Coolly, he urged the panel of officers interviewing him to change their minds. 'I begged, and said "Well, you know, if there's a real crisis, you will take me on?" They said yes. And the bloke behind me said, "What was that you had?" and I said "Allergy to feathers." So when he was asked various questions about his medical history, he said "Well I've got this allergy to feathers," and the officer said "How does it affect you?" and he said "I get this terrible pain in my back." And of course he went in A1, and was probably shot to pieces in Cyprus.'[21]

Peter was still not due up at Cambridge until October 1957, so it was arranged for him to spend the academic year of 1956–57 studying in France and Germany, as part of his relentless drive towards a place at the Foreign Office; but with six months of the old academic year still to go, it subsequently decided that a few additional months in Paris at the College Franco-Brittanique of the Cité Universitaire, starting immediately, wouldn't do him any harm. It certainly didn't; but he experienced more of a cultural and sexual awakening in those short months than any great linguistic leap. 'In the main I hung about trying to get to know women. That seemed to be the usual procedure. I was less aware of the beauty of the European landscape than the new-found qualities of womanhood,' he remembered.[22] Soon he had secured for himself his first ever proper girlfriend, a French girl; although frighteningly short of cash, he took her to the races at Longchamps and won a little more. Which was useful, as they had been forced to walk three miles from the nearest Metro station to get there because Peter couldn't afford the cab fare. At Whitsun, they hitch-hiked to the South of France, 'spending no more than our normal daily allowance in Paris,' as Peter dutifully assured his financially stretched parents.

Peter absorbed culture by the yard and reported the results back to Lyme Regis. To begin with, his reactions seem rather bemused. *The Threepenny Opera* was 'interesting but rather sordid'. Abel Gance's *Napoleon* – later to influence a parody silent film in *Not Only . . . But Also* – was 'a wonderful old film . . . really very funny.' He saw Manuela del Rio dance and Edith Piaf sing at the Olympia Music Hall, and became more enthusiastic. Piaf was 'marvellous, so good that I have been forced to buy one of her records'. He also hugely enjoyed *Les Enfants du Paradis*. Significantly for comic theorists hunting for influences, on 8 June 1956 Peter was delighted by 'a most strange play called "Les Chaises" by Ionesco, all about an old couple who are expecting hundreds of important guests who turn out to be imaginary. They hold ridiculous conversations with these non-existent people and eventually jump out of the window.'

Inspired by this surfeit of culture and by life in a Parisian garret, Peter took up oil painting. His first effort sold at a good price, but rather like the *Punch* articles, its successors failed to arouse any interest whatsoever. Unsurprisingly, Sir Arthur Streeb-Greebling seems to have shared this

period of Peter's youth. Interviewed by Ludovic Kennedy about life in
Paris he reminisced:

> *Sir Arthur*: It was a bit like London in the 60s actually, only in
> black and white and without any subtitles. I was very
> poor, had a pathetically weedy little moustache and
> I was absolutely homeless. But I was young and I
> desperately wanted to paint.
>
> *Kennedy*:   You knocked at the first door you came to.
>
> *Sir Arthur*: Yes, and I painted it. There was no answer, but the
> door swung open and there in the centre of the
> room was this most peculiar melting bed draped
> over an ironing board. I'd stumbled into the garret
> of Salvador Dali.
>
> *Kennedy*:   Fascinating.
>
> *Sir Arthur*: Yes, what looked like a melting mattress over an
> ironing board was in fact his landlady Madame
> Chevignon. Dali himself had had to leave in a
> hurry, due to an accident with a burning giraffe.[23]

Eventually, depression induced by constantly having to scrimp for cash
began to outweigh the cultural benefits of Parisian life: 'I have become
pretty fed up with my 75 franc restaurant. Invariably one starts with
radishes, then a scrap of nondescript meat followed by an apple or a
banana. Meals at the Cité Universitaire are much better value at 180
francs.' Except that Peter didn't have 180 francs, and the college was in
the grip of a German Measles epidemic. The inability to afford transport
was particularly trying: 'The other day we almost walked the length of
Paris along the side of the Seine, which was quite exhausting. One lives
and learns; I have now discovered that you are to tip the woman who
shows you to your seat in the cinema, and as far as I can see the only people
you are not expected to tip are the ticket collectors in the Metro.' Uncle
Roy and Aunt Joan came to the rescue, catching the boat-train over and
taking him out to lunch at 'Chez George's'. His parents kindly sent him *The
Radleian* to cheer him up, and Michael Bawtree wrote with the encouraging
news that he had played *The Black and White Blues* record to Sir Laurence
Olivier and Vivien Leigh. What they thought of it, he did not say. Before
his return home, Peter saved up enough cash for a last treat, and he and
his girlfriend visited the French Derby at Chantilly. 'It should be a lovely
night,' he wrote in anticipation. 'Dior clothes etc. After the recent debacles
in England I only hope an English horse runs away with the race.'

On 16 June, Peter said goodbye to his girlfriend for ever and flew home. His parents never knew about her: his letters home had always studiously avoided revealing who the other half of the ubiquitous 'we' was. He had to return, because it was almost time for the Henley Regatta. The ties of Radley were still strong – after all it had been his home for five years – and no Radley boy would dare to miss the Henley Regatta. In fact, so nostalgic was he feeling that he spent his spare time during the summer writing Thompson's Social play for the following term's drama festival. Entitled *He Who Laughs*, it was a one-act farce about a Martian spacecraft landing in suburbia, after which the entirely staid and responsible Martians become shocked by the goings-on behind the surburban net curtains. Peter never saw it performed.

Early that summer Noel Slocock's father lent his son a Hillman Huskey car, and he, Peter, Michael Bawtree, Jonathan Harlow and Peter Raby packed a couple of tents and set out to discover England. There was no set pattern to the trip. They simply zig-zagged across the country as the fancy took them, covering three thousand miles in ten days of idyllic summer weather that seemed to go on for ever. They started at Studley Priory in Oxfordshire, where Michael Bawtree's parents ran the hotel, then drove through the Cotswolds to the Forest of Dean, camped by the River Wye, then drove up to Wenlock Edge in order to stand atop it and read the Housman poem of the same name. They tracked back down to the New Forest, continued on to Devon to see Noel Slocock's grandmother, back up to Jonathan Harlow's home on the Northumberland moors, and finished the trip chewing bread and butter on Dancing Ledge at Swanage in Dorset. In the evenings, they cooked the simplest of food on open camp fires, deep in the forests. By night they sat beneath the stars in their sensible grey pullovers, drinking Benedictine, one or two of them puffing on pipes, ruminating about serious subjects, like men of the world – or at least, as they fondly imagined men of the world to ruminate. It was perhaps Peter's happiest time: utter contentment radiates from each and every face in Noel Slocock's photo album.

During the day, Peter would keep his friends amused with the usual stream of jokes. According to Michael Bawtree, 'I'm not sure that he had ever camped before, and it was quite a sight to behold this gangling, almost dandified and certainly highly urban figure crouching awkwardly beside a camp fire. He was not the best tent-putter-upper, cook or bottlewasher, but he was surely the funniest camper ever seen under canvas.'[24] Late in the evenings, however, when the pipes and the Benedictine came out, the flow of jokes dried up, and Peter talked seriously, as he only ever did when he felt very, very safe or very, very cowed.

Peter was almost certainly looking forward to spending the rest of the summer with his father, lazing on the flat grey stones of the Clapper Bridge at Postbridge, flyfishing in the River Dart, or playing mixed doubles at the Charmouth tennis club, as they were wont to do in their few precious days together. Alec had been home less than a year now, but he was bothered by the financial implications of having no job, and unsettled by the decision to put an end to a lifetime of travelling. John Stow, a Nigerian contemporary of his whose memoirs were published, considered and rejected the option that Alec had chosen, that of taking early retirement: 'When Sapper's Jim Maitland returned from abroad he was always immediately hailed as an old friend by the hall porter at his club, but this did not seem to happen to me. Since I could not pick up the threads easily with my old acquaintances, I found myself relying more and more on the friendship of those who had some knowledge of West Africa or other colonial territories. Hard as I tried to convince myself that I really wanted to give up the Service and take a job in England, I knew that at this stage I had cast off the moorings.'[25] At the beginning of June 1956, perhaps suffering from a similar rootlessness, Alec accepted an appointment to serve on the three-man British Caribbean Federal Capital Commission, charged with spending the summer touring the British Caribbean Federation in order to select a capital city. Eight days after Peter returned home from France, his father departed for the West Indies.

Instead, Peter spent a miserable summer working as a waiter to raise money. 'People are so *stupid* when they go into a restaurant. They always say things like "Is the fish any good?" As if you're likely to say, working for the place, "No, the fish is terrible, the pork is worse and the beef is disgraceful." I became so impatient. The legends about what they do when you send the soup back are true.'[26] He felt stalled. When the time came to leave for Germany at the start of his year studying abroad, he was grateful to get the train back on the tracks. Just before he did so, his father returned, in mid-September. The British Caribbean Federal Capital Commission had made three recommendations, all of which were completely ignored by the government, but the various rejected islands had composed a number of entertaining calypsos, variants on *Three Blind Mice* and so forth, deriding the Commission's choices. Alec brought a calypso record back for Peter, which became one of his favourites, along with *Why Do Fools Fall In Love?* by Frankie Lymon and the Teenagers, and *Heartbreak Hotel* by Elvis Presley. The Elvis record actually belonged to his sister Sarah: 'It was a 78, the first record I ever bought in my life, and for some unknown reason I kept it hidden,' she recalls. Peter was obviously curious enough about the rest of his family to go on little searches: 'One day at our house in Uplyme I heard it blasting out very loudly all over the house. Peter had found it, and thought it was a brilliant record, and so I felt very proud of my excellent taste.'

In October 1956 Peter set out by train for Koblenz in Germany, as he put it later, 'in an attempt to achieve sexual emancipation and to learn to speak fluent English.'[27] It was a disastrous journey, in which he was mistakenly advised to change platforms at Ostend by the stationmaster, and as a result arrived at his destination many hours late, in the middle of the night. The reality of his new billet was a far cry from the excitement he had anticipated: six months in the Koblenz suburbs with the von Wilds, a pleasant but essentially unexciting German family who lived on a hill far above the town. 'It is a very lonely view,' Peter wrote home. 'Just below us is the prison.' Every day he was taught German by an elderly lady, selected because she was charitable enough to teach him for nothing. After six months, he had negotiated an educational transfer to West Berlin.

By the time he arrived in the former German capital, still strewn with the rubble of war, Peter was crying out for a little excitement. The story of how he accidentally strayed into the East, and was arrested and jailed by the Communist authorities, is one that he often told against himself: in fact the truth is that it was a deliberate plan, devised on his first day in the city to liven things up. His new berth was another suburban family home, about forty-five minutes from the centre by S-Bahn. He discovered while riding out with his new host Herr Theile that the subway system was operated by the East German Government, and ran not just under East Berlin, but out of the city altogether on the Eastern side. After unpacking his things, he returned to the city centre and went straight to the British Embassy, to enquire about the rules governing the border. He then sat down to write to his parents. 'I asked whether it was alright to go into the East Sector of Berlin and they said yes, it was quite safe, provided I did not commit a crime, in which case, as we do not recognise the East German Government, they could do nothing for me. The Eastern 'Zone' is quite another thing; if I got into there I might well be clapped into a cell for a month or so. All the roads into the East Zone are, however, blocked, and the only way I could get there would be in the S-Bahn. I must be careful not to fall asleep and be carried on over the border.' It was as if he wanted to tell them what he had in mind, but did not dare.

A few days later, tanked up to the eyeballs on cheap booze, Peter 'fell asleep' on the S-Bahn, was carried into the Eastern Zone, was arrested by burly greatcoated soldiers and thrown into a dark cell. He was not cowed – the early days at Radley were finally coming in useful. In fact he glibly informed his interrogators that he wanted to defect to the East, because 'In the West we couldn't get these wonderful cardboard shoes and bits of string they were all queuing up for.' Peter later tended to regard this as too foolhardy a prank. 'I was such a prat. I was blind drunk and behaving like the archetypal football hooligan before it became fashionable,' he said.[28] Mercifully, after a brief imprisonment, a kindly East German not only released Peter but arranged for him to be driven to his digs in the West. He did not tell his parents where he had been, writing instead to ask if his peach trees had come up in the garden at Knollside.

Peter stayed just three weeks in Berlin, before moving on to Hamburg. Before he left, he visited the ruins of the Reichstag, saw and disliked his first opera, attended a trial – forming a habit that was to last a lifetime – and on his last night in the city, 3 April 1957, went to see Berlin's most famous political cabaret, the Porcupine Club. It was a trip that was to have momentous consequences for British comedy, for it was on that evening that he first had the idea for an equivalent British venue, that would one day become the Establishment Club. 'I thought the show was terribly bad. I spoke reasonably good German, and I thought the humour was very juvenile – says he at the age of nineteen! – but I thought, very early on, "Why isn't there the equivalent of this in London?" For a long time my major fear was that somebody would do the obvious and start it before me.'[29] Peter's own club would be more directly based, he explained later, on 'those satirical Berlin clubs of the 1930s that had done so much to prevent the rise of Adolf Hitler.'

Hamburg finally held out faint promise of the sexual emancipation that was beginning to seem such a distant prospect: 'With luck I should be able to meet some young people there, as the son of the family is about eighteen.' A few weeks after his arrival, though, this turned out to be a dead end. 'I have not really seen much of the son. I couldn't enthuse wildly over him', he wrote. Instead, he turned again to the theatre, and saw 'a very good production of *Faust*, which should be a great help for my future studies of this impossibly difficult play.' Peter later wrote the film *Bedazzled* for himself and Dudley Moore as a direct parody of *Faust*. His European trip, intended to provide linguistic ammunition for a career in the Foreign Office, was instead providing cultural reference points for a lifetime in comedy.

Peter's final port of call was Tours in France, and a course designed for English university students. It had already begun, on 11th April, but so desperate was he to acquire the company of some friends his own age that he was prepared to start late and catch up. It was an expensive course, so persuading his parents was a delicate matter. He pointed out that he could save them money in return by hiring a room and eating in the subsidised student cafeteria, rather than continuing to pay for full board with the series of dull, worthy suburban families they had helped arrange for him. That this would provide him with an added dash of independence was, of course, merely a peripheral consideration. His parents agreed to his joining the course; unfortunately, they did not look upon the other idea so kindly.

Peter arrived at Madame Bonnassin's residence in Tours one afternoon in early May with a cold and a sore throat, after a journey of nearly twenty-four hours, eighteen of them spent continuously sat upright in a train seat. He was hoping for a cup of tea, but had no such luck. 'Have you got some slippers?' barked Mme. Bonnassin, 'because we all go to bed very early and I don't want to be disturbed!' And then, without waiting for a reply, 'No visitors after seven o'clock!' 'I hardly dared ask her for my supper after that, so I went out and ate a very ordinary meal for 600 francs' wrote Peter dismally. No doubt mindful of the continued need for sexual emancipation, he went on to remind his parents how much cheaper the independent digs and subsidised student cafeteria option would be, should they ever consider it.

In fact, he did finally get himself a girlfriend, and this time he wrote to his parents to tell them about her. 'Lately I have been going out quite a lot with a very attractive Italian girl. She is very sweet and gay and what's more refuses to be paid for.' Money, it seems, was still a problem. 'The other night we went dancing at the "Paix". It was really very nice inside with a very good band, but the cabaret itself was not up to much.' The Establishment Club still hovered tantalisingly in his mind. 'We drank one glass of lemon each which cost us 600 francs apiece. Although 15% service was "compris" in the bill, the waiter looked absolutely furious when I failed to give him a further tip, and turned the empty plate upside down with a low hissing noise and a sullen expression.' The object of Peter's desire and enforced lack of generosity was called Floriana, the daughter of a Milanese shoe-manufacturer. He admitted later that it was 'a rather stilted one-way romance. One of my chatting-up techniques during that period was quoting Blaise Pascal to her. Pascal didn't have too many hints for seducing eighteen-year-olds, but he did tell me a little about getting them drunk.'[30]

Being starved of female company – and indeed of love and affection in general – for so long had created a craving that Peter was never really able to satisfy throughout his life. Being so starved of money for eighteen months, especially when he found some female company, was also to have a profound effect. Later, at the height of his fame, when he was married to or going out with some of the most desirable women imaginable, he always felt the urge to find yet more love and affection with other women;

and when he became fabulously rich, he was as likely to splash out in a fit of generosity and buy dinner for all twenty people in an expensive restaurant as he was to studiously avoid paying for coffee for two people in a corner cafe.

Peter's course ended on 30 June. On 29 June he was evicted by Madame Bonnassin. History does not record why, although it is not altogether impossible that Floriana had succumbed to his advances after 7 p.m. On 1 July, he said goodbye to her for ever and flew home to England, where Paul Butters had reserved him a place in a punt at the Henley Regatta. While he was out messing about in boats, his sister Sarah, who was obviously curious enough about the rest of her family to go on little searches, found the programme for a risqué show hidden in his room. 'It was French. There was a line-up of showgirl lovelies. I don't recall being shocked – they were so utterly, Amazonianly gorgeous and tall and sophisticated.' So it hadn't all been art and high culture then.

Peter spent the summer as a beachfront photographer at West Bay, where his charming manner earned him the then colossal sum of £20 per week. He loved every minute of it. When summer was over, and he was left with a large collection of unsold photographs, he took out an advert in a less-than-salubrious publication offering a dozen untouched original photographs in plain brown envelopes at five bob a time. The recipients could hardly complain. They did indeed receive completely untouched, original photographs, albeit of unwilling grandmothers and scowling snot-nosed kids. The dashing young entrepreneur, flushed with success, was subsequently elected President of the Torquay United Junior Supporters' Club for the forthcoming season.

Soon afterwards, in October 1957, Peter set off for Pembroke College, Cambridge, to complete the final stage of his training for the Foreign Office. Except, of course, that other attractions lay enticingly in his path.

CHAPTER 3

I Could Have Been a Judge, But I Never Had The Latin
Cambridge, 1957–60

Cambridge University in 1957 was an Aladdin's cave of opportunities, crammed with burgeoning young talents jostling for space with each other. In the field of drama, it was the generation that produced Ian McKellen, Derek Jacobi and Trevor Nunn. In the field of politics, the same generation spawned the likes of Leon Brittan, Michael Howard and Kenneth Clarke. In the field of comedy, there were John Bird and John Fortune to contend with. For Peter Cook, however, Cambridge appeared to be just another large impersonal educational institution of wooden benches, stone-flagged floors and rugby fields, of the kind he had spent his entire life shackled to. A place to be approached cautiously and respectfully, as he had approached Radley and St Bede's. Although confident of his own abilities, he was always riddled with the fear that others might not be. He was still a shy boy at heart. In its Footlights Club, Cambridge was the only university in Britain to possess a purpose-built vehicle for staging comedy revues of the kind he had made his speciality, but Peter did not apply to join. 'I didn't do too much writing in my first year, because I felt the Footlights was a tremendously elite club. I was too bashful to even consider applying for it.'[1] Such was his talent that Peter Cook could have conquered Cambridge inside twelve months, had he set himself to the task – and indeed, that is what he eventually did. But it would be a further six months before he was spurred into doing so, before he would even set foot – in creative terms – outside his college. He had been long enough in institutions to find them perversely comforting.

His first year room – on 'O' staircase, on the ground floor of New Court – was classic Oxbridge: a tall, grimy, gloomy box with two windows hewn high through the thick wall, each a twin arch criss-crossed by leaded glass, and filled to the brim with the possessions of the previous occupant who had not bothered to move out yet. He wrote encouragingly to his parents to tell them that he had been given his own gas ring, and had managed to buy a second-hand gown for 17/6 as opposed to paying 52/6 for a new one. 'I now see that I should have bought a few more pictures, as the walls seem a trifle bare – I had no idea that I would have such a large expanse to decorate,' he added. It was a cold, wet, discouraging evening, and he fell in aimlessly with John Butcher, a new neighbour. 'We trudged the streets together, rather nervous and wondering what we had let ourselves in for,' recalls Butcher. For once, Peter did not even attempt to keep his companion amused.

This reticence did not last long. That night he sat at his first dinner in Hall, amid a group of silent and directionless freshers who were clearly in need of a shepherd. Paul Sharpling sat opposite him. Peter knuckled down to the task in hand. 'Within minutes,' recounts Sharpling, 'he had become the centre of attraction, and those of us within earshot were laughing. That was a pattern which persisted for the following three years. Wherever Peter was, people laughed. At dinner a better word would probably be "choked", since listening to him and eating soon became impossible to achieve at the same time. He would seize on someone's chance remark, or a current event, allow his imagination free rein and transpose everything to a different and usually inappropriate level. When a section of one of the motorways was opened, he transposed it to the world of agriculture and gave a brilliant commentary on the opening of a new "pigway".' On another occasion, he spent the entire evening extemporising on the subject of gravel. 'His main thrust was to ridicule pomp and ceremony, and people who were carried away with it. He hated pomposity and artificiality.'

Within a few days the various political societies had come knocking on his door. As he explained to his parents, 'The Conservative and Liberal Clubs based all their appeal on their social life. The Labour Party seems to be the only one which really cares about politics.' Peter joined all of them, with the express intention of embarrassing visiting politicians, and subsequently made a fool of Lord Altrincham and Peter Thorneycroft with a judiciously constructed series of questions. 'Word filtered along that he was of course planning to go into the Diplomatic Service,' says Sir Peter Lloyd (a friend of his who became a Conservative MP), by way of explanation.

Peter also joined the Cambridge Union debating society, but after one speech, the familiar reek of the desire for power given off by his fellow members proved too distasteful: 'I remember people like Leon Brittan at

22, running around like a 44-year-old, making the same sort of debating points they're still making. It's a bit distressing when you find them running the country. They were all so self-important in their twenties that you would have thought they'd have grown out of it. I thought, I can do this, but I don't want to do this.'[2] Of course, one reason that Oxbridge has traditionally produced so many political satirists is that its undergraduates come face to face with their future political leaders at an early age, and realise then quite how many of them are social retards who join debating societies in order to find friends. Peter swiftly abandoned his foray into student politics and retreated into the insular society of Pembroke.

Tentative early friendships were formed over awkward coffees and sherries, in the manner of all first-year students since universities were invented. There was Mike Winterton, because Mike had done his National Service in Gibraltar. There was Clive Simeon, because Clive came from Eastbourne, and Peter could swap stories of eyeing up girls on the front during his trips to see Grandfather Mayo. There was Ogea Aboyade, because he came from Nigeria. There was Jeremy Cotton, who together with Peter, Ogea and a few others had a regular lunchtime competition going, to see who could eat the hottest curry at the local Indian restaurant. There was John Crabbe, who lived in the room upstairs and sometimes joined Peter for late night coffee. There were Ted Neather, Paul Sharpling, Chris Smith and Michael Wild, who shared Peter's French and German course. There were Tim Harrold, Peter Lloyd and the other members of the regular uproarious card schools that went on into the small hours in Peter's rooms. And of course, there were the members of the Pembroke College football team.

Peter was definitely at his happiest and most relaxed when playing football. He always derided his own efforts – 'I was the worst kind of player,' he once said, 'too flashy. I spent hours practising flicking the ball over my head.'[3] But his modesty and his somewhat gangly, unco-ordinated appearance were belied by a perfectly respectable level of ability. According to Tony Verity, who patrolled the opposite wing, 'He was no mean player, and galumphed sturdily up and down the left, occasionally delivering the ball to the serious pros who waited patiently in the goal area. But chiefly he made us laugh – even the pros; quite a skill on the football field.' If he fluffed a cross or missed a chance he'd simply stop, laugh at himself and apologise. Significantly, in the bar after the game, Peter wasn't the life and soul of the party. There were three much more conspicuous team jokers. Halfdan Johnson, the side's Danish captain, reckons that 'He enjoyed being one of the boys and not being expected to be the centre of attention. In fact it rather surprised us when we realised that he had this other life as a successful humorist.' It was one of the very few areas of Peter's life where he felt free of the pressure to keep the laughter going.

In many respects, being at Pembroke College was like being in the sixth form at Radley, only without the compulsory rugby. The Junior Common Room echoed with laughter as the Prefects' Common Room had done a year or so before, and people would queue up to read Peter's latest witty essay in the College Food Complaints Book. There were similar boys' excursions to the pictures. And of course, the depressing lack of female company had not changed either. 'My experience of pursuing girls was always so miserable,' moaned Peter, 'I remember so many futile treks to places in Cambridge where Swedish, French and German girls were studying English. I remember so many foul ham salad lunches, trying to strike up a conversation in various faltering tongues for a date. Also, it's rather a strain going out in the evening to parties with the avowed intent of collecting someone worthwhile.'[4]

By the end of his first term Peter was well-known throughout Pembroke College, and firmly installed as its comic heart. He continued to be both respectful to authority, and to prod it calculatedly, like a lion-tamer. One night he and a friend, Robin Voelcker, were walking through the streets of Cambridge in their gowns, as was compulsory in those days, when they had the misfortune to run into the University Proctor and two Bulldogs (University Police). Peter's shabby second-hand gown 'looked as if most of it had been left on some railings, since so much of it was missing,' recalls Voelcker. The Bulldogs ordered Peter to present himself to the Proctor, who informed him that he was to be disciplined for being improperly dressed, and demanded to know his name and college. Peter started to flap the remains of his gown slowly up and down, while the trio looked on in astonishment. Then he informed them that he was *The Vampire*, and flapped off into the dark, leaving Voelcker to explain as best he could.

On another occasion the same pair were idling away the time in the Anchor Coffee Bar when Peter noticed (perhaps a little wistfully) a courting couple gazing into each other's eyes at the next table. He began to stare at them intently, and eventually announced in the tones of Mr Boylett, 'I have been watching you.' A little while later, when they had done absolutely nothing, he said 'I saw that'; and shortly afterwards, when they had continued to do absolutely nothing at all, added 'If you do that again I shall report you to the management.' Purple-faced with embarrassment at the thought of what crimes they were presumed to have committed, the couple pushed back their chairs and fled.

Peter could invent a character and disappear into it. Perusing a theatre

programme with Michael Wild, he saw the phrase 'Printed by Smith &
Co [or some such], dramatic printers', at the bottom of the page. That
was the cue to strike an exaggerated pose and announce: 'Oh my *God*,
you've lost the galley proofs. How unutterably *tragic*.' Peter particularly
enjoyed baiting anyone blindly committed to a given point of view. He
satirised the college CND faction in the Common Room Book with an
impassioned attack on the Dean's use of string to fence off his rose bed,
raising fears of an uncontrolled string escalation. He even developed a
catchphrase, as if he were a professional comedian, which he would trot
out whenever anything went wrong: 'Oh, the shame of it.'

Robin Voelcker found him to be 'a pleasant and friendly person,
with one of the best brains and quickest wits I have ever encountered.
Having first been to Imperial College I thought I could hold my own in
conversation with almost anybody. However with Peter it was necessary
to think carefully before you spoke, since he could make fun of almost any
remark.' He could indeed be a little relentless; but he was so charming, so
good-natured, so thoughtful, so relaxed, so delighted to please, so modest
and so infectious in his humour that it hardly mattered. 'He seemed to
be fearless about speaking in public or making a fool of himself,' adds
Voelcker, which of course was the precise opposite of the true situation.
Peter was just deliberately jumping off the highest board. He had extra
cause for insecurity in that by avoiding National Service he had arrived
at College much younger than most of his year, who had seen a bit of
the world; that they generally looked up to him and not the other way
round is a tribute to his talent and his social graces. 'In fact,' says another
contemporary, Professor John Mattock, 'I suspect that most of us were
rather frightened of him, since he gave the impression of a sophistication
to which few of us could aspire.' Only when that impression broke down
would Peter be openly embarrassed. According to Chris Smith, 'I recall
him once arriving at one of our tutor's excruciating sherry parties with
his gown over his dinner jacket. It was a striking sight. And I remember
his quite bitter self-reproach at being over-dressed.' It had not occurred
to many of his colleagues that the public face of Peter Cook was partly
a means of furnishing comfort to its author. 'I realise now,' explains Paul
Sharpling, 'that his flippancy might have been a means of obscuring his
real personality.'

Like Radley College, Pembroke was possessed of first-class drama
facilities, which attracted Peter's performing instincts from the start. The
Pembroke Players, with more than a hundred paid-up members, was then
the second-largest student drama society in the country after the ADC, the
main Cambridge undergraduate theatre company that Peter was too shy

to join. Within a month of arriving at the college, he had appeared in the Pembroke Players' production of Thomas Love Peacock's *Nightmare Abbey* in the College Hall. It was not long before his fellow students were encouraging him to take centre stage and put on a comedy show of his own. There was a college tradition, somewhat dwindled, of holding 'Smoking Concerts' in the Old Reader: rather like Footlights smokers on a smaller scale, these were dinner-jacketed cabarets in which students tried out their material on each other through a thick fug of tobacco smoke. Audience members tended to mete out a warm reception, in the knowledge that the roles were to be reversed later in the evening.

Peter resuscitated this ailing tradition, with a series of shows dominated by himself; he unleashed a torrent of high-grade sketch material, much of which was to find its way on to the West End stage or into *Beyond the Fringe* within a few years. Arthur Boylett was the principal character, whose doleful monologues were edited down from long Boylett-conversations held with Tim Harrold and another friend, Jack Altman. Before long the entire college had caught the bug, and students would greet each other with the phrase 'I thought I saw it move' in reedy, nasal tones. If the characters were familiar, the subject matter was not as parochial as it had been at Radley; Peter's gallery of dullards and obsessives began to hold forth about more universal themes. He cast about for new influences to cram into the comic maw, and ordered a batch of humorous records from the States, many of them by Mort Sahl. 'He played them interminably and filleted them,' according to his occasional collaborator Anthony Garrett. Sometimes the results could be shocking, for Peter loved to rouse the complacent: as part of an outdoor fund-raising street concert on poppy day, Peter wandered about Cambridge with his Nigerian friend Ogea Aboyade on the end of a dog lead. They were begging the inevitable question 'What on earth are you doing?', to which Peter would reply, 'I'm just taking the wog for a walk.' It was an attack on racial prejudice blunter than any blunt instrument imaginable.

The dining table and the Junior Common Room served as the breeding ground for most of Peter's new material. More often than not he would sit with the leading lights of the Pembroke Players, Richard Imison, Patrick Hardy, Geoff Paxton and Clive Simeon, but it was always a loose and shifting group. Tony Verity remembers the pattern: 'Someone – not always Peter, by any means – would say something witty, facetious, acute; Peter would then, with the rest of us chipping in, develop the idea with comic logic, leaping off into the surreal world that was his trademark. He used and developed other people's material, later refining it and fitting it into his sketches. He also noticed carefully when people laughed during one of his impromptu fantasies.' When he got a really big laugh he would pause for a moment and jot the successful line down for future use.

This was how *Old J. J.*, the Initials Sketch, which eventually cropped up in *Beyond the Fringe* and *Not Only ... But Also*, first saw the light of day. John Crabbe recalls 'the embryo version being batted to and fro across the table, with some extra material being supplied by those of us who had been in the forces.' Then Peter and Tim Harrold went off to write it all down. By the mid-sixties, it hadn't changed much:

> *Peter*: What's HL up to?
> *Dudley*: Oh, minding his Ps and Qs I think. I think he's mixed up in this NEDC thing.
> *Peter*: I thought it was the EEC.
> *Dudley*: Could be, yes, could be. How's BN by the way?
> *Peter*: BN? BN? He's OK. Bit short of the old LSD. I saw TD the other day, at the YMCA.
> *Dudley*: I though he was with TWA in LA.
> *Peter*: No, he's with BEA in NW3. You're thinking of DG. DG is a VIP in the USA.
> *Dudley*: Oh, correct, yes.
> *Peter*: You heard about old HK?
> *Dudley*: No, what?
> *Peter*: Oh, he did frightfully well. Picked up the VC in Germany. At least, I think that's what his mother said.

'He held centre stage in every way,' remembers Clive Simeon. 'He had a natural, captivating ambience without being over-dominating. He had a great sense of timing, a great command of the language and was very clever in judging the mood of his audience. Above all, he was never boring.' Not everyone was so appreciative of his comic talents. Peter sent all the material he wrote to the BBC, and all of it was rejected. One of the reasons so much of it turned up later on television was the delight he took in successfully resubmitting it after he became famous.

That winter Peter's old schoolfriends Noel Slocock and Peter Raby obtained a few weeks' leave from National Service, and together with two other Old Radleians hired *The Maid Marguerita*, a 42-foot covered launch, which they navigated from Thames Ditton to Henley against the current. Peter preferred to spend an extended Christmas with his family than go on the whole holiday, but in the New Year he joined up with the party for a few days. It was a freezing January, and a series of grumbling lock-keepers had to be enticed out of their cosy bolt-holes to smooth *The*

Maid Marguerita's passage upstream. At Henley they hosted a magnificent drinks party for forty people, mostly from the Radley area; but that night there was a tremendous amount of rain and the river went into spate, crucially reducing the amount of clearance offered by the arches of Henley Bridge. 'What happened next was entirely Noel's fault,' claims Peter Raby. 'The following morning we cast off, but it was clear that we weren't going to get through the arch. So Noel attempted a turn, which merely meant that we took the bridge broadside.' The river took charge of the helpless craft and sent it spinning at full speed into the arch. With a tremendous crack of glass and splintering wood the entire cabin was ripped off, and *The Maid Marguerita* wedged itself firmly beneath the bridge.

The damage ran into thousands. The holidaymakers had to clamber up and over the guardrail of the bridge to escape to safety, where they had no option but to check into the Angel Inn. 'Our main feeling at the time was not what a disaster it was, but what a wonderful adventure,' says Slocock, the adrenalin rush and sense of relief he felt temporarily outweighing the fact that he would soon have to face his father. Two canoes and a winch operating from each bank were required to dislodge the vessel, which then took three days to patch up sufficiently to make the return trip. All the way back to Thames Ditton, the cabinless youths had to run the embarrassing gauntlet of several extremely satisfied, grinning lock-keepers.

Peter spent most of the rest of his first year at the gainful business of entertaining his fellow Pembroke undergraduates. His work did not suffer; whatever inner conflicts about his future path may have inwardly troubled him, he made it known to all that he was determined to knuckle down and make it to the Foreign Office. Cambridge University, of course, offered more academic flexibility and less immediate discipline than Radley. Paul Sharpling, who studied Racine with him, remembers 'An incisive literary critic with a very sharp appreciation of language. At one particular supervision he produced a hilarious parody of Racine's *Athalie*, in which he cast the present Queen as the heroine and Harold Wilson as the High Priest. He developed this into an equally splendid essay. His contributions at supervisions were as funny as his contributions at the dining table.' If the tutor concerned had a more forbidding demeanour, however, Peter instinctively kept his head down. Chris Smith, who studied Molière with him under the upright and daunting Dr Combe, remembers him as a quiet, unexceptional student with nothing very extraordinary to say. (He was certainly paying attention, however. Combe's favourite phrase 'La condition humaine' was to crop up, along with a number of other academic references, in subsequent Pete and Dud sketches.)

Peter's reaction to academic authority, like his reaction to most things, was to try and keep it pleased with him. At school, under the constant eye of a teacher, this approach demanded and received a high level of effort. At university, he began to realise that it was possible to slacken off a little, to enjoy himself and use his native wit to bluff his way around the odd sticky moment, without arousing any official ire. Professor John Hunter, then a medical student on Peter's staircase, says that 'After a term or so I realised that I wouldn't pass any medical exam at Pembroke if I joined the Cook entourage, however fun it might be.'

One day at the end of February 1958 Adrian Slade, the President of the Footlights Club, was sitting in his Cambridge rooms reflecting on the first, disappointing smoker of the new term, when his reverie was interrupted by the arrival of 'a long, thin, hesitant person with dashing, darting eyes'.[5] The stranger enquired haltingly about joining the Footlights. Slade enquired whether he had ever written anything. Yes, said Peter, and produced a sketch called *Polar Bores*, that affectionately mocked this country's proud tradition of Antarctic exploration. It consisted of an interview with Polar adventurer 'Scribble' Gibbons, who uttered such variations on stiff-upper-lipped clichés as 'Communications were to be our only link with the outside world.' Describing his last expedition, Gibbons explained that he had 'set up camp and prepared to set out the next morning. But we hadn't prepared for the polar nights, and for six months we waited for the dawn to break.'

Slade read the sketch and laughed. Recognising an opportunity when he saw it, he even offered to perform it with Peter at the next Footlights smoker. Where had he been since October? Slade wanted to know. 'Playing football,' said Peter. He had been 'much too frightened to approach the Footlights,' he said. Slade was intrigued by the apparent contradictions within his visitor. 'Despite the non-stop wit and nervous energy for which he later became well-known, here was a surprisingly shy extrovert. I believe he remained so. Take him off whatever stage others had put him on and he was often quiet and sometimes ill at ease. Insecurity made him his own worst, and probably only real enemy.'[6]

Slade asked him whether he had ever performed on stage – in a school show, for instance. It was as if he had lit the blue touch paper and had forgotten to stand well back. Peter was off, embarking on a two-hour Mr Boylett monologue that ranged from the methods used by ants and bees to organise their working schedules to his own plans for world domination, given that the world was about to come to an end. Slade suggested that Mr Boylett be added to the next smoker too. 'Why would anyone think it funny?' asked Peter, not at all disingenuously. Slade assured him that it was, and booked him in. A few days later, in a room above a restaurant in King's Parade, attired in a dirty mac and battered hat under the title *Mr Boylett Speaks*, Peter appeared in his first Footlights smoker. The Pembroke crowd all came along to laugh and cheer. 'The success was instant,' recounts Slade. 'A phenomenon was born and the [Boylett] language was immediately universally adopted. From that moment Cambridge cabaret and revue never looked back. A new generation of Footlights writing was born.'[7]

Never was there a better time for an aspiring comic to be joining the Footlights. Every June the Footlights Revue, comprising the wittiest material and performers to emerge from that year's smokers, was professionally mounted over two weeks at the Cambridge Arts Theatre. Both the 1954 show *Out of the Blue* and the 1955 effort *Between the Lines* had transferred to the West End of London, largely on the back of contributions made by Jonathan Miller; while the 1957 show *Share My Lettuce*, mainly the work of Bamber Gascoigne, had been purchased by the young theatre producer Michael Codron and recast in the West End with Kenneth Williams and Maggie Smith (which version Peter had been to see). Although still constrained, Radley marionette-style, by the format of rhyming couplets, Frederic Raphael in particular had contributed some biting moments to the earlier shows. The age of straw-hat-and-blazered song and dance was already coming to its end when Peter knocked on the door of Adrian Slade's room.

Peter wrote home excitedly about his first Footlights smoker, but was still sufficiently committed to the idea of becoming a diplomat to give up comedy for the duration of the summer term, when his exams were due. He spent most of May and June in a punt reading set texts, and did enough to score respectable if unspectacular grades in his first year exams, registering a 2:1 in French and a 2:2 in German. As the Pembroke first years relaxed in Hall after two grinding weeks bent over their Part 1 examination papers, Peter stood up and announced ironically: 'I must rush now. I have to swot for Part II.'

That summer saw his first ever big-screen role, as an extra in the Hardy Kruger film *Bachelor of Hearts*, which was partly set in Cambridge. Desperately short of cash, he and Anthony Garrett signed up at ten shillings a day to spend long hours hanging around in King's Parade. Garrett even volunteered to jump into the River Cam at four o'clock in the morning for a further ten shillings. Peter can be clearly seen in one scene from the film, standing in the street alongside Christopher Booker, the future co-founder of *Private Eye*. Booker remembers Peter keeping the bored extras amused with a stream of jokes.

In June, the Pembroke Players took a production of *The Merchant of Venice* on tour to Köln and Bielefeld. A letter had arrived the previous year addressed to 'The Cambridge Players', inviting them to perform to students in Germany, where Shakespeare was invariably to be found on the English syllabus. As there was no such organisation as the Cambridge Players, the postman put it through the letterbox at Pembroke, where the opportunity was seized and the German tour became a regular annual fixture. Each summer a production would be flung together hurriedly after the exams. *The Merchant of Venice* was a massive success, at least in the German sense of the word: each performance was packed out with earnest, academically-inclined students who hung straight-facedly on every word. 'It was rather intimidating,' recalls Tim Harrold. 'They had a nun at the end of each row. And the audience would all have their books out, going along following every line.' So popular was the production with public and press alike that two extra performances had to be mounted, and extracts were recorded for broadcast on German radio.

Peter played Launcelot Gobbo, delivering his lines at breakneck speed in a nasal whine. 'It was as if the part had been written for him,' enthuses his fellow tourist Geoffrey Allibone. 'His scene with Old Gobbo, played by Richard Imison [later Head of BBC Radio Drama], was a show-stopper.' In fact, Peter had not learnt his part thoroughly, owing to the lack of time involved, but he made up in bravado what he lacked in accuracy. According to Peter Lloyd, who played Solanio, 'I don't think Launcelot Gobbo stuck closely to what Shakespeare had provided for him. He would chop the lines up differently. I remember him on stage looking extremely lanky and funny, giggling, head back, and occasionally dropping into the voice of Mr Boylett' (Peter's performance was, curiously enough, in keeping with the Elizabethan practice of giving the part to the company's clown, who would improvise many of the lines). *The Merchant of Venice*, of course, was a delicate choice of text for a German audience just thirteen years after the end of the war, and perhaps it is no coincidence that the lines most likely to be 'chopped up' were the ones closest to the bone. The word 'Judes' was invariably delivered as 'Jews', elongated and emphasised for effect, with a leer at the audience. It was no doubt extremely lucky for international relations that the part of Shylock himself had been given, successfully, to Patrick Hardy. The earnest Teutonic audience, no doubt thinking they had misread the lines on their set texts, simply lapped it up.

Listening to the performances today, they are – with the exception of Launcelot Gobbo – very much of their time, the kind of high-projectile, thigh-slapping Shakespeare destroyed for ever by *Beyond the Fringe*. The Shakespeare parody in that show, *So That's the Way You Like It*, although largely the work of Jonathan Miller, undoubtedly owed a little to the Pembroke Players: not least the fact that Peter, who always liked to vary a performance from one night to the next, had shown himself reasonably capable of improvising in the Shakespearean idiom. More significantly, he had proved to himself that he could pull off a stage triumph without actually learning all his lines. It was to be a discovery that prefigured a gradual decline in application. Peter could easily have brushed up a few lines here and there during the three-week trip, but not unnaturally he preferred to revel in the party atmosphere that prevailed in the spartan former prison where the Players had been billeted.

Peter spent the rest of the summer in Uplyme, where he filled the house with music: Elvis Presley, Chuck Berry, Buddy Holly, and the Coasters' *Yakety Yak*, which was the latest thing that August. He also expanded his collection of loud rock 'n' roll ties, pride of place going to a violent pale-blue silk kipper number with musical notes on it. Such attire, it should be stressed, only came out at night; for the most part Peter dressed extremely conservatively, in the sensible pullover and tie that marked him out as the Radley boy he still was. The football season was over, so the President of the Junior Supporters' Club had missed his chance to travel down to Torquay to see United play. The 1957–58 season had been the last one to feature the old regional leagues. The brand new Division 4 had been created and Torquay were promptly relegated into it. 'I was thought to be a Jonah, so I resigned,' said Peter.[8] His ties with the region were gradually loosening.

The following October he resumed his temporarily suspended performing career at the Footlights smokers. Audiences, as before, found themselves laughing uproariously at the strange, obsessional world of Mr Boylett. Word spread quickly. Among those who came to see the much talked-about new star was John Bird, who found himself so impressed that he invited himself round to Pembroke College for tea. A Nottingham grammar school boy in his fourth year at King's College, Bird was regarded as a serious heavyweight in undergraduate drama circles. His speciality was surrealist, absurdist comedy: he had already mounted an Ionesco production at Cambridge, and was in the process of casting *A Resounding Tinkle*, the first work by N. F. Simpson. The play had already been put on at the Royal Court Theatre in London, but only in a truncated one-act form, because – after a failed earlier attempt – its director William Gaskill had become convinced that the piece was 'unplayable'. Bird had other ideas, and was determined to put on the whole work. He had seen the two 'unknowns' he wanted to cast in the lead roles – Peter and a young Newnham College Modern Languages student named Eleanor Bron – and had decided to pay each of them a visit. 'I wanted Peter not because he was one of the Cambridge actors – he wasn't then or ever really an actor – but because I thought he would understand Simpson's humour,' he says.[9]

Bird was quite astonished by his tea party with Peter Cook, who pulled out all the stops to entertain him. He found it difficult to believe the contrast between Peter's 'charming, gracious, almost courtly manners' and the ceaseless flow of humour that made Bird laugh until the tears were running down his cheeks. He told Alan Bennett later that Peter 'was utterly at the mercy of language. It was this unstoppable flow, John said, that made Peter almost to be pitied.'[10] Bird rushed straight round to his appointment with Eleanor Bron, and announced breathlessly that 'he had just met the funniest man in England'. Both she and Peter accepted their roles on the spot.

It seems bizarre to think of one student nervously regarding another student at the same university as a 'heavyweight', but such is the way college life, and particularly Oxbridge life in the late fifties, parodied the forty-year span of adult existence, compressing the transition from wide-eyed school-leaver to retiring theatrical grandee into just three or four years. Student journalists really did write about final-year actors and writers with the hushed reverence then usually reserved for national celebrities. Peter Raby and Jonathan Harlow, Peter's Radleian friends who had gone off to do National Service, arrived at Cambridge now to find their former classmate on the verge of such stardom. Not that it affected his attitude in any way: the three of them went to lunch, which Peter spent in the persona of a religious eccentric who claimed to be carrying the Holy Bee of Ephesus in a cardboard box, an insect which he said had once buzzed about the true cross, a lunch which the Radley pair spent in fits of laughter. Raby subsequently entered and won a freshman's poetry competition in *Granta*. His grand prize was to share a salad and paté lunch with the magazine's student editors, and their guest of honour John Bird. Neither Bird nor the editors passed a word in his direction throughout the entire meal.

Despite his newfound success, Peter did his best to maintain his Pembroke contacts. On Poppy Day he and Jack Altman devised that year's fund-raising outdoor college revue, *The Seventh Deadly Seal*, a parody of Bergman's *Seventh Seal* crossed with the seven deadly sins. It took the form of an extended sketch, performed four times in one afternoon on Mill Bridge, where Peter had parked a float on which a crowd of people flagellated themselves while proclaiming the end of the world. Peter himself played a Swedish subtitle. Rather mysteriously for the uninitiated, the handbills for the play consisted mainly of a list of bogus endorsements from Mr Boylett. At the end of November, he performed in *The Alchemist* once again for the Pembroke Players, this time in the character of Dapper. The College Hall was packed out for each of the three nights, and it became the first show in the history of the Players to turn a financial profit. Press reviews were good (these were the days when national newspapers covered Oxbridge student plays), but Peter's slightly camp overacted performance was one of the few not to be picked out by any reviewer.

On 17 November 1958 Peter was twenty-one, and returned home to Uplyme for a weekend birthday party. He was given a typewriter to write sketches on and a cigarette lighter, as he was enjoying a flirtation with tobacco. It was an important occasion in one unusual respect: Peter and his two sisters had each been left about £2,000 by an elderly cousin some years previously, which was to be left in the Bridgewater and West of England Building Society until their twenty-first birthdays. Suddenly, Peter had become – by undergraduate standards – immensely rich. He would never need to worry about counting the pennies again (although of course he often did from habit). He invested most of it in property in Cambridge, but was careful to set a substantial sum aside, to spend on wild parties. From this date onwards, Peter became an inveterate partygiver. The first, five days after his official birthday party, was a joint twenty-first organised with Jack Altman and Nick Fleming. The invitation read 'An Add Hock party: Social Intercourse in the Union cellars', and was accredited (in Peter's case) to 'Mr Boylett'. There followed a series of Boylett parties, always subtitled with the legend 'Social Intercourse', ranging from lunchtime drinks on the college lawns to late-night revels in Peter's digs on the Cherryhinton Road. Invitations were highly prized, as Peter's parties tended to be exciting. John Mattock remembers Peter doing an impression of his landlady's reaction to the scene of devastation in his room one morning after: 'The first thing she said to him was (and you really have to hear Peter doing his Cambridge town voice), "Oooh, Mr Cook, if I'd known you'd got friends, I'd never have had you".'

With increasing fame and riches and wild parties came all the girlfriends Peter had been forlornly missing out on for so long. John Hunter remembers 'happily bathing away in one of those bathroom cubicles in college, only to be "woken up" by a woman singing in the next door bath – unheard of in a strictly male college like Pembroke. She was Peter's live-in girlfriend of the day, a very attractive Indian girl. Apparently, he liked to spin her out of her sari.' According to John Butcher, 'There were a few quite hectic female comings and goings in his digs. I think the rear window was normally kept open as an escape route.' Peter was like a child who had finally been given the keys to the sweetshop. One girlfriend claimed to have become pregnant, and insisted that Peter – who was rather suspicious – should stump up part of his legacy to pay for an abortion. It would not be the first such payment.

The female friend who aroused the most admiration among his fellows was undoubtedly Eleanor Bron. Clever and darkly pretty with heavy-lidded eyes and a rich, seductive voice, she in turn found him 'incredibly, effortlessly charming, as well as being extremely dashing and good to look upon. He had the most beautiful blue eyes and enviably long lashes and would look down the side of his cheek at you . . . a sort of haughty, oblique, slightly distancing, testing look.'[11] He delighted in her company, and the admiring glances it aroused among his male friends from Pembroke, who observed them as they sat beside each other at the Mill Lane Lecture Rooms. Peter had not had sufficient experience of female company to suppress a little masculine insecurity: his course-mate Chris Smith remembers that 'There was a story, spread by Peter, about the use he made of her German literature notes. The only comment I can make is that if he did, it was with a bit less success than was sometimes suggested.'

A Resounding Tinkle opened at the ADC Theatre in January 1959, with Peter as Bro Paradock and Eleanor Bron as Middie Paradock. The cast also included Timothy Birdsall, later to become a regular on That Was the Week That Was, Geoffrey Pattie, who went on to become a minister in the Thatcher government, and Bill Wallis, the future Weekending regular. Wallis took on the 'strange but fairly palatable role' of a man from the Home Counties who had to spend the entire play pretending to be a member of the audience, before jumping to his feet near the end and objecting vociferously to the proceedings.

The Paradocks are a suburban couple who have an elephant delivered to their home, only to find it is bigger than the ones they have had delivered in the past:

> Middie: Tell them to come and collect it.
> Bro: And be without an elephant at all?
> Middie: We did without one the year we had a giraffe instead.

The surreal and absurdist nature of Simpson's material has led to frequent suggestions that Peter's student work was influenced by A Resounding Tinkle, and also by the work of Eugene Ionesco. John Bird is scornful of the idea, pointing out that Peter's style was already fully developed when he first encountered the play. The principal case for Ionesco as an influence rests on the production that Peter went to see in Paris in 1956. Bird is probably correct: not only was Peter's style developed early in life, but his major comic themes as an undergraduate – boredom, obsession, bees, creepy crawlies in cardboard boxes and the fantasy world of Mr Boylett – had all seized his imagination as a schoolboy.

The press were a lot kinder to the production than to N. F. Simpson himself. One reviewer complained that 'A play, like every work of art, must be composed as a logical unit and not as a haphazard succession of clever ideas which have no organic relationship to the work as a whole. It was certainly not John Bird's fault if we did not get satisfaction out of the play: if anything, his direction only added to the enjoyment of it. Still, Eleanor Bron and Peter Cook equally merit special praise for retaining fresh and alive the intentionally repetitive couple – in lesser hands they would have become tedious instead of gaining in vitality.'[12] The Royal Court Theatre was considerably more impressed, taking the production to London for a one-off performance and giving Bird the job of Assistant Director. Before leaving Cambridge to take up his post, the rising young star was prevailed upon to stay long enough to direct the 1959 Footlights Revue.

Peter wrote to tell his parents of the London transfer, in the bland, affectionate, almost schoolboyish style that was becoming increasingly distanced from the dazzlingly witty carouser and entertainer his fellow undergraduates knew: 'Dear Mummy and Daddy, I know it's a long time since I've written but as you will have guessed I have been particularly busy. The play was a great success (many thanks for your nice telegram). We played to full and enthusiastic houses, quite an achievement with apathetic Cambridge audiences. The cast were all great fun and the producer too was an extremely pleasant person. At the party after the last performance I had a long talk with the author, N. F. Simpson, a very interesting person. Our producer John Bird's flat is teeming with strange producers and writers from the Royal Court, and altogether I have been meeting some extremely interesting people.' With the exception of the achievements contained therein it was a letter he could easily have written at the age of thirteen.

John Bird and Eleanor Bron came to stay at Uplyme that Easter, and Bird was further surprised to discover the marked contrast between the Cambridge Peter Cook, who never stopped talking and making others laugh, and the quiet, affectionate, polite and indeed highly respectable Peter Cook, not necessarily the centre of attention, who nestled so comfortably in his family home. He and Peter went for a walk across the local golf course, where the Cook family were all members. Bird recalls: 'There was a howling gale blowing – it was a clifftop golf course – nobody else was around, and the wind was so loud you could hardly hear, so you had to shout to each other. And I remember stubbing my toe in a rabbit hole or something, and swearing, "Oh, bloody hell!" And Peter saying "Shhhh!" Genuinely, actually saying "Shhh! The members might hear you, you know."' The Cook family in their turn were quietly amused to discover that Bird, who always wore black, even sported a pair of black pyjamas.

Even before *A Resounding Tinkle* had opened, Peter had roped Eleanor Bron into a revue he was putting on at Pembroke. Performed over three nights at the Old Reader from 18 March, it was somewhat cumbersomely entitled *The Jolly Good Show involving (to a considerable extent) Music with some Richly Comic Interspersions by the Merry Pembroke Players (Theatrical People) and some Women too (two) Revue*. The other female cast member was Louise Burkim, whom he had spotted playing his own former role of Doll Common in *The Alchemist*. There were twenty-six sketches, all written by Peter, with the exception of a little additional material by Adrian Slade. Almost a year after their first meeting, the President of Footlights was helping out a mere College revue.

Mr Boylett was of course central to the proceedings, there was an early prototypical impersonation of the Prime Minister Harold Macmillan, and there was a Shakespeare parody prefiguring that in *Beyond the Fringe*. Entitled *The Best of the Bard*, it rolled several plays into one with Peter announcing the whole in the character of an American MC:

> An authentic anthology of genuine premasticated fact . . . cast your minds back to those versatile days when men were men and women were boys. Come with me to Elsinore, where mad, moody Hamlet paces the battlements overcome by his father's death, as was his father before him. The idle fool playfully buffets Hamlet's knee with his bladder . . .

Although well short of the heights attained by the later *Fringe* parody, the sketch contained a moment that did not fail to bring the house down each night, when Peter entered as a messenger and announced: 'I bring you safe conduct letters from the French that I may have intercourse with your Queen.'

The Revue also contained the first stage performance of a sketch that was to become a Cook favourite, *Interesting Facts*. In fact it was the earliest Mr Boylett sketch that Peter later considered good enough to perform throughout his adult life. Then entitled *Astounding Facts*, it involved Mr Boylett, armed with a diagram of the human intestine, buttonholing a hapless stranger with a barrage of useless and frequently incorrect information:

Boylett: Did you know you've got four miles of tubing in your stomach? You see how far the food has to travel? Four miles it has to go, and it takes four hours. That's a mile an hour it goes.

Man: I had no idea.

Boylett: That means you never get any really fresh food in your stomach. It's all at least four hours old.

Man: Fancy that.

Boylett: No I don't fancy that thank you very much, I don't fancy it at all.

Boylett then moved on to discuss the habits of the grasshopper:

Boylett: Do you know it has a disproportionate leaping ability, due to its very powerful hind legs, and it goes hop hop hop, all over arable land. That is land what is actually tilled by Arabs. And do you know an Arab can actually live for a whole year on one grain of rice?

Man: A whole year on one grain of rice?

Boylett: Yes . . . er, no. It's a mosquito that lives for a whole year on one grain of rice. I always get those two mixed up, because I've got them on the same page. See – that's 'mosquito' and 'muslim'.

In later years Peter improved this joke considerably, by having Boylett claim that he always got Arabs and mosquitoes muddled up 'because they were next to each other in the dictionary'. What were? queried his victim. 'Mosquitos and mosques,' replied Boylett glibly.

The show was a storming and extremely profitable success. According to one reviewer 'The cast, in which Eleanor Bron and Peter Cook were outstanding, maintained a consistently high level of entertainment.'[13] The only substandard note was Peter's determination to include a number of songs he had written lyrics for, some of which he also attempted to sing. Hugh Macdonald, who wrote the music and played the piano, says that 'On the whole he wasn't happy writing lyrics for music, in fact he had a terrible sense of pitch; I wouldn't go so far as to say he was tone deaf, but not far off, and we never gave him anything to sing if we could help it.' Eleanor Bron sang the sultry number that closed the evening, *Smoke Rings*, which was Peter's attempt to write a genuine torch song:

> Smoke rings blue, smoke rings grey
> But never so blue as I feel today.
> Smoke rings grey, smoke rings blue
> But never so grey as life without you.

Sadly, she too was hardly a diva. In a repeat of the *Black and White Blues* idea, the Pembroke Players made an LP record featuring excerpts from the show, together with a scene from *The Alchemist* and West German radio's choice cuts from *The Merchant of Venice*; Bron's decidedly flat performance was thus preserved on vinyl for eternity.

Although Peter did not know it, one member of the audience had come all the way from London to see him perform. At the beginning of term Donald Langdon, a young theatrical agent, had decided to employ a talent scout in Cambridge, and had settled on Tom Rosenthal, the Secretary of the ADC (Amateur Dramatic Company). Rosenthal, now the Chairman of Andre Deutsch books, was then a Pembroke College student, but on account of his interest in university drama had been slow off the mark in checking out the rising talent within his own college. Early in 1959 he had finally caught up with Peter's act at a Footlights smoker, and had thought him 'the funniest man I'd ever seen'. He immediately telephoned Langdon on the college payphone, and told him he had to come up and see the forthcoming Pembroke show. Langdon thought the whole idea was ridiculous. 'You must be joking, why should I come up to some tatty little college production?' Rosenthal kept shoving coins into the phonebox until Langdon's resistance was worn down. And so, after the show one night, Peter was greeted by a sleek, sharply tailored, well-fed military type in a British Warm camel overcoat, who offered to become his London agent. He accepted.

The realisation that things might get even bigger prompted Peter to conclude regretfully that he could not continue to misuse the name Arthur Boylett. Boylett was subsequently rechristened 'A. Grole'. By now, the character had become a Cambridge institution. Roger Law, the future co-deviser of *Spitting Image*, was then studying at the Cambridge School of Art, and had yet to come across Peter in person. 'But you heard Peter Cook, through the voice, before you met him. They all did the voice, all the students. You'd hear these young men in the Criterion pub doing this funny voice, that you couldn't make head nor tail of, because it was usually delivered very badly. It was an epidemic.' In fact, recalls Eleanor Bron, 'Peter's influence became nightmarish – I began to think we couldn't speak any other way.'[14]

One of the principal imitators, who even used the Boylett/Grole voice liberally in his own stage act, was an ambitious young first-year comedian called David Frost. Peter's companions were not overfond of Frost, whom they considered to be the worst sort of hanger-on. Bill Wallis, for instance: 'I remember having tea in a Cambridge teashop with Peter and a couple of others, when a frail spotty whining youth came and accosted Peter. When not offered a chair (for obvious reasons: his name was David Frost) this youth knelt at Peter's knee, and assiduously ignoring the party, gazed up wet-eyed with instant devotion; all the while making that nasal, whining, wittering sound like a chain-saw cutting into candyfloss – and which was, of course, the forerunner of the anodyne question disguised as a knuckleduster.' There was a standing joke at Cambridge, devised in fact by Christopher Booker, that the recipe for a bad joke was 'D. Frost and leave to Cook for five minutes.' Anything Peter said or did Frost would be saying it or doing it a few days later. 'They *loathed* David Frost, those Footlights people, he was a figure of fun to a whole generation for years and years,' says Wallis. They loathed everything about him, from his suburban accent to his silly little bicycle clips.

One person who didn't loathe David Frost was Peter Cook. He felt sorry for him, even affectionate towards him, according to Peter's first wife Wendy, for all the ridicule and contempt that Frost seemed to endure on his account. Of course he joked about Frost's apparent plagiarism too, but he also gave the young man a leg-up, by agreeing to appear with him at the next Footlights smoker in a double act that Frost had written. He liked it because it was funny, and perhaps because it seemed to enshrine their relationship. Entitled *Novel Reactions*, it involved Frost acting out a passage from a novel, as read out by Cook, which contained a series of increasingly unpleasant and degrading instructions. 'He bit his lips until the blood came', intoned Cook, whereupon Frost would baulk at the idea. 'Until the blood came,' Peter would intone more firmly, and Frost would take a deep breath and sink his teeth agonisingly into his lips.

Cook and Frost started to perform together in cabarets. Frost recalls: 'One of the first ones we did was at the Corn Exchange; the day before there had been a court case in which the Friar House, a rather popular but not particularly high quality restaurant in the centre of Cambridge, had been had up for only having one toilet. Peter bounded on to the stage the next night and said, "I have got good news for you. The Friar House now has two toilets. But they do the cooking in one of them." A great opening line.' Frost himself was ordered to appear before the local Magistrates' Court, to answer a charge of riding a bicycle without lights, and it took all his powers of persuasion to prevent Peter appearing as his defence counsel. Peter's intended plan was to stand up and announce that his client was not in England on the night in question, or if he was in England he was not in Cambridge, or if he was in Cambridge he did not possess a bicycle, or if he did possess a bicycle he certainly did not possess any lights; and then to become so confused that he would end up demanding the death penalty for his own client.

The Footlights Committee discussed the case of David Frost rather animatedly. 'Can we really allow this incredibly boring person into the Footlights?' was one point of view aired. Peter stuck up for him, and it was decided that even if he was boring he was at least harmless. As Peter later explained: 'They all thought in Footlights that David couldn't tell jokes, or make jokes up, or do anything funny, and therefore, because he was hard-working, he was given a job of some kind. And of course he was very good at being nice, and doing things like remembering people's names, and being industrious. He was a very bright lad, and we didn't know it.'[15]

Frost was by no means Peter's only comic partner. By now Peter was tearing about Cambridge like a dervish, appearing almost every night in some sort of show. The more people wanted him to make them laugh, the more he did his best to oblige them. He went on the road for out-of-town cabarets with Geoff Paxton and Hugh MacDonald – 'My memories of them are clouded in tears of laughter,' says MacDonald. He did a Charity Ball in front of 600 people at the Dorchester with Adrian Slade and Geoffrey Pattie, for which they were paid twenty guineas each. In Footlights smokers he tried out new characters, such as a cockney who referred to everything as 'Yer actual this' or 'Yer actual that' – a phrase that Cook invented; or Colonel Rutter, a voyeur whose accomplice kept pretty girls chatting while the Colonel lifted their skirts with his walking stick and gazed at their legs.

He also tried out new subjects for sketches, such as the Holy Bee of Ephesus, a routine based on his lunch with Peter Raby and Jonathan Harlow. The young Trevor Nunn was present when that idea made its debut: 'On the bill was a guy called Peter Cook who was doing his *Interesting Facts* sketch. He was dressed in the shabby raincoat and the shapeless cloth cap, and the sketch was a complete riot – I mean it was already a famous sketch, obviously, because there was a clamour for all of the well-known lines, you know, that Arabs live on a grain of rice a day and so on. And when he got to the end and took his bow the shouts for more were so huge and so unrelenting that Peter had to come back, and clearly he had to decide, am I going to do an encore or not? And he sat back down again, and the room went quiet. And he launched an improvisation – it was stuttering at first, it was clear that he was feeling around: where am I going to take this? After a few seconds he found a matchbox in his pocket. "I wonder whether you can hear what I can hear?" he said. There was a tremendous hush and concentration, and eventually he said "In here, in this box, I have . . . the Holy Bee of Ephesus." Which made the audience explode. That led him into this probably blasphemous improvisation, which became riotous, to the point where he said, "And the bee has told me that we are to expect a Saviour – a Messiah – who shall be called Brian.'"

Even though much of Peter's humour was indeed brilliantly spontaneous (not to mention highly influential), he liked the amazement he created when ideas and sketches seemed to spring forth fully formed. The showman in him was happy to use routines and comic flights of fancy again and again, whether the performance was a public or a private one. There are many people who cherish memories of a favourite moment of Cook spontaneity, which are in fact identical to the earlier memories of others.

Reconciling all this activity with his Modern Languages course was becoming harder and harder. 'Work is very heavy this term,' he wrote to his parents, 'as I have three full length essays to do per week and also a prose, apart from lectures and reading, so I have been burning the midnight oil a bit.' The truth of the matter was that despite even his tremendous energy, he was struggling to keep all the balls in the air at once: Chris Smith recalls 'an uncomfortable supervision when Dr Combe asked Peter whether he had in fact handed in an essay in advance, and then told him he might as well go away when he discovered he hadn't.' Peter assured his mother and father that he was keeping very fit and healthy nonetheless, and drinking plenty of orange juice. Later that Easter he was admitted to hospital with a leg ulcer so serious it required stitches.

Peter's leg was healed by the beginning of May, giving him just five weeks to prepare for the Footlights revue on 8 June, or for his exams on 4 June, but certainly not for both with any degree of thoroughness. The smokers, cabaret appearances and other work carried on unabated, including a disastrous (but well paid) performance in front of Great Yarmouth Young Conservatives, a cartoon strip in the *Spectator* co-written with Timothy Birdsall, and an appearance by a selection of Footlights performers before the Duke of Bedford at Woburn, to round off a dinner celebrating the publication of the Duke's autobiography. Peter wrote home: 'It was a very snob do, only about thirty guests including Lord Mancroft, Lady Barnett, Peter Sellers, Cyril Fletcher, Bernard Braden, Barbara Kelly etc., who had been asked more for their name than the fact that the Duke knew them; it was a marvellous dinner with more liveried footmen than guests. After dinner, that ended at 1.30 a.m., Cyril Fletcher started the ball rolling with the act that he was using at Quaglino's, very well done but rather old material. We followed and really we seemed to go down better than he; we did a special song about the Duke's eccentric ancestors, monologues and sketches. Bernard Braden came up to me afterwards and asked to see my script, and we talked for about half an hour about it and possible improvements that could be made; he was very charming and most gratifyingly complimentary; we then had a great time fooling about with Peter Sellers, who was also extremely pleasant, and what was more surprising, easily amused. I suppose we spent about an hour with him drinking liqueurs and didn't leave 'til 3.30 or so. Altogether a great experience.'

Peter was hugely taken with Sellers, one of his childhood heroes, and was to remain good friends with him.

That year's Footlights revue, *The Last Laugh*, was to be a turning point both in the history of the Footlights and in Peter's career. There would be no room for Flanders and Swann-style musical numbers with John Bird in charge. The show was set in an underground nuclear bunker, where scientists awaited the destruction of the world, and included DIY instructions on how to make your own coffin. Every sketch ended with a stated or implied death. The musical accompaniment was provided by a ten-piece modern jazz group under the direction of Patrick Gowers. The show was technically complicated, including taped inserts and back projections. There would be no easy laughs provided by men appearing in drag either; after a long campaign by Peter and John Bird the Footlights' traditional males-only rule had been scrapped to make room for Eleanor Bron.

Adopting a political stance far to the left of the Labour Party (and thereby inadvertently achieving a sort of party political neutrality), the show sought to capture and define the mood that had led 50,000 people to gather for a CND rally in Trafalgar Square at Easter. According to Roger Law, 'It is hard, looking back, to recapture the intensity and anger of that period, but I think it boiled down to a feeling that we had been hoodwinked about the nature and extent of the nuclear threat.'[16] All over Cambridge, public school students who had arrived in the city wearing cavalry twill trousers, coloured waistcoats and tweed sports coats were hurriedly casting them off along with their accents, and donning roll-neck pullovers and bogus cockney vowels instead. 'There was a feeling of throwing off our chains, our bonds,' says Bill Wallis. 'I remember being accosted by somebody who was an exact contemporary in the grounds of Pembroke College, who accused me of being a class traitor. And I said "Why?", and he said "Because all your friends are from public school."' The bomb was hanging over the world, and there did not seem to be much future for tradition.

The reason for such an all-consuming social and political shift, other than the simple consequences of world events, lay in the pattern of National Service recruitment and the reactions of those who had been put through it. It was only beginning to dawn on the powers-that-be that inculcating in tens of thousands of young men a venomous hatred of their superiors and a distrustful contempt for the military mind was not socially cohesive. Middle-class boys from schools like Radley had encountered the working classes in the army for the first time, and had experienced guilt. Full-blooded socialism, which still appeared to be a workable principle, became their absolution. Changes in working practices were having their effect too. Traditional areas of Government like the Colonial Service were shrinking, while TV and the media were expanding rapidly, with opportunities for graduates to escape their formerly predetermined lives. Peter's generation, the first to have little or no consciousness of prewar society, felt themselves in a position to become personally instrumental in sweeping away the old order.

Ironically Peter himself, whose energy and talent were to make him very much the driving force behind the early '60s satire boom, did not fit this pattern. He was comfortable with the system because he knew how to play it. He had been too smart to do National Service. The pomposity of officialdom had irked him since he was eight, so it hardly came as a revelation to him now. There was nothing to spur him politically leftwards: he was not a socialist. He disliked both Labour and the Conservatives from a position of general cynicism, as opposed to Bird's position on the extreme left. He remained conservative with a small 'c': he was not about to change his public school clothes. The only thing he changed was his upper-middle-class accent, and that is because he wanted people to like him. 'I felt daft with this peculiar voice that I had. I could have got it back in about a week if I got a job in the Foreign Office, but it was too inhibiting. Have you ever imagined an Englishman with that accent actually in bed? I can't see it myself.'[17] In short, girls in Cambridge in 1959 didn't go to bed with boys who had posh voices.

The Last Laugh was the first overtly political work to harness Peter's humour to its cause. Of course Peter's material fitted Bird's vision: his comedy mocked the characters and attitudes he had grown up with, and as he had grown up in the bosom of the establishment the match was a good one; but the motivation was different. Only a few weeks before he had been happy to play the same material, for money, to the Young Conservatives and the Duke of Bedford. Peter was not even a rebel in terms of comic taste: when other students aggressively attacked old-style comedians like Terry-Thomas, Peter would stoutly defend their professionalism and the standard of their material.

One thing Bird's revolutionary vision could not adequately cope with was the notion of Footlights-as-talent-contest, that somehow the year's best material had to be made to fit his concept. The result was an uneasy alliance between the linking device and a number of the sketches. Some ideas seemed to fit the general scheme: Peter's Antarctic sketch *Polar Bores*, a pastiche of a Prisoner-of-War film, and a parody of fox-hunting jargon penned by Peter and Adrian Slade. Other items, such as a Rodgers and Hammerstein version of *Oedipus Rex*, or the antics of Mr Grole, seemed utterly irrelevant.

According to Bird himself, 'Peter provided the only material that was actually funny.'[18] The audience certainly roared their approval for the nine sketches out of twenty-eight that he had written. Many of the sketches, such as *Guilty Party, Entitytainment* and *Mr Moses*, were veterans of the Pembroke revue. Most successful was the latest Mr Grole adventure, in which the character informed a fellow railway passenger, Mr Quorn (played by Timothy Birdsall), that the cardboard box on his knees contained a viper. It was most definitely a viper, he was at pains to point out, as distinct from an asp:

> *Grole*: If anything the viper is more voracious than the asp. My viper eats like a horse.
> *Quorn*: Like a horse, eh?
> *Grole*: Oh yes, I'd like a horse. Mind you, you'd never cram it into this little box.

It was the same verbal misunderstanding joke he had used on many occasions, and it seemed to get funnier every time.

Peter's more satirical material derived from his casting a principally parodic eye over the broadcast performances of officials. In *Don't Ask Me*, a version of *Any Questions?* questioner Arthur Grole of Hoveleigh and Gorlsden asks: 'Where are the Government road plans?' Captain L. G. Strile MP replies:

> I detest such a question. I regard it as untimely and in the worst possible taste. I refuse to descend to this level of personal abuse.

More typical of Peter's contribution was *Mr Moses*, a biblical variety turn:

> *First Man*:   Hello hello hello, who was that woman I saw you
>   with last night?
> *Second Man*:   That was no woman, that was Elosheba, daughter
>   of Amminadab, sister of Naashon, son of Mushi
>   and Jochabed.
>   (*Cue cymbal crash*)

Peter's contribution aside, the opening night was a disaster. The back projections broke down, and the show had been running for four-and-a-half earnest hours when the theatre manager came backstage and wearily told them to stop. For the first time in the history of the Footlights, the annual revue had been booed by the audience. Reeling from disastrous press reviews, Bird and the cast slashed the show to a tighter, more manageable length from the second night onwards. Luckily for Peter that was the night his parents came to see it. Luckily for all of them, the celebrated broadcaster Alistair Cooke also dropped by once it had been revised, because he wanted some visiting Americans to see what a typical Footlights revue was like. They saw nothing of the sort, but what they did get to see impressed him. He wrote in the *Manchester Guardian*:

> The whole show is acted with never a fumbling line or gesture, and since it is inconceivable that a dozen undergraduates can appear as fully-fledged professionals, the only inference is that in Mr John Bird, the (Footlights) club has a broth of a director. In fact, if the West End does not soon hear of John Bird, Patrick Gowers, Geoff Pattie and Peter Cook, the West End is an ass. In bringing in Miss Eleanor Bron, the Club has passed up the easy guffaws available in all public demonstrations of transvestism. Incidentally, they have got themselves a very fetching dish. She has a wolf-whistle figure, a confident pout, and needs only to practise singing in pitch to be something of a threat to the hoydens of the London Pavilion.[19]

Alistair Cooke's piece regenerated the considerable interest that the show had attracted before its first night, and Peter's agent Donald Langdon managed to persuade two West End producers, Willie Donaldson and Michael Codron, to come and see it. Truth be told, Donaldson was not a real theatre producer, simply a good friend of Langdon's who'd inherited a large sum of money and had ambitions in that direction.

Again, rather fortuitously for Peter, Donaldson didn't actually like his stuff, but came to the conclusion that Bird was a genius. So he bought up the sketches that Bird had written, hired him as a director, retitled the show *Here Is the News*, incorporated some new material written by N. F. Simpson and Eugene Ionesco, and reopened it at the New Theatre Oxford with a professional cast, including Sheila Hancock, Cleo Laine and Lance Percival. With disarming honesty, Donaldson admits: 'I was a complete idiot, who didn't know what I was doing. There wasn't any lighting for a start. I didn't know there was such a thing as lighting. Bird thought the designer Sean Kenny was doing it, and Sean Kenny thought Bird was doing it. It opened in Oxford with no lighting, with just the house lights on. I almost went bust.' Sheila Hancock later said that it was the angriest reaction from an audience she had ever had.

Langdon's other guest, however, did come up trumps. The altogether more professional Michael Codron, who had taken the Footlights revue *Share My Lettuce* to the West End and was looking to mount a new show, thought that Peter's material was simply hilarious. Again, fortune had smiled: Codron had already booked the star of his new show, Kenneth Williams, and was looking specifically for material that fitted the buttoned-up, boring, nasal outsider that Williams had made into a popular character in *Hancock's Half Hour*. Mr Grole, and particularly the sketch about the viper in the box, was exactly what he had been searching for. Peter, who was a big fan of Williams, jumped at the chance of becoming his writer. The actor was taken out to lunch by Codron, and confided to his diary that afternoon: 'He has found some v. good material from a boy called Peter Cook from Cambridge.' A subsequent lunch introduced Williams to Peter, who did enough to secure one of the most amazing commissions ever offered to a student: by the time he returned to Cambridge for the start of his third year, he would be the author of an entire West End show. This was not just a one-week transfer of some Footlights material for the novelty value of presenting a student show: this was an astonishing and unique offer. While it is true that *Look Back in Anger* had represented some sort of cultural watershed, and that producers were sniffing around the universities for exciting young talent, Codron was putting on a rumbustious old-style revue with dancing girls and glitzy sets. That he chose Peter Cook is a reflection both of Peter's astonishingly precocious development, the universal appeal of his material, and the tremendous coincidence that the Radley College High Table butler should have been prone to utterances that fitted Kenneth Williams's stage persona so well.

Peter was in a whirl of happiness. The rest of term passed in a haze of parties and shows, including appearances at 'May Balls' in Cambridge and in Oxford in June, where he and Michael Bawtree put on a double act at Worcester College. He was elected President of Footlights for the following year. He even stood for President of the Pembroke College Junior Parlour as well – heaven knows how he thought he'd manage it all – but was narrowly beaten to it by his friend John Dwyer. *Varsity*, the student newspaper, did a profile of Peter, listing his May Ball appearances, which was to be accompanied by a picture of Peter in black tie accompanied by a pretty young girl. Somebody on the staff of the paper knew of a pretty young girl: her name was Wendy Snowden, a student at the Cambridge School of Art with lush red hair. She was asked if she'd be kind enough to borrow a ball gown and appear in the picture. She said yes. Peter was about to meet his first wife.

'I had to sit on his lap I think, or I had to be draped around him,' she says. 'I was involved elsewhere at the time, with my first true love, and I thought Peter was incredibly full of himself. He was continually talking about himself and making a lot of jokes, and he had a bit of an acne problem. He certainly wasn't anybody that I'd have thought I'd have been spending quite a big chunk of my destiny with, absolutely not.' Peter later admitted that at that point in his life he was 'showing off to a greater degree than I ever have since. I was very, very ambitious. I liked buzzing around and being an eager beaver. Quite intolerable I should think.'[20] The pair were not to renew their acquaintance properly for another six months.

The Pembroke Players were back off to Germany to tour with *Julius Caesar* but Peter was too busy to go. He spent the first half of the summer in Uplyme, toiling away at *Pieces of Eight*, as the Kenneth Williams show was to be called. It was to be his last holiday at home with his family until Christmas the following year. The one disappointing note in all the celebrations was that Peter's father had taken a job as an Economic Adviser with the United Nations, and had been posted to Libya for twelve months. He had persuaded Margaret to come with him this time, along with their younger daughter Elizabeth: they would be gone by the end of the year. Sarah would stay at boarding school and with relatives during the holidays, while Peter would be left completely on his own. Crucially, his parents would be abroad when the time came to make the big decision about his Foreign Office career.

The script for *Pieces of Eight* was completed by the middle of August, by which time the cast had just two weeks' rehearsal time before its pre-West End tour of the provinces. Fenella Fielding was hired as the female lead, and the singer Myra de Groot was taken on to perform the songs, which were written by Sandy Wilson. It was not exactly radical stuff. Among Williams's offerings was a comic number called *True Blue Love Song*, featuring the tongue-in-cheek chorus line 'Don't let Labour ruin it.' That was the only political note. Most of Peter's contribution was based on his Footlights material, all of which had been rejected at one time or another by the BBC, for which he said he was 'profoundly grateful'. *Mr Moses* was there, and the viper-in-a-box sketch was the hit of the show. In fact this was not one of Peter's best Mr Grole sketches, containing as it did some terrible puns:

> *Man*: Would you be quiet?
> *Grole*: Bees aren't quiet.

or:

> *Man*: I'm finding your conversation a bit of a bore.
> *Grole*: There's no boar in my box.

Rather, the appeal of the sketch lay in its original conceit, and the lonely life of this strange obsessive character who put animals in boxes.

Other sketches charted a similar course. *If only* featured Williams as an elderly working-class man, so bored that he goes to the post box every day to watch the collection take place, listing all the wrong turnings he has taken during his life: if only he'd been born in Shropshire, if only he hadn't drunk milk, if only he'd had wings, if only he'd had more flesh on him ('People want to see great mounds of the stuff'), if only he'd had a glamorous name like Arthur Grangely. 'You are called Arthur Grangely,' his wife points out. 'That's what held me back,' he opines. *The Laughing Grains* was another sketch featuring an elderly working-class couple, retired music-hall artistes Mr and Mrs Fred Grain, bemoaning the decline in the theatre since the old days:

> *Fred*: They had no amplification in them days ... And do you know, when they sung, the people in the back row couldn't hear a word. That was part of their attraction – the element of mystery.

The additional material for the show was supplied by the then little-known Harold Pinter, most notably *The Last to Go*, in which Williams' elderly, bored news-vendor discusses which paper is usually the last to be sold, in an agonisingly slow, repetitive, drawn-out and pause-riddled delivery. Peter was not best pleased by the enormous length of the Pinter sketch. 'I was very cross at the time because royalties were awarded on the amount of time your contributions took up. Harold Pinter's contributions took up an immense amount of time because he'd written all these pauses into his sketches, which I called the "pay pause". I eventually submitted a sketch to Michael Codron which consisted almost entirely of significant pauses. But he knew perfectly well what I was up to, and it was rejected.'[21] Kenneth Williams also supplied an idea for a sketch, which Peter dutifully wrote up, involving a pompous military type who refuses to eat foreign food in a restaurant; no matter how exotic the dish, for instance sheep's eyes, his sole criterion for deciding whether or not to eat it is the animal's nationality. There was also one nonsense song in the show, the lyrics of which Peter was allowed to write, the slightly dubious *Onu Beeby Frisky*.

Peter was immensely proud of his work: 'I loved that revue. It was old-fashioned revue, which was eventually killed off by *Beyond the Fringe*. I found nothing wrong with it.'[22] The curtain went up for the first time at Oxford's New Theatre on 1 September 1959, just ten minutes after the end of the dress run. Peter, racked with nerves, plied himself with brandies beforehand in the Mitre Hotel and forgot to post his sister Elizabeth's birthday present. He need not have worried: the show was received enthusiastically and achieved good notices in the local press.

Peter had been paid to accompany the show on tour in order to make last-minute script revisions. After a successful week in Oxford, *Pieces of Eight* played a further seven days at the Royal Court in Liverpool and seven more at the Theatre Royal, Brighton before opening at the Apollo in Shaftesbury Avenue on 24 September. The critics were even kinder in Liverpool, where the *Daily Mail*, the *Daily Mirror*, the *Chronicle* and the *Herald* all praised it to the skies. Peter wrote excitedly to his parents from the Lord Nelson Hotel to tell them the good news. He was slightly bemused, however, to discover how bitchy the world of showbiz could be: 'Despite the fact that it has done so well and the show looks like being a hit, the cast all manage to be unbelievably fed up. Great jealousies have sprung up between Kenneth Williams and Fenella Fielding, and hours are spent altering the running order, usually for the worse.' For the first time in his life, Peter added a kiss to the bottom of the letter, although he then added a few noughts and crosses and drew a line through it, to turn it into a joke.

The London critics were slightly more reserved. Cecil Wilson was of the opinion that 'Some of the material is brilliant and some of it not funny at all', while the reviewer from *The Times* thought that the show 'tried desperately hard', but all too often produced 'the pointless joke that has failed to achieve absurdity'. J. C. Trewin of the *Illustrated London News* enjoyed himself, and applauded Peter as 'The sort of writer that hunts for haddocks' eyes among the heather bright, or goes to sea in a sieve.' One failing that would not have been apparent to them was that Kenneth Williams had failed to capture the essence of Mr Grole; the nasal whine was there, but Williams mugged, leered and rolled his eyes furiously, and performed the whole with a fixed manic smile. He had none of Peter's cold, deadpan intensity, the ability to maintain a straight face while all about were losing theirs. The supporting cast too, it must be said, were terrible. Fenella Fielding, Peter Brett and Peter Reeves played their parts with that stagy, eyebrows-raised air of forced surprise that passes for straight comic acting in the British theatre.

The rows among the cast came to a head in December when Myra de Groot vanished without trace, returning in the New Year only to be fired on the spot. It did not seem to matter. The public loved it, and *Pieces of Eight* ran for 429 performances. Among the delighted crowd were Alec and Margaret Cook and Sarah, who was thrilled to bits to be taken backstage to meet the stars. Peter went to see the show in London with Robin Voelcker, and left the theatre on a high. In the street outside they were accosted by a prostitute; Voelcker hurried on, but Peter stopped with a flourish and said 'Good evening my dear! I *do* think I have had the pleasure.' He received a torrent of abuse in return.

Peter returned to Cambridge a hero, and a well-paid hero at that, as he was now on a retainer of £100 per week; 'but he was never big-headed about it in the slightest,' says Michael Wild. He was now expected to divide his time between London and Cambridge, which was strictly illegal under university law. He was not even supposed to spend a night outside the city without special permission, and a promise to make up the extra night at a later date. So he went to see Anthony Garrett and asked if he could take over his Clarendon Street digs, which were sufficiently far out of the centre to escape the bulldogs' scrutiny. He also slipped the landlord a few quid for good measure. His tutor, Tony Camps, a kind man whose speech impediment was to crop up in one or two future Cook characters, was tolerant enough to impose nothing more than a small cash fine when he found out. Consequently many of Peter's spare afternoons were spent wandering the area of Soho behind the theatre, perusing the strip show displays and dirty bookshops, of which he became rather a connoisseur.

If anyone thought that Presidency of the Footlights Club would invest Peter with an air of responsibility, they were sadly mistaken. Bamber Gascoigne attended the first Footlights dinner of the new term, when the President proposed a loyal toast. 'The Queen, we all intoned, the Queen, the Queen. But the President was not done. He mumbled on, with the dreadful deadpan intensity which would later be known as the trade mark of E. L. Wisty, ". . . and all who sail in her.'"[23] Peter always somehow made time for practical jokes, and kept up long-running correspondences with people who put notices in the personal column of *The Times*. One woman, who announced that she was exporting ballerinas (a type of dress) to South America, was accused by Peter of being part of the white slave trade, a correspondence that batted back and forth for eight weeks.

Peter Bellwood, a new friend from the cast of *The Last Laugh*, recounts a visit to the cinema to see Olivier's *Richard III*. Arriving just after the start Bellwood went in first, and whispered to the usherette 'Excuse me, but have I missed the nude bathing scene?' The confused lady replied that, as far as she knew, there wasn't one. Bellwood took his seat, whereupon Peter came in. 'Excuse me, but have I missed the nude bathing scene?' he whispered to the same usherette. Later that evening they glanced behind them to see all three usherettes standing at the back transfixed by the film, not daring to take their eyes off the screen for a minute. Peter delighted Bellwood with his extraordinary off-the-cuff improvisations: 'The Phantom Bee-Fang Gluer, a lunatic on the loose in Amsterdam going round gluing sets of fangs onto dead bees . . . A man who was convinced the Soviets had planted a camera in his bath . . . Another who bought a walking stick because "I thought I saw it move" . . . And a man who'd managed against all odds to purchase a heap of rotting grass, only to learn that the bottom had just dropped out of the rotting grass market.'[24] Peter the showman was at it again.

By now money was coming in so fast Peter barely knew what to do with it. He bought a white Sunbeam sports car with some of it, and put some of the rest on the horses. After a big win he treated his friends to fillet steak and beluga caviar at the Garden House Hotel. A lot more cash disappeared when his room was burgled. Chris Smith recalls: 'The loot included some cheques, and Peter said, with humility rather surprising in an undergraduate in his early twenties, that he should have taken the advice of his father, who always told him to pay cheques into the bank as quickly as possible.' Another purchase was a Ferrograph tape recorder, then regarded as the Rolls Royce of its ilk, so he could stride up and down improvising sketches into it.

Despite his West End success, Peter was as prolific as ever at student level, and still found time to appear in the Pembroke outdoor revue on Poppy Day, a parody of *The Mummy* called *The Daddy*. There were smokers and cabarets aplenty, one of which was visited by Jonathan Miller. Peter was on stage performing *Science – Fact or Fiction*, a sketch he had written with David Frost. Miller recalls that 'There was this astonishing, strange, glazed, handsome creature, producing weird stuff the like of which I'd never heard before. I remember his first line when I was shot upright in my seat by him. He was playing some person in a suburban kitchen concealed behind a newspaper. He didn't say a word. But all eyes were drawn to him. Then he rustled the newspaper and simply said, "Hello, hello. I see the *Titanic*'s sunk again." One knew one was in the presence of comedy at right angles to all the comedy we'd heard.'[25] Peter went on to perform a new Grole routine, in which the character was cast as a miner who had always wanted to be a Judge but who kept failing the exams, because he'd 'never had the Latin'. After the show Miller approached Cook, introduced himself, and asked him – with reference to the sketch – whether he had ever worked with schizophrenics. Peter asked why: 'And Jonathan said, "Well you've perfectly reproduced the schizophrenic speech pattern." I wasn't aware of it at all. It came from me, it doesn't make me a schizophrenic. It just means Jonathan's wrong, as he so often is, bless his heart.'[26] It was to be on Miller's recommendation that Peter was included in *Beyond the Fringe*.

On 8 October Harold Macmillan had been re-elected, to the disbelieving fury of the student left, and Peter now elevated his impression of the Prime Minister to become a regular part of his routine. In a senile patrician drawl, he spoke of Britain's position as an honest broker ('No nation could be more honest . . . and no nation could be broker') and replied to a letter of complaint he had received from an OAP in Fife:

> Well, let me say right away Mrs McFarlane – as one Scottish old-age-pensioner to another – be of good cheer. There are many people in this country today who are far worse off than yourself. And it is the policy of the Conservative Party to see that this position is maintained.

Impressions of Prime Ministers are of course commonplace today, but in 1959 they were rather shocking. When the Macmillan monologue (entitled *TVPM*) became the centrepiece of *Beyond the Fringe* in the West End two years later, Michael Frayn was sitting behind a young couple who were 'neighing away like demented horses, until the middle of Peter Cook's lampoon on Macmillan, when the man turned to the girl and said in an appalled whisper, "I say! This is supposed to be the Prime Minister!" after which they sat in silence for the rest of the evening.'[27] Christopher Booker believes that this piece was the key moment in the birth of what was to become known as the satire movement: 'I remember seeing the first performance of Peter imitating Macmillan as the old, world-weary elder statesman out of touch. The point was that Macmillan had just won an enormous election victory. He was SuperMac. He seemed to be absolutely in command of the British political stage in 1959. Two years later he suddenly seemed to be a totally out-of-touch old fuddy-duddy who just didn't have a clue. And Peter was the first to pick up that change of mood, which actually characterised the onset of the sixties and a totally new world.' Except of course that Peter had been doing the Prime Minister for three years, not two; he may have made it seem like the first performance, but the students of Pembroke had already been enjoying his Macmillan performance for the best part of a year.

There is no question that Peter's impression was, as Booker suggests, seismic in satirical terms. It is equally true that the public outrage at the Prime Minister's performance that the impression eventually came to reflect was no part of its inspiration. According to Jonathan Miller, 'I don't think he was struck by the unfairness of Macmillan-led Conservatism, he was simply amused by the particular sort of patrician charm that someone of that sort had. I don't think he wrote that joke that begins "As one Scottish old-age-pensioner to another . . ." out of any sense of indignation about the patrician complacency of Harold Macmillan. I think he found him rather adorable really.' Peter himself concurred with this view: 'My impersonation of Macmillan was in fact extremely affectionate. I was a great Macmillan fan.'[28] For Peter, Macmillan was just another marvellous, overconfident old buffer in the Sir Arthur Streeb-Greebling mould – the sort who would come and give out the prizes at Radley speech day. Peter's comedy was in one respect a glorious wide-ranging parody of his life, and everybody and everything he came across. He was not afraid to be satirical, but moral indignation was never his prime motivation.

Peter spent Christmas in Cambridge, with the exception of a few days over New Year with the Bawtrees, much of the time in agonised indecision over his career. Should he go for the security of the Foreign Office as planned, or risk upsetting his father by gambling on a career in comedy? He confided his problem to Aunt Joan: 'Time whips by much too quickly and all the time the fearful task of choosing a job gets closer and closer. I really am no nearer reaching a decision. *Pieces of Eight* has merely served to cloud the issue even more. I saw the show again last week and all seemed well, with an enthusiastic and full house. The LP came out last week and I have heard quite a few turns from it on *Housewives' Choice*.' As if to give him a further nudge away from the Civil Service, Anglia TV gave the entire Christmas edition of their Cambridge-based magazine show *Town and Gown* over to Peter, to produce a parody version of their programme.

Sadly all copies of his television debut have long since been destroyed, but records show that Peter actually linked the programme, while most of the comic characters were played by David Frost and Peter Bellwood. Items included a football sketch and a version of the *Polar Bores* sketch from the Footlights. The list of characters shows the obvious influence of Spike Milligan in Peter's work: F. Nidgcombe, Professor Nain, Lionel Sope, Ron Plindell, Colonel Mountebank-Fowler, Larry Splutt, Mr Saffron, Colonel Nagger, W. Rupp, P. L. Wedge and Arthur Frad.

That Christmas, with most of his friends at home with their families, Peter hung around Cambridge with Jack Altman. Wendy Snowden, who had modelled for the May Ball photograph with him six months earlier, had secured a holiday job as a waitress in the trendy new Kenya Coffee Bar. 'And there I was waitressing, which I did with a bit of gusto I think despite the black nylon overall, and suddenly there was Peter, tall and debonair, in a rather beautiful wool overcoat which he was obviously very proud of wearing. And Jack was with him, who was short and swarthy, large ears and beady little jet black eyes. They were such an amazing couple. Peter had this tension around him – it was part of his magnetism, he was one of the most unrelaxed people that I've ever met. And in that kind of atmosphere it was very exciting, a creative tension. So anyway, the first thing he said was, 'Will you buy me a coffee?' He asked *me* whether I would buy *him* a coffee. And I thought this was kind of quite interesting really – because I had lots of chaps running after me at that time – this was a bit of a different approach. I paid for his coffee out of my wages. And then as he was leaving he said 'How about taking me out to the movies tomorrow?' It was going to be Sunday, my day off, and I thought 'This is novel.' I was awful, because I stood up my 'true love' to go on this date. And really that was it, because he just had me laughing all the time. I'm a rather serious, intense person – I was a bit of a religious maniac in my teens – so it was just very healing in a way, just to be able to laugh at everything.'

Despite her Christianity, Wendy was in fact of partly Jewish extraction, although her parents did not tell her this until she was an adult, to spare her the social ostracisation they feared. She was the daughter of a low-paid, intellectually frustrated civil servant from rural Bedfordshire, a philanthropist who frequently gave away his wages to the poor and wanted to change the world, but never had sufficient impetus to escape the confines of his routine life. She identified with anti-authority types and had always been the naughtiest girl's sidekick at school. Her mother was practical and independent, and her parents quarrelled frequently. Wendy herself had suffered a sickly childhood, spending months at a stretch in bed with bronchitis and TB, where drawing and painting had been her only solace. Eventually she had blossomed into a notable beauty, whereupon her father – fearful for her future financial wellbeing – had secured her a drab job as a GPO Accounts Clerk in Cambridge. She had broken free with her mother's assistance and enrolled in the local art school, where she made her own clothes and modelled herself on Brigitte Bardot, posing round Cambridge in gingham skirts, or perched on a bicycle in big tulle petticoats and a waspy waist belt. Boys adored her.

One of her first boyfriends was the huge, bear-like Roger Law: 'We called him the Tiger from the Fens or something,' she recalls. 'He'd bring whole pork chops in and munch them like Desperate Dan.' Law used to hang around with Peter Fluck – 'gangly, all nose and elbows and always sat as close as he could to the nude model' – and together the pair would go on to found *Spitting Image*. Law remembers Wendy as going through a rebellious phase: 'She was very girly, very, very lively and a bunch of trouble. She was a laugh and lots of stocking top. You'd go out with her but you wouldn't fuckin' marry her! I wouldn't, anyway. She'd spend your week's wages in one night, and expect to. Peter liked girls that were lively or tarty, and she was a flirt, a tremendous flirt, and he seemed to like all that.' Peter was certainly attracted to the apparent dichotomy between Wendy's straight-laced, spiritual side and her unabashed sexuality. His first, daring, present to her was a black nylon frilly nightie.

When she got to know Peter, Wendy found him him 'very tense, but brilliant – and that brilliance was magnetic.'[29] His childhood asthma and her bedridden youth represented a common bond: 'We both shared this incredible dark experience of illness and not being able to breathe. To both of us, I think, the night was full of fear.' By day they made an incredibly glamorous couple, and Wendy swiftly remodelled him on art school-fashionable lines. Out went the woollen jackets and ties and sensible pullovers and the college scarf. 'Peter wasn't very confident about his looks to begin with – partly because of the acne problem. He was quite sheepish with me when we were alone together.' Peter soon became a high-fashion dandy every bit as dazzling as his girlfriend, and took to gazing admiringly at himself in mirrors.

Soon he had all but abandoned his digs, and moved into the Prince of Wales, a defunct pub in Norfolk Street where Wendy lived with a crowd of friends. The bar was still operational, and the resulting parties were riotous. Unconscious bodies were invariably found curled up in corners the following morning. Wendy revealed herself to be an expert cook and natural entertainer, and Peter's non-stop monologues were the centre of attention at an innumerable series of hilarious dinner parties. It was on one of these occasions that he was eventually introduced to Roger Law, who remembers: 'Of course I realised I'd finally met the originator of the funny voices I'd heard. And of course the original was much more entertaining. He rarely spoke in his proper voice. He was very well-tailored, very good-looking, like a Regency buck. He had Italian-style clothes, box jackets with very dark designer shirts, the forerunner of that sort of snappy dressing the Beatles did. He had money coming in, and so he always had form-books falling out of his pocket – he always used to be on his way to the betting shop. He seemed very worldly and cynical. You'd say something with gushing enthusiasm, which he would then undercut with probably something nearer the truth. I mean, I really thought things could be changed a bit – a lot of people made that mistake in my generation. But I don't think Peter was fooled for a minute.'

Cynical he may have been about Law's radical politics, but he was also entertained by his radical antics. On one occasion Law had organised a raid on the Labour Party Conference, and had come up with the bright idea of sustaining the raiding party for a week by taking along a milk churn filled to the brim with cabbage-and-pig's-trotter stew. It had taken so long to cook and decant the stew into the churn that by the time the last panload had gone in, the stew at the bottom had gone off, infecting the whole brew. Law had created for himself the problem of disposing of eighty pints of stinking pig's trotter broth, and had broken into someone's garden at dead of night and buried it there.

Peter had finally found something worthwhile to do with his money. Fluck and Law moved into a property Peter owned in Park Street, and there set up the forerunner of *Spitting Image*, entitled 'East Anglian Artists' (it was just a few doors down from the grocer's shop owned by Fluck's father, from which the 'l' went missing on a regular basis). Law wanted a contract with his new landlord: 'But of course we couldn't afford a lawyer, so I went off and wrote one up as I thought lawyers did – you know, "heretofore" and all that bollocks. And of course Peter thought that was fucking hilarious.' The landlord signed it at once, but never asked for a penny in rent.

East Anglian Artists designed posters and other literature for local CND and socialist groups, but it also served as a meeting point and a place to hang around in. A frequent visitor was David Frost, who demonstrated the technique of picking up the telephone and saying 'I'll just take this on my other phone,' before making a clicking noise and continuing the conversation on the same phone. 'He was definitely on the escalator all the way to the top,' says Roger Law. East Anglian Artists straggled on until Law was finally expelled from the Cambridge School of Art, shortly after organising an Anti-May Ball with Peter Fluck. They took over an unoccupied house in a nearby village, painted the walls with satirical illustrations of establishment targets and sent invitations to every CND activist in the country. The whole thing ended calamitously in a massive police raid.

While not especially committed to the CND cause per se, Peter disliked the lies and subterfuge that characterised government nuclear policy, and could certainly be described as a sympathiser. In February he appeared with David Frost at a CND Benefit called G*A*L*A*X*Y, in which he was rude to the Queen. He also took his first straight part for over a year, appearing at the ADC in a Bamber Gascoigne adaptation of Reuben Ship's *The Investigator*, an anti-McCarthy satire starring Derek Jacobi, Richard Cottrell and Chris Kelly. In all this activity he did not forget Pembroke, and took the lead in the 1960 College revue *Something Borrowed*, although the majority of the script was written by Geoff Paxton. Among Peter's limited contribution was a sketch that was to become one of the most famous of his career.

Entitled *Leg Too Few*, but subsequently retitled *One Leg Too Few* (the show had an alphabetic theme, and it had been crowbarred in under the letter 'L'), it concerned a one-legged man's audition for the role of Tarzan. Peter often cited it as his favourite of all the sketches he'd ever scripted, and claimed in 1993 that 'I've never written anything better.'[30] Dudley Moore, who was to play the hapless auditioner Mr Spiggott on hundreds of occasions, called it 'The funniest single sketch' they ever did together, 'a real classic'.[31] Jonathan Miller described it as 'one of the most masterly sketches of twentieth century English humour.'[32] The BBC had rejected it outright.

What Moore enjoyed most was the circumspect diplomacy of Cook's theatrical agent:

Peter:	Now, Mr Spiggott, I couldn't help noticing almost at once that you are a one-legged person.
Spiggott:	You noticed that?
Peter:	I noticed that, Mr Spiggott. When you have been in the business as long as I have you come to notice these little things almost instinctively. Now, Mr Spiggott, you, a one-legged man, are applying for the role of Tarzan – a role which traditionally involved the use of a two-legged actor.
Spiggott:	Correct.

Peter: And yet you, a unidexter, are applying for the role.
Spiggott: Right.
Peter: . . . A role for which two legs would seem to be the
           minimum requirement . . .

And so on, until the most famous line in the sketch, which often elicited
cheers from seasoned Cook-watchers. It was also Miller's favourite:

Peter: Your right leg I like. I like your right leg. A lovely leg
           for the role. That's what I said when I saw you come in.
           I said, 'A lovely leg for the role.' I've got nothing against
           your right leg. The trouble is – neither have you.

It was a punchline so strong that Peter could afford to spend seven
sentences setting it up. Miller called it 'An example of language
disclosing two previously unrecognised meanings. It is the sudden
leakage that occurs between the figurative, on the one hand, and
the concrete meaning. Through Peter's comic timing, what happens
is a catastrophic and sudden and abrupt permeability between these
previously completely separate categories.'[33] Which has to be one of
the most roundabout ways ever devised of defining a double meaning,
albeit a delicious one.

Miller also pointed to the comedy created by Spiggott's 'brazen and happy
indifference to his situation . . . that curious hospitable friendliness towards
the questions . . . we are amused by the gross discrepancy between the
cheerfulness of the man and his otherwise rather painful predicament.'[34]
In short Peter had, whether inadvertently or otherwise, discovered the
virtues of engendering in the audience a feeling of sympathy towards the
comic target, allied to a sense of superiority over him. That is the key
to the sketch's enduring success, together with an entertaining parody
of the language of diplomacy, a smattering of wordplay and some good
jokes that perhaps should not be overanalysed.

His commitment to the Pembroke revue notwithstanding, Peter was
now going into College less and less. He had been demoted from the
first eleven, although he was still willing to turn out for the seconds
at the last minute if he had an hour or two to spare. He was part
of a group that sometimes met in the rooms of John Dwyer, who,
being President of the Junior Parlour, was the only third year to
live in College. He would entertain them with Mr Grole monologues
and even with early versions of the Alan Bennett sermon from *Beyond
the Fringe*. In general though, his Pembroke friends were losing touch

with him, and even getting slightly annoyed by it. The more people he
knew, the more people wanted to know him, the more he tried hard
to keep them all entertained and happy, the more he could only offer
a performance, as opposed to genuine friendship. According to Peter
Lloyd, 'He became in some respects an uncomfortable companion to
have. Eventually he monopolised the conversation in the sense that
everybody else would fall quiet and he would perform among us until
he went. Some of us, Tim Harrold was one, tried to keep up with it,
and most people were just prepared to admire the spectacle and listen.
And others would have liked to have taken some part without having
to vie for humorous lines and characterisations in which they were no
match. Latterly he would go into one of his characters, monologues or
styles of speech almost as soon as he saw you or spoke to you, and so
one ceased over the three years to talk to the Peter Cook who had come
up, and more and more one listened to, or acted the straight man to, one
of his characterisations. He must have been aware that some people were
trying to say things and he wasn't really letting them. I don't think he
tried to make anybody look small, he just adapted himself to whatever
heckling or interruption he got, and used it to develop his performance
further.'

According to Tim Harrold, who had tried to keep up, the more
he and his friends saw of Peter, 'We got to know him less and
less.'
    To some extent Peter had made a rod for his own back. Anyone who
combats loneliness and amasses popularity through being constantly
witty puts equally continuous pressure on themselves never to halt the
performance. For years people had looked to Peter to cheer them up and
make life bearable; never the other way round. The more he entertained
people, the more exaggeratedly boring his own problems must have
seemed, the less he must have wanted to burden people with his real
thoughts and fears, the more afraid he became of intimacy. Peter scented
the frustration of his old Pembroke friends but could do little, other than
cast them adrift in his wake. Later, when he was at his unhappiest, he
dismissed them all as 'mathematicians and scientists' who 'never bought
a round', who 'emerged blinking into the sunlight in their last year, all
with first class honours'[35]; but this was just reciprocal frustration finally
breaking through the barrier of good manners.
    Peter's new gang were all going places: Eleanor Bron, John Bird, David
Frost, Derek Jacobi, Ian McKellen, Trevor Nunn, Richard Cottrell, John
Fortune, Corin Redgrave, Colin Bell and Peter Bellwood would run

into each other several times a week at parties, blurring on occasion into Wendy's art school crowd. They were all confident, articulate and interesting people, and according to Richard Cottrell, who was once drunk for three days continuously, they consumed a lot of Martinis as well. Peter and Cottrell were invited – on the strength of their amusement value rather than their breeding – to join the True Blue Dining Club, a semi-aristocratic dining society at which the members had to wear historical costume. Christopher Booker remembers that 'Peter was always on show, from the moment he got up in the morning, all the way through the day, far into the night. Wherever he was in Cambridge, he would be surrounded by a group of people, all falling about with laughter.'

Peter spent his last Easter holiday before Finals visiting his family in Libya. It was an inauspicious trip; just after he departed Grandfather Mayo died, and he crossed with his mother coming back the other way to be at her father's bedside for his last few days. Sarah, who was to have gone with Peter, went down to Eastbourne instead for the expected funeral. On arrival in Libya, Peter immediately contracted jaundice and spent the holiday in bed, his little sister Elizabeth keeping his spirits up by feeding him Marmite. It was to prove a critical illness. His liver had been badly damaged, meaning that he would never again be able to drink large amounts of alcohol without seriously endangering his health.

Peter convalesced in a darkened Cambridge room with Wendy by his side. He lay yellow-skinned and sweating in his red-and-white striped travelling dressing gown, while she grilled bacon on his electric bar fire and got to know him better. There, without any funny voices or jokes but with genuine feeling, he told her of his childhood misery and nightmares, of his great dream to open a satirical nightclub like the *Porcupine* in Berlin, and his lifelong desire to tear down hypocrisy and lies and pomposity and faceless officialdom. 'He had something of my father' recalls Wendy. 'My father was all for social reform – but never had the guts to get out there and do anything about it. But here was somebody who looked like he might. Underneath it all Peter had a deep idealism. His confidence, though, was a total façade. The non-stop monologue, the needing to be the centre of attention all the time . . . he was just giving himself a feeling of security by speaking. Of course he seemed confident in front of an audience, but as the saying goes, "Everything that has a front has a back, and the bigger the front the bigger the back".' Roger Law had come to the same conclusion. 'All the voices and the entertaining a room full of people – I assumed he was quite shy. Because you don't put that much energy into something if you're supremely self-confident.'

Peter had to drag himself off his sick bed for one last gargantuan effort – to combine his Finals, from which he really needed a first class degree to be sure of a good career in the Foreign Office, with the Footlights revue that would conclude his Presidency, from which he really needed a rip-roaring success to be sure of a good career in showbusiness. Of the two, the Footlights would be the easier part. Peter's show, *Pop Goes Mrs Jessop*, which opened on 7 June 1960, was the antithesis of Bird's production the previous year. Politics was kept to a minimum, and subject to a code of strict neutrality: Peter didn't even impersonate Harold Macmillan. Instead, the sketches had titles like *The Ballad of Sir Frederick Snain* and *Pomegranates, Wild Fish and the Forest Melodies of Andalusia*. Mr Grole did his *Interesting Facts* routine, and in another sketch Peter played an equally monotonous man who expounded the virtues of training ducks:

> It's quite an achievement really. I mean these ducks are completely under my control; eating's become second nature to them now. The possibilities are endless with ducks – I was thinking, perhaps it's a bit too ambitious, but I was thinking of trying to get them up in the air – training them to fly.

Peter wrote sixteen of the twenty-nine sketches on show, of which five – including *One Leg Too Few* – had already been aired in the Pembroke revues. Eleanor Bron appeared in that and other sketches as a secretary in pebble-glasses called Miss Rigby. One of the new items was to make it as far as *Beyond the Fringe*: the anti-nuclear *Whose Finger on What Button?*, which was one of only two political sketches in the show. The other political sketch, also written by Peter, was an anti-CND satire included to maintain the political balance, entitled *Peace*. To the sound of marching music written by Patrick Gowers, an agitator chants a series of questions, which are answered by the crowd:

> Do we want war?
> *No we don't!*
> Do we want peace?
> *Yes we do!*
> Do we want worldwide complication and suffering, with women and children being knocked down by a hydrogen bomb?
> *Certainly not!*
> Do we not want peaceful co-existence with us all living happily together and having no worries at all?
> *Yes we do!*

Well what's stopping us?
THE GOV-ING-MENT!

To have included such an anti-CND item in a student show in 1960 without losing the slightest degree of audience enthusiasm ranked among Peter's more extraordinary undergraduate achievements.

Mrs Jessop herself, incidentally, was a Britannia-like figure who was persuaded by the cast to emit a small 'pop' at the opening and closing of the show. *Pop Goes Mrs Jessop* was of course an utter, resounding triumph, and Peter was very much its star. The scripts reproduced here cannot adequately capture the impact of his performance. As Christopher Booker says, 'It is quite impossible now to recreate just how Peter managed so unfailingly to inspire laughter. That is why those who did not know him in those early days will never know just why he seemed to tower over everybody else. Even the clips of *Beyond the Fringe* are only a shadow of his magic.'[36]

Peter's Finals were slightly trickier. They clashed directly with the dress rehearsals for *Pop Goes Mrs Jessop*, but he was determined not to let his father down; however he had done virtually no academic work for two years. He borrowed Michael Wild's and Eleanor Bron's notes, spread them across the floor of the bedroom he shared with Wendy, and paced the room night after night attempting to photograph them with his memory. For once, his mood was quiet, serious, almost desperate. Halfdan Johnson, the football captain, met him on the steps of the examination halls: 'He had gone without any sleep for a whole week and was completely haggard. It was amazing that he took his exams so seriously. There seemed to be a dichotomy between the very relaxed person we knew on the football field, making self-deprecating remarks, and the person who was so wound up now.'

He wasn't entirely without tricks. On the hottest day of the exams he consulted the statute book and discovered that it was permitted to bring a carton of fruit juice into the examination hall; the invigilating don, himself sweating in full rig, was furious but could do nothing about it. Peter kept up a running battle with this gentleman. The following day he openly swigged copious draughts from a bottle of brandy, informing the fuming official that he didn't want his answers to lack spirit. A day or two later his lack of sleep caught up with him: he blacked out in the middle of a paper and fell to the floor, seriously gashing his head on his desk. He was taken to Addenbrooke's hospital and reappeared with his head bandaged. The examiners said they would make allowances. Rumours flew: it was all a trick, people said, Peter had taught himself to faint at will to get out of a particularly difficult paper. Nobody believed that the dazzlingly clever Peter Cook wasn't one step ahead of the invigilators all the way.

On the day of his last paper Peter took Michael Wild home with him, and Wendy plied him with strawberries to say thank you for the loan of the notes. Had he done enough? He didn't know. It would be months before he would be able to find out.

In his heart, Peter didn't believe he had done enough either to make a career in comedy or in the Foreign Office. Discreetly, without telling anyone, he fixed up some run-of-the-mill job interviews, and was accepted as a junior copywriter in an advertising agency. A few days after the end of term, he went out for a stroll on a sunny afternoon to say a reflective goodbye to a Pembroke friend, Martin Hunter. Professor Hunter, as he now is, remembers: 'We sat together on the Mill Bridge, pondering the future over a couple of pints of Greene King bitter. I was wondering whether to embark on a fourth year at Cambridge or to start with a firm of solicitors in the City. He told me that he was starting an office job after the holidays. Slightly surprised, I asked if he had thought of taking up the stage professionally – because by then his Footlights Revue had received far more than mere local recognition in Cambridge. 'Good heavens no,' he replied, 'far too insecure. And anyway, you shouldn't allow your hobby to turn into a job, you would lose the fun of it.' I reminded him of this conversation a few years later, when he joined me at a table for drinks with some friends at the Establishment Club, after the show. He laughed, and said that the opportunity had been too good to miss; that it was still really just a hobby; and that he wasn't planning to do it for very long.'

Peter's nervousness on Mill Bridge wasn't reflected by *Varsity*, the University paper; they had him down as one of their 'Twelve Golden Boys of the Future'. They knew that through the offices of Jonathan Miller, Peter had been booked for one more revue, a small-scale Edinburgh show that summer called *Beyond the Fringe*; Miller himself had come up to do a double act with Peter at the Pembroke May Ball, to brush a few cobwebs from his own performance and to acquaint himself further with Peter's stock of material. Peter's showbusiness career, they felt, was not quite finished yet. The landlord of his digs certainly hoped not. Peter, it transpired, hadn't been there, or paid any rent, for nine months. Peter himself was simply apprehensive at leaving the scene of such enormous triumphs: 'Cambridge seemed to be the hub of the world. We didn't think that much of the outside world. When I left, I was fully equipped to stay at Cambridge forever.'[37]

CHAPTER 4

So That's the Way You Like It
Beyond the Fringe, 1960–62

Beyond the Fringe, the show that was to change the face of British comedy and West End theatre, did not, ironically, begin as an alternative to the theatrical Establishment. It was actually devised by the theatrical Establishment, in the person of John Bassett, the young assistant to the Artistic Director of the Edinburgh Festival. The official festival had been increasingly bedevilled during the late fifties by competing unofficial 'fringe' events, so Robert Ponsonby, the Artistic Director, had decided to mount his own challenge to the late-night interlopers. In 1959 he had put on a Flanders and Swann cabaret, and he was hoping to secure the services of Louis Armstrong for the following summer. When it became clear that this proposition was a non-starter, Bassett suggested actually trying to beat the amateur fringe comedians at their own game, by staging a professional revue that would unite the best Oxbridge performers of the last five years. Ponsonby gave him the go-ahead.

Not really knowing where to start, towards the end of 1959 Bassett paid a visit to Jonathan Miller, the tall, rangy, voluminously articulate star of the 1955 Footlights, whose wife's sister he had known at school. The problem was that Miller had actually announced his retirement from comedy after the 1955 show had run its course, had entered the medical profession and had since restricted his performing career to the odd radio broadcast. Bassett cornered him, sterile dressing in hand, at the University College Hospital Casualty department, and persuaded him to take a short break from his new job. 'I still fiercely regret the distraction,' says Miller. 'Much better to have been a very funny comic undergraduate and forget about it. But I got onto this terrible treadmill.'[1] Bassett asked Miller to suggest another ex-Cambridge comedian. As far as Miller was concerned, the only possible candidate was still studying there: the brilliant young man he'd seen recently in a Footlights show, Peter Cook. Bassett tracked Peter down in Cambridge early in January and put the proposition to him.

Bassett then turned to Oxford, and secured the services of an old friend from his own undergraduate days: Dudley Moore, who had played in the same student jazz band before taking his degree in 1957. Moore was a natural clown who would be able to take care of the musical element in the show. As with Miller and Cambridge, he asked Moore to recommend another ex-Oxford star, to make up a cast of four. Moore suggested Alan Bennett, a shy, bespectacled Yorkshireman who specialised in take-offs of mealy-mouthed vicars and Christmas Royal broadcasts, whom he had never actually met. He knew, however, that Bennett had done well on the Edinburgh Fringe with the 1959 Oxford revue. Bennett, like Miller, needed to be persuaded, as by 1960 he too had retired from comedy and was well on the way to becoming a medieval historian.

The four men met in a small, unprepossessing restaurant on the Euston Road, close enough to Miller's work to take advantage of his lunch hour. 'It was an Indian restaurant,' recalled Peter. 'The main thing I remember was the food. It was revolting.'[2] Bennett remembers it as an Italian meal, which suggests that the food must have been revolting in the extreme. Eight months later, when the four were the talk of the Edinburgh Festival, they informed the *Edinburgh Evening News* that they had all liked each other instantly on first acquaintance. The truth, according to Miller, was rather the reverse. 'We were all jealously guarding our own little province. I think we were tremendously suspicious of one another and very competitive.' Sartorially, Peter stood out. Bennett recalls that 'He was dressed in the height of fashion. Now there wasn't really any fashion early in 1960 – most people still dressed in sports clothes and flannels, but Peter had on a little shortie overcoat and narrow trousers, a not-quite-a-bum-freezer jacket, winkle picker shoes and a tie with horizontal bars across it; all stuff which came from a shop called 'Sportique' at the end of Old Compton Street. He took us there later, but we could never quite vie with him.' Peter was carrying a huge armful of newspapers and a book on racing form. So prolific had his comic output become by this stage that he devoured newspapers almost as ammunition: the irrelevant facts that peppered his sketches were genuine, his arcane knowledge fuelled exhaustively by yards of newsprint.

Miller, Bennett and Moore all later confessed to John Bassett that they had gone to the meeting apprehensive about who would crack the first joke. They need not have worried. Miller recounts how, 'As soon as Peter sat down at lunch, this flow of uncontrollably inventive stuff came out of him. It was impossible to compete with him, you couldn't actually participate, there was no room for one to get in, one simply had to be an audience of it. It was very exhausting. Even when in fact you were helpless with laughter, you longed for it to finish, not merely because you were exhausted by the laughter but because there seemed to be no prospect of it coming to an end at all. He seemed very threatening to us all in that respect.' Alan Bennett, who barely spoke a word, had similar misgivings. 'I had the slight feeling I was there under false pretences – a feeling that never really left me. Peter was very funny and, to my alarm, very fluent. He appeared to be able to ad lib excellent material in monologues of spiralling absurdity.'[3] Moore was feeling, if anything, even more cowed: 'I was completely mute in front of these intellectual giants. I felt I was just there to supply music more than anything. They were all six foot two, and I was five foot two, which made a great deal of difference.' When he demonstrated part of his act, in which a violin made baby sounds, Peter – who was also feeling the competition – openly laughed at it rather than with it. Moore did conclude, however, that Peter was the most approachable of the three, his manifest ambition tempered by relaxed manners and a good-natured charm. At the heart of these awkward introductions was a shared belief, later articulated by Moore: 'All of us thought we were better than the others';[4] it was a belief that was undercut, for each of them, by the fear that it might not ultimately look that way to the paying public.

A few days later, Bassett took them all round to the Edinburgh Festival offices in St James' Street, to present them to the Old Etonian and former Guardsman Robert Ponsonby. 'They came and they played the fool. I could see we were onto something'[5] was Ponsonby's bluff verdict. Miller and Bennett were still unsure about whether or not to go ahead. Peter commented that 'Jonathan had this doctor–comedian conflict, and Alan had this academic–comedian conflict. I had no conflict whatsoever, nor had Dudley. It was rather boring. We kept trying to think of something, such as "By day he is a Trappist monk, by night he is on the boards."'[6] Apparently, the fact that Peter was a full-time student supposedly bound for the Foreign Office did not represent any sort of conflict. His agent Donald Langdon had other objections. None of the other three were professional comedians, he pointed out, whereas Peter had a West End show under his belt. This tiny revue might be seen as a backward step. 'Don't jeopardise your career by working with these three amateurs,' he recommended. Peter rather wanted to fill the summer with comic activity, and dissented. The compromise they came to was that Langdon would attempt to negotiate higher wages for him. Eventually the others agreed a flat fee of £100 each for writing and performing the show, whereas Peter received £110. When Langdon's 10 per cent commission had been deducted, this left Peter with £99.

Over the next six months the four met sporadically to decide which of their favourite sketches should be included, and to write a few new ones. Occasionally they kept their hand in by performing at cabarets and balls. Wendy Snowden remembers being introduced to Alan Bennett at Lady Ismay's house party: 'He was lying on this great big four poster bed in Lady Ismay's daughter's bedroom, with his rucksack on the bed and his hiking boots by his head, reading a book on mediaeval history; and he looked up, like a little bleary badger, so unconcerned about this great party going on.' Peter enjoyed shocking Bennett – an easy matter – with smutty jokes; his victim developed the habit of stuffing his handkerchief into his mouth in a mixture of embarrassment and guilty amusement. The other three admitted that they had never met anyone quite like Peter. According to Miller, 'He ought to have been an extremely successful young diplomat – that was the world Peter came from. You felt you were with somebody from the Foreign Office who had suddenly gone completely bananas.'[7] Boarding a crowded tube with Bassett, Peter assumed a woman's voice without warning and started to shout: 'Where's my baby? I've lost my baby! Let me back in, my baby's in there!' The rush-hour crowd naturally parted to let him through.

The four held many of their initial creative meetings at University College Hospital, in between Miller's surgical operations. 'There was no unified approach at all,' says Bennett. 'We each had our own ideas of what we wanted to be funny about.'[8] Cook and Miller, both frighteningly articulate, tended to dominate and improvise. Bennett started to prepare material in order to keep pace at the meetings. Moore was simply paralysed by lack of confidence. 'I felt totally constricted and overpowered. I was totally out of place with the other three. I didn't contribute anything textually.'[9]

Apart from his lack of height, Moore felt let down by his humble beginnings. 'I came from a working-class home in Dagenham. When I went up to Oxford as an organ scholar I really couldn't open my mouth because everyone seemed frightfully suave and in control. I found that my voice started to do very strange things to toe the line. I was absolutely terrified when my parents came up that we'd all do the wrong thing. I ended up feeling very aggressive, with a great chip on my shoulder.'[10] Moore had enjoyed an awkward relationship with his mother and father, and came from a family that rarely displayed its emotions. He had been born with a club foot, and had spent most of the war in hospital, the only child in a ward full of wounded soldiers, something he never forgave his mother for putting him through. He had been bullied at school on account of his disfigurement, and had taken up 'fooling around', as he put it, to deflect the violent attentions of bigger boys. At university he had started to perform in cabaret in the evenings, and had subsequently tried to become an actor, before settling for a job as a pianist with the John Dankworth and Vic Lewis orchestras in Britain and America. His social background could not have been more different from Peter's, but otherwise the similarities were pronounced. It did not seem so at the time: Moore's childhood problems visibly informed his every move, whereas Peter's insecurities were well buried beneath layers of startling wit and social grace.

Peter supplied the bulk of the script for *Beyond the Fringe*: Moore later estimated Peter's contribution at 67 per cent, with the other third shared between Miller and Bennett. There was only an hour's worth to fill – they had been booked in to do a week at the Lyceum Theatre, following on at 10.45 p.m. from the Old Vic's performance of *The Seagull* – but there were also competing demands on Peter's stock of material. By the time the *Fringe* script had to be finalised, it became clear that Michael Codron and Kenneth Williams would be looking for a successor to *Pieces of Eight*. The latter, obviously, would be the 'senior' of the two projects. Peter saved *One Leg Too Few* and *Interesting Facts* for Kenneth Williams's use; he also split his two nuclear sketches between the two projects, Williams getting *Peace*, the cynical anti-CND item, and *Beyond the Fringe* getting the pro-CND number, *Whose Finger on What Button?* This sketch was reconstructed by Miller and Bennett, but still contained some classic Cook moments:

> We shall receive four minutes' warning of any impending nuclear attack. Some people have said, 'Oh my goodness me – four minutes? – that is not a very long time!' Well, I would remind those doubters that some people in this great country of ours can run a mile in four minutes.

John Bird later called this 'A joke which brilliantly clamped its teeth on that era's self-delusion and hopeless nostalgia for power and glory.'[11]

Peter also decided to incorporate his Macmillan impression in *Beyond the Fringe*, although in general it was not he but Miller, and in particular Bennett, who pushed the show in a satirical direction. Peter and Dudley Moore pulled the other way, which slightly grated on the other two later, when the press came to the conclusion that Peter must have been the satirical prime mover. Miller remembers that 'Peter resisted anything

which might seem to be offensive to the audience or would seem to be
upsetting the apple-cart. Alan had a harder, more satirical view.' Peter
had triumphed once in the West End with a mild, mainstream revue,
and was cautious of alienating the general public. Perhaps more to the
point, he knew that his mother would be in the country in August and
had expressed a desire to visit the show. As for Dudley Moore, he admitted
later to his biographer Barbra Paskin that: 'I was always terrified that we'd
get arrested for everything we did. I was very timid. And Jonathan, Alan
and Peter treated that fear with total scorn, thinly disguised.'[12]

There were twenty sketches in all. Only the eight solo pieces were
attributed to any author in the programme; but Peter's principal
contributions appear to have been *Sitting on the Bench*, the Mr Grole
routine in which he was cast as a frustrated miner; *Old J. J.*, the initials
sketch devised at the Pembroke dinner table; *Royal Box*, an old Footlights
piece in which Dudley played a man who'd been to see the show 497
times on the off chance that the Royal Family might pay a visit (inspired
by the faithful regular fans of *South Pacific*, as witnessed at a matinee Peter
had attended for a laugh with David Frost); *Bollard*, a parody cigarette
commercial in which the highly effeminate cast suddenly affected deep,
husky voices when the cameras rolled (this was the only sketch to be
censored by the Lord Chamberlain's office, to whom all stage scripts
had then to be submitted: the characters were not allowed to call each
other 'love' and the *stage direction* 'Enter two outrageous old queens' had
to be amended to 'Enter two aesthetic young men'); and *This is the End*
(later retitled *The End of the World*), about a dull, nasal religious mystic
and his band of followers, perched atop a mountain awaiting the final
conflagration:

> *Peter*: Up here on the mountain we shall be safe. Safe as
>   houses.
> *Alan*:   And what will happen to the houses?
> *Peter*: Well, naturally, the houses will be swept away.

There was also a fine Shakespeare parody, *So That's the Way You Like
It*, to which Peter contributed one or two of his old Pembroke lines but
which was mostly the work of the rather theatrically-minded Miller ('Oh
saucy Worcester, dost thou lie so still?'). Miller also contributed a rather
old-fashioned monologue about the number of trousers in the London
Transport Lost Property Department, which he had written in 1957 for a
radio programme called *Saturday Night on the Light*. Bennett performed his
famous sermon sketch, a variation of the act he'd been doing since 1956,

in which a vicar attempted – increasingly feebly – to identify religious parallels in a series of everyday situations, all of which were supposed to stem from the ludicrous biblical text 'My brother Esau is an hairy man, but I am a smooth man.' Moore, still worried that he was being marginalised, devised a last-minute solo spot (a Beethoven-style version of *Colonel Bogey* with a never-ending coda) on the evening before the first night. Peter tried out all the material – his and the others' – in performance whenever he could, both in public and in private. His Cambridge friend Mike Winterton remembers seeing him for the last time at an end-of-term tea party in the summer of 1960, 'when the assembled company was reduced to near hysterical laughter as he held the floor acting out various sketches. It was only after we had seen the show that we realised Peter had been giving us a foretaste of *Beyond the Fringe*.' The racing commentator Brough Scott saw a version of the complete show, minus Jonathan Miller, at Lady Ismay's ball at a country house near Cheltenham, an engagement which Peter had organised. 'He did his Harold Macmillan spoof with such cutting charm that soon even the purplest Colonel was guffawing through his moustaches. Nobody had ever heard of him, he was just a student doing a cabaret turn in front of the piano, but he was and remained the funniest person we had ever seen.'[13] Everything was set for Edinburgh.

There remained only the central dilemma of which way Peter's career would head after *Beyond the Fringe*. He still felt he owed it to his family and the hopes they'd invested in him to make it to the Foreign Office; but to be sure of achieving that, he really needed a first-class degree. Without one there was little point in sitting the FO exam. He eventually received his results in July. He had managed a lower second. It was not good enough. To all intents and purposes, he had failed. The die was cast. If he was worried that his parents might be angry with him, he need not have been; neither of them so much as raised an eyebrow. If their beloved son was happy doing what he was doing, then that was enough for them. Peter himself always felt pangs of regret though, not so much because he'd missed out on the FO – although it would have been simpler than the life of a comedian – but because he thought he'd let them down. 'I toyed with the idea of going into the Foreign Office,' he later claimed, 'but I don't think the Foreign Office toyed with the idea of my joining them. It sounds appalling, but I'd have been perfectly happy at the Foreign Office. I'd still say yes if the Governorship of Bermuda came up. I've always wanted to wear a plumed hat.'[14] He told one interviewer that he had had 'no intention of becoming a performer' until the summer of 1960 and *Beyond the Fringe*.[15]

Bizarrely, just as Peter had decided to make a go of the comedy profession, another job offer came out of nowhere. Before they left London, the *Fringe* cast recorded three sketches for the BBC TV programme *Tonight*, for use in a special Edinburgh Festival programme. The producer Donald Baverstock was so impressed with Peter's performance that he subsequently took him out to lunch and invited him to become a full-time interviewer on the show, on a salary of £35 per week. Peter hedged his bets. He would wait and see how *Beyond the Fringe* went before making a decision. In the event, the Edinburgh show's success was to make up his mind for him.

The four men set out from London by car at half past six one morning early in August. It took them eleven hours to drive to Edinburgh, stopping for a picnic on the Yorkshire Moors along the way. They moved into a rented fourth-floor flat at 17 Cornwall Street, opposite the theatre. The flat served as a rehearsal room by day, although Dudley tended to spend his nights with Robert Ponsonby's secretary Jennifer, with whom he had begun an affair. Economy dictated the style of the production: a total budget of £100 meant there could be no set, no props, just one other musician – a bass player called Hugo Boyd – and no costume changes. Cook claimed later that 'We'd have been delighted to have had a hundred chorus girls dancing about.'[16] Miller, conversely, told *The Times* that they had purposely 'tried to rinse away some of this gaudy sentiment. We abandoned decor, dancing and all the other irrelevant dum-de-da of conventional revue, hoping to give the material a chance to speak for itself.' Although Peter's interpretation of the show's staging was clearly tongue-in-cheek, a difference in outlook was undoubtedly present.

The costumes they settled on – white shirts, dark ties, sensible grey pullovers and grey worsted suits – were a highly significant choice, especially as they had to buy them with their own money. For a middle-class audience the four comedians would appear comfortingly attired, like minor public schoolboys forced to sit indoors and play chess on a wet sports afternoon. Their conservative Establishment credentials would not be in doubt. The effect would be to lend a shocking authenticity to their attacks on the society that had reared them: these would clearly not be rebellious outsiders, but young men questioning a system they had been trained to lead. The costumes were undoubtedly chosen with one eye on the minimalist approach that the cast had turned from a necessity into a virtue, but also because that was the sort of clothing they all wore anyway. Only Peter had made the recent transition into an art-school dandy. Ironically, as Miller recounts, 'He looked better than any of us did in those suits. We looked like a bunch of schlemiels, while he looked like the British Ambassador in Ankara.'

There were other problems even more pressing than the financial limitations. There could be no dress rehearsal in the theatre: the Old Vic cast of *The Seagull* refused to allow them into the auditorium until five minutes before their first performance. Ticket sales had been poor, as the Festival crowd had no idea who any of the performers were. Robert Ponsonby became convinced that he had a disaster on his hands. Then, to cap it all, with Peter about to undertake the first professional acting engagement of his career, Equity (the actors' union) informed him that he would have to change his name. There was, it seemed, already an actor called Peter Coke, and union rules were quite strict about the avoidance of confusion. Peter informed them by return that he would henceforth like to be known as Xavier Blancmange. Equity replied that it was a silly name. Peter replied that it was a silly rule. After various further suggestions, such as Wardrobe Gruber and Sting Thundercock, Equity withdrew in utter disarray.

The cast were nervous. With nine days to go, unable to sleep, Peter wrote to his mother as dawn broke over Edinburgh Castle: 'There is still a great deal of rehearsal to be done. We keep getting gloomy warnings about the legendary stupidity of the audiences up here, which is a little unnerving.' He had learnt all his lines, word for word, forwards, backwards, upside down, probably for the last time in his life. All he could do was practise them again. Wendy came up and cooked for everyone. Margaret, Sarah and Elizabeth made their way north a few days later, to lend moral support for the duration of the run. Alec Cook, thousands of miles away, sweated in Tripoli in 110°. His son was about to diverge irrevocably from the family career path. The show opened on the evening of Monday 22 August 1960. On the first night, two-thirds of the seats in the Lyceum lay empty; but from the second night onwards, the theatre would be full to capacity and beyond.

Beyond the Fringe took Edinburgh by storm inside a week. By the third night the *Edinburgh Evening News* was printing selections from the show, with the commentary: 'Are you with it? This is the sort of thing that is convulsing Festival audiences in a late-night show that slays everything it touches. The four young men who are its only begetters have come up with something fresh, something actually fresh, in revue entertainment. They are the theatrical hit of the festival.'[17] John Wells, who was appearing as an Oxford student elsewhere on the fringe, went along to see what all the fuss was about: 'It absolutely cut through all the showbiz rubbish. Other student revues, like our own, still had elaborate costume changes and make-up and pathetic opening numbers, for which we were urged to clean our teeth and grin dazzlingly into the lights. What we saw was four people of our own age slipping in and out of funny voices in the way we all liked to think we did in everyday life, being effortlessly funny.'[18] Bevis Hillier, then a student under Alan Bennett's tutelage, recalls that 'Quite as revolutionary as the assault on the Establishment was the sophistication of the humour itself. Only those who have sat through hours of 1950s radio comedy programmes will know how novel it was.'[19] The Edinburgh audiences especially adored Peter's Mr Grole character. According to Bennett; 'I had the spot in the show immediately following Peter's monologue, which was scheduled to last five minutes or so but would often last for fifteen, when I would be handed an audience so weak from laughter I could do nothing with them.'[20] Drunk on success, Peter proposed to Wendy, producing a moss agate engagement ring from his pocket. They went trout fishing on a nearby lake to celebrate their announcement. Wendy was introduced to her future in-laws for the first time. Margaret and her daughters had loved the show too, Sarah so much that she went to see it over and over again and memorised great chunks off by heart.

Journalists, agents and theatrical producers poured into Edinburgh waving chequebooks, eager for a slice of the new theatrical sensation. About the only people in the business who didn't book tickets were Peter's agent Donald Langdon, still disgruntled that Peter had ignored his advice, and his friend Willie Donaldson, still convinced that John Bird would be the hot property of the 1960s. Rather late in the week, it dawned on the pair that they were missing out. Donaldson recounts what followed: 'Langdon arrived in my office and said, 'Have you seen these reviews, for this silly little thing that's opened in Edinburgh?' And I said no I hadn't, and he said, 'Well it looks like a success. I'd better go up and see it, and I'll get it for you.' I said, 'Considering I'm the only impresario in London who's not up there, and considering I'm the only impresario in London who's just had a huge flop, I couldn't be a worse candidate.' But he was a very confident fellow, Langdon. 'No no no, I'll get it,' he said. And it was the most extraordinary achievement. The other three loathed him. Every other impresario was up there with their chequebooks out. Langdon locked these four boys in a room and he persuaded them – it took him 24 hours – he shouted at them, and persuaded them that I was the only person in London fit to do this show, on the grounds that I was so stupid and inexperienced that I wouldn't fuck it up by hiring Fenella Fielding and a band and a set. It was extraordinary. This was a sure fire hit, and they'd given it to this bloke in London the same age as themselves, who knew nothing, who'd just had a flop, who was obviously an idiot, who was teetering on the edge of bankruptcy, and who was the only person who hadn't been bothered to go up and see them!'

The deal was struck a few days after the end of the run, at the White Tower restaurant in Percy Street, after Donaldson assured them in person that he would make 'no contribution whatsoever. I think they vaguely mistook me for one of them.' The four agreed to Donaldson's proposition that they should appear in the West End for a flat rate of £75 a week each, with Bassett getting less than half that. Considering that the show eventually made its London backers close on half a million pounds, it was one of the greatest rip-offs in the history of showbusiness. Bennett remembers sadly: 'Despite the success of that week in Edinburgh, with not a seat to be had and long queues for returns, nothing seems to have alerted us to the fact that play our cards right and there was a fortune to be made here. In the worldly wisdom department we tended to look to Peter. He had already had material in West End revues and besides he wore pointed shoes and had a tailor in Old Compton Street. It followed that he must know what he was doing.' Bennett and Miller left the restaurant in a taxi: 'It was the first London taxi I had ever been in, and riding up Half Moon Street we discussed the terms. "They're very good," said Jonathan. "It's ten times what I'd be receiving as a junior doctor." It was fifteen times what I'd be receiving as a mediaeval historian but something told me even then that this was not really the point. So I kept my mouth shut, taking comfort in the illusion that the others must know what they were doing. So it is in every situation in life: somebody must know, the doctor, the surgeon, the accountant or the Prime Minister. They don't, of course. They think you do.'[21] Certainly Peter didn't know, however sharp his clothes or apparently assured his manner. Now he was in funds he was absolutely hopeless with money. It was during the London run of *Beyond the Fringe* that his car was repossessed by bailiffs acting for his unpaid Cambridge landlord.

Peter did have another lucrative source of income to look forward to: *One over the Eight*, the sequel to *Pieces of Eight*, which at this stage still appeared to be the more important project. The script had to be completed quickly, in the few weeks after *Beyond the Fringe*, in time for read-throughs by the end of September. As a consequence of the pressure on Peter's time, the additional material list was much longer this time: John Bird was roped in, along with Timothy Birdsall, John Mortimer, Lionel Bart, Carl Davis, Stanley Daniels, Kenneth Hoare and Stephen Vinaver. Sheila Hancock replaced Fenella Fielding as the female lead. Peter scribbled away furiously throughout September.

In addition to *One Leg Too Few*, *Peace* and *Interesting Facts*, he supplied *Hand up Your Sticks*, about an inept bankrobber practising at home then getting it all wrong at the bank, and *Bird Watching*, advice from a Mr Grole-like ornithologist on the best way to get close to birds in the wild:

> The first thing to do is to get right out of your house, get right out of your house, right out of it and into your countryside, and there you'll find your birds. Hundreds of 'em.

The monologue became more surreal as the ornithologist recommended disguising oneself as a tree, by standing in a rotten tree stump, holding bunches of twigs and wrapping oneself in green netting made by nuns. There was also an extraordinary sketch called *Critics' Choice*, which was a huge joke at the expense of David Frost. A writer named 'David Frost' was grilled by an interviewer about his latest stage offering, which had received a mixed critical reception, 'ranging right from "disastrous" all the way up to "abysmal"'. The interviewer, Lance Percival, went on to accuse the hapless 'Frost' of putting up highly distorted versions of these criticisms outside the theatre.

Some of the new material supplied by the other writers was chameleon-like in its mastery of the Cook style. John Mortimer's *Nightlife* featured another Mr Grole-like character, a travelling string rep who was trying to chat up a nightclub hostess on the basis that his wife had been frigid since Coronation afternoon:

> *Rep*:   I'm up for the show, String and Rope at the Olympia. I am in string.
> *Hostess*: That's interesting, darling.
> *Rep*:   Very interesting stuff, string. Very interesting varied stuff, string. It's a demanding occupation.

She encouraged him to unburden himself sexually, to 'let the words pour out in a hot bubbling stream,' but all he could do was discuss rustic twine and tarred ropette. Eventually, in an impassioned outburst disquietingly reminiscent of Monty Python's weatherman/lumberjack of more than a decade later, he shouted:

> I'm forty-one, and I've been twenty-five years in string! Twenty-five years in bloody string! I want to live! I have a right to have a life!

Perhaps irritated by all the fuss that had been lavished on Peter's performance in *Beyond the Fringe*, Kenneth Williams pronounced himself profoundly unhappy with the script of *One over the Eight*. At the end of September he demanded a 'crisis meeting' with Peter and Michael Codron, and told them – as he confided to his diary – 'It's not right that I should continually have to salvage mediocre material. We must make a stand about this.' Williams was merely being tiresomely queeny. Whatever the faults of *One over the Eight*'s script, it was of a virtually identical standard to its predecessor. To describe sketches like *One Leg Too Few* and *Interesting Facts* as 'mediocre' was nonsense. *One Leg Too Few* was in fact the sketch that Williams singled out as the worst, and his feathers had to be smoothed before he would undertake to perform it. According to Codron, 'He said he found it distasteful, hopping around on one leg.' If there was a problem, it was that Williams was still fruitlessly trying to inject some warmth into the Grole character: he insisted on simpering and adding 'mmms' and 'oohs' in between each of Peter's lines. His comic instincts were basically sound in searching out audience sympathy, but of course it took another level of skill altogether to make such a cold and unlovable creation so appealing.

Peter's principal problem now was how to fill the next seven months. Although both *Beyond the Fringe* and *One over the Eight* were ready to go into the West End, no theatre would be free for either production until the following spring. There was a danger of losing momentum. Wound up and on a roll, Peter needed to perform, to taste the feeling of having an audience weak with laughter before him. He turned down the staff job at the BBC, and did no more than a little desultory copywriting for the ad agency here and there. Instead, he returned to Cambridge and resumed life as the university's king of comedy. He and Wendy moved in together officially, sharing a flat in Warkworth Street.

Monty Python's Graham Chapman was among a new generation of Cambridge students riveted by the Cook improvisational technique: 'Although he'd "gone down", Peter had an obsessive disregard for David Frost, and came back to punish him by being funnier and more intelligent at the smoking concerts. I remember one particular sketch where Peter explained to the pilgrims that the Holy Bee of Ephesus was kept in a matchbox, and that it could cure all ills if they placed three shekels through the lid. After they'd given the three shekel piece, and weren't cured of even one ill, he explained to them that they'd probably stunned the bee.'[22] The word 'stunned' was the masterstroke in that line, just as it was many years later, in a celebrated sketch about a dead parrot. David Frost, in truth, remained one of Peter's closest friends that year, and together they wrote a tabloid parody of Britain's poor Olympic performance for the student magazine *Granta*, which Frost was editing. The location aside, it could just as easily have been written in 1996:

> On the red shale track, it was another black, black day of gloom, despair and despondency for the British lads and lassies who ran their hearts into the ground in the sizzling cauldron that is Rome. Britain must, if she is to maintain her position among the Magic 14 European diving nations, pour £48m into new heated boating rinks up and down our green and pleasant land:[23]

Frost's abiding memory of that winter is of Peter assiduously gambling away the proceeds from his two stage shows.

After Christmas there were *Fringe* cabarets to keep the cast's hand in. Willie Rushton stood in for Dudley Moore, in a performance at the Dorchester: 'I was incredibly impressed by the fact that Peter could make a whole room howl with laughter just by saying "Good evening." He'd just discovered this as a catchphrase, and he couldn't stop saying it. "Good evening, good evening." I don't know why, but it was the funniest thing I'd ever heard in my life.' Peter also got his own back on the Young Conservatives, offering them a long-winded monologue about the ins and outs of defecation; his performance was greeted with an icy silence by the Tory faithful, who had been rashly hoping for a satirical insight into the politics of the day. One of the *Fringe* cabarets was at Bennett's Oxford college, which led to a sticky moment when Peter and the others visited his room to find Mahler playing on the gramophone. Peter instantly latched on to the pretension he felt was apparent in Bennett's musical choice, and the fact that it 'just happened to be playing' as they entered. Bennett was wounded by Peter's jibes; today, he is prepared to give him the benefit of the doubt, albeit guardedly.

Peter and Wendy finally left Cambridge in March 1961. The Footlights Revue that year, masterminded and presented by its new star David Frost, was shamelessly entitled *I Thought I Saw It Move*, in which Frost essayed a passable imitation of his predecessor at every turn. Among the items was *Science – Fact or Fiction?*, now attributed solely to Frost, although it closely resembled the sketch that Miller had seen in 1959. For years, Peter's spirit would continue to haunt Cambridge. According to John Cleese, a freshman that year, 'Everybody was doing him. His presence was still very much alive. Trevor Nunn, who was directing the 1962 Footlights revue, would sit down in the rehearsal breaks and do Peter Cook sketches.'[24] Eric Idle went up to Pembroke in 1961, to find it had become 'the comedy college. His spirit lurked everywhere in the funny voices he had left behind.'[25] Clive James, who arrived at Pembroke three years later still, found that 'his legend haunted the place with an intensity unrivalled even by that of Ted Hughes.'[26]

In the discreet surroundings of the house at Uplyme, Peter's status was naturally not subject to such continuous escalation. That Christmas, Alec Cook had returned from Libya and the family had at last been reunited again, together with their future daughter-in-law. The meeting had been a reasonable success. Wendy got on well with Alec and Margaret, and was a great hit with their two girls, to whom she seemed a glamorous role model. She certainly wasn't the kind of girl they had expected their son to bring home, teetering in on high heels, but that didn't matter. She in turn found them dauntingly old-fashioned and polite: 'They were just so different from my parents, where if something went wrong the saucepans would go flying. It was as if Peter's parents were almost encountering him for the first time, each time they met.' It was difficult for a stranger to discern the deep bonds of silent affection that continued to hold the often-sundered Cook family together.

After a brief spell in John Bassett's spare bedroom, Peter and Wendy moved to a flat in Prince of Wales Drive, Battersea, along with their friends Peter Bellwood and Colin Bell. It was ensemble living, rather like the Prince of Wales pub in Cambridge, except that Peter's recent affluence and Wendy's art school pedigree were clearly on display in the fashionability of the decor. The flat was done up in a pioneering 1960s pastiche Victoriana, with polished wooden floors and solid pine furniture, dominated by a huge wooden rocking horse with a real horsehair tail. 'It was all antiqued up,' says Roger Law, who remembers it as a cross between a colour supplement and a commune. In the midst of the elegant chaos sat Peter, holding court at high-fashion dinner parties, yet always – as John Wells recalls – with the most impeccable, old-fashioned manners. 'He was very concerned that people should meet each other, and he'd keep saying "Is your food all right?", things like that.'

As soon as he'd arrived in London, Peter had set about fulfilling his cherished dream of opening a satirical nightclub, and had sat in Willie Donaldson's office telephoning around looking for premises. 'We got on very well together,' says Donaldson. 'We saw in each other two uptight public schoolboys who wanted to be attractive to women, and wished they could dance and play the saxophone and be at ease.' Before long, Peter had decided to start up his own umbrella company to co-ordinate his myriad activities. He joined forces with Nick Luard, the former treasurer of the Cambridge Footlights – whose experience in the post made him the nearest thing to a bona fide businessman that Peter had encountered – and formed Cook & Luard Productions Ltd. 'I imagined he was a financial wizard,' said Peter later, with a tinge of regret.[27]

A stack of hideous notepaper was run up, and an office was secured at 5–6 Coventry Street. *Queen* magazine ran a profile of Peter, the exciting young entrepreneur. By the time *Fringe* rehearsals started on 4 April – the day before the opening of *One over the Eight* – the rest of the cast were reasonably refreshed and relaxed, but Peter confessed himself absolutely shattered. It didn't matter. Like a catherine wheel, he continued to blaze round at full speed, sparks flying. After a few snatched days in Sardinia, he flew into Heathrow on the 4th and took a taxi straight to the Prince of Wales Theatre. The Prince of Wales was becoming something of a motif in his life.

Although the four cast members had kept their comic reflexes sharp, there is no doubt that in the seven-month layoff since Edinburgh, the *Beyond the Fringe* bandwagon had slowed considerably. People were beginning to forget what all the fuss had been about. Willie Donaldson, who had lost most of his money on his adaptation of *The Last Laugh*, had actually been unable to finance the show he had bought; in the rush of hype following Edinburgh, he had raised £7,000 of the £8,000 he needed from other enthusiastic backers. Chief among them was the impresario Donald Albery, whose £4,000 stake as good as gave him a controlling interest. Albery's enthusiasm, however, had waned severely. In an attempt to cut costs, the only rehearsal space he was prepared to offer them was the bar of the Prince of Wales Theatre during daylight hours. A few days into rehearsals Donaldson brought him along to watch a run-through. 'He thought it was terrible,' admits Donaldson. Albery asked who the fair-haired one with glasses was. Alan Bennett, replied Donaldson. 'He'll have to go,' muttered the impresario.

Although Donaldson eventually persuaded Albery to rescind that particular edict, it felt like a hollow victory. So profound was the older man's dislike for the show that he was not prepared to see it open in London. He refused to provide them with one of his theatres, which meant that they would have to set off for the provinces with no London booking. It was a depressing time for all. The newly appointed director Eleanor Fazan, who had previously directed *Share My Lettuce*, found the cast fractious and hostile to each other. 'They did not regard themselves as being any sort of team – or even comrades,' she recalls.[28] Only Dudley Moore was upset by the bickering. 'He wanted everyone to be friends, everything to be jolly and fun,' says Fazan.[29] That is, he wanted everyone to pretend to be friends, rather than face the unpalatable truth.

A pre-West End provincial tour had already been booked, consisting of a week in Cambridge and a week in Brighton, to knock the show back into shape and to give the cast a chance to try out some new material. Now they had something to prove as well. Sixty sketches had been prepared in all, including twelve of the original Edinburgh show's twenty; *Old J. J.*, the initials sketch, was among those to have bitten the dust. The sixty were reduced to thirty-eight in rehearsal, and on the opening night in Cambridge, 21 April, thirty-five of them were performed. The show began at eight and was still going after midnight. The largely undergraduate audience howled and screamed for more. Peter, in particular, was on home turf, and milked the evening for all it was worth. *Beyond the Fringe* was not going to go down without a fight.

Ten more sketches fell by the wayside over the subsequent fortnight. Among these were *Under Canvas*, a first-rate Cook–Miller composition, in which Peter (as an art expert) explained that Constable had been principally a painter of nudes, who had been subsequently compelled by the moral climate of the day to paint a lot of haystacks over all the naked ladies. 'The Hay Wain', for example, had originally been entitled 'Passionate Breasts':

> The young lady who modelled for Constable was Alice Lauderdale, who was the young lady who came in and did for Constable. Practically any woman would do for Constable.

Another of Peter's efforts to be axed was *Jim's Inn*, a more prosaic (and therefore more vulnerable) parody of a sponsored ITV show, in which product placement – then perfectly legal – played a substantial part:

Bas(Jonathan):	Good gracious me – out of the corner of my eye I thought you were wearing a good cashmere.
Nige(Peter):	I'm glad you thought it was a cashmere, but it's not.
Bas:	I'd put my money on it being a cashmere.
Nige:	You'd lose your money, Bas. It's a Nablock Histamine Non-Iron Oven-Dry Visco-Static Dynaflo, all designed to make a nice sweater with peak purchasing power.

The sketches that were to make it through to the final selection tended, as in Edinburgh, to be of a more satirical bent than these. Peter contributed *The Sadder and Wiser Beaver*, a thinly veiled and caustic

attack on a liberal Cambridge friend of his who had gone to work for
the right-wing Beaverbrook Newspaper Co., which in the light of Peter's
putative advertising career was a bit rich; *Man Bites God*, an attack on
trendy vicars co-written with Jonathan Miller, which implored people to
'get violence off the streets and into the churches where it belongs'; and
Black Equals White, an interview with a tyrannical African dictator which
owed a lot to the discussions in the Cook household regarding Nigerian
independence ('One man, one vote, that is essential – especially for the
nine million black idiots who vote for me.') Jonathan Miller confirms that
'The sketch reflected a right-wing attitude on his part, in a way which
of course is quite unperformable now. It reflected his own experience as
a child of someone who had served in black Africa, a contempt for the
hypocritical self-serving of black leaders.'

Other directly satirical items included a Miller–Bennett attack on
capital punishment, *The Suspense is Killing Me*, in which Bennett's
Headmasterly Prison Governor gave Miller's condemned man an encouraging talking to:

Bennett: You don't want to be cooped up for life.
Miller: Yes, I do want to be cooped up for life.

There was also *Real Class*, an ensemble piece which – by directly addressing
the class differences within the group – confidently satirised the liberal
pretensions of the audience.

Peter: I think at about this juncture, it would be wise to point
             out to those of you who haven't noticed – and God
             knows it's apparent enough – that Jonathan Miller and
             myself come from good families and have the benefits
             of a public school education. Whereas the other two
             members of the cast have worked their way up from
             working class origins. And yet Jonathan and I are
             working together with them in the cast and treating
             them as equals, and I must say it's proving to be a
             most worthwhile, enjoyable and stimulating experience
             for both of us. Wouldn't you agree, Jonathan?

Perhaps most controversial of all the new material was another ensemble
piece, *Aftermyth of War*, a satire – as the title suggests – on the treatment
of World War Two in flag-waving adventure films of the fifties. It seems
mild stuff today, but at the time Britain's war dead seemed too recently
laid to rest for many to stomach any sort of parody:

Peter:	War is a psychological thing, Perkins, rather like a game of football. You know how in a game of football ten men often play better than eleven?
Jonathan:	Yes sir.
Peter:	Perkins, we are asking you to be that one man. I want you to lay down your life, Perkins. We need a futile gesture at this stage. It will raise the whole tone of the war. Get up in a crate Perkins, pop over to Bremen, take a shufti, don't come back. Goodbye, Perkins. God, I wish I was going too.
Jonathan:	Goodbye sir – or is it 'au revoir'?
Peter:	No, Perkins.

Peter was extremely unhappy about the inclusion of *Aftermyth of War* in the final selection of sketches. Reducing a theatre full of Cambridge students to tears of laughter was one thing, but he feared that his parents' generation would not be so amused. This instinctive caution, born from years of experience of knowing when to stop and smile politely, came into direct conflict with his desire to tilt at established values. Despite his misgivings, he worked on the sketch enthusiastically, contributing a section concerning the switching of road signs to confuse the Germans as to the relative whereabouts of Great Yarmouth and Lyme Regis, and a character whose reaction to every military disaster is to go and make a nice cup of tea. When his wife informs him that rationing has been imposed, he suggests a nice cup of steaming hot water.

The debate about the advisability or otherwise of alienating sections of the audience divided the cast in half, with Peter and Dudley Moore still ranged against the other two. It wasn't that Peter had anything against satire; quite the reverse – he wanted to start up a satirical cabaret club of his own. But both he and Dudley, the two who had concrete experience of trying to entertain a wider public for money, felt that their own more controversial material would simply rouse a mainstream audience to anger. Satire had its place. They just wanted to get into the West End; destroying a century of theatrical tradition could not have been further from their minds. Miller and Bennett, who had other careers, were more inclined to use the opportunity to make a few points here and there.

Beyond the Fringe's disastrous week in Brighton seemed to bear out Peter's misgivings, and put a potential West End opening even further off the scale of probability. The cast performed to the sound of slamming auditorium doors throughout, as audience members stalked out in provincial disgust. One man stood up during the *Aftermyth of War* sketch and shouted: 'You

young bounders don't know anything about it!' before stalking off. Peter's
Cambridge friend Richard Cottrell, who had got a job playing Toad in a
touring production of *Toad of Toad Hall*, was playing the same Brighton
theatre in the mornings, and came to see the show on its first night: 'It
was an experience I wouldn't have missed for anything. The seats banged
up throughout the evening, it was wonderful. They were *outraged* by it.'
The reviewer from the *Brighton and Hove Herald* thought that the idea of a
sketch about the war was 'vaguely indecent', the notion of attacking capital
punishment was 'atrocious', and any mockery of Britain's preparations
for nuclear attack was utterly preposterous. 'Why be funny about civil
defence?' he asked in genuine indignation.

The show's reception in Brighton seemed to have sounded its death-
knell. Albery was content to go no further; but once more, luck smiled on
Peter Cook. Among the audience was a lawyer and small-time promoter
named David Jacobs, who was putting on a Bernard Cribbins revue at
London's Fortune Theatre. Cribbins would not be ready to start for six
weeks, so rather than leave the theatre expensively unused during that
time, Jacobs was looking for a cheaply-mounted short run production to
minimise any financial loss. He didn't think much of *Beyond the Fringe*,
but he reasoned that the excitement it had once generated in Edinburgh
would sell enough seats to turn a small profit before the show died a
death. So *Beyond the Fringe* got its London opening after all.

The contract to take the front of house pictures was awarded to Lewis
Morley, who by an amazing coincidence happened to be Willie Donaldson's
partner in a London photographic studio. He came down to Brighton to
shoot some rebellious poses on the beach and under the pier, following
them up with further shots in Hyde Park and at London Zoo. Sean Kenny's
minimalist avant-garde set, just a grand piano, a flying buttress and a flight
of stone steps leading to a platform, looking like a cross between a crypt
and a wine bar, was installed at the Fortune. Drummer Derek Hogg and
Hugo Boyd, the bass player from Edinburgh, were taken on with Dudley
as the Dudley Moore Trio. Publicity appearances were arranged with the
media, including an interview on *Tonight*. This was a disaster. Alan Bennett
stumped around the TV studio doing an impression of Douglas Bader in
an extract from *Aftermyth of War*. The audience sat in mute embarrassment.
Only then did Bennett realise that their interviewer, Kenneth Allsop, was
himself a former RAF flier who had lost one of his legs.

Beyond the Fringe opened at the Fortune on Wednesday 10 May 1961.
Around it in the West End, gaudy theatrefronts advertised comedy revues
in which heavily made-up actors stood in line to sing gang-show numbers,
where every Noel Coward witticism had to be followed by the anaesthetic

of a torch song. There were trouser-dropping farces starring Brian Rix, musicals like *My Fair Lady* and thrillers like *The Mousetrap*. There was also, of course, *One over the Eight* starring Kenneth Williams and Sheila Hancock. The age of the dinosaurs was coming to an end.

Beyond the Fringe took London by storm even more comprehensively than it had destroyed the competition in Edinburgh. Felix Barker in the *Evening News* called it 'The perfect revue, for which we have all waited through so many a groaning and fatuous night. This is the best revue I have ever seen.' Milton Shulman in the *Evening Standard* reckoned it was 'A rare delight, brilliant, uproarious and wonderfully mad.' Bernard Levin in the *Daily Express*, referring to the cast as 'The four good, great men who have done this thing to and for and in the name of us all', described the show as 'A revue so brilliant, adult, hard-boiled, accurate, merciless, witty, unexpected, alive, exhilarating, cleansing, right, true and good, I shall go and see it once a month for the rest of my life. The satire is real, barbed, deeply planted and aimed at things and people that need it.' Levin's screeches of laughter during the first night audience had been so startlingly loud that the cast had actually held an impromptu meeting during the interval to decide what to do about it. Although the show did not actually survive for the rest of Levin's life, he did have to put up with Peter repeating his screams at full volume whenever they met thereafter, preferably on a crowded pavement. The clinching review, if one were needed, came from Kenneth Tynan four days later in *The Observer*. He correctly predicted that he had witnessed 'a revolution in revue', and added that 'Future historians may well thank me for providing them with a full account of the moment when English comedy took its first decisive step into the second half of the twentieth century.' It was an analysis that only Milligan and Sellers could have quibbled with.

Beyond the Fringe's effect on its audience was no less profound. Tony Hendra, the future editor of *National Lampoon*, was actually studying to be a monk on the Isle of Wight when he dropped in at the Fortune Theatre on his way back from a trip to Cambridge. 'I went into the show a monk, and I emerged having completely lost my vocation. I didn't know things could be so funny. I didn't realise that authority was so absurd.'[30] Others whose lives were significantly affected by the show included future Pythons Eric Idle, Terry Jones and Michael Palin, who explains: 'It is not easy nowadays to convey the sensational audacity, the explosively liberating effect of hearing the Prime Minister of the day impersonated, or judges, bishops, police chiefs and army officers mocked. It was shocking and thrilling, but it was done with such skill and intelligence that it could not easily be shot down, dismissed or shrugged off. It was all the more effective for coming from within. Peter's education and background were the very epitome of the Establishment. He knew what he was talking about.'[31]

Over at the Duke of York's, the cast of *One over the Eight* were not best pleased by the reception accorded to their young writer. Kenneth Williams wrote in his diary: 'Sheila Hancock *furious* over the rave reviews for *Beyond the Fringe*. She is absolutely speechless with rage at these lovely notices for Cook, when this was the man that practically brought our show to disaster. I said it was best to be indifferent to the whole business.' In fact *One over the Eight* had received good notices – the *Evening Standard* had called it 'snappy and gay' – but the first gusts of the chill wind blowing from Edinburgh had caught it even before it could get into its stride. The *Daily Mail* questioned its 'smart frisky little dance routines', which 'swamped' the comedy. Reviewer Robert Muller complained that 'The trouble with this revue is that its chief author, Peter Cook, has failed to find real targets for his satire.'[32] Just a year previously, such a comment would have been unthinkable. Pertinently Muller singled out for praise *Bloody Rhondda Mine*, a number about miners which had been on the shortlist for *Beyond the Fringe* until Kenneth Williams had decided to go ahead with it.

In a celebrated article for *The Observer*, entitled *Can English Satire Draw Blood?*, Jonathan Miller directly attacked the production of the Kenneth Williams revues, complaining that 'The bony outlines of Peter's contributions were softened by their gay commercial setting. Tinselly dance routines, a-fidget with glow paint and fishnet would follow one of his dour, screwy little numbers and promptly erase it from the mind of the audience.'[33] The howls of protest coming from the Duke of York's were no more than the sound of people who'd backed the wrong horse. Miller was firmly behind the right horse. Peter had managed to back both horses and still turn a profit.

It would have taken a brilliant sociologist to have predicted it, but Britain was ready for the shift to *Beyond the Fringe*. Ten years of Conservative government had never really been questioned. The fear of nuclear war was magnified among teenagers facing national service in the wake of the Suez fiasco. The wave of patriotism unleashed by victory in the Second World War had receded. The new generation could only view the war at second-hand on second-rate celluloid; and the war had been the principal, if not the only reason to have felt proud to be British in the preceding sixteen years. *Beyond the Fringe* was the vanguard of a social trend, in which the first highly sceptical and aware generation of post-war-educated public schoolboys was unleashed into society. Their fearlessness came not from having surveyed a weakened political world and discovered themselves capable of mastering it, but had been instilled into them from birth by the very Establishment they now mocked, the Establishment they had been taught to assume command of in due course. It was not a revolution but a cultural coup d'état.

Within six months the word 'satire', used by some anonymous sub-editor to headline Tynan's *Observer* piece, was the topic of conversation at every fashionable middle-class dinner table in Britain. A consumer demand for satire was actually created, which became known as the 'satire boom'. *Beyond the Fringe* and Peter Cook in particular were widely regarded as the fount of all things satirical. Peter, relaxed with his amazing success, tended to allow such generalisations to flow over his head. Miller and Bennett, the two who had actually pushed the revue in a more satirical direction, tended to argue against being pigeonholed, and to attack the 'satire boom' as a journalistic construct. It was a debate that carried on right up to the night of Peter's death, when Miller and John Bird argued on *Newsnight* about whether Peter had been a satirist or not; and beyond, to Chris Morris's interjection in a Radio 4 documentary about Peter's life that the whole question was entirely semantic and therefore irrelevant.

One thing the cast of *Beyond the Fringe* was always keen to emphasise was that they had never set out to be satirical. 'We just wrote about the things that amused or annoyed us,' said Peter.[34] As a result, the satire label was slightly irritating. Bennett rather modestly contends that 'I imagine various people were doing similar sketches around the same time, and it has always seemed to me that what was subsequently labelled "satire" was simply this kind of private humour going public.'[35] Miller agrees that 'None of us approached the world with a satirical indignation. What made the show work was that we resolved not to make these conditional propositions, which were always the basis of old-fashioned revue – "Wouldn't it be funny *if* . . ." Our idea was "Isn't it funny *that* . . ." – let's observe what actually goes on. We didn't think it was a revolution. It was only when Kenneth Tynan shoved this banner into our hands – it was rather like Charlie Chaplin finding himself at the head of a communist parade.'[36] As for the notion that Peter was the most satirical of the lot, Miller snorts with derision. 'The idea that he had an anarchic, subversive view of society is complete nonsense. He was the most upstanding, traditional upholder of everything English and everything Establishment.'[37] Bennett concurs: 'He wasn't interested in satire at all. He was interested in being funny.'[38] Miller laments: 'We've been lumbered [with the satire tag] ever since. Having gone off and done something else, they say, "Oh, the old satirical verve has gone, I see. The revolutionaries have certainly found

themselves very comfortable houses to live in. The young Fringers have
gone soft." We were soft from the very start. We'd always lived in houses
like that.'[39]

It's certainly true that Beyond the Fringe did not put its case from a
left-wing perspective. Right from the start, some reviewers had drawn
their readers' attention to this apparent contradiction. Tynan, himself
a committed socialist, had raised the sole objection that the show was
'anti-reactionary without being progressive'.[40] Harold Hobson, writing in
the same day's Sunday Times, pointed out that it was 'an entertainment
founded in [the cast's] conviction of their natural superiority to all that they
discuss, attack or caricature. The close attention which I invariably give to
frivolous entertainments did not reveal to me any political principle.'[41] But
if there had been no satirical or political intent, that is not to say there was
little satirical or political effect. The Fringers may have set out to write
only about the things that amused or annoyed them, but what is satire
if not the holding up of folly and vice to public ridicule? Two principal
types of comic character dominated Peter's well-stocked repertoire, the
lonely obsessive bore and the powerful but pompous halfwit. The latter
variant especially was derived from close observation of the class that
had reared him. Of course he did not wish to overthrow his own
kind, but merely by laughing at the foolish and the morally corrupt
among their number, he had succeeded in exposing his own kind to
satirical attack.

Bird's argument was more technical than sociological: 'A satirist is what
Peter was . . . Northrop Frye wrote of satire that "It demands (at least a
token) fantasy, a content recognised as grotesque, moral judgments (at
least implicit), and a militant attitude to experience". Its distinguishing
mark is the "double focus of morality and fantasy". Cook wouldn't easily
have forgiven me for calling up this academic artillery barrage, but those
phrases perfectly describe the way his humour worked.'[42] The sketch –
and the actual joke – that Bird and Miller chose as their battleground
after Peter's death was a piece of nonsense about the Great Train Robbery
written for the show's American tour, in which Peter – as Sir Arthur
Gappy, a Streeb-Greebling variant and senior policeman – explained that
Scotland Yard had built up an Identikit picture which closely resembled
the Archbishop of Canterbury:

Interviewer: So His Grace is your number one suspect?
Sir Arthur: Well, let me put it this way – His Grace is the man
                we are currently beating the living daylights out of
                down at the Yard.

> *Interviewer*: And he is still your number one suspect?
>
> *Sir Arthur*:   No, I'm happy to say that the Archbishop, God bless him, no longer resembles the picture we built up.

The punchline was a satirical attack on police brutality, argued Bird. Just a joke, said Miller, 'a piece of inspired lunacy – I don't think Peter was the slightest bit interested in police brutality.'[43] Perhaps the latter in intent, in *inspiration*, and the former, quite knowingly, in effect.

It is worth noting what Peter himself said at the time, when asked by the *Sunday Pictorial* to define his own political perspective. 'I'm a young reformer', he replied, and suggested that he might vote Labour at the next election (although he later claimed that he hadn't done so). 'People at the top make out that they know everything. What pompous rubbish. Just because a bloke becomes Foreign Secretary he doesn't stop making mistakes. But most people think that because he's got the job he must know more than anyone. The Government and Establishment dismiss the population with a combination of arrogance and disdain. My main aim is to try to get the public treated like rational human beings.'[44] The youthful enthusiasm inherent in that manifesto is probably just a reflection of the misleadingly heady atmosphere of potential change that prevailed in the wake of *Beyond the Fringe*. What is more significant is that, insofar as Peter wished to change things, it was from a moral rather than a political perspective. The moral element that informed his humour sometimes led him down a politically satirical path. It may be oversimplifying matters to describe him as a satirist. He was definitely not a born satirist. But he achieved satire. And he certainly had it thrust upon him, a banner that he was happy to carry for a while.

Satirist or not, irrelevant semantic debate or not, the spring of 1961 and *Beyond the Fringe* marked a turning point in the attitude of the British public to its leaders. Henceforth politicians would be treated with far more scepticism and far less respect. No longer would they be free to address the voters – in Russell Davies's memorable phrase – 'as if they were a convocation of servants below stairs.' In other countries, such shifts have only ever occurred through the medium of wars and revolutions. How wonderful that in this country such seismic change could have been brought about by a comedy show.

Of course the traditional response of the British Establishment to criticism is to try to absorb its critics. Rab Butler, Iain Macleod and the Southern Rhodesian leader Sir Roy Welensky all came along to the Fortune; it was only a matter of time before Macmillan himself plucked up the courage to try and prove what a good sport he was, by turning up to see himself impersonated. The evening began well; but when Peter arrived on stage as Macmillan the Prime Minister's smile froze into an unconvincing rictus. With deliberation, Peter pointed out the presence of their distinguished visitor. Sure enough, it was not long before he began to stray, unannounced, from the agreed script:

> When I've a spare evening, there's nothing I like better than to wander over to a theatre and sit there listening to a group of sappy, urgent, vibrant young satirists, with a stupid great grin spread all over my silly old face.

The audience fell silent, but Peter didn't stop. He plunged on, more gleeful at his power to shock than disturbed by the absence of laughter.

By February 1962, when the show had been running for nine months and Bernard Cribbins had long been forced to settle for alternative accommodation, opposition MPs were getting laughs in the House of Commons by suggesting that it was Peter, not Macmillan, who had been defending the government on the TV news. On the 28th, the Queen herself came to the Fortune, flanked by the Earl of Home and the Lord Chamberlain. The management had asked Alan Bennett to delete the word 'erection' from one of his monologues, but according to Bennett, 'I priggishly refused. I cringe to think of it today. I suppose I must be one of the few people who have said "erection" in front of the Queen.'[45] Her Majesty openly roared with laughter at Peter's Macmillan impersonation. 'It proves we haven't done our job properly,'[46] said Jonathan Miller glumly.

Alec Cook finally got to see the show in London too, and was immensely proud of his son. He and his wife thought *Beyond the Fringe* was marvellous, although Margaret too found *Aftermyth of War* unacceptable. Peter's sisters were if anything even prouder: when night fell in Uplyme, Elizabeth would creep into her glamorous brother's vacant bedroom and fall asleep on his bed. For Christmas, Peter gave Sarah a letter to Kiki Byrne, who ran a fashionable dress shop in the King's Road, which read: 'Please give my sister Sarah any dress she wants from your shop.' 'I remember slipping along icy pavements to find the shop. It was just the most brilliant, exciting thing for a country-reared teenager to go into this shop, clutching this magic piece of paper.'

Peter was now extremely well off. Although the cast were only receiving a tiny proportion of the box office takings, the peripheral rewards – financial and otherwise – were considerable. In August 1961 they signed to appear in a series of five-minute spots for the ITV arts magazine *Tempo*, at £125 a time. Dudley Moore even got his own jazz show on Southern Television, called *Strictly for the Birds*. Only the BBC, it seems, were still not interested. In 1962 *The Observer* offered Peter his own weekly satire page, which he wrote with Michael Frayn and Roger Law, called *Almost the End*. Law illustrated a regular topical cartoon strip scripted by Peter, one episode of which featured two bowler-hatted, pinstriped men complaining about modern theatre:

> You know, I go to the theatre to be entertained. I don't want to see plays about rape, sodomy and drug addiction. I can get all that at home.

The page was finally scrapped after a cartoon concerning the plight of a mental patient who had escaped, committed a robbery, had been declared sane as a result, had been imprisoned for life, and then flogged for further misdemeanours in prison. The Home Secretary Rab Butler was depicted walking in a summer field with his wife, declaring that the prisoner's flogging was necessary because he had offended so regularly that 'he must be off his head'. *The Observer's* editor David Astor was so outraged at the inclusion of the Home Secretary's wife that he abandoned the satire page altogether. It was probably a relief to Peter, who by now had taken on so much work that he was meeting Law to discuss the strip during car journeys from one place to another, recycling a lot of stage material and delivering his copy at midnight on deadline day, leaving Law to draw the illustrations overnight.

Also in 1962, Spike Milligan, Peter Sellers and Harry Secombe made contact and asked if Peter and Jonathan Miller would like to take part in a *Beyond the Fringe*-meets-*The Goons* project, to be recorded for commercial release. For the Radley boy who had feigned illness in order to press his ear to the sanatorium radio so many times, this was the ultimate thrill. Entitled *Bridge over the River Wye*, it was a direct parody of the River Kwai film starring Alec Guinness. Milligan was credited with writing the script, but the mere fact that one of the characters was called Brigadier Stutling-Drobe indicates that Peter too made a contribution. Peter also introduced the record:

> It was 1962 in England, but still 1943 in Japan, such was the difference in teeth between these two great religions.

Sellers played the Alec Guinness character, who forbade his men to escape into the jungle, while Miller portrayed William Holden's single-minded American:

Holden:	One of the men has already planned to make a break, sir.
Guinness:	Is he mad?
Holden:	He has a certificate, sir.
Guinness:	It means certain death.
Holden:	It is a death certificate, sir.

Spike Milligan, meanwhile, cast himself as the Japanese Camp Commandant:

| *Commandant*: | Must – not – lose – face! |
| *Guinness*: | I think you could well afford to lose that one. |

Peter Sellers, who remembered the young student he'd met at the Duke of Bedford's bash, had already been acting as a sort of roving ambassador for *Beyond the Fringe*, persuading as many of his high-profile friends as he could to go and see it.

There were other obvious rewards for being one of the stars of the most celebrated show in the West End. Dudley Moore, who craved the company of the opposite sex even more than Peter did, made up for all those years as a club-footed outcast with a string of love affairs. Peter later admitted to being jealous of the number of women who swarmed around his diminutive colleague: 'Women, at least in those days, did have this opinion that these magic fingers, if they could weave such magic on the keyboard . . . "Would that they could tickle over my bits." It seemed an easy way of pulling birds.'[47] Eventually Moore, who had also been busy writing the music for two other stage shows, collapsed with exhaustion, and had to be replaced in *Beyond the Fringe* for three weeks by Robin Ray. He flew to Positano to recuperate. Just before he was about to board the plane he encountered John Gielgud, who recognised him and insisted on giving him a letter of introduction to his friends Rex Harrison and Lilli Palmer, who lived in Italy. Once aboard the aircraft, Moore opened it himself and read: 'Darling Lilli, This will introduce you to the brilliant young pianist from Beyond The Fringe – Stanley Moon.' Peter loved this story and often called his friend Stanley Moon thereafter. When he wrote the script for the film *Bedazzled*, that was the name he gave to the thinly-disguised Dudley Moore character.

One of Dudley's relationships was with Anna Leroy, a chorus girl from Donald Albery's production of *Oliver!*, whom he would meet discreetly in the Lamb and Flag in Covent Garden. Her chaperone was Ron Moody's understudy Barry Humphries, the future Dame Edna Everage. Humphries remembers his first sight of Peter Cook in the bar: 'An incredibly thin aquiline figure, constantly throwing back his forelock, exhibiting his profile, rather nattily turned out in a mohair suit, and quite feminine. There was nothing effeminate about Peter, but he was feminine, which is possibly the reason why so many men seemed to have crushes on him. Most of the people who worked with him had gigantic crushes on Peter Cook, and it was not difficult to see why. He was an immensely attractive figure. He was somewhat unapproachable though – he'd adopted a mocking manner, which I saw later to be a disguise for a person who was in fact quite shy.'

One crush which Peter reciprocated came from Judy Huxtable, a debutante-turned-actress from the south-west who had signed on with Willie Donaldson. She was mesmerised by his performance in *Beyond the Fringe*: 'With those daddy long legs and arc-lamp eyes he was by far the most brilliant and good looking. I can remember sitting there watching these brilliant young men poking fun at politicians, with my father sitting beside me harrumphing and saying "Absolute nonsense!"'[48] When they met, Peter in turn was knocked out by her slender beauty and her silly sense of humour. She was, according to Willie Donaldson, 'Ridiculously pretty, very shy, very timid, doll-like pretty, almost too pretty.' Peter decided to woo her in earnest. His old Pembroke friend Tim Coghlan, who lived in the flat above hers in Exhibition Road, remembers his eager pursuit.

Of course he had many rivals. Judy's best friend Gaye Brown, a large, jolly, boisterous fellow member of the chorus-line in the revue *The Lord Chamberlain Regrets*, introduced her to Sean Kenny, the extremely fashionable designer of *Beyond the Fringe*. Kenny, a guilt-ridden, hard-drinking, monosyllabic Irish Catholic, proved to be an even more irresistibly sexy figure. 'I knew that what this man, responsible for these designs, was about was the same thing I was about. And I knew that he could be my teacher,' she said.[49] Besides, Peter was engaged to be married to Wendy. Judy took up with Kenny and eventually married him. Peter remained good friends with her, and put his courtship on the back burner until a later date.

After a year in the West End, the cast of *Beyond the Fringe* were beginning to get on each other's nerves slightly, which was hardly surprising bearing in mind the artificial circumstances in which they had been thrown together. Most of the obvious sources of tension had been avoided – Oxford v. Cambridge, north v. south, middle class v. working class, tall v. short – but their four characters were so distinct as to cause complex individual frictions. Miller was getting bored with saying the same lines every night, and was tending to rush through his material: this annoyed Moore's thorough sense of professionalism. Moore came in for a degree of intellectual snobbery, the effect of which was emphasised by his inferiority complex. Peter and Jonathan Miller tended to seize control of interviews, leading the press to assume that they were responsible for the bulk of writing; this irritated the underrated Bennett. 'There was just a great deal of stand-off and subdued friction,' says Miller.

Peter tended not to reveal his feelings, but confided later to Michael Parkinson that he believed Miller and Bennett to be 'a bit phoney in a sense, a bit contrived.' He felt a distance between himself and his two colleagues; but then, says Parkinson, 'he probably felt that for the world and most of the people he met. It wasn't said in an offensive way, because he had too much natural charm and vulnerability for that.' Peter coped with boredom on stage by varying his performance every night, sometimes dangerously, taking it to the verge of embarrassment. Initially his improvisations had been hilarious: Bennett remembers that his 'frustrated miner' monologue 'was less of a sketch than a continuing saga which each night developed new extravagances and surrealist turns, the mine at one point invaded by droves of Proust-lovers, headed by the scantily-clad Beryl Jarvis. Why the name Beryl Jarvis should be funny I can't think. But it was and plainly is.'[50] (Actually one could write an essay about why the name Beryl Jarvis is funny, but there is a limit to the value of dissecting humour.) As time went on though, Peter became bored with merely being hilariously funny. According to Dudley Moore, 'The sketch got longer and longer and sometimes it got very boring. He used to be willing to bore people with endless monologues as long as he could exit on a laugh.'[51]

Drawing on his experiences from the Pembroke Players' German tour, Peter started to improvise his lines in the Shakespeare sketch. This annoyed Bennett, who was less impressed with his abilities in this area than Peter's fellow students had been: he reckoned that Peter 'couldn't do it for toffee', and that only his Elvis impersonation was more 'deeply embarrassing'.[52] Moore felt better-disposed to Peter's improvisations, and himself tended to change his lines regularly in *Royal Box* and *Civil Defence* (as *Whose Finger on What Button?* was now called). During a relatively highbrow Miller–Bennett two-hander about philosophy, Moore would sometimes stand in the wings and shout 'Nurse! The screens!' or something of that sort. 'Peter used to look forward to those moments,' recalls Moore.

Although there had been no really deep-seated problems, the show was clearly in need of a shake-up. It had won awards. The book and the record had been completed and released. The atmosphere at the Fortune was further downcast by the death of Hugo Boyd, Dudley Moore's bass player, in a car crash. Moore started afresh and formed a new trio with Chris Karan on drums and Pete McGurk on bass. It was time for *Beyond the Fringe* to start afresh as well, and the opportunity to do so arrived with an offer to transfer the show to Broadway, starting in October 1962. There was one obvious problem: Peter's satirical nightclub, the Establishment Club, was now up and running in Soho. But Peter had become known as a man who could apparently surmount any obstacle, more often than not with a grand gesture.

Author's note: *The Complete Beyond the Fringe*, published by Methuen in 1987, contains the official performance history of the show. This document contains a number of discrepancies with original programmes and contemporary press reviews. Where such discrepancies occur I have relied on contemporary sources and interviews with surviving cast members.

CHAPTER 5

Sorry, Sir, There Is a £5 Waiting List
The Establishment Club, 1961–62

By the autumn of 1961 Peter was regarded not just as the nation's foremost satirist, but also as one of its most celebrated entrepreneurs; which was ironic, as he didn't consider himself much of a satirist and didn't want to be an entrepreneur. The club he had dreamed of in Berlin, which had taken shape in late-night Cambridge discussions with Nick Luard and John Bird, had come to fruition. Peter's main reason for opening it was not to change society or to make money, just to have somewhere to go 'where we could be more outrageous than we could be on stage'.[1] In 1961 the Lord Chamberlain's Office could and frequently did censor public theatre, but the club format legally sidestepped his attentions. In the process Peter anticipated the Comedy Store and its ilk by twenty years.

Jeremy Cotton, his friend from the first-term curry club at Pembroke, had bumped into him in the early summer, loping down the Charing Cross Road. Peter explained that he was 'looking for premises'. He'd do better to return to the junction of Oxford Street, Cotton suggested helpfully, as the Cambridge Circus 'premises' were closed. Once the confusion had been cleared up, Peter explained that he was actually touring Soho's seedier parts looking for a disused nightclub. Originally his search had fanned out through Covent Garden from Donaldson's office and had settled on premises there, but planning permission had been denied; now he was tracking west to the familiar territory behind the Apollo Theatre, a tackily glamorous gangland of strip joints and sex clubs. Eventually he discovered the Club Tropicana in Greek Street, an 'All Girl Strip Revue' that had gone bankrupt after being shut down in a police raid. He cabled Luard, who was en route to a Mexican holiday: 'Have premises. Stop travelling.' Luard flew home at once, and declared it the least appealing property he'd ever seen. Within six months, Jeremy Cotton would be taking his girlfriends for nights out to the Establishment Club, and profiting from the amazing sexual kudos bestowed by a mere passing wave of Peter Cook's hand.

The club's name was of relatively recent invention: it was Henry Fairlie in the *Spectator* who had coined the term to describe the invisible nexus of power that controls our lives. Soho was the perfect place for an anti-Establishment headquarters – exotic, sybaritic, unconventional, crooked, late to bed, a place the real Establishment found difficult to control. This in itself presented a handicap, though, for a young man who on the face of it politely epitomised the real Establishment and its vulnerable good manners. There were people who would need to be paid off, people watching and waiting to see what was afoot, like cautious jackals keeping one eye on the approach of a very confident-looking giraffe to the waterhole. Mr Lubowski didn't know what to make of the cool, elegant boy who wished to negotiate a lease on his premises, and so kept 'discovering' new conditions in the lease that would hike the price up. Peter, unfazed, paid these tiny demands in a manner which signified that they meant little to him, and not at all that he was too apprehensive to protest.

In fact, raising a huge sum of money with which to start work proved no problem at all. Peter simply let it be known that he was starting a London club. One year's membership would cost three guineas – or two guineas if paid in advance – and life membership would cost a mere twenty guineas. Invitations were sent out to the famous and influential, just in case the news had slipped them by. Within a matter of weeks 7,000 people had taken out membership, including Graham Greene, J. B. Priestley, Yehudi Menuhin, Ben Travers, Lord Russell of Liverpool, Sir Isaiah Berlin, Somerset Maugham, Lionel Bart, Brian Rix and an unnamed bishop. Life members, as many of the 7,000 were, received a free pin-up of Harold Macmillan. All this in August when the Establishment was just a ruined strip joint. Virtually the only money Peter had to pay out in advance was the premium of a £50,000 insurance policy against libel damages.

His first appointment was Sean Kenny, designer of the *Fringe*, who gutted the whole place and rebuilt it using pine, hessian, steel, glass and black paint. The outside of the building was pink. 'No plush', noted *The Observer* wonderingly, 'and nothing Caribbean.'[2] A restaurant was installed, and the chef from the Mermaid Theatre lured away. The menu would feature the latest trendy middle-class dishes, such as paté and creme caramel. Peter hired his own flatmate Colin Bell as Head of Publicity. He also took on a personal secretary – Judy Scott-Fox, a jolly, oversized, upper-class woman with a hooting laugh that can clearly be heard on every *Beyond the Fringe* recording. Lewis Morley, the *Fringe* photographer, was given the first floor to open a photographic studio, and Sean Kenny started up a design studio on the floor above that. Art exhibitions were planned, along with a cinema club showing free films every afternoon, 'including the Marx Brothers, Rudolf Valentino and Adolf Hitler'. A ticker-tape machine was installed, together with a library of newspapers and journals, and a programme of informal but serious lunchtime discussion sessions was arranged, so that members could mull over the issues of the day. An advertising slogan was devised: 'If you can't join them, beat them.'

For all the bright ideas though, the club would have to stand or fall on its comedy content. Peter wanted a twice-nightly cabaret, the first bill at 9.30 featuring a resident cast of regulars, the second at half past midnight to feature the cast of *Beyond the Fringe*, fresh from their evening's performance at the Fortune Theatre. It soon became clear that this last was a pipe-dream: the others simply didn't share Peter's boundless energy, particularly when their colleague was intending to elevate himself to the status of their employer. Only Dudley Moore agreed; meek, obliging Dudley, who dutifully came to the club every night and played jazz in the basement with his trio. Jonathan Miller compromised by appearing in *Red Cross*, one of a number of short humorous films shot in the summer of 1961, which were played to the audience between sketches. He appeared as a chain-smoking surgeon who keeps flicking cigarette ash into his patient's innards. Another short featured Neville Chamberlain's celebrated prediction of peace on his return from seeing Hitler in Munich, shot over and over again by a bumbling director as Chamberlain continues to get his famous lines wrong.

One young comedian to arouse Peter's interest as a possible performer was John Wells, who had just received rave notices for a show at the 1961 Edinburgh Festival. Peter dispatched a telegram to Scotland offering to buy up his services. Wells came down to meet him amid the sawing and hammering at Greek Street, picking his way through the debris to shake his hand. Wells recalls: 'He was incredibly well-mannered. He was wearing a suit, while everybody else wore sweaters and gym shoes. I remember the formal way he shook hands, very English and polite. Even though he was exactly, to the day, a year younger than I was, I found it difficult to treat him as anything but a star.'[3] Wells, it transpired, had already secured a job as a schoolmaster at Eton, but Peter persuaded him to take the late spot on the opening night. Wells's old friend Willie Rushton, too, was to make frequent late-night appearances.

Eventually, an in-house cast of regulars was put together for the main evening performances. John Bird was enticed away from his directing job at the Royal Court and encouraged to become a performer; John Fortune, who had just come down from Cambridge, was also hired. Jeremy Geidt, a thirty-one-year-old actor and TV presenter, was taken on to provide a more slapstick element – 'He was great at falling over and farting,'[4] said Peter. There were two other short-lived professional actors, David Walsh and Hazel Wright, although in due course they were replaced by Eleanor Bron, once she had been released from her dull job in the personnel department of a large company. The jazz singer Annie Ross was hired for a short engagement; her place was later taken on a permanent basis by Carole Simpson, performing satirical numbers with lyrics by Jay Landesman or Christopher Logue and music by Tony Kinsey and Stanley Myers, the husband of *Fringe* director Eleanor Fazan. The sketches were all written by Peter himself, along with John Bird and John Fortune. Peter had perfected the remarkable knack of giving everyone the impression that his attention was fully committed to their particular area of the enterprise. Bird recalls: 'The nuts-and-bolts things had somehow been taken care of: money raised, premises organised. He was heavily involved in all this, but he must have done it in his lunchtime, or his sleep; as far as I was concerned, what he was really interested in was the show.'[5]

There were variety acts too, slotted in and around the comedy, including Norman and Laura Sturgis – banned by a directive of the American High Command from every military base in Europe – and the Unforgettable Alberts – 'Unforgettable at least to the gentleman diner who was rendered unconscious by the collapse of their half-ton exploding harp,'[6] according to Peter. Roger Law was also taken on, to produce a brand new 14-foot-by-18-inch satirical drawing opposite the bar each week. These tended to be fairly surreal: St Francis of Assisi being devoured by crows, or Sir Roy Welensky, the white supremacist Prime Minister of Southern Rhodesia, turning slowly into a pig. Says Law: 'People either liked them or they'd get cross about them and chuck red wine all over them. Colin McInnes was always getting cross about them.'

Peter appeared to be planning more of these attractions than it seemed possible for one person to organise, while simultaneously appearing in the West End's most successful show. The key to this achievement was a blitzkrieg approach to problems, knowing which obstacles to tackle head-on, which ones to skirt and which ones to ignore. Lashings of charm and a judicious assessment of when to delegate surmounted every difficulty. Finding a parking space near the Establishment, for instance, was one of those tiresome little problems that could have wasted half an hour or so of valuable time every day. So he simply parked his car illegally outside the front door, and every day the police towed it away to their car pound at Waterloo. Every evening two stagehands from the Fortune would go down to Waterloo to collect it for him. Total cost: a mere £6 a week, excepting those occasions when the police had left a ticket on the windscreen instead, which Peter would simply ignore. Eventually a constable turned up at the Battersea flat, bearing a sheaf of unpaid tickets. Peter welcomed him like an old friend, ushered him in, gave him a cup of tea and treated him royally. After about half an hour of chat and laughter, the policeman nodded sheepishly to the tickets and said: 'About these parking offences, sir. Would they by any chance have occurred during the period when your American business partner was over here and borrowing your car?' Why yes, replied Peter, that must have been the very period. 'Probably tricky to trace then,' said the policeman. 'Scarcely worth the trouble sir.'

The Establishment set its opening date for 5 October 1961. On the 4th, £13,000-worth of fire escapes were installed, forgotten in the earlier rush, and the workmen only cleared out the last of their tools on the morning of the opening. By now Peter and Nick Luard hadn't been to bed for seventy-two hours. The papers were gratifyingly full of publicity. Peter, asked about what precisely the *Fringe* cast would be contributing, as previously advertised, deflected the truth of their non-involvement with a joke. Alan Bennett would be doing the catering, he said – 'He's in favour of didactic cooking'; and Jonathan Miller would 'of course, feature his talks of old Africa centred on the rise and fall of Mr Nobitsu and his weekly encounters with the Baluba tribesmen. He will be assisted by an African waiter who will be held responsible if everything goes wrong.'[7]

Miller, in fact, wrote a huge article in *The Observer* to coincide with the club's opening. *Can English Satire Draw Blood?* expressed the hope that the club might 'develop the weapons necessary for the final overthrow of the Neo-Gothic stronghold of Victorian good taste.' England, said Miller, was still a country where the posthumous rallying-cry 'Theirs not to reason why' represented 'an expression of praise and approval rather than a signal for a rain of scorching contempt which such blinkered loyalty richly deserved. "Bloody fools" was the only healthy reply on hearing the news of the Light Brigade fiasco. It is to be hoped that when The Establishment opens its doors the cry of "Bloody fools" will ring loud and clear through Soho and down the courtly reaches of Whitehall.' Miller's hopes were not, however, entirely matched by his expectations: 'The success of this project is seriously threatened by a subtle defence with which the members of the (real) Establishment protect themselves against these new attacks. It is the threat of castration by adoption; of destruction by patronage. Cook is already somewhat disturbed by the number of applications for membership which bear the post-mark SW1. We have begun to experience the same threat in our revue. Each night, before curtain-up, sleek Bentleys evacuate a glittering load into the foyer. Some of the harsh comment in the programme is greeted with shrill cries of well-bred delight which reflect a self-indulgent narcissism which takes enormous pleasure in gazing at the satiric reflection.'[8]

It was not a problem that the Establishment Club was ever able to solve; if, indeed, it was a problem. There is always a danger that when a group of middle-class people from good homes puts on a revue, other middle-class people from good homes will want to come and see it. One might argue that it is a sign of a healthy society for its rich and powerful citizens to laugh loudly at themselves. In the radical climate of 1961, though, it was always likely to be perceived as a drawback. Peter was not entirely grateful for *Can English Satire Draw Blood?*: 'That article was very flattering, but in a way it wound up as being a disservice. The only blood drawn was from my mouth when somebody hit me round the head with a handbag.'[9]

One problem that really should have been foreseen and dealt with was that all 7,000 members would attempt to turn up on the opening night. The possibility only dawned on Peter when it was too late to stop it occurring: 'I hope we've attracted the sort of members who'll be small enough to be stacked in tiers,' he said hopefully on the eve of the opening night, before adding wearily: 'I always wanted to be my own boss, but now I'd like nothing better than to work for a large firm for £25 a week.'[10]

On the night of the 5th, Greek Street was jammed with sleek Bentleys and every other kind of car. A crowd of angry members jostled and shoved on the pavement without making any headway. The club's telephone system collapsed. Television lights blazed white and reporters pushed for quotes. Five hundred people managed to get into the performance area, which had been designed to hold ninety. Four of them were policemen. One newspaper critic, needing to leave early, had to be passed over the heads of the crowd. Among the famous who managed to gain entry were Trevor Howard, J. P. Donleavy and James Butler, the son of the Home Secretary, who arrived in black tie, laughed uproariously at a film of his father and Macmillan as nineteenth-century prizefighters, and promised to buy his father membership of the club as a present. Among those who couldn't get in were Geoffrey Johnson-Smith, MP and Jocelyn Stevens, the proprietor of *Queen* magazine; although as the harassed commissionaire was later instructed to let them both in on the grounds of their status, Jonathan Miller's worst fears appear to have been realised on the very first night. Targets for the evening included Lord Home, the Bow Group, the Trade Unions, Jomo Kenyatta (impersonated by John Bird), John Betjeman (impersonated by John Wells) and Jocelyn Stevens, lending a shred of virtue to the decision to let him in. Sarah Cook, heartbroken, hadn't been allowed a day off school to attend, but John Bassett somehow managed to get through on the phone to give her a running commentary. It was all utter chaos; but the important thing was, Peter had done it.

Over the months that followed, as the Establishment settled into what might be called a normal routine, the club really did become the place to be seen in London society. John Bird remembers: 'Socialites, cabinet ministers, fashion models, intellectuals fought to get in. Doormen were bribed. We performed twice a night, six nights a week. In May 1962, I remember walking through the audience for the second show on a Monday night and seeing two empty seats: I was appalled. It turned out that somebody had just had a heart attack and had been compelled, presumably reluctantly, to give up his place. It was filled by the time the show began.'[11] At the centre of it all shone Peter, floating between the tables, exchanging a witticism here and a word of greeting there, graciously enquiring if his guests were enjoying themselves, seeming to know everyone in the room intimately, always leaving excited faces at the tables he had just visited, like a serene yacht trailing a phosphorescent wake. 'I don't think there's ever been anybody on the London scene who had that immense glamour,' says Michael Parkinson, an Establishment regular. 'In the middle of all these long-haired girls and bright abrasive young men, he was this youthful, clever, talented, witty central figure.'

In his autobiography, Barry Humphries describes his first night at the club: 'There was a long room which had been redecorated by Sean Kenny in a kind of heavily-timbered, Tudor-Constructivist style. There was a bar at the front at which young satire groupies loitered; pale-faced girls with fringes, pearlized lips and eyes like black darns. They said "Yah" and "Soopah" a great deal and they all seemed to know Dudley Moore quite well. Late at night when the club was packed I watched the show. Eleanor Bron and John Fortune did a very funny sketch about middle-class pretentiousness, like a sort of Hampstead Nichols and May, and John Bird impersonated Harold Macmillan to a convulsed audience. I sat at the bar drinking until the late, late show when they tried out new acts, usually wags from the Great Universities. One unprepossessing fellow seemed to get a lot of laughs with a none-too-hilarious monologue about the Royal Barge accidentally sinking in the Thames. "He looks like a Methodist minister's son" I thought uncharitably, as the birds around me hooted and soopahed. How was I to know then that David Frost *was* a Methodist minister's son?'[12]

Once again Peter had held out a charitable hand to Frost, allowing him to hang about the club and appear on stage when one of the regulars was off sick. 'Frostie' learned all John Bird's lines and understudied him a few times, his performance always keenly enthusiastic; on one occasion he bounced up and down so much he broke the stage. 'He wasn't very popular,' explains one of the girls who worked in the club. 'He was so dull and uninteresting.' Pushy and eager to please he may have been, but as far as Peter was concerned, he was OK.

There was a genuine feeling at the Establishment Club that something interesting was always liable to happen. Two little-known Cockney actors, Michael Caine and Terence Stamp, propped up the bar and spoke of their future plans. Tom Driberg, the extravagantly homosexual Labour MP and double agent, gave Roger Law gossip for the wall cartoon in return for being allowed to give the impression that they were having a relationship; 'Peter always had a problem with that – he didn't like it at all,' says Law. Christine Keeler came in to have her photograph taken by Lewis Morley, now ensconced on the top floor. The resulting pose – naked and splay-legged across the back of a chair – was flashed around the world after the Profumo scandal. One night Randolph Churchill, son of Sir Winston, forced his way on to the stage and fashioned an impromptu sketch on journalism and the nature of death. Many of the female visitors headed for the basement, and Dudley Moore's jazz sessions, which usually went on until four or five in the morning. 'We paid him a ludicrously small wage,' grinned Peter, 'but he was surrounded by the best-looking birds in London.' 'It was a great scene,' says Moore. 'They came down in droves, bless their hearts.' After the show, he would usually take one of his female fans home with him, to his threadbare flat in the Kilburn High Road, where the only place to sleep was on the sofa, under a single blanket and an old winter coat. This series of inevitably short-term arrangements lasted until he seduced the model Celia Hammond over the piano keys, and began a permanent relationship.

The best evenings at the Establishment, everyone agreed, were when Peter himself decided to take to the stage. It was often an impromptu performance: an idea would occur to him while reading that day's newspaper, or he would be seized with the desire to parody someone he'd met, maybe a fashion designer, maybe a chartered accountant. Nick Luard recalls: 'I used to watch him studying them as he talked to them. There wasn't in fact a hint that he was studying them. He leant forward from his considerable height, smiling courteously, slightly stooped like a heron, his bright candid eyes never leaving their faces. Afterwards, in swift, incisive and achingly funny sketches, he'd recreate them.'[13]

Politically, Peter liked to attack both left and right in equal measure, the desire to shock as ever obliterating any thought of aspiring to correctness: 'What really annoyed people were attacks on the liberal left. If there were sacred cows at that time, they weren't Macmillan, or the Church. The real sacred cows were ladies like Pat Arrowsmith.'[14] When Peter did attack Pat Arrowsmith, a woman in the audience stood up and shouted, 'That's not what you're here for!' before clouting him – as earlier reported – with her handbag.

As Peter was an inadvertent rather than a deliberate satirist, satire rather lost out to bad taste in the long run. His material contained such characters as the lecturer on diarrhoea who walked on to the stage, opened his mouth to begin his talk, hesitated, said 'Excuse me' and rushed off again. There was also an extremely well-observed monologue about the male practice, when urinating, of trying to wash away brown traces of the previous occupant from the sides of the lavatory bowl. He devised the character of a Conservative wife for Eleanor Bron called 'Lady Pamela Stitty' (Lady Pamela's titty). During another sketch a member of the audience stood up and shouted angrily, 'I didn't drive my wife thirty miles to hear that word!' before stalking out, never to reveal exactly which word he had driven his wife thirty miles not to hear. When Peter's parents came to see the show though, the urination monologue would disappear from his act and all traces of risqué material would be cut. The contrast between the caution he exercised in selecting material for *Beyond the Fringe* and the licence he allowed himself at the Establishment appears to have derived as much from a respect for his parents' tastes as from solid commercial considerations.

As in *Beyond the Fringe*, the lack of any specific political commitment underpinning Peter's material did not mean that it was not informed by an equivalent moral commitment. After his Cambridge flirtation with tobacco he had taken stoutly against cigarette smoking, and devised a sketch that included the imprecation to 'Smoke 50,000 cigarettes and win an iron lung!' The day the government decided that Hanratty was to hang, Peter was deeply affected. 'I remember we were in a cab, where I was trying to get my *Observer* copy off him,' says Roger Law, 'and we'd just heard about Hanratty's sentence. And I've always remembered this, Peter was as cross as I've ever seen him. He wasn't being witty about it, he was very angry, and he said, "I don't think I'm going to go on tonight, as a protest."'

Ken Tynan came to review the Establishment cabaret, and commented on its position of non-party political 'radical anarchism'. He praised the three male protagonists: 'Jeremy Geidt, who specialises in sweaty brutes and insensitive rogues, begging for the extension of the death penalty, since it once deterred him from assaulting a Negro bus-conductor; John Fortune, a mop-shaped young man with tremulous lips (who specialises in) officious junior executives, edgy bureaucrats and nervous smarties, explaining in the role of a NATO instructor that the function of World War Two ("carried out", as he puts it, "with all the precision of a military operation") was to build up the economy of Western Europe in readiness for the struggle with Communism; and John Bird, a plump presence with a monkish crop of sandy hair, the most gifted of the Establishmentarians, who specialises in complacency, in smiles knowingly smiled and pipes portentously sucked.' Tynan was not, however, entirely convinced by what he had seen. 'Despite the excellence of the cast, despite the astuteness of the anonymous author and his anonymous director, something essential is lacking: a gripping, outgoing central personality for whose every entrance one waits and one on whose every word one devotedly hangs.'[15] Peter the proprietor simply could not be in two places at once.

Despite Tynan's reservations, the show at the Establishment was considered a huge success. Peter was as happy as he'd ever been. A reluctant but secretly committed nostalgist, he later described the club as 'A great place, which I still look back on with tremendous fondness. Those were tremendous times.'[16] He certainly didn't care if the real Establishment came to watch the show, as long as they paid to get in; and if the individual targets of the sketches were prepared to fork out to see themselves lampooned, so much the better. The essential criterion was that they came to him; he turned down invitations for private Establishment Club performances before the Queen and before the senior ranks of the Labour Party. For the most part, the rich and powerful did indeed come to him. Malcolm Muggeridge wrote in the *New Statesman* that 'One is struck, at the Establishment, by the general air of affluence. One looks around instinctively for Princess Margaret, or at any rate the Duke of Bedford.' Peter didn't care. 'I never suspected that workers would be coming down from Darlington saying "This is the place where the Government will be overthrown."'[17]

Beyond the Fringe excepted, Peter spent almost all his waking hours at the club, so it made sense to base his social life around it. His relationship with Wendy became strained as a result; they spent most of their evenings there, always surrounded by others. Gaye Brown, Judy Huxtable's then best friend, joined the club as an all-purpose barmaid/ticket seller/lighting operator, and Sundays were spent either in Battersea or at Gaye's little flat in Fulham, in a series of impromptu parties where Peter held court and frequently knocked over bottles of red wine with his gesticulating hands.

Eventually, whenever he turned up at Gaye's, he would bring a bottle of red wine and a packet of Saxo salt with him for the clean-up operation. In January 1962 Nicholas Garland, a lifelong friend of Jonathan Miller's, was taken on as the club's theatrical director, and he and his wife Harriet were added to the Establishment Club crowd. Harriet, and Peter's secretary Judy Scott-Fox, who was always keen to join in socially if she could, were put in charge of the club's door policy.

Although they had been confused initially by the new venture, and by the family atmosphere that seem to surround its jolly young protagonists, it slowly began to dawn on the local Soho gangsters that there was money being made in their midst. Thickset gentlemen began to pay courtesy calls, pointing out the immense structural vulnerability of a satirical nightclub to accidental damage. There was no help to be had from the (genuine) Establishment; not for any vengeful reasons, but because Soho's police force was riddled through and through with corruption, which would not be rooted out until a decade later. The local police chief, later jailed for planting a brick on a demonstrator, seemed mysteriously unable to help.

When the club didn't pay the protection money requested, the thickset gentlemen would return and start brawls, as an excuse to begin smashing the place up. Fortunately, there was always Roger Law, bigger than any local thug: 'There were always fights. I remember one wonderful punch-up like a Western. As soon as any fight started, I just went and beat the living shit out of whoever it was that started it. Peter was always crying out, "Just ignore them, Roger, don't take any notice," but I'd just fucking belt them.' Peter's tactics, naturally, were diametrically opposed, but could be just as effective. When two heavies came into the office one morning and started destroying the typewriters, Peter simply engaged them in conversation. So fast was his mind, darting ahead and charting out the path of the dialogue before they had even formulated their next remarks, that before long they found themselves outwitted, out-argued and out on the pavement. There is a famous story that two other visiting heavies met a more substantial fate: Peter ushered them into the bar while it was in the process of redecoration, and on to a tarpaulin that concealed a hole in the floor, whereupon they disappeared through to the basement. It is almost certainly an apocryphal tale, but indicative of Peter's style in dealing with threats: the criminal element simply didn't know *how* to go about leaning on this most unusual of victims.

Like a frontier saloon deep in Indian territory, the Establishment partied on. Serious drama was introduced, in March, with Sean Kenny directing. In April Peter gave the cast a holiday, and imported the pioneering American comedian Lenny Bruce to fill the gap. Bruce had developed a serious heroin addiction after being given heroin-based painkillers when wounded during World War Two, which he made no bones about. His set was peppered with expletives and explicit sexual details. In short, he provided perfect copy for a newspaper campaign, and Fleet Street was soon clamouring for this disgusting individual to be kept out of Britain. Peter managed to persuade the Home Office, entirely untruthfully, that Bruce's drug-taking days were over, and a work permit was arranged.

Peter later revealed the events of Bruce's first few days in this country: 'I'd heard his records. He was obviously a very good draw. But I had no idea what he was like. I thought – big American star arriving – so I hired a large car, Rolls Royce or something, and went out to the airport to meet him. And out came this wreck. An absolute, shambling wreck. I thought Jesus, what have I got on my hands?' A day or so later, Bruce was evicted from his hotel after a number of prostitutes had been found in his room and a number of used syringes had been discovered in his lavatory; he fetched up at Peter's Battersea flat instead. 'One of my first assignments was to go and get him some drugs, which I knew nothing about. He had this terrible phoney prescription, signed by "Dr Ziglovitz" for a heroin derivative. I thought, drugs . . . jazz. Do I know any jazz musicians? So I rang Dudley. And he only had a junior aspirin, which I didn't think would satisfy Lenny's craving.' Eventually, Peter obtained a list of supposedly crooked medical men. 'I went traipsing round London 'til about three in the morning with this tatty piece of paper, wandering round to these doctors in the middle of the night, all of whom said "piss off" in medical language. By now I had a very fixed picture in my mind that Lenny Bruce would be climbing up the wall, having the most appalling withdrawal symptoms, and screaming and yelling like in the movies. And when I got back he was sat there quietly. And I said "Well Lenny, I'm terribly sorry, I couldn't get hold of any heroin." And he said, "Oh, that's cool . . . I'd like some chocolate cake." And I got quite cross, and said "I'm willing to traipse all over London at three in the morning to look for heroin, but chocolate cake is out of the question." This of course was in 1962, when chocolate cake was not so freely available.'[18]

Peter rather grew to like Lenny Bruce over the following weeks, and found him to be a gentle person, but thereafter made sure that the hapless Judy Scott-Fox was detailed to go out looking for Bruce's drugs instead. He and Nick Luard shared the job of housekeeper–minder to Bruce for the duration of the engagement, and they and their friends received a considerable narcotic education in the process. Roger Law, for one, had no idea why Bruce kept making patterns on a little mirror with a pile of white powder. Part of Bruce's act was to tell the audience to hang on for a moment while he went off to get a heroin fix. They would scream with laughter while he left the stage and returned in a state of woozy delight, little realising that it was not an act. Sometimes he would be too doped up to perform, or would simply go missing. On one occasion Peter took the microphone to apologise to the audience and to explain that the performance had been cancelled, owing to the fact that Mr Bruce was indisposed; instead he ended up improvising a wildly successful two-hour set himself.

Bruce, whose performances were always packed out, proffered some valuable advice to John Bird and the regular Establishment cast when he saw them perform: that they should cease their obvious hostility to their well-heeled audience. 'You've got to believe that everybody in the room is sharing your opinion,' he said. 'It may be true that they don't but if you play it as if you're all in agreement, you'll come over better.' Good advice, but it did not always save Bruce from riling his own audience to the point of open hostility. Laying violently into the Catholic religion one May evening, he enraged the Irish actress, forty-year-old Siobhan McKenna, into shouting back at him, in front of her nineteen-year-old boyfriend Johnny Hippisley. When she had finished, Bruce said, 'Well if you don't like it, you must leave. And take your son with you.' Peter tried to usher them out. 'I'm glad you're going. Can I show you the way?' he said to Ms McKenna, his manners slipping slightly; whereupon Hippisley punched him in the mouth, splitting his lip, and was thrown out. Siobhan McKenna followed, flailing at Peter as she was removed. Peter pointed out that she had just scratched his face. 'These hands are clean,' she yelled. 'These are Irish hands and they are clean.' 'Well this is a British face,' replied Peter smoothly, 'and it's bleeding.' Like Peter and many others, Bruce fell heavily for Judy Huxtable, and told her she was the only girl he'd ever loved. He was no more successful than Peter in this endeavour, although he gave her some helpful advice too, on the importance of saving her virginity for the right man. When he left, everyone was sad to see him go, and promised to see him back at the club the following spring. The last any of them heard of him was when, high on drugs, he jumped from the window of his American apartment shouting, 'I am SUPERJEW!' and broke both his ankles. He died a year or two later from a drugs overdose.

The second 'holiday relief' of the year was an altogether more relaxed booking than Bruce, but no less novel. At the *Evening Standard* Drama Awards in January to pick up an award for *Beyond the Fringe*, Peter had witnessed Frankie Howerd doing the cabaret. It had been a cut-price booking for the *Standard*: Howerd's career was in the doldrums, brought down by the low-radius cycle of fashionability that has always governed British entertainment. He had not appeared in central London for many years. Peter was so impressed by his neglected talent that he booked him for a month's solo slot, starting in September, his act to be predicated on the extreme unlikelihood of his presence on the fashionable Establishment stage. It was a masterstroke, and thoroughly revitalised Howerd's career for a further fifteen years.

Having conquered West End theatre and the London club scene inside a year, Peter was keen to diversify. Soon after opening the Establishment, he had turned his attention to the magazine business, with the idea of starting a satirical publication. He had subsequently suffered rather a rude shock, when Christopher Booker, his old Cambridge friend, had turned up in the bar one evening with the first issue of *Private Eye*, a cheaply-produced satirical magazine he had put together with his old Shrewsbury friend, Willie Rushton. 'He was incredibly nice about it, far more than was justified,' says Booker. 'The one thing he immediately said was, why didn't I take a look at an American magazine, which had photo cover bubbles. He said, "Why don't you take that idea and use it on the front of *Private Eye*?"' Booker accepted the suggestion, which is still going strong today. According to Peter, 'I was actually very annoyed when the *Eye* had come out. I'd wanted to start a practically identical magazine – then bloody *Private Eye* came out and I was really pissed off.'

The *Eye* crowd, like most of the other ex-public school satirists following in Peter's wake, admired him and the rest of the *Beyond the Fringe* quartet to distraction. According to the magazine's owner, Andrew Osmond, 'These people were Gods. An image I'll carry to my grave is of Dudley and his trio at an Oxford ball – it was dawn and he was jamming away, absolutely lost in it, and he had mist, real mist, rising off the ground all around his feet, so you could only see the three of them from the waist up. They were Gods really, and of the four, Peter was the most glamorous.' However much they admired him though, they also shared his desire to shock and to go against the fashionable grain. In one of its early issues *Private Eye* confidently attacked Peter himself, satirising him as 'Jonathan Crake'. The Rushton-Booker cartoon strip *Aesop Revisited* showed Crake's triumphant passage through school and Cambridge University, to impersonating the Prime Minister in a revue called *Short Back and Sides*, before eventually opening a satirical nightclub in Fulham with stools designed by Sean Kenny. Before long, 'Crake could not open his mouth without everyone collapsing at his brilliant satirical comment.' Crowds of people fell about with laughter as he asked the way to the gents. 'Go away you ugly bone-headed bastards!' shouted Crake, but those around him simply laughed even more. He sought solace in the bottle, depressed and bereft of inspiration, unable to hold a serious conversation of even the shortest duration, before resorting to copying old jokes out of an 1890 issue of *Punch*. With the exception of the old *Punch* jokes, it was to prove a horribly accurate prediction.

Deprived of the opportunity to run a satirical magazine, Peter was persuaded instead – by Nick Luard and Colin Bell – to develop a publication based on the Establishment's flourishing cinema club, an expensive full-colour glossy called *Scene*. The project was announced in May, an office was rented off Fleet Street, and a series of impressive-looking dummies were produced. The first issue proper came out in September 1962, with Harriet Garland and the young Tom Stoppard among its staff. Entertainingly, Stoppard had applied for the job of theatre critic in the guise of William Boot from the novel *Scoop*. Luard, who could obviously be a bit slow on the uptake at times, had completely missed the allusion when hiring him. *Scene* represented something of a gamble for Cook & Luard Productions, and would have to do extremely well to repay its investment, but confidence was burgeoning.

In the summer of 1962, news reached the Establishment that Andrew Osmond wished to sell *Private Eye*. Ironically in the light of Peter's own background, Osmond was experiencing pressure from his parents to abandon life as a fledgling comic entrepreneur and resume his intended career path with the Foreign Office. His original investment of £450 – furnished merely because he was the only one of the *Eye* crowd with any money – had yielded precious little profit on a circulation of 18,000; so when Colin Bell got in touch and told him that Cook & Luard Productions would be prepared to offer £1,500 for 75 of his 99 shares, he leaped at the chance. Peter was somewhat sceptical about the deal, but told Luard to go ahead anyway, which led to a misunderstanding that would have awkward future consequences. Peter – and the grateful *Private Eye* staff – assumed that he was their new joint owner. In fact Luard had personally registered all the shares in his own name.

Blissfully unaware, Peter met the staff. 'I remember him saying, "Good evening" all the time,' says Richard Ingrams. 'It was ridiculous. Everybody went round saying "Good evening," and after a bit you thought, what a silly thing it is to say "Good evening".'[19] All were impressed by the time and charm he was prepared to lavish even on the humblest staffer. He moved the *Eye*'s offices into the Establishment Club itself – a building that was now beginning to bulge at the seams – and installed them in the waiters' changing room, a not entirely satisfactory arrangement on account of the number of waiters wanting to change. The only way out of the room was across the stage, so it had to be vacated by 6 p.m. The *Eye's* editor, Christopher Booker, was a night owl who kept erratic hours, so the system was clearly doomed from the start.

Apart from such physical inconveniences, there was the broader problem that the *Eye* lot didn't actually like the Establishment Club. According to Andrew Osmond, 'They hated it because it was very fashionable, because everybody went there to be seen or to see who else was there.' Willie Rushton reckoned that 'It was an awful place. If you went to the lavatories you were crunching over hypodermics and heaven knows what. Most of the waiters were lifting all the money. It was usually full of the very people it was targeting, all these people roaring with laughter and saying, "That's damn true about old Cyril."'

Peter's idea was to merge the *Eye* crowd and the Establishment's cabaret regulars to form a kind of 'school of satire'. He arranged a weekly brainstorming lunch at which the two groups were supposed to spark each other off. In fact, the atmosphere was queasy with mutual suspicion. Rushton remembers that 'We'd sit at opposite ends of this room in almost total silence. John Bird and John Fortune on one side used to wear black shirts and look very heavily left wing, whereas we were sort of in jolly tweeds, Viyella shirts and corduroys. We were meant to be the leading satirical wags of our time and nothing was happening at all, absolutely nothing. Then Peter would give up, and just stand up and say: "The Bee of Ephesus". And he'd set off into this thing about this holy bee, and we'd all roar with laughter and cheer up a lot.'[20] Peter reckoned that 'The *Eye* people felt the *Eye* was theirs, you know, they'd started it, so why suddenly co-operate with these other people?' The experiment was declared a failure and the *Eye* was shunted two doors down, to a cramped first floor at no. 22 Greek Street. The accounts department was left behind in the person of Elisabeth Longmore, who later fell in love with and married Nick Luard. She shared the backstage office with two beautiful and glamorous secretaries, 'both of whom Peter had decided should don pebble-glasses and answer to the name of Miss Rigby when outsiders came to visit. It was a game, all of it.'[21]

The hiccup over and done with, *Private Eye* started to go from strength to strength under its new regime. The circulation shot up to 50,000 over the summer. Peter supplied material to the magazine, including a vicious attack on the Home Secretary which accused him of being a 'flabby-faced coward'; he also found himself fascinated by the magazine's investigative side, and encouraged its expansion. Shortly afterwards the *Eye* uncovered the Profumo scandal, which did as much as anything to bring down the

Macmillan government. A number of rumours had been flying around London about the Russian spy Vladimir Ivanov and Christine Keeler, who was the mistress of both Ivanov and the Conservative Minister John Profumo. Firing blind, without having the faintest idea what they were writing about, the *Eye* satirists caricatured Ivanov as 'Vladimir Bolokhov' and Keeler as 'Gaye Funloving'. Timothy Birdsall added a cartoon entitled *The Last Days of Macmillan*, showing nude girls cavorting with cabinet ministers by the pool at Cliveden, the press as a flock of geese and a sign on a pillow reading 'Per Wardua ad Astor' (a reference to two other figures involved, Cliveden's owner Lord Astor and the society osteopath who'd introduced Keeler to Profumo, Stephen Ward). George Wigg MP raised the *Eye* article in the House of Commons. Stephen Ward was so horrified at the thought that the cat was out of the bag that he turned up at the *Eye* office and confessed all he knew. 'He thought we knew everything,' said Rushton, who received him. 'So he came and spilled the beans entirely, which was wonderful.' The government tottered, fatally wounded. The *Eye*'s circulation doubled.

With satirical publishing now firmly under its belt, the Cook empire turned its attention to television. This would be the toughest nut to crack: the BBC still refused to show any interest in Peter Cook or his myriad works. Their only concession to the satire craze had been to import the American comedian Mort Sahl for a one-off special, a quite remarkable botch job in which the Light Entertainment department had surrounded Sahl with old-style glossy dancing girls. Peter and John Bird knew enough to approach Donald Baverstock of the Current Affairs Department instead, one of the men behind the highly successful *Tonight* show. Baverstock showed interest, and invited the pair for discussions with himself and Stuart Hood, the Controller of Programmes. The negotiations were long and tortuous, but seemed to be getting somewhere: sample scripts were written and formats were drawn up. Then, out of the blue, the Establishment Show was suddenly and inexplicably dropped.

What had happened, although Peter and John Bird were as yet unaware of it, was that one of the young producers in the Current Affairs Department, Ned Sherrin, had quite independently visited the Establishment Club himself and had proposed his own satire show, along similar lines. As far as Baverstock and Hood were concerned, this gave them the moral green light to ditch the Cook–Bird proposal and go with the option that gave them greater control and fewer expenses. Sherrin was never told of the existing idea. Peter's discussions with the BBC were abruptly and completely terminated, with no reason given.

It was at this point, with Peter's plans irrevocably stalled for once in his young life, that the offer arrived to tour America. The restless desire to conquer new fields still blazed within him. The solution to the fact that he was apparently anchored to a London club was breathtakingly straightforward: he would simply take the Establishment with him to the States, as well as appearing in *Beyond the Fringe* on Broadway. He would decamp his entire lifestyle to New York. He'd get a decent salary from the American *Fringe*, too: the cast all clubbed together and put their signatures to a letter demanding a pay rise from £75 per week to £750 plus 6 per cent of the gross box office receipts, as a precondition for accepting the offer. Their demands were met, and the deal was done.

The quartet's first instincts were to shut down the London *Fringe* altogether in their absence. Peter told the *Mail* that 'This is not the kind of show which even the most experienced professional could step into. It's an amateur revue, moulded around our own personalities.'[22] The promise of residual fees changed all four minds however, and within a fortnight Peter was in Cambridge, hunting replacements among the new Footlights generation; he watched a smoker, and was unable to resist the temptation to get on stage and perform his Grole-as-miner monologue. None of the Cambridge students actually made it to the final shortlist, all of whom received an invitation to come and audition at the Fortune while Peter and co. sat in the darkened stalls. Willie Donaldson had already formulated a provisional cast of his own, consisting of Richard Ingrams, John Wells, Joe Melia and in the role of Peter Cook, David Frost; but the idea of Frost *becoming* him every night filled Peter with awestruck horror. 'Frost desperately wanted to take over from Peter,' explains Donaldson, 'but Peter said, over his dead body. That would have been the end of Frost. If I'd stood up to Peter, we would never have heard another word from Frost.'[23] A doubtful notion, but it is true that the engagement, which lasted four years, did no favours for the careers of the victorious auditioners.

Each of the four originals had their favoured candidates, and each was keen to use his power of veto. Peter didn't want Ingrams diverting his energies from *Private Eye*, nor Wells, who was also starting to contribute to the magazine; he was keen for Barry Humphries to get the job. Jonathan Miller had already independently approached Bill Wallis in a Covent Garden street. According to Wallis, 'I heard a terrible noise, and it was a Vespa or a Lambretta – one of those awful little motorcycles – and on it was this enormous figure with its knees up beside its ears, and its elbows sticking out and this great goatish face, and it hailed me and said, "Bill! Bill! I'd recognise your bottom anywhere!" And it was Jonathan Miller, who said, would I like to be in the replacement cast of *Beyond the*

Fringe? Since I'd been told a matter of minutes before by Peter Hall at the RSC that my services were no longer required, I said yes.' Wallis got the Alan Bennett part, Willie Donaldson pushed Joe Melia successfully into the Miller role, and Robin Ray moved up from understudying Dudley Moore to playing him full time. Barry Humphries won the Peter Cook role, but despite having promised to release him from his *Oliver!* contract if a good job came up, Donald Albery refused to do so when the crunch came; the part was given to Terence Brady instead.

While *Beyond the Fringe* was booked for a brief American city tour prior to its New York run, the Establishment cast would do a straight swap with the cabaret at Chicago's *Second City*, the venue that had produced Mike Nichols, Elaine May and Alan Arkin, before going on to the *Hungry I* in San Francisco, then the most famous comedy club in the US. After that there were no plans: Peter wrote to George Melly, asking him to take over as MC at the London Establishment in due course, but Melly was smart enough to realise that Peter Cook would be an impossible act to follow. Instead the fate of the Establishment would be left in the hands of Nick Luard.

All was signed and sealed, when out of the blue John Bird was contacted by Ned Sherrin. How would he like to be the presenter of a new late-night satire show for BBC Television? The two met for lunch at Bertorelli's. Bird was discomfited: he could not help but connect the proposal with the Establishment Show suggested by Peter and himself. There seemed an indecent haste about the BBC's apparent volte-face, and he did not relish the disloyalty that would be involved were he to pull out of the American tour. The US certainly provided an acceptably glamorous alternative. He refused Sherrin's offer, but agreed to help him out by appearing in the pilot show. Otherwise, his only contribution – according to Sherrin – was to think of the title, *That Was the Week That Was*. Bird contacted Peter to tell him of the offer, and they cautiously agreed to appear on the pilot together, in an improvisation slot with Eleanor Bron.

Knowing that he would be unable to get anyone connected with either *Beyond the Fringe* or the Establishment to present his show on a long-term basis, Sherrin went to see the new satirical cabaret at the Blue Angel nightclub, starring a young man who had developed a familiar-sounding impression of Harold Macmillan: it was, of course, David Frost. Sherrin signed Frost to co-present the pilot of *That Was the Week That Was*, along with Brian Redhead of *Tonight*. He also visited another new satirical cabaret, the Room at the Top, produced by Willie Donaldson in the rather bizarre setting of a chicken-in-the-basket restaurant atop an Ilford tower block. It starred Willie Rushton, John Wells, Richard Ingrams and – even more bizarrely – Barbara Windsor. So popular was satire becoming that even the Kray twins had been to watch a bit of Macmillan-bashing. As a result of his performance, Rushton too was signed up by Sherrin; and as a result of *his* performance, Wells was asked to leave his schoolmastering job by the Eton authorities.

Peter was furious with the BBC when he discovered that Frost was to present what he believed to be a thinly disguised version of his own proposal. He managed to bite his lip when Frost contacted him to ask if he'd mind their *Granta* piece, parodying the tabloid coverage of the Rome Olympics, being adapted into a sketch for the new show; but on the day of the pilot recording, Peter was too angry to turn up and do his bit. His mood was somewhat ameliorated by the fact that *TW3* didn't look as if it would ever make the screen anyway. The pilot lasted two-and-a-half hours, and the centrepiece – an argument between Bernard Levin and about forty Conservative ladies in floral dresses – was so acrimonious that Current Affairs executives subsequently decided to axe the project altogether.

The *Beyond the Fringe* cast slipped out of their roles in the West End gradually, handing over to their understudies one by one. Peter was the first to leave, and sailed for America on the SS *France* in September, confident in the thought that *That Was the Week That Was* would represent no more than a passing blip in his total domination of the British satire scene.

CHAPTER 6

Heaving Thighs Across Manhattan
America, 1962–64

'We don't want to turn this into a Dutch auction' had been Donald Langdon's considered advice, when two of America's top theatrical producers, David Merrick and Alexander H. Cohen, had put in rival bids for *Beyond the Fringe*. Cohen had got the nod, and it had only dawned on the cast afterwards that a Dutch auction was precisely what they had wanted. So keen were both promoters, they'd have paid virtually anything to get their hands on the show, and would probably have put in insane opening bids. Peter parted company with Langdon soon afterwards.

The *Fringe* quartet sailed into New York on 28 September 1962, after a week of inactivity on the *France* that was close to torture for the restless, hot-wired Peter Cook. He had been 'bored stiff,' he told his parents, on a 'vulgar floating hotel with wonderful food but no character.' Cohen knew that he had a hot property on his hands, probably in need of pampering, and moved the four first into the Algonquin Hotel, then into his mansion in upstate Connecticut, where they sat by the pool in 80°, Peter still chafing at the bit. At last, on 6 October, they got their chance. When they took the stage in Washington, in front of a packed house of 1,670 people, they were greeted like long-lost rock stars. The critics were ecstatic, including the nationally influential Jay Carmody, and President Kennedy decided to come and see the show later in the week. Although JFK was later forced to postpone his visit, the reception was even more enthusiastic in Boston and Toronto, where the cast had to bawl their lines to an audience of 3,000. Finally, on 27 October, *Beyond the Fringe* received its official premiere at the John Golden Theater in New York, by which time the show's American tour had already made Cohen a clear profit. A new Broadway institution had arrived.

The *New York World-Telegram* claimed that 'Nothing so far this season on Broadway has made you laugh so hard or so often. If only American comedians could be so devastating.' The *New York Times* assured readers that the show 'will have you shaking so hard with laughter that you'll forget momentarily to tremble with fear.' Richard Watts, much-feared critic of the *New York Post*, called it 'Immense', 'Hilarious', and 'A brilliant satirical revue'. The *Herald Tribune* credited it with being 'calmly and ruthlessly funny' on the most difficult of subjects. Summing up the American adulation for the *Manchester Guardian*, Alistair Cooke reported that 'This tumult of acceptance is a puzzle to many shrewd theatre men here who deplored the quartet's decision not to adapt their material to American themes, or their strangulated triphthongs to the ears of a people to whom a vowel is a vowel is a vowel. But they make no concessions, a British trick Oscar Wilde discovered before them. In a way their success is a nostalgic reprise of the old, and most popular, visiting lecturers, who pitied their audience, said so, and made a mint.'[1]

The four had indeed made few alterations for American ears. Jonathan Miller added an impression of Bertrand Russell, Peter changed a few lines in his miner and Macmillan monologues, and Alan Bennett made reference in his monologue to the Cuba crisis, which had rather unpleasantly threatened to kick off another World War on the opening night of the *Fringe*. (In fact Bennett was so scared that he spent the night cowering under the table in Dudley Moore and John Bassett's apartment.) The cast had cited US influences aplenty in their humour – Mort Sahl, Lenny Bruce of course, The Second City team and Phil Silvers – but the show was clearly as British as cricket and overcooked vegetables. 'The fact that it was British and we hadn't altered a word provided a sort of built-in snob merit,'[2] Peter discovered.

By the time *Beyond the Fringe* arrived in New York, celebrities such as Bette Davis, Charles Boyer and Noel Coward were already queuing up to go backstage and meet the cast. Harriet Garland went to the opening night with the grave Burmese UN dignitary U Thant, and was introduced to Lauren Bacall into the bargain. President Kennedy was still too busy with the Cuban crisis to come, but his aides telephoned the show's producer to request that a private performance be squeezed in at the White House. Like the Queen and the Labour Party leadership before him, he was crudely snubbed. 'We're not some fucking cabaret. He can come to the theatre,' said Peter, who put it slightly differently in a letter to his mother and father: 'It would have made us seem rather like performing seals.' Alan

Bennett later turned down two invitations to the White House for dinner
as well. 'Monstrous behaviour,' he now reflects. It worked, at any rate.
Kennedy duly booked seats for himself and several security guards at a
showing early in February.

Rather than simply wallow in all the adulation, Peter moved quickly to
benefit from it, and find the Establishment Club a permanent New York
home. No more than a fortnight after the opening, he telephoned John
Bird on the Chicago leg of the Establishment tour to say that he had found
an American co-producer – John Krimsky – and a venue – the dilapidated
El Morocco nightclub at 154 East 54th Street. Langdon had been elbowed
out of the deal, which had been done by an American lawyer, Jerry Lurie of
Cohen and Glickstein. Nick Garland, who was already in Boston directing
Peter Ustinov in *Photo Finish*, had been signed up to direct the show.
Gradually, the El Morocco was transformed into Strollers Theatre-Club,
host to the London Establishment, and was ready to open its doors on
23 January 1963. Much more plush, comfortable and intimate than its
London counterpart, Strollers managed – if that were possible – to create
even more excitement among New York's fashionable society than the
Soho version had done back home.

David Merrick, the producer who had lost out in his bid to stage *Beyond
the Fringe*, rubbished the new club's chances of success to anyone who
would listen. There was a newspaper strike, he pointed out, making it
impossible to raise any publicity in New York; the Establishment's opening
had already been postponed for a month as a consequence. Merrick himself
had sidestepped this problem for a show called *Subways Are for Sleeping*, by
finding ordinary members of the public with the same names as famous
newspaper critics, eliciting positive quotes from them and printing them
up on posters and handbills. Peter now struck back, by finding a shy,
middle-aged black postman in the Philadelphia phone directory who also
happened to be called David Merrick, and taking him to a rehearsal of the
new show at the Establishment. The postman pronounced it the finest
show he'd ever seen as well as the only show he'd ever seen. Thousands
of handbills were printed and distributed on the street, showing Merrick
the postman looking solemn in trilby and gabardine raincoat, a speech
bubble issuing from his mouth with the words 'David Merrick raves about
the Establishment: "I think the Establishment is the most brilliant show
in New York. It is better than *Tchin-Tchin*, *Stop the World* and *Oliver!* all
rolled into one. I wish I had a piece of it."'

Copies of the handbill were affixed to helium balloons and floated up
past Merrick's office window. Wendy and Judy Scott-Fox paraded up
and down outside theatres where the above Merrick hits were playing,

wearing sandwich boards displaying postman Merrick's eulogies. Radio commercials began with the words: 'This is the real David Merrick speaking. Don't be taken in by substitutes.' A loudspeaker van drove up and down Broadway blaring the same message to fascinated crowds. The 'real' David Merrick, furious, threatened legal action. When he found such a course would be quite unworkable, he threatened instead to take out full-page advertisements when the newspapers returned, reprinting in large type all the bad reviews garnered by the Establishment cabaret. The trouble with this idea was, it didn't get any.

According to the reviewer from the *New York Daily News*, 'Most of the show is hilarious, all of it was outrageous; I enjoyed it thoroughly'. The *Herald Tribune* called it 'Brash, bawdy and delightful'. The *New York World-Telegram* described it as 'Both outrageous and outrageously funny'. The *New York Times* said that 'The Establishment makes England's early crop of angry young men sound as benevolent as Will Rogers. Its wit is biting and its actors and talent brilliant.' *Cue* magazine, meanwhile, maintained that 'It is limp praise indeed to say we have produced nothing like it in this country. Thank you Mr Peter Cook for leading this civilised expedition to our shores.'

Peter, John Bird and John Fortune had deliberately written a harder revue for American audiences, who had some experience of satirical club cabaret. The opening number was a version of the crucifixion, with Fortune as a reasonable middle-class Christ flanked by two common-as-muck thieves. Bird explains: 'So much of the show was based on class, because class was still a defining feature of British life. We were trying to convey to American audiences the centrality of this – it was a good piece of shorthand for them.'

John Fortune and Eleanor Bron in particular specialised in English middle-class embarrassment, as in the sketch about a couple, both of whom want to go to bed with each other but neither of whom dare make the first move:

> *Fortune*: I mean, if two people are attracted to each other, I mean, why on earth can't they just go up to each other and say, you know – for example, 'You're an attractive girl, you know, and I'm – an attractive man, I suppose, you know, and why don't we go to bed?' I mean, that's the . . .
>
> *Bron*: Well yes, of course – I mean, of course, that's how it ought to be – but somehow it never is . . . Well – it's so silly, really . . .

Fortune:	Stupid, yes . . .
Bron:	Although, in fact, what you're saying isn't *strictly* true . . .
Fortune:	Oh, go on yes . . .
Bron:	It's just, in fact, a man *can* go up to a girl and say . . . that . . . but a girl, you know, poor thing, just has to sort of sit, and . . . sit, and . . . well, wait really.
Fortune:	Well, I suppose that's true, up to a point, yes . . . (pause) Where are you going for your holidays this year – have you decided at all?
Bron:	Oh, well, I'm still sort of hovering between Portugal and Poland.

It was a routine that Peter was to re-use successfully in the film *Bedazzled* four years later, with Dudley Moore playing opposite Eleanor Bron. Another of Peter's sketches that would have been too controversial for British audiences featured a blind man addressing the audience:

> Good evening. I am blind. And yet I am reading this message. I am reading it on the wonderful system known as broille . . . I'm sorry, I'll feel that again.

The punchline was a voice-over explaining that the audience had just heard an appeal on behalf of the blond. Some of them hissed, but a blind man who thought it hilarious asked to meet the author.

Moore's place at the New York Establishment's piano had been taken by the veteran jazz musician Teddy Wilson, but this did not appear to have hindered his romantic career, which pursued a course roughly opposite to the Bron–Fortune sketch. According to Alan Bennett, 'Dudley's performance on stage in *Beyond the Fringe* was often merely a perfunctory interruption of the more prolonged and energetic performance going on in his dressing room.'[3] Although undoubtedly still madly in love with Celia Hammond, upon whom he lavished endless transatlantic letters and phonecalls, Moore was desperate for female attention, and even managed to seduce Tuesday Weld, twenty-year-old star of *Sex Kittens Go to College*, in a hired limousine on the way home from the show.

Peter's personal life, remembers Bennett, 'although never so volatile nor so highly charged as Dudley's, did have its moments.'[4] On a business trip to Chicago he had already seduced a playboy bunny whom he referred to as 'Miss Kitty Nisty', whose apartment he had been forced to flee from in his underwear, when her father had burst in brandishing a shotgun.

Then, on 5 February 1963, at a dinner given by the Vice-President, he was introduced to Jackie Kennedy. He wrote to tell his parents about her, an uncharacteristic note of excitement creeping into his customarily devoted but reserved style: 'She was very sweet and she spoke in a voice like Marilyn Monroe. Two days later she came without any warning at all to see the late show at the Establishment. I sat with her at the table, plied her with champagne. She loved it and told me that [the British Ambassador] in Washington had advised her not to bring it to the White House as it was "too anti-British". She kept shrieking with delight, and saying how naughty it all was, and how Jack would never allow her up to New York again.'

Three days later JFK himself, no doubt at his wife's instigation, backed down and came to New York to see *Beyond the Fringe*. The President's red nuclear phone was installed backstage in case he needed to start World War III during the show, and the theatre was searched in advance by a phalanx of security guards. Peter left a replica pistol on his dressing room table as a test, which remained unnoticed. The security guards then attempted to blend into the auditorium during the performance, with faces of stone and bulging jackets. All eyes were on the President, which made for a slightly uneasy performance. Peter made reference to him during his Macmillan impersonation:

> The President was kind enough to show me actual photographs of the Polaris. Until we have it, we shall rely on our own missile, with a range of 150 miles. This means we can just about hit Paris – and by God we will.

The audience roared. Kennedy, who had been laughing with the rest of them, slipped easily and professionally into an expressionless mask during the Macmillan item.

After the show the Kennedys came backstage where Jackie told JFK how worried the cast were at the prospect of having to pay inflated US taxes. 'You're so naughty with your taxes, Jack!' she gushed. Bennett believes that Peter may have subsequently 'seen something' of Jackie Kennedy, who thereafter became a frequent visitor to Strollers: 'I have a vision of the presidential party in the Green Room having drinks in the interval, with Mrs Kennedy absently stroking Peter's hand as they chatted.'[5] Wendy, meanwhile, did her bit to redress the balance for British sexuality by accidentally stepping on the hem of her strapless dress as she met the President, with inevitable consequences that given his reputation he no doubt appreciated.

Peter and Wendy's relationship, which had begun to stutter somewhat under the pressure of Peter's club-owning commitments back home, underwent a revival when she joined him in America. He bought her a beautiful green Tiffany lamp as a token of his affection. It became the start of a collection, but none of the others matched the original for its sentimental attraction. It became the centrepiece of their sumptuous new apartment in the East Village, at 13 St Mark's Place. Barry Humphries, who had finally been allowed to visit America after all with a touring version of *Oliver!*, describes the decor chez Cook: 'Here and there in the rambling apartment were real Tiffany lamps, an abundance of rich textiles of crimson and mulberry silk and crushed velvet, which created an atmosphere of opulence – or so I apprehended, living as I was, only a few blocks away in an austere cold-water flat above a poodle parlour.'[6] A journalist friend was slightly less elaborate, encapsulating it as being 'decorated like a mediaeval tent'.[7] A medieval tent, that is, with subdued jazz and an octagonal sofa.

Nick and Harriet Garland stayed in the flat for a while on their arrival from Boston. Judy Scott-Fox, the faithful aide-de-camp, moved in and never moved out. Wendy, after three years of keeping open house in Cambridge, Battersea and now New York, was getting rather sick of never being alone with Peter. 'We had his secretary living with us. There were always other people around. I was actually rather scared to be on my own with Peter, because he didn't know how to be relaxed, he found it incredibly difficult.' Part of the problem was that Wendy had nothing to do in the day, other than keep house. As MC of the Establishment both in London and New York, Peter had developed a semi-nocturnal existence, sleeping in until lunchtime before dashing out to resume work on his various projects. He often had to provide his own entertainment in the middle of the night: sometimes he would phone TV stations, as when he called to complain that 'what he could only describe as a mammary gland' had just been seen on TV (at 3.30 in the morning) by his son Gary, aged seven, and his daughter Mary-Ann, aged five.

The other three Fringers lived more or less separate existences. Alan Bennett and Jonathan Miller were still haunted by their academic former lives: the former spent his days studying the life of Richard III on microfilms of medieval manuscripts he'd brought from England, while the latter researched into neuropsychiatry at the Mount Sinai hospital in Manhattan. Dudley Moore, as Bennett explains, 'would spend much of the day in bed with one or other (and perhaps both) of his current girlfriends.' Moore and Bennett developed a friendship, and would often meet at Barbetta's Italian restaurant for an unchanging supper of gazpacho, fetuccini and chocolate mousse. The doorman, who couldn't speak English properly and hadn't fully got the hang of which cast member was which, would invariably greet them in his thick accent with a cry of 'Mr Moore! Mr Cook! Behind the Fridge!' This was to become the title of Peter and Dudley's hit stage show of the early seventies. Jonathan Miller, meanwhile, had a number of friends in New York already and so enjoyed a separate social life: 'Something he tended to rather overemphasise,' says Bennett, 'which Peter would take the piss out of, as he did my medieval history.'

Peter and Wendy's social lives were centred on the evenings, after the shows. They would go out on the town with the Garlands. Peter Ustinov would come over for a late meal. They would go and watch Woody Allen perform, or he would come over to the Establishment. They would be invited to parties to meet Noel Coward, John Gielgud, Vivien Leigh. Joseph Heller, who was also being feted around New York in the wake of the publication of *Catch-22*, bumped into Peter at innumerable celebrity parties: 'You want to know what being "lionised" means? It means being invited to parties by people you don't know. Peter and I both found it funny when we discovered that neither of us knew the host or hostess.'[8] Funny maybe, but they still went. Being lionised clearly had its attractions.

By day, Wendy and Harriet Garland had nothing to do but go shopping, and spend as much money on clothes as they possibly could. Wendy kitted Peter out in the latest American fashions, including jeans, trainers and baseball T-shirts. Not only were the two women slightly bored, but they suspected that their men were slightly bored with them, so plentiful were the competing attractions. Eventually, in the cold of the New York winter, Peter and Nick Garland packed the two women off to Puerto Rico to lie about in the sun. It was a nice gesture, but it served only to paper over the emerging cracks.

Peter did not have the time to be bothered by tiny cracks in his relationship. The news from home was catastrophic. Not only had *That Was the Week That Was* been rescued from the scrapheap and re-piloted – bizarrely, at the insistence of the Tory ladies interrogated by Bernard Levin, who had wanted their case to be heard – but it had gone on to be a storming success. The entire British nation, it seemed, was now glued to its TV sets every Saturday night. David Frost had become a national institution, the new king of satire. Worse still, he had done so using a proportion of Peter's ideas. Frankie Howerd had been signed up from the Establishment, to perform exactly the same act. Frost had also been liberal in his inclusion of old sketches that he had once contributed the odd joke to, or perhaps appeared in: the first episode of *TW3*, for instance, contained Peter's discarded *Fringe* sketch *Jim's Inn*. The writing and performing element of the show had in large measure been poached from *Private Eye*: Christopher Booker, Willie Rushton, John Wells and Timothy Birdsall had all but abandoned the magazine. Richard Ingrams was practically the only person left at the Greek Street offices – and that was only because he had resigned in disgust, after Frost had ordered the *Eye* man to stand and compose sketches in front of an open lavatory door, while he sat defecating. Peter angrily coined the title 'The Bubonic Plagiarist' to describe his usurper. He also became fond of quoting Kitty Muggeridge's summary of Frost's career, that he had 'risen without trace'. Ned Sherrin, the producer of *TW3*, comments drily: 'Peter Cook was John the Baptist, crying in the wilderness, and then Frost with his fifteen million viewers came on as Jesus Christ. But John the Baptist always had a great deal more charisma.'

Christopher Booker, who had become the programme's chief writer, claimed later that 'In his genial fashion, Peter bore no obvious resentment that David Frost had turned overnight into the most famous satirist of them all.'[9] Perhaps his resentment was not so obvious at three-and-a-half thousand miles distance, but viewed from up close, Peter's famous good manners had entirely evaporated. Alan Bennett recalls: 'A regular feature of Saturday nights when we were playing on Broadway was that with the five hour time difference, *TW3* went out and had finished just before the curtain went up on our second performance; and one would find Peter in the corridor, on the phone, irate because he thought some sketch of his had been plagiarised in *That Was the Week That Was*. That was a regular occurrence. He was bothered by the money, but he was furious that Frost should be rising on his back.' Jonathan Miller reckons that 'Peter was appalled by the opportunistic – what he regarded as – theft of the idea of a satirical weekly magazine on television. I think he was shocked and dismayed, and I think that was one of the reasons why he subsequently developed a life-long antagonism to David Frost, whom I think he quite rightly regarded as simply a late-pressing of something which was vintage and really belonged to him.' In an interview for *Vanity Fair* magazine, Miller himself later referred to Frost by the slightly extended title of '*fucking* David Frost'.[10]

John Bird remembers that 'Peter was beside himself with rage the whole time we were in America. By the summer of 1963 he had built up a fearful head of steam about Frost – he absolutely fed on this long-distance resentment of him. It got down to really biological things. You only had to mention the word "Frost" and he would go off into long paroxysms of vituperation. And that summer, after the first series of *TW3* had finished, David rang me in New York and said, "I'm coming out. It would be nice,

wonderful to see you and it would be great, super to see Peter.'" At that
time Peter and the rest of the *Fringe* cast, together with Wendy and
Michael Bawtree, were taking a few days' holiday at a rented country
house in Fairfield, Connecticut. 'I rang Peter and he said, "Oh yes, bring
him down, bring him down." So when Frost arrived I drove him down,
and I thought, there's going to be a homicide.'

Everybody in the house was licking their lips and keenly anticipating
the death of Frost; but it did not happen. When Frost entered the room
where Peter sat coldly waiting for him, the Cook code of manners
reasserted itself, with a steely correctness drummed in through years
of training. Peter bit his tongue and enquired politely whether Frost
had had a pleasant journey; he was, as Bird commented, 'an *extremely*
well brought up lad'. He also suggested that, as it was a hot day, Frost
might like a dip in the pool. Frost assented, changed into his trunks and
plunged manfully into the deep end. The fact of the matter was that Frost
could not swim, but he did not want to admit this in front of Peter, so
he quietly started to drown instead. Realising what had happened, Peter,
who was a good swimmer, dived headlong after him as he went down for
the third time, and saved his life. John Bird, hearing the commotion, came
through and jumped to the conclusion that Peter was actually murdering
Frost in the swimming pool. Frost's first utterance on being brought to
the surface and rescued was: 'Super!' Peter subsequently told *The Sunday
Times* that he had assumed Frost to have been 'making a satirical attack
on drowning.'[11] He later insisted that taking the decision to save David
Frost was the one sincere regret of his entire life.

Soon afterwards, Kennedy's assassination brought the entire *TW3* team
to the States, to present an oleaginous tribute to the late President. Comedy
and satire were suspended as Frost intoned a solemn eulogy from a large
volume, a performance that wowed New York society rather as Peter had
done. Willie Rushton, who claimed to have gritted his teeth through the
whole thing, remembered that Peter 'was particularly vicious about the
Kennedy tribute. He thought it was the most appalling thing he'd seen in
all his life. He used to do impersonations of Frost doing his perorations,
in the middle of restaurants. Actually the funny thing was, I'd taken over
the Macmillan impersonations so to speak, but there was no resentment
there.' And if there had been, Rushton would have been the last to know
of it. Peter's official attitude, as expressed in quotes given to journalists and
in letters to his parents, was a polite scepticism that *TW3* would last. He told
a student reporter from *Varsity*: 'I would have liked to see the programme
– there was a lot of my material in it. But I should have thought everyone
would get tired of satire every week for thirty weeks.'[12]

The success of *TW3* strengthened Peter's determination to get into television, in America if not in Britain. In his first months in the States he had contented himself with sporadic appearances on *What's My Line* and other game shows, but in the spring of 1963 he, John Bird and Jonathan Miller accepted an offer from WNEW-Channel Five to put together a one-off satirical show. Miller directed and the other two wrote it; the rest of the cast were American, consisting of two old-time radio comics called Bob and Ray, and some of the Second City comedians from Chicago. Entitled *What's Going On Here?*, it broadcast on 10 May in America, and on 12 July on Associated-Rediffusion, London's local ITV station, and was generally well received. All trace of it, sadly, is lost.

Encouraged by the success of *What's Going On Here?*, Peter aimed straight for the top: the *Ed Sullivan Show*, America's biggest light entertainment programme, with sixty million viewers. He formed another company with two American partners, Clay Felker and Jay Vandenheuvel, and in the space of a few weeks had persuaded CBS to give him thirteen minutes of Sullivan's show every week. Again, Miller would direct, and he and Bird would write and star in the segments. The fly in the ointment turned out to be Sullivan himself: a burly, extremely conservative, Irish Catholic sports columnist, he had never been to see *Beyond the Fringe* or visited the New York Establishment, and had agreed to the newfangled satire section of his show without having a clue what it entailed. Despite the fact that the script had been – as far as Peter and John Bird were concerned – entirely sanitised by its authors, Sullivan watched the first rehearsal open-mouthed. The first sketch referred to a local news item from Maryland. 'You can't say "Maryland"!' said Sullivan, horrified.

Peter would probably have done his best to acquiesce, in order to give the show a fighting chance; but Miller was having no truck with any interference, and a series of terrific rows ensued. According to John Bird, 'Sullivan's view was that our material required cuts, starting with the first words of the script and ending with the last. My memory of Peter was that he was well aware of the impossibility of the enterprise which he had launched and rather enjoyed watching the fall-out.'[13] Miller walked out repeatedly rather than make swingeing cuts, and the satire segment was axed after two weeks. Sullivan, who was not used to being contradicted, said: 'You young men are the most discourteous people with whom I have ever worked.' Miller replied that 'You are the stupidest man with whom *I* have ever worked, and it is a pleasure to part company with you.'

Still Peter tore on, dreaming up new schemes, making new contacts, putting together new projects. He was, in Wendy's perceptive description, like a tightly coiled spring unwinding at great speed. He collected political gossip for *Private Eye*, and followed up a rumour that Kennedy had been married twice. Whenever he spotted someone whose act he felt would grace the London Establishment, he signed them up and sent them over to Luard. One such was Barry Humphries, who gave Peter a copy of a comedy record he had cut in Australia, in between appearing in the London and New York versions of *Oliver!* Peter, who by now knew Humphries extremely well (they attended Supremes concerts at the Harlem Apollo together), was sufficiently impressed to offer him £100 a week to appear in Soho. The engagement was not a success. London audiences looking for rumbustious satire were not sure how to take a nervous, skinny boy with long dark hair, dressed all in brown, in the part of a Melbourne housewife called Mrs Edna Everage. The newspapers said he 'lacked anger'. Luard released him before the end of the run.

Lenny Bruce's return performance, booked for April 1963, was even more of a disaster, in that it never took place. The newspapers had continued to campaign against him, and when he arrived at Heathrow on 8 April he was arrested by Immigration officers acting on the orders of the Home Office, strip searched and deported on the next homeward flight. Home Secretary Henry Brooke announced that it was 'not in the public interest' to admit Bruce into the country, on account of his 'sick jokes and lavatory humour', a phrase subsequently adopted by *Private Eye* on its masthead. Peter, who had been invited to Joseph Heller's that evening, spent the whole of the dinner party on the phone, frantically trying to arrange for Bruce to be smuggled back into Britain via Dun Laoghaire. It was not to be. 'I felt terrible for many reasons,' said Peter later, 'largely financial, as he had been advanced most of his money.'[14] The affair also cost Cook & Luard Productions a fortune in legal fees.

Jonathan Miller once described the *Beyond the Fringe* quartet as the Beatles of comedy, in that they appeared with the same timing and challenged similar conventions. By the same token, the Establishment Club was their equivalent of the Apple Corps – an idealistic business venture based as much upon the charisma of its founder as upon any sound management sense, and prone to consistent financial abuse by its employees. By the spring of 1963, money was beginning to haemorrhage out of the London operation. Most of the waiters had their hands in the till. There were few accounting checks. Says Luard: 'Fifty crates of wine would be delivered. Forty-nine of the crates would "walk" straight out of the cellar door. We never noticed but we paid.'[15]

The local gangsters, too, were gaining the upper hand. The removal of Peter's disarming presence had robbed the club of an invaluable bulwark against the surrounding fiefdoms. When a considerable mob invaded the building, Roger Law and the others were overwhelmed: 'I landed a few on the main protagonists – there was a little table at the top of the stairs that took tickets for the jazz club, and the table just fitted the sides of the stairwell. So I ran down the stairs with the table in front of me, and of course they all piled on top of each other like in *East End Cop*. They chased us out of the club; the guy that was driving me was an ex-racing car driver, so we got away. I got home at about three in the morning and the coat I was wearing was like a Chinese lantern. This guy had been swiping at me with a razor. I hadn't seen the razor, but when I got home I could see what he'd done. It looked all right when I was wearing it, but when I took it off it turned into one of those things you used to make at school at Christmas, with holes in the sides. I never went in to the Establishment after that. I got someone else to take my strip.'

Creatively, too, the Establishment wasn't working without Peter. Something vital was missing. The swap with the Second City performers had earned respectful reviews, but the American cast had seemed earnest and lacking in the joie-de-vivre of their British counterparts. *Scene* magazine had been the worst disaster of the lot, devouring cash at a frightening rate. 'The problem there was really my greed,' said Peter politely. 'Nick could either have done it as Cook & Luard, or he could have done it on his own, but I thought, well, it might just work.' It didn't. So little money was left in the kitty that Elisabeth Luard's jewels had to be pawned to pay *Private Eye*'s wages bill. With frightening and unexpected suddenness, Nicholas Luard Associates, the sub-company that owned *Scene* magazine, was declared bankrupt on 28 June. Three months later, Cook & Luard Productions – including the Establishment Club – folded in its wake. 'I thought I'd be a millionaire at thirty,' said Peter ruefully. 'Then I just picked up the paper one day in New York and found that the business had failed and was £75,000 in debt.'[16]

At the bankruptcy hearings, their solicitor, Mr J. A. Rose, called them 'utter fools'. Stuart Young, the chartered accountant examining the books, went further. 'The directors have acted in a stupid, foolhardy way. In fact, just think of any similar adjectives and they will apply to them.'[17] It transpired that Nicholas Luard Associates had lost £75,658, of which £39,767 had been transferred by Luard from the Cook & Luard Productions account, in an attempt to prop it up. This left Cook & Luard productions itself £65,957 in debt. Peter and Nick Luard had lost £26,957 of their own money in the crash. Rose declared that the club had been 'very badly managed' and that Luard was a man with 'no idea' of how to run a company. The Establishment Club (London) went into voluntary liquidation on 23 September, leaving 127 small supply businesses out of pocket to the tune of £24,192.

In private, Peter was absolutely furious with Luard, as well as being extremely upset. In the space of just nine months the Establishment had gone from being the most successful venue in London to the financial equivalent of the *Titanic*. The papers were laying the blame for the disaster substantially at Peter's door, even though he had been abroad since September. On brand new 'Peter Cook' headed notepaper, he wrote to his parents: 'As you seem to have gathered from the papers, Nicholas Luard has contrived to get our affairs into something of a mess. I have some very good lawyers and accountants working for me in London, who are in the process of sorting things out. The probable result will be my severing my connection with Nick. It is he who has really lost all the money, personally.' Not only was Peter out of pocket for an amount that would take several years to pay off, but he had also made a deeply unpleasant discovery: he was not, as he thought, the co-owner of *Private Eye*. This news made him 'very cross indeed. I sent over a famous New York lawyer called Sidney Cohn. I thought if anything should emerge from the shambles, I should like to retain the *Eye*. And somehow or other he did it. The *Eye* never knew how close it got to going down the tubes.' The magazine's new accountant, David Cash, remembers considerable animosity on Peter's part: 'He didn't want the *Eye* dragged down with Luard'.

The Establishment was snapped up by a Lebanese 'businessman' calling himself Raymond Nash – a former partner of the slum landlord Peter Rachman – and his associate Anthony Coutt-Sykes, who'd added the 'Coutt' in order to try and sound distinguished. 'Nash was a traditional Soho type,' said Cook. 'He never drank, never smoked, and always carried a briefcase full of cash. He was later sent to jail for gold smuggling in Tokyo. Nash came out to New York and promised me that nothing would change, but we all knew he'd wreck the place. He was a crook, and a tough crook at that. When I eventually got back it was just absolutely different – filled with very heavy men. The atmosphere was so bad.'

Nash was presented to creditors as a man with experience, who had previously co-owned the 'La Discotheque' and 'Le Condor' clubs. He offered to pay preferential debts in full, trade debts at 6s 8d in the pound, and to pay Cook & Luard absolutely nothing. They, in return, agreed to 'continue their association with the club'. The New York cast were sent over to play a few weeks there at the end of the year. 'We were surprised by the number of large Levantines in slightly iridescent suits who seemed to be in charge,' says John Bird.[18] Gaye Brown remembers that 'gambling then came into the upstairs bar, which had been this wonderful bar with nice lunches. The members hung on for dear life actually, we wanted that club, everybody wanted that club. But you can't hang on to an old result.' A few months later, Bill Wallis, from the replacement cast of *Beyond the Fringe*, was lucky enough to secure a job in the replacement cast of the Establishment's late-night cabaret. 'There were a total of three people in the audience,' he recalls. 'In fact six of us once played to a honeymoon couple. And that was it.' Nash and his fellow gangsters were utterly bewildered as to why the goose had suddenly ceased to lay the golden eggs. 'It soon reverted to a sex cinema,' noted Peter, 'dedicated to the overthrow of the government and all that it stands for.'[19]

Undeterred, Peter threw himself into the expansion of his financially separate American empire. In July he announced the construction of a new 200-seat Establishment Theatre, presenting serious drama, to be built not beside but actually on top of the Strollers Club. With *Beyond the Fringe* off the stage for its summer break, Peter and Wendy had flown back to England for the initial bankruptcy hearings, visited Peter's family in Uplyme (where 'Knollside' had recently been redecorated at Peter's expense, just in time) and had snatched a short break in Bermuda. The rest of his holiday, however, was cut short so that he could devote all his time to raising money for the theatre project. Together with producer David Balding, he secured backing from Joseph E. Levine, the President of Embassy Pictures, and Richard Burton's wife Sybil. The opening was set for the following January; Peter was so busy that he forgot his mother's birthday.

In August, the Establishment cabaret acquired a second cast: one group stayed in New York, while the other toured San Francisco, Los Angeles, Chicago and points in between. Among the new performers was Peter Bellwood, his old Cambridge friend. Peter also set to work writing a brand new show for the dual opening, and spent all his spare time in the summer shooting satirical short films to complement the sketches. Then, in early September, all his rushing hither and thither was suddenly pulled up short, by the news that Wendy was pregnant. Peter and Wendy's relationship had been wavering somewhat during the preceding months; now Wendy, in particular, wanted to make a go of it. With indecent haste – this was, after all, 1963 – they set their wedding date for just two months later.

Peter's parents, stunned by the speed of it all, dropped everything and flew out to New York, where they were politely shuttled around the expatriot comedians' social circle: supper at the Millers', lunch with Peter Bellwood, tea with Alan Bennett, to an art gallery with Judy Scott-Fox. They went with Peter to Sardi's, his favourite restaurant, and took in performances of *Beyond the Fringe* and the Establishment cabaret. When he returned home, Alec Cook gave a lecture to the British Legion in Lyme Regis about all the astonishing things he had seen in America – automatic glass doors, push button pedestrian crossings, driver-operated buses, digital temperature displays on buildings and aircraft seats with collapsible tables in the back.

The wedding took place at St Luke's Chapel in Greenwich Village on 28 October. Wendy looked stunning in a dark blue crepe-de-chine empire dress with a diamond clip, and a felt emerald trilby; she carried a bouquet of gardenias and a slight three-month bulge which did not impress the vicar at all. Peter Bellwood was the best man and Sybil Burton helped with the organisation. There was a Hungarian trio, and Dudley Moore played the organ; the reception was at Strollers. For their honeymoon, Peter took Wendy to see a double horror bill at a Times Square cinema.

Despite the aura of excitement generated by all Peter's projects, and the social novelty of his wedding, a sense of inertia was beginning to weigh upon the British satirical community. The cast of *Beyond the Fringe*, in particular, were beginning to get seriously on each other's nerves after more than three years together. Miller and Bennett's relationship was the most frayed: in one row during the interval, Miller had upended the table of sandwiches in the Green Room. Then Moore, too, fell out with Bennett: 'One evening I changed some lines in a sketch we did together and well, *we* didn't have an argument, *he* did, and I don't think we have really ever spoken much after that.'[20] Peter observed that 'Dudley had gone from being a subservient little creep, a genial serf, to become an obstinate bastard who asserted himself.' Bennett campaigned against Peter's 'vaudeville exuberance'. Miller became angry with Peter after having a furious transatlantic row with *Private Eye* magazine: a supposedly anonymous piece he'd written about 'pooves' had his name and medical title carelessly appended to it. The letter he fired off – 'You stupid bloody irresponsible cunts' it began, and continued in much the same vein – still hangs on the *Eye* office wall.

Curiously, the more irritable with each other the four protagonists became offstage, the more they began to corpse and giggle onstage. 'It got worse and worse,' says Miller. 'There were moments when the show simply didn't go on.'[21] Practical jokes became the norm. Dudley Moore would stand in the wings trying to put the others off; if they directed their performance away from him, he would dash round the back of the set and appear in the opposite wing. When Miller's wife Rachel was standing in the wings one day holding their newborn baby, Peter grabbed it, marched onstage mid-sketch and announced: 'Excuse me, Sir. Your wife's just given birth to this.' Miller replied nonchalantly, 'Oh, just bung it in the fridge.' The audience roared. In reality Miller was furious. A few days later Peter came on carrying a limp Dudley Moore instead: 'Excuse me, Sir. I've just discovered this man in bed with your wife, so I shot him.' To which Miller replied, 'Oh, well, just drop him anywhere.' The atmosphere had become semi-hysterical. At the end of 1963, Miller decided he'd had enough, and resigned from the show. 'It was a great relief,' says Bennett. 'He and I really got on each other's nerves.'[22]

Beyond the Fringe was relaunched by the surviving three cast members in a new version that began on 8 January 1964. The part of Jonathan Miller was acted by Paxton Whitehead, an English-born actor with US sitcom experience. The script was substantially rewritten to include seven new items, some of them on an American theme; Peter, more parochially, contributed topical nonsense sketches about the Great Train Robbery and the British space programme. Another of his 'new' sketches was actually *One Leg Too Few*, now resurrected once again to appear in its fourth incarnation, with Dudley Moore as the hapless unidexter. This pairing was very much the beginning of the Cook–Moore partnership that went on to dominate British comedy throughout the rest of the sixties. Moore was perfectly cast, as the sketch already seemed to sum up their offstage relationship of languid superiority versus hopeful deference. 'I think Alan tried the part first,' he says, 'but he made it too maudlin, an unhappy figure. My boundless optimism was the key.' On account of his club foot, Moore could only hop on his right leg night after night. Eventually he developed a serious water-on-the-knee problem, which persists to this day.

One Leg Too Few apart, the critics were lukewarm in their reception of the new material. *Newsweek* felt that 'The days of the show's satirical leadership are over', and that its 'original vitriolic radicalism' had been diluted. The new performer fared little better: Paxton Whitehead, according to the *New York Times*, 'reminds you of a man who isn't there'. In April 1964, after 669 performances, the American version of *Beyond the Fringe* dwindled to a halt. The British version, although it lasted longer – it was transferred to the Mayfair Theatre, where it played until September 1966 – suffered a similar slow decline. 'At first it was wonderful, and it all went terribly well,' says Bill Wallis. 'Then we discovered that things were diminishing, like laughs. We got rather depressed. Eventually we recorded a show, after a year or so, and played it sketch by sketch alongside one of our early shows, and we discovered that we weren't performing anywhere near as well as we had been, any of us. It was a most salutary experience.'

The decline of *Beyond the Fringe* was mirrored by the dramatic collapse of *That Was the Week That Was*. The satire boom, it seemed, had run into a brick wall. Macmillan had resigned in October, and his successor Alec Douglas-Home was enjoying a brief wash of public sympathy before being swept aside by Harold Wilson in the 1964 election: a *TW3* sketch which encapsulated the choice facing the voters as 'Dull Alec versus smart-alec' had received an astonishing 909 complaints from the public. One of the BBC's governors, Sir James Duff, was among the outraged. The Director-General Sir Hugh Carleton-Greene didn't want Duff to resign – 'an excellent man' he said – so he used the excuse of the impending election to announce the programme's cancellation after thirteen episodes of the new series.

As if in sympathy, *Private Eye*'s circulation suddenly crashed from a peak of 95,000 to 19,000, and London newsagents were awash with unsold copies. According to Peter Usborne, one of its ex-Oxford University founders, 'At that time the *Eye* became the last thing to be seen carrying.'[23] The staff had to take 50 per cent pay cuts and look for part-time jobs elsewhere, 'We really didn't think the magazine would last,' said Willie Rushton. *TW3* had taken a terrible toll on the *Eye*'s comic talent, and loss of morale caused by the collapse in sales compounded the problem. 'We'd almost forgotten about jokes, we were so depressed,' recalls Usborne. *The Sunday Times* described the magazine as 'The last and dying echo of the satire boom.'

Jonathan Miller once said that 'There never was a satire movement, only the Cook empire.'[24] It's not that much of an exaggeration. Peter's astonishing, virtually unchecked explosion, from tentative first year trying out his material at a Pembroke College smoker to king of satire on both sides of the Atlantic, had taken just five years. After that, it had taken less than a year for the whole edifice to crumble. He had managed to create a mass fashion across the whole Anglo-Saxon world, but had invested in it so heavily, both creatively and financially, that when the fashion passed his investment went with it. Almost simultaneously, in America and in Britain, a hiatus occurred in public cynicism. The assassination of Kennedy made it difficult, for a short while, to mock American politics or politicians. The impending and apparently guaranteed election of Harold Wilson in this country seemed to obviate satire, by convincing a new generation of naive British youth that a golden age of socialist prosperity was just around the corner. There was a sense that the satire boom had done its job, that the money changers were on the point of being driven from the temple. Of course, they would simply be back later with bigger and better pitches; and Peter, ironically, was one of the minority of young British people who had never believed or suggested otherwise.

Naturally, he kept working with the same furious energy: he and John
Bird wrote a new Establishment revue which opened at Strollers on 15
April 1964, featuring Eleanor Bron in a suit as Sir Alec Douglas Home,
in a sketch that confused many of the audience into thinking the British
Prime Minister was gay. 'Enough is enough', complained the New York
correspondent of the London *Evening News*. 'Isn't it about time that we
tried to export a little better picture of British life today?'[25] Peter was
discovering, like all empire-builders before him, that the impetus of
construction is easier to sustain than the hard slog of maintenance.
Once the empire is built, the personal charisma of its creator is no
longer enough to keep it intact, because he cannot continue to captivate
all parts of it at once.

The Establishment Theatre Co. finally presented its first production in
the new theatre in May 1964, a performance of Ann Jellicoe's *The Knack*
directed by Mike Nichols and starring the then-unknown George Segal.
Subsequent productions included *Serjeant Musgrave's Dance*, featuring the
equally unknown Dustin Hoffman, who was fired during rehearsals by
his frustrated director Stuart Burge. Peter did not stay to see any of
them. Although he claimed that he would henceforth 'divide his time
between New York and London,'[26] he actually left the theatre company
exclusively in the hands of his partner David Balding, who shepherded it
safely through the rest of the sixties. The US Establishment itself dribbled
on as far as 1965 – John Cleese was in the cast of the touring version –
but the next time John Bird visited New York he noticed that the building
had been demolished and replaced by a branch of Habitat. A Las Vegas
impresario offered Peter a lucrative contract to stay on in the States, as
a stand-up comedian working the casinos; but most of his friends were
fed up and wanted to come home, and he didn't want to be left alone.
'I couldn't face it – I didn't have the nerve,' he confessed.[27] The move
back to London filled him with no less apprehension. He later admitted
that he had been 'dreading it'.[28]

By 19 April, Dudley Moore was the only member of the *Fringe* cast
left in the USA. His girlfriend Celia Hammond had flown out to join
him, and had then left him for her ex-boyfriend the photographer Terry
Donovan; possibly because she had discovered the awkward fact that he
was also going out with another model, Cynthia Cassidy, at the same
time. So distraught was Moore at the break-up that he made his first visit
to a psychiatrist, and embarked on a course of treatment on the quite
ludicrous premise that – at the age of twenty-nine – time was slipping
by and he had not achieved anything. He finally returned to England
four months later, and was immediately offered his own BBC TV music

series, *Offbeat*. The Cool Elephant Club in Margaret Street made a home for the Dudley Moore Trio. He was sorted.

The BBC also found a job for Jonathan Miller, at the helm of the arts programme *Monitor*. Ned Sherrin employed John Bird, John Fortune, Eleanor Bron and Alan Bennett on his new venture *Not So Much a Programme* . . . a three-nights-a-week chat-cum-sketch show fronted by the brightest star in British broadcasting, David Frost. Lady Pamela Stitty, the Conservative lady devised by Peter, became a regular character; but there was no room, anywhere, for Peter himself. He was hardly a pariah, but a tainted whiff of satire continued to hang rather unfairly about him. Defiantly, he protested that 'When people talk about the satire movement being over it's like people saying that "singing is over" or "swimming is out of fashion";[29] but producers and backers were nervous of antagonising the Gods of fashion, and all Peter's ideas were quietly filed away. The only work he got that summer was when the BBC finally recorded a performance of *Beyond the Fringe* for broadcast. To make matters worse, in the autumn he slipped and broke his ankle, and was confined to a wheelchair for several weeks.

He started to work on a play set in a police station, with a cast of forty policemen, but nerves made it difficult to concentrate; he tried without success both to complete it and to interest anyone in it for sixteen months. He offered an item for inclusion in an American film, in which Jesus Christ arrives in present-day America, and runs into trouble with the Carpenters' Union. He and John Bird also wrote an adaptation of Evelyn Waugh's *Scoop* for the cinema, updated to the 1960s and featuring an African dictator who had modelled himself on Macmillan to the extent of wearing shooting tweeds and employing a ghillie in the sun-baked African landscape. The scenes were divided up between the two writers: 'I was heavily influenced at the time by Jean-Luc Godard,' explains Bird, 'so you would get a scene written by me which consisted of meticulously described camera movements, followed by a Cook scene which was pages of unadorned dialogue, sometimes without even the names of the characters. So you can imagine how difficult it was to work out.'

Another abortive film project united the *Beyond the Fringe* cast, in the story of a fiendish nineteenth-century German plot to undermine the monarchy by flooding Britain with dozens of substitute Queen Victorias. 'It never got beyond the treatment stage,' remembers Alan Bennett. 'Such writing sessions as we had were what nowadays would be called "unstructured"; as it was nobody's job to take notes, there would be lots of ideas flying about with suggestions for dialogue and so on, and when the meeting broke up we'd have the impression we'd got somewhere whereas in fact we'd got nowhere at all.' Peter recollected that 'We sat round the table simply destroying each other's stuff. I don't know if it was successful but it made us all take up smoking again.'[30] Peter Sellers and Sam Spiegel expressed interest at various times, but the quartet were past being able to work with each other again. Their later relations with each other were described by Jonathan Miller as 'distant'. When the *Beyond the Fringe* scripts were reissued in book form in 1987, Alan Bennett wrote to the publisher to say that 'Reading through the *BTF* stuff is quite painful. So relieved it's all over. I regard the book as a burial more than anything else.' Only Peter's rediscovered cigarette habit was to stick faithfully with him, despite repeated attempts to jettison it.

Peter later claimed that on his return to London from America he had simply 'sat about for a while';[31] a course of action which in actual fact would have been anathema to him. The truth of the matter was that his brain was still working on overdrive, trying to convert a flood of ideas into concrete reality; but the public were more interested in David Frost than Peter Cook. As Peter was quite prepared to admit, 'I came back expecting to be enormously well-known, and of course nobody knew me from Adam.'[32] In fact, the only thing left to him was *Private Eye* magazine. Like a tiny rodent hiding in the cracks and crevices while the great dinosaurs were brought down in massive conflagration, it had survived. It was broke, the staff were demoralised, the content wasn't very funny and nobody was buying it, but it was, at least, still there.

CHAPTER 7

The Seductive Brethren

Private Eye, 1964–70

One day in 1964, Peter Cook walked into the shabby *Eye* offices in Greek Street; it was the first time any of them had seen him for two years. One of the two cramped rooms was given over to the editorial side, and contained just Richard Ingrams, the tall, stiff, faintly dishevelled Old Salopian editor, and Barry Fantoni, a cheerful Italian-Jewish cartoonist from South London with a Beatle haircut and a big nose. On occasions, John Wells and Willie Rushton would push the quota up to four.

Peter's arrival galvanised the weary office like a bolt of electricity. Every day he would stride up and down, embarking upon impromptu lectures about enormous snakes, 'many of them millions of miles long', or he would impersonate a zoo-keeper attempting to recapture a very rare type of bee which had become intractably lodged in a lady's undergarments. He invented catchphrases: 'This man is a proven lawyer', and 'My lady wife, whose name for a moment escapes me', as uttered by the blustering writer of letters to the *Daily Telegraph*, Sir Herbert Gussett. He dreamed up topical jokes: in the wake of the collapse of the John Bloom package tour company, he put 'The Raft of Medusa' on the cover, with one of the cannibal survivors saying, 'This is the last time I go on a John Bloom holiday.' Bewildered, laughing, all Ingrams could do was write it all down as quickly as possible.

'Cook saved the day,' says Ingrams simply. 'I was very uncertain about what to do until he arrived.' Barry Fantoni adds: 'I don't think I'm being unfair, but if it wasn't for Peter Cook arriving from America and introducing all the brilliant, brilliant ideas he had at that time, we would simply have gone under.' Willie Rushton went further: 'He brought it back from the dead.' Peter introduced two series into the magazine: the *Memoirs of Rhandi Phurr*, a bogus Hindu mystic who anticipated the Beatles' antics with the Maharishi by two years; and – from Christmas 1964 onwards – *Tales of the Seductive Brethren*. The Brethren were a homegrown sect, somewhat restricted in size:

> The exact number of the Brethren at any given time is always hard to calculate but it can be safely said that a figure of two would be exact; it is our proud claim that we are far more exclusive than our religious competitors.

The two officers of the Brethren were the Holy Dragger, Sir Arthur Starborgling, and the Chief Rammer, Sir Basil Nardly-Stoads. As those titles would suggest, the purpose of the sect was 'to seize hold of young women and clamber hotly all over their bodies':

> To say that the BODILY SEIZING OF YOUNG WOMEN is at least part and parcel of our belief would be no exaggeration.

The brethren were unquestionably the spiritual descendants of the sect that had sat atop a mountain in *Beyond the Fringe*, waiting for the end of the world. Peter actually typed their adventures every week himself, with one finger. As it dawned upon him that his new colleagues were prepared to write down more or less everything that he said, he eventually confined himself to dictating his material instead.

Peter's almost biological requirement to devour the newspapers in search of raw material was an invaluable asset on a topically humorous magazine. According to John Wells, 'His jokes, like John Bird's, were fuelled with an immense amount of reading. He read all the newspapers and political weeklies and, unlike John Bird, allowed his researches to carry him into *Rubberwear News*, *The Budgerigar Fancier* and *Frilly Knickers*. He took a particular delight in misprints, sub-editors' cliche's and Fleet Street journalese, creasing up with laughter at Swoops, Grabs and Probes.'[1] Two stories in particular filled him with such delight that he would relate them again and again to anyone who would listen, improvising in a series of minute variations the possible consequences of each. One concerned the accidental drowning of a circus elephant in a swimming pool at Butlin's, immediately prior to a royal visit by the Queen Mother: Peter wanted to know what assurances Butlin's could provide that a similar fate would not befall Her Majesty. The second dated from as early as February 1962, when it had been announced that the actress Jayne Mansfield had been shipwrecked in a skimpy bikini on a desert island off the Bahamas. Her boat had supposedly capsized on a waterskiing trip, and she had been pulled unconscious from an ocean teeming with dangerous marine life by her PR man – his presence being suspiciously convenient, given that her new film was due to open that week. Peter speculated endlessly on the lobsters and other crustaceans that might have become lodged in her various orifices, an obsession that continued to grip him until 1973, when it became the basis for the first ever *Derek and Clive* sketch.

Peter was also hugely amused by a picture of the Prime Minister Sir Alec Douglas Home that had appeared in the *Aberdeen Evening Express* shortly before the election, that had been incorrectly captioned 'Baillie Vass'. Sir Alec was known thereafter as the Baillie, and Peter insisted on organising a 'Mass for Vass' protest march, which proceeded from the *Eye* offices to Number Ten Downing Street to present an ironic petition begging the PM to stay in office. On the Sunday morning of the march Richard Ingrams raised the sash of the Greek Street window to discover, with a tinge of horror, that not only had Cook's appeal actually succeeded in raising a small army of *Eye* readers, but that most of them appeared to be sporting beards and sandals. Peter, on the other hand, received them all with enthusiasm. Confined at this stage to a wheelchair with his broken ankle, he was pushed to Downing Street at the head of the parade bearing his own placard, which read 'The Baillie will no fail ye!'

Not all Peter's jokes were for the benefit of the readers. The *Tonight* programme once featured an African dance group comprising a troupe of near-naked women who jiggled around in time to music. The next day Peter rang the BBC from the *Eye* claiming to be Sydney Darlow of the Sydney Darlow Dance Ensemble, and insisted that his own troupe of white ladies be allowed to jiggle topless on the BBC as well, to the same sort of music. The Producer tried manfully to explain why it would be acceptable for black women to do so and not white women, but 'Darlow' would not let him off the hook. Peter was also fond of tormenting the Foreign Office, another organisation he had nearly joined, and would telephone to claim that the Russians were spying on him through his domestic drainage system.

As well as galvanising the humorous side of the magazine, Peter set about energetically rejuvenating its finances. He injected £2,000 of his own money, and persuaded various celebrities to lend him £100 each. Peter Sellers, Dirk Bogarde, Jane Asher, Bryan Forbes and Bernard Braden all gave generously, as did Lord Faringdon, Britain's only gay communist peer, a man who once began a speech in Parliament not with the words 'My Lords', but with 'My Dears'. Some, like Sellers, were ultimately repaid;

the remainder became 'shareholders' in the magazine, in return for a case of wine every Christmas. In October 1966 Peter took Richard Ingrams on a promotional tour of Hull, York, Middlesbrough, Darlington, Sunderland, Durham and Newcastle-upon-Tyne, to raise support from wholesalers and distributors.

While in America Peter had already made a special trip to Chicago to try and raise finance for the *Eye* from *Playboy* magazine. He had written offering them a concession on *Eye* articles written by himself and 'Willie Rushton, our fat cartoonist'. 'Hugh Hefner told me to piss off', said Peter, but not before introducing him to Victor Lownes, Hefner's British-born lieutenant. As a courtesy, Lownes was given the job of showing Peter round the Playboy Club, a five-storey private members' establishment packed with Playboy Bunnies. Members were known as 'keyholders', explained Lownes as they toured the building, and had to hand in their key to the bunny at the desk in order to book a table. 'Beauty is in the eye of the keyholder,' mused Peter. At this point a party of Chicago businessmen attempted to jump the long line of keyholders queuing for a table, and were told by the desk 'Bunny' that they would have to wait. 'Do you know who I am?' growled the lead businessman, and an angry scene was poised to erupt.

Peter seized the PA microphone and addressed the room with the straightest of faces: 'We have a problem here in the front lobby which perhaps someone can help us with. We have a gentleman here who doesn't seem to know who he is. If anyone recognises this man, will they please come down to reception and help us respond to his query?' Not daring to fence verbally with Peter himself, the irate businessman turned to the Bunny Girl and said 'Fuck You!' Whereupon, as he turned to go, Peter added: 'You'll have to wait in line for that too, I'm afraid.' He was not wrong, as the grateful girl – this was Kitty Nisty – took him to her bed that night. 'I wanted this guy for a friend,' said Lownes, gobsmacked.[2] Given Lownes's large circle of Playboy Bunny acquaintances, it was an offer Peter accepted with alacrity.

Besides the money and the jokes, high-quality contributors also flowed into *Private Eye* in Peter's wake. He encouraged Ingrams to give a regular berth to Claud Cockburn, the veteran Irish radical journalist. Cartoonists arrived, such as Ralph Steadman, Michael Heath, Bill Tidy, Larry and Hector Breeze. Barry Humphries and Nick Garland were put together, to collaborate on *The Adventures of Barry McKenzie*, a regular cartoon strip about an Australian living in Earl's Court, an idea which contributed more than anything else to the about-turn in the *Eye*'s circulation figures. 'I thought an Australian *Candide* would be a good idea,' said Peter. 'Sort of "An Arsehole Abroad".'

The character of Barry McKenzie was born on a summer holiday in Northern Brittany in 1964, where Peter and Wendy had gone with the Garlands. The LP record that Barry Humphries had presented Peter with in New York had contained a similar expat named Buster Thompson, whose entire life had been simplified into a quest for cold lager; Thompson metamorphosed into McKenzie, taking Barry Humphries's Christian name with him, and both Peter and Nick Garland spent the entire holiday in the McKenzie persona. On their return to England they contacted Humphries, and the three created the character which became such a cult figure that he eventually starred in two feature films, and heavily influenced the creation of *Crocodile Dundee*.

Despite Humphries's uncomfortable experiences with parochial material at the Establishment Club, Peter was keen to incorporate as much obscure Australian terminology as possible. Thus *Eye* readers were introduced to such colourful new phrases as 'splashing the boots', 'shaking hands with the wife's best friend', 'pointing Percy at the porcelain' and 'draining the dragon' (urinating), and such useful expressions as 'chunder', 'liquid laugh', 'technicolour yawn' and 'parking the tiger' (vomit). McKenzie's favourite lager was a deliberately obscure choice, too: a totally unheard of Australian beer called Foster's. The *Eye* readership was initially bemused, but Peter and Richard Ingrams were prepared to be patient. The Australian government was horrified, and banned *Private Eye* as degrading to the country's image; their action made the strip, if anything, more of a cult success in Australia than in Britain, and effectively launched Humphries's international career. 'Thinking about it now,' he says, 'Peter was extraordinarily generous in his encouragement of me. He must have known that I was rather downhearted in London.'

Another new recruit to the *Eye* ranks was the investigative journalist Paul Foot, an old schoolfriend of Ingrams and Rushton's. In 1964 he had just joined the *Sun* and had come for lunch at the Coach and Horses, the pub where the *Eye* staff tended to write the magazine over several pints of beer on account of the dismal state of their offices. 'There was this rather shy man at the table,' recalls Foot. '"This is Peter Cook," Richard Ingrams was saying, and we shook hands. The conversation was stilted, almost formal, until suddenly something quite mundane seemed to click in Peter's mind and he said something ridiculous. We all laughed. The laughter seemed to jolt him out of his reverie. His eyes sparkled, his face broke into a mighty grin and he was off, leaping from one glorious fantasy to another – it was something about bees. He started to talk about bees and within about thirty seconds the entire table and not just the table, but also all the pub around, clustered about and started to laugh. Every

morning after that I scuttled through my work in the hope that I might
inhale another gale of that infectious laughter.'[3] Foot joined the *Eye*
full time in 1967, and remembers that 'The joy of working there was
the tremendous amount of laughter, genuine laughter, that went on
all the time. To be in the next office and hear the laughter of Cook,
Fantoni and Ingrams . . . Peter and Richard, improvising together, were
brilliant.'

Peter had immediately hit it off with his two co-writers, who nicknamed
him Cookie. Almost uniquely in a world populated by highbrow Oxbridge
satirists, the working-class Fantoni shared his interest in sex, football and
pop music, and later went on to present a TV pop show called *There's a
Whole Scene Going On*. Together he and Peter created Spiggy Topes and
the Turds, a satire on the Beatles, and the adventures of Neasden FC, the
world's worst football team, the obsession with Neasden arising from the
fact that the *Eye*'s printers were located near there. Fantoni proved to
be a fine comic collaborator, a foil for Peter's originality and ingenuity,
and his genial enthusiasm masked a determined ability to be accepted
as such. Peter's sense of mischief – presumably – subsequently led to
a bizarre confusion about the nature of the Cook–Fantoni relationship.
Nick Luard wrote that 'One of Peter's proudest claims, a story he loved
telling, was of finding a young Italian waiter called Fantoni, who was
attending art school. Peter taught him, not very successfully, how to
play cricket and encouraged him to go on drawing. Who else but Peter
would have shown a balding Italian waiter how to bowl and helped him
to become a successful artist?'[4] Fantoni had in fact been a successful
satirical pop artist before he had joined the *Eye* of his own accord; not
only had he exhibited at the Woodstock Gallery, but he had never been
a waiter, never played cricket with Peter, and was the proud owner of a
full head of hair.

Peter's close relationship with Richard Ingrams was hardly surprising
given the similarities in their background – Ingrams's father had been
abroad for years on end, and he had been unhappily sent away to West
Downs and Shrewsbury. They shared a similar amused cynicism about the
world. Both men had a regard for the other's powers of perception when
it came to debunking pretension or dishonesty. Peter had, for instance,
cancelled an art exhibition at the Establishment at the eleventh hour when
he had discovered that the artist William Morris' works consisted of
paint-splattered sheets of paper that had been driven over in a car. 'Cook
had a very searching awareness of humbug,' says Ingrams. 'I almost always
agreed with his interpretation of people's motives. We latched onto the
slightest inconsistencies. We would almost always get a consensus about

whether someone was genuine or not.' Peter was very much one of the founding fathers of the magazine's philosophy of debunking 'pseuds', or pseudo-intellectuals.

Where the Editor and his proprietor differed were on matters of sex, bad language and jokes about religion. Peter considered *Private Eye*'s readership to be a restricted members' club in the manner of the Establishment, and gave his desire to shock free rein. In October 1964 a plastic flimsy disc was appended to the *Eye*'s cover for the first time, in which Peter appeared with Dudley Moore, Richard Ingrams, John Wells and Willie Rushton. A decade before *Derek and Clive*, Peter contributed lines like: 'As a trade unionist, people often ask me why I am voting Conservative. The answer is because I am a stupid cunt.' Ingrams complained that Peter was 'too sex-orientated. He sees wage restraint in terms of masturbation.'[5] Years later, Ingrams was to scrap the *Barry McKenzie* strip after he objected to an explicit lesbian sex scene in a dentist's chair, an action which Peter described as 'puritanical'.

The most significant attitude shared by the two men was an utter lack of interest in the administrative and financial side of the magazine. Ingrams had always espoused a patrician distaste for money-making, whereas Peter had simply had his fingers burned: 'I lost interest in business as soon as I went out of business,' he said.[6] As a consequence, Peter made himself unique among magazine proprietors by never trying to take a penny in profit or wages from his publication. 'The purpose of the magazine is to keep going, rather than to make money', he explained.[7] A company policy was implemented that advertising revenue, which accounted for 60 per cent of the income of most magazines, should be kept to a maximum of 10 per cent. If more people wished to advertise than there was space, the rates were simply increased until the 10 per cent figure was arrived at. Advertisements were always kept well away from the copy. David Cash, the quiet, dome-headed accountant who now became the *Eye*'s Business Manager, recalls that Peter's idea of a finance meeting was a hysterical lunch at his local restaurant. 'But he was a very astute man, Cook, you know, he did have a business nose.'

Neither did Peter try to interfere with editorial decisions. 'I never believed there could be such a person,' says Paul Foot. 'He was the essence of the non-interfering proprietor. Even when his best friends were attacked, or people he thought well of, never once, I am absolutely certain of this, never once did he seek to intervene with Richard Ingrams.' Auberon Waugh, who joined the magazine in 1970, says that 'He was proprietor, but his powers were never fully explained, possibly never understood, certainly never exercised.'[8] Peter, although undoubtedly the harshest of the lot when it came to attacking anyone in authority, sometimes cavilled slightly when it came to attacks on targets who had no position of power. Ingrams, however, felt that anyone in the public eye was fair game, a philosophy which became the *Eye*'s editorial policy.

When Ingrams was away Peter edited the magazine himself, assisted by Claud Cockburn, with a mischievousness bordering on recklessness. 'It was always great fun when he had an issue to edit,' says Andrew Osmond, who briefly re-joined the magazine 'because it just spun straight out of control. He would do things that Richard would never do.' One Cook cover featured a naked girl on all fours belly-up, surrounded by an admiring group of further naked girls: Peter added the caption 'And where was he standing?' Inside, he took the remarkably bold step of naming the two anonymous associates of Tory politician Lord Boothby, whom the press had criticised without daring to name: Ronald and Reginald Kray. 'Either the charges are true,' wrote Peter, 'in which case the newspapers should have the guts to publish them . . . or they are untrue, in which case they should stop scaring people with this horror movie of London under terror.' Peter took the extra precaution of making sure that he was on a plane to Tenerife on publication day, leaving Ingrams's kneecaps in the firing line. A few years later, during the *Oz* trial, Peter risked prosecution by putting a Ralph Steadman illustration of a fully-frontal nude Judge Michael Argyle on the cover.

Private Eye's old drive had been restored. Cook's energetic, surreal genius, harnessed to Ingrams's disciplined facility for building the new characters into a Beachcomberesque family, had swiftly regenerated the magazine to a position where the modern *Eye* was clearly beginning to take shape. The turnaround in sales was, however, a much more gradual business. When Harold Wilson triumphed at the polls in October 1964, it was Peter's instinct, and to a lesser extent the instinct of those around him, to attack the new regime as vigorously as they had attacked the old. This alienated the magazine's natural constituency, who were uneasy about anti-Labour jokes at the best of times and were now undergoing a protracted honeymoon period. Ingrams himself voiced the level of expectation that Wilson had aroused: 'To those like me who had been brought up on the idea that the troubles of Britain sprang from the fact that the Tories were in charge, and that they would largely disappear once the Labour Party got in, the advent of Harold Wilson was a climactic event. Consciously or not, the satire movement had been working with Wilson.'[9]

Widespread public disaffection with Wilson did not follow until the collapse of sterling in 1966, but by that time *Private Eye* had been pursuing a somewhat isolated anti-Wilson course for two years, concentrating largely on the contrast between his banal suburban Pooterishness and his Kennedyish aspirations. Peter had devised *Mrs Wilson's Diary*, a regular airing of the homespun philosophy of the Prime Minister's wife, inspired by a newspaper item he had read describing her habit of writing up the day's events. Peter recalled: 'It was my first experience of the phenomenon whereby you make something up, and Downing Street begin to think you've got inside information, that people are leaking facts to you. Harold Wilson was quite sure that somebody was informing to us, because Mary had done exactly this or thought exactly that.' Richard Ingrams and John Wells eventually took over *Mrs Wilson's Diary*, which became a successful stage musical in the West End. Mrs Wilson herself famously said that if she ever met John Wells 'she would like to bite him'.[10]

Other attacks on Wilson included a Scarfe cover cartoon showing the Prime Minister on his knees behind President Johnson, tongue at the ready, the President's trousers at half mast. 'Vietnam: Wilson right behind Johnson' ran the heading. George Wigg demanded that the attendance of his fellow Labour MPs at the *Eye's* fortnightly lunches be monitored, and was condemned as 'A slack-jawed, bleary-eyed bag of condemned offal'. Tony Benn's record was held up as 'an unmitigated disaster'. Wilson himself was livid with *Private Eye*, and thereafter regarded the magazine and all who sailed in her as lifelong enemies. He felt that *Beyond the Fringe* and the Establishment Club had been on his side, and that the satirists had now inexplicably and treacherously betrayed him. It was nonsense, of course. In 1968 Kathleen Tynan visited the 'dank and ravaged room' where Peter strode up and down dictating to Ingrams, 'sitting at his stalwart desk in a rotting corduroy jacket'. By then she found the last shreds of any political idealism Peter might once have possessed long since blown away: 'A comedian and a pessimist, he thinks the human race cannot be improved and that there's no point trying. He believes that everyone, without exception in the whole history of the world, has been exclusively motivated by greed, lust or power mania. He doesn't think anyone has ever had any other reason for doing anything else. He also thinks this is probably all right.'[11] As usual, Peter's opinion was dressed up in comic hyperbole, but the inherent sincerity with which he held it was nonetheless plain to see.

Between 1964 and 1969, a series of six further giveaway records were released – an idea devised by Peter Usborne at Oxford University and not, as often reported, by Peter himself – which in large part continued to attack the Prime Minister ('I am constantly reminded of the words of my great predecessor Ramsey McDonald: "Oh Christ, what are we going to do now?"'). John Bird came in to play Wilson; other cast members, besides Peter, were Dudley Moore, Barry Humphries, Willie Rushton, Eleanor

Bron, John Wells, Richard Ingrams and Barry Fantoni. Peter essayed rather good impressions of Enoch Powell, Dr Christiaan Barnard, the Queen, Serge Gainsbourg (to Wells's Jane Birkin) and David Frost, in an uncompromising attack on his series *Not So Much a Programme* . . . 'Peter was by far the best organised,' recalls John Wells, 'actually bringing along scripts that he appeared to have dictated to a secretary while the rest of us were in the pub.'[12]

So successful were these recordings that the decision was taken to release a commercial LP, entitled *Private Eye's Blue Record*. On this occasion however, Peter's organisational skills let him down, and nobody turned up with any material whatsoever. The whole LP had to be semi-improvised, by Peter, John Wells, Barry Humphries and Willie Rushton; the gaps were filled with excerpts from the existing flimsy records. Most characteristic of Peter and the *Eye*'s attitude was his appearance as 'John Osbum' in a pretentious debate about the artistic validity of a music-hall artist named Arthur Cock, performer of the celebrated ditty *Stick Yer Finger up Yer Bum* ('Like Zola, the Gervase syndrome was very prominent'). The LP sounded like a first rehearsal, and was so mediocre that its low sales have made it something of a valuable rarity. Peter's famous ability to improvise in leaps and bounds by sparking off his audience had simply failed to function when confronted by an inanimate microphone in an empty studio. It was a useful lesson, but sadly not one that he ever took to heart.

In 1966 Peter came to *Private Eye*'s rescue once again, although this time he was responding to a calamity of his own making. As far back as June 1962, in one of his semi-ironic, semi-libidinous trawls through a sex bookshop, he had spotted Lord Russell of Liverpool's book *Scourge of the Swastika* sandwiched between copies of *Miss Whiplash* and *Rubber News*. The book described a number of Nazi atrocities in detail, and Peter had satirised its author in the *Eye* as 'Lord Liver of Cesspool'. 'It was thoroughly prurient, full of naked people, titillating in the most horrible way,' Peter complained. Three years later, Russell sued for libel. The *Eye* had never fought a court case before.

The hearing was an unmitigated disaster. John Wells recalls that 'Peter stood in the witness box trying gamely to make jokes. In the atmosphere of the courtroom even he was like a man trying to strike matches underwater.'[13] The *Eye*'s legal team told the satirists to leave it up to them. At one point the magazine's QC David Turner-Samuels stood up and quoted *The Times Literary Supplement*: 'Lord Russell's works could be said to be pornographic.' David Hirst, QC for Russell, jumped up and finished the quotation: '. . . but they are not.' Then, as Peter recalled, 'Lord Liver produced all these war heroes in court so lots of people with no legs came in, which rather swayed the jury to some extent.' The magazine lost, and was hit with a bill for £5,000 damages plus £3,000 costs. Its total weekly takings at that time amounted to £650.

Peter immediately set to work raising the money, and dreamed up the idea of a celebrity fund-raising concert, *Rustle of Spring*. Throughout March and April 1966 he sat in the *Eye* office phoning celebrities, persuading them to give their services free; he also secured the Phoenix Theatre rent-free for the second week in May. 'There was a glittering cast', he later remembered wistfully. 'Dudley, Spike, probably Lulu and half a Bee Gee.' In fact the famous of 1966 turned out in droves to appear in the show: Moore and Milligan apart, there were contributions from Peter Sellers, Bob Monkhouse, Bernard Braden, John Dankworth and Cleo Laine, Manfred Mann, Roy Hudd, John Bird and Arthur Mullard. Peter appeared with Dudley Moore in a sketch about leaping nuns that they had performed on TV, while Willie Rushton came on as Arthur Cock and growled out *Stick Yer Finger up Yer Bum*. The audience sang along to a giant songsheet:

> When yer feeling glum
> Stick yer finger up yer bum
> And the world's a happier place.
> When yer feeling grotty
> Stick a finger up yer botty
> And a smile leaps onto yer face.

Sarah Cook, sandwiched between her parents, 'sat there dying to join in but too embarrassed to do so'. Readers, led by John Betjeman, sent in further unsolicited contributions totalling £1,325, and the £8,000 target was reached in June 1966.

From the Russell case onwards, the courts were naturally predisposed to be unsympathetic to *Private Eye*. Along with *Oz*, it seemed to epitomise the anti-Establishment swinging London culture of the late 1960s. Its attacks on the government were perceived as coming from a fashionably hard-left perspective. The judges and barristers who regarded it with contempt as a consequence never seemed able to grasp that it was staffed almost entirely by young men from their own social background, whence derived its confident criticism of the status quo. By contrast *Punch*, its chief rival and very much the favourite humour magazine of the Establishment, was largely staffed by outsiders from grammar schools. Judges felt sufficiently threatened by the *Eye* that they often tended to encourage juries to find expensively against the magazine. In 1969 two *Sunday People* reporters, Hugh Farmer and Denis Cassidy, wrote a piece about an ex-con who had used the services of a Glasgow prostitute; the *Eye* alleged that the prostitute had actually been hired for him by the reporters themselves. Farmer and Cassidy sued, employing the detailed alibi that they had been eating a quiet meal in the Epicure restaurant on the night in question. The *Eye* successfully proved that the restaurant had in fact been shut all that day. The judge nonetheless disregarded this anomaly, and ordered *Private Eye* to pay £10,000. 'This time,' said Peter. 'I'm thinking of writing a story of my life as a transvestite, or wife-swapping in Hampstead, and selling it to the *People*.'[14] In fact a reader's appeal, *Gnomefam*, succeeded in raising most of the required sum.

Despite such setbacks, the *Eye* was beginning to establish a reputation for investigative journalism. Fleet Street newspapers either rushed to set up their own investigative teams, or lifted *Eye* stories wholesale: the *People* even hijacked a story (by offering the *Eye*'s freelance reporter more money to divert it their way) which led to a corruption case against the heads of the Flying Squad and the Obscene Publications Squad, and helped precipitate the end of widespread corrupt policing in Soho. *Private Eye* readers were first to read about BP's sanction-busting in Rhodesia, the Heath government's secret talks with the IRA, Israeli links with the mafia, the 1971 Payola scandal (when disc-jockeys were bribed to play certain records) and the safety lapses that had caused the collapse of the Ronan Point tower block. The crowning glory of the investigative journalism that Peter had assiduously nurtured was the uncovering by Paul Foot of the Poulson scandal: a network of bribery which had infiltrated the Conservative Party at national level and local government level across the north of England. In 1970 the Home Secretary Reginald Maudling was forced to resign as a direct consequence of the *Eye*'s revelations. Soon afterwards the magazine's readership finally rescaled the heights it had enjoyed during the satire boom. The days when Peter would jokingly boast to the papers that it was 'The most unpopular magazine in England'[15] could be safely consigned to history.

There can be no question that Peter had come to love *Private Eye* magazine and its band of writers very dearly indeed. His joke-writing sessions with Ingrams, Fantoni, Rushton, Wells and Booker (now returned to the fold) were the highlight of his week. He felt at home in their midst. Says Wells: 'I shall always remember Peter as he was when he was imagining his own world: like a medium, head cocked, looking sideways across the room, licking his lips and then droning out some inversion of boring normality that made all our eyes flash and filled the room with laughter. Peter was unique.'[16] Occasionally Wells and the others would dare to venture suggestions: 'He only kept one or two things – he had quite strict quality control – but as I look through the things I wrote with him, I notice little chunks that clearly were mine, and I'd rather he hadn't put them in.'

A more cynical view – and Peter never objected to a cynical view – is put forward by Barry Humphries: 'I was sometimes appalled by the immoderate laughter that greeted all of Peter's *mots*,' he says. (In 1967 Peter cast Humphries in the character of 'Envy' in the film *Bedazzled*.) Humphries traces a direct lineage from *Private Eye* back to the sixth form at Radley and Shrewsbury schools: 'The magazine was run by the prefects, who were Cook, Ingrams and Willie Rushton. And the fags were people like Tony Rushton, Willie's cousin, who did the layout, and Barry Fantoni. Occasionally, ravaged schoolmasters, like Claud Cockburn and Malcolm Muggeridge, were let into the prefects' study.'[17] Certainly the Peter Cook of the 1960s seemed to display the manners of a school prefect. Humphries, who was a heavy drinker at the time, observed that 'There's no nicotine on his fingers. He never has a hangover. There's a certain austerity about him. You know, you can tell at first sight if someone looks like their father or their mother. Well, Peter looks like his auntie.'[18]

Peter always fought hard against the accusation that the *Eye* was little more than a prefects' common room for grown-ups. According to Paul Foot, 'I remember one really desperate evening at his house where the other guests were Jonathan Miller and Ken Tynan and their wives; Jonathan and Ken just spent the whole evening attacking Peter for his association with *Private Eye*. They hated the *Eye* and they attacked it from the left, from the point of view of being a rotten public school journal that only public school people would be interested in. I remember two things about his reaction to that, one of which was his intense shyness and embarrassment that the argument was taking place at all, and his rather feeble attempts to change the conversation – completely futile because they were really going for the throat. The other was his absolutely unflinching approach, which was that he was going to continue his association with *Private Eye*, and was going to continue to support it and publicise it and back it up whenever it was in difficulties, and so on.' Peter abhorred open conflict, but he was never a coward.

Later in life, whatever the vagaries of his career or the ups and downs of his personal life, however far work had taken him from London and for however long, Peter always came back to *Private Eye*. It offered him a womb-like, unthreatening atmosphere where he didn't have to prove himself, fulfil any requirements or meet any deadlines. He took no income from it so he had no income to worry about. He could come and go as he pleased – sometimes five days a week, at other times he wouldn't show for six months – write what he liked and as much as he liked, and always be sure of an enthusiastic reception. To the end of his life, he retained an absolute fondness for the place and a pride in the magazine's successful independence. The sentimental as opposed to financial nature of his ties to the *Eye* was to make the magazine his most problematic and emotionally charged legacy.

CHAPTER 8

We're Always Ready to be Jolted
Out of Our Seats, Here at the BBC

Pete and Dud, 1964–67

In 1964 a conscious decision was taken by BBC Light Entertainment to make Dudley Moore a TV star; he was charming, he was funny, and what was more important to a department with both feet planted firmly in fifties notions of 'variety', he was musically talented. His versatility had been given a thorough work-out on the successful BBC2 music show *Offbeat*, in which he played no fewer than seventeen roles, from the 'Seven Singing Viennese Sisters' to a man who falls in love with his violin. Offscreen he seemed to play the TV star role to perfection, with a flat in Shepherd Market, a black Maserati Mistrale and a glamorous new girlfriend in the shape of the actress Shirley Anne Field. At the end of 1964 the BBC offered him a one-off pilot of his own forty-five-minute variety special, *The Dudley Moore Show*.

Around the same time Peter was finally saved from his enforced comedic exile by Bernard Braden, the Canadian humorist and broadcaster, whose weekly ATV show *On the Braden Beat* was drawing a substantial audience on Saturday nights. Braden had been an admirer of Peter's material since the Footlights show put on for the Duke of Bedford at Woburn, and did not like seeing talent languish. He offered Peter four trial weekly slots to appear as the miner character from *Beyond the Fringe*. The name Mr Grole having fallen into disuse during the *Fringe* years, Peter rechristened him E. L. Wisty. The character was an instant hit with the viewers, and quickly captured the national imagination; his nasal drone was soon being imitated in pubs and offices across Britain just as it had been at Radley and Cambridge. The trial period was extended into a permanent, open-ended commission.

Wisty was tailor-made for television, perched motionless on a park bench, dressed in shabby raincoat and sombre black hat, transfixing the camera with a glazed stare as he held forth with surreal ignorance. Every Wednesday evening, the night before recording, Peter would spend five hours conversing with his tape recorder in the Wisty persona, before filleting and condensing the results:

> It there's one thing I can't bear, it's when hundreds of old men come creeping in through the window in the middle of the night and throw all manner of garbage all over me. I can't bear that. I think that's unbearable. Ghastly old men, with great pails of garbage, throwing it all over me.

Wisty and his imaginary friend Spotty Muldoon announced the formation of the World Domination League:

> How we aim to go about it is as follows. We shall move about into people's rooms and say, 'Excuse me, we are the World Domination League – may we dominate you?' Then, if they say 'Get out', of course we give up.

In 1965 Peter turned the World Domination League into a small cottage industry, producing WDL postcards and leaflets from the *Private Eye* offices. The leaflets announced 'the ten aims of the league':

1. Total domination of the world by 1964.
2. Domination of the astral spheres quite soon too.
3. The finding of lovely ladies for Spotty Muldoon within the foreseeable future.
4. GETTING A *NUCLEAR ARM* to deter with.
5. The bodily removal from this planet of C. P. Snow and Alan Freeman and their replacement with fine TREES.
6. Stopping the GOVERNMENT peering up the pipes at us and listening to *ALL WE SAY*.
7. Training BEES for uses against Foreign Powers and so on.
8. Elimination of spindly *insects* and encouragement of lovely little newts who dance about and are happy.
9. E. L. Wisty for GOD.

Peter himself described Wisty as follows: 'He is a completely lost creature, he never works, never moves, has no background and suspects everybody is peering at him and trying to get his secrets out of him. He is very keen on cosmic subjects – God, death, bees, that sort of thing. Otherwise he remains something of an enigma.'[1] Asked by journalists where the inspiration for the character had sprung from, Peter was keen to distance Wisty from his origins as a real person: 'I've never met the man. He came out of me. I'd feel a lot easier if I'd met him and imitated him, as a matter of fact.'[2] This untruthful reticence undoubtedly owed something to consideration for the real Mr Boylett's feelings, but it also acknowledged the extent to which Wisty was gradually drawing ever closer to Peter himself. 'I drift very easily into becoming E. L. Wisty' he admitted. 'I've always felt very closely identified with that sort of personality. I'm terrified I shall become some kind of Wisty figure.'[3] In many respects Wisty represented the crashing bore Peter feared within himself: many of the character's concerns – bees, newts and so on – originally belonged to its author. Peter was an easily bored man and was always strenuously careful not to bore anyone else. One way to assuage the fear of being boring was to turn his potentially dull obsessions into parodies of themselves. Even Wisty's failed domination of the world had parodic echoes of Peter's collapsed satire empire.

E. L. Wisty was signed up, almost immediately, in a lucrative deal to advertise Watneys Ales on Radio and TV. The thirteen ads were so popular that the soundtrack was eventually released as a single. They were based on a premise – revolutionary at the time – that would now be called 'deconstructionist'. Wisty would discuss the nature of advertising, some of the tricks of the trade, and his chances of landing the Watneys contract, given the huge fee that he was demanding. He himself had been compelled to go out and buy some of the beer, he explained, after seeing himself talking about it on television. Other appeals to the viewer were more straightforward, if that word could ever be used to describe Wisty's leaps of the imagination: serve your husband Watney's Brown for breakfast, he suggested, and 'your marriage will last for a million years'; drink it, he explained, and your subconscious mind 'will be visited by lovely ladies in diaphanous nighties, coming into your room and dancing about'; make sure there's some in the house, he implored, or the men from Watneys will come round, 'steal five pounds, and stamp on your glasses'.

Shortly after his initial success as E. L. Wisty, Peter received a deputation led by Dudley Moore, inviting him to be the principal guest on the one-off *Dudley Moore Show*. Moore may have been the TV star-elect, but a combination of insecurity about going it alone, and the certain knowledge that Peter would be an invaluable asset, led him to cling to

his old colleague. The other guests booked were Diahann Carroll, Sheila
Steafel, and Norman Rossington, who had appeared in the Beatles film
A Hard Day's Night. Rossington contacted John Lennon on behalf of the
production team; the Beatle agreed to appear as soon as he heard that
Peter and Dudley would be performing together, because, he said, 'I dig
what they're doing.' The large number of important guests inspired Moore
to suggest a change of title, to *Not Only . . . But Also* – as in *Not Only* Dudley
Moore *But Also* John Lennon, Peter Cook, Norman Rossington, Sheila
Steafel and Diahann Carroll.

The project was very much the brainchild of Joe McGrath, a jolly
Glaswegian producer/director in the Light Entertainment department.
Moore was an old friend of his, and in pre-*Beyond the Fringe* days
had guested on his graduation programme, when McGrath had been a
trainee at ABC Television. In between times, McGrath had pioneered the
extensive use of film in TV comedy with Michael Bentine's *It's a Square
World*. His BBC contract was coming to an end, and he wanted to move
on into the cinema: *Not Only . . . But Also* was to be his showreel, a
compendium of comedy, music and poetry with a strong filmed element
to show what he could do. The most successful creative endeavours, it
seems, are all too often born of a mixture of brilliance and accidental
circumstance.

Both Peter and Dudley Moore were determined to shy away from the
dirty word of 1964, 'satire'. They agreed that there should be no topical
or political content at all, and did their best to flinch as visibly as possible
if any journalist so much as raised the possibility. Besides, avoiding the
news of the day made the chance of a repeat transmission more likely.
Peter told the *Sun* that they would 'never mention anyone over fifty, in
case they die'.[4] Joe McGrath was in fact slated to write the bulk of the
show himself, along with his colleague Bob Fuest, but happily agreed that
Peter should write two sketches with Dudley and appear in them both.
Elsewhere, John Lennon appeared in adaptations of two of his poems,
Good Dog Nigel and *Deaf Ted, Danoota and Me*, filmed in a style parodic
of Jonathan Miller's *Monitor*; there was a parody of the Swingle Sisters
with Dudley, Norman Rossington and Sheila Steafel; and there were two
numbers from Diahann Carroll, plus one from the Dudley Moore trio.
McGrath and Fuest also devised an ingenious title sequence in which
Dudley, in full black tie and tails, went through a car wash seated at a
grand piano.

Peter naturally wanted to base his small contribution on the two
principal comic characters which had sustained him for many years.
One was the pompous aristocratic halfwit, now christened Sir Arthur

Streeb-Greebling, who was interviewed by Dudley about his life's work, teaching ravens to fly underwater:

> *Interviewer*: Sir Arthur, is it difficult to get ravens to fly underwater?
> *Sir Arthur*: Well I think the word 'difficult' is an awfully good one here.

Sir Arthur spoke of his mother, Lady Beryl, a woman so powerful 'she can break a swan's wing with a blow of her nose', and also demonstrated that it is possible to hammer a deliberate misunderstanding into the ground without compromising either humour or deftness of touch:

> *Interviewer*: Sir Arthur, where did you strat your work?
> *Sir Arthur*: I think it can be said of me that I have never ever stratted my work. That is one thing I have never done. I can lay my hand on my heart, or indeed anyone else's heart, and say 'I have never stratted my work, never stratted at all.' I think what you probably wanted to know is where I started my work. You've completely misread the question.
> *Interviewer*: (chastened) I'm sorry.

Peter's other comic mainstay was, of course, E. L. Wisty; but Wisty presented a major problem, in that he was already appearing on the other channel. Peter decided as a consequence to adapt Wisty somewhat and create an older, more downmarket version, called 'Pete'. 'As far as I'm concerned,' he said, '"Pete" was just a slightly more active extension of E. L. Wisty. He discussed the same lofty subjects.'[5] For years, one of Peter's private jokes, when ending a private telephone conversation, had been to shout 'GOODBYE! FOREVER!' down the mouthpiece and suddenly slam the phone down. Then, turning to the astonished room, he would calmly announce 'That was that bloody Sophia Loren again.' Peter now adapted this joke into a monologue for his new character. Another problem presented itself: a monologue did not allow any room for a contribution from the star of the show, something that convention demanded. So Peter divided the lines in two, and created a clone of the first character, an acolyte with a splash of Dudley about him, just as the original contained a hint of its author. Thus were Pete and Dud, TV's most successful comic characters of the sixties, if not of all time, brought into being.

In rehearsal, in the freezing billiard room of a deserted boys' club on the Goldhawk Road, the Pete and Dud dialogue simply wouldn't fire. It ran too short – under three minutes in total – and none of the production team found it funny. Essentially a long list of film starlets drawn from Lyme Regis matinees of the 1950s, all of whom had been hurling themselves unrequitedly at Pete and Dud, the sketch lacked one or two vital ingredients. 'It fell flat right through rehearsal,' says Dud, 'until we put in the physical descriptions – then everyone laughed.' [6] Then, adds Pete, 'When we came to choose costumes – it just sort of happened. They arrived fully formed.'[7]

Attired in cloth caps, old raincoats and scarves, and seated in the barest suggestion of a pub, Pete and Dud were the hit of the show. They completely upset McGrath's calculations by going on for twelve minutes, throughout which the audience roared, Dud couldn't stop corpsing and Pete – Peter Cook of the famous stonefaced stare – for once in his career was equally unable to maintain a straight face. The sketch began with Pete recounting how he had been pestered with late night calls by Betty Grable, then moved on to the appearance in Dud's kitchen of Anna Magnani in a see-through blouse. Desperately trying to improvise a witty put-down, Dud barked: 'Get out of here, you Italian . . . thing!' at which point the pair of them completely lost their composure. Recovering, Pete told of a nocturnal tap! tap! tap! at his window pane. It was bloody Greta Garbo, hanging on to the windowsill in a see-through shortie nightie, he spluttered, as they both broke into laughter again. 'I had to smash her down with a broomstick,' he explained. Dud recounted smelling a funny smell, repeating the word 'funny' over and over again, thus originating himself a catchphrase. He had climbed into bed, he explained, when he had felt a hand on his cheek. 'Which cheek was that Dud?' said Pete, in a line that he had deliberately kept from Dud in rehearsal and saved for the night. Both of them began to break up again, Dud's remark that 'It was the left upper' not helping a bit. It was bloody Jane Russell, revealed Dud, stark naked in his bed. 'Get out of here you hussy!' he shouted. 'As far as I'm concerned it's all over!'

All round the studio people were rocking with laughter, from delighted audience members to the cynical technicians who had already seen it several times. In content, presentation, and in what only the most pompous churl could have condemned as its lack of professionalism, it was like nothing any of them had seen before. Up in the gallery stood Tom Sloan, the Head of Light Entertainment, and Michael Peacock, the newly-appointed Controller of BBC2. Sloan, the only man in the studio who wasn't laughing, was deeply unhappy with what he'd seen. There were no dancing girls, no glitz, no gags, no punchlines; the whole thing smacked to him of a lack of

Peter's parents, Alec and Margaret Cook. *(Courtesy Sarah Seymour)*

Alec Cook, a lone white man in the Nigerian Bush. *(Courtesy Sarah Seymour)*

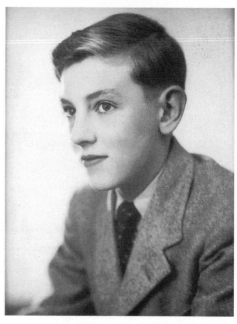

Peter and his sister Sarah in Gibraltar
shortly after the end of the war.
(Courtesy Sarah Seymour)

Peter at St. Bede's preparatory school.
(Courtesy Daisy Cook)

Peter as Doll Common in *The Alchemist* at Radley College, March 1954. *(Courtesy Sarah Seymour)*

Peter and his sister Elizabeth on the front at Lyme Regis, Summer 1957. *(Courtesy Sarah Seymour)*

Peter as Launcelot Gobbo in Pembroke College's German tour production of *The Merchant of Venice*, June 1958. *(Courtesy Tim Harrold)*

Peter as Dapper (with Richard Imison and Louise Burkim) in *The Alchemist*, Pembroke College, November 1958. *(Courtesy Tim Harrold)*

THE
RADLEY COLLEGE MARIONETTE THEATRE

PRESENTS

'BLACK AND WHITE BLUES'

BY P. E. COOK

WITH MUSIC COMPOSED BY M. BAWTREE

Wednesday, Friday and Saturday,

21st, 23rd and 24th March, 1956

Programme for the
Radley College *Black
And White Blues*, March
1956.
*(Courtesy Maurice
Friggens)*

SOCIAL INTERCOURSE IN THE UNION CELLARS

SPRINGHEELED JACK, MR. BOYLETT AND
OLD NIC

on the occasion of their 63rd Birthday
invite

Mike Winterton

to

AN ADD HOCK PARTY
SATURDAY, NOVEMBER 22nd

8.0 p.m.

R.S.V.P.   BRING YOUR BABY AND BOTTLE

McFleming.   P.Cook · J.Altman.

Peter's 21st birthday
invitation, November 1958.
(Courtesy Mike Winterton)

Jonathan Miller, Alan Bennett, Dudley Moore and Peter in *Beyond The Fringe. (BBC)*

Meeting Elizabeth Taylor on the American tour of *Beyond The Fringe. (Rex Features)*

Peter's first wife Wendy. *(Courtesy Lucy Cook)*

Publicity pose for *Not Only . . . But Also. (BBC)*

The Pete and Dud characters created for *Not Only . . . But Also. (BBC)*

Peter Sellers invites himself onto *Not Only . . . But Also*, March 1965. *(BBC)*

Peter and Dudley on location as the Finsbury Brothers in *The Wrong Box*, September 1965. *(Rex Features)*

Peter (As Hiram J. Pipesucker) and John Lennon in the *Not Only . . . But Also* Christmas Special 1966. *(Times Newspapers)*

Peter and Dudley as Jeff and Johnny Jupiter in the 1966 *Not Only . . . But Also* sketch *Superthunderstingcar. (BBC)*

Sitting on a bench: E. L. Wisty and M'Lud. *(London Features International)*

professionalism. 'If this is Light Entertainment, I'm in the wrong business,' he remarked aloud. Peacock paused and said quietly, 'I think, Tom, you're in the wrong business.' Peacock turned to McGrath. 'I want six of these,' he said. After the show Peter, Dudley and Joe McGrath stood and hugged each other with delight. They all went for a celebratory Chinese meal with John Lennon, who ended the evening sitting on the restaurant table.

The following morning the trio went to see Peacock in his office at Television Centre. The Controller wanted a series, and he wanted Peter in every one. Henceforth it would become *Not Only* Dudley Moore and Peter Cook *But Also* their guests. Peter had got his BBC TV show at last. In the curved corridor outside, the three exchanged nods and smiles. 'No running in the corridors, boys!' admonished Peter, then set off jubilantly at top speed round the bend. It would be unfair to leave Tom Sloan, incidentally, without recounting an earlier tale of his management style. After a particularly error-strewn live show in the 1950s, Peter Sellers had marched over to the caption machine, laughing, had ripped the credits off the roller and had torn them up on air. 'It's all Tom Sloan's fault, him and his bloody lineament,' he had shouted into the camera. After the show a furious Sloan had marched down and confronted Sellers face to face. 'You'll never work again,' he had spluttered, with a quite stunning degree of inaccuracy.

The one-off *Not Only . . . But Also* was set for transmission on 9 January 1965, with the other six following at fortnightly intervals. Joe McGrath and Bob Fuest conceded the bulk of the writing to the two stars, although their contribution to the script remained substantial. Peter was bursting with ideas – 'He had seventeen to my one,'said Dudley.[8] Eventually the two protagonists' names were switched round in the programme's title, to become *Not Only* Peter Cook and Dudley Moore *But Also* their guests. The natural order of things had been reasserted. 'I rearranged them in alphabetical order to avoid upsetting him,' explains Dudley sheepishly.[9]

One hard and fast rule that Peter was quite unable to overturn was the ban on him singing any songs. A mad keen fan of Elvis and the Beach Boys, he was always coming up with reasons for crowbarring a pop impression into this or that sketch, but to no avail. According to Dudley Moore: 'He always wished he'd been a pop star – he was constantly preoccupied with certain themes in the pop world, and he had this terrible impression of Elvis Presley – but he had no musicality in him, *none*. He used to play the piano like an idiot, he had no sense of rhythm, no sense of music, but he did nurture that feeling.' Joe McGrath remembers that 'Peter actually thought he *was* a pop star, but he was tone deaf, he just couldn't sing, he couldn't hold two notes. Dudley used to say "Just sing *Happy Birthday*", and he couldn't, he was just one of those guys. It's amazing really, because his other talents were so wonderful.'

Peter's only chance to sing was when he joined in, toothy twenties parody style, on the show's signature tune *Goodbyee*. The number had been improvised in one go shortly before the first recording. Joe McGrath recalls: 'I suggested doing something like *The Boyfriend*. I said "We should say goodbye." So Dudley just sat down and sang "Goodbye . . ." and that was it.' All the *fatatas* dotted through the song were originally intended to be filled in with proper lyrics later. The pirouettes undertaken by each guest during the number arose from a spontaneous little dance performed in the first show by John Lennon. 'Peter loved singing that song,' says McGrath. 'If you watch him you can see the manic gleam in his eye, and these terribly upper class movements as he tries to find the rhythm. Dudley used to say "You ain't got it, you know." But Peter would be swinging the mike and the Dudley Moore trio would have to duck.'

The *Not Only . . . But Also* studio recordings are forever fixed in the memory of everyone who was there as utterly joyous occasions. 'It was incredible,' says John Wells. 'They were like pop concerts. It was the most popular show on television. You got the impression that Peter was absolutely on a real winning streak; all the sketches were funny, everything he improvised, the audience carried him along.' Joe McGrath remembers them as 'an incredibly happy experience. When you came into the studio to do the technical rehearsal, the crew would say, "This is what we wait for every week, just to come down and see what you've done." The atmosphere was marvellous. We had to keep Dudley away from the piano during the afternoon, or rehearsals would just stop. He'd start to play, everybody would gather round, and Peter would sort of mince around, jiving in a terrible Sir Arthur Streeb-Greebling way.' The Peter Cook bandwagon was rolling again, and he was loving every minute of it. 'This is just like university,' he told McGrath, 'only the grants are bigger.'

Peter and Dudley wrote the sketches by talking them through in each other's houses, recording their conversations, playing them back, then recording them again – perhaps five or six times – until a definitive version had been arrived at. The tape would then be handed to a secretary, who would transcribe it *exactly*: Peter was most insistent that the genuine speech patterns, even the mistakes and hesitations, should be recorded precisely. By the time the sketch was actually written down, it was fully rehearsed. Dudley would then memorise it, professionally and methodically, by writing it out again in longhand until every stutter and every pause was firmly lodged in his mind. Peter, by contrast, would settle for a huge piece of card held up behind his partner, with six or seven headings scrawled on it. He used to delight in leading Dudley up hill and down dale, away from the rehearsed script and back onto it, giving him a taste of freedom then tugging him back, like a bird toying with a worm, watching him twist, turn and splutter his way back to the next familiar stretch of dialogue.

There were no punchlines to speak of. Peter hated the 'pat' line reversing all that had gone before, the brass stab from the band and the fade to black. He would rather have sketches tail away to nothing than hint at the formulaic. 'Peter would dig in on those sorts of things,' says Joe McGrath, 'so Dudley would get very frustrated. They used to have arguments.' Dudley eventually conceded the punchline debate, but in general terms the importance of the old-fashioned discipline that he contributed cannot be overestimated. Where Peter's material had previously darted about, ignoring internal contradictions – an enjoyable experience to watch but too devoid of structural interest to sustain more than a few minutes' viewing – Dudley doggedly supplied a backbone. Peter recalled that, 'Gradually, Dudley developed far more of a role in the writing. I tended to flutter off very quickly, and improvise, and ignore illogicalities . . . Dudley began, when we had an idea, to examine what was logically incorrect, right at the beginning. I would regard this as pernickety, and he would regard it as logical. So the writing process became slower.'[10] Dudley concurs: 'There were arguments about the structure of sketches – I did get very pernickety. But Peter used to be so fecund that he could put in an alternative line at the drop of a hat.' Dudley had, in effect, harnessed Peter's comic genius to the mainstream as no one had before. Nearly all great comic writing partnerships consist of one writer who takes the lead, extemporising, while the other edits and reins in excesses. Dudley had simply forced Peter into an established and successful pattern. Furthermore, Dudley's residual status as star of the show and his relationship with Joe McGrath gave his input an authority which, although technical rather than natural, could not be gainsaid.

McGrath's method of shooting happily complemented Peter and Dudley's material. He used just three cameras, and sat for as long as possible on the fascinating cat-and-mouse facial expressions of the two protagonists. Dudley, who had more TV experience than Peter, realised that there didn't seem to be as much cutting between cameras as there should be, and objected. McGrath replied that 'The whole ethos of this thing is that I'd love to do a whole Dud and Pete without a cut – just do a Laurel and Hardy – and sit on the two of you throughout.' Unfortunately he always had to have a wide shot standing by as a 'safety' shot, because Pete and Dud's sketches could march gloriously on for quarter of an hour or more. Great chunks would have to be thrown on to the cutting room floor in order to make the material fit. The shows were recorded in advance, but the idea was to make them as close to a live show as possible; there were no breaks, no going back on mistakes. Only the gravest technical disaster could bring the recording to a halt.

The show was entirely created in the fortnight before transmission: there would be five days' writing, two days' filming, and the rest of the time would be given over to rehearsals. Another radical departure was that sets were kept to minimum, just a hint here and there of a saloon bar or a sitting room. This was another happy accident that helped focus the audience's attention on the strength of the material. Even though they only had to write three sketches a fortnight, Peter and Dudley reserved the right to deliver their material late or change their minds at the last minute; frequently the faintest suggestion of a pub was all the designer actually had time to build. A little more advance preparation went into the remarkable title sequences devised by Joe McGrath. Following on from the car wash idea of the first show, six further sequences were shot, including Dudley as a one man band, Dudley as a gypsy violinist who annoys Peter as he tries to take tea, and Dudley asking Peter to remove his hat in a cinema, a shot which pulled back to reveal that they were the only two people in the auditorium.

Tragically, only the first three of the six programmes have survived, plus the filmed inserts – minus their soundtrack – of show four. Even this paltry reminder of one of the greatest television comedies of all time would not exist, had Joe McGrath not broken several rules in order to make pirate copies. 'I knew at the time that a lot of the technicians were running off copies and keeping them. So I just did one of those things you could do at the BBC in those times – I signed a form and had some of them telerecorded.' Telerecording was an immensely primitive process whereby the high-quality studio output and 35mm film inserts were preserved by a 16mm film camera, pointed at a television screen as the show went out. The blurred picture quality and furry – at times indecipherable – sound of the surviving shows bear no relation to the high standards of the original broadcasts. McGrath's three illegal telerecordings are now all that reside in the BBC library. Even the scripts were thrown away, in an act of shocking bureaucratic vandalism.

The first show had the highest concentration of McGrath/Fuest material, three sketches to Peter and Dudley's two: these included a rather old-fashioned comedy dance number with Dudley and a stripper who never finishes her act; *Tour Gastronomique de la route Circular du Nord*, in which Peter plays a French restaurant critic reviewing the Café

Fred, Dudley plays Fred ('Born within the sight of bow legs') and Barry Humphries plays the Café's filthy waiter, whose job is to decant the HP sauce; and a sketch in which Peter plays the famous artist Sir Gregory Northumberland, while Dudley plays a studio manager so eager to instruct him in the ways of television that he ends up painting his picture for him. The Pete and Dud filmstars dialogue from the pilot recording was saved until this show, to give it room to play at a fuller length, leaving Peter and Dudley with just one new sketch: a parody silent film and an interview with its star, Tarquin Mordente. This had echoes of *One Leg too Few*: Mordente, who has become a tramp since the advent of the talkies, can't see why his career has stalled despite having a ghastly throaty voice. The only other point of note was a second cameo appearance by John Lennon in the *Tour Gastronomique* sketch. Apparently he had enjoyed himself so much the first time that he had turned up uninvited for a second stab at comedy.

It was really in the second show that Peter and Dudley came into their own. This time there was only one McGrath/Fuest sketch, a parody of the BBC2 documentary series *The Great War*: a startling contribution to the programme from a visual point of view at least, as filming took place on a rubbish dump off the North Circular in the middle of a fierce blizzard; Barry Humphries (again) and Bob Godfrey appeared in minor roles. Peter and Dudley's contribution began with a marvellous sketch in which Sir Arthur Streeb-Greebling visits a tailor, because his public schoolboy son has ordered him to turn up for a half-term function in a suit that's 'with it' rather than 'without it'. Dudley, as the tailor, suggests a fourteen-inch bottom.

> *Sir Arthur:* I think you'll have some difficulty cramming my bottom into fourteen inches. I was with the camel corps in the desert and I'm afraid that rather stretched my resources.

In a delicious culture clash between two worlds that Peter knew well, Sir Arthur demands a 'sort of Tamla Motown excitement about the whole thing'. He does not, he explains, want anything effeminate:

> *Sir Arthur:* My wife is extremely effeminate you know. It's a ghastly business, I don't know where she picked it up.
> *Tailor:* Would you like a vent up the back?
> *Sir Arthur:* If you have one, yes.

| *Tailor*: | Which side do you dress? |
| *Sir Arthur*: | Nearest the window. |

Sadly, the end of this sketch is missing – the reel ends before the sketch does.

The Pete and Dud dialogue was a late night discussion, in dressing gowns, about the worst thing that could ever happen to anybody. A direct descendant of the Babar nightmare from Peter's childhood, his terrible vision of a nocturnal visit from forty-one Nazi officers – who put him in a sack full of killer ants – begins with the familiar 'Tap! Tap! Tap!' Dudley retaliates with a visit from Doctor Death: 'He comes for me when I'm getting some Spam from the kitchen and chops my head off with an axe and I run around the kitchen screaming.' Pete belittles this as a relative picnic; his killer ants have been trained to eat extremely slowly, he explains. Dud tries again, with the appearance in his garden of a female vampire who vanishes, leaving his socks turned to ice. Pete ridicules this. He once stayed at Daphne du Maurier's country house, he relates, and slept in a room where fifty years previously a nun had hanged herself – 'stupid old bag'. There he was attacked 'by a giant maneating slug of a type rarely found', an assault that made the hairs of his toothbrush stand on end.

Peter and Dudley's final contribution was an adaptation of an old standard from the 1958 Footlights written by Bob Sale – a stirring song in honour of Alan A'Dale. Performed in Sherwood Forest costumes with *Fringe* substitutes and ex-Footlighters Bill Wallis and Joe Melia, along with John Wells, this was the highlight of the programme. Alan A'Dale was essentially a musical shaggy dog story: across six or seven tortuous minutes, filmed almost entirely in a single close-up take by Joe McGrath, the song frequently threatened to arrive at some valid point without ever actually doing so. Dudley managed to extract further comic mileage from an outsized hat. Bill Wallis recalls that 'Dudley was a very disciplined showman who understood audiences – like an old pro to Peter's inspired amateur.'

Wallis was taken aback, however, to discover the extent to which Peter and Dudley had been taken over by the Pete and Dud characters. 'It was around that point that I realised how tiring it was to be with the pair of them. I mean, going to lunch with them during rehearsals in Shepherd's Bush, they'd got so hooked into Dud and Pete that they could never get out of it. I sat there expecting to have a conversation – I didn't expect to sit there watching a sort of Dud and Pete workout, and some of the sketches being formed that I wouldn't see until they appeared on television. It was just an extraordinary thing, that went on and on.' Dudley, interestingly enough, ascribes the same attribute to Peter alone: 'If he had a fault, it was that Peter was relentless in making everyone laugh. He had a verbal wit that was second to none, but sometimes he overdid it. At the parties we used to have after recording *Not Only . . . But Also*, he made sure people were laughing; but he kept on bludgeoning people with his wit. There was a certain relentless quality to him, which was not a good thing.'[11]

The fact of the matter is that Dudley did share something of Peter's compulsion to entertain those around him, to make sure that nobody was bored and that everybody was having a good time; but more importantly, he naturally deferred to Peter, and followed his lead in public. The Alan A'Dale rehearsal was the occasion for their first big row, when Dudley and the rest of the cast began to annoy Peter by clashing their staves too loudly and too often while he was trying to work at something else. When he complained, they intensified the noise dramatically as a joke. Peter flew into a terrible rage, rounded on Dudley and ordered him to shut up. It was a crucial moment: Dudley's obedience on that occasion was to define their relationship for years to come.

The third show of the series was a powerful candidate to be considered their finest ever. The programme oozed confidence in the strength of its own material right from the start, when Peter leaped on and announced:

> 372 years ago today the Sussex baron Sir Arthur Strumely-Grapps fell to his death in a ditch. Three years later war was to ravage Europe. But we're not here tonight to dwell in the past.

First up was a film about the leaping nuns of the Order of St Beryl, together with an interview with Peter as the order's Mother Superior. Originally the film had been intended to stand on its own, but Joe McGrath was in the habit of bringing Peter and Dudley into the cutting room to view the final cut of each insert; Peter would often improvise a commentary to fill the time, in this instance so amusingly that his remarks were turned into an accompanying sketch. Dudley, as the interviewer, struggled with Peter's beatific superiority:

> *Interviewer*:   Mother Superior – or may I call you mother?
> *Mother Superior*:   I think that would be inappropriate.

Peter ran through the nuns' leaping day in detail, from their breakfast of hard-boiled fish to their evening ritual of vespers and bandaging:

> *Mother Superior*:   We're early risers. We get up at four o'clock
> in the morning. Then go back to bed again at
> five, when we realise we've got up too early.

It is noticeable that Peter always played the superior character, the victor
in each sketch. If Dudley played the relative intellectual lightweight of the
two, as in the Pete and Dud dialogues, then he would lose out as a matter
of course; but if Peter played the halfwit, as in Sir Arthur Streeb-Greebling's
visit to the tailor, his character would always be blithely ignorant of his
own stupidity, usually in such a way as to leave Dudley's character tearing
his hair out with frustration.

The Pete and Dud dialogue in show three was the famous 'Art Gallery'
sketch, in which the pair established their own never-to-be-broken record
for collapsing with unscripted laughter on screen. It contained a number
of memorable slices of art criticism: that the sign of a good painting is
'when the eyes follow you round the room'; that the sign of a good
Rubens nude is 'when the bottoms follow you round the room'; that the
sign of a good Vernon Ward flying duck painting is 'when the other eye
is craning round the beak to look at you'; and that the Mona Lisa 'has an
awful sniffy look about her . . . she looks as if she's never been to the lav
in her life'. Regarding the strategically placed wisps of gauze adorning the
Rubens nudes, Dud offered up the observation that:

> It must be a million-to-one chance, Pete, that the gauze, y'know,
> lands in the right place at the right time, when he's painting. I
> bet there's thousands of paintings that we're not allowed to see,
> where the gauze hadn't landed in the right place, y'know, it's on
> your nose or something.

The sketch was an object lesson in how to make stupidity funny – by
lacing it thoroughly with genuine but half-digested, nuggets of information.
Regarding a Leonardo da Vinci cartoon that neither of them could see the
joke of, Dud offered the possibility that man's sense of humour must have
changed over the years:

> *Dud*:   I bet when that da Vinci cartoon first came out,
> I bet people were killing themselves. I bet old
> da Vinci had an accident when he drew it.
> *Pete*:   Well it's difficult to see the joke, just that lady
> sitting there with the children round her. Not
> much of a joke as far as I'm concerned, Dud.

Dud: Apart from that Pete, it's a different culture. It's Italian y'see, we don't understand it. For instance, *The Mousetrap* did terribly in Pakistan.

It was the general air of hilarity and Pete's piercing stare rather than any specific line that caused Dud to lose control for the first time:

Dud: I went up to the Manager, I said ''ere' ... I said ''ere' ...

At this point he began to laugh so much that he spat sandwich helplessly across the room. Pete moved in for the kill.

Pete: You didn't spit sandwich at him did you?
Dud: Sorry Pete.
Pete: Blimey.
Dud: I'm sorry about that. No, I said ''ere' –
Pete: You'll do it again if you're not careful.
Dud: I said 'where ...'

Whereupon Dud collapsed with laughter again, all hope of being allowed to regain his position in the script abandoned.

Pete pointed out that at a price of half a million pounds, Cézanne's *Les Grandes Baigneuses* had cost £50,000 per naked lady:

Dud: You could get the real nude ladies for that price. My aunt Dolly would've done it for nothing.
Pete: She does anything for nothing, doesn't she, your Aunt Dolly. Dirty old cow.

Dud, gurgling helplessly, attempted to force the sandwich into his mouth to stem the flow of laughter.

Pete: You enjoying that sandwich?
Dud: 'Course, you know, Pete ...

... And off he went again. The sequence perfectly demonstrated the essence of the Pete and Dud chemistry: how an audience laughed *with* Peter and *at* Dudley. Looking back, Dudley insists that 'I didn't intend to spit sandwich at him, but it was so hilarious that we just had to go on improvising from that point.' Joe McGrath remembers that 'Peter did about a minute extra on this happening, then shot a glance at the camera (me!), remarking that he wasn't surprised Dud was choking because the sandwiches were terrible.'[12] Eventually the pair went their separate ways, Peter pondering whether the bottoms would divide up amongst themselves in their efforts to follow both men around the room. Dudley Moore believes that it was their finest sketch ever.

One reason that Peter found himself able to toy with Dudley more effectively from the third show onwards, was that the shooting method had been altered to his advantage. After only half the series he was becoming blasé about the amount of graft he needed to put in, and was not bothering to learn his lines properly. If he got into difficulties he was sufficiently confident of his ability to strike out in a different direction and improvise his way out of trouble; but while this method might have suited a monologue, it would not work in a two-hander where his partner had assiduously memorised every line. Joe McGrath solved the problem of Peter's increasing laziness by putting the script on to a teleprompter where he alone could see it: 'He's actually sitting reading the lines. You can see his eyeline sometimes. In the art gallery there's a Victorian loveseat, and I sat them like that facing each other so we could get a camera right in behind Dudley, and Peter could look straight into the lens as though he was looking at Dudley. This aide memoire helped Peter a lot, because then he could leave the script and come back to it at will. Of course in those days the teleprompters were giant, they were bloody monsters, so there could be absolutely no movement out of the cameras.' In another happy accident, the need for a teleprompter machine and its lack of mobility had inadvertently helped create the effect that McGrath was trying to achieve.

Following on from the Sir Arthur Streeb-Greebling suit-buying scene in the previous programme, the third show also included a generation gap misunderstanding sketch, something that was to become a regular feature of the series, often concentrating on father-and-son relationships of awkward mutual incomprehension. On this occasion Peter played a respectable middle-aged father lunching with Reg, his unsuitable prospective son-in-law (played by Dudley) for the first time:

> *Peter*:   As a father, I have certain responsibilities towards my daughter, and I have to find out certain things about you. For example, where you went to school. Not that it matters, but it is important.

It transpires that Reg, who fidgets endlessly and irritatingly, wants to move in with his daughter.

> *Reg*:   I thought we might squeeze in, Squire, After all, we're
>   not prudes, are we, Squire?
> *Peter*:   Yes, we are prudes, Reg.

Peter's sketches always displayed a mastery of wordplay, but the distinguishing feature of his wordplay is that it was subversive of verbal convention, and therefore frequently of conventional attitudes into the bargain.

The remaining item in the show was *Incidents in the Life of my Uncle Arly*, an Edward Lear poem performed by Dudley, with Peter appearing as 'Uncle Arly'. Peter's daughter Lucy, who had been born on 4 May 1964, and to whom Dudley Moore was godfather, made her screen debut, while Barry Humphries cropped up again as a grave-digger. Humphries, like Bill Wallis, was startled by the nature of the Cook–Moore relationship: 'It was an extraordinary friendship those two men had. It was impossible to get a word in, really, because they were constantly improvising, not just on camera, but all the time. One felt sometimes that Peter – not so much Dudley, but Peter – was not going to stop being funny for a minute, in case you got a little bit too close to him. This was the carapace that he had constructed for himself.'

Among the viewers who'd been enjoying the new series was Peter Sellers, who now rang up and asked if he could come on as a guest. McGrath and Fuest nipped in and wrote two sketches for him, and he appeared in the fifth show as a boxer who uses his gloves to create abstract paintings, and in a blind tasting sketch entitled *The Gourmets*. Eric Sykes featured in the last show as a film star, and in a sketch about freemasons. *Old J. J.*, the initials sketch, also made a reappearance in one of the later programmes. All these items have since been destroyed. All that now remains of the second half of the series are the few soundless film fragments of the fourth show: a sketch in which a political canvasser knocks on Dracula's door, a title sequence with the words *Not Only . . . But Also* plastered on the side of a London bus, an attack on cigarette advertising ('Guards' cigarettes being replaced by 'Privates' cigarettes for legal reasons), and an ingenious item in which Dudley, blacked up, gets into a shower singing *Old Man River* in an Al Jolson accent, which gradually changes into his normal voice as he becomes pinker and cleaner. This last item was the cause of another sizeable row between Dudley and Peter. 'Peter didn't want to use it,' says Joe McGrath, 'because it was simply Dudley on his own. To me it was wonderful how Dudley did it, it was so simple, you could see the black going down the plug hole like *Psycho*: but Peter put the kybosh on it. They didn't include me in the debate, they would have their rows and arguments on their own, and then they'd say "We don't want to use that bit". Dudley told me, "He doesn't want to use it. I think it's wonderful, but he doesn't want to use it."' Peter was now completely in charge.

Of the other two sketches that made up the fourth show, one was later reshot for an Australian special, and concerned a young man (Dudley) who has burned his bridges and come to London to start a new job, dining with his employer (Peter), who gradually reveals that he has changed his mind about the job offer after all. It was very funny but also very cruel, and ended with Dudley having to empty his plate of spaghetti on to his own head as a mark of humiliation. The show's musical guest, Mel Tormé, begged for and got the job of playing the waiter who hands him the plate load of spaghetti. The other sketch was a Pete and Dud conversation about failing to pick up girls on buses – the script of which survives in book form – which had particular poignancy for Dudley as it was based on a real event of his youth: 'It was a dreadful thing I remembered from my school days – of a girl I could never bring myself to speak to, whom I was dreadfully in love with.'[13] The sketch was littered with the real names of girls, streets, and places from Dudley's childhood, usually subject to the merest of disguises. It began lightheartedly enough:

> *Dud*: Right, Pete. Let's go and sit up the front, eh?
> *Pete*: No, mustn't sit up the front, Dud, that's the least safe part of the bus. You ought to sit at the back, like you do in an aeroplane, that's where you're safe.
> *Dud*: Why, what's wrong with the front?
> *Pete*: Well, see, if there's a fatality, if the bus is involved in a fatal accident of any kind, it's the people up the front who get killed first, and the people up the back who get killed last.

Soon, though, Dudley is only one step away from a session at the psychiatrist's:

> *Dud*: Here, did I tell you about that bird, Joan Harold? About fourteen years ago?
> *Pete*: Joan Harold. Spring of 1948.
> *Dud*: You know she used to get the 5.45, 25B? 'Course she used to come out at 5.45 and I used to leave work about five, nowhere near where she was. So what I used to do, I used to get on a 62A up Chadwell Heath, then I used to get the 514 trolley down to the Merry Fiddlers, then I used to have

to run across that hill down by the railway bridge, over that field where the turnips were, over by the dye works, then I used to leap over the privet hedge and hurl myself onto the 25B as it came round Hog Hill. There wasn't a bus stop there but it used to have to slow down because it was a very dangerous curve. I used to lie down in the middle of the road sometimes if it was going too fast. I used to leap on to the platform and spend about twenty minutes trying to get my breath back. 'Course I never spoke to her. Actually, once she got off and I got off in front and I said "Ere' – I thought I'd tease her a bit, coax her – and I said 'Chase me', and I started running off, but I was half way across Lymington Gardens before I realised she hadn't budged an inch.

Chadwell Heath and Hog Hill were Chadwell Heath Lane and Hog Hill Road in Romford. Lymington Gardens was Lymington Road in Dagenham. Dudley's comedy was often directly, soul-searchingly autobiographical in this manner, and almost all the names he used belonged to real people (with the exception of his nymphomaniacal but non-existent Aunt Dolly). Even the characterisation he brought to the part of 'Dud' was, he said, 'drawn from various inoffensive, compliant men I'd known, including myself'.[14] The principal inspiration was 'A guy at my father's church – St Peter's Becontree – this very self-effacing man, who looked as if he felt he should know a lot, but didn't.'[15] Every week during the series Dudley would almost religiously return to this world, for uncommunicative Sunday lunches with his parents. 'First,' he explained, 'I'd have two helpings of roast lamb. Then I'd have some beer, and my father would have orangeade. Then I'd have jelly with fruit in it. Then we'd all sit in armchairs, and after fifteen minutes my mother would say: "What about a cup of tea?" Then we'd have the tea, and we'd walk round the garden. Then I'd have a packet of liquorice all sorts. Then it'd be time to go.'[16] The pain of nostalgia and unexpressed affection and mutual incomprehension seemed to inform Dudley's every waking moment. When his mother finally watched an episode of *Not Only . . . But Also*, she complimented him: 'You put me right off to sleep dear, it was lovely.'

Peter, unlike his partner, often claimed not to use his background in his material, but to draw his inspiration from a vein of English fantasy running back to the work of Lewis Carroll and Edward Lear; but this was said partly from a desire to protect his own privacy and his family's feelings.

His humour was certainly informed by his background, even infused with it; but any genuine facts present had been stretched, twisted, pulled this way and that, and made completely unrecognisable before they reached the screen. Dudley mocked his own early self in specific autobiographical detail. Peter mocked his early experiences with broad, surreal, parodic brushstrokes.

This was just one of many areas of their professional relationship in which they complemented each other like Jack Spratt and his wife. Peter's demeanour suggested breeding, Dudley's did not. Peter presented an icy calm, Dudley was fidgety and agitated. Peter's humour was mainly verbal, Dudley's principally visual. Peter onscreen was aloof, even cold, Dudley came across as eager, anxious and warm. Peter was tall and Dudley was short. Most important of all, Peter was a natural leader and Dudley was a natural follower. This aspect of their relationship was as significant in real life as it was on screen. Peter was inherently a loner both as a performer and as a writer, with a strong idea of what he wanted, so only someone prepared to defer to him could have stayed the course successfully. 'I don't know quite how Dudley managed it at times,' says John Bird, 'because Peter was not an easy person to perform with. Even if the script was one that you'd written between you and everything had been fine during rehearsal, when the red light came on a glazed look would come into his eyes and he'd be gone. He wouldn't look at you, and you would be trying to keep up. Sometimes it was a nightmare working with him from that point of view.'

Dudley admits: 'I followed Peter around like some sort of Chihuahua, with great obeisance, loving everything that Peter did and said. That was probably the way with me and my mother. So, Peter, you were a mother figure. He was the dominant one, without a doubt.'[17] He describes their on screen relationship as a continuing dialogue between 'a know-all and a yes man'; off screen, as well, 'Pete was a real know-it-all, just like his character. He did know about almost everything. He wasn't in the habit of regaling you with his knowledge, but there were times when you couldn't understand some of the things he said.'[18] Asked whether he was scared of Peter, Dudley admits only that he was 'scared of everybody to a certain extent.'

There is no doubt that Peter had a great deal of respect and affection for Dudley. 'I thought Dudley was so wonderful,' he said much later. 'He had the twitching face and projected this tremendous eagerness to show knowledge and of course humility, tinged maybe with a bit of generosity, and a little bit of savoir-faire, and all the other condiments of the elite. By God he was funny. Compared to him, even comedians like Peter Sellers and Spike Milligan seem like interlopers. Some of the funniest things we ever did – in pubs, on our way to football matches – just floated away into the atmosphere.'[19] But Dudley did not always get to witness this respect and affection. Peter needed to win admiration, and became irritated when it was too freely given. Face to face, he could often be cruel to those – like Dudley or David Frost – who doted on him.

'I used to call him a club-footed dwarf,' admitted Peter. 'I think it was good for him. Everyone else used to pussyfoot around his problem.'[20] Joe McGrath recalls: 'Even Dudley's ability to play the piano – Peter used to say, "I wish I'd been forced to learn an instrument as a child." So there was no talent, it was just that Dudley had been forced to learn. And that used to really infuriate Dudley, he used to mutter, "I'll fucking kill him".' There were ceaseless jokes at Dudley's expense, particularly at his penchant for psychiatry. Dudley took this incredibly seriously, and once told a group of cameramen that the reason he had trouble producing scripts was because of inadequate potty training. Peter used to remark, 'I don't know why Dudley took so long to find himself. I found him years ago.' Once, a *TV Times* reporter accused Peter of openly being cruel to his partner. 'You think I'm cruel to Dudley?' he replied. 'My dear, being beastly to Dudley is the only thing that keeps me going.'[21] There was, of course, one other salient reason that Peter kept up the jibes at Dudley's expense: it was funny. In fact, it was as funny when he pushed him around off screen as it was when he gave him the runaround on screen, and Peter could never resist making people laugh.

Naturally, Peter adored making Dudley himself laugh most of all. 'His main aim seemed to be to contort me into as many strange positions as he could,' says his partner. Joe McGrath remembers that 'Peter would suddenly do something totally unexpected, quite wickedly, and Dudley would break up. Dudley used to try and make Peter break up, but he hardly ever did. I think that was the whole pleasure of the relationship, the pleasure they took from playing with each other like that.' It was transfixingly enjoyable to watch Peter, his face an impassive mask, going in for the kill. The sight of Dudley giggling, wriggling and unable to escape has led some people to assume – quite erroneously – that he was the untalented one, the expendable half of the equation, that any decent comedy performer could have taken his part. Nick Luard even referred to him as 'Cook's creation'. The cartoonist Gerald Scarfe caricatured Dudley as a glove puppet, perched on the end of Peter's right arm.

In fact Dudley Moore elevated Peter's previous standards of performance quite dramatically, by bringing to them the pure essence of the one thing he had previously been unable to supply himself: audience sympathy.

Audiences had lavished Peter with laughter and admiration by the bucketload, but until the arrival of club-footed Dudley his manifestly innate superiority had not found a victim for the audience to feel sorry for, a permanent underdog for them to side with. According to John Wells, 'No-one should underestimate Dud's contribution to the partnership. The same wealth of strangely warped observation that compelled silence when Peter was inventing one of his monologues made the role of straight man in the dialogues extremely hard. Many of us tried it on *Private Eye* sound records. If you intruded on Peter's imaginary world it sounded cheap and flat by comparison, and Dudley Moore succeeded by patient repetition and support, only occasionally allowing himself a sure-fire plonker of his own.'[22] Jonathan Miller confirms that Dudley was 'subordinate to Peter in terms of invention, but I think that he was an equal partner, and it's very hard to imagine the success of the show without Dudley's talent as a performer'. Peter understood this as much as anyone. Asked about his own favourite comedy double acts, he described Ernie Wise as 'fantastic', and with reference to Dean Martin and Jerry Lewis, said: 'Most people think, oh, Jerry Lewis is the funny man – what does Dean Martin do? The answer is, he makes Jerry Lewis funny.'[23]

So bonded to Peter had Dudley become that he even began to imitate his lifestyle: 'I followed him, I suppose, I don't know. He said that when he got married I got married, when he got divorced I got divorced, when he moved to Hampstead I moved to Hampstead. Maybe that's true.' Despite the element of mutual dependence in their relationship, however, Peter did not share Dudley's ability to unburden himself emotionally. He remained as much of a closed book to his performing partner as he did to his other friends: 'I suppose I got close to Peter in the same way he got close to me – which was barely at all. You couldn't get out of him what he felt about certain things. I remember I phoned him up in trouble once; it was the only time I ever phoned anybody up in trouble. And I said, "I really don't know what to do", and he said, "Well . . ." and gave me some very general chat. It was a very stuttering reply. He didn't confide in me.'

Despite Dudley's failure to break into the inner sanctum, the recordings of *Not Only . . . But Also* were among Peter's happiest times. 'That was perfect,' he said later. 'I don't know how long it would have gone on but it just seemed by chance perfectly natural. I mean it was *ideal*. I can't imagine a comedy relationship being better. I *adored* Dudley.'[24] After the studios everyone would go, in a crowd, round to Sean Kenny and Judy Huxtable's house, or up to the Fagin's Kitchen Restaurant in Hampstead where Peter would foot the entire bill. There were some riotous evenings. For the duration of the series Peter and Dudley would spend every minute of every day together; but curiously, when they weren't working with each other, communications utterly dried up. Dudley remembers that when the series was off air 'We *never* used to talk to each other, never went out to dinner. For six months you're life and death to each other and then you're nothing. It was strange really. Peter and I had a "thing", like a love-hate relationship. Anyone else around us probably felt a little excluded, because we did exclude people. We just set each other off, we *fitted*.'[25]

Despite Peter's leading role in creating the series, *Not Only . . . But Also* was initially seen very much as Dudley's success, because it had been billed in advance as his show. In April 1965 the *Daily Mail* reported that 'The first comedy success produced by BBC2, Dudley Moore's *Not Only . . . But Also*, has come to the end of a brilliant run. So successful has it been that next month it is to be repeated before BBC1's wider audience. Dudley Moore was one of the originals of the *Beyond the Fringe* team that shattered London just on four years ago. Despite every prediction, it now seems that Dudley Moore has come the farthest. From limping along lonely in the rear, Dudley Moore has now emerged as the front runner, more consistent, more professional, more universally funny than the rest of the stable that reared him.'[26] It was not a view that would endure, but it was certainly prevalent in the press for a short while, and may have contributed to Peter's somewhat ambivalent behaviour towards his partner.

Elsewhere, reaction to the series was equally enthusiastic. *The Times* described it as 'versatile, inventive and immensely funny'.[27] *The Sun* called it 'The funniest series on television'.[28] Margaret Drabble in the *Mail* enthused that she 'found it hard to find praise high enough. Surely no two people have ever before united so many talents so successfully, the verbal wit, the songs, the visual fantasies, the expert performances have poured forth from some seemingly inexhaustible cornucopia of comedy. In comparison, other comedy writers are like that poet whose one good verse shines in the dry desert of a thousand lines.'[29] Peter and Dudley were voted 'Comedians of the Year' by the Guild of Television Producers and Directors, an award that they managed to lose during the ceremony. They were invited to appear in an 'Artists against apartheid' gala in March, they starred in *Sunday Night at the London Palladium* in September, and they performed before the Queen at the Royal Variety Performance in November. Their success had become utterly mainstream.

A special Pete and Dud royal dialogue was composed in the Queen's honour, but when he heard it at rehearsal the producer Bernard Delfont ordered some of the jokes to be cut. Lord Snowdon, for instance, was referred to as 'The former underwater wrestler, Strong-arm Jones', who prior to marrying Princess Margaret had been 'made to run from Land's End to John O'Groats in a rubber diving suit to get his weight down'. Harold Wilson was described as 'Always hanging around the palace'. The Queen herself was described, with reference to official medal ceremonies, as 'hanging one on' the recipient. Peter may have been the kind of public schoolboy who liked to shock other boys with his antics, but he also knew when to smile and back down in the face of authority. There were no Jonathan Miller-style walk-outs. All the cuts were accepted meekly. The remaining material was nonetheless very funny:

> *Pete*: Do you know that we're all in line for succession to the throne?
>
> *Dud*: Really?
>
> *Pete*: Well, if forty-eight million, two hundred thousand, seven hundred and one people died I'd be Queen.

It was also pointedly unsatirical and inoffensive:

> *Pete*: Do you know, at this very moment, Her Majesty is probably exercising the royal prerogative.
>
> *Dud*: What's that then, Pete?
>
> *Pete*: Don't you know the royal prerogative? It's a wonderful animal, Dud. It's a legendary beast, half bird, half fish, half unicorn, and it's being exercised at this very moment.

Her Majesty was observed laughing heartily in the Royal Box. The newspapers agreed that Pete and Dud had taken the Royal Variety Performance by storm – a prestigious accolade indeed in 1965 – ahead of such seasoned performers as Peter Sellers and Spike Milligan. The following year they were invited to perform *One Leg Too Few* in front of the Queen as part of ITV's rival *Royal Gala Show*. At the end of the sketch, as Barry Fantoni relates, 'an extraordinary thing happened. Dudley started to play the piano in a very Merseybeat sort of way, and Peter sang a song, a psychedelic song, about a bee. I can still clearly see him, holding the microphone in front of this large audience who had enjoyed Frank Ifield, Tony Bennett and Max Bygraves on the same bill, and there he was with his beautiful black eyelashes, acting to all intents and purposes like a pop star. The only thing was, he couldn't sing. He was dreadful.' Fortunately, the preceding dialogue had been so funny that nobody cared.

The song in question was *The L. S. Bumblebee*, a psychedelic parody subsequently aired on the 1966 *Not Only . . . But Also* Christmas special. It became one of three pop singles released by the pair, starting with *Goodbyee* in June 1965, although Dudley sang the lead on the recorded version, as he did on all their singles. As a response Peter issued a solo single in July 1965, *The Ballad of Spotty Muldoon*, in direct competition to *Goodbyee*. The two records charted simultaneously, reaching no. 34 and no. 18 respectively, making Peter the first ever comedy artist to have two hit records at once. *Goodbyee* and the *Not Only . . . But Also* album subsequently became the best-selling comedy single and album of the year. Peter had, in a small way at least, made it as a pop singer. The news that *The Ballad of Spotty Muldoon* had been banned in New Zealand, lest it offend the then Finance Minister (and later Prime Minister) Robert Muldoon, made his success even sweeter. He and Dudley performed live on *Ready, Steady, Go!* and on the short-lived pop show *Now!* (presented in his first ever TV role by Michael Palin), and wallowed briefly in the ironic adulation of the pop world. Record-buyers are of course notoriously fickle, and the two follow-up singles, *Isn't She a Sweetie?* in 1966 and *The L. S. Bumblebee* – finally released in 1967 – failed miserably. There were rumours, incidentally, which have since found their way into print, that the latter song was a John Lennon cast-off; but this was definitely not the case.

On the B-side of *The L. S. Bumblebee* was *The Beeside*, a specially recorded Pete and Dud sketch about the evils of drink and drugs, remarkable for its horribly prophetic nature. Pete told of 'A very nice family man with a lovely wife and two beautiful children what he used to dandle on his knees when he came home . . . then, one evening, he came home and looked around and said, "Nice though this be I seek yet further kicks."' The man took to the bottle and to various illicit substances, until:

> Pete: His craving got worse and worse. He got more and more drugs down his face, and eventually he became so irresponsible, he left his lovely wife and kids and home behind and went to Hollywood and lay on a beach all day with a lovely busty starlet with blonde hair what come down to her knees.
>
> Dud: That doesn't sound too bad, Pete.
>
> Pete: No, I don't think that's a very good example of the perils actually.

Dudley Moore, in fact, was not prepared to wait for any future move to Hollywood to get stuck into a series of starlets. With his celebrated compulsion for confessing all to anyone within listening distance, Dudley revealed to *The Sunday Times* in October that he was involved with 'three birds. Each of them knows about one of the others, but never the full complement.'[30] Shortly afterwards he found himself with no birds as a consequence, but he lost no time in filling the gap with the beautiful actress and model Suzy Kendall (née Freda Harrison). Peter observed sarcastically that 'Millions of women would like to adopt Dudley. Nobody wants to adopt *me* – not even the Duchess of Argyll. I wrote to her saying I was available, but not a word.'[31] Bill Wallis was even asked by a girl at a party if he would sleep with her, because he'd once been in the same *room* as Dudley Moore. Dudley himself insisted that he would continue to play the field and never get married: 'It's the one subject that terrifies me,'[32] he insisted. He subsequently married Suzy Kendall on 14 June 1968, in a secret ceremony.

With television and the pop charts conquered, Peter was keen to move ever onwards and upwards, and storm the world of films. Dudley would come with him: 'What I do in the future rather depends on what Peter does,'[33] Dudley informed the press loyally. In the summer of 1965 he and Peter signed a three-picture deal with Columbia, to carry their double act on to the big screen. The agreement sounded the death-knell, at least in his current incarnation, for E. L. Wisty; *The Ballad of Spotty Muldoon* turned out to be Wisty's last act. His final appearance in *On the Braden Beat* was a memorable occasion. Not once had Wisty's impassive expression so much as flickered during the series; that night, as the show went out live, Braden and the crew made a concerted attempt to break Peter's concentration. Cameramen, floor managers, even Braden himself crawled around the floor and popped up suddenly beside the camera, pulling faces and making rude gestures. Finally, Peter cracked, laughed heartily with everyone else, and shook his finger at his near-hysterical tormentors. 'All right you so-and-so's, you've done it, now let me finish,' he said, and did. Peter wanted the American satirist Jay Landesman to replace him, but the producers chose the home-grown talents of Tim Brooke-Taylor instead, playing a reactionary bowler-hatted city gent. No matter who replaced him, the programme would never be the same again.

In the summer of 1965 Peter formed another company, Peter Cook Productions Ltd., with secretarial help provided by the *Private Eye* staff (Judy Scott-Fox had stayed on in America to try her luck as a theatrical agent). The idea was to get his own projects on to the big screen in the wake of Columbia's interest. In October he tried to resurrect the Cook/Bird adaptation of *Scoop*, which had been abandoned in February, and also the post-*Fringe* project *The Curious Gentleman*, which had been dropped as far back as mid-1964. Neither idea excited much interest; the film business, even more than the BBC, was and remains resistant to unsolicited ideas. What Columbia wanted Peter and Dudley to do was appear in *The Wrong Box*, a camp adaption of Robert Louis Stevenson and Lloyd Osbourne's light-hearted novel, which was to be shot in Bath and at Pinewood in the autumn. An indication of the commercial importance that Peter and Dudley had attained by this time is evinced by *The Sunday Times'* reaction to the deal: 'Bryan Forbes is directing and the cast includes Ralph Richardson, John Mills and Michael Caine; with Peter Sellers and Tony Hancock making guest appearances. These are big names to brandish at the box office, but there's no doubt that Cook and Moore are the ones which matter most.'[34]

The Wrong Box, sadly, turned out to be a thoroughly incoherent and mediocre piece of work, a classic example of the British film industry's traditional custom of applying famous comedians en masse to a feeble script in the hope of papering over any cracks. Besides Peter, Dudley, Hancock and Sellers, the cast included Irene Handl, John le Mesurier, John Junkin, Norman Rossington, Leonard Rossiter, Nicholas Parsons and Jeremy Lloyd, not to mention the Temperance Seven as a group of undertakers. All concerned overacted strenuously. The result was what might be called a 'romp' (in the worst sense of the word), full of reaction shots to jokes: when one of the cast fell over, for instance, Forbes cut away to a bunch of cute children laughing. Supplying one's own onscreen approval for a joke is an insecure device that rarely works. The direction was generally turgid, the incidental music too heavy, and the film's interpretation of Victorian England strictly Carnaby Street. Insofar as it was meant to be a parody of a leaden Victorian melodrama, *The Wrong Box* failed utterly, by wholeheartedly resorting to the trappings of a leaden Victorian melodrama.

The highly complicated plot concerned the two survivors of a family 'Tontine', a lottery in which all the prize money goes to the last one of the entrants to die. Peter and Dudley played Morris and John Finsbury, the unscrupulous nephews of one of the doddering survivors (Gielgud), both of whom are determined that their uncle should win the Tontine, so that they can get their hands on the money. Unfortunately they believe him to have been killed in a train crash in which Peter loses his trousers (it's that sort of film), although in reality the dead body belongs to the escaped Bournemouth Strangler, who happened to have been wearing their uncle's coat. In an effort to conceal the death, they approach the drunken Dr Pratt (Sellers) for an undated death certificate, which they intend to fill in only after the other survivor of the Tontine has passed on. Then, due to a postal mix-up, the box containing the Strangler's dead body is actually delivered to the rival survivor's house and has to be retrieved, with extremely unhilarious consequences.

Peter and Dudley were very much cast according to type – one lordly and cynical, the other libidinous and put-upon – and encouraged to undertake as much melodramatic moustache-twirling villainy as possible. In an effort to attract TV viewers, Dudley's *Not Only . . . But Also* catchphrase – 'funny' – was incorporated into the script. Peter's role was much the bigger, and Dudley refused to sign up for the film unless his was enlarged substantially. Despite his demands being met, Dudley had an utterly miserable time; he could smell disaster looming. 'I disagreed with Bryan Forbes a great deal about his approach to comedy. He used to act it all out all the time; he used to do it for you. Unfortunately, I've done that in my time and I think it's a great mistake. I never used to find what Bryan did too easy to follow – it was like aping movement and facial expression.'[35] A bizarre method of directing two comedians who had become enormously popular in part because of their mastery of facial expression. 'I've seen the film a few times,' says Dudley, 'and I've never been able to understand quite what goes on in it – probably because I was so obsessed with the discomfort I went through.'[36]

Peter was initially delighted by the glamour of the location shoot: evidently the four hours spent in a freezing rubbish dump during the filming of *Not Only . . . But Also* had not taken the gloss off the experience. He kept visitors to the set entertained with a high-quality stream of cinematic invention: 'Remember *Ben Hur*? All those battles, with thousands of soldiers running about? Ants. Ants dressed in uniform. They make these thousands of tiny uniforms and dress the ants in them. Then they tell them to go out and have a battle, and they photograph them, and blow it up big. And Esther Williams? You know she couldn't swim a stroke. They used to drop her in a bath of gelatine so she wouldn't sink. Then they'd speed up the film. And as for Margaret Rutherford, it's common knowledge that she's four people . . .'[37] and so on, like continuous shell fire. Peter was to a great extent trying to cover his nerves about the size of the undertaking – it was the first time he had acted in anything longer than a short sketch since university; but the barrage of jokes didn't go down quite as well with a group of attention-seeking actors as it would normally have done with a more receptive audience. The feelings of unfriendly rivalry he – perhaps unfairly – discerned among the rest of the cast led him to unleash a bitter public attack on actors in general: 'The good thing about a university background is, it keeps you from getting as conceited as most actors. Unlike them, you have a period of intellectual activity. You get curious and you then stay curious. This means you're less likely to become enthralled with yourself than the actors and actresses with no cultural or intellectual background. Suddenly they're thrust into prominence. Suddenly they're told they're so important. Everything they do is reported. Usually they just get drunk. They can't cope. And actors in this country all take such a predictably *hip* line: liberal with a small "l". I think I hate them more than anybody else.'[38]

Clearly unsure about his own performance and how it would stand up in such illustrious company, Peter allowed Forbes to dictate what he should do in much more detail than Dudley ever did. The results can be seen in his scene with Peter Sellers, the only performer to emerge from the film with credit. Sellers utterly wipes Peter off the screen with a first-rate cameo performance, dripping with small visual details and verbal touches that he appears to have added himself. The drunken doctor's room is alive with cats (he was actually smeared with fish paste to keep them interested) and he uses one to blot the ink on the undated death certificate. After he has sterilised his hands, he dries them on another live kitten. Whenever Peter's lines contain the word 'Doctor', Sellers says 'Come in'.

Forbes felt that both the offscreen Sellers and Tony Hancock, who killed himself soon afterwards, 'were searching for an elusive bluebird of happiness which ultimately destroyed them both'. He also noted similar traits in Dudley Moore. 'It must be a great trial for comedians who shoot to such public fame and are always expected to be at the top of their form offstage as well as on. I had many conversations on this subject with Peter Sellers and I am sure Dudley suffers in the same way.'[39] Peter, who always was at the top of his form offstage as well as on, seemed on the surface to have fewer such problems, although Forbes said he noticed one or two 'demons' there too.

Peter's second daughter, Daisy, was born while he was on location, on 10 September 1965. Dudley bought a small refrigerator and put it in the boot of his Maserati, crammed with champagne in waiting for the news of the birth. In the event, Peter rushed to London just beforehand, and the champagne went undrunk. All day Dudley looked lost and miserable without his friend, and made a nuisance of himself complaining that his shoes were too tight. Had he known, Peter would undoubtedly have been touched, although of course he would never have dreamed of admitting so.

The Wrong Box did not do very well at the box office, but Peter and Dudley emerged with their reputations largely unscathed. It was generally accepted amid the mixed reviews that they had been hamstrung by having to perform substandard lines that they could probably have bettered themselves. The jury was still out on their film careers. Their television careers, which had remained in abeyance during the filming, resumed immediately with the second series of *Not Only . . . But Also*. So tight were their schedules that they had actually written the TV scripts on the set of *The Wrong Box* between takes. All the filming for the TV series was scheduled to take place in advance this time, so as soon as one lot of shooting was over, the next batch began, over Christmas and New Year. Time with the family was sacrificed for Peter and Dudley's booming careers. On 29 December they spent the whole day in pouring rain on Wimbledon Common, filming a boxing sketch with Henry Cooper and the former world middleweight champion, Terry Downes. On the 30th they were lowered over the side of a ship into the freezing Thames near Tower Bridge, twice, fully clothed, while playing a duet on a grand piano. At one point a steel cable temporarily slackened and managed to wrap itself around Dudley's neck. He succeeded in extricating himself, seconds before he was decapitated.

Joe McGrath had gone now – he had secured the desired job in cinema, sadly for him as director of *Casino Royale*. In his place came Dick Clement, who did little to change McGrath's successful formula: the principal difference was that owing to pressure of scriptwriting time the shows were to be only half an hour in length, the idea of a regular comedy guest being sacrificed to assist the cut. Peter claimed to find Dick Clement 'more objective' than Joe McGrath; Dudley had felt McGrath to be 'more encouraging'. In fact both producers were equally good, the comments merely reflecting Dudley's long-standing personal friendship with McGrath.

Sadly, even less survives of the second series than of the first. A new policy had been implemented by the BBC, whereby instead of wiping all comedy shows, the first and last of every series alone were retained. Jimmy Gilbert, who later worked with Peter and Dudley before becoming Head of Comedy, tries to explain: 'The Head of Comedy simply didn't know anything about tape retention. When I was Head, Bob Galbraith, who was my organiser, used to come in with these print-outs, and he would say "We're only allowed to keep eighty shows, so I'm suggesting we have the first and last of this, the first and last of that." I believe the thinking was, in a hundred years' time, you'll at least get a flavour. But the first and last of every series meant absolutely nothing.' Fortunately, the first and last shows of the second series of *Not Only . . . But Also* are two of the funniest programmes ever shown on British television. Equally fortunately, this time the BBC did not throw away the scripts of the other programmes.

The series went out weekly from 15 January 1966. The three sketches that formed the first show – slotted between songs from an impressively beehived and beak-nosed Cilla Black – enshrined Peter's power over Dudley more substantially than before. The boxing sketch, for instance, was entitled 'The Fight of the Century', between 'Gentleman Jim Cook, the Torquay stylist' and 'Dudley Moon, the Dagenham Dodger'. Dudley's character was shown training furiously for the fight while Peter's trained horizontally in bed. The commentary posed the question 'raging on everybody's lips':

> Could the Dodger's inferior height, weight, reach and ability prevail against the greater size, strength and skill of the champion? On the face of it, the answer seemed to be 'no'.

The answer was indeed no, as Dudley lost decisively.

> The moral of the fight is clear: a good big 'un will always beat a rotten little 'un.

The Pete and Dud dialogue took place at the zoo, where – as usual – Peter led Dudley off the rehearsal path into thickets of confusion:

> *Dud*:   Y'know I was here last week Pete, I dunno if I told you . . .
> *Pete*:   Yes you did.
> *Dud*:   And I saw a . . . did I?
> *Pete*:   I was here with you.
> *Dud*:   I saw . . . er . . . er . . .

Dudley resorted to chewing fiercely on his lower lip to keep the laughs down. He informed Pete that in a visit to the 'Topical Fish' department he had failed to spot a single satirical barb about the current world situation. This, explained Pete, was because he had actually misread the sign for the 'Tropical Fish' department, in which one of the letters had become dislodged by winter gales:

> *Pete*:   I was talking to the keeper about it actually, and he said that very often, during the winter months, his 'r's blew off.

– from which point on Dud was utterly unable to keep a straight face.

The third and final sketch, *A Bit of a Chat*, was a marvellous tour-de-force from Peter as a bumbling Streeb-Greeblingesque father, nervously trying to explain the facts of life to his son. It gradually transpires that he doesn't know them either. In order to have a child, he explains,

> It was necessary for your mother to sit on a chair. To sit on a chair which I had recently vacated, and which was still warm from my body. And then something very mysterious, rather wonderful and beautiful happened. And sure enough, four years later, you were born.

The solution to the mystery, it seemed, lay in the presence of their libidinous house guest, Uncle Bertie:

> *Peter:*   He's been living with us for forty years, and it does seem a day too much.

Again, Peter had created a joke from the deftest subversion of a polite cliché.

The script of the second show declared the long-suffering Dudley winner of the *Most Boring Man in the World* competition, in front of a panel of real celebrity judges – including Alan Freeman, Katie Boyle and Percy Thrower – at the Albert Hall. This was essentially a Miss World parody, in which Dudley had to take part in a mackintosh parade against Mr Switzerland, Mr Chile, Mr St Kitts ('a really first class coloured bore in a previously white-dominated province') and Mr Free China. He was judged on his banality of thought, tedium of movement, dullness of appearance and torpor of conversation. At one point Peter was handed a pair of pants:

> Well you've joined me at a very exciting moment. These are Alan Freeman's pants, which have just been bored right off him by the British contestant.

Dudley, needless to say, won the contest through his ability to converse about his specialist subjects: carpets, and how difficult it is to park in London.

There was also a sketch in which Dudley played a public school head-master and Peter his pupil – a sixth former named Rawlings. The setting obviously owed much to the Cook family's ties with Radley, and Peter's own experiences at the school, here joyously transformed by wish fulfilment:

> *Headmaster:*   As you know, three generations of Rawlings have brought distinction and credit to the school, and

your father was Head Boy for four years – giving it
a moral tone from which it has never recovered.

The headmaster explains, Dexter-fashion, that Rawlings is to be caned for
possessing a copy of *Razzle* magazine. There is, however, one problem:

Rawlings: Although you are, you know, much older than me,
                 and much more, much more experienced, Sir . . .
Headmaster: Out with it boy.
Rawlings: I would, you know, I'd just like to point out Sir,
                 I'm much bigger than you are, Sir, and if you lay
                 a finger on me, um, I'll smash your stupid little
                 head in.

Cue a huge round of nostalgic applause from the audience.

The Pete and Dud dialogue in show two concerned Dud's cold and the
plight of germs: 'They're forced to do something they don't want to. Can
you imagine having to fly up people's noses?' It contained one joke that
Peter had originally intended for himself, and had then passed to Dudley,
as it was a line written for a natural victim. Dud explained that he had
nearly died at three – he'd gone blue, he said, and no experts could find
out what was wrong.

Dud: Then they suddenly discovered the cause of it. It
             was the fact that my father had been holding me
             underwater for ten minutes.

Worse was to come for Dud, who recounted his mother's cure for earache:
having a string tied to his ear, attached at the other end to a door handle
and the door slammed shut.

The third show laid hilariously into Dudley on three more fronts. It
began with Peter as a monarch, and Dudley as a jester who wasted his
time chasing women when he should be entertaining the King. Then
Dudley appeared as a man trying to impress his girlfriend in an Italian
restaurant, a scheme ruined by the waiter (Peter), who desired that such
an obviously intelligent and well brought-up man teach him some English
phrases. As he explained, 'Is good to speak to someone who is speak well,
from Oxford.' Finally, in the Dud and Pete sketch, there were thinly veiled
references to Dud's musical ability:

> *Pete*: I often wish my mother had forced me to learn the piano when young.
> *Dud*: Yeah, me too. If only she'd forced me to play, forced me to be a genius.
> *Pete*: You wouldn't be here now, would you?
> *Dud*: No, exactly.
> *Pete*: You'd be in Vegas with some blonde girl.

There were faint stirrings here of rebellion, signs in the word 'genius' that Dud was just beginning to assert himself; but only faint ones as yet. For the moment, Dud was off on another nostalgia trip, 'cycling up Chadwell Heath to get some bananas for my mum, and on the way back down Wood Lane I could hear Mrs Woolley's gramophone blaring out Caruso.' He told of his old girlfriend Eileen, who lived near Goodmayes Park; she was disguised as 'Enid Armstrong' for the purposes of the sketch, but about half-way through Dud forgot to call her Enid and started calling her Eileen instead. Peter too changed horses with ease.

> *Pete*: Eileen had a wonderful ear for music.
> *Dud*: Yeah, oh, wonderful.
> *Pete*: Her left one.
> *Dud*: Yeah, the right one was completely useless.

A further sign that Dudley might be putting his foot down came with the inclusion, at last, of the solo item in which he gradually lost colour in the bath. After another argument Peter conceded the point, and it was reinstated in the third show. The remaining sketch, entitled *Blue Movie*, was an attack on pretentious film directors; Dudley played Dimitri Craddock, who – it soon emerged – had made no more than a tatty porn film, but who tried to justify the endeavour by using phrases like 'The divestment is symbolic of the shedding of responsibility by the young generation.'

The series sagged slightly in the middle, as comedy series tend to do. The fourth show featured several parodies of current adverts, a savage attack on slapstick comedy and the BBC executives who commission it, a not entirely successful song entitled *Isn't She a Sweetie* (based on two effete characters who sometimes populated the title sequences) and one famous sketch – *Frog and Peach*. This was another interview with Sir Arthur, whose surname had inexplicably changed to Streeve-Greevlings, about a restaurant he had started in the middle of Dartmoor which served only grotesque frog- and peach-based dishes. It is difficult to see why it has become so well known, unless for its influence on a similar Monty Python sketch about a disgusting chocolate assortment, as it was little more than a re-run of Sir Arthur's earlier futile business venture, teaching ravens to fly. It did of course contain some good jokes: the one based on Peter's wartime Torquay neighbour being blown through the window, and another based on Lady Streeve-Greevlings' experiences abroad during the war:

> My wife was a freedom fighter. She fought freedom for several years, finally won, and became imprisoned.

The fifth show continued in a familiar vein, with an attack on the film business and its stars: Dudley and Peter played leading man Stanley Moon and leading lady Titania Thurl respectively, although sadly only the first page of that script survives. There was also a sketch parodying Dudley's visits to his psychiatrist: although he appeared as 'Roger', Dudley's problems – a combination of being madly in love with a girl and various associated feelings of frustration and guilt – sounded familiar. Although the script of this sketch has also disappeared, the soundtrack survives on an LP record. Peter played the psychiatrist, Dr Braintree:

> *Braintree*: What's the girl's name?
> *Roger*:   Stephanie.
> *Braintree*: Stephanie . . . that's a lovely name. That's my wife's name in fact, isn't it.
> *Roger*:   . . . Yes . . .

By this time half the audience had guessed the twist; it took the rest of them a little longer to catch up.

The third and final sketch was an absolute corker, dealing with the Dudleyesque story of a successful middle-class boy returning to his working-class father's home in Dagenham late at night. The son handled his father's complaints with supercilious ease, making it very much a role for Peter:

> *Dudley*: D'you think I fought in the war for you to come here at four o'clock in the morning?
> *Peter*:   I don't know what you fought in the war for father, if indeed you did.
> *Dudley*: (pointing at apparent war wound) What's this, what's this then, what's this?

Peter: That's your navel, father.

Dudley's character explained that he had been 'verger at St Peter's Church Becontree for forty-five years', whereas his son never bothered to worship there.

Dudley: I got a good mind to take my bloody belt off to you.
Peter: I wouldn't do that father, your trousers will fall down again.
Dudley: (looking skyward) Rosie, d'you see, d'you see what sort of child we have, what a monster. We in our moment of joy spawned this monster.
Peter: Father I don't know why you keep looking up when you talk about mother. You know perfectly well she's living in Frinton with a sailor.
Dudley: That's a terrible thing to say, that's a bloody terrible thing to say. She wouldn't leave me, she worshipped the ground I walk on.
Peter: She loved the ground but she didn't care for you, father.

In line after line, the son rained put-downs incessantly upon his father's head, in a way that Dudley would never have dreamed of speaking to his parents in real life. Although Peter was effectively playing Dudley, he was also mocking him. But there were further signs of a stiffening of Dudley's resolve in the sixth show, with a sketch deriding – for a change – Peter's inability to play the piano. Peter played a rich, self-made man with a 'nothing is impossible' creed, who turns up on the doorstep of a Welsh piano tuner, portrayed by Dudley:

Peter: I've had no formal musical training but I have a certain sort of instinctive gift for it. My family are very rhythmical. I know about the piano, I know these are the white notes, these are the black notes. The black notes play the loud ones, I know that much.

He explains that he wishes to learn Beethoven's fifth from scratch, in order to play it as a surprise for his wife's birthday on Tuesday fortnight. Dudley points out that he will require an orchestra.

Peter: I have got an orchestra. I bought one last Wednesday.

Peter, of course, wins out in the end. He is, he explains, a millionaire at twenty-nine; and Dudley, it transpires, will do anything for a hundred guineas an hour. After that, it was back to normal for Dudley, in a Pete and Dud conversation about sex:

> *Pete*:   Have you read Nevil Shute?
> *Dud*:   Very little.
> *Pete*:   How much of Nevil Shute have you read?
> *Dud*:   Nothing.

The other item of note in the sixth show was a filmed version of Lewis Carroll's *The Walrus and the Carpenter*, which by some unexplained anomaly has survived. It was a low budget and prosaic treatment for such a surreal verse: the oysters were real and Dudley's only concession to walrushood was a droopy moustache and some stomach padding. It was also stylishly shot, intelligent and rather eerie, with only a solo violin accompaniment, and very much prefigured Jonathan Miller's acclaimed version of *Alice in Wonderland* of December 1966.

The final show of the series mercifully survives, mercifully because it contains *Superthunderstingcar*, Peter and Dudley's wickedly accurate parody of *Thunderbirds*. Hanging from obvious strings and sporting giant false eyebrows, Peter and Dudley played a variety of badly-operated puppets: father and son Jeff and Johnny Jupiter, with their flat catchphrase 'This is terrible' for every disaster; Teutonic villain Masterbrawn and his assistant Kraut; and finally, Hovis the butler and Lady Dorothy, a masterpiece of knockabout physical acting by Dudley, who poked his eye out with his cigarette holder and cleared a table of drinks with his swinging feet. Elsewhere the programme contained *Bo Duddley*, a sketch that later reappeared on the first *Derek and Clive* album, in which Peter and Dudley analysed a blues number line-by-line in earnest BBC tones, missing the point at every turn. 'You don't think any of these lyrics could be in any way connected with making love or sex?' queried Peter towards the end, fighting desperately not to laugh. The final Pete and Dud dialogue took them to heaven in white plastic macs and cloth caps, and contained the only joke that Dudley can directly remember contributing to the series:

> *Dud*:   Is this it then? Is this heaven?
> *Pete*:   Bloody hell.

'I came up with so few jokes that when I invented one I thought, "Son of a gun,"'[40] says Dudley modestly, without discussing what he thought of

Peter's decision to appropriate it. Heaven, said Peter, looked 'like Liberace's bedroom', and suffered from a predictable drawback:

Dud: I'm rather bored already.
Pete: It's a very boring place. You'll find that over the millions of years.

The reaction of the press and public to the series was more ecstatic than ever before. The BBC begged the pair for more programmes. Peter stalled. 'We don't want to become the national bores of 1966,'[41] he offered implausibly. The truth was that cracking the cinema was more important to him than carrying on with something he had already shown he could do. Finally, on the strength of the second series, he and Dudley secured what they really wanted: a deal with Twentieth Century Fox to write and star in their very own film. It was to be an updating of the *Faust* legend that Peter had once studied, entitled *Bedazzled*. This was a critical moment for the balance of power within their partnership. Dudley wanted to get going on the script immediately. Again, Peter seemed strangely unwilling to start work. He suggested that Dudley and Suzy, together with the entire Cook family, go to Grenada in the West Indies; the film script could be written there. Dudley, who had other holiday plans, reluctantly fell into line, and they flew out at the end of March. The party stayed in a pair of adjacent self-catering beach cottages, with Wendy doing the cooking as usual, and the cost was met – in return for a set of *Hello!*-style photographs – by the *Daily Mirror* and *Woman* magazine. This photo deal was something Peter later sincerely regretted: 'As soon as I saw the pictures, they looked to me as though I was trying to assert how happy I was and how gorgeous my daughters were,'[42] he complained. He resolved never to air his family, and particularly his children, in public ever again.

From the start of the trip, it was clear to Dudley that something was wrong. 'The more we stayed, the more he didn't want to work. He said, "I can't work today because of so and so," or "because of my wife," so I waited for a week and nothing ever happened, nothing *ever* happened. So I lost my temper with him – I said "You brought us out here for no good reason. What the fuck is going on? I don't understand it, you come out here ostensibly to work with me, we changed our holiday plans from somewhere to Grenada to fit in with you." And he just said "Right." So things got a little wound up.' What had happened was that despite the joint contract, Peter had decided to write the film without his partner. Dudley was being edged out. As Peter saw it, this project was his single make-or-break chance to crack the film world. He intended to get the script absolutely, scrupulously right, however long it took to write (in the event, it was to take him more than a year). He was terrified of making a mistake. He did not want to have to make allowances for anyone else's comedy judgment. He wanted that solo screen writing credit. Since his death there has been a tendency to canonise Peter Cook, who was indeed, for most of his life, extremely generous to most other performers; but he was also subject to regular human vices such as pride, envy and a highly competitive desire to be the best.

Dudley went off in a huff, took no further part in the scripting of *Bedazzled*, and wrote and starred in a film of his own: *Thirty is a Dangerous Age, Cynthia*. Co-scripted by John Wells and Joe McGrath, who also directed, and incorporating Wells and John Bird in the cast, the film was the apogee of Dudley's autobiographical tendency. He portrayed a musician named Rupert Street, who played jazz in a nightclub like he did. His onscreen Belper-born girlfriend, played by his real-life Belper-born girlfriend Suzy Kendall, was named Louise Hammond, after his sadly missed ex-girlfriend Celia Hammond and his first love Louise McDermott. The Cynthia of the title was a reference to another sorely missed ex, Cynthia Cassidy. Mrs Woolley, who cropped up in innumerable Pete and Dud dialogues, was played by Patricia Routledge. Dudley admitted that 'My mother always sent me my laundry though the mail – just like Rupert's does in the film. And like Rupert's she always included a sack of lemon drops and some bread pudding in the package.' The film flopped, which hurt Dudley bitterly.

Bedazzled, meanwhile, was also proving to be Peter's most autobiographical work. The story of a Wimpy bar chef named Stanley Moon (Dudley), who sells his soul to the devil (Peter) in return for seven chances at winning the affections of waitress Margaret Spencer (Eleanor Bron), it was an incisive and barely disguised take on Peter and Dudley's own relationship. Peter later freely admitted that Stanley Moon was Dudley, or at least an 'exaggeration' of him, shorn of his musical talents and his annoying attractiveness to women. Moon was portrayed as utterly good-hearted, but acutely insecure and lacking in self-confidence, unable to assert himself when faced with Peter's smooth-talking Satan; desperate for acceptance, he resorts to tagging along hopefully and submissively behind, and is constantly cast down when the Devil is randomly horrible to him. George Spiggott (as Peter decided to name the Evil One, after the monoped in *One Leg Too Few*), was if anything even closer to his real-life equivalent, being charming, good-looking, intelligent, perceptive, witty, and the owner of a failing nightclub with Barry Humphries in it. On the surface, he seems a decent enough sort, but he is after all the Devil, and is therefore compelled to perform constant petty, spiteful and uncharitable acts. In particular he is unable to prevent himself being nasty to Dudley's character, despite the fact that he really likes him, and despite the constant hurt look on Dudley's upturned little face. Peter's Devil is a man consumed with boredom by everyday life, something he has had to endure for millions of years; he wishes desperately to be good, to ascend ultimately to heaven, but he knows in his heart that the myriad little sins he must commit to make his daily life palatable have formed an addictive pattern that he will never escape. Worst of all, he has been condemned by God to play jokes and tricks on those around him for ever.

The script was packed full of theological debate of the most entertaining kind – evidence, believes Peter's daughter Lucy, of a degree of spiritual curiosity: 'That's not to say he had some great faith or great belief, but he pondered the question. He may have taken the piss out of it, but I think there were queries. It wasn't just dismissed out of hand absolutely.' At one point George sits atop a pillar box to explain his downfall to Stanley:

> *George*: Now then – I'm God. This is my throne, see. All around me are the cherubim, seraphim, continually crying 'Holy, Holy, Holy' – the Angels, Archangels, that sort of thing. Now, you be me, Lucifer, the loveliest angel of them all.
>
> *Stanley*: What do I do?
>
> *George*: Well, sort of dance around praising me, mostly.
>
> *Stanley*: . . . Immortal, invisible, you're handsome, you're, er, you're glorious, you're the most beautiful person in the world. Here – I'm getting a bit bored with this. Can't we change places?
>
> *George*: That's exactly how I felt.

Stanley's ordeal begins when he is stalked by George (in full cloak and fashionable sixties sunglasses), who saves him from committing suicide in return for his soul. He is given a trial wish, and asks for a Frobisher and Gleason raspberry ice lolly, which George rather unimpressively buys from a newsagent's. Patting his pockets as Peter occasionally did, George utters the immortal line: 'Have you got sixpence? I've only got a million pound note.' George takes him to the Rendezvous Club, an enterprise which is collapsing because his business partners (each representing one of the seven deadly sins) are so terminally useless. Here Stanley signs away his soul, and the contract is filed in the 'M' drawer:

> *George*: Let's see, er, Machiavelli, McCarthy, Miller, Moses . . .
> *Stanley*: Moses?
> *George*: Irving Moses, the fruiterer.

George explains that Stanley can end any wish by blowing a raspberry, and sends him on his way. His first desire is to become articulate and educated, an intellectual: this was the cue for a reworking of the old Establishment sketch where the couple grope verbally towards sex, although in the finished version Dudley based his performance on a Welsh neighbour called Griffiths. The ploy does not work: Margaret Spencer cries rape as Stanley pounces.

His first raspberry blown, Stanley returns to George's side, and receives a piece of extremely valuable (and presumably autobiographical) advice about seducing women:

> *George*: As far as sex is concerned, patience is a virtue. In the
> words of Marcel Proust, and this applies to any woman
> in the world, if you can stay up and listen with a fair
> degree of attention to whatever garbage, no matter how
> stupid it is, that they come out with, 'til ten past four in
> the morning – you're in.

Armed with this information, Stanley decides he will be Margaret's husband, a powerful, rich and influential man, with a country estate, yachts, servants and a phone in the lav; but again, the fantasy goes awry. A delightfully ingenious feature of the script is that every picture painted by Stanley contains a loophole that is exploited by a character played by Peter. It is never entirely clear whether the Devil himself is destroying Stanley's dreams, or whether, as George puts it, 'there's a lot of me in everyone'. In this instance, Margaret largely ignores her husband for the attentions of a handsome music teacher; Stanley bemoans the fact that 'I often wish I'd been forced to take up an instrument myself when I was young.' Eventually she ends up in the bath with Stanley's business associate, an arms dealer played by (and indeed named) Peter.

That night, Stanley is tempted in bed by Lust, played by Raquel Welch, who thrusts his head into her cleavage. In fact Peter wanted to call the film *Raquel Welch*, so that the posters would read 'Peter Cook and Dudley Moore in Raquel Welch', but the distributors were not impressed by the idea. Dudley eventually wore three pairs of pants to film the scene, in the (unfulfilled) hope that they would hamper his inevitable erection.

Stanley's fourth wish – to be someone women yearn after, a pop star, sexy, young and dynamic – is destroyed in the most delicious manner possible, in a scene which demonstrates that even if Peter couldn't sing, he understood the psychology of pop music absolutely. Attired in Tom Jones-style lamé, Stanley belts out a number on a TV pop show, enshrining sentiments that entirely matched Dudley's own outlook on the female sex:

> *Stanley*:   I'm on my knees, won't you please come and love me
> I need you so, please don't go, stay and love me
> Tell me you're full of yearning for me
> Touch me and say that you can't live without me
> Tell me you need me, touch me and say, oh love me!

But the next song up is by the latest pop sensation, Drimble Wedge and the Vegetations – Peter, that is – performing a psychedelic number in a flat, uninterested monotone:

> *Chorus Girls*:   You turn me on
> *Drimble Wedge*:   I don't love you
> *Chorus Girls*:   You plug me in
> *Drimble Wedge*:   Leave me alone
> *Chorus Girls*:   You switch me on
> *Drimble Wedge*:   I'm self-contained
> *Chorus Girls*:   You light me up
> *Drimble Wedge*:   Just go away.

Turning to one of the adoring girls in the front row, he sneers: 'You fill me with inertia.' The audience immediately deserts the despairing Stanley en masse.

Stanley returns defeated to George's side, in a scene which perfectly displays the mixture of charm and wickedness that Peter had invested in his Satan. Turning up at a pretty country cottage as 'the Frunigreen Eyewash Men', they offer the little old lady who lives there – Mrs Wisby – a chance to win a beautiful silver tea service and a night out with Alfred Hitchcock if she can only answer a simple question. The drawback is, she must have ten bottles of Frunigreen eyewash in her house to qualify; as she does not, George lets her bend the rules by bicycling down to the village to buy them. While she is away they mind the kitchen. George eats all her raspberries with a pound of sugar and a pint of cream, proffering Stanley a wooden spoon from inside his overall, a reference to medieval art that demonstrated a healthy variety of cultural reference points. Finally, the old lady returns to hear her 'simple question':

George: How tall is the Duke of Edinburgh?
Mrs Wisby: Ooh, I've read it somewhere . . . six foot one?
George: Alas no, it's six foot two, and this means you've lost ten pounds.

Despicably, he extracts the money from a pot on her mantelpiece and they depart, Mrs Wisby waving sweetly over the garden fence. It's impossible not to feel sorry for her, and at the same time impossible not to be secretly delighted at George's trick.

After an experimental animation sequence that ultimately fails to work – Stanley's fifth wish being a desire to become a fly on the wall – the last two fantasies are wonderfully funny. The first one seems watertight enough: George offers warmth and love, a cottage in the country, two beautiful children playing in a sunlit garden, and Margaret overcome with excitement as the car bearing Stanley bowls up the drive. The drawback is that Margaret and Stanley are actually having an affair, and that her husband Peter is in the car with him. He is Stanley's Oxford tutor, and everything in the fantasy, the house and the children, are his. He is also impossibly nice: he has bought her a present, he doesn't mind that she has forgotten their wedding anniversary, he is innocently happy to let them drive into town together while he does all the housework. Consumed by mutual guilt, Stanley and Margaret are forced to try and consummate their relationship in the car while singing Peter's praises and saying 'I love him', an enterprise which is of course doomed to tear-sodden failure. How it must have galled Dudley to film that scene, especially given the fact that during the shoot he had developed a genuine crush on Eleanor Bron.

Stanley's last chance – although he does not know it, as he has forgotten the trial wish at the start – is carefully specified. He wishes to meet Margaret for the first time, he says, and to fall in love with her – for ever. Both of them are to be young, in perfect health, and white; the surroundings are to be beautiful and peaceful; and most important of all, there are to be absolutely no other men in her life. George, apparently impressed, snaps his fingers and – hey presto! – Stanley is transformed into a lesbian Trappist nun at the convent of the Leaping Order of St Beryl. His luggage is burned by other nuns. He is shown to his cell, which has a wooden pillow and a large picture of the Mother Superior (Peter) on the wall, with the legend 'Big Sister is watching you'. The scenes which follow, with Dudley desperately trying to blow a surreptitious raspberry without attracting the attention of Peter's serene Mother Superior, are among the funniest in the history of the cinema. Stanley Donen, who eventually directed the picture, recollects that 'I had trouble not ruining the take because I kept having to laugh off camera during that scene. I was actually bleeding from biting my lip, it was so absolutely wonderful.'

Donen, whose most famous screen credit was *Singin' in the Rain*, came on board early in the scripting stage. He had been wowed by *Not Only . . . But Also*, while Peter and Wendy had been impressed by his direction of the film *Charade*, and the two sides had groped towards each other. So delighted was Donen to get the chance of working with Peter that he turned down *Hello Dolly*, for which he would have been paid more than the entire budget of *Bedazzled*. He, like Peter and Dudley, took no advance wages from *Bedazzled*, preferring to spend the limited budget of $600,000 on screen instead. It was at Donen's insistence that Peter inserted the leaping nun sequence from the TV series wholesale into the film, on the grounds that nobody outside Britain would ever have seen it. He considered that Peter's script was an absolute masterpiece, and he was right. It was episodic, which is always a weakness in a feature film, and pointed to a lack of development from Peter's origins as a sketch writer; but it was also intelligent, thought-provoking, touching and marvellously funny. The filming was set for the summer of 1967. The question was, could Donen translate Peter's first-rate script into a first-rate feature film?

Towards the end of 1967, the *Daily Express* ran a feature, along the lines of What-ever-happened-to-Peter-Cook: 'A year ago, he was a pillar of entertainment. He and Dudley Moore were the darlings of television, backing their own shows by appearing week by week as guest stars, the most original young men ever to hit the mass medium. Then, unaccountably, Cook virtually disappeared. The television companies which pursued him were largely out of luck. God and the Devil had claimed him and his typewriter. For Cook it has been a big, expensive decision at the height of his fame and earning power – for nobody is more quickly forgotten that the performer who removes his face from the fickle public.'[43] Peter himself estimated that writing the script of *Bedazzled* had cost him in the region of £50,000 in lost wages. Everything was riding on it.

In fact, in the eighteen months following *Not Only . . . But Also* and the *Rustle of Spring* benefit, Peter had taken just two jobs, so dedicated was he to his lonely obsession with perfecting his film script. One was the *Not Only...* Christmas special. The other was a cameo role in Jonathan Miller's TV film of *Alice in Wonderland*. Miller's lavishly budgeted BBC film was *Alice* for grown-ups, a visually stunning, languorous, bone-dry adaptation played to the fashionable sound of sitars, with no concessions to commercialism or to a young audience. Alice herself became a sullen, pouting, pubescent with no sense of bewilderment; the whole piece was strangely lacking in either humour or fear. 'Alice is a story of domestic strife,' Miller had explained. 'The King and Queen of Hearts are obviously Alice's parents and the Knave is her elder brother. Even the changes of size are only a child's sense of growing up. It's a marvellous, hard description of Victorian domestic life.'[44]

One of the few characters to inject humour was Peter, who played the Mad Hatter at the cobweb-strewn tea party in his 'Isn't she a sweetie' voice from *Not Only . . . But Also*. Wilfred Lawson and Michael Gough (two of the regulation star-studded cast) appeared as the Dormouse and the March Hare with no concession to mammaldom – they had been shorn of their 'disguises', explained Miller – although Peter did at least wear a top hat. 'His was a rather brilliant performance,' Miller recollects, 'but I think I probably allowed him to do too much, and it went slightly over the top during the tea party. Though there was a marvellously inventive thing which came completely unexpectedly during the final courtroom scene, when he dreamed up this extraordinary coming and going as he entered the courtroom – for which we then set up, under the pressure of his invention, a shot which would actually enhance the effect. The cameraman, Dick Bush, built himself a great swing, slung from the roof of the studio, which allowed him to swing fore and aft as Peter advanced and retreated. Peter was mainly a solitary performer; he found it very difficult to meet people's eyes. Playing the Mad Hatter, it was very fortunate that I chose (to cast him as) someone who in fact was a lunatic, who had no relationship with the other participants at the tea party.'

The *Not Only . . . But Also* Christmas Special of 1966 further exacerbated the slight *froideur* in relations with Dudley. Peter devised a quite hilarious opening sequence in which Dudley attends his first hunt with the Berkeley. Socially out of his depth and unsure what to do, he allows Peter to provide him with a large fox costume with fresh lamb cutlets pinned to it. He then sets off across country pursued by the hounds, a sequence that Peter insisted he film for real. Dudley later remarked that the sketch entirely summed up his relationship with Peter at the time: 'I thought, "This isn't massively funny." There was an element of sadism. It was Peter's idea. Peter *laughed* at that idea.'[45] So, indeed, did most of Britain.

Their disagreements, as ever, had no effect on their ability to make each other laugh. Dud spent much of the programme in tears of laughter, particularly during a Pete and Dud conversation in which Pete pooh-poohs unexplained phenomena, for instance the Surrey Puma:

> *Pete*:   There's a perfectly rational explanation, namely that a
> sheep has broken into a chemist's, got hold of some
> benzedrine, and is rushing round the countryside in a
> state of excitement.

Eventually Dud is kidnapped by aliens, the chief 'alien' being Pete with
tentacles sticking out of his cloth cap: 'I am a superior being, so watch
it,' he says before explaining that Dud has been chosen to repopulate
Pete's dying planet: 'You are to be a stud, Dud.' The Christmas show also
contained a sketch featuring Peter as a fairy cobbler whose wife, played
by Dudley, has been unfaithful to him. As always there were no retakes,
so when Peter accidentally came out with the phrase 'a cumbler's hobble
wage' he had no option but to recover his composure masterfully and
work the mistake into the script, leaving Dudley giggling helplessly.

Elsewhere in the forty-five-minute special there was another swingeing
parody of the Establishment Club, a long, rambling series of sketches
linked in an experimental, pre-Pythonesque manner. Peter played Hiram J.
Pipesucker, a thinly disguised Alistair Cooke, fronting a report on Swinging
London: 'I think it was Jonathan Miller who said, England swings like a
pendulum do.' The club in question was a converted Soho public lavatory,
with the Rolling Stones and Alf Ramsey already signed up as members, and
ten thousand people trying to get in on the first night. The doorman, played
by John Lennon, explains that there is 'a £5 waiting list'. The whizzkid
owner, played by Dudley ('Young, adventurous and horrible'), boasts that
he is hoping to open several more branches – 'A huge lavatory chain.'

The filming of *Bedazzled* took up most of the summer of 1967, and was
distinguished by its sense of optimism. Stanley Donen recalls: 'When people
ask me about the movies I have made, and they say it must have been a lot of
fun making A, B or C, I say I only had fun on one movie in my life and that
was *Bedazzled*.' Peter kept everybody in stitches, except for Raquel Welch
who did not get any of his jokes, and when Movietone News came to do a
report from Syon House (the location for Heaven), Peter and Dudley took
over their cameras and presented it themselves. Donen did, however, keep
the cast on a very tight rein. He was a professional film-maker working
on a tight budget, and permitted none of the indiscipline and messing
about that had characterised the TV series (and indeed had made the TV
series so enjoyable to watch). As with Bryan Forbes, Peter found himself
overawed by the expensive paraphernalia of cinema, and allowed himself
to be led meekly from shot to shot.

The results were excellent, but they weren't recognisable as anything
Pete and Dud had ever done before. The film was polished, fast-paced and

choppily cut, awash with Dudley's jazzy incidental music, full of visually impressive long shots. Any spontaneity had been carefully rehearsed out. Audiences and reviewers were puzzled. Where were the cloth caps and grubby overcoats they had been looking forward to? Where were Dudley's helpless giggles? Box office takings tailed off and reviews were mixed. 'Funny, but what went wrong?'[46] ran the headline in the *Daily Mail*. American reviewers were kinder, but not much. There was a glamorous New York premiere, attended by all Peter and Dudley's friends from *Beyond the Fringe* days; Peter even found time to appear as best man at Peter Bellwood's wedding. *Bedazzled*, though, was never going to do massive business in the States. A British film with an almost entirely American-free cast, whose main character was a highly sympathetic Satan, was hardly the sort to pull them in across the Mid-West, however good it was. It did respectably in the end, taking five million dollars, but as far as the distributors Twentieth Century Fox were concerned, that wasn't good enough. The intended follow-up (a medical musical called *The Whack*, about 'rejuvenation, acupuncture and spiritualism') that Peter, Dudley and Stanley Donen had already been discussing, was immediately shelved.

Dudley, naturally enough, blamed the script that he had been prevented from helping to write. 'It was rather gawkily written,' he says, pinning the blame squarely on Peter's desire to have the solo writing credit.[47] Peter preferred to point to the manner in which Donen had shot the film: 'I think we were acutely aware that the film was costing money. It wouldn't have been made if Stanley Donen hadn't directed it. I'm extremely grateful to him for making the movie; but I think we were too overawed. I don't think we relaxed enough in performing, and we did takes which we weren't satisfied with, which were too tight.'[48] Dudley concurred that he and Peter had been too timid with the director: 'Stanley Donen had a great sense of humour, but he held us down very strictly. We didn't feel the same freedom as we had in the television series. I can see why people objected to the film, it's gauche, it's awkward, it's not as flowing as our other work.'

One problem was that Peter was not sufficiently engaging when playing himself (as he was, to all intents and purposes) to attract the sympathies of a mass audience. He was a natural comic turn, but there was something too vapid and distant about his performance as a leading man. A successful leading man – as Dudley Moore later became – has to be prepared to offer his real self to the audience, and must not be afraid to show vulnerability. Peter was afraid to show vulnerability even to his closest friends. Audiences could detect his reticence, even if they did not analyse it as such. His co-stars all had concerns along these lines, which at the time they were reluctant to voice. 'It may be that essentially he was always a solo performer,'[49] reflects

Eleanor Bron. Barry Humphries is more forceful: 'He was a very bad actor. You can see it, you can even see how nervous he is.' Dudley Moore goes yet further, describing his former partner with hindsight as 'one of the world's worst film actors. He even enjoyed the idea of post-synching because he though it might improve the performance. He was much too self-aware. But he still liked the film a lot. He never brooded at all, as far as I know, about the rather iffy reviews and notices that *Bedazzled* got. He just liked the idea of being a movie actor.'[50]

Of course Peter would have been cut to the quick by the subdued reaction to the film, but he would have been keen to prevent Dudley becoming aware of any weakness. Also, he knew in his heart that the critics were wrong, that it was truly a great film. Despite the limitations that Barry Humphries discerned in Peter's performance, he for one regards *Bedazzled* as 'a very underrated, brilliant picture'. Mel Smith, a comedian whose later career with Griff Rhys Jones was unquestionably influenced by Pete and Dud, regards it as 'a terrific film. It is actually terribly, terribly funny.' Smith even believes that Peter's detachment adds to the Satanic characterisation: 'He was always slightly removed from it all, which is like a wonderful technique all of its own.' John Wells, who thought it 'a very very good film', recalls that Peter was happy with the product but not with the press reaction to it: 'He knew this was probably the crucial point in his career.'

Outside Britain, *Bedazzled* was a raging success – not that it mattered – in the rest of Europe, where they had never heard of Pete and Dud. In Italy, where the religious theme fascinated the viewing public, it became the third most successful film of the year. For a while Peter became an object of fascination to the Italian tabloids, who linked him romantically with Raquel Welch, Candice Bergen and others. Federico Fellini telephoned to offer him the lead in *Satyricon*, before subsequently withdrawing it upon discovering that he was a Scorpio. Peter was relieved when he in turn found out that the part would have required him to writhe around in manacles, stark naked. He had also been offered the lead in another European film opposite Brigitte Bardot, which he had turned down 'out of stupidity. I thought she was the most attractive woman in the world, but I didn't like the script. In those days it was almost mandatory to go to bed with her . . . and I turned it down. I mean, how fucking stupid can you get?'[51]

When the dust had settled, it was clear that the jury was still out on Peter Cook the film star. Hollywood was certainly no longer interested for the foreseeable future. Peter analysed the situation, and came up with a profoundly misguided set of conclusions: that the two things holding him back were Dudley Moore, and the need to be funny. In fact, these were the two principal foundation stones upon which his screen career was built. Peter was a brilliantly perceptive man, but perception and self-perception are two entirely different things. In the wake of *Bedazzled*, the press had often quoted Stanley Donen to the effect that Peter could become the next Cary Grant (although he now denies ever having said it). There is no doubt that the idea of becoming a romantic light comedy lead became fixed in Peter's head as the only way to make the next quantum leap forward.

Only a year previously he had rejected the possibility of diversifying in such a manner outright. Now, in an unusually revealing series of newspaper interviews, he signalled his intentions. He told the *Express* that 'You are, in fact, no more than a bore unless you have moved on and at least tried to find some different kind of comedy. I see a great danger of becoming prematurely middle-aged – an affluent gentleman completely unfulfilled simply because there was an easy route. Over the past three years I've appeared as a forty-five-year-old loony. Now I'd like to do a few things in which I appear nearer myself.' He informed the *Mail* that: 'I'd like to diversify a bit. Every time I stare at myself in the mirror I think, "Good Lord, there's a romantic lead I see peering at me."'

For a decade, Peter's career had been expanding virtually unchecked, meeting almost no resistance, like the universe spreading outwards from the Big Bang. Only the collapse of the satire boom had temporarily hindered his progress. Now, he hoped he had encountered nothing more than another minor glitch. Deep down, though, he must have feared the truth: that he had reached the limit of even his considerable abilities. The explosion was running out of gas.

CHAPTER 9

Nice Though This Be I Seek Yet Further Kicks
Family Life, 1964–71

Peter's relationship with Wendy had stuttered through the *Fringe* and Establishment years, surviving rather than underpinning the whirl of professional commitments and its accompanying sexual licence. The nature of Peter's work entailed his being surrounded by a permanent crowd of friends and admirers, and he made sure that his home life was not dissimilar. He preferred, if at all possible, not to be left alone. Wendy, by contrast, had long yearned for a more conventional marital existence. The arrival of their two daughters Lucy and Daisy had forced Peter's hand; but any doubts he may have entertained about the appeal of domesticity were dispelled by the lavish outpouring of love and affection for his children that welled up within him. He was fiercely protective of his girls, especially where the press was concerned. He explained: 'I'd rather my children were known for what they did and what they were, than as Peter Cook's daughters. One of the moments in my life when I felt most ashamed was when someone came up to my father and said, "You're Peter Cook's father." I felt ashamed because he wasn't just my dad – he was Alexander Cook.'[1] Alec Cook's asymmetrical ears, a trait shared by his son, were inherited by Daisy. Otherwise, the two girls received the best of their parents' good looks.

On returning from America, the family did not go back to Battersea – Peter had found South London 'drab and seedy'. Instead they moved in with the Luards, then to a rented flat in Knightsbridge, until such time as Wendy's daily house-hunting yielded a permanent residence. On 24 September 1964 they completed the purchase of 17 Church Row, NW3, a splendid, black-railinged, seven-bedroomed early Georgian terraced house that had once belonged to H. G. Wells. Situated in a gentle, secluded, hilly part of Hampstead, Church Row is a broad, elegant, tree-lined street that slopes downhill into the Churchyard of St John's, and is dominated from below by its graceful spire. Any lingering notions that Peter might have harboured a secret, radical desire to destroy society would have been dispelled by the discovery of his next-door neighbour's identity – it was the Home Secretary, Sir Frank Soskice, complete with permanent police presence – and by the extremely substantial purchase price of £24,000. Although the money was handed over in September, the family did not move in until April 1965; in the ensuing seven months Wendy set to work with a team of workmen, to gut the house and create her dream home.

First, all the pine had to be stripped. The heavy front door, the floorboards, large areas of wall panelling on five floors, even the kitchen furniture, all was stripped to the natural wood. Where there was no wood, dark, thickly patterned William Morris wallpaper went up instead. To add light and space by way of compensation, windows blocked up in the days of window tax were re-opened, and smaller rooms were knocked together to make bigger ones. An aga was installed in the cavernous basement kitchen, which was also fitted with a vast table and two refectory benches so that dinner parties could be held there. At the time, these were all radical, free-thinking ideas in home design. The old dumb waiter, which had once transferred food to a ground-floor dining room (and elsewhere in the house) became instead a taxi service used by Lucy and Daisy to ferry themselves around the building. Virtually all the fixtures and fittings were genuine nineteenth-century antiques, with the exception of the built-in wardrobes, which were treated to look like genuine nineteenth-century antiques. Converted Victorian oil lamps supplied pools of soft light in the evenings. The kitchen was dominated by the huge industrial wheel of an antiquated coffee grinder. In the knocked-through ground-floor drawing room where two cats prowled, a bright yellow Victorian mail cart stood before the fireplace. An ancient sofa had been re-upholstered in olive velvet, a buttoned Chesterfield in tobacco-coloured corduroy, a Victorian armchair in printed plush. The sideboard was early English. On the first floor was Peter and Wendy's bedroom, dominated by a darkly polished nineteenth-century American bed, with a stripped pine rocking cradle at its foot. The huge en suite bathroom featured a free-standing bath with marble slab surround, carved wood sides and an overhanging wall of Edwardian ceramic tiles. The second floor was the nursery floor, an entire storey given over to the children and their nanny. On the third floor, up a steep and creaking wooden staircase, was Peter's rooftop den, an attic conversion with marvellous views over London and a huge old desk, where he would closet himself in the afternoons to work with Dudley, and from which the sounds of helpless laughter would filter down through the house.

Peter took very little part in all this redecoration. 'Anything you like, I chose it. Anything you don't, Wendy did it,'[2] he informed a visiting reporter. In fact, his *pièce de résistance* was situated in the spacious paved garden, under the pear tree: an amazing, detailed, multi-storeyed Wendy House he had commissioned for his adored daughters from a carpenter friend of Harriet Garland's. There the children would sit for hours and play bankers, using autumn leaves to represent huge sums of money. It was an opulent, stylish lifestyle, that Peter would have been unlikely to have emulated at the Foreign Office. It did not, however, give callers a feeling of ostentation: 'The only extravagance,' according to family friend Sid Gottlieb, 'was this *beautiful* Tiffany lampshade they had brought from the States.' Everyone who visited the house remarked on the lamp's loveliness. The idyll was complete, the only fly in the ointment being the fact that the telephone number closely resembled that of the local cinema. Anyone who called enquiring if they had got through to the box office was answered in the affirmative by Peter, using his E. L. Wisty voice. When they went on to ask for programme information, he would reply: 'Mind your own business.'

The basement kitchen became the setting for a series of huge dinner parties, hosted by Wendy with almost military precision. As often as three times a week, every week, up to twenty guests would gather round the big dining table, which literally creaked under the weight of ratatouilles, moussakas and quiches lorraines. Peter, a self-confessedly awful cook, would take no part in the preparation of the feast; instead he would sit and hold court at one end of the table, ensconced in a large Windsor chair. Wendy would sit at the opposite end, on a slightly smaller seat. Lined up between them on either side of the table were London's famous, celebrities of all shapes and sizes assembled in a deliberately eclectic mix. Regular guests included John Lennon, Paul McCartney, Charlotte Rampling, Peter Sellers, Cat Stevens, Peter Ustinov, Ken Tynan, John Cleese, Paul Jones, John Bird, Eleanor Bron, Willie Rushton, Michael Foot, Bernard Levin, Jay and Fran Landesman, Malcolm Muggeridge, Victor Lownes, and of course Dudley and Suzy Kendall. Most of the guests were purposely selected for their fame and interest value, but they were almost all distinguished by the fact that they had sought Peter's friendship, rather than he theirs. As Barry Fantoni points out, 'Peter was *the* sixties icon. Pop stars were presented to him at parties, not the other way round.'

Harriet Garland remembers 'Wonderful, happy, happy evenings at

Church Row, with John and Cynthia Lennon and Paul McCartney. Lennon was there a great deal. Wendy would do this wonderful spread – she was incredibly ambitious – she'd think nothing of roasting a whole boar for instance, and putting it on the table; and it was all wonderfully decorated, with fantastic puddings. I've never laughed so much in my whole life – Peter and Lennon were just frightfully funny together. The two of them would do an act: Peter was always becoming somebody, Barry McKenzie or E. L. Wisty or whoever.' John Lennon, in fact, told Peter and Wendy that he had written the song *Lucy in the Sky with Diamonds* for their daughter. Wendy herself remembers the dinner parties as a source of 'non-stop, freewheeling hilarity'. She was even approached by *The Observer* to write a hostess page for them, detailing the secret of her success.

Most of Peter's old school and university friends had long since fallen by the wayside, unless they had gone on to become involved in the entertainment industry. There were a few unfamous guests, though, in the shape of the cleaning lady and Reverend Hall, the local vicar. Wendy explains that 'I've always been – and still am – fascinated with putting people together who don't normally meet each other, whether it's a Majorcan peasant or somebody who's written an opera, just to see the alchemical reactions.' The pronouncedly cockney world middleweight Champion Terry Downes, for instance, found himself seated next to Bernard Levin. Downes insisted that 'Peter gives the finest parties I've ever been to. It might be Michael Caine or John Lennon, or one of these top people you see on TV, but everybody's mixin'. It boils up to a great evening. Peter never makes himself too busy, never makes himself Jack the Lad. He looks after everybody, especially the women, gives them that little bit of extra attention. My bird's knocked out by Peter. He's a real hundred per cent diamond person.'³

Downes was present at an evening described by Nick Luard in a recent book, *Something Like Fire*: 'For one of Peter's birthdays, Wendy gave one of the finest dinner parties I've ever been to.' Luard recounted how he and his wife sat down with John Lennon and Paul McCartney, the columnist Bernard Levin, the actors Peter O'Toole and Tom Courtenay, the poet Christopher Logue, the designer Mary Quant, Terry Downes, and half a dozen more. 'We sat up into the early hours playing music and talking – about politics and prize-fighting, painting and poetry, theatre, de Gaulle and President Kennedy, the Chelsea Flower Show and the summer sun in Spain. Peter, in an ancient wooden rocking-chair, presided . . . I and my wife Elisabeth were living in Hyde Park Square near Marble Arch. Normally we'd have taken a taxi to get back. That warm summer night we strolled home together beneath the stars, arriving as dawn was breaking.

It seemed the only fitting end to a bewitching evening which belonged partly to the mood of the times. When since has a brilliant acerbic Jewish intellectual broken bread and discussed the meaning of life with a couple of Beatles and a flattened-nosed Bow Bells-born pugilist, to the equal enchantment of all four?'[4] Hopefully never, one is tempted to respond, but there is no doubt that Peter and Wendy's dinner parties warmed the memories of all those who attended them for years afterwards. No doubt it was this effect that kept the Luards so cosy on their dawn stroll home, rather than the summer weather, as Peter's birthday generally tended to fall on 17 November.

Not all the dinner guests shared the Luards' unabashed enthusiasm. While acknowledging that it was 'the party invitation to receive', the American satirists Jay and Fran Landesman, twenty years older than their fellow guests, were initially curious as to why they had been invited. Eventually it dawned on Jay Landesman that 'the reason why Peter and his wife were attracted to middle-aged people like Fran and myself, was because we were the sort of niggers of showbusiness, we were very exotic to England in those days, being from America and having the background that we had. I didn't have a particularly good time.' Paul McCartney was present at the first dinner party the Landesmans attended, and he had been tracked to the house by a gaggle of fans. 'The scene was reminiscent of pre-French revolution days when the hungry masses beat on the windows of the rich, demanding food.'[5] Wendy showed McCartney a copy of the Landesman LP, with its Jules Feiffer illustration on the cover. 'That's . . . that's, er, a nice drawing,' the Beatle offered uncomprehendingly. The party then repaired to a disco in St James's Place, where McCartney recited a few lines of a song he was working on, about a girl named Eleanor Rigby.

A few weeks later John Lennon was the star guest at an even less relaxed occasion attended by the Landesmans. Wendy insisted that Lennon try her Salade Niçoise, but he became embarrassed and refused to touch the dish, because he had never heard of it and couldn't pronounce its name. Then Christopher Logue criticised him for turning down Peter's request for the Beatles to play at the *Private Eye* benefit *Rustle of Spring*. The party had no recourse but to repair to the same disco in St James's Place. 'I got the impression,' says Landesman, 'that Wendy would have liked a little more privacy. But that was Swinging London, that was what you did in those days. You had a lot of people over, you got drunk and had a lot of good times. But in general it fucked Wendy and Peter up, all that, no doubt about it.'

Jonathan Miller's comparison between the *Fringe* quartet and the Beatles still held true to some extent: Peter and John Lennon had become drawn to each other because of their profound similarities, both being sharp, cynical, witty and the brains of their respective writing partnerships. Dudley and Paul McCartney were in each case the housewives' choice of the duo, their wholesome, sympathetic, and in some ways greater mainstream appeal providing a slight source of irritation for their more caustic and dominant partners. In each case, however, the relationship was symbiotic; both Peter and John Lennon knew, deep down, that they performed better with their sidekicks than without. It is interesting too that both men, unaccustomed to deferring to others in public, did so in each other's company, giving each other space in which to perform. The Cook–Lennon dinner party double act gave Lennon more room than Peter ever afforded Dudley. A further similarity, of course, was that by the mid-1960s both Peter and John Lennon's marriages were, although they were unaware of it, on course for disaster.

For a few years from 1965, though, Peter and Wendy were as glamorous as any couple in England. They both looked terrific. One journalist described Peter as resembling 'a dandified giraffe', always kitted out in the latest Carnaby Street fashions. According to Sid Gottlieb, Wendy was 'entirely responsible for his beautiful clothes at that time. She was very very insistent, forever driving him on. Wendy herself was incredibly exotic in those days. She had the most wonderful hair, which she grew down to her hips, and she was always very, very exotically dressed – a lot of long Indian skirts. She was always very carefully presented, but her dress was never ostentatious and never synthetic.' Her hair was by Vidal Sassoon; there barely seemed to be an item Mary Quant had designed that was not in her wardrobe; her shoe cupboard included zip-up platform boots, direct from New York. She was even said to have worn false eyelashes when she gave birth.

The Cooks were right at the top of the 'A' list for parties and premieres, as much for Peter's entertainment value as for their social prestige. Journalist Bill Calthrop remembers Peter turning up for Terry-Thomas's party, lounging indolently in the back of an open-topped prewar MG driven by a producer friend, cigarette in one hand and unspilt drink in the other. At the premiere of Peter Hall's *US*, an avant-garde anti-Vietnam play devised for the RSC by Peter Brook, the cast put brown paper bags on their heads and descended into the auditorium, silencing the audience hubbub; the hush was broken by Peter, sitting in the circle, who provoked a laugh by shouting, 'Are you waiting for us, or are we waiting for you?' Peter was the driving force behind an Oxfam charity concert at the Albert Hall, with Wendy and Elisabeth Luard in charge of the post-show catering; among the guests were Tom Wolfe, David Hockney and the Rolling Stones. When not attending functions, he would relax at his local pub the Flask, and entertain the regulars, who happened to include John Hurt, Robert Powell, Patrick Wymark, Ronald Fraser and James Villiers. 'It was not that Peter had a nose for the centre of things,' explains Elisabeth Luard, 'he *was* the centre of things.'[6]

Behind the glamorous public lifestyle, Wendy laboured tirelessly to keep the whole show on the road. The wild girl of Cambridge had revealed a talent as something of a domestic drill-sergeant. Even the children were pressed into service, contributing half a day's house-cleaning a week when they were old enough, in return for their pocket money. Peter, according to Dudley Moore, was treated with housewifely 'disdain' in private. Barry Humphries, who felt that Peter was 'henpecked' by his wife, recalls that 'It was always quite a surprise, when one rather idolised him, to hear someone speaking to him as though he were a kind of fool.'[7] Wendy was still capable of romantic gestures: she commissioned a life-sized model of Spotty Muldoon for his Christmas present in 1965, and once hired a skywriter aeroplane to emblazon the words 'I love you P. Cook' across the Hampstead sky, although that idea was vetoed by the Board of Trade. Some of their friends, though, believed that she felt out of place in the world she had created; that she had given herself the role of supporting her husband and organising every detail of his life to perfection, and was probably working too hard at it. A slight resentment of Peter's languid and lazy ease had begun to build inside her.

Peter's only escape from the twenty-four-hour showbiz lifestyle was to go and watch Tottenham Hotspur, which he did every time there was a home game, in the company of Sid Gottlieb. A doctor specialising in problems of drink and drug addiction whom Peter had met at a party, Gottlieb occupied the curious position of official doctor to Ronnie Scott's nightclub. A man with many friends in the entertainment world, he instinctively recognised Peter's need for approval and reassurance, and freely gave it. Soon the two became best friends. 'You couldn't have a straight conversation with Peter, but you could have a very illuminating conversation. He knew his stuff, he read masses of newspapers, and was able to tell you what was going on in his particular way. There were one or two voices he used to speak in. A cockney would always creep in, and a totally effete aristocrat, like Streeb-Greebling but more pathetic. That was the one that always creased me.' Like an eager child, Sid Gottlieb would urge Peter to repeat his finest moments, slices of old sketches or former conversations, performed for Sid alone in the car on the way to the game.

Peter had adopted Tottenham partly because they were John Bird's team and partly because they shared their first two letters with Torquay, for whom his support gradually waned into a weekly result check. Sid

Gottlieb didn't actually care much for football, but Peter was not going to attend football matches alone when he could have his best friend by his side. 'I went along because it was immense fun to travel to and from the game,' explains Gottlieb. 'This was an hour or more's entertainment in itself, and what entertainment – passing comments about people in the street, names of streets and all that stuff – he just took off. On arrival at the ground Peter's conduct would be completely different from that of all the other stars who supported Spurs: most of those guys sat in the Directors' Box, and went into the Directors' Office for tea at half time, and had a parking lot. No way did Peter have any of these privileges, nor did he seek them. I would pressurise him for my own comfort. "Oh, we'll sort all that out," he'd say – but in fact we never did, and Peter and I would drive Christ knows where to park the car, and invariably he'd say, "I haven't got any money, can you . . ." Then he'd be hailed all the way from the car park to the ground, by supporters and antagonists alike – of course everybody recognised him – and he'd be besieged by autograph hunters. He did it beautifully, graciously actually. The extraordinary thing about Peter, which impressed me most of all, was his genius for identifying with whoever he was talking to, down to the merest local kid.'

Peter sat in the old stand, where he trained a group of some ten or twelve local kids to embarrass the officials of the away team, who sat below them. The rest of the time he spent shouting and screaming at the players and the referee at the top of his voice, with fervent sincerity. Northern sides, especially, were dismissed as peasants and barbarians. Dudley Moore, who hated football, came along once or twice and was stunned by Peter's behaviour: 'We were at that end of the goal field [sic] and he shouted *continually*. I had to stop up my ears because he was so vociferous.' The only time Peter didn't muck in with the rest of the supporters was when a really big game was on: for the 1967 Cup Final, he and Sid Gottlieb hired a Rolls, and after Tottenham won 2–1, drove round the West End hooting the car horn. Similar celebrations followed the 1966 World Cup Final, at which he had been sitting next to a northern fan; with England leading 2–1 shortly before the end of normal time, the man opened a bottle of champagne and announced, half an hour ahead of Kenneth Wolstenholme, 'It's all over.' When the Germans equalised, Peter turned to him and said, 'If you open your fucking mouth in extra time I'll kill you.' Peter was a truly passionate fan. 'He would go into a very serious depression for hours after a defeat,' recalls Sid Gottlieb. 'We would always go to my home after the game where tea and cake was laid on, and Peter would go straight to the television and turn it on, just to see confirmation that we really had been beaten. Then he'd go home.'

For big away games the pair would travel up in the early morning and sit in the home end of the ground, at Peter's insistence, where Peter would continue to scream abuse at the home team at the top of his voice. He seemed to lead a charmed life, probably because every adult football fan in Britain knew who he was, knew that it was Peter and that he didn't really mean it. 'I saw it hundreds of times,' says Sid Gottlieb. 'He could never accept that the opposition fans could really dislike him.' Peter's run of good fortune came to an end on 27 January 1968, at a third-round FA Cup tie at Old Trafford, when Spurs equalised late in the game. He, Sid, Sid's son Peter and Frank Cvitanovich, a Canadian film-maker, had been standing in the Stretford End, where Peter had kept up a ceaseless barracking of the 'northern brutes' who made up the home team. On their way out Peter and Cvitanovich, who had become separated from the other two, were surrounded by a group of some fifteen to twenty adolescents, aged about thirteen or fourteen, one of whom stepped forward to ask for Peter's autograph. As he obliged he was kicked in the groin and fell to the floor; he curled into a hedgehog ball while they kicked him, splitting his forehead and booting his front teeth clean out. Cvitanovich, who was a huge former American football player, six foot six and sixteen stone, fought furiously and was even more badly beaten. Youngsters, it seemed, were not party to the national consensus of affection for Peter Cook. Eventually the pair were rescued by the police and escorted to the station, where the boys in blue rather needlessly cleared the platform of all non-Londoners by means of a baton charge. Sid Gottlieb was surprised to note that Peter, 'as a sort of upper-class public school character, totally identified with all this action.' His missing teeth, no doubt, were helping to inform his opinions.

Outside football, Peter's hobbies were few. He often recommended books to friends and family – Fran Landesman was urged to read Thomas Mann's *Magic Mountain* – but nobody ever actually saw him read anything other than the papers. Conscious of the need to make Wendy's life as busy as his own, in Autumn 1965 he presented her with the funds to start her own fashion business; the up-and-coming Royal College of Art design graduate Hylan Booker was taken on to design clothes, with Wendy doubling up as boss and assistant designer. 'Peter and Wendy were an idyllic couple really,' cliams Sue Parkin, the children's nanny. 'She'd have presents and flowers. I really think he worshipped her then. I know he worshipped the children. I just think he really worshipped the whole family idea. He was happy in Hampstead with his children and his beautiful wife and success. It was just a really brilliant time.'

Sue Parkin was Wendy's right-hand girl, recruited through a personal

ad in the *Telegraph*. 'I arrived at number 17 Church Row and this, well,
I can only describe her as a dolly bird really, answered the door. Big
eyelashes and loads of hair tumbling over, she really was quite striking,
and I thought she would be the au pair. Anyway, I said, could I speak to
Mrs Cook. And she said, "I *am* Mrs Cook."' Sue Parkin was appointed in
spite of her *faux pas*, and more or less became a fifth member of the family.
At Wendy's insistence, she had to address her employer as Mrs Cook; Peter
preferred to be called Peter. Immediately, the young nanny found herself
pitched into a living and breathing *Who's Who* of British entertainment:
flirting at the door in *Upstairs, Downstairs* mode with Dudley Moore, or
serving breakfast sausages to Paul McCartney and his enormous Dulux
dog. 'I just didn't believe it was happening really.' The only visitor to
whom Peter utterly and completely deferred, she noticed, was Kenneth
Williams: Peter would become part of the audience, in fact, while his guest
turned the tables on him. 'I'd never seen Peter laugh so much as he did
that night,' says Sue Parkin, 'listening to all Kenneth Williams's hilarious,
wonderful voices.' Gaye Brown observed the same phenomenon on a
separate occasion: 'Peter sat at Kenny Williams's feet and this guy
entertained us until I was *ill* with laughter. And I said afterwards as
we were going home, "I've never seen Peter quiet before, listening."' Sid
Gottlieb remembers Kenneth Williams imposing a serious conversation
on the Cook household one evening, a trick that he had only ever seen
Jonathan Miller pull off, of Peter's other friends. 'Both he and Miller
simply refused to be entertained by Peter,' he recalls.

By the beginning of 1967 Peter was contentedly pronouncing himself
middle-aged. He had taken to attending the opera, something he had
openly scorned in the early sixties. The money was flowing in, some of
it salted away in overseas bank accounts. He smoked and drank, but not
to excess: he managed long periods off the cigarettes, and never once got
drunk – 'He was terrified of being drunk,' recalls Wendy, 'because he was
scared to lose control.' He kept himself fit, going for tennis weekends with
the Garlands at Harriet's family home in Great Bardfield. He was a dab
hand at entertaining the children, not just his own but the Gottliebs',
always being ready to start an impromptu game of cricket on the lawn
or a game of football on the beach. He never forgot his parents, and took
the whole family to see them for a week's holiday twice a year, in 1965
and 1966. His sisters were treated royally when they came up to London,
lent the latest fashions by Wendy and packed off to exciting nightclubs.

In September 1965 he spoke of his contentedness to the *Sun* newspaper
(in its pre-tabloid days), in an interview which hinted that the opposite
sex was still, in many respects, a foreign country to him: 'I don't think

I could operate at all unless I was well looked after, which I am. Of all the things I dread, the worst is that awful bachelor state – making the phone call at six in the evening: "Hello so-and-so, you don't remember me, but . . ." You take a girl out and at the close of the evening she says to you indignantly: "You take me to the theatre, you take me to dinner, then at the end of it – in addition to my company – you expect me to indulge in some vile act with you! Do you think you can buy my kisses?" And here is the poor man left on the doorstep, counting out his change and confirming that the evening has cost him £17 18s 6d. "What does this girl think?" he shouts to himself, "that I'm going to spend the whole evening listening to this rubbish pour out of her mouth for nothing?" Everybody ends up hating everybody. Thank God that's behind me. I have my cosy domestic life.'[8]

Dudley envied Peter's cosy domestic life so much that in February 1967 he moved out of his Cheyne Walk flat and bought a seven-bedroomed Georgian house of his own, just round the corner from Church Row, into which he moved with Suzy Kendall. But for all the apparent rock-like contentedness of the family structure that Peter and Wendy had built, it was clear from the *Sun* article at least that theirs was not a meeting of minds. Their relationship was founded initially on love, sex and mutual regard, but they had very little actually in common. In particular, Wendy was becoming increasingly interested in the alternative beliefs, philosophies, diets and lifestyles that became popular in the mid-sixties, which were meat and drink to Peter's comic imagination. She was a serious soul at heart, without a highly developed sense of humour, whose enthusiasms solemnly mattered to her; from that point of view, Peter was probably the worst person in the world for her to have married. At one stage, she believed that she had witnessed an alien spacecraft; she also believed that their house was haunted by the ghost of H. G. Wells. These were the sort of claims that made Peter snort with laughter. Sometimes, she would inadvertently speak in feed lines: 'I'm a romantic about furniture. Look at that chair – who knows who has sat in it?' Such hanging questions were irresistible targets for her husband. 'To begin with it was probably quite healthy to be made fun of,' she admits, 'but eventually it began to erode my self-confidence. I think it was the same with Dudley.' Within the marriage, the appeal of Peter's wit wore off.

'When Wendy told Fran how lucky she felt to be married to such a funny man, we suspected the marriage was really in trouble,' recalls Jay Landesman. 'Fran couldn't believe there could be anyone funnier than Peter Cook. By then, neither could he. Having watched the disastrous effect success had had on so many of our friends in the same situation,

I warned him of the perils which lay ahead. "It'll never ruin me," he said. "I'll have the same wife and friends that I have now. I can handle it." We wanted to believe him, but as his career moved from strength to international recognition, we watched the tiny cracks form in their once-idyllic marriage. I told them the reason we were still married was because neither of us had ever had a success that had lasted more than fifteen seconds.'[9]

'We married very young,' said Peter haltingly, in an unhappy attempt, many years later, to explain what went wrong. 'And we weren't very good at being married. I don't know why. We just started not getting on.'[10] He admitted later to Eleanor Bron that 'women had always been a bit of a mystery to him', on account of his isolated start to life; he had, for instance, found it a distressing experience to be present at his children's birth. According to Bron, 'I think his being really rather beautiful and very attractive didn't make that side of his life any easier.'[11]

Wendy's unhappiness began to communicate itself back to Peter. 'He was in fact nervous of her, let it be said on the record,' maintains Sid Gottlieb. 'His jokes at her expense were never meant to hurt, I don't think, but she could put him down devastatingly and he would go down.' According to Willie Rushton, 'I think she gave him a bit of shit really. And when you're doing rather well the last thing you want to do is go home and be beaten up. After the adoring millions have just been hailing you and waving their hats in the air, to get back and be reminded of your various shortcomings – not the sort of thing he was looking for.' Thus are relationships distorted by fame. The children sensed that something was going wrong. Lucy Cook remembers that 'one morning Daisy and I both literally dragged on his trouser legs, not wanting him to go to work. I'm a great believer that children feel a lot more than they're given credit for, perhaps not on a conscious level, but they're sensitive to emotions that run underneath. And I think perhaps there was stuff going on then between Mum and Dad that was not spoken, and we just didn't want him to leave, we didn't want him to leave the house.'

Wendy turned to Sid Gottlieb for advice and therapy, followed by her husband. Sue Parkin – who had herself become distressed by the turn of events – followed suit, giving rise to an absurd situation in which every adult member of the household was going to the same person for counselling. It was all to no avail. 'I don't think it was conceivable that Peter could have been happy,' explains Sid Gottlieb. 'I don't think he knew what it felt like. If you take the start, if you take the outlines of his evolution from a young boy, sent away, millions of miles away to England, to a residential public school; never any length of time of association with his parents or with his sisters even, or with chums in a home setting. This was a child alone, this was a boy alone, this was a man alone, he was *always* alone, from whatever time it was that he signed off from entertaining people.' Loneliness was perhaps the only thing in the world that Peter feared, but he always carried his loneliness within himself. 'Alone together, I could no longer be comfortable with Peter,' relates Wendy. 'He was never rude, or abusive, or sullen. He was polite. But I never knew what he really felt about anything. Humour was his way of keeping the world at bay, and he never let anyone, not even me, right inside.'[12]

Even when he had found love, Peter continued to search for it. Sexual infidelity bedevilled the marriage, both his and Wendy's. She blamed him for having been the first to stray from the relationship; he claimed that she was at fault, for having been the first to transgress after the actual wedding. In fact it wasn't really important whose fault it was. What mattered was that they were both looking for something that they knew the other could not provide. Peter's was a lifelong, hopeless quest for reassurance. With his looks and his fame he was not short of willing conquests, but the fact that they found him attractive and desirable in the first place was what mattered. 'I would have said that Peter was looking for instant adulation rather than instant sexual gratification,' suggests Barry Fantoni, 'and there is a big difference.' Wendy confided in Willie Donaldson at the time that she had considered hiring a barrage balloon, and flying it across London with the words 'Peter Cook is an attractive man' emblazoned across the side. All of which is not to say that Peter was incapable of straightforward lust; but there is no doubt that his behaviour was principally governed by a longing for intimacy. He might be faulted for amorality, rather than for immorality.

This was partly, but not entirely, conditioned by an absence of childhood cuddles. Peter also had a profoundly addictive personality, and had not yet come to realise it; the rush, the 'fix' itself, was what he sought, over and above the general pleasure to be derived from taking part in an activity. The rush of onstage adulation, the thrill of the horse race finish after an hour of moiling tedium, the romantic 'fix' that comes with finding a new lover. Peter was addicted to being wanted. Actual drugs, the chemical means of creating or prolonging a rush of excitement, had only just made an appearance in his life through showbiz contacts; from being profoundly disapproving of them at first he quickly became hooked. Speed was widely prescribed as a slimming drug in those days, and he took to 'borrowing' it from his female friends' medicine cabinets. He began scoring purple hearts in Soho and was totally hooked by the end of the decade.

'You could always tell, on television, when he was on amphetamines,' remembers Sue Parkin. 'He'd have a dry mouth and you could see him licking his lips.'

Wendy, by contrast, temporarily diverted her unhappiness into drinking too much. Peter's racing buddy, Jeffrey Bernard, later boasted in print how he had dropped round one night, seduced her, then robbed her when she was drunk: 'I tapped her for some money. So she started to write me a cheque for £5, and as she wrote the "fi" – of "five" I got hold of her hand and guided it into another "fty", so that the cheque was for £50, and I was at the bank the next morning at one minute to ten to cash it. She was pissed but she was loaded. He was very mean, Peter.'[13] Dudley Moore reflects pertinently that 'Peter certainly had a lot of acquaintances, but not many deep friends.' With a few glasses of wine inside her, Wendy was liable to attack the superficialities of the showbiz lifestyle. At dinner with Mr and Mrs David Niven, for example, she laid into her hostess for boasting that they had had to hire an extra suite at Claridges, simply to house all their Christmas presents.

There were rows, walkouts. Wendy turned up at Roger Law's house in Cambridge, having pranged the car on the way up: 'My wife never wears make-up, so my daughter was fascinated by Wendy's cosmetics. Wendy slept on the couch, and the little girl kept getting out of bed and going downstairs to check Wendy out because of all the make-up. And she had a suitcase which was half full of clothes and make-up, and the other half full of bottles of drink. The whole thing was getting out of hand.' When she was absent, Wendy had to leave the children to be looked after by someone else, which bothered Peter because Daisy was asthmatic and liable to serious attacks. Under normal circumstances Wendy was an excellent mother who doted on her children, so the extent of these dramas reflected the depths of her collapse in morale. Peter was frantic with worry and full of reproach. Wendy was not impressed by this aspect of his concern for the children: 'He'd never got up in the night or gone to the doctor's with them. I'm sure he *loved* them, but what is love?' It was all getting horribly messy.

As early as December 1966, Wendy had begun to look for a way out of their dream lifestyle. She admits to having an inner restlessness that militates against domesticity: 'I see a pattern in myself that when things feel settled, I think, "This is incredible, this is awful, is it going to be like this for ever?" And one sort of starts to try and shake things up. That was the start of my going abroad.' She began looking for a holiday home in Provence – no more than a holiday home at this stage – but by the time her search shifted to Majorca in 1967 she had one eye on a permanent move. That Easter the whole Cook family took a holiday at the Villa Colina, along with Wendy's sister Patsy and her husband. The adults would lie in every morning, while Sue took the children to the beach; an experience that Wendy enjoyed so much, she decided to come back out for the whole summer while Peter filmed *Bedazzled*. The authoress Nell Dunn lent her a villa owned by her father, the steel millionaire Sir Philip Dunn, for a month; thereafter she moved into a third villa for the rest of the summer, with Peter paying just one brief visit. 'She was so happy over there, we all were,' recalls Sue Parkin.

An extremely attractive, well-off and manifestly unaccompanied twenty-seven-year-old woman with her own villa naturally became a magnet for the young men of the neighbourhood; especially as the presence of Sue, who had rather modelled her image on that of her employer, doubled the attraction. The local pop group, in particular – three young men named Francisco, Santi and Eusebio – were unusually keen to have their lyrics translated into English. Peter told friends that he was unhappy about the possibility of various Spanish men playing with his children; the story began to find its way around the entertainment world, and one morning a tabloid reporter, sweating in black suit with briefcase, stepped from nowhere on to the terrace of the villa. He had come, he said, to investigate reports that the Cooks' marriage was in difficulties. Wendy sent him away with a flea in his ear.

Towards the end of the year she put in an offer of £3,000 for a picturesque but semi-derelict 300-year-old sandstone farmhouse, and in January 1968 announced publicly that she and the children were moving permanently to Majorca, to cultivate fig trees and olive groves in the sun. 'I'm tired of London,' she told the *Sunday Express*, 'it's a ghastly scene at the moment – like living in a goldfish bowl. How much time I spend on the farm is something Peter and I have got to work out. It will mean being parted at times but that is nothing new – Peter's work often takes him away. The atmosphere will be more conducive to peaceful thought. And I will find the self-discipline to do some writing. Peter and I will divide our time between London and Majorca.'[14]

In fact it would have been patently impossible for Peter to have operated professionally from Majorca for any length of time, but Wendy was happy enough to see less of her husband. By the time the article appeared she had already departed, driving south in a car packed with as many belongings as would fit in. Sue Parkin and the children travelled separately, flying out on the 9 January along with Peter, who was coming for a fortnight's inspection of their new property. On the trip down he confided that he objected to the 'laissez-faire attitude' that prevailed in Majorca, and that he wanted other people prevented from picking his children up and playing with them. 'He adored those children, absolutely adored them,' says Sue.

Wendy and the children moved into temporary accommodation while the interior of their farmhouse was gutted and redesigned, a process that took the best part of a year. Lucy and Daisy were enrolled in the local (Spanish-speaking) school, which they enjoyed, although Daisy has profound memories of nuns jabbing huge needles into her bottom, as she had to endure a course of injections to counter her asthma. Eventually, however, the 'laissez-faire lifestyle' and the amount of work it entailed for Sue Parkin began to pall on the nanny. 'I was getting too fond of the children. Me and these two little girls, we did everything together, we were together all day, every day. They were darlings, absolutely gorgeous children, but I was so fond of them that I felt it was time to go really.' Sue walked out in the summer of 1968 and found a bar job. Wendy was very upset and phoned Peter, who flew out and demanded to know what had happened, to no avail. Sue never saw the children again, although when she had her own daughter, she named her Daisy.

Back in London, Peter was drifting further and further away from his wife. One day in May 1967 he was hailing a taxi outside Turnbull and Asser, when he ran into Judy Huxtable, whom he had not seen for a couple of years. They chatted for a bit. The old spark was still clearly there. A few days later Gaye Brown gave a dinner party and invited them both. 'I don't go to parties, but she said Peter Cook would be at this one, and I went,' recalls Judy. 'I may add, she was setting me up a bit, mind you. She said, "He's going through a bad time right now with his marriage." Things weren't so hot for me either.'[15] The dinner party was a riotous one, and at the end of the evening Judy invited Peter back for coffee. Her husband Sean Kenny was away, and Wendy and the children were in Majorca. She drove home in her white E-type, while Peter followed in his Citroen convertible.

Judy remembers that 'I was twenty-three or twenty-four then, very grand to be inviting married men back to my place. I just was not one of those ladies that bopped around the town. I'd been faithfully married to a Catholic Irishman all this time. I was living in Cheyne Row. I gave Peter whisky after whisky and he seemed quite happy. There were general gropings around but, in fact, I was known in those days as "Untouchable Huxtable". Finally, he went up to bed and I slept on the sofa, because I thought if you got in the same bed with a man, that's it. I didn't know at the time Peter had quite a few famous girlfriends. In the morning he came down and said, "Where am I?" So I made him a very proper breakfast,

with fresh orange juice. He was very straight, which I liked: he told
me his wife was in Majorca and seeing other people, and he was
in London seeing people – he could fit me in between the others
if I liked. When we started going to bed I had to explain that I
didn't sleep around, and it was a traumatic experience as far as I
was concerned.'[16]

Since her Establishment days Judy Huxtable had become a reasonably
successful actress and model, appearing in *Those Magnificent Men in Their
Flying Machines*, *Nothing But the Best* (a 1964 film with Willie Rushton)
and taking the lead in the successful short *Les Bicyclettes de Belsize*. She
was described by one observer as 'remarkable to look at, face wide at
the cheekbones, chin narrow, a tilted nose, a thousand curls.'[17] Slight
of frame and always immaculately presented, her appearance put one in
mind of Pete's ideal woman, as described to Dud in a *Not Only . . . But
Also* sketch:

> Pete: Above all others I covet the elfin beauty, very slim, very
>   slender, but all the same, still being endowed with a certain
>   amount of . . .
> Dud: Busty substances?

Both Peter and Judy had the weakness of vanity, and revelled in their
mutual good looks. Barry Fantoni recalls that 'with those two, there'd
often be a fight as to who could get to the bathroom mirror first. Peter
found his looks fascinating, and he looked at himself in the mirror as if
he was looking at a stranger.'

Their mutual attraction was, however, based on a lot more than physical
beauty. She was scatty, elusive, charming, sensitive, and behind a shy public
persona, extremely witty. She made Peter laugh, and of course he did the same
for her. After years with Wendy, the idea of a girlfriend who shared his sense
of humour was immensely appealing. It was to form a deep bond between
them. Furthermore, Peter fitted the pattern that Judy unconsciously sought
in all her men. Her father, a Lloyd's underwriter, had been a heavy drinker,
and her husband Sean Kenny likewise. Their marriage was turbulent, and
on Kenny's part, jealous, accusatory and threatening. Eventually he was to
drink himself to death. Although neither of them yet knew it, Peter too
had an extremely addictive personality: the exact statistics are disputed, but
the proportion of women with fathers who have a tendency to alcoholism
who grow up and seek out partners of a similar nature is extremely high.
There was, incidentally, one other unexpected quirk that united the pair:
Judy, like Peter, was fascinated by bees, and enjoyed stroking them.

Judy fell madly in love with Peter, and he with her. 'I remember once seeing him with his kids Lucy and Daisy,' she says. 'They were these two exquisite little things. He was bathing them and making them laugh and put their knickers on their heads because they'd lost their bath caps. I thought, "Here is this bright, intelligent, witty, sexy man, and it's ridiculous, he is so *nice* too, cooking and coping," and other *Woman's Own* thoughts of that kind.'[18] Gaye Brown remembers that 'Peter flipped for Judy, completely and utterly. He really wanted her. She was a bit like a drug in a way.' At the end of 1967, Judy became pregnant by mistake. Peter arranged for her to get rid of the baby, but they resolved that one day they would have children together. Peter's marriage, meanwhile, was deteriorating further. Judy recalls that: 'He and Wendy had been to a party near Clapham Common – they were having an argument driving home, and he opened the car door and fell out. He turned up on my doorstep at 3.30 a.m. He later told me that when he returned to Church Row the next morning she was furious and worried, but he deflected it by saying he'd spent the night on Clapham Common doing his best to find shelter.'

With Wendy remaining in Majorca from the beginning of 1968, the relationship became a permanent, if discreet, part of their lives. 'Peter, with all his silk-lined Savile Row suits and Turnbull and Asser shirts, would wash his socks in my bath as I didn't have anything like a washing machine,'[19] Judy remembers. The affair was carried on both in her house and at Church Row, where Peter was supposed to be living alone, but where she would occasionally stay the night. 'Once I had come back with him after the theatre. The next morning we heard the cleaning lady coming in with his breakfast, and he pushed me under the white fur rug on the bedroom floor so she wouldn't see me. Another time John Cleese came bounding up the stairs saying: "Peter, Peter, where are you?" and Peter pushed me into the wardrobe. The wardrobes were very elegant mind you, and Peter had some wonderful clothes, so John started going through everything in the cupboards while Peter got dressed. He was flicking through the suits and suddenly he came to me. "What are you doing there, Judy? Do come out, dear girl!" So I did, and Peter of course made a joke of it. One night Sean, who could get very drunk, came banging on the door in the middle of the night. Peter just got up out of bed, nipped out of the back door, and took me to Dudley's house. It was three in the morning and Peter just said: "We need a bed." Dudley didn't ask any questions, he just showed us to the spare room. When I woke up in the morning it was really spooky because the room was identical to Wendy and Peter's house. The house was a complete replica of Peter's, down to having the same William Morris wallpaper.'[20]

In the autumn of 1968, Judy had to go to America to shoot a British film entitled *The Touchables*. On her return, she moved out of the house she shared with Sean Kenny. He was distraught, having discovered a photograph of Peter in her washbag. She moved into a flat in Redcliffe Gardens with a girlfriend of Mike Nichols, before purchasing a little house in Ruston Mews in North Kensington, the former Rillington Place. By the end of the year, when Peter had been seeing Judy in secret for more than eighteen months, he realised that he would have to tell his wife what was happening. He broke the news to her at Christmas. 'I thought we were going to have our first family Christmas in Majorca,' recalls Wendy, 'away from the telephones amongst the fig trees. And . . . you know, I'm no saint, we'd both had relationships on the side, but this was obviously something serious. He came and said that he'd fallen in love, and it didn't take me too long to say, "Well I want a divorce." I don't think he was ready for that.' Peter was indeed not at all ready for that, not in any way, shape or form. He was utterly, completely stunned. The prospect of losing his children struck him like an ice-cold knife through the heart. The idea virtually paralysed him with fear. But Wendy was adamant that there could be no point in continuing.

Lucy Cook recalls that 'When mum left him, dad wrote *pleading* letters to my grandmother – I think she's still got a couple – begging her to persuade Mum to come back . . . He probably wanted it all, is the answer. He probably wanted sexy Judy Huxtable, the comfortable wife and children and family home – the stability of that – probably wanted it all, and he couldn't have it.' In fact, it is quite impossible to see how Peter could have expected to keep it all, but he did not yet seem to have faced up to the fact. *Private Eye's* Andrew Osmond came across an assessment of Woody Allen provided by Mia Farrow that bears some similarities to Peter's behaviour at this time:

> He lived and made his decisions while suspended in a zone constructed and controlled almost entirely by himself . . . He did not acknowledge other beings except as features in his own landscape. He was therefore unable to empathise and felt no moral responsibility to anyone or anything.

Peter, although acting entirely without malice, had imposed similar limits on his own field of vision. 'He couldn't find it in himself really to forgive me,' reflects Wendy.

Ironically, Peter was an adept, decisive solver of other people's problems, a knight in shining armour to whom his friends would repeatedly turn for help in a crisis. When Nick Garland left his wife Harriet in July 1967, she fled to Peter's: 'He was wonderful, he was very, very good,' she says. He took charge of the situation and got the two sides talking. Similarly, he looked after Gaye Brown when her relationship broke up. Other female friends came to Peter to arrange their abortions, at a time when abortion involved considerable social stigma and immense legal problems. Peter was always soothing, urbane and quietly efficient, and of course paid for everything. He was able, it seemed, to carry out difficult tasks effortlessly, a degree of control far removed from the bewilderment he felt when the parameters of his own world were breached.

Peter demanded that Wendy return from Majorca to live at Church Row so that he could see the children more often, although she continued to take holidays in Spain whenever possible. Lucy and Daisy were transferred to London schools, after one or two arguments as to the religious element in their upbringing (Wendy wanted one, Peter didn't). Peter moved into Judy's Ruston Mews house, taking only the Tiffany lamp and a few clothes. The press did not catch on until late in the year, when Wendy was forced to announce that Peter had moved into another flat 'for work purposes', in order to 'write in peace and quiet'. As far as possible, appearances were kept up. In the first week of March 1969, Peter and Wendy took the children on a family holiday to see Peter's parents. On account of the Majorcan adventure, it was their first visit as a family unit for two-and-a-half years. It was also to be the last. There were no more glamorous dinner parties at Church Row. Peter and Wendy's friends began to polarise into two groups: the great majority gravitated towards Peter, leaving a bitterly upset Wendy with one or two loyal diehards. 'All the more well-known ones wanted to be with Peter. That was really incredible to me,' she reflects. 'I was devastated by the shallowness of the thing showbiz people call friendship'.[21]

It was a terrible time of rows and dramas. Wendy walked out of a screening of Peter's latest film. She accused him of getting their Swedish au pair girl pregnant, incorrectly as it turned out. She was also injured in a car crash. 'The two of them seemed to be off their rocker,' says Richard Ingrams. 'Wendy came here with the two little girls and started barricading herself in – she thought that Cookie was going to come down here and break into the house in the night.' Lucy recalls that 'Mum became absolutely paranoid – she thought that dad had all this wealth and notoriety, and she thought he had a strong possibility of being able to get hold of us. She used to scare us that we might be kidnapped from school one day. Meanwhile, he was a bit scared of her. There was a statue, an iron cast statue of an African head that they had bought when they were together; and I think she thought that Dad admired it, so she sent it to him, and Dad thought it was black magic or voodoo or something. He said, "Get it the hell out of the house, I don't want it."'

Both sides believed that the children would be better off with them – 'Judy and Dad at that time were very much holding out, trying to get custody of us,' says Lucy – but custody was only ever going to be awarded to Wendy. Peter turned to drink and drugs to blot out the awful black misery of losing his daughters, and to help him go on with his job of trying to keep the public entertained. An ex-girlfriend who came with him on a shopping trip to help him buy jewellery for Judy remembers that he was shaking uncontrollably from the amount of speed he had taken. Eric Idle and Bill Oddie bumped into him, tipsy in the Fulham Road, drinking from a silver hip flask after a Chelsea v. Tottenham game. Peter's Citroen convertible, filthy, undriven for two months and covered in catkins, was driven away by a passer-by. Finding an envelope addressed to Peter inside, the man wrote offering to dispose of the car for him; he was arrested (coincidentally by a PC Peter Cook), charged with theft and subsequently acquitted.

'It was all very traumatic, with both of us going through the hell of separation and the misery it caused,' remembers Judy. Peter lived for the days when he could see his daughters. Judy was good with the children, and they became extremely fond of her; Daisy remembers Judy taking her for an emergency asthma injection, and keeping her spirits up by getting her to sing in the doctor's surgery. But Wendy was resentful of the fact that she had been forced to leave Majorca, and of the relative financial superiority that enabled Peter to lavish the children with expensive presents. 'The relationships between he, Judy and myself were not easy or supportive,' she admits.

Eventually Dudley Moore persuaded both Peter and Judy to go into psychoanalysis, and they enrolled with a celebrated Kensington psychiatrist, Dr Stephen Sebag-Montefiore. Dudley and Suzy Kendall came along for the ride. Peter explained: 'I wanted to talk to someone who wasn't involved and who had no bias, so I could sort of talk about how unhappy I felt without being a burden on friends. From my experience, most people I've known going through a difficult time in a relationship only want you to say: "Yes, you're right, how could she do that, isn't it awful?" I didn't want to burden my friends with that. Terribly English thing to feel. But the psychoanalysis helped.'[22] It may have helped to talk about things, but Peter was too smart for the psychiatrist and played intellectual cat-and-mouse games with him. 'He used to come back and say, "I bluffed him,"' reports Dudley. 'And I'd say, "How can he know anything about you then? What is the point?"' Also, Peter simply could not take the whole procedure seriously. When Peter and Judy saw the psychiatrist together, they got the giggles. Eventually, his innate resistence to the whole procedure tended to find its way into sketches:

Peter: Right you are Sonia, will you send in the next patient please.
Sonia: This way please Mr Withersgill.
Peter: Ah Mr Withersgill, come in five guineas, sit down ten guineas, how are you fifteen guineas.

Michael Bawtree, who had not seen Peter in a long while, was surprised to discover that his old friend was seeking psychiatric help, and asked him why. 'I have been talking in other people's voices for so long that, when I don't, I have a terrible sense of emptiness. I don't know who I am,' Peter confessed.

In May 1970 Peter and Wendy's separation was formally announced. By this time they were getting on so badly that he was not sorry to split up with her; but the destruction of his family as a unit still troubled him deeply. He and Judy flew to Jersey just before the news was made public, to avoid the attentions of the press. Judy was due on location in Portugal to film *Die Screaming Marianne* with Susan George; she and Peter spent part of the summer there, and the rest of it house-hunting. In August they moved into Kenwood Cottage, a detached house opposite one of the ponds in Millfield Lane, Highgate. 'What more can I say but that I love Judy very much, and we're living together?' he told the journalists when they finally caught up with him. 'Judy found this place, an old farm cottage. I couldn't believe my luck. I was the first one to call here, and the owner said he didn't want all kinds of strangers tramping over his house. We fixed up the deal at once. I've turned myself into a do-it-yourself man. I moved in with a bed, a cooker and a fridge, started chipping away at the plaster, and discovered a mass of beautiful oak beams which we've varnished.'[23] Peter's flirtation with manual labour completed, Judy was left in charge of the decoration. When she suggested putting up William Morris wallpaper, he replied: 'Judes, I'm sick of it. I don't ever want to be asked about wallpaper and dinner parties and curtains and carpets. Just do whatever you like.'

There were no celebrity evenings, as there had been at Church Row. 'We lived like lovers,' explains Judy. 'We were very close'. They sat and enjoyed each other's company in a haze of smoke. Only a few close friends like Sid Gottlieb received a dinner invitation: 'They'd entertain in the local restaurant,' he recalls, 'Take you to dinner, reciprocate. You'd have them home, they'd take you back. Judy wasn't an entertainer. She was a funny, amusing girl, but it was a totally different lifestyle from the Wendy era.' Without Wendy organising his wardrobe, Peter's natural lack of sartorial elegance began to show through for the first time in over a decade. Ray Connolly, writing in October 1970, found him attired in a T-shirt, the bottom half of a smart pin-striped suit which had split at the crotch, a jean jacket and a pair of lace-up wrestler's training boots. Another journalist remarked on his elegant suits, but noticed that the cuffs and trouser hems were badly frayed. One night Peter went to the Savoy Hotel, late, by himself, looking so scruffy that the Head Waiter felt obliged to inform him that the myriad empty tables were all booked. 'D'you mean to tell me that hundreds of people are going to descend on sixty-five tables at eleven o'clock at night?' asked Peter. Yes, replied the Head Waiter, they were expecting a large party at that very moment. Peter strolled out to the telephone booth in the lobby, phoned the restaurant and said, 'This is Peter Cook speaking, could I have a table for two?' 'Yes, of course, Mr Cook, at what time will you be arriving?' they said. 'In ten seconds,' replied Peter, and strolled back into the restaurant. The Head Waiter didn't say a word. Whatever traumas he had been through, Peter had certainly not lost his sense of panache.

He spent his spare time working on a book of children's verse, because it was in his nature to fill his every working hour with new projects, but he never finished it, or looked like finishing it. The coiled spring was unwinding more slowly now. He eventually converted the most successful poem into a television sketch instead. He also took up playing golf on the local course, for its reflective qualities, even though he admitted he'd always hated the types he met on golf courses. That year he became an uncle, which cheered him up a bit: his sister Sarah, now married to Mike Seymour, produced a daughter named Aletta, whom Peter said resembled Bill Oddie at birth.

Peter was still desperately in love with Judy, and extremely happy to be with her, but he had become profoundly sick at heart at the collapse of his family. He took the extraordinary step of publicly attacking those, like the Underground Press, who advocated the use of drink and drugs: 'To preach drugs is, I think, very sick. I doubt if anyone would approve of a magazine which preached the use of alcohol. What annoys me particularly is that they print all kinds of information about what things give the best trips, without also printing, or even knowing about, the findings of medical research which point out the dangers.'[24] It was a surprising statement, perhaps brought on by a desire to make a good impression in the divorce courts, because his own use of drugs – and particularly drink – was getting out of hand. In November 1970 he was arrested, hopelessly drunk at the wheel of his car, and given a year's driving ban the following April.

Peter's divorce came through on 11 January 1971. He did not try to defend Wendy's petition, which cited his adultery with Judy, although Wendy admitted adultery as well. Judge Curtis-Raleigh formally awarded custody of the children to their mother. Again, Peter flew out of Britain for the announcement, on a filming trip to Australia with Judy and Dudley Moore. The following day Peter and Judy posed for pictures in Sydney and announced their engagement. Judy's divorce from Sean Kenny was harder to arrange, as Kenny had proved difficult to track down, but eventually went through with Peter named this time as the third party. In April 1971, Peter went to visit his parents. It was the first time he had been able to face them for two years.

The divorce, sadly, was not the end of it. A furious campaign of attrition followed through the spring and summer, over the details of Peter's access to the children. Neither he nor his wife could bear to see them leave, when they visited the other. Wendy, who had given up the fashion business and thrown herself into voluntary work with the Hampstead branch of Task Force, an old age pensioners' charity, remained extremely fearful that one day Peter would not bring her daughters back. One afternoon, when he picked up Lucy and Daisy and took them out for a permitted access visit, she telephoned the police in a panic. He then had to spend some time explaining himself to policemen and sorting out the mess. Eventually, Peter became too upset to cope. 'Although he didn't want to leave his children,' explains Judy, 'he really wanted to get out of the country because the divorce was making him feel sick. He needed a change of scene.' Peter packed his bags, and prepared to flee.

CHAPTER 10

Learning to Fly Underwater
Pete and Dud, 1968–71

In the wake of *Bedazzled*, Peter rather enjoyed hoisting the devil's banner sympathetically around town. He appeared in a lunchtime debate at St Mary-le-Bow Cheapside against the Rector, Joseph McCulloch, and put up a spirited defence of Lucifer and his forbearance in the face of the raw deal handed down to him by God. A packed congregation heard the Reverend McCulloch counter with the argument that 'Jesus was, in a way, the greatest satirist of all time,' thereby proving that Alan Bennett's contribution to *Beyond the Fringe* had changed nothing. The Rector, who had expected to face a wild, angry, irreligious subversive, was so surprised by Peter's gentility, humility and excellent manners that he actually wrote to Margaret Cook to compliment her on the way she had brought up her son. 'I'd rather go to hell with Peter Cook than to heaven with the Archbishop of Canterbury,' he confessed.

On 28 January 1968, the day after losing his front teeth at Old Trafford, Peter bravely fulfilled a commitment to defend Satan's point of view on a BBC religious programme: 'I don't believe those fellows were the instruments of God's revenge,' he remarked cheerfully. It began to dawn on TV producers and the organisers of public events, rather belatedly, that he was an absolute natural at the chat show game – witty, articulate, combative and bursting with amusing anecdotes. The organiser of a symposium entitled *This Is England* managed to lure Peter, Alan Bennett and Jonathan Miller up to Manchester later in the year, an event that caused Bennett to reflect in his diary: 'Seven years since *Beyond the Fringe* have hardly altered the relationship between us. We still retain much the same characteristics we had when we first worked together, only in an intensified form. Jonathan is voluble and lucid, Peter seizes opportunities for laughs and delivers good cracking insults, while I make occasional heartfelt but dull remarks. The difference between 1961 and 1968 is that all feeling of competition between us has gone.'

From the beginning of 1968, Peter became a regular and much-requested guest on *The Eamonn Andrews Show*, the principal TV chat show of the time. One of his earliest appearances, recorded at the Royal Lancaster Hotel on 8 January, set the tone for the rest of the series: Andrews spoke to each of the guests in turn, soliciting bogus showbiz compliments for the Hollywood star Zsa Zsa Gabor, who sat alongside him blushing, batting her eyelashes and stroking the small dog that sat sweating in her lap. 'Who do you think is the *real* Zsa Zsa?' gushed the Irishman. The other guests obliged with suitably fulsome remarks before Peter, reclining languidly, fag in hand, replied that the *real* Zsa Zsa was almost certainly a vain, untalented non-event. He was not in the best of moods: his family was due to emigrate to Spain without him the following day. The fur flew, literally in the dog's case, Zsa Zsa pointing out that Peter was the rudest young man she had ever met, who would do well to get his hair cut. 'It doesn't matter, because I'm a raving poof anyway,' retorted Peter to a round of audience applause. The row continued for weeks afterwards by telegram, and Peter later predicted that when he finally expired the newspaper headlines would read 'Zsa Zsa man dies'. The show's producers were delighted, and made his a semi-regular booking as a consequence.

Peter enjoyed appearing on chat shows: they involved little by way of preparation and it was usually easy for him to steal the scene. Once, for instance, he persuaded Dudley (who'd come along to watch) to walk onstage instead of him, to Eamonn Andrews's utter bewilderment. The shallow nature of the programme's remit – in one show he was called upon to debate hanging with the actress Dora Bryan – did not seem to bother him, and may even have perversely appealed. It was all just harmless image-building. After almost two years out of circulation, writing and filming *Bedazzled*, it was time for another co-ordinated assault on the British public. For a while Peter and Dudley had considered having a direct crack at America: Alexander Cohen had offered them a run on Broadway in their own two-man stage show, which they had provisionally entitled *Good Evening*. From there a further assault could be mounted on Hollywood. 'I wouldn't mind being a West Coast blond God,' Peter admitted, 'although I'd be coming in on a piddling little wave.'[1] But experience told him, in the end, that the idea was likely to prove little more than a sideways step, a career-freezing move like the US tour of *Beyond the Fringe* a few years previously. The plan was shelved in favour of a British-based campaign.

One thing Peter and Dudley agreed was that they should move on from *Not Only . . . But Also*. The BBC's offer of a third series was rejected. 'We're bored doing quick little sketches on television,' announced Dudley, who explained that they wanted to make 'a bigger splash'.[2] Peter opined that 'I would rather take the chance to do something I really want to do than work myself into a withered rag by the time I'm forty doing things which I despise.'[3] It was a harsh analysis, and one that indicated a creative burning of boats. The cinema was the thing, and Peter signed no fewer than three film deals: a straight role in *A Dandy in Aspic*, Anthony Mann's film of Derek Marlowe's ingenious spy thriller; an appearance alongside Dudley in Richard Lester's version of the Spike Milligan–John Antrobus play *The Bedsitting Room*; and a reprise of his moustache-twirling antics of *The Wrong Box*, again alongside Dudley, in the Franco-Italian comedy *Monte Carlo or Bust*. All of these were essentially compromises; what Peter really wanted was to star as the lead in his own light comedy vehicle. Sadly, his commercial clout at the box office was considered insufficient to secure him a deal. The most likely possibility in this direction was *The Rise and Rise of Michael Rimmer*, a script by John Cleese and Graham Chapman, about a talentless but two-faced young go-getter who rises to become Prime Minister. Ironically, given that the project had been devised and commissioned by David Frost, the two writers had actually fleshed out the central character as a vicious parody of Frost himself. Apparently oblivious, Frost was set on making the film with Peter in the lead, but he was finding the fundraising a slow and tortuous process. In the interim. Peter decided unwisely to 'keep his hand in'.

The first of the three to be made, *A Dandy In Aspic*, was bedevilled by bad luck from the start, when the director Anthony Mann fell ill and died halfway through shooting; the film's star Laurence Harvey completed the job. Harvey played Eberlin, a British spy charged with tracking down and assassinating Krasnevin, a Russian agent in Berlin. Eberlin was placed in something of a dilemma, as he actually *was* Krasnevin, operating under an alias. Derek Marlowe's script was clever, if labyrinthine; Mann's directing style, faithfully mirrored by Harvey, served only to muddy the waters. The result was impossibly mannered, full of odd angles and sudden zooms, jump-cutting wildly from handheld to still shots and from wide angles to close-ups. Harvey's performance was dour and resolutely wooden, while that of his co-star Tom Courtenay was as camp and mannered as Harvey's direction. In fact the only two of the contributors to emerge with any credit were Mia Farrow, strangely cast as an English debutante, and Peter himself, who enjoyed fifth billing just ahead of John Bird.

Peter was appropriately cast as Prentiss, a vacuous, effete FO type instructed to look after Eberlin; who appears to be interested only in chasing women, but who in fact knows more than he is letting on. His was an entirely respectable performance, but viewers couldn't help wondering what he was doing wasting his considerable abilities on a small hack film part. Peter later described it as 'a mad decision. I don't think I was that embarrassing, but I was slightly embarrassed by it. Luckily, not many people saw it.'[4] The opportunity afforded by the film to revisit Berlin was not as enjoyable as it should have been: nerves about his performance got the better of him, and he finally lost his up-and-down battle to control his smoking, moving to a permanent forty-a-day habit. An air of impending disaster hung about the location, an apprehension which was to be amply borne out at the box office. For many years Peter claimed to have forgotten *A Dandy in Aspic* and its title altogether, but when he did finally bring himself to discuss it in 1980, he reflected that 'I had the idea of becoming a romantic lead, so I did a film which had me running around with a gun in my hand. But I looked such a berk I couldn't carry on.'[5]

The Bedsitting Room was to encompass yet further personal disasters. A bleak satire on bureaucracy's attempts to administer a Britain destroyed in a three-minute nuclear holocaust, the play was sufficiently hard going on stage to make it an extremely risky proposition to put before a mass cinema audience. Although the script was brimming with ideas, Spike Milligan's inability to handle the conventions of plot structure, so charmingly quirky a feature of his work over the course of a half-hour *Goon Show*, made for a relentless and tiring ninety minutes. One look at the cast should have kindled immediate forebodings: it was the usual British stellar band-aid, consisting of Peter and Dudley, Spike Milligan, Harry Secombe, Arthur Lowe, Rita Tushingham, Roy Kinnear, Ronald Fraser, Jimmy Edwards, Michael Hordern, Dandy Nichols, Ralph Richardson, Frank Thornton, Bill Wallis, Jack Shepherd and Marty Feldman. Many of the characters underwent surreal nuclear mutations during the course of the film, Arthur Lowe becoming a parrot and his wife a cupboard, Dudley turning into a dog and Ralph Richardson into the Bedsitting Room of the film's title. Peter and Dudley played two policemen, operating for the most part from a squad car suspended from a hot air balloon, whose job entailed instructing the nuclear survivors ceaselessly to 'Move on.' Peter was given the closing speech, which he was allowed to adulterate personally: 'The earth will burgeon forth anew . . . the lion will lie down with the lamb, and the goat will give suck to the tiny bee.'

The film was only made as an emergency measure, after Richard Lester had been given a million dollars by United Artists to make a

Mick Jagger musical scripted by Joe Orton. Orton had been murdered by his homosexual lover in the project's early stages; once the money had been allocated, though, it had to be spent, so Lester had hurriedly bought up *The Bedsitting Room* as an alternative. His solution to the film's lack of commercial viability was to punctuate it with 'comedy' brass musical stabs. Dudley Moore found him a difficult director to work with: 'He gave peculiar instructions which were hard to follow. He was a very nice man, cheerful and affable, but there was nothing you could do to please him. He wanted different opinions but rejected them all, which was very disconcerting.'[6]

Filming took place in a disused quarry at Chobham in Surrey, from May to July 1968. In the first week of June the wind began to pick up. The ballooning expert crouching in the bottom of the basket, suspended high over Chobham Common, remarked to Peter and Dudley in the car below that he 'wouldn't go up on a day like this'. Peter pointed out that all three of them were, indeed, up on a day like this. 'Well, it's just for Mr Lester,' explained the expert, 'but I wouldn't normally go up – we're at the mercy of the winds.' At which point, with remarkable comic timing, a sudden gust seized the balloon and the battered car suspended from it, and dashed them a hundred feet to the ground. By a miracle, Dudley and the balloonist escaped completely unhurt. Peter was less fortunate. He was taken to the Nuffield Hospital in Bryanston Square, where an entire cartilage was removed from one knee in an emergency operation. He subsequently had to learn to walk again using crutches, which took up the four weeks' holiday he had intended to spend visiting Wendy and the children in Majorca. His future sporting activities would be severely curtailed. The episode put a dampener on Dudley's wedding to Suzy Kendall on 14 June, which Peter was unable to attend. The atmosphere was then even further cast down, with the news three days later that Pete McGurk, bassist of the Dudley Moore trio, had killed himself following his girlfriend's decision to leave him for the group's drummer Chris Karan. *The Bedsitting Room*'s release was delayed until 1969, but everybody concerned suspected from the start that it would be a commercial disaster. In the event Richard Lester was not given another film to direct for almost five years.

The residual prestige attached to the stage play meant that Peter and Dudley's reputations were not unduly damaged by their participation in the failed film version, but they did their best to make up for this with *Monte Carlo or Bust*. A limp Italian-produced attempt to recreate the box office success of *Those Magnificent Men in Their Flying Machines*, the film was originally entitled *Quei Temerari Sulle Loro Pazze, Scatenate, Scalcinate Carriole*. Twenty replica vintage cars with modernised Fiat engines were entered into a fictionalised, slapstick recreation of a Monte Carlo rally of the 1920s. Part of the action took place in Italy and Sweden, the rest in front of a blurred back projection. Every character was a national stereotype: Tony Curtis was imported to play the victorious American, with a clear eye on transatlantic sales, Gert Frobe played the evil German and Terry-Thomas appeared as the dastardly Brit. Peter and Dudley, hired on the strength of *Bedazzled*'s performance in Italy, played two twittish British officers, Major Dawlish and Lieutenant Barrington. The film was not too badly received by the critics, but like the preceding two projects it bombed utterly at the box office. 'Peter acted terribly I thought,' claims Dudley dismissively. 'Really badly. He couldn't deliver other people's stuff at all.' Peter's film career was beginning to resemble a bull trapped in a bullring, charging furiously hither and thither, trying to break through the encircling walls, growing gradually weaker by the minute. Increasingly, the David Frost project *The Rise and Rise of Michael Rimmer* was taking on a crucial significance, outstripping even that of *Bedazzled* to Peter's future prospects.

While waiting for Frost to get the funds together, Peter and Dudley had been approached by Lew Grade, whose ATV company was due to take over the Midlands ITV franchise as of August 1968. He wanted to poach *Not Only . . . But Also* and take it to ATV. Peter and Dudley had already turned the BBC down, but the sums being offered by Grade were considerable. They gave in to his overtures, and agreed to make three one-hour specials, to be entitled *Goodbye Again*. At Peter's insistence the old-fashioned torch singers of the BBC series were to be replaced by a reasonably fashionable selection of rock bands. The first show was scheduled for transmission on 18 August 1968, on a Sunday night, with the next show going out the following Saturday and the last a fortnight later. The intention was to book an American celebrity for each show, with a view to selling the programmes to the States.

ATV have proved better than the BBC at looking after precious old programmes. The first two episodes of *Goodbye Again* have survived, together with an LP record. The third show, together with a fourth programme commissioned and recorded in the summer of 1969, exist in a condition that could easily be restored for transmission if any of the TV channels see fit to pay for the work. What remains, though, is ample proof of the commonly held perception during the 1960s and 1970s that successful BBC shows invariably lost something in the big money transfer to ITV. Shaun O'Riordan, the producer, was not of the comedy Premier League like Joe McGrath or Dick Clement, and clashed with Peter and Dudley, especially when he preferred to reshoot sketches that had not run entirely smoothly the first time. Much of the genuine spontaneity that had characterised the two BBC series was lost. Also, despite the increased programme budget available, studio sizes were roughly the same, so O'Riordan still had to face the perennial sketch-show problem of cramming a number of items into a relatively confined space. Unlike McGrath and Clement, who had opted for a series of intimate and suggestive sets, O'Riordan instead went for one cavernous and detailed set that would encompass every item. The design was specifically linked to that week's Pete and Dud dialogue: thus when Pete and Dud found themselves arrested in the first week, the entire show took place in a huge prison; the second week's show, in which they discussed medical matters, was played out in an enormous functioning hospital ward; and the third show, in which they pontificated about each other's physical fitness, took place in a spacious and well-populated gym. It was a profound misunderstanding of the importance of physical intimacy to the Pete and Dud act. It was also extremely confusing, as the dialogues did not take place until the second part of each show, so there was absolutely no explanation as to why Ike and Tina Turner were belting out *River Deep Mountain High* against a background of nurses, drip-feeds and elderly patients.

The need to fill sixty minutes each week told on Peter and Dudley's creative abilities and busy schedules. As a result sketches which they once would have pruned were allowed to run too long, giving the shows a slight air of slackness. The rock groups and the long hair that Peter and Dudley now sported did not help either: their cast of elderly upper-class twits and sad working-class bores took on a more subversive air when acted by well-spoken, clean-cut, short-haired boys performing within the then still dignified and old-fashioned surroundings of the BBC. Their comedy now seemed to be coming from outside the Establishment rather than inside, culturally as well as geographically. All of which is not to deny that *Goodbye Again* contained some marvellous moments: it was the overall framework that was lacking.

The first show, as far as can be pieced together from newspaper reviews and gramophone recordings, introduced a sophisticated Chelsea version of Pete and Dud named Peter and Dudley, and featured a version of *The Trial* in which the original Pete and Dud found themselves under arrest without knowing why. Pete chose to defend Dud, an idea inspired by his Cambridge notion of defending David Frost against the charge of having no bicycle lights:

Judge: Where were you on the afternoon of the alleged offence?
Pete: My client refuses to answer that question – on the grounds
            that he has forgotten.

The judge, incidentally, was also played by Peter, a performance which very
much prefigured his triumphant parody of Mr Justice Cantley's summing
up in the Jeremy Thorpe case, at an Amnesty revue some years later.

The first show was chiefly remarkable, however, for an astoundingly
confessional sketch which broke – for the first and last time – all Peter's
previous unwritten rules about directly airing his personal life in public.
Peter and Dudley played themselves – retitled for the occasion as Peter
Rae and David Moon – in a thinly disguised rehash of their real love
lives. Facts, names and places were chopped up, mixed and doled
out arbitrarily between the two men, but were clearly recognisable
as facts nonetheless. The sketch opened with Dudley grappling with
a Spanish-speaking operator as he tries to contact his girlfriend, who
is living not in Majorca but in Acapulco. The girlfriend, named Penny
Garland (an obvious reference to Harriet Garland), turns out to be taking
advantage of her freedom in the Latin sunshine to sleep around, and is
having an affair with a photographer named Terry (another clear reference,
this time to Dud's ex-girlfriend Celia Hammond, who had left him for the
photographer Terry Donovan). What Penny does not know, however, is
that Dudley has begun an affair with a lover called Judy. 'I imagine your
relationship with Judy in no way alters your very deep personal feelings
for Penny,' remarks Peter sarcastically. Dudley has enlisted his friend's
help to provide bogus alibis – late work meetings, and so on – to enable
him to continue the affair with Judy, undetected at long distance.

Peter: Is she very suspicious?
Dudley: No, it's just that I sound guilty when I'm on the
            phone to her.
Peter: You sound guilty? Do you think it's anything to do with
            the fact that you are guilty? Could those two be possibly
            linked together, do you think?

The sketch then continues to its denouement, a long-distance telephone
argument in which the two cheating lovers accuse each other of infidelity
while protesting their own innocence.

This was playing with fire, as Wendy had just returned from eight
months in Majorca and was actually sitting in the audience. It was this
risk factor, the desire to see how close to the edge he could go without
falling over, that had no doubt motivated Peter. At this stage, although she

knew that he had been unfaithful, Wendy had absolutely no idea about his relationship with Judy Huxtable. Peter later explained what was going on to BBC Producer Jimmy Gilbert: 'He used to say that Wendy disapproved of the whole thing of going to ATV, and didn't like the series. She was in the audience, and it was pretty obvious that she wasn't enjoying herself. So he used to try and get some sort of reaction. I don't think the ATV series was a very happy or successful one.'

The second *Goodbye Again*, starring Ike and Tina Turner and Donovan, survives intact, and affords a clearer opportunity for analysis. The most innovative element is that the show contains no punchlines: every sketch, including the musical items, is linked into the next in a continuous and consequently surreal stream. This was a technique first pioneered during an extended sketch in the 1966 *Not Only . . . But Also* Christmas special, and later adopted by the Monty Python team (who have generally been credited with conceiving the idea) in 1969. A great chunk of the budget was blown – as it was in each programme – on a huge troupe of dancing girls who came on and performed for no more than a few seconds. This was something of a satirical response to the financially enforced minimalism that had previously characterised every show Peter and Dudley had ever done: 'We've always had this fantasy of having about thirty seconds of a hundred girls dashing across the stage, just for no reason at all,'[7] Peter admitted later. Each show ended, as the BBC shows had done, with a performance of *Goodbyee*.

The first item in the second show was an extended sketch entitled *Sherlock Homes Investigates . . . The Case of the One-Legged Dog*, with Peter naturally playing Holmes and Dudley a faintly sarcastic Dr Watson: 'I realised for the eight millionth time that I was in the presence of a genius.' The whole sketch took place on film, apparently shot in double-quick time in the same patch of woodland. Thereafter, most of the second part of the show was occupied by that week's Pete and Dud dialogue, which soon drifted away from its supposed hospital theme into a description of a Black Mass hosted by the ubiquitous Mrs Woolley:

> Pete: She moaned and she trembled – and suddenly out of her mouth came a strange tongue.
> Dud: Somebody else's tongue, Pete?
> Pete: No, her own tongue came out, but she spoke in a strange ethereal mystic voice that was not her own. And suddenly she said—
> Nurse: (behind Dud)   The doctor will see you now.
> Dud: That's uncanny! I didn't see your lips move!

> *Pete*:   Well, as in most of these cases, Dud, there is a rational
>   explanation for that fact. The reason my lips didn't move
>   was, I wasn't speaking.

There followed a parody news report based on the Aden crisis, featuring
Rodney Bewes, John Wells and Brian Murphy as various soldiers and
journalists. Dudley, as Sergeant McPepper, is trying to launch a surprise
night attack on the Arabs, but finds himself under intense media pressure
to wait until daylight when filming conditions will be better.

The final sketch, occupying the bulk of the third part, was the one
intended to 'get some reaction out of Wendy' that week. A man, played
by Dudley, goes to see his Teutonic psychiatrist because he is bored sick
with his wife of seven years, who is mother to his two children. He has
fallen in love with a girl called Jane and has begun an affair, and officially
cannot decide between the two, although every time he is shown a picture
of his wife he screams. The psychiatrist suggests Aversion Therapy: he will
be given a tub of strawberry yoghurt every time a picture of his wife flashes
up on the surgery's slide projector, whereas every time his girlfriend Jane's
picture appears he will be smacked around the head with a cricket bat.

> *Psychiatrist*:   You will sensate – or rather feel – I use the word
>   'sensate' advisedly, and wrongly indeed . . .

At this point both Peter and Dudley began to get the giggles.

> *Psychiatrist*:   It seems to amuse you . . .?

Dudley was lost from this moment on, and soon collapsed into hysterics
when a picture of his wife appeared and Peter tried to cram Turkish
Delight into his mouth. Shaun O'Riordan had the good sense not to try
to re-shoot this scene.

The third show began with another filmed sketch, this time a Sherwood
Forest parody with Dudley as Friar Tuck and Peter as Robin Hood, the
leader of a merry band of in-laws ('Outlaws, Tuck', corrects Peter). The
language was cod Shakespearean and the attack on the abilities and
values of 'straight' actors implicit. The action then moved indoors to the
'Sherwood Forest Health Club', a transparently flimsy device to excuse
the as yet unexplained gym setting, where Peter, Dudley, Rodney Bewes,
John Wells and John Cleese performed the Alan A'Dale number from *Not
Only . . . But Also*. This demonstrated in microcosm what was wrong with
Goodbye Again: not just the fact that there was insufficient new material

to fill a whole programme, but also the fact that the direction was failing to reflect the intimacy of the comedy. Whereas Joe McGrath had filmed 'Alan A'Dale' head on, concentrating closely on the earnestly optimistic faces of the performers as they sung their hilariously directionless twaddle, *Goodbye Again* saw the piece filmed largely in wide shot from the side, with a background of parallel bars.

The second full-length sketch in the show, another parody news report on the subject of violence, showed yet more pre-Pythonesque touches. Dudley appeared as a Mrs Pepperpot-style old lady with headscarf and screeching falsetto, and the sketch investigated the problem of senile delinquency via the case of Fred and Deirdre Nimble, an elderly couple who are machine-gunned to death in slow motion after stealing a number of milk bottles. Dudley also appeared as football hooligan Ted Stagger, in a section based on Peter's encounters at Old Trafford, while Peter appeared as Inspector Knacker of the Yard, a Richard Ingrams character borrowed from *Private Eye*. Again the direction let the joke down: Knacker was pictured expressing absolute confidence in the police's ability to tackle crime, while a smash-and-grab raid on a jeweller's took place in the background beyond his right shoulder. The basic rules of comedy direction dictate that the shot should have stayed fixed and the burglary kept as a background detail to undercut what the speaker was saying. O'Riordan cut away to big close-ups of the jewel raid instead, thereby utterly destroying any humour present in the scene.

Sandwiched between a number by Traffic and a three-second performance by the all-girl dance troupe, Pete and Dud discussed physical fitness. As with all their *Goodbye Again* dialogues, the conversation soon rambled away on to a completely different topic, albeit a highly amusing one. Pete expressed the opinion that throughout the anals of history (sic), all the truly great men, like Mahatma Gandhi, have been extremely skinny. By the same token, he reasoned, Twiggy must therefore possess one of the most brilliant minds of our age. From Twiggy it was but a short leap to eastern religions, and the steps required to go into a mystic trance:

> *Pete*:   Let your mind go blank. Have you done it?
> *Dud*:   Oh, yeah.
> *Pete*:   Not a very difficult step for you, I imagine.

The final item was another father and son sketch, which drew heavily and rather desperately on the films that Peter and Dudley had recently been making. Peter appeared as a rich upper-class businessman, John Cleese as his butler Gattis (a character from *A Dandy in Aspic*), and

Dudley as his son Edward, who is planning to leave home in order to get married:

Peter: Is there any particular reason for your going so suddenly? I mean, you've been with us for a long time, haven't you?

In a development redolent of *The Bedsitting Room*, Dudley's fiancée is then ushered in by Gattis, and turns out to be a large box (or she is contained in a large box – it is purposely not made entirely clear which). Peter's wife is then brought in, and proves to be an identical box. The boxes proved difficult to hide on the night, and the audience was able to register their presence long before O'Riordan was able to get his cameras on to them.

Peter freely admitted later that the scripts for *Goodbye Again* were not up to his usual standard. The party atmosphere of the *Not Only . . . But Also* studios had given way to a more subdued ambience: when Tina Turner shouted 'Everybody help me one time!' not one member of the audience joined in with the chorus. Press reaction was ambivalent: the *Daily Mail* spoke of 'a show that glittered at every moment with the old originality, literacy and wit';[8] but the *Daily Sketch*, under the headline 'ITV puts a damper on Pete and Dud', complained that 'Cook and Moore seemed slightly subdued . . . they performed timidly, as if they were bashful maidens not quite sure whether their slips were showing, and frightened if they were.'[9] The set design came in for general criticism and the whole attracted unfavourable comparisons with *Not Only . . . But Also*. Peter and Dudley resolved not to make another series with ATV, although they consented to do a further one-off special the following year, when Anne Bancroft was offered to them as a special guest. That show, produced by Garry Smith and Dwight Hemion, was closer in concept to the BBC series: Mel Tormé provided the music, Anne Bancroft appeared in a parody of *The Graduate*, and also as Dudley's mother, taking him to see a child psychologist played by Peter.

By the autumn of 1968, following *Goodbye Again*'s lukewarm reception, *The Rise and Rise of Michael Rimmer* had begun to take on even greater significance to Peter's career. In early December, David Frost announced that he had raised sufficient backing to make the film, with his customary mixture of smooth persistence and blithe self-confidence. Columbia-Warner had been persuaded to fund the project: they had Peter under contract anyway, making this the third (after *The Wrong Box* and *A Dandy in Aspic*) of his three-picture deal. John Cleese and Graham Chapman had originally written the script in a three-month sojourn on

Ibiza in 1967, paid for by Frost; it was now in need of updating, so Peter himself set to work rewriting it with the two authors and the director Kevin Billington. As with *Bedazzled*, Peter was determined to put in far more time and effort than was normally the case, in order to be sure that the script was absolutely right; and as with *Bedazzled*, there was no room for Dudley on the writing side. He went off to star in a disastrous adaptation of *Play It Again Sam* at the Globe Theatre, produced by David Merrick of all people, Peter's arch enemy from the Establishment days. Woody Allen's script was anglicised at Merrick's instigation, the action was transplanted from Manhattan to Swiss Cottage, and all traces of Jewishness were removed from the play, which was missing the point to say the least.

The satirical thrust of *The Rise and Rise of Michael Rimmer* was to demonise opinion pollsters with the same wary distrust often lavished on spin doctors and PR executives today. The science, if one can call it that, of opinion polling was a relatively new one, and was held in some quarters to have influenced Labour's victory at the Kingston-upon-Hull by-election of January 1966, in which large numbers of undecided voters had supposedly reacted to the pollsters' findings, rather than the other way round. David Frost had devised the story of a smooth opinion pollster who becomes a politician, and takes over Britain by asking the public's opinion on everything from devolution to road-widening in the Scilly Isles, until they are so sick of giving it that they are happy to abdicate all democratic decision-making powers to his dictatorship.

Gradually, it began to dawn on Frost that there was something familiar about the manner in which Rimmer's character had been fleshed out, especially since Peter had added his contribution to the script: Rimmer liked to stroll about saying 'Super to see you' to everyone, and was portrayed hosting a celebrity party at London Zoo which was uncomfortably similar to a celebrity party that Frost had organised at Alexandra Palace. At the time, Peter vehemently denied to inquisitive journalists that these parallels were intentional: 'There are obviously similarities with someone who gets on very successfully like David in the character of Michael Rimmer, but I think it would be odd if there weren't. Honestly, the film isn't really supposed to be about anyone. Anyway, David says "Gorgeous to see you" now.'[10] Later, Peter admitted that he had been telling a little white lie: 'Frost got quite paranoid in that he thought we were exactly mirroring his career, which to an extent we were. Some of the character was based on David. The ultimate irony was that the set designer, who had never seen David's living room, and which we'd never talked about to her, produced an almost exact replica of David's room.'[11] Certainly there are multiple ironies present in the fact that Frost, who had modelled his early career on Peter, was paying Peter to parody that career on film.

The script was completed by the middle of 1969. The plot was utterly linear, following Rimmer's progress upwards from his first mysterious appearance, as a junior pollster who is appointed Managing Director of his firm on the strength of a secret time-and-motion study he carries out on his colleagues. He subsequently discredits a rival firm by rigging their poll on the religious habits of Nuneaton: a series of stooge interviewees claim to be Muslims or Buddhists at his instigation. His own firm gains a reputation for accuracy after they interview *every* voter at a by-election. Rimmer then offers to publish a fraudulent poll showing a national Tory lead, in return for the safe Conservative seat of Budleigh Moor (geddit), and swiftly becomes the party spin doctor. Simultaneously, he persuades the Labour Prime Minister (George A. Cooper as a thinly disguised Harold Wilson) to take part in a deliberately clumsy TV broadcast. So soulless is Rimmer that he even selects his wife from a national popularity poll. Eventually the Conservatives win the 1970 election, and Rimmer is appointed Chancellor, after the original candidate appears in a selection of gay photographs (this was based on a real incident, although the photos – of a senior Tory politician – were offered to *Private Eye* but never published). A vicious monetarist, Rimmer even cuts conventional military spending in favour of cheaper germ warfare. He finally murders the Prime Minister by pushing him off a North Sea rig, accedes to No. 10 and moves swiftly towards dictatorship.

The script was quite remarkable in its predictive qualities. The election result, the rise of monetarism and classless Toryism, the sacking of Enoch Powell and the increase in media manipulation by politicians were among the wide range of the film's satirical targets. But there should also have been warning signs. Cleese and Chapman were not screenwriters – not at that stage, at any rate – and neither, in all honesty, was Peter himself. Their speciality was sketch material, and the script was full of verbal gags. Funny situations were thin on the ground. The linear progression of the storyline contained no surprises, no subplots, no dramatic tension and no emotional involvement. There was not a likeable or even put-upon character in sight to engage audience sympathy; Dudley's absence was to prove telling. All the writers involved were naturally funny men, but the writer has not been born who can create a great film script instinctively. Writing a successful film script involves a substantial learning process, as Cleese later discovered when he attended a screenwriting course before writing *A Fish Called Wanda*. Instinctive and natural wit like Peter's was just one part of the equation. The result was that the script for *Michael*

Rimmer put immense pressure on its lead actor to produce a charismatic performance which would hold the whole enterprise together. Perhaps mindful of these deficiencies, Kevin Billington hurled famous character actors at the project, a sign of impending doom as clear as a plague cross painted on a front door. Arthur Lowe, Denholm Elliott, Ronald Fraser, Dennis Price, Ronnie Corbett, Michael Bates, Jonathan Cecil, Diana Coupland, Norman Rossington, Frank Thornton, and John Cleese and Graham Chapman themselves took part, and there were cameo appearances from Harold Pinter, Joe McGrath and Percy Edwards.

Filming took place in the autumn of 1969 at a disused Masonic Temple in St John's Wood, and was completed by the beginning of December. The film was due to be edited for release the following month. Then, the bombshell dropped. There was a change of management at the studio, and the new bosses weren't keen on *Michael Rimmer*. Specifically, they felt that it was too sensitive a topic to air in the run-up to the general election, and that it would be best if the film were responsibly postponed until after the end of the campaign. The whole point of the film, of course, was to predict the course of the election, but studio heads have often been and often will be morons. 'We were in despair,' recalls David Frost. 'Peter in particular. He really wanted people to see this film before the election. He suggested a simultaneous premiere in Huyton, Harold Wilson's constituency, North Devon, Jeremy Thorpe's constituency, and Bexley, as Edward Heath's constituency was then known. Now that was a great idea, but still they wouldn't do anything.' The disappointment was utterly, completely crushing. *Michael Rimmer* was shelved until further notice. Peter's film career continued to hang in the balance.

In the final weeks of 1969, BBC producer Jimmy Gilbert got a call from the Head of Light Entertainment. Peter Cook and Dudley Moore, it seemed, were unexpectedly available in the early months of 1970, and wanted to fill their time with a third series of *Not Only ... But Also* (Dudley, in fact, was not free at all, as *Play It Again Sam* was still running at the Globe, but Peter had persuaded him to record the series on Sunday nights, which were his only evenings off). The BBC, Gilbert was told, had commissioned a series of seven forty-five-minute shows to be transmitted at fortnightly intervals, with a week's filming and a week's rehearsal before each show, as in the first series. He was to produce it, and he had approximately one month in which to put it all together. 'I was appalled that we had to do it as quickly as that,' remembers Gilbert, 'it was so fast. There was no time to do any casting for guests. I booked a middle-of-the-road singer called Nanette for the whole series, a pretty

American girl, merely on the basis of a photograph. Peter was intrigued because of her looks and because her father had played the piano in the pit in the Chicago of *No No Nanette* back in the twenties – which is how she got her name.' Peter insisted that there should be rock groups as well, and Gilbert managed to book Joe Cocker and Yes.

Peter and Dudley went in to the scripting process immediately. There were no more relaxed, laughter-filled sessions like those at Church Row in 1965; there was no time for that. The two men sat in an office at Television Centre and dictated straight into a tape recorder, which was then given to a secretary for transcription. 'A lot of things used to go on too long; they could have done with a bit of cutting, but they weren't keen on that,' says Gilbert. 'I tried to direct them, because I always feel that until actors have roughly learned something you can't direct, but it was all so late. The first Pete and Dud sketch we did was one of the strongest, because they'd written it far enough ahead to be able to rehearse it. So of course I said to them "This is great," and they'd agree, "Yes, yes, great, OK, we'll do it every week." But of course they didn't. They *always* left everything to the last minute, including all the filming. We'd start each fortnight with nothing, nothing to film.'

Peter, with Dudley tagging along at his side, was just filling in time. Not with any great motivation, as he had done before, his ambition driving him onwards and upwards, but for the sake of it, for the need to work. His heart was no longer in it, his private life lay in tatters. 'I thought it was rather sad,' remembers Gilbert. 'He told me, "All my best work was done before I was eighteen, or before I was twenty anyway." He was talking about the sketches that he did for the stage revues. Those were the ones that he was most proud of, the ones with Kenneth Williams.' Awash with sentimental nostalgia, Peter must have known that his bandwagon was slowing to a halt. And yet, despite the personal sadness that underpinned this lack of conviction, and the physical weariness that told on Dudley's contribution, Peter, Dudley and Jimmy Gilbert produced a fine television series. It did not quite scale the heights of the first two series – that would have been impossible given the lack of preparation – but there was no question that Peter and Dudley were back doing what they did best, in the place most suited to harnessing their talents.

Incredibly, every single programme in the third series of *Not Only . . . But Also* was subsequently destroyed by the bureaucrats. Mysteriously, even the regulation first and last shows were not kept. Just a few of the film sequences shot in advance remain; they are virtually the only surviving examples of Peter and Dudley's work recorded in colour. The unedited scripts, fortunately, are still with us, enabling an approximate picture of each programme to be built up. The principal innovation that distinguished the series from its predecessors was *Poets Cornered*, a regular finale devised by Peter in which he, Dudley and a comedy guest sat perched on stools above a tank of disgusting sludge. A rhyme would be improvised by one of the participants, the verbal baton passing to the next man whenever Jimmy Gilbert up in the gallery pressed a buzzer. Failure to come up with a rhyme, or undue hesitation, resulted in the performer being catapulted forward into the tank. Eventually one poet would be left, ploughing on desperately until he too was plunged into the sludge. It was a brilliant idea, both comically and because it enabled Gilbert to adjust the show to fit its forty-five-minute slot. If Pete and Dud had been overrunning earlier on, he could easily shorten *Poets Cornered*. Spike Milligan was the first guest on the *Sludge Poetry Competition*, as it began its life. Subsequent poets were Willie Rushton, Barry Humphries, Frank Muir, Ronnie Barker, Denis Norden and an extremely reluctant Alan Bennett. Sadly, because it was entirely unscripted, nothing whatsoever remains of *Poets Cornered*, but it is still fondly remembered by all who saw the shows go out.

Gilbert continued and improved upon the sequence of remarkable title sequences devised by his predecessors. The first programme, recorded on Sunday 1 February, began with Peter and Dudley leaning over the rail of Tower Bridge, which proceeds to open between them, sending them skywards and away from each other as a giant *Not Only . . . But Also* banner unfurls between the two arms of the bridge. The first sketch on the show trod familiar ground – Dud played a libidinous piano tuner ('Just like a piano, women need to be tuned very regularly, kept up to concert pitch and as many hands over their keys as possible') who visits the house of a Latin teacher played by Peter. It transpires that the piano tuner knows far more about the teacher's wife than he does, namely that she is extremely promiscuous, and that far from being on a visit to her flu-ridden mother, as her husband supposes, she is walking the streets wearing thigh-length boots, micro-skirt, see-through blouse and an Indian head-band. 'Dressed up the way she was to kill, something might have happened to her,' Dudley suggests. 'She could have just sort of gone out the door, crossed the road and fallen under a West Indian.' The unusual outcome of this sketch was that for the first time ever, Dudley emerged as the clear victor over Peter. Partly, this reflected Peter's sense of defeat in his personal life, and partly the fact that Dudley had now developed a far more dominant role in the writing, as Peter subsequently admitted. Dudley now estimated his contribution to the script as being about 30 per cent. The balance of power was shifting back between the two men.

Dudley was fast becoming dissatisfied with the media perception of him as Peter's lovable glove puppet: 'Cuddly I am not,' he barked at one reporter. 'I highly resent being considered as some sort of human Sooty, a plaything for doting matrons. It was an image that grew on me like fur. I now want to shave it off.'[12]

After a terrible song by Nanette, the second of the three sketches in the opening show was one of Peter and Dudley's finest ever, a cod Hollywood documentary about the life of Greta Garbo, which – as it was shot on film – survives intact. Dudley was made up to the nines as Joan Crawford, while Peter played the mysterious Emma Bargo, from her earliest film role in *Three Thousand Girls Jump into the Sea*, to her later life as a recluse, driving down the high street atop an armoured car shouting 'I vant to be alone!' According to Jimmy Gilbert, 'By this stage Peter didn't enjoy the hard work of having to write it all, but he loved all the performing of it. He and Dudley were incredibly flamboyant and extrovert together when they got into the studio, and gave the impression of a huge sense of enjoyment there. Peter *adored* the Greta Garbo bit. I remember Peter and I sitting in Lime Grove looking at old Garbo movies; he postponed the actual sitting down and writing of it until the last minute but he loved the dressing up.' Peter himself concluded, entirely erroneously, that 'I looked incredibly beautiful – I fancied myself rotten. I thought I looked rather better than she did.'[13]

The third and final sketch, after a couple of nonsense songs from Spike Milligan, was a Pete and Dud dialogue that was once again heavily influenced by the plot of *The Bedsitting Room*. Dud had been having recurrent dreams about climbing into a wardrobe:

Pete: The wardrobe represents your mother, and your desire to get into it shows an infantile yearning to return to the warmth and security of your mother's womb.
Dud: You're wrong there, Pete. I have absolutely no inclination to get back into the confines of my mother's womb.
Pete: Not consciously. I'm not suggesting that you go round to 439 Becontree Avenue and ask your mum for readmission. It's three o'clock in the morning and anyway it's illegal.

Gradually Pete's analysis is accepted so completely by Dud that he comes to believe that his mother actually is a wardrobe.

Dud's newfound mood of confidence ('You're wrong there, Pete') was evident elsewhere in the sketch. A question about the extent of his reading did not lead to the ritual humiliations of previous series:

> *Pete*: I don't know whether you're familiar with the works of Freud.
>
> *Dud*: I do have a cursory knowledge of his theories. I recently skimmed through his lectures to the students of Heidelberg on the phallic implications of the penis.
>
> *Pete*: An interesting, if superficial study. Did you read it in the original German?
>
> *Dud*: No, I read it in précis form on the back of a box of Swan Vestas.

The second show of the series opened with a blistering attack on the Tom Sloan style of running BBC Light Entertainment. The writer of *'Til Death Us Do Part*, Johnny Speight, had been undergoing his customary battles with the management over the number of swear words permitted on air, as indeed had Peter and Dudley themselves. Knowing that the BBC would seek to remove some of the swearing as a matter of course, they and Speight tended to include too much to begin with, then negotiate down to their originally desired position. The sketch featured a thinly disguised Speight, played by Dudley, doing a deal with Peter's Head of Light Entertainment in his office:

> *Johnny*: Look, tell you what I'll do. I'll lose ten bloodys if you give me two more bums and an extra tit.
>
> *Head*: Right, that leaves you seventeen bloodys, eight bums and a pair of doodahs.
>
> *Johnny*: Hold on, how many bloodys are there to a bum?
>
> *Head*: Let's say ten.
>
> *Johnny*: I raise you one bum.
>
> *Head*: You're really pushing me into a corner . . . but what's the point of letting one bum stand between us? Another bum it is. I'll whip the script off to Sooty this afternoon.

'That sketch was based on an actual meeting,' recounts Dudley, 'negotiating tits and bums. We got away with it, though I'm amazed we did. Peter *loved* it when we got away with things.'[14] In fact Peter had rarely needed to resort to swear words to make people laugh at any point in his career, but the notion of smashing the BBC's swear word record in such a deliciously ironic manner appealed to him. In a further comment on the whole situation the show's opening and closing titles promised 'lavatory humour' – in fact a series of elderly and inoffensive music hall jokes told in stopframe animation by a row of talking lavatory seats.

That classic sketch apart, the rest of the second programme all too clearly revealed the lack of preparation that had gone into the series. A Joe Cocker number punctuated a feeble Pete and Dud dialogue about Dud's chances of becoming the new James Bond, and *The Glidd of Glood*, a filmed version of one of the poems from Peter's abortive book of children's verse. The *Glidd* poem was actually rather good – it too survives to this day – but was only included out of desperation because Peter and Dudley had been unable to write anything else. Filmed at Bodiam Castle, it featured Peter as a medieval ruler so mean that he dresses in a brown paper parcel, and forces his subjects to eat slabs of wood for dinner. Dudley played Sparquin, the tiny jester whose job it is to entertain the Glidd, but who succeeds instead in escaping with all his master's money. As with the Piano Tuner sketch and the Johnny Speight sketch, Dudley's character emerged as the unquestioned victor.

The third show in the series also failed to live up to the standards of Peter and Dudley at their best. A title sequence displayed on a station destination board led into a long sketch in a railway carriage that would have better served *The Two Ronnies*, in which Peter and Dudley held a conversation synchronised to the rhythms of the rattling train. Sir Arthur Streeb-Greebling then spoke of a life spent observing worms, quite a neat idea in which he displayed a series of identical slides purporting to show worms in various states of anger, distress, ecstasy, and so on.

> *Sir Arthur*: Would you like to see one of my worms leap through a flaming hoop?
> *Dudley*: Yes indeed. I would.
> *Sir Arthur*: So would I . . . but they won't. Damned things won't even try.

It was a funny sketch, but was essentially a retread of Sir Arthur's earlier attempts to tame recalcitrant nature.

The Pete and Dud dialogue dealt with racial prejudice, Dudley having blacked his face to discover what it is like to be on the receiving end of bigotry. It was an extremely well-meaning item, but would probably not be transmittable today.

> *Pete*: Both black and white have individual talents. If the white man is good at one thing then the black man is good at the other.
> *Dud*: Yer. I heard they were good at that.

And that was one of the less controversial jokes. The final item in the programme, a rambling dialogue between two Streeb-Greeblingesque buffers in a club who have forgotten each other's names, was little more than space filler, a sketch that was all middle but had no real beginning or end.

By the fourth show, Peter and Dudley seemed to have recovered from their mid-series stutter. Although the Hitchcockian opening titles ('Not Only . . . But Psycho') did not live up to the promise of the idea, all three sketches were high-quality stuff. The Pete and Dud dialogue found Pete, like his alter ego, in a fit of depression:

> *Dud*: You know what my mother would say?
> *Pete*: No.
> *Dud*: 'Somebody has got out of the bed on the wrong side this morning.'
> *Pete*: If your mother said that to me today, I'd smash her in the teeth with the coal scuttle.

Dud tries to analyse Pete's general malaise:

> *Dud*: Spring is here and perhaps disquieting emotions are seething beneath your mackintosh.
> *Pete*: Nothing is seething beneath my mackintosh save for a general feeling of despair and futility and boredom with you.

What, Pete asks, can be the purpose of life?

> *Dud*: The purpose of life? Well, we are here on this earth for a brief sojourn; life is a precious gift; the more we put into it, the more we get out of it; and if on the way I can have spread a little sunshine, then my living shall not be in vain.
> *Pete*: Thank you, Patience Strong. Have you ever thought about death? Do you realise that we each must die?
> *Dud*: Of course we must die, but not yet. It's only half past four of a Wednesday afternoon.

The sketch was a parody, but an accurate one, of relations between Peter and Dudley's real selves at that juncture. A genuine sense of pointlessness had settled like a pall over Peter's life.

An excellent and perceptive father and son sketch followed, in which Dudley played a sixteen-year-old who asks his father – Peter – for permission to get married. You're not emotionally mature enough, explains Peter, whereupon Dudley points out that his supposedly emotionally mature parents regularly throw crockery at one another. Thereafter, the final item in the show was a piece of pure Python: a filmed cricket match between Good and Evil (both Terry Jones and Terry Gilliam later admitted that similar Monty Python sketches had been heavily influenced by *Not Only . . . But Also*). The Evil XI, captained by Adolf Hitler, featured Attila the Hun, Goliath, Long John Silver, Goebbels, the Marquis de Sade, Bluebeard, Al Capone, the Goddess Kali, Stalin, Salome, and Jack the Ripper as twelfth man. The Good XI consisted of Lord Baden-Powell (captain), Gandhi, Albert Schweitzer, St Paul, St Francis, Matthew, Mark, Luke and John, Florence Nightingale and Cliff Richard. The umpires were Doubting Thomas and Pontius Pilate. Peter opened the batting as the Marquis de Sade with an enormous spiked bat, which he used to pummel Florence Nightingale's gentle underarm lobs: 'He's punishing the bowling, and he's even punishing the bowler' ran the commentary, as the Marquis took Florence (Dudley) over his knee. After a disagreement as to whether Long John Silver's wooden leg constituted a leg for lbw purposes, Evil declared on 564–4 and quickly reduced Good to 2–9. To save the day, Albert Schweizer prevailed upon his black runner Jomo to do a Zambezi rain dance, in the hope of a postponement. Jimmy Gilbert had the hoses at the ready, but as the rain dance began, a remarkable thing happened: the heavens opened and snow began to fall thickly, quickly carpeting the entire field in white. The script was hastily altered to take account of what had become a spectacular meteorological finale. Bizarrely, when the surviving *Not Only . . . But Also* material was packaged for reshowing in the early 1990s this first-rate sketch was missing, although it was certainly present in the BBC Archive when the author of this book viewed it in 1982.

Another filmed item, of which only an unedited fraction has survived, formed the centrepiece of the fifth show: a wonderful, sprawling solo piece by Dudley (something that would have been unthinkable five years previously) in which he portrayed Ludwig van Beethoven as the star of his own Tom Jones-style variety show, and played a symphonic version of *Delilah*. Peter appeared in brief cameos as Francisco Goya and as William Wordsworth, surrounded by Young Generation-style dancers dressed as daffodils. The other filmed item in the programme has long since vanished, an ingenious title sequence devised by Peter in which Sir Arthur Streeb-Greebling planted a row of seeds, which flowered to form the words *Not Only . . . But Also*. The necessary time-lapse photography proved almost – but not quite – beyond the capabilities of the show's cameraman.

Elsewhere in the show there was an excellent sketch in which Peter played an elderly, dying man who refuses to see a doctor, while Dudley played the local GP, who has to pretend to be an electrician to get in to see him, and has to improvise an electrical reason for each of his various medical procedures. The Pete and Dud dialogue was less successful, consisting of the plot details of a Harold Robbins-style potboiler that Dud has started writing, full of racy scenes ('Heaving thighs across Manhattan'); it concerned a porn magnate who has made his fortune selling 'a combination of nude ladies and intellectual articles by Jonathan Miller and Kenneth Tynan' – two targets that Peter never lost the opportunity to have a dig at. 'We did run out of material for Dud and Pete to discuss,' confesses Dudley, 'maybe because we always chose subjects like Sex and Art and Religion.'[15]

In keeping with the up and down nature of the series, the sixth show included one of the finest ever *Not Only . . . But Also* sketches, a savage attack on small-minded, self-aggrandising bureaucrats, entitled *Lengths*. Peter and Dudley played George and Reg, two nasal, suburban telephonists who have mislaid some (unexplained) 'Lengths' and are trying to engender a little self-important panic by using phrases such as 'We're up to our eyes', 'We're going mad here' and 'We're working like beavers up here love':

> *George*: Sylvia, get me Bernard, would you please, on green. Bernard, it's George here. Sorry to trouble you but we're in a bit of trouble re. these Lengths. I've got Alan on my back. They've been through Transit Control and on to Admin but they haven't been roneoed and there's no dockets.
>
> *Reg*: Er Bernard, it's Reg here, sorry to interrupt.
>
> *George*: It's Reg on green, Bernard.
>
> *Reg*: Yes, I've just had a look through here at what we've got but there's nothing at all. We haven't got a trace of a docket either. Unless we have a docket we can't move.

In addition to whipping up a little drama in their professional lives, the two are equally busy trying to conduct their private lives with discretion. Almost every caller is greeted with the hissed explanation: 'I can't talk now, 'cos he's here.' The cumulative effect of seven or eight minutes of spiralling bureaucratic absurdity is to create a genuinely original and fiercely well-observed slice of social satire. Eventually George has a brainwave:

George:	There's no trace of the dockets and no sign of the Lengths. I don't know where to turn.
Reg:	No, it looks pretty black, doesn't it.
George:	We might try Lengths, I suppose.
Reg:	It's a shot in the dark, isn't it.
George:	Still, give it a whirl. Brenda, get me Lengths would you love. On purple, yes.
	(*Reg's phone rings. He answers it.*)
Reg:	Hello, Reg Lengths here.

By contrast, the other two sketches in the show were half-hearted: a long-vanished film item in which Dudley, as a conman, rings on Peter's door with a wholly unconvincing sob story, and a rambling Pete and Dud dialogue about health foods.

For the final programme in the series, Jimmy Gilbert pulled out all the stops. The opening title sequence featured the words *Not Only . . . But Also* painted in huge letters on the deck of HMS *Ark Royal*, a task that took the ship's crew three days; the closing sequence saw a pair of tailor's dummies dressed as Peter and Dudley, together with an upright piano, catapulted up the aircraft carrier's take-off ramp and into the sea. The latter stunt was the idea of the ship's captain, who had used the catapult to fire elderly second-hand cars over the side as a means of entertaining his men in the South China Sea. The ship's officers were delighted to try anything to drum up televised publicity, to ward off the threat of imminent decommissioning. The stunt had a sad ending, however, when one of the *Ark Royal*'s jets crashed into the sea shortly afterwards at the same point, killing both pilots; the wreckage of the plane unfortunately became intermingled with the wreckage of the piano. A one-hour thank you concert for the crew, which Peter and Dudley had been rather dreading, was cancelled as a result.

The centrepiece of the final show was a huge documentary attack on the world of films, which Peter had found so impossible to crack. Entitled *The Making of a Movie*, it tore not just into Great British Acting – a favourite target of Peter's – but into the self-regarding pomposity of directors, producers and screenwriters as well. Peter played Robert Neasden, a ruminative, pipe-smoking writer redolent of Robert Bolt, while Dudley played the suspiciously Bryan Forbes-like Bryan Neasden, director of the smash hit *When Diana Dors Ruled the Earth*:

Voice-Over:	Neasden describes how the idea for his new film came to him.

Robert:	I was in the cinema at the time . . . and I was watching this film, and suddenly I felt, 'That's it, a film. A film. A film.' It was so simple I almost wept.
Voice-Over:	Robert Neasden took his idea to famed producer–director Bryan Neasden.
Robert:	I see it as a film about people.
Bryan:	Yes.
Robert:	People who need people.
Bryan:	People who need people . . . yes.
Robert:	Big people, with universal emotions.

Eventually Peter O'Neasden (Peter as O'Toole) is cast as the Archbishop of Becontree and Richard Neasden (Dudley as Richard Burton) takes the part of King Henry VIII, in what has become a historical epic:

| *Richard*: | I've always wanted to work with Bryan, and when I heard that Robert had written the script I didn't need to read it. The money's neither here not there. It's in Geneva. |

A number of marvellous mock-Shakespearean scenes follow, in which Peter and Dudley rail against each other in a variety of roles, always employing that booming, stagey, projected delivery that characterises Great British Acting, a thespian tradition once described by Peter as 'rubbish'. Much of the dialogue is suspiciously familiar:

| *King Henry VIII*: | Please, release me, let me go, for I don't love you any more. Her lips are warm while yours are cold. Release me my darling, let me go. |

Eventually, when the epic is complete, Bryan returns home with Robert:

Bryan:	Oh God, it's marvellous to be home. Help yourself to a drink. I'll go and get Vera and the kids. (*Hegoesupstairsshoutingforhiswife,andcomes down again.*) That's peculiar, she was here three years ago.
Robert:	There's a note here.
Bryan:	(reading) 'Goodbye for ever, love Vera . . .' My God, what a fantastic title for a film.

> *Robert*:   Yes, I see it as a very contemporary film.
> *Bryan*:   A film . . . a film . . .

Peter was obviously in a biting mood. One of the two other sketches in the show was an equally savage attack on a middle-class dinner party, the well-heeled guests discussing au pairs and the children's education. The subject matter was uncomfortably close to home, especially when Dudley outlined his character's marital situation:

> *Dudley*:   Verity and I have a very honest relationship. She knows
> perfectly well that from time to time I may have a bit
> of a fling, but she also knows that I'll never get seriously
> involved with another woman. I mean, I've never got
> involved with her.

The final sketch of the series was a Pete and Dud dialogue, extremely tired by now, that began by half-heartedly retreading the ground of the famous Art Gallery sketch, drifted off into a discussion of a porn mag ordered by Dud, and ended up dawdling round the houses of Dud's youth once more. These two characters, at least, had come to the end of the road.

Peter was not happy with the series, probably because he was just not happy, and described it as 'textually messy'.[16] Certainly Jimmy Gilbert was happy to get the chance to re-edit the programmes down to thirty minutes each for repeat transmission – 'It was just a matter of cutting the dead wood out. It became a very tight show then, I thought it was great.' The press reaction had been muted – 'A disappointment on the whole,'[17] said the *Daily Mail* – which was perhaps fair by comparison with the first two series, but not in any other context. The series had been a definite improvement upon *Goodbye Again*, and knocked spots off almost every other comedy show on TV at the time. Much of the disappointment stemmed from the dwindling appeal of the Pete and Dud double act. Shortly afterwards, Dudley acknowledged the negative part that he had played in this decline, by altering the chemistry between the two: his character was no longer prepared to be kicked like a faithful dog. He had become 'too intelligent, too well read. I think at one stage the reactions to things weren't quite so primitively funny.' Although he did add, somewhat contradictorily, that 'Peter's sarcasm was detrimental to the relationship,'[18] referring no doubt to their offstage rather than their onstage relationship.

Pete and Dud aside, today Dudley believes that 'We did some of our best work in that series,' and it would be impossible to contradict him.

Willie Rushton, a guest on *Poets Cornered*, called it 'excellent, a really good series'. If anything had been lost, other than the amount of preparation time available in previous years, it was a degree of warmth visible in the earlier shows. What it had gained by way of compensation was a slightly experimental quality, as if Peter was restlessly and unconsciously pushing against the boundaries of the sketch show format. There were fewer overt jokes than before, and more in the way of character study. John Wells's memory of that period is that 'Peter was constantly pushing, but didn't know in which direction he ought to push; but he had to push in some direction constantly to try and see which would finally ring a bell. A lot of those sketches like the Greta Garbo one almost weren't comedy, they had the air of an expressionist film. I think he'd been slightly seduced into believing that he ought to move into a slightly more serious realm. He thought he couldn't just go on sitting in a chair making jokes for ever.'

The whirling social life and after-show parties that had accompanied the first two series had been revived third time around, but perhaps with a slightly more forced air than before. Sid Gottlieb, who came to three or four of the recordings, remembers that 'Judy was very energetic about those shows, very encouraging, and always very well spruced up, she'd make a great fuss of Peter going to the studio and at the dos afterwards at the Fagin's Kitchen Restaurant.' At the parties, Peter and Dudley were more exhibitionist than ever before. Jimmy Gilbert recalls that 'Peter was very much into attacking Great Acting at the time, so at one party he leaped up onto the table and Dudley onto another – we hadn't taken the whole restaurant over, there were some rather astonished guests there as well – and they started improvising all these Great Shakespearean speeches in that Great Acting style. In fact it went down exceedingly well with all the diners.' But when the performance was at an end, Peter sat sadly in a corner with Jimmy Gilbert and mourned all those lost improvised lines that had floated off into the air. 'He told me, "My greatest tragedy is that I haven't got a Boswell, if only I had a Boswell going around, because that's the only way I can write. I invent it, it all happens, I don't know where it all comes from, but it's there and I really need a Boswell to write it all down."'

Everything now seemed to depend on *Michael Rimmer*. The BBC wanted another series of *Not Only . . . But Also*, and American Television too came in with an offer of a 26-part series, but Peter demurred. To do further TV shows, he made clear, would be to stand still, to tread water, to become *boring*. According to John Cleese, 'After his great stage and TV successes, he had nowhere to go, because basically the way up was via film'[19] – which is not to say that making films is intrinsically more important than achieving success on stage or on TV, merely that artistic convention was channelling Peter's need to face new challenges along a predetermined career path. *Michael Rimmer* was finally released in November 1970, five months after the Conservatives' victory, and billed as 'The film they wouldn't let us show until *after* the election.' Much of what it predicted had come to pass. From being an ingenious satire on what might happen, it had become a limp reflection on what had already happened. Far, far worse than that, Peter's performance in the lead role was an unmitigated disaster. Rather than holding the whole thing together, his was a performance of glassy emptiness. You could tell that – beneath Rimmer's nonchalance – Peter was trying desperately hard, but he was insufficiently sincere at being insincere. John Cleese felt that 'Although he was a great sketch performer, he wasn't a very good actor. I would suspect that it was something to do with the fact that he wasn't very comfortable with his emotions, and as an actor you have to be able to access your emotions. In the milieu where he grew up, emotions were kept very much out of the way.'[20] Peter himself was his harshest critic: 'I was suffering from Cook's disease, which involved that terrible glassy-eyed look. I belong to the school of acting which consists of doing nothing in particular. The variety of my expressions between shock, joy and terror are very hard to define.'[21]

The man from the *News of the World*, who called upon him at Kenwood Cottage to check on the progress of his home improvements, found Peter to be a bag of nerves, waiting for the press reaction. Unfortunately, there was to be no quick execution. The film garnered the worst possible critical reaction from Peter's point of view – one of barely concerned ambivalence. Under the headline 'Too many cooks spoil the Cook' Cecil Wilson in the *Daily Mail* described the film as one that 'involves with uneven results . . . the laughter never really comes to the boil.'[22] The *Liverpool Echo*, one of the few other papers to give it a lot of space, reported that the first half of the film was good, after which 'it tails off, unfortunately, just when it is building up'.[23] Peter knew full well what it all meant. His career as a leading man of the cinema was over. For the first time in his life, he had failed. His next film, which had already been announced – he was to star in *Easy Does It*, directed by Jerry Epstein – was quietly cancelled. Another screenplay he was writing for himself was left on his desk, unfinished. In December 1970, unsure of where to go or what to do next, he accepted an invitation to appear as E. L. Wisty on *Holiday Startime*, an ITV Christmas variety programme. He was well down on the bill, below Max Jaffa, Les Dawson, Thora Hird, Kenny Ball, Reg Varney and Ted Ray. The middle-aged audience tittered in bemused fashion. It was a backward step, the first of his career, and in terms of the company he found himself in, a humiliating one. In Peter's heart, it must have been the clearest possible admission of defeat.

He was not poor, but then money had never really been the issue. He and Dudley were still in demand for commercials: they filmed one for Harvey's Bristol Cream and another for a failing soft drink, with Ursula Andress. He lived a relatively restrained lifestyle, travelling everywhere by tube, keeping no credit cards. As long as he had enough to afford a copy of every newspaper every day, that side of his life was not a problem. The guiding principle behind Peter's career at this stage was the need to progress, to meet new challenges and to stave off boredom. Unfortunately, 'up', as John Cleese put it, was now barred to him. Gaye Brown, who was seeing Peter more frequently on account of her friendship with Judy Huxtable, believes that professionally speaking he needed the thrill of the chase to stimulate him: 'Only there was no chase left for him, he was already famous. That was the problem.'

A year or two previously, when Peter had first begun to show signs of uncertainty as to the direction in which he should proceed next, Nick Garland had expressed a confident verdict to the *Evening Standard*: 'Peter can now choose what he'll do, whether he'll be a performer, a publisher, or a producer. He said to me the other day that he admired Orson Welles and Peter Ustinov not for what they do but for what they are, that they could afford to fail on a gigantic scale and survive, that they take risks. You know there's this view about the famous Portland Vase in the British Museum, that it's improved since it was smashed. Well, Peter has not yet been smashed.'[24] In fact, emotionally speaking at least, Peter was in no position to fail and survive. One serious fall was always likely to bring the roller-coaster ride of his career juddering to a halt – not from the public's point of view, but from his own. The next career decision he took was to prove his most disastrous. He was about to get smashed, in more ways than one.

In the wake of the mediocre reception accorded to *Michael Rimmer*, the BBC's new Head of Comedy Michael Mills sensed that it would be a good time to entice Peter back to television. The carrot that Mills held out to the reluctant star was a substantial one: he could do anything, any programme he liked, as long it was a comedy show. Peter imposed certain conditions. He did not want to do another series of *Not Only . . . But Also*. He did not want to do anything with Dudley. After dipping his toe back into satirical waters with *Michael Rimmer*, he did not want to do anything remotely connected with politics, the news or the 'artificial indignation',[25] as he put it, that had characterised *TW3*. He was keen for his new show to be live and dangerous: 'I wanted to restore that embarrassing element that there used to be on television, when sets fell over and people forgot their lines and things went wrong.'[26] Also, he wanted the programme to have a serious element, to show that he could do more than just tell jokes. He wanted to present his own chat show.

The inspiration for this came partly from his success in livening up *The Eamonn Andrews Shows* in 1968, and partly from his friends, who were always telling him what a fabulous conversationalist he was; if he could capture the magic of all those impromptu conversations in the pub or around the dinner table, he would be on to a winner. There was also a subconscious motive, according to Ned Sherrin, who appeared as one of Peter's guests: 'I'm sure there was an element of "If Frost can do it, I can do it."' David Frost was by now the widely acknowledged King of the TV chat show, and Sherrin believes that 'Because Frost had attained celebrity as a chat show host, somewhere at the back of Peter's mind, although he was infinitely more humorously clever than David, he thought, "Obviously I must be a chat show host. It's easy." Being a chat show host may be pretty negligible compared with being a comic genius, but it does require certain skills.'[27] Peter had indeed made a terrible wrong turning. 'He wasn't cut out to be a chat show host,' explains Jonathan Miller. 'He was cut out to be a chat show guest; a chat show guest who is bound to overwhelm and completely obliterate the host. And therefore to cast him in the role as the hospitable host of a chat show was a fatal choice on his part, because it simply misidentified what he brought to the occasion.' All those enthralling conversations in the pub were driven by Peter, darting from subject to subject in a dazzling show of verbal agility: there were very few people so fascinating to him that he was prepared to sit back and listen to them quietly.

Peter was breezily confident that he could emulate Frost, and this confidence communicated itself to Michael Mills. Peter asked for a pilot programme; even he was taken aback when Mills insisted that no pilot would be necessary, and commissioned a series of twelve prime-time Friday night shows for BBC2 there and then. The show was to be called *Where Do I Sit?*, to be produced by the young *Monty Python* producer Ian MacNaughton, and would combine a chat show element with various live comedy sketches. Peter had one further request, which was granted without demur: he wanted to sing a pop song every week. It was a classic example, emulated many times since, of BBC management being happy to commission a famous comedian to do something entirely outside the scope of their proven abilities, with absolutely no evidence whatsoever that such a switch might succeed. Peter was about to deliver 'that embarrassing element' with knobs on.

Advance filming began in late January 1971. With Ian MacNaughton and the crew disguised as GPO engineers and hidden in a striped workmen's tent nearby, Peter leaped out to confront unsuspecting drivers at a Batley filling station, dressed as Cilla Black. 'Hello! Do you know who I am?' he asked in a camp falsetto. 'Morning Mr Cook,' replied one Yorkshireman flatly. 'Go away,' responded another. 'What's going on?' the man from the *Radio Times* asked Peter. 'Nobody knows,' he admitted. A few days later, he was to be found lying across a muddy brook in Black Park, Fulmer, Buckinghamshire, while Judy, resplendent in white fur coat, miniskirt and long black boots, walked across his body. The scene was shot to illustrate Peter's recording of *Bridge Over Troubled Water*, as well as being a mark of his utter devotion to his girlfriend. Ahead of the series, the journalist Ray Connolly found Peter in cautiously confident mood about his singing ability: 'I'd love to be able to sing. I think if I get into the right state of mind I can. Some people say I can and some say I can't. Come in here and listen to this . . .' (At this point Peter proudly played Connolly a tape of himself singing a self-penned composition called *Mother's Knickers*, and did his Elvis Presley impression.) 'I would secretly like to have been a pop singer,' he confessed. 'Wouldn't every man?'[28]

For the first show in the series, transmitted on 11 February 1971, Peter decided to do an impression of Johnny Cash. The guests in the chat show element were to be the *Private Eye* columnist Auberon Waugh and the elderly American humorist S. J. Perelman. A few days before the recording, Claud Cockburn invited Willie Rushton to a dinner party: 'Claud said, "You must come around, because I've got S. J. Perelman coming and this will be tremendous." Now Perelman had once been very funny, let's be fair, but I should say possibly his brain had gone. He just sat there yawning heavily and dropping off. Then I discovered, shock horror, that he was going to be the first guest on the Cookie chat show. It was dreadful. He was not a very amusing man, and Cookie was on the wrong side.' Peter had done no advance preparation at all, by way of planning or researching questions. He wasn't the sort to plod away at something; it either came naturally or – as in this case – it didn't come at all. Faced with an inert Perelman on the night, for the first time in his life, Peter froze.

Auberon Waugh watched the disaster unfold with a fascinated horror. 'It was terrible, terrible. Oh, it was awful. It was totally disorganised and pathetic and didn't work at all. Peter had insisted on being live, but he'd had no experience at all in anything like that, so he was just dithering around and interviewing you badly, then standing up and wandering around the studio. There was no shape or form. It was just a disaster.'[29]

Willie Rushton, who had switched on in eager anticipation, remembered later that 'It was the worst thing he ever did, worse than the stuff he did when people said he was the new Cary Grant. He thought he could sing like Johnny Cash – this was a major error – and he sang this Johnny Cash number which was terrible, it was really awful. Nobody knew whether he was joking or not. It just wasn't working and he knew it. What you could see was a man not entirely happy about this particular period of his life, who'd embarked on a dreadful idea.' After the show Peter recovered his composure sufficiently to entertain a crowd of admirers in the BBC bar, laughing and joking nonchalantly about how dismal the recording had been, and thereby proving that in his private life at least he could act when he needed to.

The following day he was utterly crucified by the press. Chris Dunkley in *The Times* labelled the show 'dismally embarrassing' and the Perelman interview 'truly pathetic'.[30] Peter's inability to disguise the mechanics of the chat show host's job, such as knowing where to stand or when to bring an interview to a close, came in for particular criticism. 'I mean, we've got past the days of saying, "I'm sorry, I'm getting the wind-up signal from the producer,"' complained the *Daily Telegraph*.[31] The BBC admitted officially that there had been 'teething troubles'. The round of parties and meals that had characterised the *Not Only . . . But Also* recordings continued – Gaye Brown attended dinners at the Ark restaurant off Notting Hill Gate where Peter and Judy performed impromptu routines just as Peter and Dudley had once done – but beneath the jollity Peter was gripped with nerves. He took to drinking heavily before recordings.

The second show lurched from bad to worse. When the star guest Kirk Douglas walked on, a tipsy Peter rose to his feet to ask the question 'How are you?' Unfortunately, it came out as 'Who are you?' Unfazed and smoothly professional, Douglas replied, 'Well, Peter, I'm extremely well.' 'Hello Kirk,' said Peter nervously. 'Hello Peter,' replied Kirk. There followed a long, awful silence. Later in the show Peter asked his second guest Johnny Speight a question, only to cut Speight off abruptly just as he began his answer, as the interview had run out of time. The comedy content of the programme consisted principally of a sketch performed with Spike Milligan, which led Mary Whitehouse to telephone the Chief Constable of Worcestershire and ask him to prosecute Peter for blasphemy. The two men had walked on stage dressed as tramps:

Peter: I'm God.
Spike: Oh, Christ! Oh dear . . . I'm sorry, he's your son, isn't he.

Peter's character went on to claim that the Universe had fallen off the back of a lorry. Only the most narrow-minded person could have found the piece offensive; but what bothered most viewers was that after the sketch, Peter had actually asked the audience whether or not they had been offended. One young man had tentatively admitted that yes, he had found it a bit strong. Peter had then proceeded to humiliate and ridicule him live on air. The television critic of the *Daily Mail* reported that the answer to the programme's title *Where Do I Sit?* was 'As far from the television set as possible . . . I have the feeling that fame has gone to Cook's head, and he feels that his mighty presence is enough to rivet millions to the screen. He sits scriptless, jabbering mindlessly to baffled guests.'[32] Philip Purser in the *Telegraph* pointed out that when interviewing Johnny Speight, Peter's voice had gradually and unconsciously assumed Speight's cockney tones: 'He is always playing some part. We're not sure he's capable of being himself.'[33] Michael Mills's boss, the Head of Light Entertainment Billy Cotton, warned that unless there was a considerable improvement the show's days were numbered.

Like a rabbit caught in the headlights, Peter seemed transfixed, completely unable to sidestep inevitable disaster. 'There was a gathering sense of panic, and futility, and the knowledge that I couldn't do it,'[34] he admitted later. Judy recalls that 'He had thought that a chat show would be a piece of cake, and didn't realise until after he got involved that it wouldn't suit him; but by then it was too late and he had to go through with it. Peter was a very proud man and he couldn't handle the stress of realising that he couldn't do the show. The emotional odds started to bank up against him. He was drinking too much, and abusing prescriptive drugs. In fact he was using a whole cocktail of drugs to cope, mixed with alcohol.' Ned Sherrin, who was the chief guest on the third show along with starlet Julie Ege, remembers that Peter was doped to the eyeballs on drink and drugs that night: 'He was in a terrible state. He was frightened. It was chaos.' The previous week, one viewer had written in to complain that Peter was clearly a drug addict, so Peter had conceived the idea of telephoning him live on air. The phone was answered by the complainant's wife:

Peter:	Could I speak to Mr Wentworth please?
Mrs Wentworth:	Ooh, I'm very sorry, but Mr Wentworth's in the bath.
Peter:	Well this is Peter Cook speaking. He just wrote in to the show and said I was a drug addict and I'd like to talk to him.

Mrs Wentworth:	Ooh, fancy that! Well, I'll just see if I can get him out. Are you on at the moment?
Peter:	Yes.
Mrs Wentworth:	I'll just switch on the telly to see if we are on, you know. It takes a little time to warm up. (*shouts*) George!
Mr Wentworth:	(off) What?
Mrs Wentworth:	It's Peter Cook on the line! He says you said he was a drug addict!
Mr Wentworth:	What? I'm in the bath!
Mrs Wentworth:	Well, we're on!
Mr Wentworth:	We're on what?
Mrs Wentworth:	We're on the television!
Mr Wentworth:	I'm in the bath!

Peter, meanwhile, sat smiling helplessly on camera, twiddling his thumbs. There followed a long, agonising pause while Mr Wentworth came to the phone:

Mr Wentworth:	Who's that?
Peter:	Peter Cook. You said I was a drug addict.
Mr Wentworth:	Yeah ... I was ... er ... lost for words. Anyway, I can't linger now 'cos I'm dripping wet. And I'd like to watch the rest of the show.

The exchange had a certain Mike Leigh charm but it had not really been worth the wait. Peter was left, as he put it in his own idiosyncratic rhyming slang, 'looking like a right Sir Anthony'.[35]

Ironically, Peter had been correct to a certain degree, in that the public did enjoy watching disaster unfold – or at least they enjoyed being appalled by it. The audience had actually risen in size across the three episodes. In a rare display of unity, both the nation's television critics and the viewing public were later to vote *Where Do I Sit?* the worst programme of the year, by an overwhelming margin. 'I loved it,' recalls Gaye Brown, 'because it was two fingers up; it enshrined that rather extraordinary amateur quality that he had.' The BBC was not so impressed. On the Monday morning following the third show, Billy Cotton summoned Peter and Ian MacNaughton to his office and informed them that the remaining nine shows had just been cancelled. It was an achievement almost unique in broadcasting history. Peter railed bitterly at Cotton's decision, but to no avail. The official announcement declared that: 'After a great deal of consideration, we have decided that the programme was not doing the job it set out to do. We felt that we had to protect Peter Cook's reputation and that of the BBC.' The Corporation's chat show policy now changed tack, and the young journalist Michael Parkinson was hired to replace Peter.

'We were all very upset,' remembers Gaye Brown, 'but Peter was *terribly* upset. It was very important to him that it would work, that he could be recognised for himself away from Dudley. He was *desperately* upset. It didn't matter how much love everybody gave him, and told him how brilliant he was; I don't think he ever really recovered.' At *Private Eye*, Barry Fantoni recalls that 'I noticed the first major change in Peter after the chat show thing, in which he had his first genuine taste of failure. It presented him with nowhere to run. It was difficult I think for him to talk about it to his friends. I think he laughed it off a bit in the pub, when he would come in and not unnaturally blame other people for the failure, unable to see that he was simply not fit to be a chat show host; and this increased his sense of loneliness and isolation.' Willie Rushton remembered, too, that 'Cookie was absolutely amazed by the scale of the reaction.' A wave of belated press sympathy did little to assuage the pain. Most hurtful of all must have been the *Daily Express* post mortem that concluded that Peter simply did not have the all-encompassing talent of David Frost.

In later years his chat show flop became one of his favourite anecdotes, a form of anaesthetising self-deprecation. The programme had, he acknowledged, been 'disastrous', his own performance 'hopeless'. Peter's personal analysis of the failure, as expressed to Michael Parkinson in 1975, was that 'I'm very bad at being interested in people.' He told the *Illustrated London News* that 'From the first minute of the first show I realised that I was not going to be interested in anything the guests said.'[36] It was a verdict with which others, such as Ned Sherrin and Dudley Moore, were inclined to agree; but perhaps one that is a little unfair. Peter the devourer of newspapers was fascinated by other people and their doings, however trivial. In a one-to-one conversation he was usually solicitous of others' news, and genuinely cared for his friends and loved ones. But Peter the performer was a man possessed, locked off almost into a trance-like state, unable to interact successfully with those around him unless they were prepared to go with his flow, as a number of performers like John Bird and Dudley Moore had discovered over the years. It was for the same reason that Peter was not a particularly good actor. Like many great comedians, he was a solo performer at heart. The BBC promptly destroyed all trace of *Where Do I Sit?* soon after the series was axed, leading to rumours that the programme was in fact a lost comic gem. Nonsense, says Auberon Waugh. 'It was total rubbish'.[37]

Given the embarrassment Peter felt following *Where Do I Sit?*, the only other project he had on the stocks came as something of a relief. This was a pair of special Australian editions of *Not Only . . . But Also*, requested by ABC in Sydney where Peter and Dudley's TV shows had become immensely popular. The intention was not to write anything new – the commission was accepted more as a paid holiday than anything else – but to put together a greatest hits package. The project served as an escape, both from the pressures of Peter's dying marriage and the perceived humiliation of his chat show failure. There was a brief filming trip in early January, to take advantage of the Australian summer weather, where one new sketch was recorded with the touring England cricket team. It was here that Peter's divorce was announced.

Peter, Dudley and Barry Humphries then teamed up to record the shows proper, and added a further splash of new material. There was a sketch in which Pete and Dud were stopped by an Australian immigration official (Humphries), demanding to know whether they had 'any lizards or water buffaloes about their person'. Sir Arthur Streeb-Greebling too made an appearance, in an interview about his plans to domesticate the funnel-web spider, wherein he repeatedly crossed his legs in a violently exaggerated manner, a joke later appropriated by Kenny Everett for his 'Cupid Stunt' character. This sketch made plentiful use of the verbal misunderstandings so common in Peter's earliest work:

> *Interviewer*: Sir Arthur, what is the porpoise of your visit to Australia?
>
> *Sir Arthur*: There is no porpoise involved . . . I have never become involved with a porpoise. What I think is happening is that you are misreading the word 'purpose'. The porpoise is a mammal. It suckles its young.
>
> *Interviewer*: Like a whale.
>
> *Sir Arthur*: Yes I'd love a whale.

The bulk of the shows, which were transmitted in this country in June 1971, consisted of old favourites such as *One Leg Too Few*, *Bollard* and the Beethoven version of *Colonel Bogey* from *Beyond the Fringe*. It is a measure of how completely the press in this country had turned on Peter that the material received mediocre reviews, the critics seemingly unaware of the established pedigree of the sketches they were watching. Australia, by contrast, feted Peter and Dudley in delirious fashion, and they loved every minute of their trip. Peter was on top form: 'I went on a number of car journeys with him in Australia,' says Barry Humphries, 'and he would look out of the window of the car and start reciting the names of shops and the words on advertisements, an endless litany which, just because it was his observation of the world, was so funny.' The contrast with the relentless misery afforded by England could not have been more pronounced.

On their return, Judy fell seriously ill with peritonitis, and had to be taken into intensive care at one point. Dudley's marriage, meanwhile, had followed Peter's into severe difficulties: he had moved into a small, grubby flat, while Suzy Kendall had begun a much publicised affair with Michael Caine. In a telling diary entry, which revealed that any emotional disturbances bedevilling Peter's life were as nothing compared to the profound malaise lurking beneath his partner's jolly exterior, Dudley wrote of his wife: 'How does one replace one's mother with the person she should have been, and get one's feelings to recognise this new face and ignore the old?' To cap it all, Dudley's father had suddenly been taken ill with cancer that spring, and had died soon afterwards. Like Peter, Dudley was beginning to find life in England increasingly trying.

Peter rather drifted through the rest of the summer. In July, he and Dudley appeared in a late-night television play by John Antrobus entitled *An Apple a Day*, with Spike Milligan and Kenneth Griffith. Long since wiped, it told the story of a frustrated young accountant (Dudley) who wishes to become a doctor, and the reaction this inspires from his father (Peter); the programme passed largely without comment. In August, Peter edited an issue of *Private Eye* in Richard Ingrams's absence; this was the occasion when he put a full-frontal nude drawing of Judge Michael Argyle on the cover. The face alone was obscured, by a black rectangle, and the caption read: 'To avoid prosecution under the Obscene Publications Act, the obscene parts have been blacked out.' Browned off and disillusioned with his life though Peter may have been, he never lost his sense of style, his charm, or his generosity. Attending a charity auction at the Theatre Royal in Stratford, he was asked at ten minutes' notice to stand in for the host, Spike Milligan, who had not turned up. Improvising swiftly, he invited anyone in the audience who had one of the new 50p pieces to try and hit him with it, by flinging it at the stage. Peter went down in a hail of 50p coins, and raised £60.

Australia continued to beckon. After the success of their TV specials there, the offer came through for Peter and Dudley to embark upon a five-month tour Down Under. They had received many similar offers to tour America during the late sixties and early seventies, and had always turned them down. This time, the circumstances were different. Both men jumped at the chance to get out of Britain. The only problem was, they would actually have to sit down and write a stage show first. They set to work with the tape recorder at Kenwood Cottage, Judy ferrying in an endless supply of tea and biscuits. They decided to call the show *Behind the Fridge*, after the doorman at Barbetta's strangled attempts to get his tongue around *Beyond the Fringe*.

Creatively, Peter was at the end of his tether, and found it difficult to motivate himself. The coiled spring had almost uncoiled. 'It was difficult to write with him', recalls Dudley. 'He could get very distracted by horses. He loved horse racing, he was always betting. If that was the television and that was me, he used to be, like, "Wait . . . wait . . . wait a minute . . . shit!" And this distraction to me was endless. At one point I remember saying: "Well, I'd better go." We'd had a miserable morning trying to think of something and couldn't think of anything at all. And I remember standing by the door, saying "Well I'll see you later." And he said, "What about – why don't we do that thing about the . . ." And we started talking – actually doing it. So I could quite often do something directly I was on my way out, but generally it involved me standing at the door saying: "I can't stand it." Sometimes we used to fall about endlessly and sometimes, sometimes it used to be miserable.'[38]

Some of the material that resulted was extremely black indeed. *Mini Drama* was a bizarre, bleak sketch about a Lord (Dudley) in the back of a minicab, the driver of which (Peter) begins to display indications that he might be a homicidal maniac. Peter wore the sunglasses that Satan had sported in *Bedazzled*, a single black glove in homage to *Dr Strangelove*, and kept a gun in the dashboard. The car radio referred continually to other weird jobs being carried out that night, including the collection of bits of people's bodies. The statutory father and son sketch, *Closer to Home*, featured Peter as a successful film star visiting the home of his working-class parents, only to be told by his father (Dudley) that his sick mother has died before he could get there:

> *Son:*   I couldn't get back because if I'd come back we might have lost the snow.
> *Father:* What do you mean, son?
> *Son:*   Well you see, Dad, if I'd gone to Mum's funeral, by the time I got back to the location, maybe the snow would have melted and the continuity would not have worked out and the film would be messed up.

Father:　Of course . . . I understand, son.

The autobiographical element, as far as Dudley was concerned, was plain to see.

Hello was a satire on shallow manners, consisting of a dialogue between two people who have clearly never met, but who are afraid to acknowledge the fact in case it turns out they have merely forgotten a previous meeting. Another sketch, *Gospel Truth*, was designed to rile the Mary Whitehouse element of the audience. It consisted of a newspaper reporter from the *Bethlehem Star* – Dudley doing an impression of Peter's impression of David Frost – interviewing one of the shepherds who had been present at the birth of Christ, a Mr Arthur Shepherd. The Dud and Pete sketch – as it turned out, the last proper dialogue between the two characters ever written – was also slightly nearer the knuckle than most of their TV material had been:

> *Dud*:　A lady is peppered from head to foot with erogenous zones.
> *Pete*:　Have you seen this diagram?
> *Dud*:　I daren't look.
> *Pete*:　It's like a map of the Underground.
> *Dud*:　I mean, a man is very hard put to know where to start his sexual voyage.
> *Pete*:　Well not the Northern Line. You end up in Crouch End.

The marvellous setting for this sketch was Dud and Pete's living room, where Pete sat watching Dud iron his plastic mac.

The material was by and large of a high standard, if not quite their best. There was not a huge amount of it. They had composed perhaps a dozen sketches, topped up with a smattering of old material: for instance, Dud expanded a Brecht-Weill routine he had devised during *Fringe* days into a full-length number. Such instances of recycling could be forgiven: in the circumstances, to have devised an entire stage show of such quality was a Herculean effort on the part of both men.

At the end of July 1971, Peter put the Church Row house up for sale for £45,000. It was snapped up quickly. Dudley gave his Hampstead mansion to his wife. In September Wendy and the children moved into Kenwood Cottage, the little house that Peter and Judy had shared, that he had laboured on so uncharacteristically and painstakingly. Peter and Judy put their bulkier belongings into storage, packed their bags, and together with Dudley, set out for Australia and a new life on the road.

CHAPTER 11

3-D Lobster

The Humour of Peter Cook

By the time he left for Australia in September 1971, Peter had completed the last truly substantial piece of work he would ever write. The rest of his career was studded with individual instances of genius, and he continued to be a dazzlingly funny social companion to his friends, but from this point onwards he seemed incapable of sustained artistic effort. His fragile self-confidence was such a fundamental part of his make-up that when it was damaged, his will to achieve went into a tailspin every bit as irresistible as the ascent that had preceded it. He was later fond of telling people that he had 'run out of ambition at twenty-four', to which Dudley would retort that he hoped this wasn't the case, as their double act hadn't even started out until Peter was twenty-seven. In fact, Peter's ambition died when he was thirty-three. *Where Do I Sit?* had been its last decisive flicker, although the corpse would occasionally twitch in the years ahead.

In little more than a decade he had cut a remarkable swathe through British comedy. There was some good fortune, naturally, in being part of a generation which was crying out for iconoclastic heroes, but one suspects that he would have shot to the top in whatever milieu he had found himself. Never can there have been a comedian who combined such speed of thought, such power of spontaneous invention and such sheer tangential originality. The incredible rapidity with which his mind worked, darting ahead and examining possible avenues and opportunities for wit, is well illustrated by a two-line encounter he once had with a fellow guest at a party. 'I'm writing a book,' the man remarked. 'Really? Neither am I,' Peter replied. He had mentally edited out the next five or six lines of conversation almost instantaneously, thus creating a marvellous joke that depended on nothing more than anticipation for its comic impact.

It was his spontaneity, though, and the relentlessness of it, which most impressed his colleagues. 'It was almost discouraging,' explains John Cleese. 'Whereas most of us would take six hours to write a good three-minute sketch, it actually took Peter three minutes to write a three-minute sketch. I always thought he was the best of us, and the only one who came near being a genius, because genius, to me, has something to do with doing it much more easily than other people.'[1] Friends speak of the extraordinary rococo palaces of absurdity that Peter could construct from a single word, such as 'jojoba'. The constraints of television meant that his most elaborate constructions were reserved almost exclusively for private performances, and the enjoyment of those closest to him. Max Beerbohm once wrote that 'laughter becomes extreme only if it is consecutive': on these occasions, Peter's ability to create laughter was invariably cumulative, joke piled upon joke until those present often found it difficult to stop laughing long enough even to catch their breath. Jonathan Miller likens the effect to those bombing raids that created firestorms – eventually no more ammunition was needed, the flames became self-fuelling until the supply of oxygen was exhausted. Frequently, Peter's audience laughed so much that the following day they found it hard to recall what he had even said to have sparked off such a reaction. And all of it seemed so controlled, so effortless on Peter's part.

An impression of effortlessness, of course, is rarely achieved without some effort. At school and at Pembroke College, Peter had paused naively whenever he got a laugh, in order to jot the successful line down on a scrap of paper for future re-use. These jokes would crop up again not just on stage, but in conversation elsewhere. There are probably more people who believe that they were privy to the first ever improvisation concerning the Holy Bee of Ephesus, than there are supposed fragments of the true cross. This was not a habit that Peter subsequently abandoned, merely one that he resorted to more discreetly. His daughter Daisy confirms that at home he jotted jokes down continually, on napkins and empty cigarette packets. As late as 1970, he confessed that 'My cheque book is covered with illegible notes which are supposed to remind me of things. This morning I woke up and saw "teeth" written down. Couldn't think what it was.'[2] In public, though, he was enough of a showman to wait until nobody was looking before scribbling down these notes.

Dudley Moore was among those dazzled by his private performances. 'Peter comes out with these sentences perfectly formed, like the best jazz,' he said wonderingly. 'How it happens is totally mysterious.'[3] But Dudley was not Peter's only writing partner: throughout the 1960s the staff of *Private Eye* also had the opportunity to scrutinise his methods at close quarters. Andrew Osmond points out that 'You couldn't conceive of Peter doing ordinary things, like filling in his tax return or talking about the best way through Basingstoke. You could make a huge list of things that clutter our lives – bills, babies, getting the car fixed – which he seemed to dispense with. Or if he dealt with them, it was certainly under a tight security blanket. No-one ever caught him at it. But I think he probably didn't do those things at all. Just being Peter Cook required a sort of intensity of concentration which eliminated all the rest. The usual assumption is that he could turn it on, just like that, if he was in the mood. But who knows how much he prepared of any of it? How did the spring get coiled?

My feeling is that he may have been a bit like one of those artists, or chess players, whose mind is so completely used up by the concentration of producing those moments of brilliance in the twenty-four hours of the day, that there was nothing left for anything else. What was he doing when he was walking along the street not talking to anybody, just catching a bus or something? He was running those monologues in his head so that when the moment was right he could reach for a tape off the shelf in his mind. Not exactly that it was memorised or rehearsed, but he'd prepared it – he had a whole comic character ready for exposure, an invented personality that he'd been living with and testing for weeks or even months. The business of being Peter Cook, I suspect, was a full-time job; a full-time, exhausting, demanding job which sort of wore him out. I never heard Peter mention a book of any description, never heard him talk about music, never heard him talk about painting. Football, yes; but football, for Peter, was probably a bit like Wittgenstein going to the Cambridge cinema every night to watch Marilyn Monroe films. It's what you do after a hard day's philosophising. Genius – the exercise of genius – takes concentration. It's strange to me that, in all that's been said about him since he died, nobody has placed him in the ranks of those people who were worn out by the demands of their gift.'

Osmond's perceptive analysis is shared by Richard Ingrams and John Wells: 'For all his apparently free stream of warped, boredom-racked consciousness, he had some intricate design at the back of his mind which he was slowly and often quite laboriously working towards,'[4] recalls Wells. 'You would often see the same jokes, or patterns of jokes, re-appear elsewhere in a different context. The other thing is, Peter was famous for never writing anything down, but in fact he did write down a lot of scripts at home – I've only recently discovered that. There are whole

film scripts even, which were never published.' All of which is not
to deny that Peter was a brilliant improviser – he was, of course –
but many of his most impressive performances were voyages between
islands that he had already charted in his imagination. He could vary
the route or add in new and interesting detours, but he had already
discreetly consulted the map before setting out. Something akin to this
mental process could be observed during the run of *Beyond the Fringe*,
when Peter would vary the Mr Grole monologue (about the miner who
wished he had become a judge) every night; eventually it had almost
completely metamorphosed into a different sketch, but the improvisation
was never allowed to stray too far from the successful sections of the
previous night's route.

Peter could be irritable with interruptions, humorous suggestions
thrown in by others for a change of direction, that threatened to divert
him from where he was intending to go. Sometimes he would ignore
them, and plough on regardless; at other times he would twist away in a
new direction altogether, take a different route to his destination and try
to shake off his pursuers in the thickets. Only if the interruption actually
assisted him in his progress – if, for instance, it was the broadest or most
general of helpful questions – would he be delighted to incorporate it into
his flow. 'Most of the *Eye* gang got the hang of it eventually,' explains
Osmond, 'the hang of it being that you had to be the straight man. You
had to keep saying things like "What do you mean, newts, Peter, what
newts? There aren't any newts." You just had to keep putting the plain
man's point of view – protesting, if you like, on behalf of the rational
world – if you wanted to trigger this flow. If you got good at it, you
could keep him running for hours. "Do you dream about these newts,
Peter? I mean, how big are they?"' It is paradoxical that later in life,
when Peter ceased to make such a concerted effort to be blindingly
funny all the time, the impression of absolute effortlessness began to
slip occasionally.

Peter had a compulsion to be funny, which in Christopher Booker's
words, 'overrode everything else so that it sometimes seemed like a
Frankenstein's monster.'[5] Dudley Moore recollects that in conversation,
Peter would try to go out on a laugh line just as if he were on stage.
He needed to have an audience, and to make that audience laugh. It
didn't matter if there were two people listening or twenty million, he
applied maximum energy to the task. Fame, as sought after by the
majority of performers, was not centrally important to him; success at
what he was trying to achieve, on the other hand, was paramount. Of
course he enjoyed being recognised and feted by the public, but what

gave him a kick was that they enjoyed what he was doing, that he had made them feel happy.

Even in one-to-one conversation, Peter would endeavour to entertain the person he was talking to. He actually communicated through jokes. Very, very few people, most of them blood relatives, crossed the divide and attained that inner sanctum of intimacy where he felt secure enough to relax and chat naturally for any length of time. Even friends and colleagues that he knew as well as Alan Bennett and John Wells found the way barred to them. 'Alan and I were talking about it the other day,' reflects Wells, 'and I was saying how difficult I used to find it being alone with Peter, because it was very difficult to manage any kind of small talk. Generally speaking he was performing, and you could either compete or drop out, as competing was almost impossible. Alan said that he too found going to see Peter very difficult, because – in spite of his politeness – he didn't seem to have the normal social apparatus.' In this respect Peter led a slightly solipsistic existence: he tended to be interested in the rest of the world in so far as he could relate it to his own world, appropriating parts of it as fuel to feed the furnace of his mind. If a person wasn't in some way feeding his imagination, unless they were one of his loved ones, he wasn't really interested in discussing the details of daily life with them. As a result, very few among the hundreds of friends who adored him ever got truly close.

Peter's compulsion to entertain was only counterbalanced by a delight in shocking people. 'He used to shock the shit out of me,' says Dudley Moore. 'I used to drop my head in sheer exhaustion at the prospect of what he was about to say. Anything could set him off – it might be this wine glass – and before you knew it, he could be on a tour of every orifice in the human body. I never succeeded in shocking him, though I used to try all right. I could never match him for speed, for one thing.'[6] When Peter famously described Rab Butler as 'A flabby-faced coward' in the early days of *Private Eye*, it was not because he hated Butler, or because of any profound political grievance against the Conservatives, or even – probably – because he believed Butler to be a flabby-faced coward. It was because he wanted to shock, to elicit the reaction 'They can't say that about the Home Secretary.'

This is not quite as contradictory as it seems. Generating laughter and generating shock are both ways of creating an effect, of making a splash. Sometimes the latter could be used as a substitute for the former; if an early cabaret in front of the Young Conservatives wasn't going terribly well, Peter would prefer to stun them into horrified silence than to depart unmemorably as the purveyor of an indifferent evening. His celebrated

rudeness to Zsa Zsa Gabor was more of the same, a calculated decision
to overturn *The Eamonn Andrews Show*'s atmosphere of mediocre showbiz
complacency. Even if nobody there had been impressed by such a gesture,
it would have banked future stocks of entertaining material in the form
of a good story, and – just as importantly – it would have amused Peter
himself at the time.

It must not be forgotten that Peter needed to entertain himself as
relentlessly as he needed to entertain others; he required constant
stimuli to ward off the boredom of everyday life. He had an intensely
low boredom threshold. He once got so bored at the cinema, during
a showing of *A Clockwork Orange*, that he jumped up, stood in front
of the screen and despairingly shouted 'Why don't you all go home!'
at the audience. There was a brief smattering of amused applause, but
nobody followed him through the exit door. 'And once you've decided
you have a low boredom threshold,' Peter complained, 'you just become
more and more bored.'[7] Comedy was his chief means of blotting out the
ennui of everyday existence, both during his hectic early career and his
more sedate later years.

Vast tracts of Peter's comedy concerned itself with boredom. Take E.
L. Wisty on royalty:

> Even if it's the most boring thing in the world, people still say, 'Isn't
> it interesting that a royal person is doing something boring?'

Or the *Beyond the Fringe* miner on his fellow miners:

> Very boring conversationalists, extremely boring, all they talk about
> is what goes on in the mine. Extremely boring. If you were searching
> for a word to describe the conversation, 'boring' would spring to
> your lips. Oh God, they're very boring. 'Hello, I've found a bit of
> coal.' 'Have you really?'

'The key to Peter – and this can go straight into *Pseud's Corner*,' reflects
Ian Hislop, 'is a sort of existential boredom from an early age. People
have said, "Oh, he's an absurdist playwright who appeared in sketches,"
but there's a sense in which all those grotty people he invented – the
Pete and Duds, and Derek and Clives – were just hanging about, filling
in time.'[8] Pete, indeed, once complained to Dud about the futility of a
life which consisted of 'cups of tea, interminable games of Ludo and the
occasional visit to your Aunt Dolly.'

Peter had been immersed in boredom from an early age – it was rooted in his childhood existence, and he feared it. He could identify it in others, and chase it away. John Wells recalls a feeling 'almost like being X-rayed'. But Peter could never clear out the reservoir of black boredom that bubbled deep within himself: he could only open the vents to release some of the pressure. 'Engaging and fascinating as he was as a raconteur,' remarks Hislop, 'at the end of it a look would come over him, which would indicate that in a sense, he too had just been filling in time.' When he was forced to talk seriously, by a persistent or humourless journalist for instance, Peter would often make up serious-sounding lies instead, to keep himself entertained. He once claimed, for instance, that he had been a promising junior amateur wrestler for Devon.

Analysing humour is, of course, a dangerous and frequently self-defeating business. Enquire too closely into how an illusion has been performed and the mechanics will draw the attention fatally away from the results. Peter himself refrained from self-analysis, fearing that if he managed to identify the source of the flow it might dry up. 'I think he probably analysed his humour less than almost any other comic I've ever come across,' says John Cleese, although Dudley – for all his psychiatry – must have been a serious rival in this regard. Perhaps the most concise analysis of Peter's style is provided by John Bird: 'it wasn't really a style, it was the way his mind worked.'[19]

Let's try, anyway. Essentially, the characters that Peter performed can be roughly divided into two principal types. First, there were the droning, nasal, lower-middle-class obsessives like Pete and E. L. Wisty, their lives trapped in empty boxes like the animals on Wisty's lap, their minds free to roam across the vastness of space and time, always unencumbered by the mental apparatus needed to make such a trip. As Bill Wallis observed, 'They were like the train guard you meet who can quote reams of Shakespeare and who has opinions on everything, but they're all dreadful opinions.' As early as 1959, in one of his earliest interviews, given just after the opening of *Pieces of Eight*, Peter explained: 'Sometimes I think of old men who live in single rooms. I see them listening to their portable radio sets and charting news bulletins, which then take on great importance in their pathetic little lives. They become amusing, not because one pokes fun at them, but because they make unimportant things seem important and base their lives on false premises.' Their failure was not the point of the comedy, rather their confident lack of awareness of their own shortcomings; although, as the journalist Ed Porter has pointed out,

'Their lack of self-knowledge was usually so vast as to represent success of a sort.'[10]

Someone who continues to speak to you, while remaining unaware of the gap between how interesting they think they are and how interesting they actually are, is the very essence of a bore. These characters were the boredom that haunted Peter made flesh, and the straight men trapped with them were that side of himself which could never escape. Sometimes, if he was minded to be contrary, Peter actually made these characters boring on stage, quite deliberately, as if to emphasise that however frequently he exorcised the demon of boredom by laughing at it, it would ultimately be impossible to subdue.

Peter's other principal character was the pompous authority figure, usually upper or upper-middle-class, equally confident and unaware of his own shortcomings, equally sharply observed, equally capable of seizing control of Peter for an hour or two, but in other respects the reverse of Pete or E. L. Wisty. These were men like Sir Arthur Streeb-Greebling, who enjoyed power or material success or both, frequently conferred on them by accident of birth, and who were free to do anything they wished with their lives. Unfortunately, it was their minds that were trapped in boxes, unable to grasp the notion that there was a simple alternative to the futility of their existence. In the words of John Cleese at Peter's memorial service, these were 'men, particularly English men, so trapped by their culture that they never knew how to live'. They were of course autobiographical characters, parodic of the milieu in which Peter grew up, the traditional educational institutions where unthinking adherence to the established pattern of life was prized above all else.

Peter was sometimes at pains to deny that his upbringing ever surfaced in his humour – 'I don't use my background,' he told one reporter bluntly – but this was just another instance of his protectiveness towards his family, and his keenness to distinguish them (for whom he felt nothing but love) from the institutions they sent him to (for which he felt nothing but amused disrespect). Peter never parodied any members of his family, and if they did crop up in his humour it was in the most incidental manner, not as the target of the joke. Take, for instance, this wonderful passage from *A Life in Pieces*, the televised autobiography of Sir Arthur Streeb-Greebling:

> My mother was a saint. Whenever I think of my dear mother I have an abiding image of a small, kindly, plump, grey-haired lady pottering at the sink. 'Get away from the *bloody sink*,' my mother

> would yell at her, 'and get out of my kitchen you awful plump little kindly woman!' We never found out who she was.

Peter's abiding image of his mother was, indeed, just as Sir Arthur had described. The rest is comedy.

In contrast to his public remarks, Peter was happy in private to acknowledge the link between his humour and his past. *A Life in Pieces* producer John Lloyd recalls that 'Peter said to me once, "Everything I've ever written is autobiographical, it comes from my own life, it's about who I am, where I come from."' Wendy Cook, certainly, would agree, reflecting ruefully that 'I've seen quite a few sketches that are based on incidents with me, like the one in the Amnesty show where Eleanor Bron has a balloon up her jumper and says she's pregnant.' Wendy's alien encounter in the late sixties turned up many years later on a *Clive Anderson Talks Back* special, in the mouth of a character who claimed that his wife had been abducted by aliens.

It was when drawing on his background, and specifically when amplifying the inherent ridiculousness of the class and authority structures that he had been funnelled through, that Peter inadvertently crossed paths with political satire, and indeed practised it more effectively than many a radical comedian whose sense of ire clouded his comic judgment. As Jonathan Miller says, 'He wasn't springing away from and repudiating his background. He came from a very conservative background and he brought to his conscious life most of the prejudices and commitments that such a background would imply. He imitated much of what he knew in his background, but he didn't really attack it.' Thus were judges and politicians humbled, knowledgeably and therefore more comprehensively than by most of his more radical rivals.

Politically, Peter's preferences were as elusive as his views on the autobiographical content of his work. Partly because he was a very private individual and partly because he did not like to displease his friends, he was something of a chameleon in this respect. People tended to see themselves in him: according to Richard Ingrams, 'I would define Cook as conservative, Christian and anarchist too, like myself, except that he would deny the Christian bit. But he was obsessed by religion. He was very bothered by it.'[11] Fascinated perhaps, but certainly not a believer. Richard Ingrams was given every indication by Peter that he was 'pretty keen on Thatcher', a Hampstead rightie alone in Glenda Jackson country. Auberon Waugh – who is very very far to the right – goes further, believing that Peter was 'very very far to the right'.[12] In fact, Peter even accepted an invitation to Sun City in apartheid South Africa, and told the *Radio Times* in 1977 that he was 'right wing through and through, probably through sheer greed'. Writing in 1996, Nicholas Luard spoke enthusiastically of Peter's 'contempt for socialism, the deceitful flatulence of its rhetoric, its spite and envy against the world'.[13]

Then again, Peter took part in frequent anti-apartheid, CND and Anti-Nazi League benefits. He told author John Hind in 1987 that he found the Thatcher government 'more offensive than any other', and that Mrs Thatcher herself was 'the Prime Minister that he had most disliked'. He also claimed that the Macmillan government of the early 1960s 'needed taking apart'.[14] He once described the Young Conservatives as 'awful', and in 1976 wrote a letter to *The Times* defending the activities of Militant. He told his friends that he had voted Labour in 1959 and 1964, and on the latter occasion he held an election night celebration party to mark Labour's victory. In 1970 he assured the journalist Ray Connolly that he had voted for Ben Whitaker, his local Labour councillor. Only seven years later he would tell the *Radio Times* that 'I have never voted socialist in my life'.

The Liberals were so convinced that Peter was one of theirs that they kept inviting him to become a Liberal parliamentary candidate. In 1970 they begged him to contest Epping on their behalf, although he respectfully declined, having assured them of his full support. In 1992 Adrian Slade, the former Footlights President who had gone on to become a Liberal councillor, tried again. 'Peter had always felt more at home with the Liberals than any other party,' explains Slade, 'and he told me that he relished the idea of taking on Glenda Jackson. The Hampstead Liberal Democrat candidacy was still vacant and for a short time he was on the verge of being persuaded by me to put himself forward for the next General Election.'[15] Peter was busy entertaining himself again, but the idea of him genuinely becoming a Liberal candidate – he was by this time a severe alcoholic – is too fantastic for words.

In fact Peter barely had a party political bone in his body. He was conservative with a small 'c', in that he felt the status quo was probably better than the alternative, and that he didn't want to have to pay 93 per cent income tax; but his political views were in the main motivated by moral considerations. In particular, he detested hypocrisy, the exercise of authority for its own sake, and any kind of corruption (other than obvious and massive corruption – he found pantomime villains like Robert Maxwell so hilarious that their comedy value overrode his sense of indignation). According to Paul Foot, 'Peter was suspicious of rulers of every description, but in particular he detested the secrecy, pomposity and hypocrisy which sustains them. The point about Peter – and the point about *Private Eye*

– is that they spotted a simple and very elementary fact, which is that the world we live in is run by hypocrites and humbugs, who are mainly helping themselves to money which has been provided by someone else, and then slapping themselves on the back for this brilliant achievement. Whatever his political approach, he recognised this fact, and he also recognised that the most powerful weapon to use against such people, the one that goes really deep into them, is mockery. Nothing hurts important humbugs more than the sound, the huge roar of people laughing at their absurdities.'[16] Paul Foot, incidentally, was one of the few people that Peter admired unequivocally, on account of his brilliant journalistic exposés of political corruption in the *Eye* and elsewhere.

These sentiments applied not just to Peter's perception of the wider world, but to his personal life as well. Peter's own personal morality was absolute – not his sexual morality, for he quite clearly distinguished social mores from professional and financial probity – but his application of the standards he expected from those in positions of authority to his own behaviour. Roger Law remembers discussing *Spitting Image* with him: 'I said, "You know, no-one's ever offered me a fucking bribe not to do something. Wouldn't that be great? They give you the money and you don't have to do it. It actually happened in the past – I mean, satirical cartoonists like Gillray and Cruikshank were paid not to attack people." And he got quite sniffy about that idea – like, "Don't talk rubbish, of course you couldn't do that" – at which I was really quite surprised, because I thought it was quite a funny idea.' Alan Bennett recalls that Peter was deeply intolerant of humbug in those around him, and that if he felt he had detected it, 'He would fly into a huge self-fuelling rage which propelled him into yet more fantasy and even funnier jokes.'[17]

In some respects, Peter subscribed to the almost puritanical morality of *Private Eye*, which he shared with Richard Ingrams and Claud Cockburn; again, not (on his part) a sexual puritanism, but a belief that nobody's feelings must be spared, no reputation should be left unscathed, in the pursuit of a comic target which deserved attack, on the basis of moral criteria. 'He used to reiterate his theory on satire,' says Roger Law, 'which is that you should be completely and utterly unfair.' Peter himself insisted that there was not a person alive or dead, or institution, or any subject matter, that qualified for exemption from genuinely merited humorous attack: 'I don't think there's *any* subject which cannot be funny,' he opined.[18] This fierce morality, coupled with his innate sense of mischief, were responsible for Peter's most satirical moments.

However scathing or pointed his wit, there was never any personal malice behind Peter's comic attacks on public figures, in *Private Eye* or elsewhere. His humour utterly embodied George Lichtenburg's maxim that 'The finest satire is that in which ridicule is combined with so little malice and so much conviction that it even rouses laughter in those who are hit.' Clive Anderson records that 'Without wishing to trample on Peter's reputation as a savage wit and satirist, I am bound to say that I found him to be not only one of the funniest men in England, but also one of the nicest. This may seem an odd thing to say of someone who once described David Frost as the "Bubonic plagiarist" and who kept up an endless string of insults at the expense of Dudley Moore's size, class and physical condition, for no real reason except that it was amusing. But there was no malice in his method.'[19] Andrew Osmond concurs: 'He was an immensely kind guy. In other words, I don't think I ever saw him put down someone to their face, never. He would meet all kinds of absurd or simple people but he would never mock them or wound them in any way. He would do imitations of Macmillan and so on, but I never saw him exercise his wit at the expense of any vulnerable person.'

In fact, Peter was perfectly capable of hurting people quite viciously if he chose; but it was a capability he resorted to only rarely, and when he did so it tended to be at the expense of those he loved the most and was closest to. During the 1970s, Dudley Moore and Peter's second wife Judy would come in for particular verbal punishment. According to Barry Fantoni, 'He reminded me of when I've been in the company of very, very strong men; I met Mohammed Ali once, and you got the feeling that he had the physical power to destroy you absolutely, I mean, three good punches would see you off the planet. Peter had that in an intellectual sense. Now, there was no more gentle man than Mohammed Ali in the right circumstances; and Peter was gentle, like that, when he sensed that he had power over someone.' In a perverse way, Peter's verbal cruelty to Dudley and Judy marked a loss of power: it was an unfortunate testament to the increasing dependence he felt towards them. Without realising it, he came to fear the intimacy and vulnerability present in his associations with his wife and his partner. As his self-respect dwindled along with his immediate career prospects, he lashed out at those closest to him in a classically self-destructive pattern.

Although the course of both relationships was to become sticky and complicated, there was never the slightest suggestion of enmity. Peter, in fact, was remarkable in that he was a man without enemies. Partly this was because people feared his wit, partly it was because they admired him, partly it was because they feared the social consequences of placing themselves in an opposite camp, but principally it was because the absence of malice that generally characterised his humour unconsciously communicated itself to his targets. He might write something for *Private Eye* with Richard Ingrams, and invariably the aggrieved victim would make Ingrams into a lifelong enemy while privately exonerating Peter. When the magazine took on huge, powerful and rich enemies like Maxwell or Sir James Goldsmith, Peter was usually at the forefront of the campaign. Such adversaries were vengeful, and keen to crush the *Eye* men individually, one by one; but always, Peter was discreetly exempted from their retributions. David Frost, a regular *Eye* target, explains: 'If somebody wrote something in *Private Eye* that you didn't like, or even loathed, everybody would say, "That wouldn't be Peter, it must be somebody else you know." You just had this warm, kindly image of Peter, which was true. He was never abrasive or acerbic in real life you know, he was warm, and generous, and kindly, and that was what everybody wanted to remember about him.' Frost's spectacles were rose-tinted indeed.

Being a cynical man, Peter had no illusions about the powerlessness of humour to damage its targets. He shared none of Paul Foot's 'We'll-get-them-this-time' optimism. Barry Humphries spoke of his 'rhapsodic cynicism', and called him 'a bracing influence for sanity in the sloppy sixties'.[20] By and large this was a healthy and intelligent cynicism, but there were times when it threatened to overwhelm him, when he felt that any stance, however heartfelt, was ultimately pointless – that nothing could be achieved. Griff Rhys Jones believes that 'He was haunted, like so many comics, by the inner demon of nihilism.'

Peter was profoundly disinclined to take anything seriously; this too was fundamentally healthy, but like his sense of nihilism, it was an attitude that conspired against hard work and conventional success. In many respects it is remarkable that he managed to get as far as he did, and a tribute not just to his talents but to the protestant work ethic which had been drummed into him from his earliest days in the public school system. Referring to a comment by Christopher Booker that Peter was secretly 'extremely proud' to have saved David Frost from drowning, Alan Bennett remarks that 'Peter wasn't extremely proud of *anything*, and not to appreciate that or to see how drenching irony and a profound sense of the ridiculous informed everything he thought and did (and sometimes blunted his best endeavours) is to miss the point of the man.'[21]

In that respect, his humour served as a defence against commitment, just as it served as a defence against so many things. For example, it was a highly effective barrier against personal revelation, 'the classic way of jamming intimacy'[22] as Barry Humphries observed. Asked if anyone or anything truly inspired him or fired his imagination, he would generally reply, 'Dorothy Squires'. When Peter came into *Private Eye* after a long absence, there would be no word about where he'd been or what he'd been doing. 'He wasn't one to confide,' says Richard Ingrams, 'although to be fair he probably thought we might find it boring.' As a result, Peter could be a nightmare for inquisitive journalists. 'You won't get me to say anything. Not me. I know what comes of it,'[23] he leered with a cockney accent at a lady from the *Sun* in 1965. Of course there is no reason why he should have discussed his life with the *Sun*, even in its pre-Murdoch days, but there were a number of occasions when he quite happily agreed to take part in searching biographical interviews on television, deflected all the questions with jokes, and ended up sitting in an atmosphere of strained hostility with his interviewer – most famously with David Dimbleby in 1979. 'Nobody can be themselves in public,' Peter explained defensively. 'Even if they appear to look natural and use their own voice, they're still not behaving as they would at home.'[24] Then, once in a while, usually when he was profoundly depressed in his later years, he would be unable to erect the barriers and it would all come tumbling out, great reams of his innermost thoughts that he had denied to his friends, printed in a newspaper for all to see.

Under normal circumstances, though, he defended himself expertly against analysis, turning everything into a joke. No one would ever have dared to analyse him to his face, for they would immediately have been shot down in a fusillade of withering humour. 'It's not that *everything* was a joke to him,' explains his sister Sarah. 'When our parents died he did show his feelings. He just had the ability to use humour as a coping mechanism if necessary. From my own experience, such reticence is an old boarding school habit: when you were young, if there wasn't anybody to talk to when something was really upsetting you, then you got into the habit of not confiding, or thinking that you were being frightfully boring if you went on about it.' It was this refusal to show vulnerability that prevented him from engendering the sympathies of a mass audience, which was why Dudley's presence became such a vital part of his comic armoury. But the vulnerability was there, all right. Horace Walpole said that 'This world is a comedy to those that think, a tragedy to those that feel.' In Peter's case, it was both.

So where did Peter's comedy come from, what was the source? One certainty is that it was entirely original, entirely personal to him. Of course he was lonely and bullied at school, of course he was part of a confident, iconoclastic generation, but these were shaping influences, not causes. He never sat down to learn how to be funny, either. 'I didn't really have any ambitions to learn my craft as a performer,' he admitted.

'If it had involved any hard graft I'd have given up very early on. That sounds appalling, I know.'[25] He did have a repertoire of comedic tricks, but these were almost certainly instinctive. For instance, he knew how to use comedy specifics – that is, the application of an unnecessarily detailed piece of information to create a joke. In *Bedazzled*, when Stanley Moon queried the suggestion that Moses had sold his soul to the Devil, and George Spiggott explained that he was referring to Irving Moses, the fruiterer, the basic fact of there being two Moses was transferred into a good joke by the application of the irrelevant but intrinsically funny word 'fruiterer'. The blizzard of information that Peter absorbed from publications great and small helped in the application of such comic trivia – he knew, for instance, an inordinate amount about the life and marriages of Gracie Fields.

He also knew the value of repeating an amusing word or piece of information until the very relentlessness of the repetition added to the humour. Stephen Fry noted a perfect example of this, when someone remarked to Peter that it wasn't Elizabeth Taylor's fault that she was putting on weight, it was her glands:

> I know. Poor woman. There she is, in her suite in the Dorchester, harmlessly watching television. Suddenly her glands pick up the phone and order two dozen eclairs and a bottle of brandy. 'No,' she screams, 'please, I beg you!' but her glands take no notice. Determined glands they are, her glands. You've never known glands like them. The trolley arrives and Elizabeth Taylor hides in the bathroom, but her glands, her glands take the eclairs, smash down the door and stuff them down her throat. I'm glad I haven't got glands like that. Terrible glands.

Jonathan Miller points out that perhaps more than any other comedian, Peter could 'extract peculiar surrealistic effects from an endless repetition of lower-middle-class clichés.'[26] Indeed, the humorous contrast achieved by juxtaposing suburban banality with surrealism was one of Peter's chief comic weapons.

Subverting as well as repeating clichés was of course one of his favourite methods of making people laugh; as in this extract from the *Behind the Fridge* sketch in which Peter, as Arthur Shepherd, is being interviewed by Dudley's reporter from the *Bethlehem Star*:

> *Shepherd*:   Er, basically what happened was that me and the lads were abiding in the fields.

Reporter:	*(writing)* Abiding in the fields, yes . . .
Shepherd:	Yes. Mind you, I can't abide these fields.

. . . whereupon Peter went on to repeat the word 'abide' over and over again in different contexts. Deliberate misunderstanding was often used to subvert a cliché, or just as a joke on its own. Asked for a capsule description of Dudley Moore, Peter replied 'He's a capsule.' The Great Train Robbery sketch from *Beyond the Fringe* featured a whole sequence of deliberate misunderstandings:

Interviewer:	So you feel that thieves are responsible?
Sir Arthur:	Good heavens, no, I feel that thieves are totally irresponsible – ghastly people, who go around snatching your money.
Interviewer:	I appreciate that, Sir Arthur.
Sir Arthur:	You may appreciate that but most people don't. If you like your money being snatched, you must be rather an odd fish, I think.
Interviewer:	Who do you think is behind the criminals?
Sir Arthur:	We are.

Then there was the self-undermining statement, the apparently minuscule qualification which destroys the confident pronouncements that have proceeded it. Peter's *Beyond the Fringe* miner, for instance, spoke favourably of the leisurely lifestyle enjoyed by miners: a mine being a place where you can do almost anything you like, he explained, as long as you have collected several hundredweight of coal by the end of the day. One could go on listing such comic devices, but ultimately they were all salad dressing. The secret of his humour lay in his bizarre and original mental processes. Peter himself had no time for comedic theory, precisely because comedy came so easily and instinctively to him, although he did derive considerable enjoyment from portentous Californian and East European analyses of jokes.

As a genuine original, Peter had been directly influenced by very few other comedians – Milligan, Sellers and J. B. Morton (Beachcomber) perhaps being the most important. He deferred to few of his colleagues in company: Milligan and Sellers again, Kenneth Williams, Peter Ustinov and Mel Brooks were among this select group. Interestingly, those comedians he cited as his favourites often tended to be old-fashioned gag merchants, capable of doing something that he couldn't do and therefore worthy of admiration: Groucho Marx, Abbott and Costello, Jerry Lewis. In performance Peter was closer to a comedian like Harry Enfield, able to come up with a stream of funny lines without actually resorting to wisecracks. A number of commentators have observed that most of Peter's humour was verbal, which is true, but then a lot of it was to do with the expression of immensely visual ideas, which could never be realised except in the imagination. Sometimes, as with the leaping nuns or the Good v. Evil cricket match, the ideas were filmable, but enormous snakes many millions of miles long or saintly bees were condemned to remain forever locked into Peter's mesmeric, droning delivery.

Peter knew full well that he was in the front rank of British comedians. Asked by David Dimbleby how he felt about being 'probably the funniest Englishman since Chaplin,' he replied: 'Well, this is no time for false modesty.'[27] Peter enjoyed compliments, and grew irritated when critics dismissed his humour as 'schoolboy' or 'undergraduate'. This, he reasoned quite correctly, was a feeble device used by those who have failed to understand or appreciate a joke, to endeavour to raise themselves above it. 'I don't go round saying "That's senile humour", do I?'[28] he protested. This confidence in his own ability, as every comedian knows, had nothing to do with the confidence – or lack of it – that it will be all right on the night. 'Professional confidence combined with a personal un-confidence' is how his fellow-sufferer Dudley Moore summarises it. According to his first wife Wendy, 'His outer confidence, at least to begin with, was just pure delight at being able to share his inner community of these characters that inhabited his imagination. But it was a total façade. Somebody who smokes three packs a day is not confident.'

In Peter's case, these fears became self-fulfilling. With every triumph, the effort required to equal it or better it became greater, while the thought of just giving up and allowing his best work to pass into history became ever more seductive. In attempting to better what he had already achieved, he drove himself to try and succeed outside the confines of that area in which his genius enjoyed total command, with the result that failure became inevitable. The loss of momentum in his career around the turn of the 1970s, together with the upsetting upheavals in his personal life, combined to create an especially vulnerable state of affairs in which he was overwhelmed by that depression which had always been present in his make-up.

His second wife Judy remembers that throughout their time together in the 1970s, Peter's moods would alternate: at first he would be elated, and increasingly so, which was when he would be at his funniest, most extrovert and most convivial. Then, like a plane rising into an ever steeper

ascent until it stalls, he would plunge rapidly and without warning into a
black, inconsolable depression, accompanied by bitter reproach for himself
and those closest to him. Gradually, he would emerge from these depths,
normality would re-assert itself, and then the build-up of elation would
begin again. These are, in fact, the classic symptoms of manic depression,
and it now seems likely that Peter was an undiagnosed manic depressive.
Certainly Judy now believes that this was the case.

Depression of this sort is often hereditary, and let us not forget that
Peter's grandfather was a charming, convivial, witty man, doing well in
his job, who inexplicably went into his garden one day and blew his brains
out; nor the fact that Peter found the discovery of these events so profoundly
disturbing. Manic depression is endemic, too, in comedians, often going
undiagnosed in milder cases. The wave-pattern of the depressive, from
elation to depression and back again, is more pronounced than that of
the normal human being. Very often, rising into the crest of a wave, the
depressive's enhanced extroversion and predilection for laughter will lead
him to put on a performance for those around him; in time, those who have
the ability to become professional comedians learn to control the depression
that follows, to suppress it while putting on a realistic semblance of the
entertaining 'high' that characterised the previous upswing.

This, perhaps, is one clue to the elusive wellspring of Peter's humour.
Consider this personal description of the early onset of manic depression,
provided by expert and sufferer Kay Redfield Jamison:

> An intoxicating state that gave rise to ... an incomparable flow
> of thoughts, and a ceaseless energy that allowed the translation of
> new ideas into papers and projects ... ideas were coming so fast
> that they intersected one another at every conceivable angle.

Later on Ms Jamison found herself becoming:

> Increasingly restless and irritable, and I craved excitement; all of a
> sudden I found myself rebelling against the very things I most loved
> about my husband: his kindness, stability, warmth and love.[29]

Consider also this description by Oliver Sacks of one Mr Thompson, a
patient in an institution, suffering from a degenerative disease connected
to alcoholism:

> He is driven to a sort of narrational frenzy, of ceaseless tales and
> confabulations. Superficially, he comes over as an ebullient comic.

People say, 'He's a riot'. And there is much that *is* comic, but not just comic: it is terrible as well. For here is a man who, in some sense, is desperate, continually inventing, throwing bridges of meaning over the chaos that yawns continually beneath him. After finding him 'a riot', 'a laugh', 'loads of fun', people are disquieted by something in him. 'He never stops', they say. 'He's like a man in a race, a man trying to catch something which always eludes him.'[30]

This example is, of course, not directly relevant: Peter was not suffering from the same complaint (Korsakov's syndrome), nor did he even faintly require the services of an institution. But indirectly at least, there are undoubted similarities present. Both men were driven to fill their lives with comedy because they were afraid of what would be left if they did not. The inner demons Peter wrestled with may have been greater and more fundamental to the inspiration of his humour than many of his friends realised. In the years following 1971, they were to gain the upper hand.

CHAPTER 12

I Can't Talk Now, 'Cos He's Here

Behind the Fridge, 1971–75

Australia was fun at first. Peter and Dudley were 'lauded and applauded and loved,' as Judy put it, and the show was a triumph. 'A supremely well-worked evening' said the *Herald*, and the Melbourne *Sun* reported 'a brilliant night'. The show opened in Canberra, before moving on to Melbourne, Sydney, Wellington and Auckland in New Zealand, and finally Perth. Peter, Dudley and Judy travelled around in a gang together, although Dudley was quick to find a female companion in the shape of Lyndall Hobbs, a local journalist. 'It was like being in a band,' recalls Judy with fond nostalgia. 'We all got to know each other very well indeed. There were lots of car journeys and plane journeys, and we were always mucking about. Peter and Dudley used to improvise routines about the boring shops and suburbs we used to pass through en route.' Dudley remembers 'Nights when I couldn't think of anything being more enjoyable. It was such tremendous fun, and you came off absolutely ecstatic and jumping about the place. We'd hit a peak and it was just hurtling along.'[1] Disastrous chat shows and arguments with ex-wives seemed a million miles away.

On 21 September they appeared as guests on a special Australian TV edition of *The Dave Allen Show*, and shocked Australia by saying the words 'bum' and 'piss', and performing the Bethlehem sketch *Gospel Truth*. More than 650 people telephoned to complain, causing Sir Frank Packer, the Chief Executive of Television Corporation Ltd, to describe the show as 'a vulgar programme in bad taste', and his son Clyde Packer, who by an amazing coincidence was the Managing Director of Channel Nine, to complain that it had contained 'offensive and irresponsible remarks'. The

Australian Broadcasting Control Board moved quickly, and handed Peter, Dudley and Dave Allen lifetime bans from all 47 TV and 116 radio stations throughout Australia. Peter and Dudley were stunned at first, and rather ungallantly issued a statement seeking to blame Dave Allen for allowing the show to go 'beyond the bounds of decency'.

They need not have worried. The incident made them into national heroes, and ensured that every night of the tour was a complete sell-out weeks in advance. Just eight days later Channel Nine ignored the ABCB ban and televised a charity gala in aid of the Freedom from Hunger Campaign which starred Peter and Dudley. The Board was dealt a fatal blow from which it never recovered. Shane Maloney, who was a student at Melbourne University at the time, recalls that 'when the terrible duo appeared on campus in the midst of their battle with the forces of puritanism and cant, they were greeted as heroes. The hall filled to capacity as soon as the doors opened. Speakers were rapidly set up outside to cater for the overflow. When these proved insufficient, the show was piped campus-wide on closed-circuit television.'[2] Peter sent a telegram to the head of the Australian Broadcasting Control Board thanking him for all the free publicity.

Unfortunately, this high-spirited escape from the pressures of home was to be short-lived. On 2 October 1971, the day of their Melbourne opening, Peter received a cable from Wendy informing him that Daisy was in the process of having a severe asthma attack, and that specialists had ascribed it to the painstakingly installed decor and furnishings of Kenwood Cottage, which she was about to rip out. Distraught, he sat down to write as restrainedly as he could to his parents:

> Darling Mummy and Daddy,
> . . . I've had a cable from Wendy about the house and Daisy. I didn't reply as I think it's just her usual game of trying to get at me – I'm sure if anything was really wrong you could let me know. Perhaps you could give her a ring – I don't want to get involved with telephone chats with her at this distance.
> Judy and I send lots of love,
> Peter

Whereupon he sealed the envelope, put the letter in the post box, drank himself almost insensible, and walked fully clothed into the swimming pool of the President Motor Inn. Eventually, he had to be fished out by the hotel staff. 'He was in agony,' remembers Dudley. 'To my mind, he became an alcoholic from that moment on.'[3]

Somehow Peter stumbled through that evening's performance, but it was the start of a downward slide. 'Peter really started drinking then,' says Judy. 'He was missing his two children terribly, and that's what cracked him, but Wendy kept writing these angry letters. Peter hadn't actually told her that he was going away to Australia until the last minute. Wherever we went there would be messages from Wendy saying "The kids miss you", and the fact that he was so far away made him feel powerless and guilty. He absolutely adored his children and was a very emotional man, much more so than Dudley. When Dudley got divorced it was upsetting to him, but the absence of children meant it wasn't so traumatic. The strain nearly cracked Peter and it nearly cracked me. I don't think Peter had realised the grief involved in the break-up of a marriage.' Peter felt that he was being subjected to a particularly carefully timed campaign of mental torture. Entirely reasonably, Wendy saw things from a totally different perspective: 'Daisy was ending up in oxygen tents and having adrenalin injections and being sent home from school regularly, and the doctors were giving her steroids and telling me that I had to get rid of the cats and soft furnishings, and make the house plastic so it could all be sponged down.'

On 21 October the tour moved on to Sydney for four weeks, where Michael Parkinson was among the audience. He was amazed to see that 'Dudley was literally holding Peter up on stage. If Peter couldn't grab the furniture he'd grab Dudley; he was pissed all the time. I felt very, very sorry for Dudley – he was trying very hard, but Peter's drinking was destroying their relationship. Of course the Australians were so chuffed to see people like Peter and Dudley out there, there was a kind of forgiveness. Peter and Dudley were allowed to pretend it was all part of the act. In fact they'd have had to dismember their grannies on stage to have had anything like a bad review.' Dudley himself remembers that 'Peter was drunk for the whole of the first week in Sydney. I didn't know how to stop him, I really didn't. I remember saying then for the first time that I wanted to put an end to the partnership.'

It was while the pair were in Sydney that Lewis Morley, the photographer who had taken the publicity pictures for Beyond the Fringe ten years previously, invited them to a dinner party. Everyone had a little too much to drink, and Peter sat there slapping mosquitoes, quietly murmuring to himself, 'Things have changed, things have changed.' Dudley started to read out some John Betjeman poems, then stopped and burst into tears. 'The other guests at the party were a little confused,' says Morley. 'They had expected an evening of jollity with a never-ending stream of Pete and Dud-isms. It was a very quiet car that drove back to their hotel.'[4]

By the time the show reached New Zealand, the alcohol problem had become a permanent feature of their professional relationship. Dudley explains that 'I had to ignore it. If I had acknowledged it, that would have turned all our sketches into something else – me and my drunken friend, me and the drunken clergyman. He was drunk every night.'[5] The trouble was, Peter kept wandering off the script into random cul-de-sacs from which he could not always retrieve himself. 'He would come on so hopelessly drunk and start ad-libbing on something that had nothing to do with anything we'd ever performed – imagine being in front of 1,500 people and trying to get through it, never knowing what you're going to get.'[6] Massive rows followed. Peter really needed time off to sort himself out, but theirs was a show which could never incorporate understudies. Dudley dreamed up a practical demonstration of what Peter was doing to their act: 'One night *I* got drunk, which I had never done before a performance, and afterwards he complained, "That's the worst performance you've ever given." So I said, "Now you know what it feels like."'[7]

Later, Peter tried to dismiss his drinking on the tour as a bit of a lark at Dudley's expense, brought about by the abundance of local hospitality, but it must have been clear to all present that something was seriously wrong. Any thoughts that Dudley might have had of splitting the partnership, however, were fatally undermined by the mutually dependent relationship between the two men, both onstage and offstage. 'They were obsessed with each other,' relates Judy, 'they were like brothers. Everything one did, the other had to know about. There was an extremely competitive element in their relationship, and neither wanted the other to get further ahead.' Dudley has always been painted as the hapless victim of Peter's excesses, and it is true that Peter's drinking was extremely hard to cope with on stage, but Judy feels that she witnessed a different side of Dudley at close quarters – a man expert at using the appearance of emotional vulnerability to get what he wanted, from sympathy to sex. 'He was very manipulative – he could be cold and withhold his love if he wanted to. Dudley always wanted information about Peter, it was part of his manoeuvring; he would phone me solicitously to see whether Peter and I had had a row, but I felt that it was really just prurience masquerading as concern. But then Peter would also want to know what I had learned about Dudley.' Being together twenty-four hours a day, every day, had become a stressful experience; sometimes their exchanges were hilarious and delightful, at other times they circled each other warily.

One night in New Zealand, when Peter had got blind drunk and collapsed into bed, Dudley sat seductively playing the piano in the locked-up hotel bar; around him lounged a collection of adoring waitresses, and Judy. It was five o'clock in the morning when Dudley's performance was interrupted by the sound of the hotel lift going up and down, apparently at random. The culprit proved to be Peter, dressed only in his underpants, too drunk to find the right lift button, jabbing randomly at the control panel in the hope of finally arriving at the ground floor. He was absolutely livid at the thought that his girlfriend might have been left unaccompanied with the sexually rapacious Dudley – although his furious entry into the bar was somewhat undermined by his attire, and by the method of his arrival. Giggling, Judy scuttled upstairs. 'Life with Peter and Dudley was *so* complicated,' she says. 'I'd been wary about the Australia idea. It was fun for a while and the shows went well, but in some respects it didn't work in the end.'

The question of what to do next was a vexed one. Alexander Cohen wanted to bring *Behind the Fridge* to the United States. Donald Langdon, Peter's former agent, wanted to mount it in London first. The BBC wanted another series of *Not Only . . . But Also*. That, decided Peter, would be utterly pointless. In the end Langdon proved persuasive once more, and got the nod because, as Peter put it, 'I'm damned well not going to miss another football season here.'[8] And of course, there was also the small matter of seeing his daughters again. As it turned out, Langdon did not get his production together until November, giving Dudley the chance to appear in an absolute abortion entitled *Not Only Lulu But Also Dudley Moore* for BBC TV. It was Dudley's way of testing the waters of a career without Peter, but he soon realised that he had made a terrible mistake. He found it impossible, for instance, to write alone. 'I hated it, and I didn't do it very well. I'd always coasted in before on the tails of Peter.'[9]

Peter returned to London at the end of February 1972, to play a small cameo role in *The Adventures of Barry McKenzie*, a film version of the cartoon character that he had originally created in *Private Eye*. Barry Humphries and director Bruce Beresford had somehow managed to elicit a quarter of a million dollars from the Australian Film Development Corporation, and had telephoned Peter while they were in Australia securing the money, to ask him to take part. Peter was to play a BBC TV director in the climactic scene, in which a fire at Television Centre is extinguished by a group of Australians drinking Foster's lager and urinating onto the flames.

When Peter arrived at the Soho location, he was drunk. Humphries, who had cured his own drink problem, remembers that 'I was absolutely horrified. I hadn't seen him for a long time, there I was back in London in terrific health, all ready to make this film, and I'd been thinking, how great to welcome this man without whom we wouldn't be making this movie. He was affability itself, but as a friend of Peter's I was quite shaken and distressed to see him like that.' Despite an engaging

amateurishness and some delicious moments, the film garnered terrible
reviews and did nothing for Peter's career – 'The worst Australian film
ever made,' complained Max Harris – but the efforts of the Australian
Film Development Corporation to restrain the language ensured that it
became a cult success. It eventually made a 500 per cent profit and
provoked Foster's Lager, who had spent a decade trying to market a
sophisticated image, into changing their advertising strategy altogether.
There was, incidentally, a failed sequel that Peter had nothing to do with,
entitled *Barry McKenzie Holds His Own*, that was notable for a cameo by
the Australian Prime Minister Gough Whitlam. In a scene with Barry
Humphries's Melbourne housewife Edna Everage, the PM improvised the
line 'Arise, *Dame* Edna!', and a character was reborn.

Peter and Judy bought a four-storey house in Denbigh Terrace in
Notting Hill Gate – Wendy and the children were still living in the
re-upholstered Kenwood Cottage – and settled down there. Peter had
absolutely no intention of doing any work. All he really wanted to do
was see his children, and they were frequent visitors. The rest of the
time Peter and Judy sat, surrounded by stripped pine, picture mirrors,
oil lamps, pot plants and of course the green Tiffany lamp, gazing into
each other's eyes. They really were hopelessly in love with each other.
'Peter was a very easy person to live with,' says Judy. 'We could laugh
together about anything, just the two of us. We thought we would be
together forever. I really loved him and he really loved me. I want to
remember him as I knew and loved him, before things got so distorted
by the drinking. There was a sweet, quirky gentle side to him which
people don't know, intellectual, spiritual and a little bit dotty.'[10]

The drink had yet to destroy Peter's looks, and the drugs were keeping
him slim. He and Judy still made a remarkably good-looking couple. He
developed a passion for odd accessories – coloured shoes, interesting
sunglasses, bizarre hats – and always wore a French gendarme's hat in
bed. He was invariably an interesting person to live with, on account of
his unpredictable behaviour. One night a local West Indian household
held a party, with reggae blasting out well into the small hours; a gang of
youths shoved smoke bombs through the letterbox. Peter got out of bed,
and marched across the street to sort things out. He returned at breakfast
the next day, having had the time of his life.

Peter and Judy were happy together, but his depression and sadness were
never far from the surface. 'It was very sticky with Wendy,' explains Judy,
'there was so much tension. She resented the way Peter had dropped in and
out of the children's lives.' Wendy developed an interest in macrobiotics,
with particular reference to treating Daisy's asthma, and took her daughters

to stay at the vegetarian commune at Findhorn in Scotland; she liked it so much that she decided they would go to live there permanently. Peter had to take out a court injunction preventing his family from moving so far away. 'He was very controlling,' objects Wendy, 'he wanted to have us nearby.'

Peter took solace, as ever, in alcohol. In April, he was invited to a banquet at the Grosvenor House Hotel to celebrate the tenth anniversary of *The Sunday Times* colour supplement, in company with six hundred others who had 'made news during the sixties'. Judy, because she was not Peter's wife, was not invited. Peter got drunk, and worked himself into a self-propelling rage at the slight to his girlfriend. He stood up, grabbed the microphone and shouted a tirade of abuse at *The Sunday Times*. Unfortunately – or perhaps fortunately – he had forgotten to switch the microphone on. 'I have never known anything like it. It was the most embarrassing few moments for everyone,' one of the waitresses told the papers.

In the summer, Paul Foot decided to leave *Private Eye* after a row with Richard Ingrams. An ardent socialist, Foot had been unable to come to terms with jokes about left-wing figures such as Bernadette Devlin, Angela Davis and the striking dockers. Peter was inordinately upset at the loss of the journalist he admired so wholeheartedly. The *Eye's* Managing Director David Cash remembers that 'We had this farewell lunch, at the Terrazza in Romilly Street, and it was the one time I saw Cookie *totally* legless. He got very emotional about Footie going, and then he collapsed in the gutter outside.' Peter got drunk, too, at a *Beyond the Fringe* reunion staged for the *Parkinson* show. 'There was an awkward feeling about the meeting,' reflects Michael Parkinson, 'a sense of time erecting fences.'

Peter only took on one professional engagement in the nine months between *The Adventures of Barry McKenzie* and the London opening of *Behind the Fridge*: a leading role in *Mill Hill*, a thirty-minute theatre presentation for BBC 2 at the end of May. *Mill Hill* was an embarrassingly weak John Mortimer farce in which Peter played Peter Trilby, a nervous dentist who is having an affair with the wife of his partner Roy, escaping to see her in the afternoons through the pretence of attending cricket practice. The other performances – by Clive Revill as Roy and Geraldine McEwan as his wife – were even worse than Peter's. The script levered in plot details with an industrial lack of subtlety, as in the scene establishing the situation and the names of the characters:

Denise: Oh, Peter.
Peter: Yes, Denise.
Denise: Of course, it's been wonderful having lunch together –

they must think we're married at the trattoria – but this
is the first time we've been really alone.

Peter: How long have we got?

Denise: The whole afternoon. Isn't it marvellous?

Peter: Until Roy gets back.

Creatively, everything Peter touched – with the exception of his collabo-
rations with Dudley – seemed to turn to mud.

Dudley was undergoing similar problems. He spent the summer
appearing as the Dormouse in a film version of *Alice's Adventures
in Wonderland*, which was as mawkish and misconceived as Jonathan
Miller's TV version had been dry and clever six years before. He too
was experiencing severe depression: his divorce from Suzy Kendall came
through on 15 September 1972, an upsetting situation only partially
alleviated by his affair with the singer Lynsey de Paul. He spent much
of his time on the psychiatrist's couch. 'I just didn't want to be funny any
more. Trying to be funny to protect myself was rather annoying to me.
I didn't know what I wanted to be. Peter was some support. He felt that
this was just a normal condition, and why did I have to go through all
these contortions to figure this out, when to him it was self-evident.'[11]

It was in such sober circumstances that Peter and Dudley drifted back
together for the London opening of *Behind the Fridge*, at the Cambridge
Theatre on 21 November. They had decided to write some new material
for the show, and to include a selection of short films, but when it came
to it Peter was no longer prepared to sit improvising with Dudley; he just
wanted to stay at home. They wrote the new material separately, on paper,
and posted their work to each other. Peter proffered the vague excuse that
good ideas were 'altered' by improvising on tape; Dudley complained to
a *Times* journalist that he was finding the new method 'more difficult . . .
it's harder to become colloquial from a written script than it is to keep it
natural by continually improvising it.'[12] Neither was Peter even remotely
interested in the staging of the show. Dudley complained testily of his
partner's 'sheer laziness', recounting how 'the staging somehow got into
this extraordinary business of Peter sitting on his bottom and me doing
all the work.'[13]

Peter maintained that it didn't really matter how the show was staged.
'They'll be coming from north of Watford in coachloads,' he predicted
confidently. 'Mark my words, the bookings will be good, regardless of
what the smart West End crickets say.' 'Crickets' was Peter's term for
the critics, a group of people whom he had come to dislike and distrust
over the preceding few years. He was right, insofar as the show was

sold out for months even before the opening night. Dudley, however, wanted reassurance, not a repeat of the onstage chaos that had marked the Australian tour, and invited Joe McGrath to direct both the show and the new film inserts. McGrath was surprised to find how much had changed since he had produced the first series of Not Only ... But Also: 'In the early days Peter had seemed very much in charge of the two of them, but by the time of Behind the Fridge Dudley seemed to be gaining the upper hand. Peter was occasionally in a very bad way.' Partly on the advice of his psychiatrist, Dudley had become – in Peter's words – 'No longer such a servile little creep.'[14]

Eventually, very little new material was added. There was a sketch about Idi Amin and a song about Ted Heath entitled Heath, based on Isaac Hayes' Shaft. Resting, a sketch that had been improvised in the final weeks of the Australian tour, was now officially included: it concerned an unemployed actor who takes on domestic work in the home of a High Court Judge. Peter explained that 'I have had actors who are resting doing domestic work for me, and on the whole it's been remarkable how little domestic work has been done, and how much talk about the state of the theatre, ducky.' In keeping with the bleak tone of the show, the sketch ended on an unpleasant note with the murder of the Judge by his cleaner. The promoters – Donald Langdon for Hemdale, and Colin McLennan – were unhappy about the amount of black humour in the show, and argued for the removal of the sketch about the minicab driver. The arguments continued until a few weeks into the run, when Harold Pinter inadvertently settled matters by attending a performance and pronouncing it the best thing in the show.

Most of the specially written films were based on old ideas. Shot in the late summer and performed by Peter, Dudley and Judy, they included the 'Diarrhoea Expert' sketch from the Establishment Club – in which the speaker dashes offstage before he can begin his speech; the shower sketch from Not Only ... But Also – in which Dudley's voice and skin change colour; a musical number in which Peter got to dress up as Marlene Dietrich; and a new sketch written by Dudley, about an appeal on behalf of the Spooch Ompodiment Society, which was basically a rewrite of Peter's Appeal on behalf of the Blond from the days of the New York Establishment.

The pair composed amusing essays about each other for the programme. Dudley wrote of his partner that:

> He pretends that under his glassy exterior is a heart of gold. The exterior is just the tip of the iceberg. Rumours that we have split up are true.

Peter replied that:

> Like many smallish men (Napoleon, Adolf Hitler, to name but two) Dudley has a superficial charm and warmth that deceive many. Underneath lurks a demented sadist, capable in private of unspeakable deeds.

As the date of the opening night approached, Peter was seriously afflicted by nerves. According to Judy, 'Peter hated the Cambridge Theatre – he thought it would be the kiss of death. He thought that it was too big and had no atmosphere – it was like a barn. He also began to fear the vitriolic things the critics might say; he was always more affected than Dudley by what the critics wrote. He had to be the best, he had to be seen to be the sharpest.' Joe McGrath too found conditions at the Cambridge extremely difficult: 'They never got the lighting cues right, not once in a whole year. The stage hands would work for a few days, then a whole new group would come in. We rehearsed for days before the first night, and half an hour before curtain up a new group of stage hands came on, who hadn't even seen it. The guys we'd been rehearsing with just left. I said, "What's going on here?" They said, "We'll tell the new lot what to do. Don't worry guv, they know what they're doing." They didn't, of course.'

That was the least of the disasters that were to beset the opening night of *Behind the Fridge*. The *This Is Your Life* team, headed by Eamonn Andrews, had decided to surprise Dudley with the famous red book. With almost unbelievable stupidity, they arrived with the cameras just as Peter and Dudley were about to go into the dress rehearsal. Dudley was whisked off to the TV studios in a car. Peter, smiling politely for the cameras but crumbling inside, went with him. There was no dress rehearsal. Joe McGrath, furious, refused to come along. Nobody had thought to discuss it with any of them. 'You should come Joe,' begged Dudley, 'you're part of my life'; but McGrath stayed where he was, fuming, alone on the stage. At the TV studios, Dudley was hurried in front of the audience and the usual phalanx of friends and relatives. Peter, already a bag of nerves, was left alone in the green room with the drinks trolley.

Inevitably, by the time they got back to the Cambridge Theatre, Peter was virtually insensible. The audience began filing in after 6.30 p.m. and by seven the auditorium was packed with 1,200 people. The show was due to start, but Peter had passed out backstage, as Dudley, Joe McGrath and various frantic theatre staff tried to slap him awake. McGrath dressed him while he was still unconscious. Black coffee was literally forced down his throat until he began to come round. In the auditorium, the first slow hand claps began to start. An Assistant Stage Manager was sent onstage with a made-up story about a technical hitch in the projection equipment, to try and buy more time.

After twenty minutes, Joe McGrath came up on to the stage and peered through the side of the curtain. He could see Sean Connery in the front row. 'I thought, that's all I need, bloody James Bond. Dudley came over and said, "Somebody has to tell them," and I said, "Well I'm not," and he said, "Well neither am I." Eventually the audience began to sing "Why are we waiting?", and Dudley began to dance around the stage behind the curtain in time to the song, and he grabbed me, and started waltzing with me. There we were, waltzing to "Why are we waiting?", and Dudley was pointing at the curtain and singing "I'll-tell-you-why-we're-fucking-waiting, the-cunt-is-drunk, the-cunt-is-drunk, he's out of his fucking mind." Then he unzipped his trousers, pulled them down and mooned at the curtain, in the direction of the audience.'

Finally, Peter was resuscitated to a point where it was just about possible to start the show. The curtain went up, and he and Dudley went on stage to a tumultuous round of applause. The very first joke in the show consisted of Peter and Dudley entering from either wing, as if to meet in the middle of the stage, but continuing past each other and into the opposite wing; then re-entering, this time for real. The first pass was greeted with a huge laugh. Then Dudley returned to the centre of the stage alone. Peter, in the far wing, had not moved. Joe McGrath, who was standing just a few yards away, went across to him to see what was the matter. 'Peter turned to me and said, "I can't do this, I can't fucking do this." And then he started to cry. He just said, "I'm sorry Joe, I'm so sorry."' Peter Cook, *the* Peter Cook, who had taken British comedy by storm with *Beyond the Fringe*, the Establishment Club and *Not Only ... But Also*, was standing in the wings of the Cambridge Theatre, with big helpless tears running down his face.

McGrath grabbed him roughly by the shoulders, turned him round, and propelled him on to the stage; for a few minutes, he seemed stunned, but then, for the rest of the evening, Peter did not put a foot wrong. It was Dudley, in fact, who perpetrated the odd slip, so fearful was he that Peter would suffer another breakdown. 'The next day,' relates McGrath, 'Michael Billington wrote this review saying that Peter had been magisterial and wonderful, and that Dudley had been very very nervous. Dudley went completely mad. He told me, "I've had it. I'm getting out of this. It's driving me up the fucking wall. I can't be dealing with it. It's totally out of control, and I've got to make my own future." After that, Dudley began to take

over and become very strong.'[15] In the bar after the show, all the talk
had been of Peter's dazzling performance; the 'technical hitch' had all
but been forgotten. Sean Connery, though, had smiled a little smile at
Joe McGrath, and said with reference to Peter: 'Wee bit o' trouble, Joe,
eh? Wee bit o' trouble there?'

In general, the 'crickets'' response to the show was not terribly
enthusiastic, as Peter had predicted, although the reference to *Beyond
the Fringe* in the title had naturally provided a clutch of rather limited
minds with the same obvious blunt instrument to beat the show with.
Jack Tinker in the *Mail* spoke sarcastically and camply of the 'clever
young men' who had killed off good old-fashioned revue. John Barber
in the *Telegraph* complained that the 'anything-for-a-laugh gagging was a
poor exchange for the hard, eye-on-the-ball savagery of the quartet who
gave a new meaning to the word satire.' Elsewhere, Herbert Kretzmer
in the *Express* called it 'A curious little revue . . . curiously devoid of
adventure or audacity.' Sheridan Morley in *Punch* pointed out that 'A
few of the sketches are not exactly in mint condition.' All were agreed
that the longer sketches could do with a few cuts. But *Time Out* called it 'A
good show', and Irving Wardle in *The Times* described it as 'An outpost of
original and intelligent fun in the West End.' Audiences certainly seemed
to be enjoying it, which was what mattered.

After the first night, Dudley demanded a summit meeting to discuss
Peter's drink problem. The result was a deal whereby Peter promised to
limit himself to just a couple of glasses of wine before going on stage.
To enable him to keep his word, Judy was taken on as the show's dresser
from January, with the specific job of measuring out Peter's drinks by
hand. Peter enjoyed having his wife as his dresser: 'He used to swap
his trousers for Dudley's as a joke. Anything that made life difficult for
Dudley would crease Peter up.' The arrangement seemed to work: for
the rest of the London run Peter was sober on stage, and if he wanted to
hit the bottle he had to do so after the show. The show was deemed a
great success, and Peter and Dudley were considered sufficiently famous
to be asked to switch on the Christmas lights. Peter even dreamed up
a new sketch, although he didn't put it in, about a nervous comedian
who keeps suicidally changing his punchlines at the last minute. The
BBC televised the show one night, although Joe McGrath – who as a
mere ex-employee was not allowed to produce it – was annoyed by the
cack-handed editing.

In the long run, though, Peter and Dudley gradually became more and
more bored, both with each other, and with the material, which was now
almost two years old. With a degree of control restored, Peter resumed

his old habit of trying to make life difficult for Dudley onstage. 'Peter had the ability to wing it,' says Judy, 'while Dudley had to stick to the script. Peter loved to have the audience in the palm of his hand giggling, Dudley wriggling, as if to say, "Look, I've cut the little bugger right up." Sometimes that could be very cruel – if Dudley didn't want it to happen – and sometimes Dudley laughed his head off. It went full circle between the two.' In one sketch where Peter's character smoked a cigarette, he would often deliberately annoy Dudley by blowing smoke into his face. When he succeeded in making Dudley cross, Peter said that his partner's eyes took on the appearance of 'hen's arses'. Judy believes that 'Ultimately, the antagonism between them was inevitable given the circumstances. Peter's drinking gave Dudley ammunition, but if Peter hadn't got drunk the arguments would have been about something else.' Once the show was finished for the evening, the pair would go their separate ways. There was no socialising together, as there had been during the *Not Only . . . But Also* days. Curiously, the more strained their relationship became offstage, the more giggling and corpsing occurred onstage, rather as in the dying days of *Beyond the Fringe*. This was hysteria, rather than genuine enjoyment. 'Dudley's hysterical laughter became an act,' admits McGrath.

In 1973, Peter and Dudley were interviewed for daytime television by Mavis Nicholson. It was one of those remarkable occasions when, for whatever reason, Peter lowered his defences and both men spoke quite openly about their true feelings – about the lack of communication between them, for instance:

> *Dudley*: I think we are terribly opposite, actually, opposite to the point where it becomes difficult to communicate I think at times, wouldn't you say?
>
> *Peter*: Sometimes when we're working it is disastrous. It's like the worst kind of polite marriage. You sort of sit round, and neither of us is really very good at coming out with what we really think.

Peter confessed to having been 'arrogant' and 'cruel' to his colleague. On the subject of alcohol, he added:

> *Peter*: I tend to drink too much.
>
> *Mavis*: Why?
>
> *Peter*: I don't know. I think it's a symptom of boredom really. And my mind can drift off. And Dudley won't actually speak to me.

Dudley: So why do you do it? Why do you in fact not concentrate for two performances in a row? Why do you make me get into this state?

Peter: I don't 'make you get into this state'.

Dudley: Yes you do. I think you're playing at it.

Peter: I'm not at all. It's just, I'm aware afterwards that at a certain moment, my mind has wandered off onto something else.

Nicholson asked Peter what he did during the daytime:

Peter: I get bored very easily. I tend to get up late, I read the newspapers, I sort of hang around the house. I sometimes – very occasionally – go out shopping with my girlfriend. I do very little during the day, and I'm very much aware that I'm doing nothing, which annoys me. Yet so far I haven't actually done anything positive about it.

Mavis: Can you live alone?

Peter: I don't want to try.

Dudley admitted that he, too, had been affected by ennui to the point where he sat in his flat doing nothing; he had even given up playing his beloved piano.

Mavis: How happy are you both?

Dudley: I'm OK these days, I think, I'm gradually getting calmer, I'm getting to myself, getting to know what I want (*gradually Dudley has been putting on the voice of an American psychiatrist*).

Peter: You see, this is what you're doing the whole time, you're evading it. You're putting on a funny voice.

Dudley: I'm not evading it! You know that the truth is there. I'm not evading it, I'm *saying* it, but in a funny voice. (*Dudley repeats his earlier sentence laboriously, in his normal voice.*)

Peter, meanwhile, had successfully managed to evade the question by concentrating on Dudley's struggles to answer it.

It was clear that they were coming to the end of the road as a double act, but also that they would be completely locked into the partnership, unable to get out, until it finally hit the rocks. What they probably needed was an enforced break from each other's company. What they got was another, more forceful, more lucrative offer from Alexander Cohen, to shut down the London production and take the whole show to New York. Peter was keen: he was bored with London, bored with Denbigh Terrace, bored with fighting with Wendy, bored with life. New York offered a nostalgic, sentimental attraction, stirring happy memories of the golden days of 1962. Dudley was wary, convinced that it could end up becoming 'hell on wheels'. The offer of $7,000 a week each, plus a percentage of the box office, swayed him; he was still recovering, financially, from the decision to give Bentham House, their Hampstead mansion, to Suzy. He and Peter agreed to fly out in September 1973.

There would have to be compromises: Alexander Cohen didn't like the *Behind the Fridge* joke, and wanted to revert to the title of the abortive 1968 tour, *Good Evening*. Idi Amin and Ted Heath had to go. 'We started getting all this "Gee guys, could you change this, they're never gonna understand it" stuff,' recalls Joe McGrath. 'Of course they're gonna fucking understand it! It's *English*, and Peter and Dudley had been there before with *Beyond the Fringe* and succeeded on their own terms!' But Peter was in no mood to resist this time, and made all the changes that had been demanded. The resultant gaps were filled with four old sketches, *One Leg Too Few*, *Frog and Peach*, the miner monologue from *Beyond the Fringe*, and *Six of the Best*, the TV sketch in which Dudley's headmaster tries to cane Peter's cocky schoolboy.

Before leaving, Peter and Judy sold the house in Denbigh Terrace to Richard Branson, and bought a large property in Hampstead. Peter had also been feeling nostalgic for the old days in Church Row, and wanted to move back there. Eventually, after much searching, Judy came across a spacious, discreet, comfortable, three-storey mews house in the next street along. It had gothic, lattice-worked windows, like Peter's old college room. He wrote excitedly to his parents to tell them the news:

> I've bought a super Queen Anne Coach House in Perrin's Walk, which is a lovely cobbled mews at the back of Church Row. I just know you'll love it. It has a big garden at the back with a fishpond, 3 bedrooms, a huge living room, a garage, 2 bathrooms and 2 loos. It really is great and I'm very pleased and excited about it. I hope I never have to move again. I've had enough of upheaval. I hope you won't tell Wendy, who'll immediately turn green with envy and start screaming for more money. She's done very well, what with Kenwood Cottage plus her farm in Majorca, but I'm sure that won't stop her being outraged.

Judy wanted to write affectionate messages all over the walls, as she had done at Ruston Mews, but Peter was feeling too houseproud to have any of that sort of thing.

Peter discovered a further, unexpected attraction in the shape of one of his new neighbours, George Weiss, an ageing hippy who was gradually working through the money his father had amassed during years in the diamond trade. 'Rainbow George' kept open house (not that he owned his house – he had no idea who did and had certainly never paid any rent), and suffered a constant haemorrhage of belongings as a result. He was always full of wild schemes and plans, very few of which ever came to fruition. Although theirs was a brief acquaintance at this stage, Peter was to form one of the most entertaining friendships of his life with his eternally, hopelessly optimistic neighbour.

After a farewell visit to his parents, Peter jetted off to America with Dudley on 25 September, leaving Judy behind to complete the purchase and oversee the redecoration of Perrin's Walk. She had suggested putting William Morris wallpaper in the bathroom, but Peter had been stirred for once to express a decorating option: 'Absolutely not! I never want to see another piece of William Morris wallpaper as long as I live.' Judy gave pride of place to the Tiffany lamp, and planted a fig tree in the garden to symbolise their love.

On the plane over, Dudley tried to have an earnest talk about the importance of not drinking in the United States, but Peter was inconsolable at the thought that he would hardly see his children for another two years. By the time they touched down in New York he was hopelessly drunk again, and Dudley had to fill in both their entry forms at immigration while Peter sat in the corner, crying. 'I don't know why he was crying this time,' says Dudley. 'He had a lot of angst but he didn't talk about it. Just like I didn't talk about mine to him. His was an anxiety that was inexpressible.'[16]

America – and particularly American society – was delighted to welcome back the dazzling young men who had so enlivened New York in the early sixties. Jackie Kennedy – now Jackie Onassis – was overjoyed to see Peter again, and brought her sister Lee Radziwill along to meet him. Alone, inebriated and craving female companionship, Peter was in no mood to resist, and immediately began an affair with Radziwill. Tuesday Weld, meanwhile, was keen to renew her acquaintance with Dudley Moore, and telephoned their hotel. Peter intercepted the call, got talking, and soon began an affair with her as well. Not that Dudley was short of female company; when his current girlfriend Lysie Hastings (who also happened to be his best friend's wife) flew out to join him, she promptly flew home again upon discovering quite how many girlfriends Dudley had already managed to accumulate.

By the time Judy arrived, Peter's love life was in a hopeless tangle. He immediately gave his two girlfriends up and told Judy all about it – theirs was a painfully honest relationship – but he had proved himself utterly incapable of being alone. Judy says that 'Women responded to him off stage like audiences responded onstage. But I knew I was the one who was with him in the end.' Judy offered Peter uncomplicated love without reproach, which was difficult given his ways; whether it was beneficial to him or not is perhaps open to debate.

On stage, *Good Evening* was a colossal triumph, outstripping even the reception it had been accorded in Australia. Peter and Dudley opened with a preview stint in Boston on 12 October 1973; the house was packed with a raucous, knowledgeable, anglophile audience. When Peter launched into his miner monologue, they applauded the first line and joined in with some of the subsequent ones. Even when Peter fell off the stage into the orchestra pit, severely bruising his leg, they laughed heartily because they thought it was part of the act. On 10 November the show moved to New York's Plymouth Theater, on 45th Street, west of Broadway, where the reception was equally huge. The critics raved. The *New York Daily News* thought the show 'immense'; the *New York Post* called Peter and Dudley 'two of the funniest and most inventive men in the world'; while the much-feared Clive Barnes of the *New York Times* thought them 'mad, funny and truthful'. The US correspondent of the *Daily Mail* reported that 'New York has gone bananas over them and one of the more absurd sounds to be heard round the town is that of Brooklyn gentlemen trying to do a Pete and Dud impersonation.'[17]

The only sour notes came from the veteran British radical film maker Lindsay Anderson, who publicly bemoaned the absence of satire; from a woman called Jane who wrote in to complain about the Tarzan sketch; and from the religious lobby, who objected to the nativity sketch. The Anti-Blasphemy Movement credited Peter and Dudley with 'opening the floodgates of satanism', but nobody turned up to their demonstration outside the theatre. Celebrities queued up to go backstage and meet the two stars, including Cary Grant, Charlton Heston, Walter Matthau, Tennessee Williams, Henry Kissinger and Groucho Marx, who invited Peter and Dudley back home with him. It transpired that he was deaf, hadn't heard a word of the show and wanted a private, extra-loud performance of the material at his house. He later pronounced them 'two of the funniest performers he had ever seen'.

Peter eschewed the round of late-night dinners and parties that had characterised his last visit to New York, and the roster of schemes and projects that had occupied his days. He rented a quiet apartment from Tony Walton, the Old Radleian stage designer, as well as a large, three-storied clapboard house in Nutmeg Drive in the Connecticut suburbs, with wide grounds and a swimming pool. The children came out for a holiday in the summer of 1974, which was when Peter was at his happiest. 'It was a fabulous house, with peacocks roaming round the gardens,' remembers Daisy. 'We had a really lovely holiday – we went to the circus and Dad was very good at barbecuing chicken. I just remember lovely languid summer days, and him being at the barbecue and making us laugh all the time.' Peter played pool with Lucy, gave his daughters money to place on horse-races and organised world record attempt frisbee-throwing competitions.

The rest of the time, he sat and did very little, the boredom eating slowly away at him. He wrote to his mother and father:

> I think both Judy and I find New York rather dull and exhausting. We both miss England a lot. I wish I could persuade you both to fly out here for a week or so. I have forgotten both your birthdays again but I have a feeling that one of them is imminent so please let me know – so your uncommunicative son may remember for once. I'm on a ghastly diet (I've put on about a stone and none of my trousers fit). It does seem to be working but I can't say it does much for my temper. What's worse – instead of melting away from my waist I think all the weight must be coming off my feet and knees. I haven't really seen much of the people I used to know here and we are leading a very quiet life. Sorry to have so little news, but apart from doing the show nothing much happens. I miss you both very much and will write again soon.

But things were happening; things were gradually beginning to go wrong. Joe McGrath became very upset after Peter gave a TV interview describing the London shows as 'rather lazy', the American shows as 'much, much better' on account of Alexander Cohen's input, and claiming that they had needed 'a stronger director' all along. Dudley told McGrath not to worry, but enough was enough, and the director flew home. He was replaced by Jerry Adler, the stage manager. Judy, meanwhile, had fallen ill with a serious internal infection, and had to spend increasing amounts of time in London for treatment. She had been intending to fly back to New York for Christmas 1973 with Gaye Brown, but was too unwell to make the trip. Gaye – whose ticket had been paid for by Judy – decided to travel without

her and spent Christmas with Peter; they went to the Russian Tea Room with
Woody Allen on Christmas Day. She and Judy never spoke to each other
again. In fact, says Gaye, 'Peter couldn't bear it without her. He was going
slightly crazy – very different, rather manic, rather strange, and very very
possessive of his friends. I spent a day with Dudley, just wittering, and Peter
was absolutely furious. I got an extraordinary call from him, very drunk . . .
I've never heard so much abuse. Looking back now I realise that he was
incredibly unhappy.' Peter didn't like to be himself, and would keep his stage
make-up on all day, his deep, dark eyes lined with thick black mascara.

He was now more firmly in the grip of drink and drugs than ever. One
dinner invitation that he and Judy did accept was from Joseph Heller, who
recalls that 'Peter was terrified all the time that he was going to run out
of pills. He had brought a supply of uppers and downers from London,
but he only knew what they were called on his London prescription. He
didn't know the generic name or how to replenish his supply. I would say
that he was in terror about them.'[18] In a bizarre reversal of Lenny Bruce's
visit to London, it was now Heller's turn to spend the night hours trying
to find a doctor flexible enough to assuage his guest's craving. A few days
later, Heller brought Dustin Hoffman to see *Good Evening* and to meet
Peter afterwards. Peter occupied the entire conversation, as was his wont,
while the taciturn Hoffman said next to nothing. As soon as he arrived
home, Heller got a call from Peter. 'It was late and this was about one hour
after we had parted at the entrance. He was very distraught. Not only had
Hoffman not talked at all. He had never said that he liked the show.'[19]

Drink had once again started to affect his stage performance. 'I was
getting really peed off with his getting sloshed every night,' says Dudley.
'I didn't like working with him in this way. He'd changed a great deal
from what he had been, and had become much slower. Everything was
slower; oh it was painful, painful. I remember one day he didn't turn up
at all, and people were having to break down the door of his apartment
and drag him out. He was really out of it and he was saying "I'm fine."
I had to entertain the audience by playing the piano for about forty-five
minutes.' An announcement was made that Peter had been delayed 'by
a traffic accident'. Eventually, he appeared in the wings 'like a ghost',
and gave Dudley the thumbs-up sign. 'And the funny thing was, there
were people in the audience whom I'd invited, who didn't notice Peter's
drunkenness.'[20] Either that, or America didn't seem to care.

Alexander Cohen, however, was furious, and became increasingly
disillusioned with his star. 'It was unheard of in the theatre' he told Moore's
biographer Barbra Paskin. 'It was irresponsible and unprofessional – which
is the worst thing I can say about a human being. After the performance,

Dudley remonstrated with Peter and it was a very ugly moment. It was horrible and terrible, and you could tell that this was going to be a tough go. But I think part of what held them together was financial. I was paying them a great deal of money.'[21] Cohen allocated Peter a minder called Tommy, to ensure that he got to the theatre on time in future. Peter, who had lost none of his charm or sense of mischief, merely enlisted Tommy as a drinking companion instead. Dudley suggested psychotherapy; Peter refused outright. 'I have a feeling that what I'd find I wouldn't like in the least, and nobody else would either,' he said.[22]

There was still a great deal of affection between Peter and Dudley, but the counterbalancing friction had begun to outweigh it. Judy remembers that 'Peter and Dudley would be arguing as they left the stage, and they could keep it going across New York, in the cab and into the restaurant: Peter was angry at Dudley getting a joint writing credit, as he wanted recognition that he was the main writer. It *really* fucked him off that Dudley wanted to take that credit, and that Dudley refused to acknowledge that Peter had written nearly all the stuff. So that was the basis of a burning resentment and an enormous antagonism. But the irony was, Peter couldn't do it without Dudley, and Dudley used to tell him so. And of course, Dudley needed him too. This row had begun as a mild grit in the wheels in Australia, and had built up in London. Like a problem in a marriage, it took a while for it to build up into a full scale row. The trouble was, they were both completely right.' Peter's increasing desire for a solo writing credit was a measure of a growing insecurity, directly connected to his increasing inability to generate new material.

To complicate matters, Dudley had now begun an affair with Tuesday Weld. A Hollywood starlet with a severely disturbed childhood, she had been a heavy drinker at ten, had lost her virginity at eleven and had made her first suicide bid at twelve. She had already been married once, to the screenwriter Claude Harz, and had an eight-year-old daughter. Although intelligent, she could also be childishly petulant and provocative. Her past romantic history with Peter brought an uneasily flirtatious and incestuous atmosphere to the occasions when Peter and Dudley had to go anywhere with their respective partners, and so helped curtail their joint social life. Judy remembers having to go to a party given by Lee Radziwill: 'On the way both Peter *and* Dudley played footsie with Tuesday in the cab, right in front of me. It wasn't a normal situation. I just accepted it as part and parcel of a star's lifestyle.'

Peter and Judy's wedding, which had already been scheduled once for the spring of 1973, and cancelled because of difficulties in finalising

Judy's divorce papers, finally took place on Valentine's Day 1974 amid the red leather banquettes and theatrical prints of Sardi's, their favourite New York restaurant. Peter did not ask Dudley to be his best man – Alexander Cohen stood in – because Judy thought it was all getting too incestuous. Dudley was bitterly upset, and refused to come. There was a scrum of cameramen and television crews, who demanded the ceremony be restarted because the lights needed to be re-adjusted, but otherwise the day passed off well. As soon as the ceremony was over, Peter had to leave at once to do a TV appearance; but despite this apparently unromantic gesture, he was still very much in love with his bride. When Judy's medical problems resurfaced and she had to return to London, he missed her so much that one night, after the show, he had the New York police stop the traffic, sped to the airport by taxi, flew to England, crept into her bed, then flew back a few hours later in time to catch the next night's performance.

He could also be unkind to her when depression gripped him. On one occasion he took her to a peep show in Times Square and was ejected for trying to chat up one of the strippers. He admitted too that 'I can be verbally very vicious. I can be extremely nasty. I said to my wife: "You know nothing. Keep it to yourself." It doesn't make you very happy when you're told that.'[23] On another occasion, when Peter was entertaining a dinner table, Judy was laughing so much that her mascara was running down her face. Peter suddenly stopped in mid-flow and said coldly, 'I wouldn't laugh like that unless you intend to change your make-up.' According to Gaye Brown, 'When Peter got angry during the 70s there was something acidic about him, wicked, unnecessarily so. But we all know what that is. It's hitting yourself, when you're being that vile to people.' Michael Bawtree, who saw Peter for the last time in New York, had also noted a change in his old school friend: 'The bitterness that haunted his talk in later years had already begun to gnaw at him, I think: the satirical cast of his humour had become a little blacker and more hurtful.'[24]

On stage, meanwhile, *Good Evening* was going from strength to strength. By January 1974, it had broken the Plymouth Theaters box office record. In April, Peter and Dudley were presented with a special Tony award, and a Grammy for the show's soundtrack. On 30 November, by now transferred to the Lunt-Fontanne Theater, they clocked up their 438th Broadway performance, a record for a two-man show. On 14 February 1975, in another ironic reversal, the Foreign Office feted Peter with a special lunch to celebrate his first wedding anniversary, hosted in his honour by the British Ambassador Sir Peter Ramsbotham. The BBC, whose attitude to Peter had also come a long way since the early sixties, was now openly begging him and Dudley to do more episodes of *Not Only . . . But Also*. The pair agreed only to provide linking material for a compilation of old material, entitled *Pete and Dud in New York*, to go out as a Christmas special in 1974.

Jimmy Gilbert flew out to direct the show, but soon ran into unexpected problems. The US broadcast trade unions refused to allow a BBC entertainment crew to operate on American soil, so the entire programme had to be shot on board the *Jonathan B*, an elderly tug, in the middle of the Hudson. Peter and Dudley dressed up in their cloth caps and plastic macs, and Dudley's piano was loaded aboard. Peter constructed an elaborate plot about the Isle of Wight ferry getting lost and finding itself off Manhattan but, admits Gilbert, 'It was so convoluted that it didn't really work.' It was around this time that, unknown to Peter, Gilbert made the horrible discovery that most of the *Not Only . . . But Also* programmes had been wiped. 'People were asking "Where the hell is it?" – and it was all gone,' he recalls uncomfortably. Similar union problems were encountered, incidentally, by another BBC crew who came out to film a special documentary celebrating Peter and Dudley's theatrical success; they were not allowed into the theatre, and had to film the entire programme on the pavement outside, and at Sardi's restaurant.

After breaking the New York performance record in November, both Peter and Dudley were weary and bored and keen to come home; but Alexander Cohen badgered them persistently to stay on and undertake a national tour of the USA. 'Dudley truly didn't want to go on,' remembers Cohen,[25] but somehow the reluctant pair found themselves persuaded. Fortunately for Cohen, they feared that they would lose the proceeds of all their hard work to the Labour Government's 90 per cent tax rate on high earners. Peter and Dudley were given two months off, after which *Good Evening* would resume in Washington, DC. Their director Jerry Adler held a big Christmas bash, at which Peter had too much to drink and asked Tuesday Weld loudly in front of several people, 'How does it feel to be the only woman in town who's fucked the entire company of *Good Evening*?' Relations with Dudley descended another notch. The straight-laced Alexander Cohen was horrified.

In January, Peter flew home to see the children, and took them to see his parents, where he, Lucy and Daisy camped in the back garden. He didn't know them well enough at the ages of nine and ten to guess what sort of presents they'd like. 'He bought us these ridiculous capes,' smiles Lucy, 'like bicycle capes, but they were sort of Army surplus – he thought we'd be really chuffed with those.' Then it was back to life on the road, and the claustrophobic boredom of touring in front of all those unchallengingly delighted American audiences. Peter kept up a running commentary to his parents by mail. From the Jefferson Hotel, Washington, he wrote to tell them unenthusiastically of the show's massive, sold-out success. They were off to Detroit next, 'God help us.' From the St Regis Hotel, Detroit, he wrote: 'Believe me, this is the ugliest, most boring city I have ever visited. I feel I have done five years' penance in four weeks.' Judy remembers that 'In Detroit we were so bored we used to lie in the hotel room, taking bets on lifts going up and down. Peter's drinking had led to him over-eating and putting on weight. He kept going on these "death diets", in which he allowed himself one steak and one salad a day. Then we went on to Toronto, and Tuesday joined us. Suddenly there were four of us on tour, and that completely altered the dynamic.' The incestuous feeling intensified. 'Peter and Dudley's obsession with each other increased. Whatever Dudley had for breakfast, Peter had to know. Whatever Peter was wearing, Dudley had to know.'

By the end of April the tour had reached Philadelphia. Dudley wrote to his mother: 'Frankly, I wish the show were over. I have performed it enough times to satisfy my wildest enthusiasm.' They had been reciting the same lines now for three and a half years. Peter and Dudley took bets from each other on anything they could think of – for instance, a thousand dollars on whether Vichy water was naturally or artificially carbonated. Tuesday announced that she was so bored she was going home to her mother; it later transpired that, without telling Dudley, she was actually going home to have an abortion. Judy, who continued to commute between England and the States, flew home at the same time. Left to their own devices, Peter and Dudley did what they always did in such circumstances, namely give in to their insatiable, almost narcotic craving to sleep with as many women as possible. On one occasion, Peter phoned Judy in London, only to be interrupted by another woman's voice on the line, shouting 'Get your arse out of here if you're going to call your wife!' Peter apologised to Judy: 'He was telling me how awful she was, and how much he loved me, and how he couldn't remember how he'd got there. Later he phoned when he got home and said he was sorry, and he was so funny that even though I was taken aback and shocked, I couldn't help laughing. I suppose part of me was excited by him, although I'm not sure it was a healthy excitement.'

Peter had begun to make an increasingly severe distinction between the females he loved – his wife, his daughters and his mother, whom he worshipped and adored – and the females who threw themselves at him in bars or after the show, for whom he had virtually no respect, and whom he regarded as worthless. He took to picking up such women by abusing them, as if to make clear from the outset that what followed would mean nothing whatsoever to him. 'Peter and Dudley had very different attitudes to women,' explains Judy. 'Dudley was very charming to all women and talked psychotherapy, wanting to know their real feelings and their problems. He would listen all night if necessary. It was a very seductive method. Peter could be insulting to women, and some women actually liked this. He had this devastating combination of amazing good looks and a mind too fast for his own good. He read them very quickly and then got bored with them. Peter and Dudley had a ghastly rivalry between them to pull the birds; they were always insulting each other as well.' Their behaviour had absolutely come to mirror that of the two conflicting pop singers in *Bedazzled*.

Soon after the end of the tour, Peter and Dudley gave a remarkably frank interview to *Penthouse* magazine, in which they openly argued in front of the interviewer about each other's method of picking up women:

Peter:	The secret of success in the States, in my limited experience, is to be fucking rude. The only method. Kindness and civility and everything else was treated as a waste of time. Tell them they're dirty fucking cows and stupid to boot. That's because the American male has spent the last fifteen years reappraising his role in society, and getting more and more nervous about how badly women have been treated.
Dudley:	It doesn't seem to me to be true at all – I mean, your attitude seems to be quite exceptional. I don't know many men who go up and say 'You're a dirty fucking cow,' and then expect them to go to bed with you. That wasn't my experience at all. I said, 'I think you're absolutely—
Peter:	– a marvellous human being—
Dudley:	– and they go to bed.
Peter:	Yeah, but it takes longer.
Dudley:	Speak for yourself.
Peter:	If you go through your whole life history – this tedious tale – also get into what star sign she has,

	read their fucking palms, give them your psychiatric history, then at about four o'clock in the morning there's a possibility that you might be able to meet her next weekend for a cosy tea.
Dudley:	Speak for yourself, I've had no trouble. If the only way you can get them into bed is by saying, 'You're a cunt'—
Peter:	Not the only way, it's the quickest.
Dudley:	Speak for yourself, dear.
Peter:	Who else would I be speaking for?
Dudley:	Well, you're speaking to me about it, you're saying it takes me until four in the morning, star signs and telling them about my psychiatric treatment, I don't know where you get all this fucking—
Peter:	Private detectives.
Interviewer:	Let me ask you about something else.
Dudley:	No, no, why? The atmosphere is thickening like the gravy.[26]

The partnership was becoming strained to breaking point.

The tour ploughed on through Chicago, where Peter woke alone in his hotel bed to find two black men going through his luggage. 'I was fully armed with one soiled Kleenex,'[27] he explained later. He remained calm, let them escape with his valuables, then fainted with fear at five o'clock that afternoon. The experience crystallised his dislike of America. Unlike Dudley, he had become desperately homesick. He devoured English newspapers, any English newspapers, wherever and whenever he could find them. He missed going to the football terribly, and on one occasion pretended to be ill, cancelled a performance of *Good Evening*, and flew to London in order to go to White Hart Lane with Sid Gottlieb. He brought with him a magnum of champagne, to toast Tottenham's victory. The magnum still sits, undrunk, on Gottlieb's windowsill, in memory of a Spurs victory that never took place. Peter had tried to fill the long American days by writing a film script about Queen Victoria's gynaecologist, which he hoped to direct himself in due course, entitled *Dr Jekyll and Mrs Hyde*. The inspiration came from Richard Ingrams, whose grandfather actually was Queen Victoria's gynaecologist. As he explained in a letter to his mother and father, 'Instead of turning into a monster he changes into a woman. The female role will not be played by WENDY.' It was never finished.

Finally, the tour reached its grand finale, with a six-week run at the Schubert Theater, Century City, Los Angeles, from July to August 1975.

Judy and Tuesday were reunited with their respective partners. 'The drinking had got much worse,' remembers Judy. 'It had finally become a way of life, it had got under his skin and he was trapped by it. Day had become night for Peter. He would sleep all day and eat just before he went on stage. By the time he got to LA he often couldn't remember what he'd done the previous evening, and kept having to apologise to me. He started promising not to drink, and breaking those promises. Peter wasn't in control any more.' In a final, extravagant gesture he rented a huge mansion on Roxbury Drive. The children came out for the summer, and he stirred himself to sober up long enough to be a good father. 'The house was an absolute palace,' remembers Lucy. 'We were just blown away. It was in one of those streets where Lucille Ball lived, just so wealthy, and everywhere a limousine. He took us to Disneyland and we went on all the rides and everything; the one he enjoyed most was a pirate trip, into a dark tunnel with all these pirates and silly, jolly music.'

It was in Los Angeles that Peter finally attempted to realise one of his lifelong ambitions, by making a pop record. Keith Moon, drummer of The Who, had remarked to him that 'Anyone can sing.' Peter had replied that 'there's one person in the world who can't.' The debacles of *Where Do I Sit?* still hung heavy in his memory. Moon, however, had been insistent: 'No. Ringo can't sing, I can't sing, but we all have hits.' Moon had just released a quite dreadful solo LP, *Two Sides of the Moon*, and he was determined that Peter could emulate his achievement. 'So Keith and I went along to where there were some demo discs, and picked out one called *Rubber Ring*. Quite a nice tune. Come the night, Clover Studios are booked, along comes a fleet of Cadillacs containing LA's best musicians – The Band, Ricky Nelson as vocal adviser, Keith as drummer and producer, about twenty musicians, every drug in the world available. You only had to loosen your throat and something would go down. All we got done in twelve hours was a three-chord backing track, because the musicians were all going off shooting up in the toilets, and I conclusively demonstrated that I could not hit a note. If I'd tried each individual word and put them together, it still would not have come out.'[28] Peter never attempted to sing in public again.

Around the same time, Tuesday Weld presented Dudley with a double surprise: not only did she confess the story of her April abortion to him, but she informed him that she was pregnant again – and that this time she intended to keep the baby. For months, their relationship had been shuddering like a tall building in a high wind, on account of Dudley's serial infidelities and his girlfriend's volatile, childlike behaviour. They were clearly on the verge of splitting up. Now, Dudley felt he had no

option but to do the decent thing – something he'd sworn to himself
he'd never do again – and get married to Tuesday. At the end of the
tour they drove to Las Vegas without telling anyone, and were wed in
a quiet, impromptu ceremony. Peter was not invited.

When the curtain came down on the last performance, and the last
eager standing ovation had dispersed, Peter did not have the faintest
idea what to do next. He looked to Dudley for a lead; but Dudley, to
his horror, wasn't interested: Dudley had reached the end of the road. It
was all over, he told Peter. The partnership was finished. He was going
to stay on in Hollywood, settle down with Tuesday and the baby and
try to make it as a film star. Peter was stunned, aghast. Deep down, he
must have been afraid of such a development – after some of his more
wretched episodes of onstage drunkenness, he'd muttered 'I suppose you
won't want to work with me any more' – but he'd always rather hoped
that Dudley would continue to cling to him as he clung to his partner.
Dudley, however, had reached the point of no return.

In fact, Dudley did have some extremely presentable reasons for splitting
up: he did indeed want to make it in Hollywood ('I didn't want to do
sketch material any more, I wanted to do material where I could act'[29]);
he did feel a responsibility to his wife and unborn child (the version Peter
gave out to the press); and unlike Peter, he'd never felt truly at home
in the predominantly middle-class world of British TV comedy. 'Peter
misses London,' explained Dudley. 'Hampstead, the corner paper shop,
his mates. I don't. Not at all. I've spent the past seven months in hotel
rooms, and really rather enjoyed it. The anonymity of life like that appeals
to me. I suppose I am rather like some cheap old whore, being seduced by
hotel after hotel.'[30] America, he thought, 'had a certain friendliness that
I couldn't get hold of in Britain.'[31] Ultimately, however, these were all
attempts to rationalise Dudley's unhappiness with the partnership. Peter,
refusing to believe what had happened, insisted on telling journalists that
they were merely 'having a bit of a rest from each other'[32] and that they'd
be 'back working together by the following summer'. But when Jimmy
Gilbert, at the instigation of a BBC encouraged by such pronouncements,
flew out to the USA to persuade Dudley to come and do another series
of *Not Only . . . But Also*, Dudley's response was blunt. 'I'm not working
with that man again,' he said emphatically.

In later years, Peter admitted that the split had left him 'bereft . . .
It produced a gap in my life which is probably still there today. When
people asked, "What are you going to do now?", I really didn't know. Still
don't really. I've written with many other comics, but I couldn't imagine
doing four series with *them*.'[33] Barry Humphries believes that 'Peter had

too much of a sense of cosmic joke to ever reveal self-pity. But I got the feeling of sorrow – sorrow about the end of the Dudley Moore alliance. Peter felt enormous frustration. I think rage is not an exaggeration.'[34] Dudley later acknowledged that Peter felt 'betrayed'. Wendy believes now that 'Splitting up with Dudley was more painful than any of his divorces.' 'The impact of Dudley's refusal to work with him was massive,' confirms Judy. 'Peter was devastated when Dudley turned him down. He felt misery, resentment, anger and hurt pride. He had to face the fact that he needed Dudley more than Dudley needed him.'

It was perhaps the sense of frightening directionlessness that gripped Peter most acutely. Judy recalls that 'I wanted Peter to be offered jobs in LA to widen his horizon, but I also wanted him to come home and lead a normal life and get away from the craziness of LA. He had desperately wanted the show to come to an end, but he had been frightened of it ending too. When it finally came to a close it was difficult for him to get back into a normal life again. He said "Judes, I just want to sit in a bar and drink. I don't want to be here. I don't want to go back to London. I just want to sit here and drink." He had no one to debrief him. He was burnt-out, lonely and addicted.'

Judy took Peter home to Perrin's Walk, where two years' mail was waiting for him. He refused to open any of it – in fact, he refused to open any mail ever again. In the 1990s, his third wife found letters in his house containing royalty cheques that were twenty years old. It was only when he got himself another agent (he signed up with David Wilkinson Associates soon afterwards) that he managed to sort out his income. There were other unpleasant surprises waiting for him back in London: Wendy had taken the children away from Kenwood Cottage, to the very edge of the area allowed under the terms of Peter's injunction, to the village of Forest Row in rural Sussex, three hours from Hampstead by car. Through her interest in macrobiotics she had been persuaded of the benefits of the Rudolf Steiner method of education, and had enrolled Lucy and Daisy in the Michael Hall Steiner School there. 'It was very painful when we went to Sussex,' recalls Daisy. 'Dad was very sad about that, I don't think he wanted us to leave town.' To make matters worse, a burly criminal, wanted for GBH and on the run from the police, had broken into Kenwood Cottage; posing as a respectable householder, he had had the electricity supply transferred to his name. He made it clear to Peter that if anyone called the police, he would torch the house before he could be arrested, whereas if Peter did nothing, he would leave of his own accord eventually. Defeated, Peter chose the latter option.

Peter tried taking himself off on holiday. He went to see Claud Cockburn, the veteran *Eye* columnist, at his home in Cork. On the way back he stopped off in Dublin, where his neighbour Rainbow George had moved for a while in pursuit of a girlfriend. 'We went to a club together,' says George, 'but they wouldn't let him in because he was so drunk he was staggering about. I said, "This is Peter Cook the famous comedian," but it didn't make any difference. He was meant to be staying in Dublin for a few days, but the following morning he was woken up by a phone call. Judy was in hospital.' Finally, the health problems that had plagued her for so many years had come to a head. The cause, it seemed, was that a contraceptive device, inserted after the embarrassing unwanted pregnancy of their extra-marital affair, had caused a serious and persistent infection. The result was that Judy would never be able to have children. George remembers that when Peter discovered the news, 'He was very distressed, crying. He threw his things into his case and raced to the airport. I knew he desperately wanted to have a family with Judy because she was so special to him.'[35]

Peter was at the end of his tether. 'I suspect that he had a breakdown,' recalls Judy. 'For the best part of a year he couldn't eat or sleep. He just sat crying. Sometimes I cried with him. He was too frightened to admit to himself that he'd become an alcoholic. He'd crash out on the floor at nights, insensible. I kept talking to him, telling him that he had to admit his alcoholism and ask for help. We had awful rows about it – "You don't know what you're talking about," he'd say. Then, soon after we got back to London, he collapsed. Lying there, he finally admitted that there was a problem. So I rang Sid Gottlieb.' Life had battered Peter to a standstill.

CHAPTER 13

I Don't Want to See Plays About Rape, Sodomy and Drug Addiction – I Can Get All That at Home

Derek and Clive, 1973–79

In the autumn of 1973, shortly after arriving in New York, when boredom had already set in but daily drunkenness hadn't, Peter had turned up on Dudley's doorstep with a proposition: he wanted to go into a recording studio 'just for fun' and improvise a sketch. When they used to sit ad libbing together as Pete and Dud on long car journeys or in hotel bars, the conversation often took a scatological turn; it was something of this kind that Peter wanted to improvise now. He had already booked the Bell Sound Studios, he explained, so Dudley obliged. They drove down to the studios, two microphones were switched on, the tapes were set rolling, and with no warning at all Peter launched into a routine:

> *Peter*:   I tell you the worst job I ever had.
> *Dudley*:   What was that?
> *Peter*:   The worst job I ever had was with Jayne Mansfield. Y'know, she's a fantastic bird, y'know, big tits and huge bum and everything like that, but I had the terrible job of retrieving lobsters from her bum.

The lobsters, Peter went on, had 'shot up there when she went bathing in Malibu'. Dudley was taken completely by surprise. 'I was just stunned,' he recalls. 'It came out of nowhere. I had to do a very hasty, improvised response – it was all about the worst job I ever had, which was picking up Winston Churchill's bogeys. It was out of desperation, it was somewhere to go.'[1] And that, Dudley discovered, was that. 'That was all he wanted to do, the first and only item.'

The Jayne Mansfield sketch had not been improvised on the spot, of course. It was an old routine that Peter had been doing around the *Private Eye* office since 1962, although Dudley was not to know that. Because it was unbroadcastable, Peter had not been able to find an outlet for it in the eleven years since first devising it. He had simply decided to commit it to posterity in the form of a private tape, kept in his possession, and had taken the now indispensable Dudley along as his foil. In fact at one point in the recording, when Dudley had attempted to divert from the preplanned path, Peter had told him to 'shut up'. Nonetheless both men had rather enjoyed their day out, and subsequently decided to take the experiment a little further. The two characters were given names and identities, to distinguish them from Pete and Dud, their more wholesome alter egos. They became Derek and Clive, a pair of toilet cleaners at the British Trade Centre in New York.

It was not the first time that Peter and Dudley had gone into a recording studio to amuse themselves by taping unbroadcastable material. In 1963, when the US tour of *Beyond the Fringe* had begun to pall, they had produced *The Dead Sea Tapes*, a series of quite unusable interviews with people who had known Jesus. This time they went one further, hired the Bottom Line, a small club in Greenwich Village, and invited an audience of friends to witness the performance. Some of the material was old stuff: *Bo Duddley* from *Not Only . . . But Also* and the *Appeal on Behalf of the Blond* from the US *Establishment* cropped up, while Dudley performed two risqué traditional ditties. But there were also a number of new Derek and Clive dialogues, some of which later had to be wiped, because they contained libellous references to such luminaries as Harold Wilson and Kirk Douglas. Six routines survived: *Top Rank*, a surreal ramble in which Derek visits the Top Rank ballroom to find his wife being 'fucked by a gorilla' and complains to the manager, who is having oral sex with an ant; *Squatter and the Ant*, in which a second ant is hunted down by a military type; *Cancer*, a maudlin list of Derek and Clive's acquaintances suffering from the disease; *Winky Wanky Woo*, in which a pervert who has been in prison fory-four times for offences against Anna Neagle tries to persuade another man to play with his 'doodah'; *This Bloke Came up to Me*, a list of strong expletives uttered in meaningless aggression by two complete strangers; and the self-explanatory *In the Lav*. It was all fairly harmless stuff, largely inoffensive in intent and also – for those who had no problems with the swearwords – in execution. Peter and Dudley subsequently recorded a second version of the same material at the Electric Lady Studios, without an audience. Soon afterwards, though, ennui and depression overcame Peter, and his enthusiasm for the Derek and Clive project dwindled to zero.

There it would have ended, but for the fact that the recording technicians had bootlegged a selection of various live and studio sketches, a tape of which did the rounds of New York's other recording studios and quietly began to breed. At some point, an unknown tape editor added it to a compilation bootleg, featuring the famous studio argument between the members of the Troggs, Orson Welles's audition for the part of a frozen pea in a commercial and an out-take of Harold Wilson shouting at David Dimbleby, 'You wouldn't ask Edward Heath about his yacht!' Word of the tape got around the rock fraternity, and before long bands like Led Zeppelin, The Who and the Rolling Stones had scrounged copies. As Peter and Dudley toured America in 1975, it dawned on them from chance contacts in hotels and airports that they had become the rock world's favourite entertainers. In LA they met and became friends with numerous rock stars as a result.

On one occasion Peter was drinking on board a plane with the members of Led Zeppelin, when the stewardess decided to close the bar. 'Now miss,' said one of the band, 'you wouldn't want us to start behaving like a fucking pop group, would you?' The cabin staff decided instead to leave the bar open. Unfortunately, on landing, the band did behave in exactly the manner described: the actor Telly Savalas, who had been on the same plane and had been playing cards with Peter at one point, was surrounded by camera crews on the tarmac, whereupon Led Zeppelin started shouting ribald abuse and pointing out that they were just as famous as that bald git. A fracas ensued before the assembled press, with Peter caught in the middle. It was a testament to his popularity in opposite camps of the entertainment world that both parties came out of the scrap fully convinced that he had been firmly on their side.

By the summer of 1976 the Derek and Clive tape was so widely available that it was being offered for sale in the personal columns of *Private Eye*. In previous years that wouldn't have mattered very much – it would have been no more than an irrelevant splinter from Peter's usual raft of projects – but at the end of a year in which he felt directionless and shorn of inspiration, Derek and Clive represented a useful stopgap, a ready-made, off-the-shelf entertainment that could be released without undue exertion on his part. A deal was done with Chris Blackwell of Island Records, who issued *Derek and Clive (Live)* – the original title had been *Derek and Clive (Dead)* – in August.

Perhaps unexpectedly, the record was a huge worldwide hit, albeit

mainly among adolescent boys. In Britain and America it far outstripped
sales of any of Peter and Dudley's previous LPs, thanks in no small measure
to the number of radio stations – the BBC included – that banned it. In
the UK alone it sold 100,000 copies. Peter made some solo promotional
appearances, tried to interest Jonathan Miller in mounting a stage version,
and attempted to sell the LP to Polygram in Canada, in the person of his
old Pembroke College friend Tim Harrold. Harrold's principal reaction to
meeting Peter again was sadness at the changes wrought by the previous
fifteen years: 'I was really shocked to see the comparison of his physical
condition. He'd put on weight, his hair was going grey, he was very grey
in the face and ashen. I really was amazed at how he'd transformed.'

There remained the problem of what his mother and father would think
of *Derek and Clive (Live)*, a difficulty that Peter sidestepped by ordering
them not to listen to it under any circumstances; cloistered in their new
retirement home in Milford-on-Sea they remained blissfully unaware of
its content. Wendy, on the other hand, made her displeasure known:
'I just felt that it was completely not what he was about – just couldn't
get it. Being the mother of young, impressionable children at a Steiner
school where it became a cult, I just found it incredibly distasteful.' The
LP carried a disclaimer instructing adults not to play it in the presence
of children, but Peter himself reported that he had been surrounded, at
a football match, by eager nine-year-old Derek and Clive fans: 'Instead
of saying, as usual, "Where's your mate, Pete?", they were saying, "Here
Clive, you're a cunt." So all these kids not allowed to hear the record have
obviously been getting hold of it.'[2]

Peter remained cool and amused by the ripple of synthetic journalistic
outrage that followed. The record, he explained, was about 'inarticulate
frustration: Dud and Pete hadn't met anyone, but these two have, and
they take offence at everyone. They are always angry. It's Dud and Pete on
speed.'[3] He agreed heartily with a *Sunday Times* journalist who suggested
that the record was actually satirical of people who swear every other word;
an argument which certainly held water in the case of *This Bloke Came up
to Me*, but which could only be tenuously applied to any of the other
sketches. 'I don't find it shocking,'[4] Peter stressed, although he almost
certainly enjoyed the fact that others did.

The release of *Derek and Clive (Live)* had presented Dudley with a
difficult dilemma, quite apart from the problem of preventing his mother
from getting hold of a copy ('The first "cunt" would give her a heart attack,'[5]
he predicted). On the one hand, he had told Peter that he did not want
to work with him again, and that he was going to stay in LA to try and
make it in Hollywood. On the other hand, he had just completed a year of

dismal unemployment, sitting in his garage playing the piano and waiting for the phone call that never came. Nobody in the film business, it seemed, was interested in one half of a theatrical double act with a commercially dubious record on celluloid. *Derek and Clive (Live)* had suddenly rekindled an enormous amount of interest in the Peter and Dudley partnership, and had invested them with a sense of youthful rebelliousness at a time when they had produced no new material for five years and seemed in danger of slipping out of fashion. Guinness offered the pair a lot of money to do a TV ad campaign, but far more importantly, Michael White's company let it be known that they would be prepared to finance a Cook and Moore film. It was the opportunity to revitalise their careers that both of them had been waiting for, and Dudley had no option but to climb ruefully back on board. He returned to Britain, underwent a *Derek and Clive* promotional tour in the Autumn, and then sat down with Peter to write *The Hound of the Baskervilles*, a parody which took as its starting point the Sherlock Homes sketch from *Goodbye Again*.

The therapeutic effect of Dudley's return was astonishingly swift and dramatic. Suddenly, Peter's life was looking up again. The blanket of gloom that had swathed him for so long was suddenly lifted. With the help of Judy and Sid Gottlieb, he finally found the will to kick his booze habit. He lost weight, dyed his hair a virulent orange-brown ('Peter's gone prematurely orange' reported Jonathan Miller's wife Rachel) and prepared to take on the world again.

Since returning from America, Peter had endured a terrible year. He had not done much work, and the only concrete project he had committed himself to had been a disaster. At the end of 1975 he had obtained a part as the chief baddie in *Find the Lady*, a quite wretchedly unfunny British–Canadian comedy film starring the young John Candy as one of a pair of inept cops. It was the kind of film where the female cast members frequently found themselves gratuitously stripped to their underwear, where a Chinese character's every entrance was greeted with the sound of a gong, and where car crashes involved a vehicle being driven out of shot, followed by a crunching sound effect and a single tyre rolling back into frame. To add insult to injury Dick Emery and Mickey Rooney were cast as a pair of violin case-toting Italian mobsters without the slightest attempt to change their accents. The film predictably bombed at the box office.

Apart from impersonating Harold Wilson on a *Private Eye* floppy disc, a stint helping to organise the War on Want Christmas appeal, and a failed attempt by TV producer Dennis Main Wilson to interest the BBC in a satirical show consisting of Peter, Marty Feldman and Spike Milligan sitting in a pub commenting on the week's news, Peter's only other project that year had been a collaboration with screenwriter Claude Harz, the ex-husband of Tuesday Weld. Together they sat in Peter's house and wrote a doomed film script entitled *It Sucks!*, about a hoover that takes over the world. Peter had met Harz in America in 1973 after the writer had started seeing Dudley's ex-girlfriend Lysie Hastings. He felt that Harz might be just the man to galvanise a depressed comedian back to work. 'He was trying to get back into the process of writing,' explains Harz. 'He was totally different from me – I'm very disciplined, I turn up every morning and I write solidly for five hours. Peter wanted someone who could make him do that. He was also looking for a transcriber – he found typing things out very boring; even going back to revise material was dull to him. He used to march round the room improvising. Even when he was drunk he could be the funniest person in the world ever, but that wasn't consistently the case: some days he was just *too* drunk. He was fantastic company and incredibly generous – he once bought Lysie a transatlantic air ticket so that she could join me – but he was *terminally* bored with life. Sometimes you'd see it in his eyes. No matter what happened, however exciting, however funny, the break in the boredom was only momentary for him.'

When not writing with Harz, Peter maintained a small but respectable income by appearing on chat shows. He told Russell Harty in October 1975 about his lack of energy. 'Have you come back to England to recharge your batteries?' asked Harty. 'If I could find them, I'd recharge them,' Peter replied. Four months later he turned up on *Parkinson* in a safari suit and Donny Osmond cap, his hair noticeably greyer and his waistline thicker, shaking visibly. 'It was a mixture of nerves, alcohol abuse and various other substance abuses,' recalls Parkinson. Peter explained that since returning from America he'd 'just been inside watching the telly and reading the paper,' and that his plans for the future involved 'doing some more resting.' Admittedly the house in Perrin's Walk was taking up some of his time, partly because it had started to slip slowly down the hill and needed reinforcing, and partly because he was engaged in a topiary sculpture on the tree outside the front door, turning it into a two-fingered gesture to the world. Also, the criminal occupant of Kenwood Cottage, despite having kept his promise and departed, had simply given way to a further bunch of squatters; whom Peter only managed to evict after a protracted negotiation involving an extremely large builder friend before finally being able to sell the property.

In the main, though, Peter's relative inactivity was symptomatic of an ever-deepening malaise. 'He was a classic example of the addict not being able to tell his doctor the extent of his addiction,' explains Sid Gottlieb.

'He might say to me, "God, I had a rough night last night, you know I must have killed half a bottle of vodka." And I would say, "Peter, for Christ's sake, why do you talk to me like that? You must have half a bottle of vodka before brushing your teeth every day. If you're talking about a rough night last night, that means, what? Six bottles? Why can't you just tell me? I need to know, because it's a measure of the danger to your liver.' Gradually Gottlieb and Judy had worked on Peter, steadily chipping away at his fatalistic desire to continue drinking.

It was a huge task. On his visits to the *Private Eye* offices, Peter had fallen in with a journalist named Martin Tomkinson, a big, burly, bearded northerner who alone among his colleagues liked to go out for a lunchtime drink; the magazine was no longer put together in the pub, because most the the rest of the staff had been forced to give up alcohol on medical advice. Once in his cups Peter's charm would evaporate, and he would rile Tomkinson deliberately, almost as if he were trying to goad the journalist into punching his lights out. Tomkinson had an Asian wife, and on one occasion Peter purposely went into a tirade about the benefits of apartheid, which was not a cause for which he had ever shown the slightest sympathy. 'He went on and on about it, like a dentist with a drill who's found the weak spot,' recalls Tomkinson. Eventually, Tomkinson lost his rag and attacked Peter with a bar stool, but was so drunk that he missed his intended target and completely destroyed one of the Coach and Horses' chandeliers instead; which was fortunate, as Peter was far too drunk to move out of the way. The following day Norman the barman, who had barred Tomkinson on the spot but had subsequently relented on account of the journalist's size, explained: 'You're a stupid cunt. Peter *always* does that to people. He just winds them up.' A sober Peter did at least telephone to apologise.

On other occasions Peter tried to persuade Tomkinson to come with him to tacky massage parlours after lunch, and find the most unattractive, unappetising girls they could. 'I refused, and he would say, "You've got to come with me, I can't walk." I would assist his stumbling figure to the entrance of these establishments, push him through the door and then flee. It was actually quite frightening sometimes to observe the intense loneliness within him. I think he felt a huge inner void that terrified him. Booze went some way to palliating this terror, though it may well have provoked different fears and terrors. He was finding it increasingly difficult to interest himself in himself or anything else. Horses, girls, football – nothing really seemed to work.' Another fellow *Eye* journalist of the period, Peter McKay, remembers not only that Peter visited massage parlours, but also that 'he knew to the nearest comma the humbug phraseology to condemn such behaviour.'[6]

To add to Peter's depression, *Private Eye* itself was seriously threatened with closure in 1976. The magazine had libelled the millionaire James Goldsmith – who had been a friend of the murderer Lord Lucan – by repeating a mistaken assertion from *The Sunday Times* that Goldsmith had been present at a meeting of Lucan's friends convened to help the fugitive peer escape justice. Goldsmith, who had ambitions to start up a news magazine of his own, decided not just to sue for damages in the conventional manner, but to crush *Private Eye* utterly with a massive legal salvo. In his first barrage of writs no fewer than sixty-three wholesale newsagents were sued for distributing the magazine, including three which had never stocked it and one which was owned by Goldsmith himself. Richard Ingrams, the editor, and Patrick Marnham, the offending journalist, were sued for the antiquated offence of criminal libel, which carried a custodial sentence. No one was quite sure why Goldsmith was pursuing the case so ferociously. There were various theories: the *Eye*'s investigations into his financial dealings were thought by some to have angered him; others believed David Frost's assertion that Goldsmith had offered to assist his friend, the much-satirised Prime Minister Harold Wilson, by ridding him of 'this turbulent magazine'. Certainly Wilson attempted unsuccessfully to ennoble Goldsmith soon afterwards. Whatever the reason, Goldsmith was a fearsome opponent. He proceeded to sue over further allegations that the *Eye* was confident of defending, whereupon key defence witnesses hurriedly reversed their testimony or fled the country.

Peter's traditional behaviour when *Private Eye* was threatened with legal disaster was to ride to the rescue, dispensing confidence and bravado all round. On this occasion, however, there were fears in the *Eye* office that Peter might be at too low an ebb to resist the enemy. 'The regular staff were concerned that Cookie might sell them out,' recalls Martin Tomkinson. 'When he came round to visit there was an undoubted tension.' A friend of Goldsmith's, Simon Fraser, contacted Peter to say that he wanted to buy the magazine. Peter – although suspicious that this was a Goldsmith bid in disguise – went along to see what terms were on offer. Discreet measures were taken by the magazine's accounting staff to hinder any sale. Fortunately for *Private Eye*, Simon Fraser brought a business partner with him, whose name was also Simon Fraser. Peter was quite unable to take seriously the idea of negotiating with two men called Simon Fraser, so the meeting dissolved into farce. Subsequently Peter went to see Goldsmith himself, without telling anyone, to see if he could identify the source of the millionaire's extreme displeasure. 'He was a very unpleasant man,' Peter decided. 'He wanted an eye for an eye, a tooth for a tooth.' Peter's resolve was stiffened by Goldsmith's attitude, and any hope the tycoon might have had of acquiring the *Eye* was lost.

In the event the case simply became bogged down in the Dickensian procedural mire that passes for a legal system in this country, and Goldsmith had to settle out of court for £30,000 in damages. He had set so many actions in train that the lawyers would have been able to keep the various cases going for decades. The 'Goldenballs' readers' appeal raised most of the money, with contributions coming in from such notables as Sir Alec Guinness, the Earl of Lichfield, Professor Hugh Trevor-Roper, Reginald Bosanquet, Tiny Rowland and several local Liberal and Labour parties. Peter, his spirits recovered, had taken to betting on the outcomes of the various hearings, and had devised a plan to place the entire 'Goldenballs' Fund on Goldsmith to win at evens. That way, if Goldsmith won, the fund would have been doubled, and if he had lost, it would not have been needed anyway. When the case collapsed, Peter contented himself instead with organising a fundraising concert to pay off the remainder of the debt, at which he finally and joyously resumed his double act with Dudley.

Peter had only seen Dudley once since leaving him behind in Los Angeles twelve months previously. At Christmas he and Judy had holidayed in Montego Bay, and had called in on Dudley – who was staying in New York – on the way back. There they had agreed to make a 'farewell' appearance on US TV's *Saturday Night Live*, hosted by Chevy Chase, and had performed *One Leg Too Few*, *Frog and Peach* and an impression of Sonny and Cher. Peter had continued trying to persuade Dudley to come back, and had even come up with a film idea which he wanted to direct, starring Dudley as a murderer; but to no avail. In April he had tried to entice his former partner back to appear in the Amnesty International benefit *A Poke in the Eye with a Sharp Stick*, but Dudley didn't come. Peter did his miner monologue, appeared in a Monty Python sketch, and took part in the *Fringe* Shakespeare sketch *So That's the Way You Like It* with Jonathan Miller, Alan Bennett and Terry Jones.

The change in Peter after Dudley's return was immediately obvious. He dieted enthusiastically from December 1976 onward, losing thirty pounds in three months; and the next time he appeared on *Russell Harty*, he was conspicuously drinking from a can of Fresca Sugar-Free Lemon ('It causes death in rats,' he announced cheerfully). Derek and Clive were put into abeyance – they had, after all, served their purpose – and Peter and Dudley immediately set to work on *The Hound of the Baskervilles*. They were both pleased to be writing together again on a major project, and worked enthusiastically and committedly for eight hours a day, dividing their time between London and Los Angeles so that each man could spent at least some time with his family. The script, they announced, would reinterpret the tale from the hound's point of view. Certainly, Peter felt the weight of expectation ('What would you like to be when you grow up?' Russell Harty asked him; 'A little boy,' replied Peter) but he was also hopeful that this time they could come up with a genuinely popular, mainstream product.

Suddenly, Peter's old drive to work all the hours that God sends was back: from 31 January 1977 onwards he contributed an entire page of jokes every week to the *Daily Mail*, entitled *Peter Cook's Monday Morning Feeling*, filing it from California if necessary. It came complete with his own badly-drawn but witty cartoons, under the heading *I Can't Draw Either*, which tended to be high-quality one-liners in speech bubbles rather than visually based ideas – for instance:

> 'The problem is that my wife understands me.'
> 'I like a man who can hold my drink.'
> 'I went to the University of Life – and I was chucked out.'
> 'I'm leaving my wife.' 'Who to?'
> 'If there's such a thing as a racing certainty, it's that there's no such thing as a racing certainty.'

The text of the column was primarily news-based, and substantially right-wing in tone. Targets included the Labour Party, the new PM James Callaghan, the Liberals, Peter Jay, Marcia Williams, Jimmy Carter, the Grunwick Trades Unions, the Social Contract, the EC, free collective bargaining, declining manners, the 'well-known murderer' Yasser Arafat, the Sex Pistols, pornography (while simultaneously defending the right to publish it, and with no mention of Peter's own avid consumption), further immigration, and the notion that the problems of Africa are entirely the result of racism and colonialism as opposed to tribalism. Although Peter was always fairly conservative with a small 'c', in this instance he was almost certainly emphasising his more old-fashioned opinions in order to satisfy his employer's editorial policy. 'I felt bogus about having opinions,'[7] he admitted when asked about the column years later. The *Mail*'s management was pleased, especially by the lack of swear words. They cut almost nothing from it, although the famous LBJ assertion that Gerald Ford couldn't fart and chew gum at the same time was deemed too strong for the paper's readers.

The rest of the column was taken up with genial showbiz taunts. Peter offered to pay £5 to charity every time Michael Parkinson managed to get through an entire programme without saying the word 'Barnsley', which earned him a further booking on *Parkinson*; and he initiated a debate as to whether Russell Harty had ever seen his own bottom, which earned him another appearance on Harty's show too. After discussing the lives of the early saints, including one named 'Sexburga', Peter rechristened his wife 'Judy Sexburga Cook' and made her into a regular character in the column (she, in response, called him 'Your Holiness'). There were also one or two wild mental leaps more characteristic of the familiar Peter Cook: the suggestion that 'God is a benign drunk and the world is his hangover', for instance, or the assertion that 'I am gay and have not always been faithful to Dudley'. Peter was getting so keen on the journalistic idiom that in March he tried his hand at writing a major story for the news pages: an exposé of expense-fiddling by the Labour MP Gwyneth Dunwoody. Sadly, this experiment ended in disaster, when Mrs Dunwoody successfully initiated legal action. The fact that she was later revealed to be an inveterate expenses-fiddler was little consolation.

Peter and Dudley's performing partnership, meanwhile, was back in full swing. Early in 1977 they appeared in a televised charity gala before Princess Anne. Peter recalled later that 'She passed gracefully down the line and paused briefly in front of Dudley and me looking understandably baffled. After a few moments' silence I decided to break the ice and said: "My name is Stewart Granger and this is Mickey Rooney." She smiled, and quipped: "You're not."'[8] The pair went on to perform *One Leg Too Few* in an ATV special, *Once upon a Century*; in May they appeared together again in *The Mermaid Frolics*, that year's Amnesty International show; and in the same month they recorded some sketches for an American TV special about the Queen's Silver Jubilee.

By this time the backer of *The Hound of the Baskervilles*, Michael White, had selected a director to start work on the film. It was a highly unusual choice, but one that Peter and Dudley liked the sound of: Paul Morrisey, an American former protégé of Andy Warhol, who was chiefly famous for making independent art house pictures, but whose hobby was his detailed passion for British film comedies, particularly the *Carry On* series. Morrisey's involvement promised to contribute both kitsch intelligence and an awareness of mainstream tastes; at least, that was the idea on paper.

Morrisey's first act was to rewrite the script substantially, and award himself a writing credit. He wanted *The Hound of the Baskervilles* to enjoy the good-natured innuendo and groaning wordplay that had characterised the *Carry On* films. He also demanded that one quarter of the script at least be made up of classic Peter and Dudley sketches, such as *One Leg Too Few*, which had absolutely nothing to do with the plot. 'That was

Paul's idea,' confirmed Peter apprehensively. 'We were very worried about that, because we said, "It will just look like we're rehashing old material," but he said "No, it's stuff which works. If you look back to the Marx Brothers, they did stuff on film which they'd done on stage for years and years, and they did it on film because it worked." I hope he's right.'[9] Morrisey also had the novel idea of flinging a cast of well-known British character actors at the project: Kenneth Williams, Denholm Elliott, Joan Greenwood, Terry-Thomas, Max Wall, Irene Handl, Hugh Griffith, Roy Kinnear, Prunella Scales, Penelope Keith, Spike Milligan and Josephine Tewson were all signed up, along with the singer Dana and the Page 3 girl Viv Neve. The warning bells were already beginning to ring ominously in Peter and Dudley's minds.

By the time the final draft of the script was completed, it contained some quite excruciating jokes, such as:

> *Watson*: What time does the train leave for Baskerville?
> *Mortimer*: Twelve o'clock tomorrow, Victoria.
> *Watson*: Oh no, you can call me John.

Or for instance:

> *Watson*: I saw someone signalling across the moors.
> *Barrymore*: It's moors code.

Joan Greenwood had the unenviably embarrassing task of delivering the line: 'Sir Henry, we were just discussing your uncle's willy – I mean will', while Kenneth Williams was given the scarcely superior line: 'All the Baskervilles have hearty dicks – dicky hearts, I mean.' There was also a minor subplot about a party of nuns trying to recover a stolen religious relic, 'in the name of all the flocking blind cripples'. At the end of May, Morrisey sent scripts off to the agents of the cast members. 'It made me laugh out loud,' wrote Kenneth Williams in his diary. 'Some of it is very funny.' The actor told the *Evening Standard* even more enthusiastically that the script was 'screamingly funny'.

Whatever merit may have remained in the script after Morrisey's revisions was to be utterly extinguished by his disastrous attempts at direction. Melvyn Bragg's *South Bank Show*, excited at the presence of the great US director Paul Morrisey working in this country, filmed an entire documentary about the making of *The Hound of the Baskervilles*. Despite its respectful tone, it must surely have been obvious to the film-makers that they were watching one of the greatest disasters in British cinema history unfold. Viewing their efforts today, Peter and Dudley's palpable unhappiness radiates from every interview, while it is abundantly clear from the minute he opens his mouth that Morrisey's understanding of comedy was at best theoretical and divorced from reality, and at worst non-existent.

Morrisey brought his personal analysis of the success of the *Carry On* films to the *Baskervilles* set: 'The emphasis was on the performers, with the most routine, sloppy, slapdash plots,' he said. The characters, he went on, should be 'cut off from analysis of what they're doing. I think a director is an aid, that's all. But he doesn't create the film, that's the performer.' As far as Morrisey was concerned, the bigger, the more extreme the performance, the better. Kenneth Williams, whose vanity had been stroked by the favourable comparisons, agreed wholeheartedly that casting and not scripts had been the key to the *Carry On* films. The two men's joint philosophy was to prove mutually supportive and extremely damaging to the project. In fact, any weaknesses in narrative tension in the *Carry On* films had constrained rather than underpinned their success. Williams's assertion to the *South Bank Show* crew that 'There's something basically funny about people who are able to handle comedy – the persona is the essence of comedy' ignored the fact that almost all successful comedy films (including the *Carry Ons*) employ a range of character types, from the most straight or sympathetic to the most comically absurd. The eye-rolling grotesques that Williams had made his speciality only worked as a contrast to the other characters. A whole film full of eye-rolling grotesques, as Morrisey intended, was a recipe for disaster.

Every cast member was given a comedy characteristic, which they were required to demonstrate as loudly and ostentatiously as possible throughout. There was no sense that actors had been cast in appropriate roles, rather that the film was a series of attention-seeking cameos competing against each other. Peter's Holmes was a comedy Jew. Dudley played Watson as a high-pitched Welshman, and Watson's mother Ada as a screeching parody of his own mother (who shared the same name). Kenneth Williams, Spike Milligan, Max Wall and Terry-Thomas all played exaggerated versions of their famous comedy roles. Prunella Scales played a postmistress who could only speak in opposites, like a *Two Ronnies* character. Even the famous sketches that had been crowbarred in, like *One Leg Too Few*, had to be performed in silly accents – entirely removing, in the case of that particular sketch, the contrast between Dudley's tentative optimism and Peter's restrained delicacy that had made it work in the first place.

Kenneth Williams adored Morrisey's desire for huge, theatrical reactions, and poured scorn on the conventional wisdom that good film acting involved the deftest of touches: 'It's the conviction that matters, not the style,' he pronounced. Clearly unconvinced, Peter had doubts about the director's insistence that he emphasise his own performance: 'Paul Morrisey has made me as grotesque as I've ever been, apart from in private life, which is almost continuously. It's been very hard to do a take which was over the top for him, because my philosophy was, it's Clint Eastwood time, the less you do the better, and Paul kept saying "Come on Peter, a slightly bigger reaction"; so I'd go "RUARRGH!" and he'd say "That's good!" . . . I think in comedy you have to make yourself ridiculous. Which is what I am in life.'[10]

By the time filming had kicked off at Bray Studios in early July 1977, with an audition for the part of the hound got up mainly for publicity purposes, Peter had already started back on drink and drugs again. Judy was in despair. 'He was collected by car every morning at 6.30 a.m. and he would drink a bottle of wine on the way to the set every morning. He was on uppers all the time. Eventually I asked him to move out for the duration because he was driving me mad, he'd be up all night retelling old jokes.' Peter refused her request. He had also begun to make public jokes at Dudley's expense once again: 'Dudley is still not quite sure how to play Dr Watson. I tell him that Dr Watson is basically a small, bumbling, ineffective fool, but Dudley has some objection to playing himself.'[11]

Kenneth Williams's diaries detail the film's gradual descent into catastrophe. As early as 4 July, Peter was trying to undermine Morrisey's direction. 'Peter Cook reiterated: "Sir Henry must be very mild and vulnerable . . . be careful you don't get that *edge* into your voice." It's ludicrous the way he and Dudley talk about *truth in characterisation* the whole time . . . the seriousness with which everyone sits around discussing the merit of this word or that word for inclusion in this hotch-potch of rubbish is the sort of thing Cook would have ridiculed in his undergraduate days.' For all his bluster, Williams was now actively dissociating himself from the script. On 13 July, he wrote: 'I was surprised watching the rushes today. I looked very good, the light blue summer suit photographed well . . . of course the dialogue is lousy a lot of the time, but the look and the manner are OK. Critics will say "Tired, laboured, unfunny" etc., but it don't matter, and I do need the money.'

On 21 July Williams received a surprise. 'Peter Cook said on the phone: "John Goldstone (the producer) and Dudley and I agree that Paul has made you do things which are over the top and bogus, and we must put it right. I want this picture to be really good. Dudley and I have had a row with Paul about it, but he was the only one at the rushes who was laughing at your

stuff." He certainly threw me for six.' On 2 August Morrisey contracted
hepatitis and filming was suspended. There were sixty-three minutes in
the can so far, and three days later the cast gathered in Central London
to view their efforts. Williams reported that 'It was all rather depressing.
Again and again in this script, I've thought "That is hilarious", yet the
fact remains, there is nothing hilarious in any of the stuff I saw in the
cinema today. There were certain bits (e.g. the one-legged man) which
don't really belong to the story at all.' Peter kept the idle cast entertained
with improvisations and jokes at Dudley's expense; explaining why Dudley
enjoyed life in California, he said, 'It's the space you see. He loves the space.
Californians have a lot of space. Most of it's between their ears.'

Behind the barrage of jokes, of course, Peter was extremely upset. When
Morrisey finished the film, Peter, Dudley and John Goldstone rejected the
cut. 'I thought it was very bad,' explained Peter. 'It was a mess, with some
funny moments. The script was a very bad compromise between Dudley,
myself and Paul. Dudley and I edited the final version, which I regard
as marginally better, but there's still no making it any good.'[12] Peter and
Dudley laboriously removed all their old sketches, with the exception
of the perennial *One Leg Too Few*. The film was eventually re-edited yet
again for the American market, with several of the sequences put into a
different order; the mere fact that such a thing was possible says a lot
about its construction. Morrisey had delivered one of the all-time turkeys
of the cinema. 'He was *terrible*,' groans Dudley today. 'I thought he was
going to be terrific, but he wasn't, he was unbelievably strict.' Dudley
thought his efforts 'dreadful, raucous and unfunny'.[13] The film's release
was postponed until further notice. All Peter and Dudley could do was wait
for inevitable disaster at the box office. Of course Peter blamed Morrisey,
but he also blamed himself. He was incapable, he decided, of coming up
with an idea that would sustain for more than five minutes.

The revitalised Peter had committed himself to so much work at the
end of 1976, that in 1977 – in between cameos for *The Eric Sykes Show*
and others – he found himself working flat out on another full-scale project
at the same time as *The Hound of the Baskervilles*. This was *Consequences*, a
triple concept LP by Godley and Creme. The two musicians had invented
the 'gizmo', a mechanical device that clipped on to the bridge of a guitar
and made a variety of sounds using different combinations of tiny wheels;
their idea was to use the album, which they had started work on while still
members of 10cc, to promote the invention. Unfortunately the concept,
such as it was, barely filled a sentence, let alone a whole LP: it was to
be a gambling game at which each of the four participants corresponded
to one of the elements. After they had completed the first side of the

first disc, tunefully but with little sign of the concept in sight, Godley
and Creme asked Peter to write a comic play that would run between
the tracks and flesh out their idea. Peter's first act was to change the
concept entirely, replacing it with a divorce negotiation taking place
at the end of the world. Property would be divided inside the room,
entirely pointlessly, as the land outside the room would simultaneously
be divided by earthquake and conflagration.

Peter's script, when he finally delivered it, was a thinly veiled and
bilious attack on the petty and acrimonious legal arguments surrounding
his own divorce. As the atmosphere cracks and groans outside, the hapless
Mr Stapleton, who is due to be divorced from his wife Lulu, is being interrogated at length by her lawyer Mr Pepperman about his financial assets:

> *Pepperman*:   I'm only too aware of one glaring omission. In this
>   list I can find absolutely no mention whatever of
>   hairpins.
> *Stapleton*:   Well, if there are any hairpins, they're, er, Lulu's.
> *Pepperman*:   (triumphantly) Which is *exactly* what I've been
>   trying to establish!

Stapleton's lawyer Hague counters by demanding that Lulu Stapleton
hand over her teeth:

> *Stapleton*:   I don't want her teeth.
> *Hague*:   You may not want them now, but who knows what
>   the future holds.

An argument follows about the number of Mrs Stapleton's teeth. At one
point, Hague's secretary interrupts them via his desk intercom:

> *Secretary*:   Just to remind you, Mr Hague, to feed the goldfish.
> *Hague*:   Er, let me have that in writing, later.
> *Pepperman*:   Have we agreed that the teeth are *ex parte*?
> *Hague*:   *Ex parte* teeth? I'll have to drink about that.

There was also a surreal second strand to the plot concerning Mr Blint, a
menacing, middle-aged idiot-savant with strong overtones of E. L. Wisty.
Blint is a pianist, who refused to move out when the block was taken
over by lawyers and now lives with his piano in a tarpaulin-covered hole
in Hague's office floor. Whenever the word 'hole' is mentioned, a holy
choir sings. 'I'll be downstairs if you need me,' says Blint darkly, 'and

I'll still be downstairs even if you don't need me.' Eventually it dawns upon Mr Stapleton that the increasingly apocalyptic weather pauses every time Blint plays his piano; only Blint has the answer which will save the world. In a shaggy dog finale, which predated *The Hitch-Hiker's Guide to the Galaxy*, the answer is revealed to be seventeen.

Unfortunately, unlike *The Hitch-Hiker's Guide to the Galaxy*, where the numerical punchline was ingeniously set up throughout the plot, Peter's use of the number seventeen was no more than a device to hide the fact that he couldn't think of a way to resolve the storyline. He had become increasingly depressed by the *Baskervilles* fiasco throughout, and the quality of the script audibly subsides during the album, until it meanders, drink-filled, into its puzzled cul-de-sac. This decline was parallelled by an even more pronounced falling-off in the quality of the music, from its pleasant, melodic beginnings, to a series of overblown, overlong, pretentious and tuneless finales. 'Most of the time we spent during that album we were stoned out of our minds on various substances, both Lol Creme, myself and Peter,' confesses Kevin Godley with disarming honesty. 'It turned into a fourteen-month recording session, which cost a fortune and produced a very pretentious album. We didn't know what the fuck we were doing.'

Peter was involved for a three-month period during the summer of 1977, coming up to the Manor Studios in Oxfordshire whenever the *Baskervilles* film schedule allowed it. The original idea had been to cast Peter Sellers and Peter Ustinov in the main roles, but Peter made everyone laugh so much reading out the script that he was given all the male parts, with Judy playing Lulu Stapleton. 'We were never totally in sync,' remembers Godley, 'because Lol and I would work until quite late, one, two or three in the morning, and get up quite late. Peter was an early riser, he'd be up and around by eight, bathed, showered, fresh as a daisy. And he'd be in the studio ready to boogie by the time we staggered downstairs for breakfast at half-eleven, looking like shit. By the time we finally came to, he was going out of it, because he'd start drinking around midday. He was going down as we were coming up, so we'd meet for maybe an hour or so in the middle.'

Phonogram records, who had been hoping for another *Tubular Bells*, and who had already begun to plan the stage version, found themselves saddled with one of the biggest and most costly disasters in the history of popular music. It was a turkey as massive in the music industry as *The Hound of the Baskervilles* was to become in the film business. Today the record has a cult following, and – remarkably – its own website, its small but devoted fanbase dedicated to working out what it all means.

'I wouldn't try and read much into it,' offers Kevin Godley, 'apart from the fact that there's three people totally out of it. I don't think we acted as any kind of restraining or disciplinary force on what Peter was doing, which might have been a mistake.' Or vice versa, one might add.

Quite apart from the project's artistic failures, two other developments doomed it from the start. First, the invention of the gizmo coincided with and was made redundant by the invention of the low-cost, mass-produced synthesiser. Secondly, as Kevin Godley relates, 'About six months before we finished the project, enter the Sex Pistols. Oh-oh. Sudden removal of carpets. It suddenly became apparent that we were no longer creating the ultimate record; ourselves and the project had been instantly invalidated. At that moment a little bit of the heart went out of it. I know it did for me. In fact it was such an incredible failure that it forged a sort of bond between the people that were involved.' Peter remained fiercely loyal to the two musicians: at the LP's launch in Amsterdam, where the pair were greeted cynically by Dutch journalists, he interrupted one hostile questioner by asking him what he did with his time. 'I do nothing,' replied the Dutchman. 'Well fuck off home and do it,' said Peter angrily.

The year that had begun so brightly, promising so much, had tailed off into disaster. His home life, which had seemed so jolly and full of optimism, had slipped back into despondency and depression. Peter's daughters, who spent a lot of time at Perrin's Walk, were now old enough – they had been twelve and eleven at the beginning of 1977 – to appreciate their father's mood swings. Before the calamities of the summer, Daisy observed that 'Dad and Judy were lovely together. She was very funny, they had the same sort of wonderfully idiotic sense of humour. They just seemed to laugh at the same things and to make each other laugh – they had a real rapport, they would make each other shriek. She was a really lovely gentle soul, and she looked after us very well, spoilt us completely rotten.' Judy would take the two girls shopping, while Peter specialised in home-made entertainments. He produced three skateboards, including a giant surfboard-on-wheels for himself, and took his children whizzing through the gravestones in St John's churchyard at the bottom of Church Row, or speeding down Hampstead High Street, himself in the lead wearing a policeman's helmet.

He also devised imaginary characters, like Blind Willie Lemon, who was so blind he was invisible, whom he blamed for every mishap; he would draw Blind Willie as a solitary lit cigarette in the middle of a blank page. He tried to interest the two girls in televised football, by getting them to root for one particular player. And always, when it was time for them to go, he would be in floods of tears. 'He was very soppy,' recalls Daisy. 'He would get quite emotional. It was a real wrench when it was time to leave. I felt it very much, just hating to leave really.'

Even when his daughters weren't there, Peter in a good mood behaved as ebulliently as if they were. Once he taunted four large Manchester United fans in the High Street, then hared off on his skateboard when they tried to attack him. He and Spike Milligan improvised the game of indoor candle-lit ping pong in his garage, played with two six-foot builders' planks and a tennis ball; Peter's World Championship-winning smash actually destroyed the table tennis table. One evening, looking out across the garden at the back of the houses in Church Row, he and Judy spied an opulent dinner in progress. Peter went down into the garden, vaulted the wall, knocked on the back door of the house and joined the party. Judy watched him all evening through the window, having the time of his life entertaining a roomful of strangers.

Peter needed his constant fixes of adulation. His self-confidence was like a drain, impossible to fill to the brim however many compliments were poured into it. Sid Gottlieb worked hard at the job of pouring: 'Peter needed affection and admiration in spades. You can't give someone in his predicament enough reassurance. In fact the general content of my conversation was boring, repetitiously but deliberately so, just reinforcing my conviction of his genius.' As far as Gottlieb is concerned, Peter's need for reassurance regulated his womanising; as professional disaster set in over the summer, this increased sharply. For a start, there were always the au pair girls. 'I insisted on choosing them,' says Judy, 'and I found someone very serious and plain, a student, thinking I'd be safer with her than the long-legged Swedish variety who would drop by for a spot of light dusting. But before I knew it, she told me she was in love with him. It happened all the time.'[14] When famous women came to call, such as Germaine Greer, Peter could flirt so furiously that he barely spoke to his wife. 'I remember going upstairs and putting different clothes on and thinking, I wonder if he'll notice me now. He didn't.'[15] On another occasion he took Raquel Welch out for the evening, leaving a surprised Judy at home on her own; Peter and his date were photographed by paparazzi, entering the Savoy Hotel. A few months later he repeated the trick with Ursula Andress.

At the end of August Peter took his daughters on holiday to Cornwall with the Gottliebs and their seven children. Judy decided not to come, which was the first public sign of a rift in their relationship; but Peter was happy enough wallowing in the company of his kids, whom he introduced to the sport of 'grassboarding' down a hill at midnight on a silver tray. 'Peter was an absolute wizard with all those children,' remembers Sid Gottlieb. 'He'd get up a squad of footballers or cricket players, and he'd be in the middle getting as worked up and partisan as they were – there was absolutely no question of the sports master in charge or any of that stuff. He'd take sides, and cheat, and argue that somebody hadn't put their bat down in the crease. Then sometimes he'd invent a character, and this character would take over for the day; for example there was Mr Sharkey, who operated the electric chair. And so he would set up an imaginary electric chair in the garden, and the kids would be in fits of laughter. Then in the evening Peter and my wife and I would go to a restaurant, and he'd hold court non-stop. The other diners all used to be quiet and lapped it up, killing themselves with laughter.' The holiday, which Peter made into a regular fixture, provided a welcome escape in the shape of an affectionate, uncritical audience, whom he could entertain without having to accommodate the whims of colleagues or the conforming pressures of a career path.

Back in London things were not going so well. By the autumn of 1977 Peter and Judy had begun to quarrel 'endlessly and magnificently'.[16] Judy would point out in no uncertain terms that she had once had to get rid of a baby for him. On one occasion she refused to talk to him for three days. She became ill with bronchitis and went to sleep in the spare bed: 'He came and shouted into my ear that if I was set on this course, I had better pack all my things and be gone.'[17] On his fortieth birthday Peter telephoned the *Daily Mail* in a fit of gloom and told them he wouldn't be writing his column any more. When someone from the *Mail* came to call, Judy had just thrown a cup of scalding tea over Peter. Dudley Moore is in no doubt that 'Judy worshipped Peter,' and that he had driven her to it deliberately. He was sabotaging a perfectly good relationship as a perverse means of self-protection, getting his rejection in first before it inevitably happened to him. His self-respect was so low that, to paraphrase Groucho Marx, he didn't want to join any club prepared to have him as a member. Even his children began to feel the rough edge of his tongue, a sure sign that something was very wrong. Lucy remembers that 'It would be something really silly, like he'd be fixing a plug – he wasn't the most practical of men – and he'd be getting terribly impatient with it. You'd go to help him and he'd say something very sharp and make you feel just awful. It wouldn't be a joke, it would be sarcastic and cutting; sometimes not even that, it would be just his tone and his look, making you feel not so much scared, but certainly intimidated.'

By the end of 1977 Peter and Dudley found themselves right back where they'd been twelve months previously, with only Derek and Clive for company. The follow-up album was the only arrow left in their quiver, and they convened, depressed and ill-prepared, at the CBS studios in London's

Whitfield Street, to record the whole thing in one day for Christmas release. It was entitled *Derek and Clive Come Again*, and contained precisely two jokes, both of which were to be found on the sleeve notes: one described a vicious assault on Clive by an octogenarian who had previously been keen on the pair – 'That's when the fan really hit the shit' – and the other referred to their huge cult following in North Korea – 'Unfortunately one of the huge cults followed them back to their hotel and beat the shit out of them.' The content of the album was a vicious, bleak outpouring of genuinely inarticulate, pent-up rage and frustration. There was nothing funny whatsoever about it, and it bore little relation to the subversively good-natured original.

The bulk of the rage was Peter's, and much of it was directed at Dudley; his partner tried to match him obscenity for obscenity, like a small boy trying to impress a gang leader with his loyalty, but Peter was always going to be the victor on that score. In *My Mum Song*, for instance, Dudley improvised a rhyme about his mother sucking his penis, to the tune of *My Old Man's a Dustman*. Peter countered with:

My old man's a dustman
And he's got cancer too
Silly fucking arsehole
He's got it up his flue.

Peter knew perfectly well that Dudley's father had died of cancer of the colon, and that it had been the single most devastating event of Dudley's life to date. The reference was not intended to be therapeutic. Peter was, of course, extremely drunk indeed. Dudley, however, was stone cold sober, and co-operating out of a sort of horror-struck, fascinated loyalty. The pair ploughed on with *Back of the Cab*, an analysis of Picasso: 'You take shit out of other people's arseholes, shove it on the canvas and send it to other cunts.' *In the Cubicles*, a routine about gay sex carried out through holes drilled in lavatory walls, degenerated into a slanging match where the pair merely shouted 'You fucking cunt' at each other. *Having a Wank* concerned Dudley's mother catching him masturbating over his father's photograph, his explanation being that he had 'cancer of the knob' and 'had to get the pus out'; Peter replied that he was suffering from 'cancer of the wife'.

Not to put too fine a point on it, *Derek and Clive Come Again* was rubbish, and nasty rubbish at that. It is of purely historical interest only, a laboratory slide showing that day's cross-section of a life in despair. Of course a number of wide-eyed students became excited by the daring and splenetic nature of the content, but that hardly represents a thoughtful endorsement. According to Dudley, 'Peter wanted to shock people with it and did. There's no doubt he shocked me, and it seemed that was his main source of pleasure – shocking me. He was pushing me to go further too – I don't know what his plan was with that. I didn't enjoy it as much as doing Pete and Dud. Also I think we were running out of material.' Peter claimed defensively to the press that the record 'broke new ground by tackling subjects that we all dread.' But he knew that his nihilism functioned as a kind of defence mechanism, by furnishing an inbuilt excuse for any bad reviews. He insisted that 'I've played it to people I love and respect and they've found it very releasing.'[18] In fact Peter had held a party at his house and had played the record to the assembled guests, but after putting it on the turntable he had retired to the bathroom, to stare at his forty-year-old face in the mirror.

Island records were not responsible for *Derek and Clive Come Again*; no doubt in anticipation of further substantial profits, Peter had set up his own Lichtenstein-based company to publish it, named Aspera, with the release being handled by Richard Branson's Virgin Records and the distribution by CBS. Such financial planning was to prove largely unnecessary. There were problems with the content from the start, when staff employed to test the quality of the pressings refused to listen to the LP. 40,000 advance orders were shipped to record stores, but after that CBS refused to go on with the distribution, when they discovered that they would be jointly liable for any prosecution under the obscenity laws. In a mix-up far more amusing than anything on the actual record, a saboteur with a sense of humour at Kay's, a Worcester-based mail order firm, put 700 copies of *Derek and Clive Come Again* into *Black Beauty* cassette boxes, and vice versa. Peter wondered who would be more upset, the 700 bewildered children or the disappointed Derek and Clive fans. The shambles continued when Ron Matthews, a twenty-year-old petrol pump attendant from Oxfordshire who had managed to get hold of a copy, was dismissed from his job for possessing it, and took his case to an industrial tribunal with Peter's help. Licking their wounds, Peter and Dudley absented themselves from press attention by accepting a private cabaret booking in Bermuda on the album's official release date. Of course, because the sales had been frozen there was no telling what the actual demand for the album would have been; Virgin gave the pair the benefit of the doubt, and commissioned a third Derek and Clive album for the following Christmas.

The Hound of the Baskervilles, meanwhile, was finally due out in April 1978, but it was so awful that the distributors kept postponing its release in the hope of finding an extremely uncompetitive month in which to slide it quietly into the cinemas. There was no straight-to-video option in those days. A summer release was postponed, officially, because it would 'coincide with the World Cup'; eventually a date was chosen in November. Dudley, who was utterly fed up, flew back to Hollywood in the interim to continue his hitherto fruitless search for film work there. His marriage, which had been tempestuous at the best of times, had not been helped by his long absences in England, and in the spring of 1978 he and Tuesday Weld split up. She subsequently gained custody of their son Patrick in the divorce courts.

By the summer, Peter – who had done very little but drink himself insensible and argue with Judy for six months – contacted the BBC to offer them a new series of *Not Only . . . But Also*. He even announced it to the press, while bemoaning the show's title as 'lousy – the worst ever. It was, of course, one of Dudley's plodding ideas.'[19] Dudley, however, was having absolutely nothing to do with it. He was committed to the third Derek and Clive album, and that was it. Over and over again during the next few years Peter was to arrange a new series with the BBC and announce it to the papers: in November 1978, April 1979 and again a year later, but always without Dudley's agreement, and therefore without any realistic chance of success. After Dudley's first refusal to take part, in June 1978, Peter defiantly announced instead that he was writing a new solo TV series to be called *The Wonderful World of Wisty*: but a year later, he had managed to accumulate just fifteen minutes of material.

That spring though, the rebellious image of Derek and Clive had actually yielded a job offer, when Peter had been asked to appear as a weekly guest on *Revolver*, a brand new ATV show highlighting punk and new wave music. *Revolver* was presented by Chris Hill and Les Ross, and produced by Mickie Most. When they had met to discuss his involvement, Most had been extremely impressed by Peter's knowledge of the punk scene: 'He knows more about it than I do. I hadn't even heard of some of the bands he mentioned to me,' he said. 'That was probably because I made some of them up,' Peter later confessed. 'They didn't exist.'[20] The conceit of the show was that the ill-tempered manager of a dilapidated dance hall, played by Peter, had been forced to let out his premises to the TV company; this allowed him to make regular abusive interjections about the standard of the music on offer. Given Peter's current nihilistic state, it was the perfect job for him. He genuinely thought that some of the punk bands were 'dire', and said so. 'That was rubbish,' he would pronounce emphatically as Eater or the Lurkers finished their set. The Only Ones, he announced, were 'direct proof that there is unintelligent life in outer space.' Pete Shelley of the Buzzcocks remembers Peter distributing porn mags among the audience, and encouraging the recipients to hold them up when the cameras rolled, in order to put the band off.

It was, of course, a performance entirely in the spirit of punk. The audience would shout 'Off, off!' whenever Peter appeared on screen, seated behind a desk with a big-breasted stripper perched on it. 'Learn a language,' he would retort, then – to the stripper as she removed a stocking – 'Thank you Jill Tweedie.' His jokes went down well, including the one about the man at a Sex Pistols concert who attacked Sid Vicious (a rare instance of the fan hitting the shit) and the one about his huge cult following (everywhere I go I have a huge cult following me). Peter became the favourite comedian of another generation of rock bands, most notably the Sex Pistols; Johnny Rotten and Malcolm McLaren consulted him at various stages of the group's development, and Rotten assured him that one of their songs had been based on his Drimble Wedge and the Vegetations number from *Bedazzled*. 'I don't know which one,' Peter told the *NME*. 'I was too pissed to remember.' *Revolver* was charmingly disorganised and rather enjoyable to watch, the first decent new material that Peter had been involved in creating since the early seventies.

The critics naturally detested the show, not because of any humorous failings but because they both feared and failed to understand the musical concept. Philip Purser in *The Sunday Telegraph* called it 'a deplorable entertainment', while *The Sunday Times* suggested that encouraging the Sex Pistols in this way might lead young people into a life of crime. Peter wrote to the letters page in mock appreciation, claiming that 'I myself turned to crime on learning that my idol, Robert Mitchum, had been convicted on a drugs charge.'[21] The barrage of criticism had its effect, though. After a successful pilot in a prime Saturday evening placing in March, the series proper was moved by frightened TV executives to a late night ghetto slot in July which varied from region to region; the resulting paucity of viewers in relation to the size of the programme budget inevitably condemned it to be viewed officially as a failure. Peter, who had only signed up for *Revolver* on the basis that it would be a Saturday evening primetime show, was furious and depressed. Just as luck seemed to have been on his side throughout the early part of his career, it seemed now to be deserting him utterly.

Martin Tomkinson observed his drinking companion's mood and behaviour becoming increasingly black and vicious throughout the year. The famous absence of malice, which as far as Peter's old friends were concerned had always solidly underpinned his humour, was showing clear signs of weathering under the pressures of a difficult twelve months. After a spell in the wake of the first Derek and Clive release when Peter had bounded into the pub and ordered triple tomato juices in the brightest of moods, he had returned to his former practice of deliberately looking for trouble. In September 1978, Dudley returned to Britain to record the third Derek and Clive LP, and Peter invited him along to one of his drinking sessions with Tomkinson, at a small club in Gerrard Street: 'Peter ordered trebles for himself – he only drank spirits now – and singles for Dudley and me. The atmosphere was very uneasy and the two bosom companions seemed to me to have nothing in common. They just growled at one another. Conversation was stilted, if not non-existent, and it felt like being between a warring married couple. When Dudley was out of the room Peter called him 'a horrible little shit'. Never a hail-fellow-well-met drinker, his influence that day was positively malign. He seemed to relish the *froideur* in proceedings. People say that Peter was incapable of malice, but I'm afraid that's bollocks.'

Peter's comic contributions to *Private Eye* had been taking on an increasingly savage tone; his visits were as welcome as ever but it was clear that Richard Ingrams disapproved of the indiscriminate drinking and casual sex that seemed to constitute Peter's social life. Martin Tomkinson was working on a series of articles about casinos, and as part of his researches travelled to interview the British head of the Playboy Club, Victor Lownes, at his country mansion Stocks. Peter, who was keen to renew the friendship that had begun in Chicago in 1962 and the company of the Bunny girls that came with it, accompanied Tomkinson on the trip. Lownes's hospitality was lavish and the two men swiftly became regular visitors. Peter often went on his own, and Tomkinson remembers that 'He would regale me with the sexual goings-on he had either witnessed or participated in.' Judy, whom Tomkinson remembers as 'fluttering nervously' when he visited their house, came to dislike and distrust Peter's visits to Lownes's mansion.

It was Stocks that was to mark the end of the friendship between the two men. At three o'clock in the morning at an especially licentious party, Tomkinson was frolicking in the jacuzzi with three bunny girls. Peter suddenly appeared with an Instamatic and gleefully snapped the proceedings. 'Ha ha, wait 'til Ingrams sees *this*!' he crowed. Later on, when Peter had passed out from drink, Tomkinson searched his pockets, found the offending film and destroyed it. 'I wouldn't hazard a guess as to what interior demons drove him to such behaviour,' says the journalist. 'Certainly they were intimately tied up with his brilliant humour. He was at his happiest making people laugh, and he could be side-splittingly funny. But in the long watches of the night I think he had to confront a deep and truly terrifying emptiness, which vodka could assuage but never permanently dispel.'

Derek and Clive Ad Nauseam, a record which came with a free sickbag, was scheduled for recording over three days from 8 September 1978 at the Town House Studios: it was the day of Keith Moon's death, which cast a pall over the proceedings, not that any pall was required. The LP was even more of a primal scream of rage than its predecessor, if such a thing were possible: at one point Peter did an impression of Moon's death throes, crawling across the floor and pretending to vomit. Moon had been one of his closest friends. Richard Branson, in his undergraduate enthusiasm for the whole project, had proposed making a film of the recording session. Peter had readily agreed; he knew that *The Hound of the Baskervilles* was due to be released any day, and wanted to counter it by having a celluloid alternative ready as soon as possible. Dudley, who still had hopes of a mainstream film career in Hollywood, was annoyed to find on the second day that Peter had hired three cameras and the director Russell Mulcahy without obtaining his prior approval. 'That was a very bad night for us,' said Peter, 'because I was rather cross that Dudley wasn't eager and he was being moody in return.'[22] Peter was also, of course, hopelessly drunk on whisky. There was only one sketch prepared, a vaguely amusing horse race commentary in which most of the horses were named after sexual organs and took up humorous positions in relation to each other. The remaining two days' worth of material (Dudley failed to turn up on the third day) contained almost nothing of merit, the supposed highlights of which were boiled down to make an hour-long LP, a ninety-minute film entitled *Derek and Clive Get the Horn*, and a few bonus tracks which were later added to the reissued second album. There was surprisingly little material common to both the film and LP versions. The content of the film seemed nastier, perhaps because the accompanying visuals matched the soundtrack for unpleasantness, but the LP was not without its share of items that would have benefited from being quietly jettisoned. *The Horn*, for instance:

> Clive: You know that big nigger that lives down the road . . . the
>   black cunt, Ephraim . . . I said, 'You like cannibalism, don't
>   you, you like eating people alive in a frying pan.' I said,
>   'Go round to the BBC with some of your mates, dressed
>   up in your loincloths and that, and paint yourselves up in
>   different colours, whatever you cunts do back in Africa,

> go berserk, tear the fucking place down, spunk all over
> the Director-General.' Y'know, he got about forty of these
> coons gathered together to rush round to the BBC.

Clive then related with disappointment how 'the cunt black nigger black
poof' had failed in his task. On the subject of Dudley/Derek, Clive
claimed that 'I've never seen anything more stupid in my life than
you' and explained that 'It would amuse the world to see you burnt
to fucking death for a fucking laugh.' Other recorded items included
an endorsement of rape, and a sketch about cutting your wife's hymen
out with an electric carving knife.

Peter's aggression towards Dudley seemed even more pronounced in
the sketches chosen for the film version. When Dudley, in the character of
Peter's mother but in the voice of his own mother, asked his little boy to
get his penis out, Peter refused, 'because, Mother, you're being very stupid.
You're a stupid old fucking cunt. Why don't you shut your FUCKING face
and DIE. Best thing you could FUCKING DO.' Later on Peter produced
an inflatable woman, which served to represent Clive's wife Dolly, who
he said had interrupted his attempt to get into the Guinness Book of
Records by creating the world's longest uninterrupted trail of snot. He
related the ensuing conversation:

> *Clive*:   'Shall I tell you what I'm going to do now? I'm going to
> get the Guinness Book of Records to recognise me as the
> No.1 cunt kicker-in in the world.' And I spread her legs
> apart. And I kicked her and I kicked her in the cunt for
> half a fucking hour 'til I was exhausted. And then I said
> 'Dolly – will you get a Polaroid of THAT!' And the cunt
> wouldn't even get up!

Peter went on to illustrate his 'cunt-kicking' abilities with a vicious assault
on the inflatable woman.

Dudley today is deeply embarrassed by the whole project, which he
says he loathed taking part in. 'That film is so hostile to women that
I shudder at times – my head obviously drops a few times during the
filming. I think his hatred for women was fairly apparent there. He had
a very garbled attitude towards them. He could be very hostile, like in
the bit where he's kissing a woman and he's kissing her with a cigarette
end. It's terrible.'[23] Judy, who was present in the studio throughout the
filming, says: 'I couldn't stand it, especially the bit with the blow-up doll.
The Derek and Clive film was a complete nightmare session. But Peter's

apparent misogyny on show wasn't a hatred of women – he was just afraid of women.' He hated himself, rather, for his dependence on women. 'Also, he was flailing at women because he was flailing at everybody in sight. Nothing was safe from his bitter rage. He was very pissed indeed when he made the film. He'd come out of that initial deep depression over Dudley leaving him, but now he was going at Dudley out of bitterness at that rejection. He was flailing at him like a wounded animal. Dudley was still holding himself up as a twinkling little star who could get the girls; "I'll get you this time you little cunt" was the feeling I got from Peter when we got home. He was trying to drain his soul of the hate and loathing and anger he felt at everything. Afterwards he just passed out, totally drained. Dudley probably went off and played the piano in a bar.'

Looking back with a clearer head many years later, Peter described the film as 'A document about two people who are at the end of their rope with each other. I saw the whole of it recently. God, it gave me nightmares. A friend of mine said it was just a wonderful evening of excess – I'm not sure that's the whole story. I think we were scraping the bottom of several barrels. It's only when I saw it all through again that I realised what a bully I was. I know I'm impatient, but it gave me no pleasure to see that I was that much of a bully. When you see yourself being yourself, it's like seeing my golf swing on video: I had no idea I was so dreadful.'[24] Dudley told Barbra Paskin that 'Everyone thought we'd taken something, but we hadn't – we just got very belligerent with each other. Peter's rage was quite bitter and seemed directed at me a bit. He always appeared to be trying to get a rise out of me. I didn't know why, and I didn't confront him.'[25]

At the time, and for about a decade afterwards, Peter's public attitude to the LP was extremely protective and defensive in the face of generally hostile questioning: 'Maybe people resent that we aren't seen to labour over these albums. But I think if we worked any harder at it, they wouldn't get any *better*. If we were recording for four months, it wouldn't make the album any *better*. But people say, "Oh, Ron and me in the pub do better stuff than that." But we aren't stopping Ron and anybody from doing it . . . As for making money out of something that's usually dismissed as smut, well, there are countless comedians and entertainers who do filth. They just don't put it out . . . You get all these complaints about language on television – and there, at 10.30, which is reasonably early, you have all these fucks and shits. And because it's *Pinter* coupled with two very distinguished knights of the theatre it's somehow tolerable. "An arsehole is acceptable in Richardson's mouth." Or, "Sir John can handle a prick with delicacy and taste." Well I think that's bullshit.'[26] This latter argument mirrored one put forward in a sketch on the LP, but like the others in Peter's defence it was flawed and largely irrelevant to the reality of *Derek and Clive Ad Nauseam*.

Bizarrely, Peter sought in all seriousness to blame Dudley for many of the record's excesses: 'Dudley, especially, is incapable of preventing himself from filling everything with swearing and farting noises. He's dreadful.'[27] Dudley, who had indeed tried hard to match Peter for shock value, put the blame squarely on Peter. In so doing they reduced themselves to the status of two small boys caught writing obscenities on a wall. Dudley was the one saying, 'He told me to do it, sir,' a statement which rarely serves as an acceptable defence but which is nonetheless usually accurate. In the film itself, their exchanges had been rather less evasive. Dudley had asked Peter, 'You know what's going to happen when you get to heaven? You're going to have this tape played endlessly as you burn.' 'You don't burn in heaven,' Peter had replied. 'We will, mate,' Dudley had asserted. 'Breaking up is so easy to do,' he had muttered elsewhere.

Two practical jokes played by Richard Branson punctuated the recording session, both of which appear in the film. He hired a strippagram, whose only interesting act was to remark confidentially to Dudley, 'You're my favourite. *He's* horrible'; and rather more successfully, he staged a bogus police raid, with two Virgin Records accountants posing as plain-clothes men from the Drug Squad. Judy and Dudley were totally taken in, and Dudley pushed the still-smouldering joint he had been smoking down his boot. Silent and crushed, he could see his Hollywood film career going up in flames. Peter was incredulous, his mind clearly working at high speed, examining all the angles, trying to decide if it was a hoax or not, buying time with jokes ('That's the last time I do the police ball'). Someone asked Dudley to play a tune at the piano while he waited to be interviewed. 'Nah, nah,' he replied disconsolately. When Branson leaped out like a grinning Jeremy Beadle, Judy admitted that she had been 'quaking', while Dudley confessed: 'I'd shit myself.' It said something for the quality of the rest of the film that a practical joke devised by Richard Branson should be its most fascinating moment.

Today Peter's friends, fans and colleagues are divided into two distinct camps on the Derek and Clive question. Tellingly Adrian Edmondson, the purveyor of *Bottom*, found the film offensive. All the *Private Eye* writers, with the exception of Barry Fantoni, find Derek and Clive regrettable. According to Ian Hislop, 'Peter was much more talented than that. It did nothing for me, and I don't buy the interpretation of it as breaking down cultural norms and being a forerunner of punk and that sort of thing. It was rubbish, it was Peter and Dudley swearing at each other in a studio.' Reviewers at the time agreed: the *Daily Telegraph* condemned its 'unpleasant moments of nasty nonsense' and 'violently misogynistic outbursts'; Stephen Pile in *The Sunday Times* said that 'It goes beyond humour or satire into abuse and cruelty'; Brian Case in the *Melody Maker* spoke of 'Fine minds at the end of their tether . . . Pete and Dud are settling for out-takes.'

In the opposite camp, comedian David Baddiel says that 'I loved the sheer unadulterated, graphic ugliness of it, and when Peter Cook died I was angry that Derek and Clive were glossed over in the hit list of his achievements.'[28] Barry Humphries claims that Peter 'elevated scatology to a lyrical plane'[29] and that Derek and Clive 'are among the funniest of Cook and Moore's virtuoso turns'.[30] The writer John Hind describes the three albums and video as 'arguably Cook and Moore's finest captured moments', while one of his interviewees in the book *Comic Inquisition*, the comedian Gerry Sadowitz, assesses their dialogues as 'the poetry of comedy. It's like beautiful music really, like Lennon and McCartney in tandem – Peter Cook plays rhythm and Dudley Moore harmonises, adds melodies.' A more profound and pretentious misunderstanding of the furious, barely articulate outpourings of a man at the bottom of a black trough of depression would be hard to imagine. *Derek and Clive Ad Nauseam*'s only real virtue was its honesty; but while most good comedy contains an element of honesty, that does not make unadulterated honesty funny.

This time round Dudley made it clear to Peter that he definitely wasn't going to work with him again, and this time round he definitely meant it. 'I just didn't like where Peter was going. I couldn't do those sort of sketches any more,' he says. Furthermore, he told Peter that he didn't want *Derek and Clive Get the Horn* to be released under any circumstances. The British Board of Film Censors agreed with Dudley, pointing out to Peter that the film would be liable to prosecution under both the obscenity and blasphemy laws, and refusing it even an '18' certificate. Peter moved instead to have it released on the relatively new home video format; Dudley fought him successfully in America, but in Britain Peter finally won the battle (and exacted a measure of revenge) by releasing it on the eve of the British premiere of *10*, Dudley's first major Hollywood film, in February 1980. It was to be a short-lived triumph, as the Chief Constable of Greater Manchester James Anderton – the infamous 'God's Copper' – impounded all eight hundred copies due for sale in his area under the obscenity laws. 'He never returned them, the cunt[31] said Peter afterwards. The film's release was rapidly halted while the legal position was clarified, and very few copies made it as far as the public. The delay put too much of a strain on the cashflow of the fledgling video company handling the distribution, which quickly went bankrupt. All remaining copies of *Derek and Clive Get the Horn* were impounded as assets, and the film did not see the light of day again for a further thirteen years. Peter Cook, the man who had been famous during the 1960s for being able to surmount virtually any obstacle, had been soundly defeated in the 1970s yet again.

Dudley stayed in England until November 1978, long enough to publicise the British release of *The Hound of the Baskervilles*. (Fortunately for his US career the American distributors were to wait a further two years before showing it.) He and Peter appeared on *Parkinson* together, Dudley stealing the scene, Peter subdued in formal attire, his hair dyed a virulent blond. It was his third image overhaul in six months. 'Peter dyed his hair because he was hitting his forties – he was quite open about it,' recalls Judy. 'He had it permed to look like a footballer soon afterwards. He kept changing it in search of youth. He would discuss his image in detail and wasn't at all embarrassed to do so, but he wasn't actually very good at maintaining any image. So after a while his roots would show.' Michael Parkinson asked Peter and Dudley about the status of their relationship:

Peter:	There are storms, there are tantrums.
Dudley:	It's like a marriage.
Parkinson:	How is it like a marriage?
Peter:	We're getting divorced.

The pair then performed *Goodbyee* together, without anyone present realising that they were watching a genuine farewell.

The Hound of the Baskervilles was released in November, sent to its doom like a reluctant soldier at the Somme ordered over the top into the machine-gun fire. It was slaughtered by the critics and by the public alike. Kenneth Williams recorded in his diary that Peter 'sat smoking fags and gleefully relating the worst notices he'd read.' This was trench humour indeed. 'Peter was putting on a front to cover his defeat,' confirms Judy. 'He couldn't accept defeat, and he was bitterly hurt and wounded by the rejection. I could see the man I loved disintegrating, and I didn't know what to do about it or who to ask for help. Of course there were doctors – Peter saw lots of different doctors and tried different drying out schemes, but with no success.'

Throughout the tail end of 1978 and the early part of 1979 Peter made a series of valiant but entirely unsuccessful attempts to kick the booze. At

one point he booked himself into a hotel in Park Lane to dry out, and
Judy hired a suitably fat nurse to look after him. Peter had the nurse
replaced by a pretty Australian girl, with whom he promptly began an
affair. After he had checked out of the hotel, he started sneaking her
into Perrin's Walk when Judy wasn't there. Becoming suspicious, Judy
announced one night that she was going out, but hid in an upstairs room
until Peter in turn left the house. Then she concealed herself in a
large suitcase in the living room and waited for him to return. Sure
enough, he arrived in due course with the Australian nurse and Judy's
worst suspicions were confirmed. Unfortunately, having decided against
a theatrical eruption from the case, she had to remain there until Peter
took the girl up to bed several hours later. Emerging, cramped and stiff,
she startled Wiggins the cat, who turned tail and fled, straight into a
paper bag. The panic-stricken cat then began to charge about the house
with the paper bag stuck on its head. While Judy let herself swiftly and
silently out of the front door, Peter became convinced that he was being
burgled, and got up to search the house. He found only two empty coffee
cups that Judy had drunk earlier, in the upstairs room where she had
waited, and came to the conclusion that someone had broken into the
house solely for a cup of coffee. 'As always, it was impossible to be angry
with him, because we ended up in tears of laughter about it,' she says.

Such instances of laughter were getting fewer and further between. In
a haze of depression and alcohol, Peter accepted just the occasional day's
work over the next few months. He presented the Melody Maker readers'
poll awards with Janet Street-Porter, for which he had the excellent idea of
arriving dressed as Janet Street-Porter, only to find that Bob Marley refused
to accept any award from a man dressed as a woman. He also appeared as
'Prince Disgusting' in a radio pantomime for former Cambridge Footlights
performers, entitled Black Cinderella 2 Goes East. This was devised and
produced by Douglas Adams, later to become the author of The Hitch-
Hiker's Guide to the Galaxy, and written (largely at the last minute) by
Clive Anderson and Rory McGrath. Also in the cast was David Hatch, the
Head of BBC Radio Comedy, who continually demanded that innuendoes
and double entendres – of which there were many – be removed from the
script. 'Peter was such an ally,' recalls McGrath. 'He'd say, "No, I think
this is the funniest bit in the whole show, and unless it's left in I'm going
to walk out." So good for you, Peter.'

Early in 1979, Peter's behaviour became somewhat erratic. Johnny
Rotten and Malcolm McLaren telephoned him to see if he wished to take
part in their film The Great Rock 'n' Roll Swindle, and subsequently paid
a visit to Perrin's Walk. Rotten recalls that 'When we went round to his

house, he was so deeply insane. And just taking the piss out of the whole idea, it never got off the ground with him. He would do things, like, if we walked in the door, he had a big basket full of sweeties. And you put your hand in, and there was all these syringes underneath, and he'd go, "Yes, we're all into heroin in this house." Absolutely threw Malcolm for six.'[32] Judy explains that 'Peter's manic depression was making him *so* high and *so* low by turns, and uppers, downers and drink just exacerbated the condition – taking them was the worst thing he could have done. When Peter was down he just wouldn't speak at all. Age was making his depression harder and harder to tolerate. His weight was shooting up and down, governed by his mood. I understood his pain, but I know now that I was too passive. I didn't fight his self-destruction enough.'

The rage that had spilled out into Derek and Clive began to infect Peter's personal life. 'Most people didn't know how bad he could be,' says Judy, 'what rages he could fly into, his furious anger at the world. Being an actor and a funny comedian, he could almost always put a good face on things in public. He could be in the process of destroying me, then the phone would go and he would be civilised beyond belief. Also, Peter's career could have been ended if the truth had got out. I was never able to admit anything to anybody. These days it would be easier to get help, but then it was all a huge secret, which made it more of a strain. In the end I could cope with the other women but not with the bottle. I lost that battle because Peter didn't want to win it. He made it clear that he wanted to drink and nothing would stop him, even though he knew it would kill him – it was a vicious circle. That knowledge was so awful it just made him want another drink.'[33] In March 1979, Judy moved to a separate part of the house, but Peter's violent rages pursued her there. On the 24th, she was granted an injunction restraining Peter from molesting her, and he was ordered by the court to stay away from his wife within their marital home. She put in train the first steps to sue him for divorce in the High Court before the end of the month. Peter had already driven away Dudley for good. Now it seemed that his wife was about to suffer the same fate.

CHAPTER 14

You Are to Be a Stud, Dud

Dudley's Hollywood Success, 1979–83

Judy's injunction could have destroyed Peter, but it didn't. Instead, it jolted him to his senses, and forced him to realise what had become of him. In one of his sporadic outbursts of frank public confession, he told the world: 'I've made many, many mistakes. I know I've been destructive. What I do reflects the idiocy and chaos within myself. I don't think I fit in anywhere comfortably. From time to time I'm contented, but that's the best I've ever achieved. That well-known saying "If only I had my life over again I wouldn't change anything" is rubbish. Lies. I do a lot of "if only". Maybe that's me – the "if only" man. I suppose one of my "If onlys" is that if only my personal life had worked better . . .' The last thing he wanted, he explained, was to return to bachelorhood: 'I need people near me. I don't like being alone. I've nearly always been with someone. I enjoy that kind of lifestyle. Why meddle with a losing formula?' On the subject of Derek and Clive, he added: 'I do worry about what people think. I don't want to be disliked. It's just that sometimes I put my foot in it. On every level. I make a couple of records and suddenly I'm supposed to swear wherever I go. It's got to the stage where people come up to me and say, "Peter Cook isn't it? You're the one who goes f— this and f— that". It really isn't me at all. I suppose I find humour a protection against unpleasantness. In a way I reflect my own confusion and ignorance. I'm very ignorant. Everything seems muddled up.'[1]

Judy never went ahead with the divorce hearing. The details of the injunction, which were meant to be confidential, were sold to the *Sun* newspaper by one of the courtroom clerks within minutes of the end of the hearing. For a fortnight afterwards a small troop of press photographers camped out in Perrin's Walk, and Peter and Judy had to come and go through a neighbour's house over the garden wall. Judy felt sorry for what she had done: 'I felt as though I'd created a nightmare. It had backfired in the most terrible way,' she admits. Peter was even more profusely apologetic, and resolved to make a new start there and then. They were to stay in separate parts of the house, however, for another three months. A *Daily Mirror* journalist who came to interview Peter found him 'deeply sad and lonely',[2] surrounded by comforting pictures of his wife. Eventually, in June, they came to an agreement: Judy would give him one last chance, while Peter would stop drinking for good and enrol in Alcoholics Anonymous. Furthermore, they would give some thought to moving away from London, to a house in the country. Judy wanted to get him away from the sex clubs and the ready supply of drugs and drink available in the capital, to a place where they could be alone together and rekindle their romance, where she could keep a protective eye on her husband's progress.

Peter swallowed his pride and signed up with the Hampstead AA clinic run by Max Glatt, throwing himself wholeheartedly and unashamedly into their day-to-day work. Past history suggested that it wouldn't succeed. According to Alan Bennett, 'I remember hearing he'd gone to Alcoholics Anonymous and thinking, well it won't work, simply because his sense of the ridiculous is so strong that he won't be able to get through the meetings.' The spiritual aspect of the AA recovery programme must have proved an especially difficult hurdle for Peter's cynicism; but he surmounted it. 'In the past,' remembers Judy, 'he'd always been so charming and one step ahead of the doctors, so he was always able to hide the truth from them. But this was the year he finally admitted it to himself.'

Not only did Peter attend AA meetings, he also became an exceptionally able and kind counsellor of others. He would invite his fellow victims back to Perrin's Walk for tea and coffee afterwards. He also perfected an extremely accurate and hilarious imitation of Max Glatt's accent, with which he would regale Sid Gottlieb. Judy was delighted to have her 'wonderful, passionate, funny, insanely good-looking guy' back. She explains that 'He found it impossible not to take *anything* – he didn't stop taking drugs – but he looked better and was much more hopeful. There was a childish glee to him and he seemed happier with life.' Judy herself joined Al Anon, the sister organisation for the partners of alcoholics. 'They asked me what I missed about Peter being drunk, if anything. I said it was seeing him trying to get out of his trousers.' Peter never once became censorious, and was happy to furnish his guests with drink without touching any himself. He liked to conceal his ups and downs from his family, but his parents, who were very fond of Judy and who kept in regular touch, were delighted that an obvious difficulty had been resolved.

The immediate effect on Peter's work was electrifying. The first job of his new regime was the 1979 Amnesty International show *The Secret Policeman's Ball* performed over four nights from 27 June at Her Majesty's Theatre. It was to become one of the highlights of his career. He was slated to perform three items: the E. L. Wisty/Mr Grole *Interesting Facts* routine, with John Cleese appearing as the straight man; *Pregnancy Test*, a John Fortune sketch with Eleanor Bron playing an eccentric wife (believed by Wendy to be a pointed reference to herself) who puts a balloon up her jumper; and the old *Fringe* sketch *The End of the World*, with a celebrity-packed supporting cast including Cleese, Bron, Michael Palin, Terry Jones, Rowan Atkinson and Billy Connolly. After the first night, however, one or two newspaper critics suggested that the show was too cosy and unsatirical. Peter responded the very next evening, by arriving with a newly composed piece he wanted to try out: a parody of the Judge's summing-up in the recent trial of Jeremy Thorpe for conspiracy to murder, that he had been working on that day at *Private Eye*.

The story of the Thorpe conspiracy was a bizarre one that had been running in the *Eye* for four years. A professional hitman, Andrew Newton, had been arrested after trying to execute a male model named Norman Scott on Exmoor; he had shot Scott's Great Dane as it tried to defend its master, whereupon his gun had jammed, enabling Scott to flee and raise the alarm. Scott subsequently claimed to the police that he had recently ended a homosexual affair with the leader of the Liberal Party Jeremy Thorpe (he was able to produce Thorpe's love letters), and that Thorpe had hired Newton to kill him in order to prevent him from going public. Newton confirmed the story, and a senior Liberal, Peter Bessell, added details of how Liberal Party funds had been used to finance the plot. The police wanted a prosecution, but the Director of Public Prosecutions Sir Anthony Hetherington did not seem to want to rock the Establishment's boat. So the police had leaked all their information to *Private Eye*, until the weight of public interest forced the DPP's hand.

Thorpe's trial – at which he was acquitted – was a celebrated farce. Thorpe, after all, was a prominent Oxford-educated politician whereas Scott was an avowed homosexual and Newton – who deliberately sabotaged his own testimony in court – was a criminal. The matter of whether or not Thorpe had paid out Liberal funds for a contract killing was skated over in a judicial summing up that instructed the jury not to believe a word that any prosecution witness had said. Scott, concluded Mr Justice Cantley, was no more than 'a crook, a fraud and a sponger'. Cantley's summing up had been published just a day or two before the Amnesty Concert, and in one of the finest satirical attacks in the history of British comedy, Peter tore it to pieces. He took his title, *Entirely A Matter For You*, from the constant disclaimers that peppered the judge's assaults on the characters of Bessell, Scott and Newton:

> We have heard for example from Mr Bex Bissell, a man who by his own admission is a liar, a humbug, a hypocrite, a vagabond, a loathsome spotted reptile and a self-confessed chicken strangler. You may choose if you wish to believe the transparent tissue of odious lies which streamed on and on from his disgusting, reedy, slavering lips. That is entirely a matter for you . . . We have been forced to listen to the whinings of Mr Norman St John Scott, a scrounger, a parasite, a pervert, a worm, a self-confessed player of the pink oboe. A man who, by his own admission, chews pillows . . . On the evidence of the so-called hitman, Mr Olivia Newton John, I would prefer to draw a discreet veil. He is a piece of slimy refuse, unable to carry out the simplest murder plot . . . You are now to retire, as indeed should I, carefully to consider your verdict of Not Guilty.

Michael Palin remembers that 'Peter was still honing it in the wings as he waited to go on. I remember him desperately asking around for an original euphemism for a homosexual. Eventually Billy Connolly, with the air of a scholar remembering some medieval Latin, ventured that he'd heard someone in Glasgow use the phrase "player of the pink oboe". Two minutes later Peter was on stage as the judge, adding his own twist to Billy's contribution by referring to the witness as a "*self-confessed* player of the pink oboe". It was the "self-confessed" that made me laugh most of all.'[3]

The audience roared throughout, and cheered Peter to the rafters at the end. His sister Sarah found him in his dressing room afterwards, beaming with delight: 'He was smoking the biggest joint you ever saw and was on tremendous form. I only had a puff or two but laughed uncontrollably all the way home.' So successful was Peter's performance that it was released as a mini-LP of its own, entitled *Here Comes the Judge*, together with some hastily-improvised sketches co-performed and produced by the young *Not the Nine O'clock News* producer John Lloyd. ITV had already negotiated a deal to televise the concert as a Christmas special, but amazingly decided to drop Peter's judicial summing-up from the edited version. Their pompous programme buyer Leslie Halliwell ruled that 'It is quite obvious who this sketch is about. It is not suitable for television.'[4] The uncut version did, however, go on to be released in British cinemas the following year, where it achieved good reviews and respectable ratings, largely on the strength of Peter's performance. Incredibly, it was the first time he had managed to achieve such a thing in fifteen years of trying.

A much healthier Peter started throwing himself energetically into sport. He played tennis – describing his game as 'contentious . . . like Nastase's without the shots' – charity football – 'I was kicking the players not only after the ball had gone, but long after the game had finished' – and televised celebrity golf. The BBC2 series *Pro-Celebrity Golf* invited him up to Gleneagles, where nerves overcame his desire to do well on his first outing: he made the green in one stroke, then took six putts to reach the hole. He soon relaxed, though, and became a regular and enthusiastic participant in the show. The racing driver James Hunt, for instance, insisted on being accompanied by his alsatian Oscar, so Peter brought along his own pet, a goldfish called Abe Ginsberg; he would place Ginsberg's bowl alongside the tee and instruct the fish to watch for infringements. During one series he found himself on the same programme as Ted Dexter, the first time they had encountered each other since Radley. Peter exacted the best possible revenge for his miserable childhood by insisting upon being match referee for Dexter's round. Whenever Dexter – who was a superb golfer and knew it – played a shot, there would be Peter on camera behind him, dressed in knee-length boots, jodhpurs, leather jacket, scarf and gloves with a First World War flying helmet and a riding crop, his cheeks rouged, his mouth lipsticked and his eyes mascara'd from a nearby pensioner's make-up bag, announcing another erratic refereeing decision. Some people chose to question the apparent incongruity of the Amnesty International satirist involving himself in so mainstream an activity as celebrity golf: 'What you must remember,' explained Peter, 'is that Swift was an extremely keen golfer who kept the fact carefully concealed from his public.'[5]

Peter's ability to make himself at home at either end of the showbiz spectrum was never more graphically illustrated than by his role at a giant party given by Victor Lownes on 7 July 1979, to celebrate the twenty-fifth anniversary of *Playboy* magazine. This was one event that Judy was definitely not invited to, new start or no new start. Peter was one of the meeters and greeters – along with Ingrid Seward and Dai Llewellyn – at a twenty-five-hour extravaganza in which Stocks was crammed to capacity with a thousand guests. Eight thousand bottles of champagne and five hundred bottles of whisky had been ordered, but when the champagne ran out Ingrid Seward simply sent a Rolls Royce to the Clermont Club in London and told them to fill it to the roof with Lanson Black Label. There was a fairground, a roller disco, a

Peter as The Mad Hatter on the set of Jonathan Miller's *Alice In Wonderland*, 1966. *(BBC)*

Peter and Richard Ingrams on a *Private Eye* promotional visit to Durham University, October 1966. *(Courtesy Private Eye)*

Judy Scott-Fox (on a visit to London), Wendy, Peter, Daisy and Lucy Cook, circa 1967. *(Courtesy Daisy Cook)*

Peter as the Devil (George Spiggott) in *Bedazzled,* 1967. *(BFI)*

Peter and Dudley as leaping nuns of the Order of St Beryl in *Bedazzled,* 1967. *(BFI)*

Peter and Dudley suspended from a balloon in *The Bedsitting Room*, June 1968. Immediately after the photograph was taken, Peter was injured as the squad car plunged to the ground. *(Rex Features)*

Peter as Greta Garbo in *Not Only . . . But Also*, February 1970. *(BBC)*

Peter's girlfriend (and later wife) Judy Huxtable on the location shoot of *Where Do I Sit?*, January 1971. *(Sun Group Newspapers)*

Peter imitates Elvis Presley on *Where Do I Sit?*, February 1971. *(BBC)*

Peter, Dudley and Spike Milligan on stage in Australia in *Behind The Fridge*, November 1972. *(Courtesy Judy Cook)*

Top, left: A promotional shot for the *Behind The Fridge* stage show. *(Scope Features)*
Main picture: Peter and Judy pose on a building site opposite Ruston Mews, 1970.
(Courtesy Judy Cook)
Above, left: Peter, Lucy and Daisy in New York, summer 1974, during the
American tour of *Good Evening*. *(Courtesy Judy Cook)*
Above, right: Publicity pose for *Revolver*, March 1978. *(Brian Moody/Scope)*

Peter and Dudley as Derek and Clive. *(Courtesy Ciara Parkes)*

Peter briefly adopts a footballer's perm, June 1979. *(BBC)*

Peter with Dirty Bertie, one of Judy's lambs, at Mitchell Leys Farm in Wingrave, 1981. *(Courtesy Judy Cook)*

Publicity pose for *The Two Of Us* with Mimi Kennedy, April 1981. *(Transworld Feature Syndicate)*

Rainbow George with a tiny fraction of his cassette collection. *(Courtesy George Weiss)*

Peter and Ian Hislop face the media following the Sonia Sutcliffe libel verdict, 1989. *(Courtesy Private Eye)*

Peter with his third wife Lin Chong Cook, 1993. *(Rex Features)*

Peter with his daughters Lucy and Daisy at Daisy's wedding, September 1994. *(Courtesy Daisy Cook)*

Peter and Sting at the annual celebrity Perudo tournament, November 1994, just a few weeks before Peter's death. *(Rex Features)*

fashion show, aerobatic displays, horse riding and a giant jacuzzi filled with Bunny girls. 'Peter was wonderful,' says Ingrid Seward, 'bouncing around with his funny voice, in a huge checked cap, shouting into his micro-phone.'[6] The celebrities he had been asked to corral were distinctly B-list: Kenny Lynch, Nicky Henson, Michael Winner, Reggie Bosanquet, Bernie Winters, Jonathan Aitken MP and Gary Glitter, four years after his last top ten hit. One wonders what some of Peter's more radical friends, such as Malcolm McLaren or the Sex Pistols, would have made of it had they known. His charm and social versatility were admirable qualities, as perhaps was his loyalty to his host, but Lownes's party was a grimly tacky occasion, which – if one is not to be too judgmental – was well beneath his dignity. In fact, so successful was Peter as an MC that he was employed soon afterwards to host the Disco International Awards at the Bond Street Embassy Club, thereby proving that dignity was the last thing on his mind.

Most of Peter's work in the first half of 1979 had been fragmented and directionless. Before his reconciliation with Judy he had taken part in *Why Vote, It Only Encourages Them*, a Radio Four election night special, and had appeared as 'Count Yourchickens' in *Tales from the Crypt*, a failed radio pilot put together by Griff Rhys Jones and Rory McGrath. 'He had been very crabby and uncommunicative,' recalls McGrath, 'and worried that people were trying to rip him off. He spent most of the time on the phone to his agent saying "What if this thing takes off – should I be on a merchandising deal?"' In the summer, when things had begun to look up, he had agreed to take part in *Person to Person*, a series of full-length individual interviews hosted by David Dimbleby. The programme contained one hostile exchange, much commented upon, which was to prove a turning point for Peter. Dimbleby attacked *Derek and Clive Ad Nauseum* as 'disgusting', and suggested that he and Dudley had run out of material; Peter denied it, and hinted strongly that another series of *Not Only . . . But Also* was in the offing.

Dimbleby:	But that's all come to an end, your relationship with Dudley.
Peter:	No, no, his number one priority at the moment is to make films, but there is no actual end to the partnership. We'd both like to do a series over here. We will fairly soon, I hope.
Dimbleby:	But haven't you been left high and dry, in a sense?
Peter:	It's a remarkably comfortable relationship, because it all comes so naturally.
Dimbleby:	But that's not what I mean.

An argument ensued as to whether or not Peter had been left 'high and dry'.

>   *Peter*:   ... It doesn't leave me high and dry, in that I can write a series for myself.
>
>   *Dimbleby*:   But you haven't.
>
>   *Peter*:   I haven't done it yet, no. I've written fifteen minutes of the first thirty minutes, with E. L. Wisty as the central character.

Peter was stung by Dimbleby's accusations, particularly the fact that they were all true (unlike many of his answers). He vowed there and then to create something worthwhile, to knuckle down and turn *The Wonderful World of Wisty* into a viable and successful TV show without Dudley's help. 'It was a sort of challenge to prove I could still do family entertainment,' he told the Daily Express. 'I thought, I'll show *you*, David Dimbleby.'[7]

In the autumn of 1979 Humphrey Barclay at London Weekend Television received a call from David Wilkinson, Peter's agent. 'He said, "Peter would like to come and talk to you about doing a special for London Weekend." So I thought, "Oh, how lovely, hurray," you know. I didn't know Peter at the time. It was when he'd suddenly become acceptable again after *The Secret Policeman's Ball*, and he'd been reclaimed as an object of worship by all the up-and-coming people, so he was able to bring in various performers as new as Rowan Atkinson, for example. He came in to see me, and I felt I was on trial a little bit, because he would be saying some of his stream-of-consciousness nonsense in that laconic way, with his lips curling into a smile, and always looking at me to see whether I was picking up on it. I gathered that the show was rather important to him, that he was trying to re-establish himself.'

Dimbleby's goading was of course not the only factor inspiring Peter to revitalise his career. Dudley himself, after three years of trying, had made a small but significant breakthrough in Hollywood in the summer of 1978, which ironically enough had owed something to the revival of interest inspired by the first Derek and Clive album. Chevy Chase was making his screen debut opposite Goldie Hawn in the comedy thriller *Foul Play*, a film that included a cameo written for Tom Conway about a diminutive sex-mad orchestral conductor who attempts to seduce the heroine. When Conway turned the role down, Chase – who had met Peter and Dudley on *Saturday Night Live* in 1976 – suggested that the success of Derek and Clive made Dudley a commercially worthwhile risk once again, especially as the role was such a small one. Dudley accepted the offer only reluctantly – 'I didn't want to play *another* oversexed undersized twit,' he explains – but a job was a job, and he did well in the role. The film was immensely successful, and suddenly Dudley was bankable again.

In December 1978 Blake Edwards, who had met Dudley in psychoanalysis, was writing and directing a comedy about another libidinous musician, *10*. The film's star, George Segal, walked out on the first day of shooting in protest at the amount of artistic input Edwards was conceding to his wife, the film's co-star Julie Andrews. Dudley, who had just returned to the USA from recording *Derek and Clive Ad Nauseum*, jumped at the chance of another substitute appearance. So closely did the role mirror his own life that he was able to play the part straight, and effectively appear as himself. *10* was a massive worldwide hit, making 1000 per cent profit on its $6 million production costs. Dudley's abortive seduction of Bo Derek to the sound of Ravel's *Bolero* made his reputation as a vulnerable sex symbol, prompting the Hollywood Women's Press Club to present him with the Golden Apple award as 'Male Discovery of 1979'. In the space of a year, he had gone from being a virtually unemployable English comedian whose best days were presumed to be behind him, to a millionaire film star with countless female fans. Peter's 1965 prediction that Dudley would enter middle age as the 'cuddly funster at the piano of the Edmonton Empire' had gone hugely awry.

Peter was, not unnaturally, stunned. There were similarities with the case of David Frost, seventeen years before: both Frost and Dudley had used comic characters and voices devised by Peter as a launching pad to go on to bigger things. Significantly, however, both men had made their quantum leap by abandoning Peter's comic voices and appearing as themselves. In both cases, Peter's attitude was ambivalent: he felt affection tempered with disbelief and an enormous frustration that they and not him had been catapulted to such seemingly uncritical acclaim. It was not that he wanted to be the star of *10*, or indeed that he could ever have made a success of the part – that was not the point. He was angry that after all those years of trying and failing to carve out an equivalent success for himself and Dudley, his subordinate partner should have had fame, fortune and female attention seemingly handed to him on a plate for taking part in what was frankly a mediocre film.

At this early stage of Dudley's Hollywood career, Peter contented himself with one or two mildly sarcastic jokes when journalists quizzed him about *10* – as they did, endlessly and irritatingly. He suggested that Dudley must have slept with Blake Edwards to have got the part. He dismissed his ex-partner as 'A power-crazed ego-maniac, a kind of Hitler without the charm,' and explained that 'Women want to mother him in some way. But I'm not envious.'[8] Asked to review the film he groaned, 'Does that mean I'll have to see it *again*?' With reference to Dudley's glamorous new six-foot girlfriend Susan Anton, he expressed sardonic surprise 'that Dudley should choose a girlfriend who sings country and western, when I know for a fact he can't stand that type of music.'[9] (Peter's next door neighbour Rainbow George points out, incidentally, that after the pair went their separate ways, all Dudley's girlfriends were at least six foot tall, while most of Peter's measured approximately five feet two.)

Even now, Peter's friends disagree profoundly with each other about the true nature of his reaction to Dudley's success. Stephen Fry, for instance, states that 'When Dudley Moore became a film star there were many who believed Peter was jealous, and that must have been deeply hurtful, for nothing could have been further from the truth. He was sorry not to have his great collaborator around for more fun, but jealous, never.'[10] John Lloyd begs to differ. 'Was Peter Cook unhappy, was Peter Cook jealous? Well, inevitably – you know, your best friend becomes one of the biggest stars in the Hollywood universe. For most people it's very difficult to feel very jolly about your friends being enormously successful. I think Peter's thing was, he thought that Dudley wasn't a sex symbol. By all that is just, it was a ludicrous idea.'

The reason for the apparent discrepancy is that Peter lived his life in a series of pockets: his myriad friends and acquaintances did not all see the same side of him. He liked to please the person he was with, so if a friend like Stephen Fry or Sid Gottlieb offered him almost unqualified admiration, he would try to live up to their proud picture of him. 'He was so incapable of the least snide remark about Dudley, or any one of the *Fringe* cast for that matter,' insists Gottlieb. In the privacy of the *Private Eye* office, though, he behaved differently. Willie Rushton remembered Peter being 'faintly furious' about Dudley's film success, and his remarking bitterly that 'It doesn't matter how much therapy Dudley goes to, how many psychiatrists he sees, he'll still be short and thick.' Richard Ingrams concurs: 'He was cut up about Dudley's success. He started talking about him in a disparaging way – calling him a deformed dwarf. There's no doubt that one of Peter's fantasies was to have been a Hollywood film star. It must have been very galling to him when Dudley succeeded. He was supposed to be the glamorous one of the two, and Dudley was this comic figure from Dagenham. If you'd said, which of these two men is going to be a Hollywood sex symbol, we'd all have said Peter – and it didn't turn out like that. I always thought there was a strong similarity between the Cook–Moore relationship and the Milligan–Sellers one – Spike experienced that same kind of resentment. I've experienced this with John Wells too: you're resentful of the fact that you rely on this other person, so you resent their individual success. You can see what's missing that you would have put in, and you're annoyed that people are raving about something they've done which is actually slightly less good than what you've done together.' It is in such circumstances that the partner who has been left behind rationalises the success of his departed colleague as a form of 'betrayal'.

The almost schizophrenic mixture of pleasure and displeasure that Peter felt with regard to Dudley's achievement must also have contributed to the surprising disparity between different assessments of his state of mind, deriving from apparently similar sources. Alan Bennett, for instance, maintains that 'Peter didn't resent the fact that Dudley had taken off,'[11] while Jonathan Miller is sure that 'Peter wanted to be a movie star, and envied Dudley that particular success.'[12] Perhaps the definitive answer, if there can be one, is that offered by Michael Parkinson: 'I think he was slightly peeved, because I think Peter would have loved to have been that Hollywood superstar if only to have knocked it. He would have loved it because it would have appealed to his sense of style, but he would have needed to have been a maverick within that.' As Peter himself said, 'There's two kinds of fame. There's fame like Charles Manson and there's fame like Dudley. There has to be something between the two.'[13]

It is undoubtedly significant that before the release of *10*, Peter had missed Dudley so much that he had even taken to telephoning his partner's mother. He had also written frequently to Dudley to tell him that he was sober and happy again: 'I do think that when we manage to do another series, your mother should become a regular along with Dud and Pete. I don't want to press you when things are obviously going so well for you in the States. I like to think that when you become "hot" and "enormous" it will make it easier for us to do a decent movie together with our choice of director.' Rather hopefully, he had assured Dudley that *Derek and Clive Get the Horn* 'works really well visually . . . some of the stuff is hilarious.' After the release and massive success of *10* however, Peter never once contacted Dudley to congratulate him, nor made any comment to him, adverse or otherwise, about that film. When Dudley was paid a considerable sum to fly to Britain in October 1979 to appear as a guest on *The Muppet Show*, there was no contact between the two.

What is also significant is that Peter's next step, in February 1980, was to fly to Hollywood in search of work. He had been invited by CBS to take part in a charity show for Cambodian refugees, but stayed in Los

Angeles for a month, locked in discussion with various major studios. His explanation was that he was short of money, but he was already in the middle of his perfectly lucrative project for London Weekend back home, which showed every sign of having the potential to become a long-running success. He admitted to reporters in LA: 'Yes, I would like to be a sex symbol – who wouldn't? Someone here said today's male stars are the non-macho types who don't present any threat. Well, I always used to think Dudley didn't present a hint. So there should be hope for me.'[14] The trip had not begun in the most auspicious manner: boarding a taxi at the airport, he had found himself trapped in a terrible traffic jam as he entered the centre of town. After his cab hadn't moved for some minutes, the driver had got out and walked along the line of cars to see if he could find out what was causing the hold-up. Eventually he had returned in a state of high excitement. 'Hey, you'll never believe this,' he had shouted at Peter. 'It's Dudley Moore up there! DUDLEY MOORE!' Peter slumped back into his seat, lost for words for once in his life.

Thereafter, things started to look up. After sifting his way through some 'lousy' film scripts, he was offered the starring role in a CBS-TV version of *Two's Company*, the successful British series about an American woman and her English butler (originally portrayed by Elaine Stritch and Donald Sinden). The show had been retitled *The Two of Us*, had been relocated to New York, and the middle-aged Stritch character had been recast as a pretty young talk show hostess with a precocious daughter. Peter later nonchalantly claimed that he had got the job 'almost by accident . . . I was on holiday in Los Angeles when I was asked to do it.'[15]

This was disingenuous to say the least. The actress Brenda Vaccaro, who threw a 'Derek and Clive' party in Peter's honour, reports that Peter was very excited to have landed *The Two of Us*: 'He had been a bit sad that his career wasn't taking off, and he felt a strong competitive strain with Dudley. He very much wanted to work here and be successful, even though he always said he didn't, and now he was getting his shot at it. He was in the best shape ever, and Dudley was happy and proud to see him in such great condition.'[16]

Before he left for home Peter took part in a successful pilot of *The Two of Us*. He made a curiously camp and aggressive butler, and the sartorial elegance of his youth was clearly on the wane, but as far as the American TV executives were concerned, he was the very essence of Englishness. They were happy, to believe, in fact, that an English butler might be called 'Brentwood', and that upon being asked to go into the kitchen to prepare a meal, he might reply, 'I'll just go check your utensils'. In the name of gravitas Peter was required to abandon the hair dye he had favoured for the past three-and-a-half years; he never wore it again. He claimed to find the role of a sardonic butler easy enough: 'This is not acting. I'm just being English. I don't have to dredge deep within my resources to be sardonic. In a way I find many things in America ridiculous and say so. So it is nice to be playing somebody who is a slightly more ridiculous version of myself.'[17] CBS had yet to decide on a suitable co-star, so Peter agreed to return to LA later in the year to record further pilots.

Back in London Peter set to work enthusiastically on his Wisty special, now renamed *Peter Cook & Co.*, which he recorded at London Weekend in June 1980. 'There is a whole generation now who can only identify me with the "foul-mouthed" Derek and Clive records. I want to put that right,'[18] he told the *Daily Mirror*. His competitive instincts were faintly cheered by the disastrous reception accorded to Dudley's new film, the biblical comedy *Wholly Moses*. Asked for the thousandth time if he envied his former partner, he replied: 'I'm not envious of Dudley. I certainly wouldn't like to have made *Wholly Moses*, which nobody has ever heard of.' Peter was now writing sketches with the experienced Bernard McKenna, and described the process as 'easier and more enjoyable without Dudley. He was so pernickety. I'd want to start a sketch with two blokes sitting in a railway carriage and Dudley would say, "How did they get there?"'[19] The absence of Dudley's restraining hand was considered less of a boon by Humphrey Barclay, who had become executive producer on the programme: 'The difficulty as always with Peter's writing was finding a punchline. You wander down this wonderful meandering path taking whatever route takes your fancy, and then you suddenly think, "We've been going for five-and-a-half minutes, we've got to get out of this somehow."'

This lack of discipline apart, *Peter Cook & Co.* turned out to be a funny, interesting and original programme which comfortably sustained an hour's viewing. Rather than attempt to replace Dudley on screen with a single performer, the producer Paul Smith had persuaded John Cleese, Rowan Atkinson, Terry Jones, Beryl Reid and Paula Wilcox to partner Peter in turn. There was no last-minute script panic as there had been on *Not Only . . . But Also*. Cook and McKenna prepared everything meticulously, well in advance. Their linking device was an American cabbie, a character based directly on Peter's experiences in the USA in February, with whom the viewer was trapped as he enthused hoarsely about 'wet blouses' and 'big gazonkers'. The first item was a solo piece too, a parody of Roald Dahl's *Tales of the Unexpected* entitled *Tales of the Much As We Expected*, with Peter in the part of Dahl delivering a confidential fireside chat:

> *Dahl*:   Ronald was a pretty ordinary name, and until I dropped the 'n' nobody took a blind bit of notice. But 'Roald' makes me sound mysterious and important. If Ronald Biggs had called himself 'Roald', like me he could have got away with daylight robbery.

As he spoke, the crackling log fire slowly spread across the carpet beneath his armchair.

The second item was a perfect example of a good idea being allowed to meander too far from its original premise. Beryl Reid appeared as Elka Starborgling, a twenty-four-hour emergency plumber who arrives for a job dressed as a huge bee: 'I know. You weren't expecting a woman. Or a bee.' What began as a very funny satire on expectations then turned into long monologue about her life on an Arctic trawler, before wandering into a sketch about control of the country being seized by thousands of bee-people. The closing item in part one was tighter, a *Not Only*-style father and son sketch with John Cleese as an upper-class gentleman trying to initiate his son into the mysteries of girlfriends; the twist being that his son, played by Peter, is forty-two.

The second part of the show indicated Peter's determination to emphasise his versatility. He appeared first as Professor Heinrich Globnick, a marvellous teutonic ant expert whose central premise was that 'ant society is a shambles'. Give an ant a bottle of vodka, he explained, and it will become incapable of operating heavy machinery. Questioned about the sex life of the ant, he replied: 'Basically . . . it is a shambles.' The presenter, played by Rowan Atkinson, finally tried to wind up the interview:

> *Presenter*:   Well Professor, I'm sure we could go on all night talking about ants.
> *Globnick*:   No we couldn't. We've hammered the subject into the ground.

Peter re-appeared next as cowboy Lee van Wrangler in a musical number during which he related his drunken father's dying advice – advice which went on and on, getting more and more useless and specific. The song even had a punchline, the final piece of advice being 'If you've got any sense son, don't take my advice.'

As if to prove that Peter had moved beyond revisiting old ideas and characters himself, the next sketch actually cast Rowan Atkinson as E. L. Wisty, or at least an ill-disguised version of him, buttonholing Terry Jones in a railway compartment:

Atkinson: Hello . . . Are you gay?
Jones: No . . . no, I'm not gay.
Atkinson: Nor am I.

The next sketch, however, actually did revisit an old idea, being a straight remake of the Establishment Club film purporting to be the out-takes of Neville Chamberlain's return from Munich in 1938. Peter appeared as the camp film director and John Cleese played Chamberlain, utterly unable to grasp the required sequence of: 1. Getting out of the plane; 2. Waving the piece of paper; and 3. Making the speech.

The third and final part contained two new items and one old. *The Amnesiacs* saw Peter and Beryl Reid as a television-obsessed couple who could never remember any actor's name or what else they'd been in, while their son (who knew all the answers) couldn't get a word in edgeways. 'I really adored that,' says Humphrey Barclay. 'It was delicious, partly because it was kept to a reasonable length.' Another sketch followed with Rowan Atkinson playing a part that Peter might have been expected to take: that of a creepy, sex-fixated rural shopkeeper who intimidates a customer newly arrived in the village from London, played by Paula Wilcox. The idea clearly derived from Peter and Judy's agreement to move towards a rural lifestyle. The grand finale of *Peter Cook & Co.* featured E. L. Wisty at last, singing *Lovely Lady of the Roses*, the B-side of his 1965 single *The Ballad of Spotty Muldoon*. After a brief ramble about his paranormal powers, seated at his customary park bench, a huge pink set populated by an all-girl dance troupe – the Wistyettes – was unveiled. A giant rose bloomed open to reveal a pink-clad Wisty, who sang the words: 'Underneath the mac and trousers is a wonderful human being, if you just treat him right.'

Peter worked furiously hard at promoting the show before its September release. He took Stephen Pile to a Tottenham game for *The Sunday Times*, and surprised the writer not just by screaming abuse at the players and the referee, but also by shouting 'Millwall supporters! Hooligans!' at a party of sedate old ladies stepping on to a zebra crossing on the way to the game. He sat down and wrote an E. L. Wisty article for the *TV Times*, to tie in with the routine about the character's paranormal powers:

All of us at one time or another have had a sense of *déja vu*, a feeling that this has happened before that this has happened before.[20]

As it turned out, the critics were divided on the subject of *Peter Cook & Co.*, but most agreed that it had been a triumph. 'Twice as fresh and twice

as funny as the usual jaded junk' said the *Daily Mail*. 'He could not have
done better' said the *Guardian*. The *Express* called the show 'dazzling' and
claimed that 'It restores hope for the survival of television comedy', before
predicting that 'Mr Cook will rapidly be restored in the nation's affections.'
The Times offered the opinion that 'Cook writes sketches as brilliantly
as ever (though he badly needs an editor).' The *Telegraph* dissented,
complaining that 'Every sketch went on too long and fizzled out in
an unconvincing or routine pay-off', while the *Evening News* summed
it up as 'a series of overlong sketches which didn't sustain the interest'.
America, though, lapped the show up unconditionally, and showered
Peter with trophies, including a gold medal at the New York Film and
Television Festival and an International Emmy Award Nomination. The
resurrection of Peter's career was proceeding apace. London Weekend
was naturally delighted, and asked for a whole series of *Peter Cook & Co.,*
but Peter stalled. Hollywood still beckoned, an unwanted but nonetheless
unfulfilled challenge. Like a spider making a final, brave effort to climb
out of the bath, he was determined to give it one more try.

While waiting for work on *The Two of Us* to restart (it had been delayed
by an American actors' strike), Peter and Bernard McKenna, together with
Graham Chapman of Monty Python, negotiated a contract with Orion Films
to write *Yellowbeard*, a spoof pirate epic in which Chapman would take the
lead and Peter would co-star. The project had been around for a while –
it had originally been suggested many years previously by Keith Moon –
but finance now became available following Chapman's success in *Monty
Python's Life of Brian*. The trio set to work immediately. There was plenty
of other work over the summer: Peter when sober and in a good mood was
a fearsomely energetic figure, every piston and cogwheel racing full steam
ahead. He became involved in Spike Milligan's BBC series *Q9*, and wrote
a foreword for Paula Yates's book *Rock Stars in Their Underpants*, which
included such gems as 'Some men are born in their underwear and some
have underwear thrust upon them', 'It is a measure of our liberty that such
a work would not be allowed in the Soviet Union', and, with regard to
the long-lost art of pantie-reading, 'As a Matelot on the cusp I have never
really been compatible with Dudley Moore, who is a typical Boxer with
Y-fronts rising.'

He also got a last-minute job as the star of the Barclay's Bank commercials,
following the death of Peter Sellers in July, playing a conman called Harry
Hodgers. Sellers' death badly upset him, and he fired off a furious letter
to the *Guardian* after the paper published an appreciation by the Boulting
brothers which he felt to be insufficiently generous. He was hardly better
pleased to be offered the part of Inspector Clouseau in the *Pink Panther*

film that Blake Edwards and Peter Sellers had been planning, especially when he found out that Dudley had already turned it down. 'Nobody takes over from Sellers,' he insisted, before going on to point out that he would, however, be perfectly happy to take over from Jacques Cousteau.

Somehow, Peter found time to write yet further letters to the press, of a more light-hearted nature, such as this offer to the *New Statesman:*

> I would be interested in financing the film being prepared by the Agnes Varda Women's Collective. Ms Lloyd outlines a scene in which 'a literary editor of middle years is stripped naked, covered in warm honey and suspended by his genitalia from a chandelier; whereupon a swarm of bees flies in through the window.' Before sending a cheque I would like an assurance that this is not to be yet another bee-ist exploitation movie like *The Swarm*. I would not be a party to any endeavour that perpetuated the sexist myth of the idle drone and I trust that the film will depict the profoundly matriarchal society of bees in an accurate light. There must of course be no cruelty to the bees.

Perhaps most incredibly of all, given the amount of work he was doing elsewhere, in August 1980 Peter presented Judy with a surprise: Mitchell Leys Farm, a beautiful country cottage in the quiet Buckinghamshire village of Wingrave. There was stabling for horses, and plenty of room for the menagerie of other animals that Judy required to occupy her time and her unemployed maternal instincts. Peter had discovered it himself, he explained, and arranged the entire purchase through his offshore company. 'I was really touched,' says Judy. Peter pronounced himself thrilled. 'It's exactly what we have been looking for. A middle-class dream come true,' he said.[21] The landlord of the Rose and Crown pronounced his new tomato juice-drinking customer 'a super bloke'. Coming from someone so city-bound that he regarded Tooting as the equivalent of West Africa, the purchase seemed a remarkably generous gesture on Peter's part. Of course he spent most of the week working in London and living at Perrin's Walk, but he came up every weekend; however he had developed the habit of playing a lot of tennis on Saturdays and Sundays, and Judy did not see as much of him as she would have liked.

That autumn, she made a rather unpleasant discovery. Wingrave, it transpired, was quite close to Stocks. It had not been Peter, but Victor Lownes who had found Mitchell Leys Farm. It was Lownes that he had been playing tennis with – if, indeed, that is what he had been doing. 'I hadn't seen the wood for the trees,' she says regretfully. Peter was

desperately keen to show her that all was above board, and took Judy
with him to Stocks, where there were indeed tennis courts – as well as
scores of Bunny girls. Despite his protestations, the discovery could not
help but throw a dark shadow across their relationship; Peter had always
previously told Judy the truth of his indiscretions, even if it sometimes
took him a while to get round to it. This seemed underhand.

America remained a further point of unease between them. Peter sat
idly waiting for the call throughout the autumn, before finally being asked
if he'd like to return to LA just after Christmas. The fact of the matter
was that he didn't really want to go. He explained: 'When I signed for
the pilot of this series, I was told: "If the show succeeds, you are locked
in for five years," which I consider to be a cruel and unusual punishment.
I did the pilot never believing for a moment it would go into a series –
the chances, I was told, were 100–1 against. Then I could get home to
my wife Judy and my two daughters. My only hope is that after thirteen
weeks and vast critical acclaim it will be cancelled, with a terrific row.'22
Peter was being disingenuous again; faced with a direct choice between
The Two of Us and making further episodes of *Peter Cook & Co.*, he had
deliberately chosen the former, even though he knew he would hate it,
because it was a nut he just had to crack (and also because CBS were
prepared to pay him £400,000 to crack it). Both Judy and his friends
from Alcoholics Anonymous were apprehensive about his going. 'He'd
built up such a good back-up in London,' explains Judy. 'He hadn't had
a drink for nearly two years. But he needed to be in touch with people
who could keep him on the wagon. For Peter, America could be like a
candy shop. We had big discussions about it. He was seriously depressed
about it – he really didn't want to live over there.' Compelled to give it
one more try nonetheless, Peter left in January 1981. Judy did not go with
him – she had her animals to look after, and anyway, she could not face
America again after the tribulations of the previous trip.

At first, *The Two of Us* went well. Peter made two more pilots, with
a view to selecting a co-star, and Mimi Kennedy was chosen from the
second of them. Four trial shows were transmitted in April, garnering
excellent reviews and big audiences. It shot to number four in the ratings,
bringing in thirty million viewers a week, and a further twenty-four shows
were scheduled for September. He stayed with Brenda Vaccaro rather than
hiring a hotel suite, a domestic environment which shielded him somewhat
from the more obvious temptations on offer, and he telephoned Judy every
night. When he returned to Wingrave in the summer he admitted to his
wife that he had indeed started drinking again – but only a small amount,
he said, and it was all under control. One day the telephone rang, and

Judy answered it; it was Mimi Kennedy, ringing to thank Peter for the flowers. 'She didn't even know he was married,' says Judy. 'When I asked him about it, he said, "Judes, I just had a crisis." I don't think they'd had an affair – he just had a crush on her. It wasn't a sex thing any more with other women. He just needed affection. He constantly needed people to let him know he was worth being around, to bolster his confidence.'

In September, Peter returned to Los Angeles. Still on the crest of a wave professionally, he was reunited with Dudley for an interview with the *Daily Mirror*. There were jibes – 'What's a small, stunted ugly little Dagenham git like you doing here in this living temple to Gloria Swanson and Mary Pickford?' – but there was also a tremendous chemistry, that made a mockery of the two years they had spent apart. As Pete and Dud, they improvised an updated version of their first ever double-act:

> *Dud*:   Farrah Fawcett-Majors managed to slip away from Ryan O'Neal the other evening, Pete. She said to me: 'Come and be mine tonight.' So I said to her: 'Look here Farrah, we've had our laughs. On yer bike.'
>
> *Pete*:   Know just what you mean, Dud. There I was watching the baseball and sucking an ice lolly in my hotel room the other evening, when there came this scratching at the window. 'Who's there?' I enquired. 'It's me, Brooke Shields. Let me in, now.' So I said: 'Hoof it, Brooke. I'm busy, and what is more I'm expecting a discreet visit from Linda Lovelace.' So she went, broken-hearted of course.
>
> *Dud*:   Funny you should mention that. There I was the other evening, sitting there being barely entertained by the *Jerome Carson Show*, when I suddenly feel this hand on my cheek. I look up and Gawd, it's Dolly Parton. So I says: 'Get out of here, you hussy!' and I throw that great, huge bra of hers . . .[23]

Dolly's bra was too much for the pair of them, and they fell about laughing. The humour was only slightly undercut by the fact that what had been a series of absurd fantasies in 1965 would not actually have been such unlikely occurrences had Dudley experienced them in 1981.

Peter's jollity, sadly, did not last. In the autumn, over its longer run, the all-important ratings of *The Two of Us* plummeted as fast as they had risen. Mysteriously, it failed to re-enter the top twenty, and by Christmas it had fallen out of the top forty altogether. This time, staying in a hotel,

Peter was alone with his failure. His performances began to be affected by alcohol once more. He continued to talk to Judy on the phone every night, and one night she broke the news to him that her mother had died. She had been left a considerable amount of money, and she wanted to return to her Devon roots. She planned to sell the house in Wingrave, and move to the isolation of Exmoor: 'I decided I wanted to try real countryside,' she says. 'At first Peter was shocked, but he came round to the idea.' The switch was achieved extremely swiftly: Judy bought almost the first house she could find, an isolated building called Blagdon Close at Wheddon Cross. Peter nicknamed her 'Baroness Blagdon'. It was arranged that he would take a few days out of his punishing, fifty hours-a-week schedule at Christmas 1981. A chauffeur-driven car picked him up at Heathrow and drove him straight down to Devon. When he arrived, he had to be poured out of the car. He was blind drunk.

The Two of Us staggered on to the end of its run at the beginning of March 1982, when it was scrapped by the network for the candid reason that it was 'not doing well enough'. Exhausted and seriously dependent on the bottle again, Peter returned home to London. He was, according to his American agent John Gaines, 'very disappointed'.[24] Questioned about the failure of his sitcom, he tended to react bitterly and defensively. He insisted to the *Sun* that the series had not failed at all: 'My career is certainly not a flop. I can only tell you I have never been so lavishly over-praised by the critics.'[25] On *The Late Clive James*, he claimed that he had left CBS, not the other way around, after his agent had disputed the size of his salary for the second year of recordings. He informed John Lloyd that he had 'absolutely hated' doing the show, and that he had done it as badly as he could in the hope that it would be scrapped. He suggested to the *Sunday Express* that he had deliberately left his golf clubs at the Chateau Marmont Hotel, in order to ensure that sod's law would dictate the cancellation of the series and thus the loss of the clubs.

In the months that followed, Peter gave Hollywood and its 'face-lifted androids' a veritable tongue-lashing. 'There's an elitism and a snobbery in LA which is pretty insufferable,'[26] he complained. 'People are only interested in what you are doing, and they are always lying about what they are doing. Saying they're busy. The people who work on films go to bed early so they'll look good for early call in the morning. And those out of work don't go out in case anybody accuses them of not working.'[27] Peter liked to tell a multi-layered anecdote which encapsulated the world he had just left behind, about a charity benefit he had taken part in at the Radio City Music Hall, called *The Night of a Hundred Stars*. Gina Lollobrigida, it appeared, had claimed to have been mobbed by adoring fans. 'What actually happened is that she tripped over her own dress. The truth is, hardly anyone recognised her. The only person who was mobbed was Larry Hagman. There was an acute shortage of liquor backstage. About halfway through the evening you had all these big, big stars knocking on each other's dressing-rooms to see if anyone had half a bottle of vodka to spare. The only guy who had the good sense to bring some booze with him was Larry Hagman. No wonder he was mobbed.' After the show there had been a cast party, at which the chief topic of discussion had been the sentimental standing ovation accorded to the wheelchair-bound James Cagney, which had caused the actor to cry. At about 3 am, it was realised that Cagney had not actually shown up at the party, and a search party was dispatched. An hour or so later he was found in the basement: he had left the stage by lift to tumultuous applause, but once in the basement he couldn't get out of the lift unattended, and had been left there for hours.

The following day, Peter had paid a visit to Elizabeth Taylor in her hotel suite and found her in floods of tears. She told me that the worst thing that had ever happened in her life had just happened. "Elizabeth," I said, "knowing *your* life, that must be pretty bad." Well, it turned out that five minutes earlier, Jane Russell of the outsize boobs had come into Elizabeth's suite and for no apparent reason had picked up an ashtray and flung it at Elizabeth's left breast. Elizabeth started shrieking, and Jane had to be sedated and carried off to hospital. That's the tacky side of showbusiness I loathe.'[28] Pete and Dud themselves could hardly have composed a more ridiculous sequence of events. It was indeed a world that Peter loathed; but he had wanted to conquer it sufficiently to be in a position to reject it. Instead, it had rejected him.

Dudley felt that Peter's dislike of his surroundings had affected his performance: 'The trouble was, Peter was apologising all the time for being here and it showed in his work.'[29] It did not help matters that Dudley was now enjoying another massive success with *Arthur*, his portrayal of a drunk whom he admitted basing – in part – on 'this man out there who's an alcoholic whom I know'. Arthur was rich and successful enough to have his own butler, which made Peter's failure in the part of a butler all the more embarrassing. In November 1981 Peter had endured another galling humiliation, when he generously agreed to appear live by satellite in a London Weekend special tribute to Dudley's success, made while Dudley was on a visit to England. The announcer trumpeted: 'Hollywood's newest screen sensation . . . from humble beginnings in his home town of Dagenham he's stepped out to conquer the world of entertainment. Musician, composer, comedian and now international

superstar, will you please welcome: Mr Dudley . . . MOORE!' This was the
cue for Peter to do his bit, and he appeared on a large screen describing
Jayne Mansfield's affair with a starfish; but there was a cock-up on the
studio floor, and someone cued the Dagenham Girl Pipers to begin their
'Tribute to Dudley Moore' before Peter could finish. The resultant round
of applause drowned him out, so the director cut his losses and switched
Peter's feed off in mid-sentence.

Everywhere he went, Dudley's success was gleefully rubbed in. More
often than not Peter smiled, and said nice things. 'I'm delighted for Dud.
He's a brilliantly funny man and it couldn't have happened to a nicer
guy,'[30] he told the *Sunday Express*. He informed the viewers of *Parkinson*
that he was 'delighted – very pleased. And Dudley's revelling in it, having
the thoroughly good time he deserves.' Dudley, he told the *Evening News*,
was his 'best and oldest friend'. At other times, his patience would snap.
Brutally, he informed the *Sun*: 'Perhaps if I had been born with a club foot
and a height problem I might have been as desperate as Dudley to become
a star. That's all he ever wanted. I'm not trying to copy Dud because I
don't have the same need to prove myself. We're totally different people
and we have very little in common. I don't know how we ever agreed
on anything like writing scripts together. I've not bothered to go and
see *Arthur*. I thought I'd wait until it came on television in America, but
when it did I watched a football game on another channel. I appeared on
The Night of a Hundred Stars show recently – and do you know who got
the loudest cheers from the crowds? Television stars like Larry Hagman
and Linda Gray. Movie stars like Gregory Peck went almost unnoticed,
but the people went bananas every time a telly star walked in.'[31] Later
on, Peter told the same paper that 'Dudley hasn't changed a bit in more
than twenty years – he's still selfish, vain and greedy. At one time he
wanted to be a pop star you know. He did once complain to me that
he is surrounded in Hollywood by fools and sycophants who laugh at
everything he says. I reminded him that when he was living here he was
surrounded by intelligent people who kept telling him what a little toad
he was.'[32]

Dudley was suitably hurt by all these negative remarks. 'I don't
understand why Peter constantly vilified me in the press, and said
unnecessary things about me,' he complains. When he telephoned Peter
to discuss it, he got no reply, and his messages were not returned. A few
years later, Peter told him he had not enjoyed *Arthur*, but that he had
rather liked *Arthur 2*. 'Now why exactly he liked my character in *Arthur 2*
I can't imagine,' ponders Dudley, 'because they were the same.'[33] *Arthur
2*, in fact, differed from its predecessor in that it was a failure at the box

office. Most of Peter's own failures at the box office had been shared with his partner, or at least paralleled by a simultaneous Dudley flop. Their chagrin and their determination to do better next time had been an experience shared between two friends. Now, for the first time, Peter was shouldering the burden of failure entirely alone.

Dudley, of course, could be just as cutting in his assessments: 'He wasn't as good from the time that we broke up. He wouldn't have admitted it, but that's what it coincided with.'³⁴ Outwardly, at least, Peter was still determined to prove that this was not the case, and that he still possessed the ability to show Hollywood a thing or two. He still had *Yellowbeard*, and he had a host of other plans. Asked about his career in 1982, he replied defensively: 'You mean the things I do when I'm not playing golf or breathing in the fresh country air at our place in Exmoor?' After discussing *Yellowbeard*, he continued, perversely: 'There's talk about a TV series called *Cook for 45 Minutes*, and I'm also busy working on a screenplay set in the States. Ideally it should be filmed over there.'³⁵

In truth, though, Peter was spent. He did not do a stroke of work in the six months until October 1982, when *Yellowbeard* was due to be filmed. Instead, he made a brave attempt to move to Exmoor, and to go for long walks in the country. He joined Minehead golf club and opened local bazaars. He made frequent visits to see his parents, and they to see him and Judy. He named all Judy's animals after the main protagonists in the Falklands War. 'He talked to the cats and dogs as if they were people and made up stories about them,' recalls Judy fondly. 'He was very whimsical. Peter was a very loving, affectionate man who was desperately in need of love and affection himself. When my animals had to be put down he'd cry more than me. Once we sat up all night with a dying lamb, night after night. I had a grouchy alsatian, which I'd actually saved from being put down, and the dog always sat on the sofa between us. Peter was scared of alsatians, but he never once objected to its presence – in fact he eventually became friendly with it.'

But it was not to be. After two months, Peter knew that he had to move back to London. 'He needed to be near his fixes, and the bright lights of the city,' says Judy regretfully. She refused to allow alcohol in the house, which made him extra miserable, his mind transfixed by the prospect of his next drink. He found Blagdon Close cold and lonely, and urged her to buy somewhere prettier, with a stream, like the one he and his father used to fish in when he was a child. He begged her, also, to divide her time between Exmoor and London, but she was determined never to return to the city. He continued to visit her for a few weeks at a time here and there, but for the most part she lived alone. Emotionally,

Peter and Judy were still dependent on each other, and spoke at length on the telephone almost every evening; but in terms of living together as a couple, their marriage was effectively at an end. Many years later, Peter explained that it had failed because 'I didn't want to live in the country and she did. Prosaic, but very important. I'm not really much good at talking about farm subsidies with someone who lives twenty miles away, however delightful their labradors.'[36] The reality had been so, so much more complicated than that.

Peter didn't tell his daughters that Judy had gone; they had to work out for themselves why she and her belongings had just vanished. 'I remember arriving at Dad's and she wasn't there,' says Daisy. 'He didn't offer much of an explanation. There were some subjects it didn't occur to you to broach, and that was one of them.' Lucy remembers that 'He kept a message on his answering machine saying "Peter and Judy aren't here at the moment" for about seven years afterwards. We never dared talk about it because we thought he was so devastated by it.' Richard Ingrams recalls that 'If you went to the house she just wasn't around, like Mrs Mainwaring. He said she'd become agoraphobic, which was his excuse as to why she would never come to *Private Eye* parties.' Peter could not bring himself to discuss what had happened with anyone but Sid Gottlieb: 'He would have given God knows what to get her back. He realised he'd lost someone he loved very much. In his mind I think the feeling was "I lost her, and I bloody well deserved it yet again."' Perrin's Walk became something of a shrine, with a huge picture of Judy taking up one wall. A second wall was plastered with a selection of family photographs devoted to Lucy and Daisy's growing up.

Fate then delivered a cruel blow, one which was especially harsh given how much Peter's family meant to him and how difficult he found it to cope with emotional setbacks. In the summer of 1982 his father fell ill with Parkinson's disease; it was, effectively, a death sentence. The local G.P. decided that his mother was not in a position to cope with such a progressively disabling condition unaided, and committed Alec Cook to St George's Hospital in Milford-on-Sea. Peter immediately rode to the rescue on his white charger: he drove down to the hospital, discharged his father, brought him home, hired private nurses to look after him and cheered everyone up into the bargain. He, Sarah and Liz stayed at the house on a rota basis, sometimes in pairs; there were giggly occasions when Peter and Sarah tried to give their father a bath, Alec still correctly attired in soaking pyjamas. Peter invented a character, an imaginary Auntie Flo, who could be held responsible for any mishap. 'Peter was tremendous,' says Sarah. 'He just became completely involved.' Later, in his father's distressing final days, when his condition worsened to the extent that home care became impossible, Alec Cook was so heavily sedated by hospital staff that his mind wandered erratically; Peter argued with the doctors about what drugs they were giving him and how much of it was necessary. Always, throughout, he was a pillar of strength, and always he was of good cheer; but back home in Hampstead, George the next door neighbour would find him sitting alone, sobbing helplessly about his father's impending death.

In October, when he really wanted to be at his father's side, he had to go to Mexico to film *Yellowbeard*. There too, he managed to be the life and soul of the party, standing in the hotel swimming pool, philosophising as E. L. Wisty about the speed of darkness relative to the speed of light. He was sufficiently determined to turn in a good performance that he managed to give up alcohol for the duration, but as a consequence he sought consolation in marijuana instead. Eric Idle volunteered to go with him on a grass-buying expedition: 'Where to look? 'No problem,' said Peter, 'we shall find the nearest bordello.' My wife gave me an old-fashioned look, which Peter intercepted, reassuring her with his incredible charm that I should come to no harm. So off we drove to the local Mexican bordello. A small door in a white-walled street led into a cantina, a square open to the sky with a band and a bar and lovely girls who were happy just to dance, or there was a low *cabaña* with discreet rooms if you wished to dance horizontally. There were tables for drinking and strings of coloured lights and when we entered it had the air of a private party where the guests had yet to arrive.

Peter was an instant hit. He ran in shouting loudly in cod Spanish, shook the hand of the barman, seized a beautiful tall girl in a shiny red bathing suit and stormed onto the deserted dance-floor where he began the most unimaginable shaking jitterbug boogie. The girls went nuts. They danced around him and he boogied with them all, flinging his arms around, his hair wild, occasionally sinking to his knees or exaggeratedly twisting low. I sat quietly by myself in a corner sipping beer and cursing my inability to cut loose and join him. Everywhere he went he brought joy with him. One minute it was a slow night in a naughty night-club and the next it was a one-man fiesta . . . My last sight was Peter leading a line of ecstatic ladies in a conga line. He waved cheerily, tapped his nose and yelled, 'No problem, Eric, we're in . . .'[37]

On screen, Peter played Lord Lambourn, a bumbling aristocrat, to Graham Chapman's Yellowbeard, pirate and serial rapist. Lambourn has unwittingly brought up Yellowbeard's son Dan as his own, training him to be a far-from-ruthless landscape gardener, little suspecting that

Yellowbeard's treasure map is tattooed on the boy's scalp. After twenty years in prison the pirate escapes, makes contact, and together the three set sail for the Caribbean aboard the *Lady Edith* (actually the *Bounty* from the Marlon Brando epic). There were some very funny scenes, notably when the crew attempt to smuggle women on board in defiance of the *Lady Edith*'s captain, played by James Mason. The Captain has failed to notice that one of the ship's officers obviously is a woman in disguise, named Mr Prostitute; although when a sailor laughs at the mention of the name, he has the man's foot nailed to the deck. There were also a smattering of old *Not Only . . . But Also* jokes and some dismal puns, for instance:

> *Blind Pew*:   I may be blind, but I 'ave acute 'earing.
> *Sailor*:   I'm not interested in your jewellery.

The main faults of *Yellowbeard*, however, were structural ones. Peter and his writing colleagues still had not mastered the creation of dramatic tension to counterbalance the comedy, and the attempt to create a sympathetic love interest echoed the failure of *The Wrong Box*, by introducing a thoroughly insipid and uninvolving hero and heroine in Dan and his girlfriend. Peter was wasted in his one-joke supporting role, while Graham Chapman mugged furiously. The rest of the cast, predictably, was top-heavy with competing celebrity cameos: apart from Eric Idle and James Mason, there were John Cleese, Spike Milligan, Kenneth Mars, Nigel Planer, Beryl Reid, Susannah York, David Bowie, Cheech and Chong, Madeline Kahn (a quite disastrous Cockney accent), Michael Hordern and Marty Feldman, in his last role. *Yellowbeard* was a collection of unlearned lessons, a project doomed to failure from the first sentence of its first draft. Peter later described it, unconvincingly, as 'A great script, which was damaged . . . by the director I suppose.'[38] But he had cried wolf once too often. *Yellowbeard* was both competently and indeed lavishly directed by Mel Damski. Peter must have realised in his head, finally, that his particular genius was simply not suited to the cinematic format. His humour was too immediate, too instinctive, too indisciplined to be harnessed to the big screen. It was part of his tragedy that the cinema is regarded by most people – Peter among them, for a long while – as the peak of the entertainer's profession. While that is certainly the case financially, the notion of a creative progression towards Hollywood is one that has needlessly constrained and damaged the development of many artists, Peter included.

By 1983, as a result, his career had utterly stalled again. John Wells bumped into him in the reception of BBC Broadcasting House: 'He dropped into a louche BBC tobacco-throated drawl to tell me, with real warmth and affection and delight in the shared joke, that the Light Entertainment Department was "tremendously excited, really tremendously excited" by a little idea for a programme in which he would appear, and that "With any luck, we should be able to put it out at something like four in the morning with a view to reaching a really substantial audience." He never heard any more about it, and scheme after scheme collapsed in the same way.'[39] Peter actually didn't mind any more. He knew that as far as the industry was concerned *Yellowbeard* had been his last chance at writing a film script, and that nothing remained professionally but to drag his tired frame back to television or the stage – areas where he had triumphed conclusively again and again, and which he had nothing to gain and everything to lose by revisiting. Frankly, there was no point. He didn't have the energy or the inclination to do it all again. He had not so much run out of ambition as run out of room to expand, but the effect was much the same. He was like a much-decorated General who has advanced as far as he can and realises that it would be futile to remain in the front line. His last big push was over. Work, henceforth, would either be small and interesting or irrelevant but extremely well paid.

Work, furthermore, had to take second place to helping his father die with dignity. When he was not with his family, Peter was now very much alone. There would be no more joyous weekends entertaining the children to look forward to: for the children had grown up. Lucy was 18 and Daisy was 17, and Wendy had encouraged both girls to enrol in cookery school in Alfriston. Thereafter Daisy travelled the world before going on to art college, while Lucy became a chef at the Carved Angel in Dartmouth. Inevitably they saw less of their father. Judy, of course, had gone too. Dudley, naturally, was never coming back. Even Stocks had ceased to be one long party: the Playboy Organisation had fired Victor Lownes while Peter was away in America, and the endless supply of money had dried up. There was just Peter, and the booze, and Rainbow George next door for company.

CHAPTER 15

Whereupon I Immediately Did Nothing
The Single Life, 1983–89

One afternoon in 1983 Peter came bounding up the stairs of Post House Productions, a film editing company in D'Arblay Street in Soho, carrying with him a can of unedited 16mm film. The young office assistant Ciara Parkes showed him to one of their suites, where an editor loaded the reel on to a viewing machine. It contained a sketch, shot a year previously in Venice Beach California, in which E. L. Wisty sat on a park bench extolling the virtues of the What? Party, a new force in politics not dissimilar to his World Domination League of two decades before. 'It was just him rambling, but it was very funny,' remembers Ciara. Like Derek and Clive or *The Dead Sea Tapes*, this was just a private joke, intended for Peter's own amusement. Unlike Derek and Clive, it would never see the light of day. Peter's professional frustration had receded, like a great wind abating, and he was happy that his best work should now be entertaining a film editor and an office junior rather than millions of American cinema goers.

The film took three days to knock into shape. While it was being edited, Peter asked Ciara to transcribe the soundtrack for him. 'So I started typing, hours and hours and hours until late at night. I mean no one discussed money or anything, everybody was so bemused that Peter Cook had walked in off the street. And then he started to tell me, sitting by the typewriter one day, dictating more things to me, all about the What? Party. And he told me all about George, who was his neighbour, who was Minister for Confusion, and he asked me to be the Party Secretary.' Peter returned to the post-production house day after day, until it became clear to all that he had developed quite an attachment to Ciara. She was eighteen, blonde, pretty and clever, and wore a tiny red mohair jumper; his nickname for her was 'Red Fluffy Jumper'.

'Finally,' she remembers: 'he phoned me up one morning and said, 'Right, I've got the What? Party sorted. I'm going on *Wogan* tonight, at the Shepherd's Bush Green Theatre.' He was phoning up about eight times a day at this point on What? Party business, and I was trying to do my job. Anyway, he said, 'I need some badges made. What? Party badges for everybody to wear and one to give Wogan. Can you make some?' So I had to get a cab and buy those badges we used to have at school races, and colour them all in and do What? Party logos. Then he phoned again and said, 'I can't go on by myself, you've got to come on the show with me. Don't forget to wear your red fluffy jumper.' I told him that I simply wasn't going on the show. He said, 'I've already told them that you're coming on, to talk about the What? Party.' I said, 'I don't know anything about the What? Party.' And he said, 'That's exactly right. There's nothing to know.'

To Ciara's immense relief, her increasingly frustrated employers forbade her to leave early.

Her parents were not very impressed by the burgeoning relationship either. 'Peter used to phone me incessantly at home – my Mum was going, "What on *earth* is Peter Cook doing phoning you?" and Dad was having fits.' Peter dipped into his reservoir of natural charm. 'He phoned up one day when I wasn't back from work, and spoke to my Mum. She knew that Dad didn't approve of him phoning me up, but more to the point she couldn't get him off the phone because she was laughing so much. When I came home she said, "Peter's given me a job". And I said "My God, what are you doing?" And she said, "I'm Minister for Lifts."' Ciara became a regular visitor to Peter's house. He would send a car to pick her up from work, which would then drive her all the way home to Reigate at midnight. If she refused to go, saying that she needed an early night and had to get home on the train, she would arrive home to find the car waiting for her outside her front door.

Throughout, Peter was a perfect gentleman. 'He'd say, "Please come on over, we've got What? Party business to discuss. George will be there and there'll be about ten other people."' Ciara would arrive to find Perrin's Walk jostling with random passers-by that Peter had accumulated, none of whom she had seen before or would ever see again. He was filling his

lonely life with home-made entertainment and providing himself with
a ready-made audience. 'More often than not, though, it was just me,
George and Peter, sitting round talking nonsense, drinking and eating
takeaway food. If there was something he didn't like on television he
used to make George and me phone the duty office and complain. He
had two telephones, one for incoming and one for outgoing calls, so we'd
just sit there endlessly complaining to the BBC in different voices.' On one
occasion Peter made Ciara and George go down to TV-AM in the middle
of the night, in a fruitless attempt to persuade the station to transmit a
What? Party promotional video he had made.

Of course there was never any serious intention to enter the What?
Party for the next election – it was just another of Peter's comic fantasies.
Rainbow George, however, was a genuine fantasist, and saw in Peter's
creation the capacity to change Britain for the better. He called Peter
'The Wizard' – 'because I associated him with magic; he was somebody
that could make things happen' – and began referring to Perrin's Walk
as 'The Magic Mountain'. When Peter refused to put forward a What?
Party candidate in the 1984 General Election, George formed his own
political party instead – Captain Rainbow's Universal Party (CRUP) –
and contested the Enfield and Southgate by-election in December 1984
on a platform of abolishing Parliament. 'Midway through our earthly
association,' he explains, 'I found myself being directed by the Wizard
to venture out into the world beyond the Magic Mountain, to cause
as much confusion as humanly possible.'[1] The CRUP, he said, was
'an idealistic, futuristic, mystically motivated movement that aspires to
create a Lennonesque world.'[2] Britain would become 'Rainbowland', a
country organised according to specifications laid down to George by a
spirit guide over nine years of detailed conversations. George, who took
a lot of drugs, was totally and utterly stunned when he polled just 48
votes, to Michael Portillo's 16,684. 'I was convinced I was going to sweep
to victory,' he confesses. 'Also, I was foolishly anticipating that Peter would
get involved, but of course that didn't happen. That was the beginning
of ten years of me trying to get Peter involved. We had this running
agreement, that if I dropped his name to the press, or associated him in
any way with the Rainbow movement, he would deny all knowledge of
what I was talking about.'

Peter found Rainbow George endlessly amusing, particularly his utter
conviction that political success and huge wealth were just around the
the corner. His neighbour had returned from his sojourn in Ireland in
1979, but was only a part-time resident of his house in Perrin's Walk
until early 1984, because somebody else had started living there while he

was away. From 1984 on, after moving back permanently, George's life was consumed by a variety of schemes and dreams, all of them doomed to failure from the outset. Although he was not the dirty mac and trilby type – he sported a grey beard, a wool jacket and bottle thick glasses – there was something distinctly Wistyesque about George's touching optimism and his belief in his own visionary powers. His principal ambition was to stage a gigantic 'Rainbow concert' at Wembley Stadium, but he was aware that having absolutely no cash at all presented one or two minor obstacles to his dream. He saw the answer in a competition in the *Independent* offering a first prize of £30,000 to whoever could best describe in not more than 150 words how the money would change their life for the better. If he could win that, he reasoned, he could easily turn the sum into three million pounds. 'I would convert the £30,000 into pennies, three million pennies, you see, then we could sell three million "Penny Dream Tickets" for a pound each, and raise three million pounds that way . . . it was just a question of what we would attach these dream tickets to.' George found himself in a state of amazed disbelief when he failed to win the *Independent*'s cash prize.

'Peter was interested in the whole scheme,' insists George, 'but he was interested to the extent that he said, "You get hold of the £30,000 and we'll go from there."' George conceived the idea of staging a huge party that would cost only a penny to get into, but three pounds to get out of. No one would be able to resist the lure of such a low entrance fee, he reasoned, and would have such a good time that they'd happily pay three pounds at the end of the evening; if ten thousand people turned up he'd be quids in. He hired the Camden Palace on tick, and in the event fifteen hundred people turned up, including Peter, for what all were agreed was an excellent party. Everybody happily paid the 1p entry fee, but unfortunately almost everybody except Peter then refused to pay the exit fee. There was, after all, nobody to prevent their departure, and no sanction that could be applied to make them pay. George ended up with £150 in pennies and a bill for nearly four thousand pounds. Peter was in hysterics. 'He enjoyed the spectacular nature of my failures really,' says George. 'He got great fun and enjoyment out of them.' George appealed to his mother for financial assistance, even though he'd already devoured a great part of the family fortune; she insisted instead that he see a psychiatrist. Peter eagerly volunteered to play the part of a Teutonic psychiatrist in a series of rehearsals, to get George's performance up to scratch in readiness for the real thing.

George continued to fight elections and by-elections up and down the land as Captain Rainbow, cadging the money for deposits from various amused friends. Peter helped him devise policies, such as closing the country down for redecoration for one year. Drumming up publicity was a problem – during one Euro-election campaign George failed to raise any interest whatsoever, even from local radio or the local press. 'I got increasingly upset, so a few days before the election I hit upon the idea that the way to get publicity was to get myself arrested.' George rolled the biggest joint imaginable, made his way to Parliament Square, and proceeded to smoke it in front of the police guarding Parliament. None of them was even slightly interested, so he repeated the experiment outside Downing Street and in Leicester Square, again without success. After a dispiriting and arrest-free day, he marched into Hampstead Police Station the following morning and set fire to another enormous joint. 'Do you know what this is?' he asked the desk sergeant. 'Yes, sir,' the sergeant replied. 'It's an illegal substance,' George pointed out superfluously. 'Yes, sir,' said the sergeant. 'So are you going to arrest me?' 'No, sir.' 'Why not?' 'We're not looking for smokers, sir, we're looking for dealers.' Eventually, on George's insistence that he was in fact a dealer, he was offered a caution; this was no good, he insisted, only an arrest would do. Finally, he was detained at his own request for a few hours, then released on the promise that he would be contacted in three months' time, to be informed whether any further action was to be taken. He never got the call. His efforts secured him a small paragraph in the local paper, published the day after he had been thrashed in the by-election. 'Peter had a really good laugh at that one,' recalls George. 'I loved seeing him laugh, I loved to be able to make him laugh. He was such a sweet man. I was very, very fond of Peter.'

Inevitably, everything George touched turned to dust. If money did come in, he often gambled it away in the hope of increasing its value. Peter made huge sums simply by placing bets on the direct opposite of whatever George had predicted. Sometimes he helped his neighbour out financially in return: when the Rainbow Party found itself £1,000 in debt, Peter put £1,000 at evens on a horse called Rainbow Quest that was running in the Arc de Triomphe. Rainbow Quest won, and he donated his winnings to George. On another occasion, George managed to lose a further £1,000 on another fund-raising event, the 'Give Peace A Chance' party; Peter quietly covered his costs.

Perhaps George's finest failure came when he attempted to accompany Peter to an orgy. Peter's interest in sex remained constant: beneath the pedestal upon which he had placed Ciara Parkes, he was also enjoying a rather earthier relationship with a black model called Sandy Grizzle, who had once had a bit part in *EastEnders*. He had also taken to attending regular orgies in Muswell Hill. George was always pestering Peter to invite him along, and when Peter drove off with his keys one day he had the perfect excuse to follow. In turn, a friend of George's begged to accompany him to the event, and volunteered to furnish the transport. When the two men got there the orgy was already underway. The door opened, and their identities were demanded. George explained that he was Peter's esteemed friend Rainbow George Weiss, and – in one of those bizarre lies that spring needlessly to mind when responding guiltily to sharp questioning – he explained that the man with him was 'the minicab driver'. A quick visual assessment was made by the assembled guests, and 'the minicab driver' was eagerly accepted into the orgy; but George was unanimously rejected. He had to sit in the kitchen drinking a cup of tea until proceedings had exhausted themselves.

When not flirting with Ciara or seducing Sandy Grizzle, Peter would spend much of his time lounging on George's floor (most of George's furniture had been 'borrowed' or repossessed), chatting to whoever happened to be passing through the house at the time. Among the regular visitors were two golfing friends, Lawrence Levy and Howard Baws. They were Jewish, so Peter purchased a record entitled *Hitler's Inferno*, a collection of the dictator's favourite tunes, and gleefully put it on the turntable whenever possible. 'He used to have it blasting out when he knew I was coming round – I'd love to have been left it in his will,'[3] laughs Baws. Peter had discovered that his own paternal grandmother had been associated in some unspecified way with an organisation called the 'British Israelites', and derived a humorous fascination from the notion that he himself might in fact be part-Jewish.

Another regular visitor to George's house was Bronco John, a local tramp festooned with used tea bags, whom Peter appointed Minister for Tea in the What? Party. Until 1986, when he ran out of space, George recorded every word spoken in his house on the portable cassette recorder which was his only possession; one wall of his living room was blotted out by a giant stack of cassettes. Among the more entertaining recordings is one of Peter, George and Bronco John attempting to cook a tin of beans that Peter has brought round from his house at three in the morning; unfortunately, none of them has the faintest idea how to operate George's cooker. 'Peter never knew how to operate any cooker,' says Ciara. 'I offered to warm up some croissants I'd bought him one day for breakfast, and he said, "I've no idea, you sort it out."'

Few of the tapes in George's possession are worth listening to today. There is the odd enjoyable moment – 'In the beginning was the word,' says George in an argument about scripture; 'and the word got about' replies Peter – but for the most part Peter sounds drunk or out of his head on drugs. Although George didn't drink, drugs were all too often suspiciously available at his house. 'Peter was doing quite a lot of coke,' George admits, 'and a bit of Ecstasy. Personally I liked him drunk, he was more accessible when drunk than sober, but of course he could go over the top. Someone once parked an open-topped Rolls Royce across the front of Perrin's Walk, blocking the entrance. He emptied a dustbin of rubbish into it.'

Both Peter and George had difficulty sleeping, and became obsessive listeners to LBC, the London radio station. It was George who first had the idea of trying to wangle his way on to the airwaves, to promote his political career: 'I became a fanatic,' he explains. 'In the early days, before they realised, I could be on several times a day on different people's programmes.' From there it was but a short step for Peter to begin contributing as well. As E. L. Wisty he telephoned the Steve Jones show to claim that the What? Party had seized control of the media, and that George (who was in the studio with Jones) was 'holding a gun to your head and making you sound natural. Anyone listening would think you were fully in charge of the programme, as opposed to the What? Party; and to maintain that illusion, I shall shortly get off the line and pretend that you're getting on with it under no duress whatsoever.'

It was all too easy, though, to get onto a radio phone-in as a famous Peter Cook character. There was no challenge involved. So Peter set himself the task of interrupting George's political appearances in a variety of disguises. 'He really loved doing that,' says George. 'I've got some early tapes of him trying to get on to phone-in programmes and not being allowed to speak. When they were debating abortion he called in as a priest who had left the fold; then he phoned the Pete Murray Show as a German called Fritz, and started going on about breeding budgerigars.' Eventually both George (as a guest) and Peter (as a bogus caller) concentrated on the Clive Bull Show, which went out between 1 a.m. and 4 a.m. on LBC. Bull was the only presenter prepared to offer George repeated airings, as one of the cast of nocturnal regulars who gave his show a family atmosphere, along with such luminaries as Babs from Bermondsey and Ray and Jan from Rayleigh with their organ requests. He was also individual enough to allow regular calls from Sven of Swiss Cottage, a mysterious Norwegian fisherman who began ringing in soon after George made his debut.

Sven was one of Peter's finest creations, enjoyed – in many cases unwittingly – by no more than a few thousand listeners, and preserved for posterity only because Peter had finally found his Boswell, in the shape of George and his cassette recorder. Sven was lonely and upset because he had been abandoned by his wife Jutta – the similarity of her name to Judy's was no coincidence – and blamed himself thoroughly for her departure. To compensate, he picked up a series of girls in launderettes, but found no lasting happiness there either. Clive Bull remembers that 'It was a sort of growing soap opera. It became a kind of agony hour, and callers would call in advising him on what he should be doing; but the predominant theme was always fish, which would somehow be wangled into every conversation. He started off with this stuff about how men in Norway were judged by women according to how many fish they caught. I knew it wasn't a real Norwegian fisherman – he was very quick-thinking for a start – but at three o'clock in the morning on that sort of programme it was nothing out of the ordinary to have somebody on claiming to be a Norwegian fisherman.'

Sven: I'm only a visitor here, from Norway, and I listen to the phone-in and think wonderful things, because in Norway these phone-in is mainly devoted to the subject of, you know, like . . . fish.
Bull: Like *fish*?
Sven: Yes, we have a phone-in—
Bull: That's a *fish* phone-in?
Sven: That's Norway time, when people ring up for one hour, and the gist of it is, things about, you know, is a carp very big, or is a tench very big, or you know, how big is a—
Bull: Very interesting.
Sven: It goes on, all night. And it's so nice to come to this country and hear people talking about, well, you know, Parliament, and taking clothes off, and singing. In Norway all we get is this fish stuff going on and on.

Whenever Peter travelled abroad, he always sent Bull a postcard from Sven detailing his worldwide search for his wife, and whenever he returned home, Sven would call to complain about the country that he had just visited. He was also a keen contributor to specific debates, such as drug-taking ('The gudgeon is more harmful than cannabis') or football hooliganism:

Sven: I know it's a very serious subject tonight, but in Norway we have no hooliganeering, I think because we have so many fish programmes on. Every day we have programmes on fish, on TV and on radio. And at the football too. Before the

	match, people come on, expert fishermen, showing how to catch chub and roach and everything like that.
Bull:	So it's more of a family occasion.
Sven:	It calms people down. In Norway, we have no hooligans at all, at football. We have no-one at football. Because of the fishing that goes on before.

Much of Sven's agonising concerned his various launderette-based girlfriends, all of whom – despite their various names – seemed to represent one woman, a young and unapproachably fashionable girl. He wondered whether he should bone up on youth culture to attract her, by finding out about 'hip sounds' like Chubby Checker, or Joey Dee and the Starlighters. He didn't seem to know how to chat her up.

Sven:	Just as an icebreaker I went up to her with some socks and some underwear, and said, 'You know, this could be the start of something'. And she burnt them. She does not understand Norwegian humour.

Sometimes, Sven could get quite depressed. 'When he was down he was very down,' recalls Bull. 'There was an inkling there of what he really felt as opposed to what Sven thought. When you hear those calls in isolation they sound a bit weird, and not particularly funny.'

Sven:	I just wanted to say, Clive, I mean, I have been so gloomy in the past, always talking about how miserable my life is and how these women are making me miserable, but it is up to me.
Bull:	It is, yes.
Sven:	It is up to me to just go out and say, 'Look, I am alive, I am a man, I have a mackintosh.'
Bull:	So you're going to go out there and grab life by the—
Sven:	Grab life by the throat, wrestle it to the ground and kick it to death.
Bull:	Well we're all thinking of you.
Sven:	Because I get miserable and I feel my mood switching at the moment, I could go downbeat any moment.
Bull:	No, no, you hang on upbeat.
Sven:	For goodness sake try and keep up my confidence Clive.
Bull:	Hang on there upbeat, we're all rooting for you.
Sven:	Thank you Clive.

By this stage Clive Bull had become aware that his late-night caller was really Peter Cook. Perhaps unfortunately George had told him the truth, out of a well-meaning desire to make sure that the switchboard operator would put the calls through. In fact when LBC lost its franchise and Bull's programme was axed, then reinstated after complaints from his fans (including Peter), the centralised switchboard system at the new company made it very difficult for Sven to get through, and his calls became less frequent. Peter came clean to Bull (who did not let on that he had known the secret for some time) and invited him to tea at Perrin's Walk.

'Although one should be extremely wary of the autobiographical line of enquiry,' says Peter's sister Sarah, 'I think these calls contained a lot of truth about Peter. Late at night he was often lonely and unhappy. A lot of it was done for the fun of it of course, but they should not be regarded as "performance" in the usual sense.' It was perhaps inevitable that Peter's emotions should come out in some sort of performance, because he was so addicted to performing that it was often his only means of expression. Frequently, when he wanted to speak to Judy, he would ring her on one of his phones, then hold the receiver up to the other phone while he telephoned the Russian Embassy or the BBC Duty Office in an assumed voice with some frivolous complaint. One of his favourites was the routine devised in America in which he objected to a pornographic film having been shown on TV too late for his children to see it. The BBC were completely taken in of course, and responded to this parade of bogus obsessives and halfwits with the profound reverence normally reserved for genuine obsessives and halfwits.

When not phoning radio stations or the BBC Duty Office, he would assuage his boredom by phoning his friends at length. He would ring Barry Fantoni, for instance, during football games or boxing matches on TV, and stay on the phone throughout. He would ring Rory McGrath, an Arsenal supporter, whenever Arsenal got a bad result, especially against Spurs. 'The minute the game was over,' recalls McGrath, 'he'd phone immediately. So if Arsenal won I'd phone him up and say, "Hi Peter, it's Rory. I've been out of the country and I wonder if you know what the Arsenal–Spurs result was?" Once I saw him walking towards me in Hampstead High Street and then suddenly he disappeared, and I realised he was crouching behind a pillar box. I thought, "That's very odd. Is he avoiding me? Have I got one of his porn films?" Then it dawned upon me of course that Arsenal had beaten Spurs that week.'

Harry Enfield recalls that 'I would know when Cookie had rung, when the answerphone screen said "one message", but the 30-minutes'-worth of tape was used up. I would rewind to find him skimming through the day's events as covered by the tabloids, or questioning the legal validity of Noel Edmonds' beard. Once he began whimpering like a dog for a full five minutes before finally confessing to visiting Threshers' off-licence several times and begging me to relieve him of his post as Chancellor of the Exchequer. If I had received a juicy bit of bad press, I could rely on Peter to ring up and relay it to me. "I think it's outrageous that everyone thinks you're a cunt. Guffaw, guffaw.'"[4]

As the evening wore on, Peter's phone calls would often become more maudlin. 'It's a well-known boozer's trait for some reason, to ring people up late at night,' suggests Richard Ingrams, who along with Paul Foot received a great many nocturnal calls. According to Barry Fantoni, 'On a very lonely night he might ring up all his *Private Eye* mates. I'd speak to Ian Hislop and say, "Did Cookie phone last night?" And he'd say, "Yes, he was quite pissed. I didn't say much."'[5] Peter's was a loneliness that could be assuaged but never cured. He made calls for company – never from a need to speak intimately or revealingly of how he felt. 'Even in the middle of the night, he always put up barriers to any attempt to find out what was really going on inside him,' remembers Paul Foot. Reunited many years later with Dudley Moore, the two of them discussed the subject of phoning people. Dudley ventured the opinion that 'People who indulge in comedy tend to be more and more isolated as the years go by. The end product is to be on their own. I rattle around on my own. Do you have any close mates? Do you phone them up when you're in pain or in trouble? I don't.' Peter replied that he wouldn't phone anybody on those terms, 'because I haven't had anything that has happened to me that they could help with. And I don't like people ringing me up with some ghastly problem, because all I can do is listen. I've got no advice to give them.'[6]

Occasionally Peter's boredom spilled over into frustration. He would stand in his living room, legs apart, tapping endless golf balls across the carpet into a plastic cup, then snap. 'I'm so fucked off,' he announced once to Ciara Parkes, then 'Catch this!', with which he tossed a huge, heavy radio at her, which she only just managed to catch as it slammed into her chest. 'I shouted, "What are you doing?"' recalls Ciara. 'He said, "Chuck the radio, see who drops it." I was livid and chucked it back really hard at him. "You're just being aggressive," I said.' Most of the time, however, Peter fed his boredom with a relentless supply of information, fattening it like a goose into an immobile torpor. He would sit inert in front of the television, devouring everything from *Good Morning with Anne and Nick* to hardcore porn videos. 'I have very little social life,' he said in 1986.

'It's mainly peering at Brazilian soap operas on television and wondering why the telly closes down.'[7]

Peter became an expert at minority sports, from world championship darts to truck-racing live from Idaho on satellite. Stephen Fry recounts how he would open a conversation with 'Hope you caught Keith Deller's nine-dart finish against Jocky at the Lakeside on Saturday.' His least favourite sport was Rugby League, but he watched even that assiduously enough to acquire an encyclopaedic knowledge. The fact that he actually sat down to watch it at all suggests that he was innately bored, in the way that people who sit through entire TV shows in order to write outraged letters of complaint about them are innately outraged. He also masochistically liked to watch bad sitcoms, and tried to pre-empt the punchlines. According to Alexei Sayle, 'I only got 100 per cent of his attention when I told him about the late night programme *California Highway* – three Germans inexplicably cruising the eponymous Highways of California, visiting and badly filming various tourist sites and interviewing minor celebrities such as Lee van Cleef and the woman who was the lead singer with the Fifth Dimension. Peter was truly taken with the idea of the programme and was deeply sorry that he'd missed it. Also, when I mentioned David Stafford, he not only knew that he worked on the Channel Four consumer programme *For What It's Worth*, but he also knew the names of the other presenters.'[8] As far as Peter was concerned, the more dreadful and lowbrow the programme the better. 'My idea of hell would be watching an endless series of films recommended by *Time Out*,'[9] he once remarked.

Peter's floor was a mass of videotapes, unlabelled blank ones in a state of hopeless disorganisation and pre-recorded ones hired by the dozen from Video Video in Heath Street. He acquired his hardcore videos – oriental porn was his favourite – from Supermags in Old Compton Street. Rory McGrath used to borrow them in turn: 'I said to Peter, "What do you feel like when you go into Supermags? Because you must be recognised." And he said, "Well I go in and they say, aren't you Peter Cook, and I say yes – have you got any porn?" He was always very upfront about things like that: "I don't want any kinky stuff, or animals. I want dicks and cunts." "Oh yes, Mr Cook, we'll get you that."'

On one occasion McGrath briefly lent some of Peter's porn videos to John Trotter, a drummer friend. 'Peter always left his answerphone on and sat beside it on the sofa, so I rang up and said "Hi Peter, it's Rory here. I've just got your films back and Spurs are fucking useless and you're a cunt—" So he picked the phone up. I said, "We're going up to the Three Horseshoes for a drink, d'you wanna come?" So we're sitting in the Three Horseshoes, and Peter comes in wearing flip-flops, shorts, a very loud shirt, a baseball cap and sunglasses. And he walks in brandishing this cassette and calls out, "Is *Kowloon Cunt* any good to you?" And the packed pub turns round and thinks as one, "That's Peter Cook, isn't it?" Then John said he'd got hold of some cannabis, and he wanted to make some cakes – he makes exceedingly good cakes, electric Kiplings. We went back to Peter's and John said, "Have you got a pan?" And Peter didn't have any pans in his kitchen. We got them made eventually, I don't know what we used, we managed somehow. Then we sat upstairs watching the cricket, and Peter had two cakes, which I thought was a bit of a mistake. And it was rather disquieting, because I didn't see Peter for another four days. I was rather worried, so I phoned John, and Peter had just rung him. He'd said "Is that John?" John had said yes, and he'd said, "You fucking cunt. I've been stuck on the sofa for three days, watching the room move around.'''

Such was Peter's daily life by the mid-1980s. In many respects he cut a dashing figure to his friends and colleagues. According to John Wells, 'If the more puritan elements at *Private Eye* disapproved of some aspects of his life, others saw it as charmed. There were tales of multiple Bunnies, and when he and I went together to his favourite strip-club in St Anne's Court, I was deeply impressed when the stripper winked at him and threw him her bra.'[10] When Peter listed his top ten pleasures for the *Independent*, he discreetly left out matters sexual. But the remaining pastimes constitute an accurate picture of a prosaically leisured lifestyle:

1) Gossip.
2) Reading books.
3) Watching sport, and occasionally playing it.
4) Late-night radio phone-ins.
5) TV.
6) Comedy (especially Harry Enfield).
7) Newspapers (especially the *Sun*, and the Matthew Parris and Alan Coren columns in the *Times*).
8) Food and Drink.
9) Cigarettes.
10) Other people's pedantry (specifically the kind of people who write to the BBC to say 'Dear Sir, LNER did not have lamps on Pullman carriage tables in 1923').

Item (2) was the surprising one, as barely anyone alive had ever seen Peter read a book. He claimed to like Simenon, Dick Francis, Graham

Greene and John le Carré, and always gave books as presents; but when he contributed book reviews to the *Literary Review* it was clear, according to the magazine's editor Auberon Waugh, that he 'plainly hadn't read them'. He did tell *The Sunday Times*, however, that 'If I really want to go to sleep I read one of Clive James' long, boring poems.'[11]

The most obvious omission from the list was gambling, for Peter would bet on anything to alleviate the boredom. 'I remember going round to his house once,' says Ian Hislop, 'and Miss Singapore 1978 was on cable, and we just started betting on it. I mean it was just the sort of thing he did.' Certain superstitions accompanied his betting habits. Ciara Parkes remembers that 'I moved a chair once, and he said, "Don't move that chair, it's my lucky racing chair!" He'd put this chair next to his precious Tiffany lamp and sat in it to pick his horses. He and George used to bet on racing every day; he never knew whether he'd won or not, he just found out at the end of the week if he was up or down.' If he cared about a result, for instance if Tottenham were playing, he'd back the opposition, to give fate no chance of beating him on both counts; to help his team's chances he also had a selection of lucky hats and other accoutrements. He could be quite an astute gambler. He correctly forecast the results of general elections throughout the 1980s and early 1990s – he wagered £1,000 each time – and would annoy his left-wing friends by punching the air with delight on election night when the Tories won. He was, however, conned out of £10,000 by a bogus bookmaker, who persuaded him to invest in a non-existent company in the early 1980s. His favourite gambling occasions were big race days, when he would actually raise himself to visit the course, often in the company of Mel Smith, and combine a little light betting with colossal amounts of alcohol.

About once a year, Peter made valiant but increasingly doomed efforts to kick the bottle. There were periods of abstention in 1984, 1985 and early 1986, the first of these in a brave response to his father's death; but more often than not the sense of crushing depression brought on by remembering that unfortunate event sent him spinning the other way. In November 1983 he was invited to the new Nicholson Suite at Tottenham, and spent the game crouched behind a pillar. In 1984 he attended a celebrity golfing weekend in Spain with Ian Botham, Patrick Mower and Lennie Bennett, and got so drunk that the police had to be called, after he punched a German tourist. At the New Year wedding of Rolling Stones guitarist Ronnie Wood, he attempted to seduce the bride, then got into the wrong limousine in the car park. The Stones, of course, were delighted by these antics, and they and Peter formed a sort of mutual appreciation society. He described the band as 'proper stars: Brian Jones did the right thing for a rock 'n' roll person, drowned in his own swimming pool. And Keith Richards, he's a proper star, because although he's alive, he's nearly dead. Give me *Ruby Tuesday* over *Yellow Submarine*, all that garbage. I don't like these fucking kids who don't smoke, don't drink and don't sleep around. I mean, what kind of a rock star is that?'[12]

In November 1986, on his forty-ninth birthday, he acquired a brand new Honda saloon and drove it drunkenly into the back of a police car on a zebra crossing. He was subsequently fined £200 and banned from driving for a year. By this stage he was drinking triple vodkas for breakfast, or several bottles of Holsten Pils, while simultaneously chain-smoking Superkings. He seemed to be pushing at the boundaries of alcoholism just as he pushed at the boundaries of everything else. His face puffed up, his looks faded and his weight ballooned: during the 1980s he expanded to 16½ stone. To Jonathan Miller, he seemed 'a swollen, smoked, rather spirit-logged figure'.[13] Drink, Peter admitted, had become 'not a pleasure but a necessity'. According to Sid Gottlieb, 'Once he'd become established as an alcoholic there was no gainsaying. The pattern is always pretty well the same. You have to drink to relieve the awful collywobbles and nervous tension, and the drink sets you up, so you drink some more, but then you pass out. And then you wake up awful, so you've got to start again. That's the classic pattern and it was invariably Peter's pattern.'

In some respects Peter had probably been heading towards alcoholism all his life. An American expert, Gilman Ostrander, explains that: 'Alcoholism is basically a disease of individualism. It afflicts people who from early childhood develop a strong sense of being psychologically alone and on their own in the world. This solitary outlook prevents them from gaining emotional release through associations with other people, but they find they can get this emotional release by drinking. So they become dependent on alcohol in the way other people are dependent on their social relationships with friends and relatives.' The prevailing medical view is that factors in infancy or early childhood lay the foundation of a personality vulnerable to alcholism. Interestingly, the *Encyclopaedia Britannica* points to 'inconsistency in rearing practices' as a major factor, and suggests that the potential alcholic would begin to demonstrate 'defiant exhibitionistic deviance' from an early age.

Sid Gottlieb tried putting Peter on Antabuse, a drug which makes the user horribly sick if it is combined with alcohol, but its side effects were awful to behold. 'It made him slur his words as if he were dragging them up from the cellar,'[14] recalls John Wells. As a result, Peter seemed drunker on the drug than he did when he was actually drunk. The inebriated – or apparently inebriated – figure of Peter Cook became a familiar sight shuffling down Hampstead High Street, often in his carpet slippers, always with a stack of newspapers under his arm, slurring his requests in shops. His lack of sartorial co-ordination was famous. One journalist described 'a pair of multi-coloured surfing slacks only a madman or an Australian would wear, having a major argument with his shoes. He looked like a confused package-holiday tourist who's lost his group in the arrivals lounge.'[15] He did not, however, cut a pathetic figure – there always seemed to be a humorous twinkle in his dissipation, and his collection of loud hats, sunglasses and coloured sneakers were clearly deliberately mismatched.

His antics were frequently eccentric. Once he went into his local off licence and demanded a bottle of wine which was not on the shelves. The assistant went into the storeroom to find it, leaving a steaming cup of fresh coffee on the counter. When he returned with the wine, Peter was gone and so was the coffee, the empty mug sitting forlornly in its saucer. Only once was Peter bested, by a member of the public in the local ironmonger's. Taking the man, a Mr Bevan, to be a member of staff, Peter posed the one-word question 'Secateurs?' To which the man replied, instinctively rather than intentionally, 'Non sequitur.' Peter left the shop giggling.

The house at Perrin's Walk was as unkempt as its owner. Gone were the days when a houseproud Peter had forbidden Judy to write on the walls. Now he scribbled all over them himself – favourite words like 'oxymoron', for instance – and blu-tacked up vital documents like his passport and driving licence so that he could find them easily amid the chaos. Elsewhere he stuck up pictures of his childhood home and of himself as a brilliant young man, a photograph of John Lennon over the headline 'I don't feel 40 – I feel like a kid', pictures of famous alcoholics like George Best and Jimmy Greaves, Pete and Dud photos, cuttings and memorabilia, and a tabloid double-page spread headed 'The day Peter Cook became a drunk, by Dudley Moore'. A second-hand fruit machine stood next to the sofa, for in-house gambling. The floor was strewn with old newspapers. When *Hello!* magazine asked to do a photospread of his home life, Peter turned them down on principle; but principles hadn't really been necessary to reach a decision. Ciara Parkes remembers that 'When I first went to his house, there were huge piles of mail behind his door up to waist level – it was almost impossible to open. Old birthday cards, bills, going back months. He had a huge row with Sir Iain Vallance at BT after his phone was cut off.' Peter told John Wells that his bureau had become completely filled with demands from the Inland Revenue, so he had simply bought another bureau. It was a joke, but not too far removed from the truth. Peter lived his life in a state of stunning financial disorganisation. Despite his having offshore funds, his credit card was sliced up in the supermarket.

'On a few occasions the house was in such a mess, I'd just start tidying it up,' remembers Ciara. 'I came in one day and said, "Peter, what is all this white stuff?" There were mounds of white powder all over the carpet. He said he'd just sacked his Portuguese cleaner when she was halfway through putting Shake-'n'-Vac on the carpet, and he couldn't be bothered to do anything about it. Then on another occasion I was meant to feed the fish; Peter had rigged up this sound-and-light show for the fish, and had imported these expensive fish flakes from America. I said, "Where are all the fish flakes?" And he said, "I got so hungry last night I ate them."' It was probably another joke, but one that was also uncomfortably close to reality. Peter enjoyed cooking, and boasted an extremely limited but effective repertoire, but the sinkfuls of filthy crockery that characterised his kitchen in the early 1980s gradually gave way to an absolute reliance on takeaway food or eating out. 'When Peter was lonely he used to go and sit in the Villa Bianca Restaurant, where Alan Clare played the piano, and hold court,' remembers Barry Fantoni. His other favourite restaurant was the La Sorpresa, on the corner of Perrin's Walk, where he also ate alone on many occasions. He always ordered a side plate of spinach, which he detested. 'I hate spinach. I get my own back by leaving it,' he explained.[16]

Peter did not get much exercise. 'I do fifty eyebrow-raises a day,' he said sardonically when asked. In 1986, though, he sobered up sufficiently to partner Annabel Croft in a celebrity tennis tournament. 'I'm a "touch" player,' he explained. 'Not for me the dull serve-and-volley game adopted by the Hoads and Lavers of this world. The greatest pleasure for me at least is to touch the ball, preferably with the racquet.' There was also golf of course, usually in competition with Lawrence Levy and Howard Baws, or with his agent David Wilkinson; or pro-celebrity golf, with adoring chums like Jimmy Tarbuck, Bruce Forsyth and Kenny Lynch. Peter was a member of the exceptionally straightlaced Highgate Golf Club, where he was not always popular with his fellow members, for both sartorial and protocol reasons. He was totally immune to club etiquette: when asked to remove his cap, he demurred on the grounds that he was an orthodox Jew. He hated losing, so his friends often lost to him deliberately. Once, when on the brink of defeat at the 18th, he set fire to the rough so that the game had to be abandoned.

An occasional golfing companion was Michael Parkinson. 'He was extraordinary. You used to dread waiting for him, he used to bring out all the worst things in a human being – 'I hope this person doesn't make me ashamed of him,' you know. But you never knew how he was going to turn up at a golf club, and they're very formal places. He turned up at my club at Temple with a pair of trainers, and this bloody big pink 'Sloppy Joe' shirt right down around his knees, and jeans. He broke three dress rules before he got out of the car. I had to go up to him and say 'Peter, for Christ's sake, you might think that dress rules are dozy but there *are* dress rules.' He had to go to the pro shop and buy a pair of trousers, it was a kind of ritual we went through every time. Anyway, we got down to the second tee and he said, 'Would you like a drink?' And he opened this big clanking golf bag, and it was full of cans. I thought 'Oh dear,' and I said, 'I don't think so Peter.' He pulled out this can which looked like a Coke can – it was white and blue and had identical markings – and I thought, 'Oh that's all right, it's Coke.' He had one every hole and after about four he was pissed. So when he picked a fifth one out, I said, 'Can I have a look at that?' And they were tins of Bacardi and Coke. I think we made it round to the tenth, by which time he didn't know where he was, so we went back to the clubhouse, and he'd started sweating profusely. He had this huge dinner plate of sweat on his shirt, and I remember thinking to my eternal shame, 'I hope to Christ the Captain doesn't come in.' It was like bloody school. Eventually he started talking about drugs in a loud voice, and there were several old ladies playing bridge, absolutely frozen. In fact the entire room was absolutely enchanted by him. He was an amazing bugger, it was never easy to be with him. He challenged you all the time, he didn't believe in rules or conventions.'

Whether Peter's friends appreciated him drunk or not varied considerably according to personal taste. 'Drunks are usually bores,' reckons Harry Enfield, 'but Peter's drinking affected his health more than his personality. He was never a bore.'[17] Paul Foot disagrees: 'He could be very dull, as people who drink too much often are, when he just wanted to have a chat about some trivial matter at two o'clock in the morning.' Stephen Fry insists that 'Peter never yielded to the dark side, never once turned aggressive or rude or loud or bullying or vain.'[18] Rainbow George, on the other hand, contends that 'Everybody who really loved Peter also on occasions really hated Peter. He could be very sharp.'[19] It all depended on his mood, who he was with, and what he wanted them to think of him. Certainly he could be a frustrating person to be with when drunk: on the way to an England–Italy international at Wembley, he and Barry Fantoni abandoned their car in heavy traffic and set out to walk to the ground; Peter was waylaid by the first pub they came to, went in for a drink and didn't emerge until closing time.

Gradually, news of Peter's condition filtered through the British television industry. Willie Donaldson, whose Henry Root books had been put forward for television adaptations, recalls that 'We had lots of plans to do things together, but his name killed them stone dead. I wanted him in *Root*, but people in television just went white as a sheet and said "Over our dead bodies". I had this TV sex comedy project called *The Karma Chingford*, devised with Geoff Atkinson, starring a thinly disguised Major Ron Ferguson figure played by Peter. BBC Light Entertainment asked for a pilot budget, then sent a letter rejecting it, on the grounds that Peter was in it – that collapsed it.'

Instead Peter and Donaldson spent afternoons sitting on park benches like two E. L. Wistys. 'He got me into Ecstasy,' says Donaldson. 'These two old arseholes, taking Ecstasy. The only difference was that I wasn't drinking, whereas he was shaking whenever we met. He said, 'You'd even like Richard Ingrams if you tried Ecstasy.' I'd never heard of it, I didn't even know what it was. In fact all we talked about were drugs and pornographic videos. He'd tell me about gay sex and scoring cocaine in New York at four in the morning. These two sad old addicts stumbling around, bored in the afternoon. I think I understood. I know all about boredom, and Peter was bored. He'd do *anything* rather than be bored. Drink, drugs and dirty sex was one answer. If you're not bored yourself, I don't think you'd understand that sort of despair. It was three o'clock in the afternoon and he couldn't bear being alive, in his head, without taking drugs. If you cannot bear the fact that somehow you've got to exist for two-and-a-half hours until *Neighbours* starts at 5.30, hard drugs or alcohol snaps you out of it. Peter took cocaine, he tried everything, but I think the fact that he was an alcoholic basically saved him from being into much harder drugs.

Once the drugs are on the way, the boredom goes. If you see a drug addict, they cannot bear the prospect of having to get through the next twenty minutes. But the second you tell them the drugs are on their way, they're OK. It's the same with porn, it's a cure for the horror of getting through the next five minutes. Sex is the greatest instant anti-boredom treatment. You can't be bored and have sex at the same time. Peter was actually sexually very attractive but insecure; I think he resented Dudley's 'sex thimble' tag. I used to say to Peter, how can someone as talented as you be so bored with the idea of sitting down and writing? But that sort of pull-your-socks-up approach is no use. You can't jack yourself up like that. The dream dies in your head. You get bored with your own brain. He wanted to scream. There was something he couldn't express. He thought everything was ludicrous – that's why he watched terrible television. We appeared on a *Literary Review* panel at

the Cheltenham Festival, with Auberon Waugh, Willie Rushton, Anna
Ford and Keith Waterhouse, where the audience were supposed to ask
questions. He told me he had this overwhelming urge to swear at his
polite questioners, to shout 'You fucking cunt!' at a middle-aged lady. It
amused him, like all depressed people, the thought of doing something
absolutely frightful to cheer himself up. I remember asking him about
Judy, though, and that was the one thing he'd never talk about. He'd
never say *anything* about her.'

Peter did not like what he had become. If his daughters tried to
telephone him when he was drunk or depressed, he would sit by the
phone without answering. If they came to the door he was too ashamed
to answer it, because he did not want them to see him in his distressed
state. 'He was obviously going through a difficult time, and feeling lonely,'
says Lucy. 'In the mid-eighties he was doing a short stay at Champney's,
a bit of a health boost. I remember I'd done this long trip down, a 2-hour
drive, and I hadn't seen him in quite some time. When I arrived there,
we had a cup of coffee in some quiet private little place. And we were
just talking about this, that and the other, when his eyes started welling
up with tears, and mine did too. Then he cut the conversation short,
and said 'Well, you'd better be going now.' I'd only been there about
half an hour, and I'd driven two hours to be with him. I think he just
couldn't bear it, he couldn't bear feeling so emotional. He was such an
incredibly vulnerable man. Most of the time he did quite a good job
of covering it up and being very funny, but underneath he was hugely
emotional and couldn't deal with it. I wasn't angry with him, I just felt
so sad. I thought, 'This is just love we feel for each other, it's OK to
be a bit sad, it's OK to show vulnerability.' But for him it was almost
impossible. So I have a lot of regrets, a lot of things I suppose I wish
I'd said.'

Even though he was sometimes too embarrassed to face his family,
Peter could always be relied upon to come to the rescue in a crisis. 'Even
if I hadn't been able to get through for months,' says his sister Elizabeth,
'I always knew that if I was in trouble he would be there immediately.
I could leave message after message saying "Hello, hope you're OK,
this is your sister", and nothing would happen. But if I left a message
and he could hear that I was near tears, he'd be there at once.' When
Lucy was about twenty-four, she suffered a terrible eczema attack. 'I
felt like a leper, it was all over my face. And I'd heard about a miracle
cure that could help, but it was quite an expensive treatment.' Peter
came to the rescue at once, and the whole thing cleared up inside ten
days. There were, however, limits to the emotional assistance he was

capable of providing. When his daughter Daisy had a nervous illness in the mid-1980s, she went to stay with the Gottliebs for a few months. 'Peter would come and see her very often,' recalls Sid, 'and you could see he was distressed. But he found it difficult to show affection. It would have been nice for Daisy if he could have put his arms around her and cuddled her, but he couldn't bring that off. I think he would rather that he'd enjoyed a more conventional relationship with his daughters than he had, that it didn't have to consist of way-out jokiness a lot of the time. He would cry about it – he was a very, very shy and lonely person.'

Family life was not all gloom and despondency, of course. Peter still kept in close touch with his mother, who looked forward excitedly to his visits. Impractical as he was at home, he liked to perform odd jobs for her around the house, such as effecting the bi-annual switch between her summer and winter curtains ('Curtains down, curtains up. Son exhausted' ran the comment in her visitors' book). He spent Christmases with the family. He also took holidays at the farm in Majorca. Wendy had moved back to the island, although to a different house, while Lucy and Daisy had abandoned the catering trade and settled into adult life as an aromatherapist and an EFL teacher respectively. In 1985 Peter went to Majorca with John Gilbert, the manager of Dire Straits; one morning the pair got up at 5 a.m. and paid for every sunlounger on the beach, to forestall the German tourists who always got there at dawn. In 1988 he went there with Daisy and her boyfriend Simon Hardy, and met Wendy for the first time in almost two decades. 'It was an awkward meeting in the town square, where we had all turned up to the regular Sunday morning market,' recalls Hardy. 'I think Peter would have avoided it if he'd possibly been able to. Wendy had started a project in the Majorcan hills where she, her partner and another couple were building up an alternative centre for agriculture and the crafts. I remember Peter saying he was thinking of going to take a look, but he was worried about being confronted by a gaggle of people waving vegetables at him.'

When Peter was up, and in a relatively good mood, he would emerge from Perrin's Walk and spread laughter and mild anarchy. When he was down, he would lock himself away in retreat from the world, sometimes for weeks. His mood swings were getting wider and wider, gaining momentum like a Newton's cradle in reverse. Most of his friends simply assumed during his long unexplained absences that he was simply off seeing other friends. After all, he never discussed what he did or who he'd seen, preferring to talk about what was in the papers or on TV. As a result, he left some people with a false impression of constant jollity and happy drunkenness. Part of the problem was that Peter had set himself the lifetime task of cheering other people up: he was almost fated to entertain everyone he met. But there was no one to cheer him up, to lift his spirits when he was down. He always had to entertain himself.

Gradually, it filtered through to the public and the press that Peter Cook was no longer attempting to produce any worthwhile work. He appeared, in the words of John Cleese, 'to have lost it'. Peter himself repeatedly insisted that it was a matter of simple indolence. 'Work is for grown-ups,' he'd say; or, on the prospect of kick-starting his career again, 'The idea that you should work like a maniac until you are sixty-five and then take time off is crazy – I'd much rather take time off along the way. Idleness comes naturally to me.' He added that 'It made me ill to hear them complaining at the Tory conference about shorter working hours and longer holidays on the continent, as though that's something dreadful.' When Jonathan Ross invited him to lunch to discuss the idea of collaborating on a new show, and suggested making a non-broadcast pilot, he replied: 'I was rather hoping that we could make a non-broadcast series.' The coiled spring had completely unwound.

Unfortunately, very few people actually believed that the problem was one of inclination rather than inspiration. According to Jonathan Miller, 'The thing about comedy, and why so many comedians are driven mad and driven to the bottle, is that it's an extremely rare commodity, this laughing gas. When it dries up you have nothing to fall back on, and there's nothing worse than drilling and finding that the well is dry.'[20] Peter had not run out of ideas though; if anything, the *fear* of running out of ideas was a stronger influence on his decision to take a step back. Confidence drained out of him by the day. 'The most ordinary thing, like appearing on *Clive James*, fills me with panic,' he admitted. 'I'd rather do it for a few people socially, but it would be a bit rude to take up a collection after dinner . . . if others say I'm good at comedy, they probably mean when I'm out to dinner, or with my friends at home, not when I'm performing on stage.'

There was fear, too, that he could never match past glories. In his foreword to the reissued *Beyond the Fringe* scripts in 1987, a page that took him four months to write, he said: 'There is only one depressing side effect of re-reading the text – I may have done other things as good but I am sure none better. I haven't matured, progressed, grown, become deeper, wiser, or funnier. But then I never thought I would.' The degree of satisfaction expressed that he had fulfilled his own expectations was outweighed by the 'depressing' limits he had set on those expectations.

Dudley said that the sentence had 'moved him to tears'.[21] The point, of course, was that he had long since hurtled to the limits of his considerable capabilities. 'He wasn't just a genius,' says Clive James, 'he had the genius's impatience with the whole idea of doing something *again*.'[22] And not just impatience, but also a fear that he wouldn't enjoy himself in the process. It simply wouldn't have been *fun* to try to do it all again. Given Peter's natural contrariness, the more that people pushed him to get off his backside and 'do something worthwhile', the more they impressed the virtues of the 1980s hard work ethic upon him, the more disinclined he became to stir himself.

To be frank, it is doubtful, also, whether he actually could have matched his past successes, bearing in mind his physical condition. His professional self-discipline was shot. 'The wit was never diminished,' says Sid Gottlieb, 'but there was a lack of physical will.' The alcohol had undoubtedly taken the edge off his performance. 'There's a Dr Johnson quote about Congreve,' remembers Richard Ingrams, 'to the effect that he'd never found him actually drunk but that he was always "muddy". When Peter used to appear on *The News Quiz* on Radio 4 with me, that's what I felt, that he was always "muddy". He wasn't quite sharp. And you notice it on a programme like that, because it's a question of knowing when to stop.' As Willie Donaldson had discovered, there was also a temporary lack of interest in Peter's work among commissioning editors; not just because he was drunk, but because in the mid-80s surreal comedy was out of fashion, supplanted by a wave of conventional joke-heavy material brought into television by a generation of ex-radio producers, through *Not the Nine O'Clock News* and other programmes. Professional rehabilitation, if such a term can be applied to such a brilliant and celebrated performer, came in the wake of a renewed interest in Peter's work inspired by young comedians later in the decade.

Peter did, of course, do some work in the 1980s. The proceeds of his American sitcom *The Two of Us* had been ample, but insufficient to allow permanent retirement. 'So I sell my body, mainly on the streets of Hampstead,' he claimed, 'but that's not very profitable. I always have to buy it back.'[23] Some of the projects he undertook were interesting or worthwhile, but some were indeed only one step removed from walking the streets. In 1983 he did four jobs, the first of which fitted the former category: *An Evening at Court*, a celebrity benefit concert for his old Footlights companion Adrian Slade, at the Theatre Royal on Sunday, 23 January. Slade had been falsely accused by the Conservatives of corruption during his successful election campaign to the GLC for the Richmond Liberals, but had been saddled with a huge legal bill in defending himself. Humphrey Barclay directed the show, which also featured Rowan Atkinson, Eleanor Bron, John Cleese, David Frost, John Fortune, the Goodies, Willie Rushton and the young French and Saunders. Peter actually wrote a new E. L. Wisty sketch for the evening, performed with John Cleese, which proved that the well of comic inspiration was far from dry. It was called *Inalienable Rights:*

Wisty: Hullo. I see you're reading *The Times*.

Cleese: Yes.

Wisty: As you are fully entitled to do. That is one of your *inalienable* rights. Aren't we lucky in this country to have *inalienable* rights?

Cleese: I suppose so.

Wisty: You only suppose so? In Russia you wouldn't be allowed to sit on a bench reading *The Times*. You'd have to sit on a bench reading *Pravda*.

Cleese: Or *Isvestia*.

Wisty: Or *Isvestia*. And they are both pretty dull reads. Unless you speak Russian. Do you speak Russian?

Cleese: No I don't.

Wisty: No you don't. And you have an *inalienable* right not to speak Russian in this country. In Russia they have to speak Russian. I have a smattering – well, just the one word actually.

Cleese: Just the one, eh?

Wisty: 'Nyet'. Do you know what that means?

Cleese: 'No'.

Wisty: Neither do I.

The sketch was a classic example of Peter's ability to hit the same word again and again, making it sound more ludicrous with every repetition, the level of audience laughter rising like compound interest each time.

Peter was sufficiently inspired by its success to revive Wisty for a weekly appearance on *Russell Harty and Friends*, an early evening BBC chat show, from 21 September onwards. He sat oddly among the recipes, celebrity interviews and cute stray dogs, though, and seemed ill at ease. His first appearance, talking about the What? Party, was punctuated by stumbles and losses of concentration, although he did manage to announce one or two amusing policies: capital punishment for parking offences, and clamping for muggers and murderers. *The Sunday Times* reported that 'E. L. Wisty's resurgence was not the hoped-for smash. So the problem of finding Peter Cook something suitable to do on television looks like going unresolved again.'[24] In June, he received good notices for a cameo appearance as Richard III in the pilot of *Blackadder*. In November, he had nothing better to do on his forty-sixth birthday than appear on *After Midnight* with Janet Street Porter and Hunter Davies, reviewing the sixties: he was in a bad mood, and expressed the opinion that nothing of any value had taken place since 1973 except the invention of Blu-tac.

In 1984 came what was perhaps the nadir of Peter's cinema career: an appearance as Nigel the Warlock in *Supergirl*, a failed female version of *Superman*. His contribution took four months to film at Pinewood, was extremely well-paid, and was so atrocious that the details are best omitted. In a career littered with 'lots of trash', as Peter put it, *Supergirl* was the only film he was prepared to concede that he sincerely regretted doing. 'It was awful,'[25] he concluded. The death of Peter's father brought a brief burst of sobriety and an accompanying determination to achieve something worth while. He set to work on a golfing sitcom, *The 19th Hole*, starring himself as an up-market con man, and wrote a funny article for *The Sunday Times* about his life:

> I'm a fairly moral person. For example, in all my arms dealings I've always sold faulty equipment to the side that I wish to lose. I sold a huge consignment of those rockets that didn't work in the Falklands to Gadhaffi. He said to me rather touchingly over the phone: 'My bodyguards are your bodyguards, Peter.' Of course, they're not much use to me, being in Libya, but it's a nice thought.[26]

By the end of the year, however, he still had not finished the sitcom script, and it dribbled away to nothing like so many other projects.

Peter returned to the bottle in the autumn to make a remarkable, drunken splash at the Nether Wallop Arts Festival. This arose from a newspaper article by Stephen Pile, asking why arts festivals always had to take place in glamorous places: An organisation called Charity Projects answered his challenge by mounting a festival in the Hampshire village, which became the forerunner of Comic Relief. Peter, Mel Smith and John Lloyd devised an act in which Peter and Mel would appear in rubber hats and bathing costumes as a pair of lesbian synchronised swimmers. 'We drove down in a limo,' recalls Smith, 'and we had a fifty quid bet on exactly when we'd arrive. And Peter *purposely* misdirected the limo in order to win the bet. I couldn't believe it, because it was late at night and we wanted to get there; all for the sake of fifty quid. We spent half an hour piddling round Middle Wallop and Nether Wallop until he won his bet. He'd bet on anything actually, like how long he could keep an ice cube balanced on a baby's head.

Anyway, having attended to all the writing and rehearsing, which Peter did pretty well under the circumstances, the minute we got on stage in these stupid bathing costumes Peter was immediately off the script, and it was totally and utterly scary to me. I was hanging on by my fingernails. What should have been a two-line speech with me coming in neatly on cue became a sort of monologue; the audience pissed themselves, so I had no complaints. But the really funny thing was trying to do this little bit of synchronised swimming on stage: that took longer to rehearse than the rest of the thing took to write, and he never got it right.'

After the show Peter sat drinking in his hotel with John Wells: 'Very slowly he had the idea for a practical joke. As we all watched he got up, none too steadily, and closed the door. Then, chuckling to himself, he found a chair, propped it with the back lodged under the handle of the door, and rang for the waiter. A few moments later the waiter tapped on the door, Peter shouted "Come in!", convulsed with giggles, and the door opened easily, pushing the chair smoothly back with it. Peter said "Damn!" and ordered some more drinks. He fixed the trap, as far as I remember, at least twice more, and every time it failed, the waiter as far as I could see unaware that the chair was even there.'[27] Eventually, overcome with frustration at the failure of his joke, Peter smashed the chair.

In January 1985 he appeared as a guest on *Bob Monkhouse's Comedy Showcase*, performing *Frog and Peach* as Sir Arthur Streeb-Greebling with Monkhouse as straight man. The critics couldn't help noticing that almost every time he appeared on TV, it was to perform something from the early 1960s. 'Golly, I thought I was seeing a ghost,' scoffed the *News of the World*, which described his contribution as 'dated, dull and desperately duff.'[28] Peter, who paid a cuttings service to send him a copy of everything written about him, must have been wounded. In February he trotted out an old E. L. Wisty routine (it was either that or the Macmillan sketch from *Beyond the Fringe*, he admitted) for a charity show. He informed *The Sunday Times* that otherwise, he was 'doing bugger all at the moment'.[29] The rest of the year saw appearances on *Tell the Truth*, a downmarket ITV game show, *The Late Clive James*, *Who Dares Wins* and *Kenny Everett's Christmas Carol*. In August he resurrected E. L. Wisty once again for *Twenty Years On*, a sixties retrospective presented by David Frost that ran for five weeks, then for a further four in 1986. The irony that he should be reduced to appearing as a minor character on a show presented by Frost could not have been lost on him. The only interesting project on offer, a suggestion from the producer of *South of Watford* (presented by John Lloyd) that they should make a special edition of the show entitled *Peter Cook's London*, concentrating exhaustively on the forty yards between his house and the newsagent's, expired from a lack of application on Peter's part.

If *Supergirl* had been the nadir of Peter's film career, then the nadir of his television career, perhaps even more so than *Where Do I Sit?*, was the chat show *Can We Talk?* in 1986. The BBC had no interest in Peter presenting a chat show of his own – that lesson had been learned – but they were keen to entice the American comedian Joan Rivers to do so. Rivers agreed, on the condition that she be allowed to choose her 'second banana' – that is, a straight man who takes part in an introductory chat, then sits on the end of the sofa throughout, a post which was standard on US chat shows in pre-*Letterman* days. She wanted Peter, to inject a bit of 'British class', and Peter had no work. He and Neil Shand, who had been asked by the BBC to be one of the show's writers, flew out to Lake Tahoe to meet Rivers in December 1985.

It was not an enjoyable trip. The BBC had hired a cut-price helicopter to ferry the two men over the last leg from Reno to Lake Tahoe. Shand, who had actually walked unscathed with David Frost from a helicopter crash in Central Park in 1972, was unimpressed by the size of the vehicle and the shabbiness of the pilot's T-shirt and jeans. As they flew off into the sunset, the pilot handed Peter a torch, and asked if he would train it on the dashboard instruments; none of the on-board lights were functioning. As they attempted to gain altitude to fly over the mountains, it dawned upon the two passengers that they didn't seem to be moving. A downdraft was overwhelming the tiny helicopter's rotor and holding it stationary, facing a wall of rock in the dark. 'I was going crazy. Peter was calming me down,' says Shand. Only a fortuitous change in the wind saved them, sending the little craft suddenly plunging over the mountains and down into Lake Tahoe.

The six shows were eventually recorded over six days at Television Centre in January 1986, and transmitted weekly from 10 March. Peter's contribution was an utter disaster. The producers, unfamiliar with the American template they were working from, scheduled precious little by way of opening chat; instead Peter sat at one end of the sofa throughout like a stuffed bear, contributing nothing. No one asked him any questions and he couldn't think of any questions to ask. The notion that he could have functioned as anyone's straight man was absurd enough, and made doubly so by the fact that he barely knew Rivers and was given no time to establish a comic relationship with her. Barry Cryer, who also worked as one of the show's writers, remembers that 'Peter was very unhappy. He got very depressed and didn't try very hard in his bits. He rang me in a very emotional state one night, and said "More people have seen this fucking show than anything else I've done!" He affected not to care about things, but he *did*. He used to *dread* the recordings.'[30] One evening Bernard Manning appeared as a guest on the show and remarked: 'You used to be very funny, Peter.' Then, turning to the camera, Manning added bluntly: 'He can't remember his lines, you see. *I* work every night.'

The newspapers administered a severe beating, like muggers kicking their victim while he lies in the street. The *London Daily News*, referring to his 'impersonation of a heavily doped Chinese illusionist', described Peter as 'a man with a great future behind him'. *The Times* spoke of a 'fiasco' containing nothing but 'showbiz flatulence'. Peter blamed the tight recording schedule, and excused his reticence by explaining that 'I was there to help Joan out if she got into trouble, but she never thought she was in trouble, so I never helped her out.'[31] In private he admitted to Barry Cryer that he was 'devastated' by his reviews.

Perhaps the only positive thing to come out of *Can We Talk?* was the appearance of Dudley Moore, flown over at great expense as a guest. The angry frustration with Dudley that had characterised Peter's American failure had receded, and he offered his former partner the apologetic hand of friendship. They went out together after the show, and had an enjoyable evening, even if it was slightly clouded by a guardedness on Dudley's part, and the knowledge on Peter's part that another of his projects was headed for disaster. Dudley's fellow guest on *Can We Talk?*, who hadn't seen Peter since the *Baskervilles* fiasco nearly a decade previously, was Kenneth Williams, who confided the details of the evening to his ubiquitous diary: 'When P. C. was out of the way I told Dudley, "I find one always gets an *act* from Peter and therefore I'm obliged to act back, but there isn't the fundamental ease in the relationship which I used to know."'

The disaster of *Can We Talk?* was a great pity in more ways than one, for it obscured a superb performance by Peter on Channel Four's *Saturday Live*, which went out on 22 March. He presented the show on a one-off basis, and appeared in a number of sketches – as President Marcos, as German bandleader James Last (a quite devastating imitation) and as Lord Stockton, slumped fraudulently in a chair: 'There is no more ardent opponent of apartheid in South Africa than myself. Except possibly the 27 million black people who live there.' Instead, Peter knew that 1986 would be remembered as the year of *Can We Talk?* He did no further work over the summer; his mood plunged and his weight ballooned.

He was rescued from that particular depression by the nostalgic idolisation of the younger generation of comedians now coming through: he secured a major part as the Prime Minister, Sir Mortimer Chris, in the cinema version of the TV series *Whoops Apocalypse*, released in March 1987. Owing little to its televised origins and a great deal to *Dr Strangelove*, the film told the story of a Falklands-type conflict which escalates into full-scale nuclear war because the Prime Minister is gradually going mad. Peter played Sir Mortimer as 'Sir Anthony Eden on speed' with Mrs Thatcher's resolve added: 'I let my moustache do the work actually. The only thing I felt absolutely certain about was that I had to have a moustache. I don't think Anthony Eden would have invaded Suez if he hadn't had a moustache. Look at Margaret Thatcher – a triumph of the depilator's art. Moustaches give you the confidence to invade people.'[32] Peter had, in fact, only narrowly got the part. David Renwick, the co-writer, explained that 'Dudley Moore had become a big film star and Peter hadn't, and we had to ask ourselves whether there was any reason for that. In the end, though, it was one of the most significant things he's done over the past few years.'[33] Because Peter was playing what was essentially a comic cameo, albeit an extremely substantial one, with lines that could have been written for Sir Arthur Streeb-Greebling, his weaknesses as a leading actor never entered the equation.

The film contained some high-quality jokes. The Soviet leader proclaims that he has 'the heart of an elephant', whereupon an aide proclaims that 'the elephant was honoured to part with it'. When the President sustains a fatal heart attack in a hospital bed the Vice-President is sent for, at which command another decrepit pensioner is wheeled in on a trolley. Gearing up to attack them, Sir Mortimer announces that 'The time has come to be resolute. But you can't be resolute without being strong. And you can't be strong without blowing people up.' For every decent joke though, there was a good minute or so of sub-Ben Elton rant. What was intended as a satire on the Falklands War was actually little more than an exaggeration of it, and elsewhere real characters and events were 'satirised' by nothing more inventive than a negative portrayal. Suggesting that the SAS are in fact fantastically incompetent did not actually satirise the regiment or its dealings in any way. Nor did the random idiocy of Peter's Prime Minister bear comparison as a satirical device with the escalating paranoia of *Dr Strangelove*'s base commander. The authors betrayed their background in TV sitcom by omitting to provide a central character that might involve the audience, and by failing to sustain dramatic tension for any length of time.

Whoops Apocalypse made few ripples at the box office, and most reviewers were unimpressed. 'The audience at which this woeful entertainment seems to be aiming is one which finds the phrase "fucking dickhead" funny in itself and funnier still if reiterated at a shout several times over,' wrote the *Guardian*. *The Sunday Times* was kinder, describing it as 'a smart comedy, hardly satiric – satire makes you think, this doesn't – but frequently sublimely funny.' Peter alone emerged with credit: the *Daily Telegraph* reckoned that he 'held the film up by its knicker elastic'. In fact, there seemed to be a wave of all-round affectionate relief that he had turned in a funny performance. He had succeeded in losing weight for the part, and was looking good again. Immediately after the filming, he threw himself into another round of optimistic activity.

He began work on a screenplay, and on another TV special, which would be linked by a Teutonic psychiatrist who would scientifically attempt to work out what is and what is not funny: if 4,000 men slip on banana skins, for instance, is that 4,000 times funnier than one banana-related incident? The character would examine the role of Germans in the development of modern comedy, concentrating on the invention of the joke by two men called Fritz and Boris. On top form, Peter then pretended to be Jonathan Ross's father on *The Last Resort*, where he was asked about his hours in front of the television: 'It's so much better than a relationship,' he said. He appeared, too, on *Clive James*, where he confessed to having been in negotiation with the Kremlin about a possible defection. In April he flew out with Barry Humphries to open the inaugural Melbourne Comedy Festival, where he performed a version of his judicial summing-up in the Thorpe case. Shane Maloney, who was helping to organise the festival, recalls how Peter immediately reduced his reception committee to hysterics on arrival at the airport: 'When informed that the hotel manager, a Swiss gentleman, had requested an autographed photo for the "celebrity guest" wall of the hotel bar, Peter immediately launched into a twenty-minute dissertation on the role of the Swiss hotelier in the development of modern comedy. It was, he explained, entirely due to the influence of the Swiss that housemaids announce their arrival with a brisk "knock knock". And it was the hotel management schools of Zurich that first came up with the idea of leaving a small joke on the guest's pillow at night.'[34]

Peter also appeared in two films in 1987. One was Rob Reiner's well-regarded *The Princess Bride*, in which he played a very small part as a camp bishop, 'somewhere between the Archbishop of Canterbury and a female sheep',[35] as he put it. The other was a short film by the Comic Strip, *Mr Jolly Lives Next Door*, which was funded by Channel Four and televised by them shortly after its cinema release. In a small but excellent cameo Peter played a blood-drenched homicidal maniac in the adjoining office to that in which the main action took place; despite the sign on the door advertising fluffy toys, he had a picture of Adolf Hitler on his wall and always seemed to be chopping up innocent visitors with a meat cleaver to a deafening soundtrack of Tom Jones hits. Peter was chosen, according to the Comic Strip's Adrian Edmonson, because 'We were aware that there was quite a lot of Pete and Dud in what we did. We were in awe.'[36]

Not just Edmonson but a whole generation of 1980s comics had grown up in awe of Pete and Dud. A cameo appearance from Peter Cook was endorsement indeed. His apparent lack of drive appealed: it created an entirely uncompetitive atmosphere around a relationship of mutual respect. Peter's generosity towards younger comics was almost unique among his generation. According to Mel Smith, 'Performers of my age and younger who met him were just bowled over by the fact that he was so interested in what we were doing, and that he was so relaxed about it.' When Jay Landesman bumped into Peter for the first time since the 1960s in the newly opened Groucho Club, he found him surrounded by an adoring group of aficionados led by Robbie Coltrane. Peter made an especially attractive role model for young comedians: effortlessly and brilliantly successful in his youth, iconoclastic, self-destructive, and an avid consumer of their televised work into the bargain.

Perhaps the first manifestation of this had been an appearance on the chat show *Friday Night Saturday Morning* in November 1979, a programme which had been handed over to the Cambridge Footlights to present: Emma Thompson and Hugh Laurie had been among the reverential hosts. A couple of years later more Footlighters of the same generation, including Stephen Fry, had come across Peter dining alone in the La Sorpresa restaurant, at a low ebb – had they known it – following Judy's move to Exmoor and the collapse of *The Two of Us*. They had been amazed when he had amiably returned with them to their modest little flat, and had then consumed everything with even the slightest alcohol content on the premises. In due course Fry became one of Peter's greatest friends, and purchased for him a fax machine named Betty, with which a delighted Peter bombarded both his friends and various world leaders with absurd messages. Fry himself owned a fax machine called Hetty, and the two machines kept up a long and involved correspondence.

'He was accessible, friendly, he had time and he was generous with it,' says Ian Hislop, another fan-turned-friend. Hislop encountered Peter in the early eighties, when he wrote from Oxford University to ask for an interview for his humour magazine *Passing Wind*. Peter readily agreed to meet him for lunch; Hislop, who was not a great drinker, recalls that 'We got completely pissed, and got thrown out of this restaurant at about

3.30. Peter said, "I think you should go home and sober up, and come back and do the interview at six."' Staggering down the white line in the middle of the road, it occurred to him that Hislop showed promise. He subsequently recommended him to *Private Eye*'s editor Richard Ingrams, which led Hislop to a career on the *Eye* and his eventual appointment as Ingrams's successor.

The retirement of Ingrams in March 1986, after a quarter of a century on the magazine, came as a shock to both proprietor and staff; still more unexpected was Ingrams's unilateral decision to appoint Hislop to take over his job. Still only twenty-five, Hislop was regarded very much as Ingrams's personal protégé, and the appointment enraged many of the old guard. Auberon Waugh, referring to the new editor as 'Hinton' and 'Driscoll', described the change of editorship as 'in tune with the *Eye*'s misguided policy of seeking the custom of yobbo readers'. The magazine's gossip columnist Nigel Dempster called Hislop 'a deeply unpleasant little man who knows nothing about journalism'. Journalist Jane Ellison called him 'a ludicrous figure'[37] while her colleague Peter McKay challenged the legality of the appointment, asking how 'a tired editor was able to choose his successor without consulting anyone'.[38] McKay wrote a column in the *Evening Standard* demanding that Peter, as proprietor, should step in and sack both Ingrams and Hislop.

Even though he had introduced Hislop to the magazine, Peter was put out that he had not been consulted over his appointment. 'He was very upset about it,' confirms Richard Ingrams. 'He thought I should have consulted him, but I just thought if I'd started consulting people it would never have happened.' An anti-Hislop lunch was convened at the Gay Hussar restaurant, consisting of Auberon Waugh, Patrick Marnham, Richard West, Peter McKay and Peter, together with the magazine's managing director David Cash, whom Peter had persuaded to attend. Over several bottles of wine the issue was debated, until eventually an election was held to appoint a replacement editor, and Peter McKay was voted in. Peter and David Cash then set off for the magazine's new offices in Carlisle Street to confront Ingrams.

Unfortunately for the conspirators, Peter – who was still in a bad way following the failure of *Can We Talk?* – was now blind drunk. He may have set off from the restaurant with the best intention in the world of removing Ian Hislop, but by the time he had staggered across Soho Square, into Carlisle Street and up the stairs to Ingrams' office, he had completely forgotten why he had come. Hislop was there too, and Peter recognised him through an alcoholic blur. 'Welcome aboard!' Peter said, clapping him enthusiastically on the back. This left Cash on his own.

There'd been a sort of vote, he explained, and Peter McKay . . . Like the Mekon, Ingrams turned his piercing blue eyes onto Cash and shrivelled him to a crisp.

When he sobered up, Peter laughed uproariously at the failure of his abortive mission. Relations between the new editor and his proprietor remained cordial thereafter, and Peter conceded publicly that Hislop was the right choice. 'Ian is our concession to youth,' he said, 'he being all of fifteen. And I believe he's a woman as well, so that helps.'[39] Hislop cemented the new alliance by inviting Peter to his wedding. Of course, even if he had been sober, Peter would not have been able to exercise any authority over Ingrams, for the simple reason that he had never once attempted to establish any. Hislop believes that Peter had never sought to make any money from *Private Eye*, or to exercise any control over it, partly because he viewed the magazine with nostalgic affection as the last surviving independent remnant of his satire empire. Tongue-in-cheek, Peter described the *Eye* as 'a monument to my lack of financial acumen'.[40]

Before the end of 1986, the magazine came under an even greater threat than it had done from James Goldsmith. The aggrieved litigant this time was Robert Maxwell, then proprietor of the *Daily Mirror*, who had been the victim of a photographic lookalike comparing his face to Ronnie Kray's, and who had also been accused of funding the Labour Party in the hope of one day securing a peerage. '*Private Eye*,' thundered Maxwell, 'is a satirical magazine whose proprietor is in the habit of going after innocent people. I am one of those. But he knows if he steps out of line (here he thumped the table top) he'll be swatted like a fly. Does it really make a valuable contribution to our society to destroy both in our own eyes and in those of the world at large our major national asset of incorruptibility in public life – to replace it with a belief that the instincts of the piggery motivate our successful entrepreneurs?'[41]

Peter had crossed swords with Maxwell already, when the Mirror Group had put the *Sporting Life* up for sale a year previously; Peter had attempted to buy it, but had been rebuffed on account of his ownership of the *Eye*. Now he threw himself into the legal hostilities with relish, revitalised physically by the enjoyment of making *Whoops Apocalypse*. As Maxwell gave evidence on the witness stand, Peter waved his cheque book scornfully at him across the courtroom. As usual, he provided the downcast *Eye* staff with moral support. 'Whenever I was in court and about to lose a million, he would turn up and take me out to lunch, and say that it wasn't too serious really,'[42] remembers Ian Hislop. The magazine lost, of course. A weeping Maxwell told the court that 'Mrs Maxwell and all of our children were utterly shocked to have me, their father, compared to a convicted major gangster.' In November 1986 the *Eye* was ordered to pay him approximately a third of a million pounds, which all but cleaned them out at the bank.

Maxwell was not finished, and neither was Peter. The tycoon diverted the *Mirror*'s presses to produce a million copies of *Not Private Eye*, a bogus issue featuring large pictures of Nazi leaders conversing, doctored to include Richard Ingrams chatting with Hitler. He then bullied W. H. Smith into banning *Private Eye*, and selling his alternative version instead, before flying off to New York to see his mistress. Ian Hislop remembers: 'We had this vague idea that if we could get hold of the dummy of *Not Private Eye*, we could persuade Smiths to reverse their decision – but how to get it? So Cookie said, 'Let's send a crate of whisky over to the people who are putting it together, because they won't want to do it, they'll have been ordered to do this.' So we sent this crate of whisky over. About two hours later, Cookie said, 'Let's phone them up and see what's happened.' We phoned up, and the four people doing it were completely legless. So Cookie said, 'Sounds like really good fun there, we're coming over,' and they were so drunk they said, 'Yeah, fine.'

So we all got into a taxi and went down to the Mirror building; and it was the first time I realised that if you're very famous you can do anything, because security stopped us and said, 'Have you got passes?' and we had to say 'No.' Then Cookie appeared and said, 'We're just going upstairs, lads, is that all right?' And they said, 'Oh, it's Peter Cook' and let us in. So we went up to Maxwell's suite, where they were all lying across the floor, and stole the dummy'.

The others were keen to head for the exit, but Peter had only just begun. He sat at Maxwell's desk, rang the *Mirror*'s catering department and ordered champagne. Then he telephoned the photo desk, and ordered them to come up and take a picture of the *Eye* party relaxing in Maxwell's suite. He graffiti'd the walls and windows with crayons, writing 'Hello Captain Bob' everywhere. Then he telephoned Maxwell's mistress in New York, and got Maxwell himself on the line to explain what he had done. Maxwell went ballistic, and telephoned *Mirror* security at once. Before long a party of security men burst into the suite; such was Peter's charisma, however, that before long they too had joined the party. In due course W. H. Smith were shown the *Not Private Eye* dummy and were persuaded to reverse their decision, on the grounds that Richard Ingrams was an elderly retired man who would almost certainly sue over the Hitler picture. It was a famous riposte.

A year after Maxwell had emptied the *Eye*'s bank account, an even worse legal disaster befell the magazine. Sonia Sutcliffe, wife of the Yorkshire Ripper, suddenly and unexpectedly sued over a 1982 article alleging that she had taken money from a *Mail* journalist for information about her husband. The jury, insanely, awarded her £600,000 for her injured feelings, a sum far in excess of that awarded to any of the Ripper's victims or their families. Mrs Sutcliffe subsequently sued the *News of the World* for making a similar allegation, and lost, when the paper was able to prove conclusively that the *Eye's* report had been largely correct. Not without a certain glee, the legal establishment refused the *Eye* leave to attempt to reverse the original decision.

Peter was filming a Wispa chocolate advertisement at Shepperton with Mel Smith when news of the record libel damages came through, in May 1989. 'He got the phone call at lunch time,' recalls Smith. 'He was *really* flattened by it – I mean it took him an hour or so to come round.' Peter went straight to the pub and drank himself into oblivion; but the following day, nursing a terrific hangover and tucking into burger, chips and lager for breakfast, he was laughing, joking and lifting everyone's spirits again. He told the *Sun* that the magazine was 'planning a big story on a vicar who has a nice day out in Bournemouth. Of course, we will not name the vicar.'[43] He even offered to go on a sponsored slim to raise the money, in order to get rid of three unwanted stone that he had recently acquired. 'He was great,' recalls David Cash. 'He made a rather sombre occasion rather jolly. He came to all the meetings we had with the lawyers, he spent a great deal of time in court and he phoned me several times a day.' Fortunately for the magazine, the sum was eventually reduced to a relatively manageable £60,000 by the Appeal Court.

Peter still came into the *Eye* to write jokes, although not as often as he used to; in periods of depression, he could be absent for months without warning. His appearances were great events though, always unannounced except for his annual Christmas appointment to help write the 'Gnome Xmas Mail Mart'. This was a parody of the low-budget small ads for implausibly miraculous products that litter the pages of *Exchange and Mart* and elsewhere. Peter was genuinely fascinated by them: 'He got very excited once by a magic mail order mollusc which was going to hoover up all the gunge in his goldfish pond,' remembers his sister Sarah. He and Michael Winner had a competition going as to who could purchase the most useless product. The parody versions in the *Eye* allowed his imagination to run riot: Ian Hislop recalls that 'Richard's ads were always about ingenious pencil sharpeners. Cookie's were about screaming Hawaiian grass that yells at you to cut it when it reaches a foot long. Ants on ice was another of his, these Torvill and Dean ants on an ice cube – you could always spot Cookie's jokes.'

Both Ingrams and Hislop kept a tight rein on Peter's scatological tendencies, and edited out any swearwords that crept into his contributions. 'I'd have loved to get Barry McKenzie back,' said Peter wistfully. 'I had vague talks with Barry Humphries, but he's a superstar now, and anyway Ian didn't want it.' Peter always carried with him a tattered copy of an ancient spanking mag, containing a picture of a man whom he swore looked like Ted Heath. Hislop didn't want that either. When explicit nude photographs of the Duchess of York did the rounds (long before the Duchess's infamous toe-sucking incident) Peter was mischievously desperate to publish them; again, the proprietor was overruled by his staff.

Obviously, Peter's alcohol intake tended to regulate both the quantity and the quality of his *Eye* work. Barry Fantoni believes that the Sir Herbert Gussett letters, which parodied pompously old-fashioned letters sent to the *Telegraph* and tended to begin with phrases such as 'Those of us who have died in two world wars', actually got drunker as their author did. Peter would come into the office clutching a briefcase containing a bottle of vodka in a brown paper bag, which he would drink during writing sessions. He liked to sit in the corner of the room, perched on the back of a swivel chair that was as well-lubricated as he was, and when sufficiently drunk would sometimes find himself facing the wall. 'To be honest, if Cookie was pissed it was a complete waste of time,' admits Ian Hislop. 'I mean whatever the rumours, people that are completely pissed just aren't funny.'

When Peter was on song, though, he was as funny as he'd ever been in the early sixties. Whenever there was a formal dinner or leaving do he would stand up and deliver an impromptu speech, an event which the staff would anticipate with enormous eagerness. One such performance concerned a bottle of aftershave called 'Mandate' that he'd found in the office, which he accused Christopher Booker of slapping on indiscriminately in search of added masculinity; another placed the journalist Francis Wheen in an itsy-bitsy teeny-weeny yellow polka dot bikini, enjoying a sexual encounter with a fat colleague on the London to Oxford train. Peter's finest speech, however, was undoubtedly the one he delivered early in 1987, at the Grand Hotel in Brighton, at *Private Eye*'s delayed twenty-fifth anniversary lunch. 'There were all these other speeches first,' recalls Ian Hislop. 'I'd given this rather wooden one which I'd prepared too hard. But Cookie had been reading the menu during the speeches, and one of the items on the menu was sautéed potatoes. Instead of talking about the *Eye* he got up and did twenty minutes on sautéed potatoes. It was just brilliant.

I was sitting next to Willie Rushton, who was crying with laughter and saying, "This is the funniest man alive."' Rushton himself remembered 'looking over, and there was Andrew Osmond. He was staring, his veins were standing out and he had that sort of righteous grin that chimpanzees used to have when they were fired into space: it was fear, fear that he was going to die laughing because he couldn't breathe anymore.' According to Auberon Waugh, 'It was *absolute* genius. Every single line was totally inspired. And I can't remember a word of it.'[44] Ian Hislop, who also cannot recall a single joke, points out that 'Everybody else had put a huge amount of effort into these speeches, but Peter just did it straight off the cuff.'

Or did he? 'Brilliant, hilarious stuff it was,' agrees Andrew Osmond, 'but here's the interesting thing. Just before the speech I was talking to him, and I noticed that under his arm, among the newspapers, was an A4 pad with pages and pages of fast, messy handwriting. He'd written the whole thing out beforehand – probably that very morning.' It was a conjuring trick; Peter had secured a copy of the menu in advance. A few years later, Osmond observed the same phenomenon at the *Eye*'s thirtieth anniversary party, at the National Liberal Club in 1991: 'I happened to be standing beside him again, just prior to the speeches, and there again were the pages of writing. This time he was visibly nervous, edgy, perspiring. Peter was supposed to follow Ian Hislop, who went on rather long and got a few laughs. But when the moment came, Peter just signed off with a one-liner. Something in the atmosphere, the huge boring room, I don't know what, had convinced him the magic wouldn't work.' For all his apparent nonchalance about whatever project he was working on, Peter's general confidence level was, in fact, usually conditioned by patterns of success or failure in his professional life; 1987 was one of his better years, 1991 one of his more disastrous. Also, that year saw an acrimonious court hearing in the wake of his second divorce. But the fact that he was putting so much clandestine effort into preparing the speeches at all, in Osmond's opinion, 'makes his life, his achievement, all the more splendid and heroic. A huge, fantastic, all-consuming work of art.'

That Peter was still functioning at all by the late 1980s was much to the credit of his new girlfriend, Lin Chong. A Malaysian Chinese with a handicapped daughter, and separated from her husband, she had met him as far back as 1982 at Stocks, where she had been invited as a friend and former assistant to Victor Lownes. She had been playing backgammon, and he had come over and moved the pieces. 'He was drunk, very drunk,'[45] she says. Peter had discovered that she lived close to him, in Old Brewery Mews in Hampstead. She was, he said, 'a nerveless gambler',[46] a freelance property consultant who invested acutely in Cameron Mackintosh musicals such as *Cats*, *The Phantom of the Opera* and *Les Miserables*. She was also a 'name' at Lloyds. She was discreet, strong-willed, proud, quiet, affectionate and possessed of a fearsome temper when roused. Their relationship did not start properly until a year-and-a-half later, in November 1983. Before then they would bump into each other in Hampstead from time to time, until eventually she invited him for coffee at her 'doll's house' and he returned the favour.

Lin was stunned by the chaos of Perrin's Walk. 'How could anyone live in this mess? I felt it was so sad to live in a beautiful house this way. I felt so sad for the man. His wife had left him to live in the country. He had no-one giving him any family life.'[47] Unaware that he had all but driven his wife away and that he was too ashamed to let his daughters into the squalor of his house, it seemed to Lin that Peter had been abandoned by his loved ones. She started tidying up after him; he told the other women in his life that she was a cleaner. He was alternately grateful and abusive for her efforts. 'He could be very aggressive. He would tell me to eff off or mind my own business. It hurt at the time, but he was sorry afterwards.'[48]

Gradually, Peter's annoyance at the woman who had determinedly appointed herself to look after him turned to dependence, and dependence in due course to love. She became part of that select group of women who received his undiluted affection rather than a defensive barrage of humour. 'In a funny way I had become a part of his life that he valued. For the first time, he opened a tiny door to himself. We talked like normal people about our families. He wasn't being funny or hyperactive; he was just vulnerable. When it was time for me to go home, he didn't grab me or fall over me, he just reached out his hand and said, "Please stay". I regretted it the next day. Inevitably, I started getting hurt and jealous. A lot of his girlfriends were Bunnies. He admitted that he liked tarts: blondes, short skirts, fish-net stockings. I just didn't fit into his girlfriend mode.' Lin made it clear that if he wanted to go out with her, the other girlfriends would have to go. 'He said he would give them all up – except for two. It seemed reasonable at the time, but I found I couldn't cope. On the nights I wasn't with him, I would be eaten up with jealousy in my own little house.'[49]

The two girlfriends in question were almost certainly Ciara Parkes and Sandy Grizzle, who provided friendship and sex respectively. Ciara, the object of his romantic infatuation, solved the problem herself by changing job and moving into her boyfriend's house, and then failing to pass on her new numbers. The situation, she felt, was getting too complicated, and she was after all the same age as his daughters. Peter was extremely upset: one of Sven's depressed nocturnal calls to LBC complained that Ingeborg, his girlfriend from the dry cleaners, had found someone else and that he 'didn't know what to do':

Bull: Maybe we'll play you a little record to cheer you up later on.
Sven: Not fish.
Bull: No no, no fish.
Sven: No Marillion.

Sandy Grizzle was dropped soon afterwards, and marked the end of their affair by telling all in lurid fashion to the Daily Star. In a two-page spread headed 'Captain Kinky – He And His Porno Pals Wanted A Gang Bang', her story related a legally cautious non-event of an orgy that had taken place in 1985, just after she and Peter had split up. 'What the lusty showbiz rich and influential men had in mind is what's known in porno circles as the "chocolate sandwich" – a black and white girl together having a bonk, or a black girl between two men,' breathed the paper excitedly. The mysterious 'Captain Kinky' was, apparently, the anonymous organiser of the orgy. 'Stunning Sandy Grizzle' told the Star: 'Although I'd finished with Peter, the Captain asked Amanda and me round to his house for a party, and he told us Peter would be there. But when we got there it was just all men. Me and Amanda were the only girls there.' The writer of the piece added: 'What those men – all prominent film directors – had in mind for the two girls was nothing short of disgusting. "It wasn't Peter," says Sandy. "He was a bit drunk in the corner. It was the other blokes."'[50]

The mysterious 'Captain' was, in fact, easily identifiable as Rainbow George. The Daily Star had got it horribly wrong, accusing George – who had failed even to get a look-in – of being the sexual mastermind behind the whole thing. The idea that his house was populated exclusively by prominent film directors, as opposed to tea-stained tramps, was even more fantastic than the notion that the Rainbow Party might one day win a by-election. An aggrieved George sued for libel, but had neither the financial resources nor the organisational capacities – he tried to represent himself – to mount a successful case; the action was finally struck out for 'inordinate and inexcusable delay'. Peter thought that his first ever kiss-and-tell was hilarious, especially the fact that George had managed to lose out yet again. Judy, who still regarded herself very much as a married woman, found the piece humiliating, and the episode drove another wedge between them. 'I felt belittled,' she says. 'I overreacted to it, and I wish I'd reacted differently.' Nonetheless Peter continued to visit his wife, and to ring her every day.

According to George, 'Judy was definitely the love of his life, and I don't think he ever got over their relationship coming to an end really. He used to keep all her clothes, and shoes, and photographs.' Once, George came upon Peter sitting on his bed sobbing, all Judy's clothes laid out on the bedsheets around him. 'Lin was perfect for Peter because he was already on a self-destruct course with drink, and she was very good at looking after him. He loved her, make no mistake about that, though she could never stop his drinking. But Judy represented something different from Lin, and he could never get her out of his bones. He said to me many times over the years that Judy was the ultimate love of his life.'[51]

Gradually though, Lin squeezed out the competition with a combination of unconditional love and sheer determination. George recalls that 'one row was so big that the police were called. Theirs could be a very stormy relationship.' Lin admits that 'I left him so many times you can't imagine – but Peter usually asked me to come back.'

According to Sid Gottlieb, 'Lin and Peter were two different species biologically, let alone culturally, let alone in terms of their sophistication. It was a measure of Peter's despair that at his most abject there was Lin, and there were no conditions attached to her love. She gave everything and he appreciated that.' Peter himself said that 'very simply, it's nice to have a person you love around you. God, this sounds boring, but she's very good for me because she cares for me. She's very different, but touch wood without legs on, it works.'[52] Lin herself admits that she knew nothing of *Beyond the Fringe*, or *Private Eye*, or the Establishment Club: 'I knew who he was, of course, but I didn't really know his work, so there was nothing for me to be in awe of. To me he was a lonely person who needed someone to talk to at 3 a.m.'[53] She did his washing, his ironing, his gardening and his typing. When he appeared on TV, she sat behind the camera, quietly encouraging. She followed behind him on the golf course, absorbing his every word 'as though it was the Bible'.[54]

According to George, 'I honestly believe that if it wasn't for Lin, Peter wouldn't have lived to see his fiftieth birthday, let alone his fifty-seventh.'[56] She set herself – as so many had done before her – the fruitless task of helping him combat his drink habit. She telephoned friends like Barry Fantoni for advice, and during the great trough of depression that accompanied the illness of his father, she took Richard Ingrams out to lunch in search of assistance, before finally persuading Peter to go back into the *Eye*. She found it difficult to believe that so many people, including Peter himself, appeared to have abandoned him to his fate. 'Peter would notice my tears – I couldn't help it – if I came in and saw a bottle by his side, and he would go and put it in the fridge. He did try. I could understand what he meant when he said he could tolerate people better when he had a few drinks. He was easily bored.'[56] Lin proudly refused to admit the seriousness of her boyfriend's condition in public. 'If you mentioned the word alcoholism to her, she would have an absolute fit,' says Richard Ingrams. 'She seemed to regard it as a slur.'

Lin tried, too, to effect a reconciliation with Dudley. Unknown to Peter, she contacted his former partner when he came over to appear on *Can We Talk?*, went to see him at Claridges and tried to convey the true level of Peter's affection for him. During the early 1980s, Dudley had not contacted Peter when he visited Britain. It was largely thanks to her efforts that Peter and Dudley saw each other socially on that occasion and thereafter. Dudley stopped short, however, at the idea of working with Peter again, which was what Peter openly wanted ('I'd like nothing better,'[57] he had repeatedly told the papers). Alexander Cohen arranged a meeting between the pair to discuss a new two-man stage show: 'Dudley told me, "I can't do it and I won't do it,"' recalls the impresario, 'although he'd been gentlemanly enough at least to meet with Peter as I had asked.'[58]

In public, Dudley's tone was different: 'We could work with each other tomorrow. All one of us has to do is pick up the phone,'[59] he lied to the press. Encouraged by such pronouncements and by the renewal of social contact, Peter tried to spring a surprise reunion on Dudley in Bermuda in December 1986, on a TV show hosted by Mike Bishop. 'But the TV company couldn't get past Dudley's entourage of secretaries and business agents,'[60] Peter admitted dolefully. Dudley regretted their split – 'The stuff we did towards the end of our careers was not really the essence of us,'[61] he later confessed – but he was not about to put himself through the mill again. He telephoned Peter and left a message suggesting that he should throw himself into his individual work instead, and realise 'his wasted potential'. It was a message that Peter never once acknowledged having received.

The following year, Peter contributed by satellite to a US version of *This Is Your Life* for Dudley; then he flew out to Los Angeles to perform *One Leg Too Few* with him on the US TV version of Comic Relief, an occasion at which they were billed as 'Dudley Moore and Peter Cook' for the first time since 1965. After the show, Peter and Lin went for dinner at Spago's restaurant with Dudley and his third wife-to-be Brogan Lane, and Peter finally apologised formally for his rudeness over the years. 'Dudley had to get used to a new Peter who wasn't saying hurtful things any more,' explains Lin. 'A Peter who was capable of sending him a fax to say "I love you" instead of teasing him about his height and his foot. I think they grew closer after that, and maybe my little intervention acted as a catalyst.'[62] This analysis was somewhat undercut in 1988, when Peter flew to the USA to play a suave estate agent in a Diet Coke ad. He had got the job under false pretences, by sending a picture of himself looking younger and fitter than he actually was; he was so racked with nerves during the shoot that the director had to pretend to rehearse him and film that. His abject performance may have contributed to an interview he gave to *Vanity Fair* magazine about Dudley and his new wife. The article portrayed the pair's house as a 'Munchkinland' filled with toys, china ornaments, rag dolls and teddy bears. Brogan was encapsulated as being part baby doll and part nanny. Peter's contribution was to describe her as 'vacuous' and to point out her physical resemblance to Mick Jagger. 'She has had a special boot made for Dudley's foot. She marches him up and down the side of the Grand Canyon before breakfast,' he added.

The piece left Dudley 'severely pissed off – I'm getting fucking tired of it,'[63] he snapped. Peter tried to explain that his remarks had been made off the record, but Brogan, according to Dudley, thought that his contribution was extremely insulting: 'You know, when you're very liberal and straightforward and sincere, and just plain nice from Virginia, that sort of thing, well she thought it was quite evil.'[64] When Dudley flew over to Britain for his sister's sixtieth birthday in 1989, he was asked to appear with Peter at that year's Amnesty show, *The Secret Policeman's Biggest Ball*. He really didn't want to do it, but John Cleese wrote to him to demand 'if your Eminence would be prepared to show up at this thing; or are you the contemptible little piece of shit that the Archbishop of Canterbury says you really are?' Cleese's apparently primitive psychology succeeded, and Dudley reluctantly agreed to appear in yet another performance of *One Leg Too Few* and *Frog and Peach*. Brogan, however, refused to attend the event.

Peter and Dudley appeared in a reunion interview with Mavis Nicholson on ITV that summer, filmed at the Villa Bianca restaurant, and spoke amusingly but ruefully of their 'acrimonious divorce'. They also did an interview for the December issue of *Harpers & Queen* in which Peter made Dudley roar with laughter as he imitated a retired colonel:

> I don't mind telling you the Japs were jolly stern taskmasters. When I started the war I was 93 stone and by the time I finished that bridge I was down to 3lbs 4oz. Looked lovely in a swimming costume.

Not long afterwards Dudley returned to London to film a series of Tesco ads, and this time Brogan agreed to join Lin, Peter and her husband for dinner. Lin said that 'It filled my heart with joy when I listened to the two of them, because they always said just the right thing to each other and it would be so funny. They were both incredibly clever with words. I've never met two people who were quite like that, the way they talked to each other. They came out with the funniest things, and it sounded so natural even though it was so crazy.' Brogan, however, detected 'an awkwardness between the two . . . they seemed uncomfortable with each other.'[65]

Peter's family were initially delighted that he had found a partner so obviously devoted to him. In 1988 Lin 'came out' in public as Peter's consort – the papers reported seeing him around town with a 'dusky beauty' – and he took her down to Milford-on-Sea to meet his mother three times that year. 'Lin wanted to become part of the family', says Lucy, 'and she did things for us in Dad's name: like, on my birthday, she bought tickets for a musical in the West End, the best seats. It was obviously her, not Dad, because Dad was totally disorganised, never remembered to send a birthday card. And then there'd be invitations to go out to dinner or to lunch with them. I think it probably felt to her like we excluded her when we met, because we were just *starving* to spend time with him. It's not that we didn't like her or were uninterested in her, but we so wanted to spend time with him that it might have appeared that we were excluding her. Then she seemed to hold that as a grudge, and our family seemed to become her enemy. It created a conflict for Dad, because he would have liked to spend time with us, but I should think any time he did, he probably went home to a sour face. I think she thought we shouldn't have let him get into that condition, that we'd always just waltzed in, had a good time and left, and that we'd always left the place looking like a tip when we came and went. In fact whenever we'd got in we'd done a massive rally round with dustbin liners, doing the washing up and trying to make it look a bit more respectable.'

Lin never returned to Milford-on-Sea; Peter explained to his mother that she was allergic to cats.

Some of Peter's old friends also found relations with Lin less natural and easy-going than with his previous wives. Claude Harz, for instance, remembers that 'We had dinner a couple of times with Peter and Lin but it wasn't like the old days. She made it clear that she was taking care of him now, and he was falling into that psychology. We felt very excluded.' Neither did Lin entirely approve of Rainbow George and his circle. For every old friend who felt excluded, though, there was a new one, encouraged by Lin, to take their place. She helped Peter to reconstruct his social life, and telephoned people she liked the look of, like Stephen Fry, to encourage them to invite him out. She persuaded Peter to start holding parties again, for instance on his fiftieth birthday in 1987. For the first time since the 1960s Peter's life was filled with celebrities, and he saw a lot more of people like John Cleese, Stephen Fry, Harry Enfield, David Baddiel and Jonathan Ross. This is not to say that Peter consorted with celebrities for celebrity's sake. Famously, David Frost (now Sir David) telephoned him to announce: 'Peter, I'm having a little dinner party on behalf of Prince Andrew and his new bride-to-be Sarah Ferguson. I know they'd love to meet you, big fans. Be super if you could make it, Wednesday the twelfth.' 'Hang on,' Peter replied, 'I'll just check my diary'; and then, after a few rustles, 'Oh dear. I find I'm watching television that night.'

Nonetheless, the number of famous people in Peter's social circle at the end of the 1980s significantly outweighed the number present at the start of the decade. Harry Enfield remembers him being nervous before one birthday party, 'because Julian Clary was coming. He admired Clary, and hoped that Clary would admire him.'[66] Clary was coming to Peter's birthday party – he was one of about twenty guests – and Peter had never even met him. Peter Fincham, the Managing Director of the TV company TalkBack, recalls meeting a 'bizarre' selection of celebrities at these parties, from Eric Idle to Soraya Khashoggi. There would also be a smattering of everyday locals – the video store owner, the chemist – to provide a faintly self-congratulatory social mix. Peter, at least, would chat to such people as openly and at length as he would to the famous (Graham Chapman, who had similarly impressed his celebrity acquaintances by inviting the local baker – an elderly lady – to one of his parties, was extremely relieved when Peter, alone of his guests, was prepared to talk to her for an hour). The echoes of the highly organised Church Row dinner parties of the 1960s were plain. The court of King Peter was being reconstituted.

Peter's fellow celebrities were all too happy to pay homage. As Clive James put it, 'His superiority was easier to take after he ceased to exercise it. In his last years, when he sat at home reading newspapers while defying alcohol to dull his brilliant mind, he was a cinch to love. Early on, when we were all struggling to get started and he was effortlessly up there dominating the whole picture, to feel affection for him took self-discipline. Admiration was too total. You couldn't write a line without imagining him looking over your shoulder, not very impressed.'[67]

Sadly, however much he enjoyed the company of his revived social circle, deep down they were no substitute for his family. Lin's had been a remarkable achievement, to have rescued Peter, to have recognised his craving for love and support and to have fulfilled it; but one of his principal problems, that of being unable to communicate his love to his family successfully, had not been solved (if indeed it could ever have been solved), merely brushed aside. After Peter had failed to return Daisy's calls for some while, a family friend arranged to take her round to Perrin's Walk and hammered on the door until he opened it. A few moments of stilted conversation ensued, until finally the ice began to melt, and Peter and his daughter began to communicate. Daisy's friend absented herself, and left Daisy to rebuild bridges. Then, she recalls hearing 'an incredible noise from downstairs and the sound of breaking crockery and shouting. I gathered Lin had returned home; she told us to leave, telling Daisy that she had no right to make demands on her father. We left immediately.' Peter found himself in an awful cleft stick. Brenda Vaccaro, who saw him soon afterwards, remembers that 'He was very sad, and he broke down and cried, and there was nothing I could do. He said the people he loved the most would probably never see him again.'[68] Slightly bewildered, she assumed that he was talking about Dudley.

Lin wanted Peter to marry her. 'I was happy for a while after he gave up the remaining two girlfriends,' she says. 'I never thought I would feel the need for us to be a conventional couple, but as our relationship grew, no matter how much he said he loved me, I wasn't family. He said it didn't matter. But it hurt. I was not Lin Cook but Lin Chong. At the end of the day, I was looking after someone else's husband. He was anxious. He didn't want to make another mistake. Eventually I said: "If you love me enough to want to be with me all the time, you have to accord me the dignity of being your wife."'[69] Lin urged Richard Ingrams's girlfriend Deborah Bosley to persuade Ingrams into marriage as well: marriage, she said, conferred a status and respectability that might otherwise be lacking from their relationship. When Lin read in a newspaper that Mel Smith was to get married, 'Tears just came to my eyes as I sat next to Peter on the sofa', she says. 'It wasn't as though Lin was trying to take a piece of Peter's life,' says Mel Smith, 'she just wanted to sort of stand guard over it really.'

'Peter never wanted to marry,' claims George, no doubt blinded to Lin's sincerity by his sadness at being edged out of her husband's life.' 'He never wanted to get divorced from Judy, he held out for ages and ages. But Lin from day one set out her stall that she was going to marry Peter. I never thought he would, I really never thought that he would succumb. I used to tell her that on regular occasions – "he'll never marry you".' Peter told Ian Hislop that he could only attend the Hislops' wedding reception and not the church service beforehand, 'in case it gave Lin ideas'. On the other hand, he was genuinely in love with Lin, and she had made her wishes clear. He had also become utterly dependent on her: when she went away for a week, both his gas and electricity were simultaneously cut off the day she left – he had been under the erroneous impression that she had arranged for the bills to be paid to prevent such an occurrence – and so he sat forlornly in the cold and dark, in too disorganised a state to organise reconnection. Eventually, he took the plunge and asked Judy for a divorce.

In 1989, he booked a week's stay at the Cedar Falls Health Centre near Taunton. Judy picked him up from the station, and when he got into the car he started to cry. He was obviously in a bad way. At the health centre, where he was supposed to be drying out, he circumvented the problem of restricted alcohol supplies by drinking the Listerine from the bathrooms. Eventually, he came out with it: he had come, he confessed, to get a divorce. 'Do you actually want a divorce?' Judy asked him. 'No,' he said, and wept; but he felt he no longer had any alternative.

'The divorce from Judy threw him terribly,' says Sid Gottlieb. 'The fact that he'd finally lost her, there was no way he was going to get her back.' Judy was equally upset. They had stayed in close contact throughout the 1980s, and Peter had sometimes visited her in the new house she had bought near Minehead, after selling Blagdon Close at his request; but just as his devotion to Judy had enabled him to part company with his children in the late 1960s, so his devotion to Lin enabled him to sever the last bonds with Judy. Again, there were doubts, recriminations and regrets, but Peter's need for constant love, support and affection proved the stronger of the conflicting forces involved. 'I've practically always been married and I really can't imagine not being married,'[70] he said. 'I think he woke up and saw I *was* his wife,'[71] explains Lin.

In the autumn of 1988, Rainbow George fell prey to another of life's little calamities. He obtained a hundred tabs of acid, and – in an attempt to raise the deposit for a Rainbow Party candidate at the Govan by-election – resold them for £150 to two men who turned out to be *News of the World* reporters. The paper splashed on the story, revealing George to be a millionaire drug mastermind with a haul of 200,000 LSD tablets hidden in his house, which he intended to sell for £5 each. George was promptly arrested, sent for trial, and in the summer of 1989, imprisoned in Wormwood Scrubs. 'I asked Peter if he would look after all my tapes for me,' explains George, 'so I stored them all in his garage.' Peter, however, was at heart a thoroughly respectable citizen. 'When I was in Wormwood Scrubs he panicked and got paranoid, and thought that I might after all have concealed a stash of acid in the tapes, so he called the police.' The officers dismantled and reassembled every one of George's myriad cassettes in search of the non-existent drugs. 'He was really ashamed of himself for having done that afterwards,' says George.

By the time George was released from prison at Christmas, Peter had decided to marry Lin, written to his mother to inform her of the forthcoming event, and just eight weeks later had tied the knot at a small, impromptu family ceremony. Unconvincingly, George believes that his absence was crucial to the weakening of Peter's previous resolve. Peter returned to his south-west roots for the wedding; just four people attended the Torquay registry office, where he and Lin were married by registrar Steven Lemming on 18 November 1989. The reception, for family only, took place at the Imperial Hotel, a large, undistinguished pile enjoying fine views across the bay. None of his friends even knew the wedding was taking place. Only Judy knew it was imminent, and even she was unaware of the exact date. Minutes after saying 'I do,' Peter phoned her. 'I could hardly believe it,' she says ruefully. 'He said to me, "Judes, I've just got married again."'[72] Lin insists, rather mysteriously, that 'He was not being cruel. He didn't want her to read it first in the papers.'[73]

Lin was overjoyed: she had married the man she loved at last. She believed him to be 'indestructible'. Sadly, they were to have just five years together.

CHAPTER 16

Now That the World Is In My Grasp, It Seems a Fitting Time To Go

The Final Years, 1989–95

Peter took Lin to the Ritz Hotel in Paris on a sort of honeymoon, but the trip was hardly any more romantic than his previous two efforts – David Cash, the dome-headed Managing Director of *Private Eye* came with them. He and Peter were already booked to go and see the Paris-based *Eye* shareholder Anthony Blond, to discuss his stake in the magazine. It was a nostalgic journey: on the plane over, Peter reminisced about his first girlfriend, whom he had courted in the city forty-two years before. The trip was also eventful. After a meal at a restaurant in the Sacre Coeur, Peter led the party to a sex club, where he misread the decimal point on the drinks menu and ordered several bottles at a thousand francs a time. When the time came to pay the bill, a huge bouncer stood over the three until they had emptied their pockets. The following day they became caught up in an armed robbery while walking down the street, and Peter had to push Lin into a doorway to avoid the flying bullets. There was also a faint disagreement between the newly married couple: 'Over dinner, Lin suddenly started talking about the *Eye*,' recalls Cash, 'and saying that Peter, as proprietor, should be getting a lot more out of it, that the current set up was quite wrong and that he should be benefiting financially. He said to her, "You just don't understand how the *Eye* works. It isn't like an ordinary company."' The conversation moved on, but a few seeds of future discord had been sown.

Such minor anomalies aside, there is no question that Peter and Lin made an extremely affectionate and devoted couple. When Roger Law visited Perrin's Walk, he came across love notes from Peter scribbled on tiny pieces of paper and stuffed between the sofa cushions for her to find. On their wedding anniversary, Lin opened the front door to discover a blackboard in the hall with 'Happy Anniversary darling wife' chalked on it, a row of wobbly kisses scrawled below. Eleanor Bron spoke of the 'great pride and astonished affection'[1] with which Peter described his wife. In *Something Like Fire*, the book of essays Lin commissioned after his death, she herself spoke of their mutual love for the Perrin's Walk garden in terms which amazed many of his long-term friends: 'In one year it might be me, and in another Peter who said, "I saw the first ladybird today." We left bread for the robin and cheerily greeted him with "Hello Robin" whenever he hopped into sight . . . Peter took boyish delight in netting the larger goldfishes from the pond to transfer them to his new pond. I said he might be separating families and we'd be having lovesick goldfishes, which made him call me a "daft sausage" and smile indulgently at me.'[2] This image of Peter as a kind of pastoral Fotherington-Thomas sat ill with the picture many had of his garden as a venue for wild parties and experimental newt-breeding; but he had been emotionally bruised and battered over the years, and almost certainly did need to start again at the simplest level.

'I think as far as Peter was concerned,' says Mel Smith, 'she was just very solid, a real unmovable centre to his life. She was never a very social animal, she was always quiet whatever the circumstances, she never pushed herself forward at all. They definitely had a relationship that was more important to them when they were alone. In public, Peter was still basically let loose at the front of the team with everybody else hanging on to the reins, and Lin was very quiet and supportive.' Peter, in turn, became an affectionate stepfather to Lin's handicapped daughter Nina. 'I guessed that Peter would not be able to cope with that at all,' admits Sid Gottlieb, 'but in fact he impressed and surprised me with his solicitude.' He always held Nina's hand when they went for walks around Hampstead. Peter and Lin chose to live apart, and although she moved a number of times during their relationship, they always maintained their separate houses; his untidiness and insomnia would certainly have been difficult to live with, although with his wife around to tidy up after him, some of the mess in his living room could latterly be attributed to contrariness. Despite this apparently divisive arrangement they saw each other nearly every night.

It was generally agreed among Peter's friends that Lin had changed him for the better. According to Eleanor Bron, 'He was much mellower, talked about himself in ways he never had done, and even expressed one or two things I'd always wondered about: that partly because of his upbringing and schooling women had always been a bit of a mystery to him, and I suspect the source of quite a lot of grief. The way he talked about his wife suggested that she'd contributed a lot to the change.'[3] According to Jonathan Miller, 'I think he finally came to terms with the fact that for a long period he had not been approved of and applauded in the way that he had been when he was young, beautiful and wonderful to listen to.' Barry Fantoni remembers that 'He became, when intimate with you – if he felt confident enough to be intimate – absolutely open about his genuine feelings and genuine loves, and the funny voices would be a million miles away. The jokes of course never would be, though.' At one point Fantoni became suicidal, and turned up on Peter's doorstep announcing that he was going to kill himself. Peter took him through to the garden. 'He said, "I must show you the pond. I've got these fish. They're extraordinary. If they get too near the edge, they jump out of the water and commit suicide . . . Ah," he paused, "that's not a very tactful way to start."' Fantoni started laughing, and of course didn't stop for the rest of the evening, all thoughts of self-destruction chased expertly from his mind.

Peter and Lin's relationship remained stormy; often the arguments concerned his drinking. Roger Law walked into the middle of one, as Peter brought a period of self-enforced abstinence to an end. 'It was a rather upsetting evening. He hadn't drunk for ages, but he chose that evening to drink in the restaurant, and then he really went at it with a fucking bucket. The wife left. Smacked the keys down on the table. I wasn't sure how to deal with it. When we got back to his place, she'd gone. I said, "Well I ought to go," and he said, "No, no, don't go." And I said to him, "Well, why the fuck did you choose tonight to get back on the piss?" And he said, "I lost this job." I said, "What, a really important one?" He said, "No, just some commercials." So I asked, "Well, what are you pissed off about then?" And he said, "Because it would have meant I wouldn't have had to work for a year." And I couldn't get my head round that.'

Like Judy before her, Lin took Peter to see Sid Gottlieb: 'I was forever talking to him and Lin about his liver. They came to see me professionally, for a serious new beginning. I said, 'Right, what you've got to have, urgently, is a baseline. You've got to establish the current state of your liver. There's nothing sentimental about this problem of alcoholism; it has to do with encroachment on the liver, and I will tell you precisely, after the tests are done, what the degree of encroachment on your liver is.' And the encroachment was substantial, and I told him. I said, 'You have enough liver to survive on, but you've got to stop drinking *completely*.' And in the same breath I went on, 'Look, I say this sort of thing so many times to so many people, and I realise it's not the point. The point is not telling you what you already know. The point is trying to find a way of your *absorbing* this piece of information, that you're killing yourself

with these massive doses of alcohol.' Of course he knew that, absolutely.
I don't believe that people sit there dousing themselves with alcohol
because they want to die, because Peter always showed the appropriate
terror when confronted with an alcoholic crisis. There was no question
of joking about that.'

Terrified or not, Sid's strictures were powerless in the face of the inexorable
pull of alcohol. Peter insisted in a magazine interview that tests had shown
his liver to be 'undamaged', and he continued to drink heavily. He made
frequent attempts to give up, of course, but in the long run he always
found his way back to the bottle. The year following his divorce and
remarriage was one of the worst; despite having gained Lin, the prospect
of losing Judy had plunged him into a pit of depression from which he
took years to emerge. 'Happiness is one of the great delusions of living,'
he claimed. 'You think back on the times when you think you were happy
– but you probably didn't notice it then. You remember the unhappiness,
though.'[4] John Cleese believes that 'Peter almost took the choice that he
would rather live a shorter time and drink. That was the great sadness,
because his close friends – and latterly, I counted myself as being very,
very close with him – made some feeble attempts to say something. He
responded not in an unfriendly way but with slightly humorous defiance.'[5]
Reminded by another journalist that he had assured her he was on the point
of giving up drink, he replied: 'Giving up drink? I never said that. If I did, I
must have been drunk.'[6] So out of condition had he become by 1991, that
when the author of this book interviewed him one lunchtime for a radio
documentary about *Private Eye*, he was barely able to stand unaided. 'I
really thought he was going to die,' reflects Jonathan Ross.

The divorce settlement had hit Peter not just emotionally but financially.
He had chosen at the last minute to desert Wright Webb Syrett, his
solicitors of many years' standing, and to employ Lin's solicitors instead;
Judy, represented by Anthony Rubinstein, had rejected the terms on offer
and had chosen to contest the matter in court. The case was not completed
until November 1991, when the High Court awarded her a settlement of
over £200,000, with costs going against Peter. After the hearing was over, he
shook her hand, and said, 'Well done.' An anonymous caller subsequently
telephoned the *Daily Mail* to inform them that Judy was 'nothing more
than a gold digger'. It was not the only financial blow to hit Peter and his
wife: Lin, in her capacity as a Lloyd's 'name', lost £32,000 after a bad year
on the insurance markets, and her brother Yin even more.

For the first time in his life, Peter approached *Private Eye* for money. He
was reluctant and embarrassed to ask, but there was absolutely no reason

to feel so. The Editor and Managing Director, after all, paid themselves handsomely. Andrew Osmond explains that 'For many years, we always said, "Peter, take some money." We were drowning in the stuff. But he'd always say, "No no, I don't need it. You guys pay yourselves." So the tradition that the loot was distributed among the doers rather than the owners was at his urging.' Now, Peter requested a salary of £30,000 a year for his contribution. 'They would never have thought of resisting, even if he'd asked for twice as much,' insists Osmond. Some felt, probably correctly, that £30,000 per annum undervalued his input over the previous three decades.

In the year before his divorce, Peter had been making good money with a series of undemanding film cameos. He appeared in three films released in 1989, playing a slimy bit-part character in each. *Without a Clue* was a Sherlock Holmes comedy almost as dire as *The Hound of the Baskervilles*, with Ben Kingsley portraying Dr Watson as the secret mastermind behind the dazzling successes of Michael Caine's dim-witted Holmes; Peter played the editor of the *Strand* magazine who forces Watson to go through with the deception. *Great Balls of Fire* was a Jerry Lee Lewis biopic, with Peter as the cynical leader of the Fleet Street ratpack, who exposes the true age of the rock singer's child bride. *Getting It Right* was a rather pointless British romantic comedy that actually began with a shot of a red London bus; Peter played the smarmy, unpleasant owner of the hairdressing salon where the romantically undecided hero of the film earns a living. All three were extremely passable comic turns. There was also a TV appearance that year, playing Craig Ferguson's vaudeville-obsessed father in Channel Four's *The Craig Ferguson Story*, a live stand-up concert packaged with a series of framing biographical sketches. The results were so hopeless that transmission was delayed until 1991, in the forlorn hope that the impact of reputations falling on to concrete from a great height might be dulled by a suitably obscure placing. Like the films, it was just another routine piece of work for Peter, in the persona of the jobbing actor he had become. Only his witty and self-deprecating appearances on chat shows served to remind the world of his true abilities – on *Aspel & Company* he claimed to have secured a job as Raymond Burr's stunt double and forecast a bright future for Dettol as a social drink.

In the year following his divorce and remarriage, Peter did no work to speak of. In March, however, he was invited by the Australian Associated Press, at the suggestion of Michael Parkinson, to give a fundraising speech in Sydney and to take part in a pro-celebrity golf tournament. The deal was that in return for the speech and the golf, Peter and Lin would receive first-class air travel to Australia, plus two weeks' all-expenses-paid holiday prior to the event. 'They bought the idea,' recalls Parkinson, 'and Cookie flew in with Lin and they had a wonderful time – they went right up to Northern Queensland. And the first sign of anything amiss was when the Associated Press got a bill from a helicopter company for $12,000. Peter was flying round looking for property, would you believe? He bought two properties – God knows what he did with them, he tried to sell me one.' Mel Smith, meanwhile, was driving round the Daintree rainforest near Cape Tribulation in a rented four-wheel drive, looking for film locations and listening to the radio, when to his astonishment he heard the familiar tones of Peter, who had wandered into the local radio station in Port Arthur. Smith rang in, made contact, and spent a drunken evening with Peter at his hotel: 'We sang the only line we could remember from *McArthur Park* over and over again until we cleared the entire lounge.'

Back down in Sydney, the organisers of the fund-raising event were getting nervous; but not as nervous as Peter was himself. Michael Parkinson, who had the task of going onstage to introduce him, remembers his arrival on the night: 'I thought, there's no way he's going to perform, because he looked absolutely awful, he was very pissed. His tie was dishevelled and he wasn't quite together – he looked like three different men had been assembled. But he had got with him – which I thought heartening – a big pile of notes which he'd written in longhand.' Peter walked out in front of a thousand people and placed his notes carefully on the lectern in front of him. 'Good Evening,' he said. At this point the notes slithered off the lectern on to the floor in a disordered heap. Laboriously, he bent down and collected them all up, trying desperately to get them back into some sort of order. As he gathered the last sheets he straightened, and cracked the back of his head underneath the lectern, which toppled off the stage into the front row of the audience, causing him to drop his notes again. 'Oh, fuck it,' he announced, before walking off. 'Now I worked out that that was the highest-paid speech in the history of speech-making,' laughs Parkinson. 'Typically, there was no scandal about it – it was just "poor old Peter". If I'd done it, it would have been in all the bloody newspapers, I'd have been called this and that, they'd have withheld payment and probably sued me. But Peter got away with it.'

As so often when he was drinking heavily and finding it difficult to work, Peter turned to the repackaging of old material as a source of income. For seven years, since the trough of 1983, he had been sporadically negotiating with the BBC for the release of a sell-through video of classic *Not Only . . . But Also* sketches, supported by TV repeats. It was his mother who suggested a way out of the bureaucratic impasse that was bogging him down. 'Why don't you write to the Chairman of the BBC,' she said, 'and tell him that your mother is now very old and that she would very much like to see the shows again before she dies?' Peter did as suggested, and two days later Marmaduke Hussey wrote back sanctioning the project. In the summer of 1990 Peter flew out to America to persuade Dudley to lend a helping hand.

He found his old partner rueful, down in the dumps and glad to see a friendly face. Dudley's marriage to Brogan Lane had collapsed and his career was in free-fall. 'Most actors, if they are lucky, last five years,' Dudley said bitterly. 'I was tops for around two years, then one morning I woke up and found I was on the B-list and falling. I tell you, Hollywood is a great place in which to get cynical about human behaviour.'[7] Dudley produced some Ecstasy and the two men sat in Peter's hotel room avoiding reality. 'I was very surprised at Dudley coming out with these little tablets,' Peter later told Rory McGrath, swiftly adapting an old joke, 'because I always thought Junior Disprol was the limit of his drug-taking activity. The trouble with E though, is that you do want to fuck everything – I started looking at the Corby trouser press in a different light.' Peter's life seemed to Dudley to be happier than his own, and Dudley admitted to a certain jealousy. He had even followed Peter's example by suggesting that his new girlfriend Nicole Rothschild live in a separate house.

Putting together the video – *The Best of What's Left of Not Only . . . But Also* – was to prove an illuminating and nostalgic experience for the two men. Peter knew the material well; he confessed that he often sat alone and watched his tapes of the old sketches, especially *The Glidd of Glood*. It was only from viewing the material again, he admitted, that he had realised '*just* how much I bossed Dudley about.'[8] They chose fourteen sketches and two title sequences for the video, having to leave out only the John Lennon material, as they could not come to a financial settlement with Yoko Ono. They also recorded a new Pete and Dud sketch to introduce the tape, which simply did not match up to the material that followed:

> *Pete*: We have not spoken for twenty years and now we have broken the silence – or rather, I have broken the silence whereas you are sat there and not talking.
> *Dud*: It's because I can't get a word in edgeways.
> *Pete*: Which word would you like to put in?
> *Dud*: Maybe I would like to put in the word 'edgeways'.
> *Pete*: Feel free. Where has it got you?
> *Dud*: Nowhere. I think I will put 'nowhere' and 'edgeways' in.

The problem was, manifestly, that the dynamic had changed. Dud was no longer the subservient acolyte, hanging on Pete's every word. He was an equal partner, questioning, disagreeing, almost churlishly so at times.

Off screen, though, relations between the two men were at their best for twenty years. They underwent the usual round of promotional interviews together, including an appearance on the *Wogan* programme on a replica pub set, where Dudley and Terry Wogan sat with their pints untouched while Peter ripped through his. There was a big party to celebrate the video's release on Bonfire Night, at which the Rolling Stones were honoured guests. Peter was disappointed, though, that unlike the Stones' royalties, the financial rewards due to him from re-releasing 1960s hits were proving rather limited. 'He was rueful about that particular comparison at the time,' says TalkBack television's Peter Fincham. 'I didn't get the impression that he was earning an awful lot of money from the video. In fact he gave the impression that he was getting rather short of cash.'

Peter's income was a subject of increasing concern to him. Mel Smith remembers that 'he'd had a lean year, and I'd had a good couple of years, so when Cadbury's wanted to reshow our Wispa commercial, my office was saying, "No no, forget it, you'll have to come back with something better than that." And Peter used to keep ringing me, saying, "What are we doing? I mean, what's happening? We'd better take this money." And I was saying, "Peter, Peter, relax, don't worry about it, it'll be fine," which it was in the end. But he was beginning to panic slightly.' The journalist John Lahr remembers visiting him at Perrin's Walk, 'when the sound of the doorbell sent him lurching to the window to peek out in case it was the tax collector, to whom he owed, he said, seventy thousand pounds.'9 The continuing costs of the divorce case were beginning to worry him too, so at the end of 1990 he began to look actively for work. He secured TV ads for Nat West Bank (with Harry Enfield and Jennifer Saunders) and Panama cigars (with Ronnie Corbett, Frank Carson, Frankie Howerd and Bruce Forsyth). He also did a deal with Mel Smith's TV company, TalkBack, to write and star in a series of short programmes for the BBC.

Peter Fincham, who produced *A Life in Pieces*, explains that the series was originally Griff Rhys Jones's idea. 'He said we should do a programme called *The Twelve Days of Christmas*, but he didn't explain what he meant by the idea, so in characteristic style he left us sitting round saying "What should we do?" And somebody said, "Let's get Peter Cook in."' Peter and John Lloyd, who was hired as director, suggested twelve five-minute programmes in which Sir Arthur Streeb-Greebling would be interviewed by Sir Edward Heath about each of the twelve gifts in the song. Heath turned the proposal down point blank, and was replaced by Ludovic Kennedy; BBC 2 bought the idea, which didn't cost much, for late-night transmission at Christmas. Conscious of the fact that Peter would probably be insufficiently self-disciplined to sit down and write an hour's worth of material, TalkBack took on Rory McGrath as scriptwriter/transcriber, to knock Peter's taped improvisations into shape.

Even though it was only a late-night fringe programme, *A Life in Pieces* was Peter's first solo TV vehicle for a decade, and he found himself in a state of nervous indecision. He expressed his worries to McGrath: 'Peter insisted that it should be just him talking; he said, "I don't want it to be an interview." So I said, "Great, I'll tell them that it'll be just you talking to camera then." Whereupon he said, "No, I think it should be an interview."' Similar problems bedevilled the writing process. 'We had these fantastic lunches together. He said, "Come round first thing in the morning." And I said, "What time is that – nine?" And he said, "No, one o'clock." "One o'clock in the *morning*?" No, one o'clock in the afternoon.' So I'd turn up at lunchtime, he'd sit there with a can of cider, improvising, and it was hilarious, I was just pissing myself laughing. When I got home and sobered up it was still magic to listen to, but I couldn't make it into a series. I was supposed to be doing twelve episodes, each with a self-contained story, and this was just the ramblings of a crazed comic genius. I tried to hone it into shape, but whenever Peter saw something written down he tended not to like it. He said, 'This isn't very funny,' and I'd say, 'Well this is what you said,' and he'd say, 'No, it's not good enough.' So I rewrote it completely and junked all that stuff. And he said, 'This *is* funny, it made me laugh a lot, but I don't want to do it because it isn't me.'[11] The week of recording loomed nearer, and still there was no script.

Peter, John Lloyd and Peter Fincham improvised further material in the more ordered surroundings of Lin's house, and Lloyd turned his hand to cramming the autobiographical wanderings of Sir Arthur into the 'Twelve Days' format. Eventually the scripts were prepared and transferred to autocue, and a manor house was booked for three days' filming in early November 1990. Peter Fincham recalls that 'We were in the hotel one night, looking at the scripts for the following day, and Peter said, "One of these isn't good enough" – it was for the third day of Christmas. So we went to his room and turned on the tape recorder; and he started going into this extraordinary tale about being in Brussels, and falling in love with a girl called Rochelle or something, whom he took back to his flat, and it's the most touching and funny thing.' In fact the programmes were a mine of semi-autobiographical material – reminiscences about Sir Arthur's childhood, family history and student days that bore uncanny similarities to Peter's own.

In so far as the programmes were noticed in their late-night eyrie, they attracted kind notices: 'Supremely diverting,' said the *Daily Telegraph*, for instance. Even those involved, however, admitted that they had not really succeeded. The improvisatory feel of the material was smoothed away by the single-camera mode of filming: Peter and Ludovic Kennedy never appeared in shot together, their questions and answers were recorded separately, and no relationship between the two was ever built up. The material only dimly fitted the format: *Ten Pipers Piping*, for instance, was connected to *The Twelve Days of Christmas* only in that the subject of Peter's monologue was a man named Piper. A faint atmosphere of nostalgic regret hung about Peter's performance, that sat ill with Sir Arthur Streeb-Greebling's traditionally obtuse confidence. 'It had a slightly pointless feeling about it,' admits Rory McGrath. 'I think if it wasn't Peter Cook you probably wouldn't have forgiven it.' John Lloyd reflects accurately that 'It's got some wonderful things in it, but it was done for its own sake.' Justin Sbresni, a student handing out flyers for his fringe show in Hampstead High Street, gave one to Peter, who stopped to chat for fifteen minutes about Sbresni's material and about his own; *A Life in Pieces*, he said with regret, was really not very good.

Peter did at least come away from the project having cemented his friendships with his three colleagues. 'I'll always remember him playing cricket in Regent's Park with my then three-year-old son and an entire family of passing Pakistanis,' says John Lloyd. 'And going to the Limelight Club with him, half-cut, in the middle of the night, where nobody except the doorman recognised him, where he was, nonetheless, instantly surrounded by gorgeous bimbos drawn to his unshielded charm.'[10] Lloyd remembers Peter as a man capable of enormous merriment, as distinct from happiness. 'He was also a gracious person, which sounds ridiculous to say about somebody who was often six stone overweight and somewhat lumbering and frequently didn't wash his hair; but there was a grace about him.' Externally, Peter's looks may have changed, but the grace he was now displaying was very much the rediscovered grace of the young Peter Cook. Peter Fincham remembers lunching with him in Hampstead, 'when a bloke came up who was almost the classic sort of bore who confronts a celebrity – a would-be comedy writer who'd sent some scripts to the BBC, that hadn't been sent back. Peter dealt with it so completely gracefully and without betraying any impatience or condescension whatsoever; he was utterly charming to this man.' It was with equal charm that Peter tried to persuade Fincham to buy some of his daughter's paintings – Daisy had taken up a new career as an artist – which he said were typical of her 'expensive period'.

The divorce settlement of 1991 left Peter in further need of money, but the disappointment of *A Life in Pieces* and his continuing 'broken-heartedness' – as John Lloyd put it – over his divorce made work a difficult proposition. It was to be a year before he undertook another job, putting in a 'muddy' performance on *Have I Got News for You* (after smuggling a carrier bag of booze into his dressing room) and doing the voice-over for the TV version of the *Viz* cartoon strip *Roger Mellie*. As he arrived at the TV studio for the *Viz* job, a producer greeted him insincerely with the words: 'Peter, you're looking great! You've lost weight, haven't you?' – to which he replied: 'Yes. Another few stone and I'll be a sixties cult figure again.'

Patiently, Lin began to build him up again, weaning him off alcohol and getting him back to work. In 1992 Jonathan Ross bumped into him in a bar drinking a 'Lite' beer. He had secured a major role in the ITV comedy drama series *Gone to Seed*, starring Jim Broadbent, Warren Clarke and Alison Steadman as triplets who feud over the running of a garden centre in the London docklands. Peter played Wesley Willis, an unscrupulous property tycoon who plans to turn the place into a helicopter pad, for which performance he received extremely respectable notices.

That spring Peter and Lin were among a large, celebrity-heavy party treated to a Nile cruise by John Cleese and his third wife-to-be Alyce-Faye Eichelberger, following the success of *A Fish Called Wanda*. Peter was on top form, and dazzled the likes of Eric Idle, William Goldman and Stephen Fry with his powers of invention. Standing by the swimming pool of the Royal Simbel Hotel he devised 'The Royal and Not Noticeably Ancient Game of Abu Simbel', which consisted of two teams bowling beach balls through the loop of the pool handrail, as regulated by an encyclopaedic array of jargon-heavy rules. Before long he had cajoled the entire hotel, staff included, into taking part in a tournament. The men's team was captained by another member of the Cleese party, Mrs Thatcher's former adviser and confidant Sir Charles Powell, while the women's team was captained by his wife Carla (Peter was undoubtedly mellowing with age, as these were the types he would have mocked gleefully during his *Beyond the Fringe* days). His invention was such a success that on his return to England, despite a bout of dysentery, he attempted to interest various games-makers in marketing it.

As Peter's spirits continued to recover, 1993 saw him undertake a battery of work. First was an appearance as the recently deceased Robert Maxwell in *The Bore of the Year Awards*, written and produced by Ian Hislop and the author of this book; in search of a noble Maxwellian gesture, he stood on the deck of his yacht and forced a servant to commit suicide. This was followed by a second appearance on *Have I Got News for You*. Then, after a holiday by Loch Lomond with Lin and Nina, he flew to Portugal to take part in *One Foot in the Algarve*, a Christmas special of the Richard Wilson sitcom *One Foot in the Grave*; he appeared as Martin Trout, an accident-prone freelance photographer who trails Victor Meldrew in the belief that he is carrying a valuable roll of film. The Algarve trip was chiefly remarkable for an incident in which Lin overheard a tourist passing an adverse comment about her husband's work. Later, when she saw the man in the village square, she walked across and punched him. Eleanor Bron subsequently remarked that 'it was lovely to see Peter's delight and pride that anyone could leap to his defence in this way.'[11] Nobody had ever defended Peter before, probably because nobody had ever thought he needed defending. Peter spent the rest of the summer with Eleanor Bron, filming a cameo appearance in the cinema version of *Black Beauty*, a telling choice given the videotape mix-up with *Derek and Clive Get the Horn* all those years previously. He turned in a decent performance as Lord Wexmire, to Eleanor Bron's Lady Wexmire, the first time they had been cast together since *Bedazzled*. The pair spent a great deal of time in Bron's trailer talking in the personae of two extravagant foreigners, and promised each other that one day they would turn the conversations into a two-person stage show.

In August 1993 Peter filled a double-page spread in the *Evening Standard* with a hoax article claiming that the Ryder Cup might be attracted to Hampstead – a sort of delayed April Fool. The accompanying photograph of the 'Hampstead Heath Ryder Cup Committee' showed himself, his golfing pals Lawrence Levy and Howard Baws, and Rainbow George. The piece claimed that the entire Heath could be covered in a giant perspex dome within which any weather condition could be simulated. The centre of Hampstead village would become a huge car park – 'as cars would be unable to move in any direction'.[12] So pleased were the *Standard* with this piece that they commissioned a further page a fortnight later, on England's chances in the forthcoming football international against Poland. Peter showed that he had lost none of the mastery of jingoistic tabloidese that he had parodied so expertly in 1960:

> The game will be won or lost or drawn in midfield, but ironically the goals (all-important under FIFA's crazy system) will almost inevitably be scored at the extremities of the pitch. England will be forced to kick the ball towards the ludicrously placed opposition goalmouth and then, if they fail to score, run hundreds of yards in the opposite direction to defend their own net. Believe me, the Poles are ruthless and cunning enough to exploit this state of affairs.[13]

Peter's own physical fitness had recovered to the point where he actually won a pro-celebrity golf tournament that year, in South Carolina.

In the autumn, Peter recorded *Radio Night*, a BBC2-themed evening transmitted later in the year, in which he played the part of 'Radio'. He also chose his favourite comedy clips of all time for *Junkin's Jokers*, a BBC radio show: all of them were childhood choices, the most modern being excerpts from *Pieces of Eight* and *Bridge over the River Wye*, with one exception – a solitary piece from the first *Derek and Clive* LP. This was by way of a shameless plug, for the autumn of 1993 also finally saw the unopposed video release of the film *Derek and Clive Get the Horn*. It was a project about which Peter had become ruefully nostalgic; the law having relaxed somewhat since the late 1970s, he was re-releasing it partly because he needed the money, and partly because it was not in his nature to leave loose ends untied. He admitted that he had been 'quite shocked' to view it again after fifteen years, and that it was indeed 'horrible. But on the other hand, you can't re-edit it to fit with fashion. It's like all those Bogart films where he's smoking,' he told an unimpressed reporter from the *New Musical Express*. 'This video is rubbish.'[14] concluded the paper tartly.

Polygram, who were marketing the video, put Peter in touch with Public Eye, the PR company they had appointed to handle the release, and fixed up a lunch meeting between him and the woman who owned the company. 'Hello Red Fluffy Jumper,' said Peter when she walked in; it was Ciara Parkes. 'Peter and I had a long, funny lunch talking about old times,' she recalls. Their friendship was instantly rekindled: they developed a private joke based around hidden satanic messages, and Peter devised a secret satanic sign which he would make to Ciara during the round of TV and press interviews she arranged. He also came up with some novel PR ideas for her, such as Rizla papers with a 'Derek and Clive' slogan typed on them (by Lin). One reason Ciara had been hired was that by chance, she had recently done some work with Dudley Moore. 'So my job was basically to get Dudley involved,' she says, 'which was very difficult. But we managed it finally.' Dudley's film career no longer presented an obstacle, as it was all but over; but *Derek and Clive Get the Horn* still held unpleasant associations for him.

Perversely, a bonus reason for re-releasing the film was that it gave Peter the chance to work with Dudley again. 'There's no one better than him to have by your side,'[15] he told the press. Dudley recalls that, once again, 'Peter wanted me to come back and do some more revue-type material with him. I think he was quite keen for that but I didn't want to do it.'[16] Dudley was, however, reluctantly willing to oblige his old friend to the extent of allowing the release of the Derek and Clive video, and of adding his weight to the PR effort. Peter was overjoyed. Daisy's then boyfriend Simon Hardy remembers that 'The liveliest and most invigorated I ever saw Peter was at that time. Daisy and I met him for lunch and he seemed a different man. He was drinking very little and gone was that air of melancholy and ennui. He was buzzing. He was in the midst of a succession of press and television interviews, making plans for his post-launch party, and, most important of all, he was working with Dudley again. He had great plans to get a piano put in his garden so Dudley could play.'

The launch party was held on the top floor of the Cobden Working Men's Club in Kensal Road, now a permanent media hangout. 'We spent days going round before we found the place,' says Ciara. '"This is it", we thought. "This is Peter".' A huge cavalcade of celebrities was invited, including Alan Bennett, Jonathan Miller, the Rolling Stones, the Monty Python team, Paul Merton and Ian Hislop, Rory McGrath, Mel Smith and Griff Rhys Jones, Julian Clary, Alan Bates, Ian Dury, Dave Stewart, Sam Torrance, David Gower and his fellow England cricket captain Chris Cowdrey, Roger Law, Mariella Frostrup, and – naturally – Kenny Lynch. 'Lin did the guest list,' explains Ciara. 'She was very involved – she wanted to be a part of it. There were so many top-flight celebrities there. Their coming was a big tribute to Lin.' Peter rang his sister Sarah in a state of high excitement to invite her and a guest. She asked her daughter Aletta, by now a student at Newcastle University who caught the train down. On the morning of the party, however, Lin discovered that Peter had invited his young niece, and telephoned Sarah to rescind Aletta's invitation. 'Is this your wish, or Peter's wish?' asked Sarah. Lin put the phone down. Sarah and her daughter spent the evening at a comedy evening at the Riverside Studies instead.

'It was one of the best parties ever,' says Ciara. 'The Stones turned up in a handbuilt white 1930s coach. The paparazzi went mad. Every comedian in the world was there virtually.' According to Griff Rhys Jones, there was 'a whole room of comics all performing at each other.' Two huge bouncers brought by the Rolling Stones stood at the door to repel non-celebrities, but even so, the party was so packed that Alan Bennett and Jonathan Miller never even got to see their host. Peter was in his element, surrounded by his adoring colleagues. At one point he announced, 'Oh fuck this, let's go down the pub,' and led a stream of admirers down the stairs into the members-only bar of the working men's club. Not wanting to be left out of the chance to drink in the bar of a genuine working men's club, the entire throng of celebrities poured after him. A clutch of bemused pensioners enjoying a quiet drink were amazed to see the doors fly open and a huge crowd pour through. 'Suddenly Peter and the Stones and everybody else just burst through the door,' recalls Ciara, 'singing, dancing, Dave Stewart was there, and he was singing, and some of the Python lot too.' Mel Smith believes that 'Peter loved showbusiness – he was a real tart, really. He didn't take it seriously, but he was always very much at home with the idea of all those famous people – I think he loved it all, actually.'

When the party at the Cobden Club ended, Peter held another party immediately afterwards at Perrin's Walk. Lucy and Daisy, who had also found themselves excluded from the Cobden party, were reunited with their father. 'We felt rather sad,' confesses Lucy. 'Daisy talked to Bill Wyman and said, "Would you like a drink?" and he just thought she was the maid.' Simon Hardy, however, reckons that 'The party was great – I remember turning round and seeing Ronnie Wood of the Stones ensconced on a sofa with his legs open, scratching his scrotum, while next to him sat Sir Charles Powell, Mrs Thatcher's former foreign policy adviser.' Trying to light some outdoor candles in the garden, Peter managed to set fire to his trousers by mistake, and had to jump into the fishpond to extinguish himself. The party was still in its drunken death throes at breakfast time, Peter racing up and down Perrin's Walk after Keith Richards and Ronnie Wood, brandishing a video camera.

It had all been a huge success, at least in terms of achieving its stated PR aims. The press coverage was enormous, and 'sales went mad', as Ciara put it. 'It was probably the happiest I ever saw Peter,' says Rainbow George. 'He'd have been quite happy to die that evening.'[17] George was still at the Perrin's Walk party at 9 a.m., a fact that Peter pointed out to him at the time. 'That's rock 'n' roll man,' said George aimlessly, a statement which elicited a tart response. George was becoming annoying; suddenly he seemed an irritating embodiment of a depressing period of Peter's past life.

Peter was on a roll again. At a *Private Eye* party he fell into a discussion with Clive Anderson, and came up with the idea of a special edition of Anderson's chat show in which all the guests would be fictional characters played by him. Anderson, who knew Peter as an entertaining if evasive guest, thought that the conversation had just been party talk; but by the following morning Peter had managed to find out his home telephone number and had made contact, bubbling with enthusiasm and throwing around ideas for possible characters. His original plan was to make two half-hour programmes, punctuated by topical jokes; the end result was simpler, a single Christmas edition of *Clive Anderson Talks Back* populated by just four characters. Both Peter and Clive Anderson were keen to make the shows genuinely improvised, avoiding the semi-preparation that characterises most TV comedy panel games, but in the event this proved impossible – Anderson needed to be aware of the characters' fictional backgrounds to be able to interview them. So, after a few initial meetings, a researcher was assigned to each character as if they were real chat show guests, to talk to them in advance and to come up with a suggested set of questions and a structure for the interview.

First up was Norman House, a Wistyesque biscuit quality controller who believes he has been abducted by aliens: 'I felt at the same time strangely calm and horribly terrified.' His wife Wendy has taken various incomprehensively blurred pictures of the event, which, he says, have made him appreciate just how insignificant the aliens are. Second, and by far the best, was football manager Alan Latchley, an emphatic, emotional and inarticulate bundle of beautifully observed clichés: 'Football is about nothing unless it's about something'; 'Football is all about motivation, motivation, motivation – the three Ms'; 'I can look myself in the mirror in the morning and say, "There is a man".' Third (and very much Arthur Streeb-Greebling to the first character's E. L. Wisty) was overenthusiastic judge Sir James Beauchamp, who has been suspended for shooting a defendant in court. Finally came rockstar Eric Daley, formerly of the Corduroys and now a member of supergroup Ye Gods, recently emerged from alcoholism treatment at the Henry Ford clinic: 'It's a much tougher regime than the Betty Ford clinic. You have to build a car before you can get out.' Daley obviously owed something both to the rock stars of Peter's acquaintance, and to his own experiences: 'I love the country,' he remarked. 'We were lucky enough to find a place in the country very near town.'

Peter looked better, fitter and slimmer than he had done for some time, although his cigarette-throated tones constrained his former vocal versatility. There was an air of successful collaboration and improvisation about the show that had been absent from *A Life in Pieces*. The critics loved Peter's performance: 'Brilliantly fleshed out', remarked the *Mail* excitedly; 'A classic', said *Today*. Peter's friends were even more enthusiastic. 'Absolutely brilliant,' said Richard Ingrams. 'Just like the old Peter Cook. He was absolutely on the ball, his timing was excellent and he was clearly off the booze.' Jonathan Miller found it 'remarkably inventive. Every piece of his invention was there in untarnished abundance.' John Bird regarded it as an improvement on the old Peter Cook: 'There was something new here – an insight and even a sympathy in the way in which he approached his characters. The comedy had become more humane.'[18] It had indeed been a good show, but these assessments were not without an element of hyperbole, brought on by the sheer relief of seeing Peter back to what looked like good health and his best form. This time, though, Peter had achieved success through furious concentration: his characters' po-faced stares were real po-faced stares, never threatening to collapse into relaxed laughter as they used to in his heyday. Be that as it may, his friends now willed him to take this success and run with it, and not to sink back into illness and depression once more. 'Peter was set on a new course onwards and upwards,'[19] suggests John Cleese, who described the *Clive Anderson Talks Back* episode as the start of a renaissance cruelly interrupted by his divorce settlement, among other personal tragedies. This re-ordering of history was wishful thinking indeed, as Cleese desperately wished happiness and success on his old friend.

Peter entered 1994 in optimistic mood. 'For years I used to think I can't really act. Now I think I can,'[20] he told the *Independent*. He embarked upon *Why Bother?*, a series for Radio 3 that was essentially a retread of *A Life in Pieces*, but with Chris Morris taking the Ludovic Kennedy role. Morris was one of the few performers able to match Peter for speed of thought and surreal invention, giving the programmes a collaborative edge; furthermore, despite the recording of more preparatory improvisations with Peter Fincham, the programmes were largely improvised in the studio. Morris himself cut the five eight-minute shows from eight hours of recordings. As a result, the series was a considerable improvement on its televisual predecessor. Fincham recalls that: 'Chris would take Peter off down completely bizarre avenues. For instance, one of them starts with Chris asking about Sir Arthur Streeb-Greebling's discovery of the fossilised remains of the infant Christ, which bowled out of nowhere. When I heard that broadcast, I thought, "I'll never work again," because it's so blasphemous. It was all about cloning Christ, and faxing him in DNA form, and about his various dry runs for the resurrection. We didn't have any complaints, which is a reflection, presumably, of the size of the Radio 3 audience.'

Like its predecessor, *Why Bother?* was packed with parodic autobiographical material; even the title referred to its author's attitude. Sir Arthur, for instance, discussed his stint as a co-chat show host with Joan Rivers, whom he described as 'a pain in the arse'. With reference to his childhood, Sir Arthur explained that he once had to spend an entire winter standing in the middle of a frozen lake:

> *Sir Arthur*:   It was a learning experience to be a child in my father's household, or whichever household he put me in. He felt that the best education I could possibly have was to be put in prison and raised by hardened murderers. We were woken at dawn by the sound of hanging.
>
> *Morris*:   Did you hold this against your father at all?
>
> *Sir Arthur*:   We never spoke about it.

Sir Arthur's Munchausenesque tales, consisting mainly of extreme hardship, exploration, discovery, bizarre medical experiments and inept or criminal commercial ventures, were generally considered to be up there with Peter's best work. The *Daily Telegraph*, among other publications, pronounced them 'very funny'. Nonetheless, an air of regretful weariness continued to hang about them. Discussing his role in mowing down 'as many whites as blacks' during the LA race riots, and asked the question 'Do you feel any pride in that now?', Sir Arthur replied:

> I feel nothing but pride. That's all I do feel. An empty pride . . . a hopeless vanity . . . a dreadful arrogance . . . a stupefyingly futile conceit . . . but at least it's something to hang on to.

The wave of energy that had carried Peter through 1993 was beginning to subside. The success of *Why Bother?* led to a second series commission for its TV stablemate *A Life in Pieces*, but Peter had neither the inclination nor the application to see the project through. When Mark Booth of Century Books met him for lunch to discuss commissioning his autobiography, Peter arrived claiming to have the finished book with him in his bag. He produced a few pages of notepaper covered in rough scribbles. 'Is that it?' asked Booth. 'I thought we might flesh it out with a few photographs,' smiled Peter. If he was disinclined to finish a series of short, collaborative TV scripts, the chances of him sitting down alone to write an entire autobiography were practically non-existent. Peter had been threatening to write the book for years: he had informed viewers of *Aspel & Co* that 'I'm not going to tell all that old stuff that everybody knows, about being Golda Meir's toyboy: "She was a fearsome and aggressive lover." But any person who's wittingly slept with me – or unwittingly slept with me – thirty grand in Deutschmarks, large denominations, will probably hush it all up.'[21] Joking aside, Peter confessed to Booth that he wouldn't even consider such a project while his mother was alive.

Peter still visited his mother regularly and devotedly. He would frequently take a black cab to Waterloo station to catch the Hampshire train, but more often than not, once ensconced in the back with a pile of newspapers, he would order the cabbie to drive him all the way to Milford-on-Sea. Margaret Cook remained active and intellectually alert in her eighties; she took part in regular literary group meetings at which the novels of Trollope, Jane Austen and Bruce Chatwin were discussed. In 1993 she had fallen seriously ill, and for a brief period had not been expected to live. Peter had rushed down to her Southampton hospital in the middle of the night; 'He came into the ward,' remembers his sister Sarah, 'and said

"Mum, you're so *pretty*." It was probably the best kind of magical medicine anyone could have administered.' His mother made a full recovery.

Soon after being allowed home, she travelled to the Chewton Glen Hotel in the New Forest where Peter was trying to write the second series of *A Life in Pieces* with Peter Fincham. The three lunched together. Fincham remembers above all that 'Peter was absolutely devoted to her, and utterly charming to her. He was extremely solicitous, especially as she'd been unwell. She was a very sweet lady – and I remember thinking what a bizarre son he must have been for her, to have enjoyed such fantastic success at such an early age, and then to have gone through such strange changes in his life. He cut a very rococo figure – he was very large, with grey hair, he was wearing bright pink tracksuit trousers with an old jacket, which didn't go together at all except in his mind, he was trailing cigarette smoke, and in a posh hotel in the middle of the country he presented a pretty weird sight. In fact it was a weird but entirely charming lunch; they just seemed completely devoted to one another.'

Peter continued working into 1994, and after *Why Bother?* he appeared in the first ever episode of *Fantasy Football League*; but his heart was not in it. As a celebrity manager he'd been determined not to take the selection of his notional eleven seriously: at the advance auction he'd spent £4.5 million on the unknown Ipswich keeper Craig Forrest, and he also played his top signing Eric Cantona in goal. On the night, though, he seemed rather overwhelmed and out-of-sorts, unable to get a word in edgeways against the quick wit of Frank Skinner. He dropped out of the series soon afterwards. He was tired. He arranged to meet Ciara Parkes but cancelled, explaining that he was exhausted, and 'off for a few days' rest'. George remembers that 'Often I'd go round and ring on his buzzer and say, "Hello Wizard, it's Wicked" [Wicked Weiss' was the name given to George by the *News of the World*]. And he'd say, "Oh Wicked, I'm tired. I'm going to bed."' Lin informed George that Peter didn't enjoy his company any more. 'He became quite reclusive in 1994, and I think he must have known that he was not well,' reflects George.

Peter sat at home, watching *Harry Enfield*, *Blackadder* and *Have I Got News for You* and ringing his friends. Michael Palin remembers returning home to an elongated answering machine message about a newspaper story that had accused him of cheating at conkers. 'Why had I done it so publicly? Was it a cry for help? It was the sort of message only someone with time on their hands would have bothered to send.'[22] Peter telephoned Dudley, too, in another forlorn attempt to persuade him to come back and do some sketch material. *Not Only . . . But Also*, he said, was one programme that he was 'not ashamed of'. Dudley turned him down again.

Peter drifted back onto the booze, not that he had ever truly left it during his exertions of 1993. 'He had cut right down,' explains Jonathan Ross, 'but then he cut back up again.' He missed a deadline for a further sports article for the *Evening Standard*, after a drunken night out with Keith Richards and Ronnie Wood. He took part in a pro-celebrity golf tournament in Malaga, clanking round the course with two golf bags, one of them entirely full of booze, and had to be rescued by a greenkeeper in a van. One night, drunk, he telephoned one of his old AA friends out of the blue and asked for help. He wanted to go to hospital, he explained, and insisted on ringing the Wellington Hospital to demand admission. When they asked why, he said that he just wanted to lie down. As his liver deteriorated once more, he was twice admitted to hospital for more concrete reasons.

The reason for this latest downturn, if reason were needed any more, was that his mother had fallen ill again. In April 1994 she woke to find that she had lost most of the sight of one eye, but insisted on driving 28 miles that day to a lunch appointment. Her optician could find nothing, and the problem appeared to pass. In May, she and Peter's sister Elizabeth travelled to Dartmoor for a short holiday, where they stayed at the Lydgate House Hotel in Postbridge, scene of many a family holiday when Peter was a child. One night, she suffered a severe stroke and was rushed to hospital in Exeter. For the following month Elizabeth, Sarah and Peter kept vigil by her bedside on a rota system, as they had done during Alec's final illness. Peter deflected his pain into jokes. 'The trouble with my mother,' he told Barry Fantoni, 'is that she will insist on driving even though she is completely blind. Of course, she knows the town very well.' Margaret Cook died a month later, on 6 June 1994.

Peter was utterly destroyed. He found himself full of stupid remorse that he hadn't been there at her bedside when she'd gone. At her funeral he said that any success he'd had, anything he'd ever been, he owed entirely to his parents. And he cried; he cried and cried, his puffy cheeks soaking up the tears like blotting paper. Meeting Ciara Parkes one morning, he stood racked with helpless sobs in the street. 'You're broken-hearted, aren't you?' she asked. 'Yes I am,' he replied, and pushed his way numbly into Safeways for another bottle. Corinna Honan, a journalist who had come to interview him, happened to mention his mother: 'whereupon he began to weep. Big, shocking tears blurred his vision and then slid slowly down his face. "Hit me for six," he said, gulping for breath. "Of course, losing your mother is normal, but . . ." For several minutes, he stared at me unblinkingly as I tried to calm him down and return his thoughts to happier memories. The pain in his eyes reminded me of a child's uncomprehending grief, but he listened almost beseechingly to my inadequate words of comfort.

Was she proud of him? He nodded, speechless with grief.'[23] He was in a terrible state, recalls Honan: knocking back triple vodkas at 11 a.m., his hair overgrown and standing up in curious tufts, his gait reduced to an inelegant shuffle.

'Why are you crying?' asked Barry Fantoni one day. 'I don't think I've been a very good son,' replied Peter. 'I asked him whether he loved his mother,' says Fantoni, 'and he said yes. And I asked if she loved him, and he said yes. And I said, "So in what sense do you think you haven't been a good son?" And he said, "I . . ." and left the question hanging in the air.' According to Lin, 'His mother's death completely crippled him emotionally. He couldn't quite cope with that grief and probably took less care of himself. I could ask him not to drink and nag him to look after himself, but there's a limit to what someone else can do to help a person. A lot of it is up to that person.'[24] Alan Bennett was surprised to find that after his mother's death Peter regularly referred to himself as an 'orphan'. 'This seemed to me so strange and uncharacteristic, both in Peter or in any man in his mid-fifties, that it made me feel that I perhaps hardly knew him at all.'[25] That was as confessional as Peter got. 'I remember just wanting to talk to him about Mum so much,' says Sarah, 'but he just wasn't able to.' As his mother's belongings were gathered up and cleared away, Peter asked for just two items from the family home: his father's desk; and most important of all, the CMG that had been presented to his father by the Queen.

Peter now threw himself into a little flurry of work, as he had done after his father's death a decade before. He telephoned Eleanor Bron about the long-forgotten plan of mounting a stage show, and instituted weekly meetings to improvise material into a tape recorder. He appeared on *Room 101* to list his pet hates, making a truly brave stab at being funny about cotton wool, push taps, John Patten, low-quality German soft porn, a Nationwide Building Society ad, Gracie Fields, the TV programme *Watchdog*, unopenable cellophane packaging, pink-eyed pet rabbits and of course the countryside. Host Nick Hancock played him a slowed-down film of the countryside: 'You've deliberately speeded this up!' accused Peter. Hancock inquired if rabbits' eyes ceased to be pink in flash photographs. 'Yes,' drawled Peter, 'the only place a rabbit looks really good in is a disco.'

He also made a Christmas sell-through video, entitled *Peter Cook Talks Golf Balls*, which was heavily based on his *Clive Anderson Talks Back* appearance. This time the four characters were Alec Dunroonie, an old, bearded, retired caddie, who told tall tales of ants that attack people in tasteless golf trousers; Dr Dieter Liedbetter, a Teutonic golf psychiatrist who set out to prove that golf was played by prehistoric man; Bill Rossie, a wildly overequipped American caddie with a golf bag full of drink; and best of all, Major Titherly Glibble (Sir Arthur Streeb-Greebling again), misogynistic Chief Secretary of the Antler Room, a satire on the type of pompous golf club official likely to raise objections to Peter's attire:

> In the rules of golf there is no mention of women as such. The rules of golf are enormously long – as indeed is my wife. We have a working arrangement. She works and I arrange things.

As he became drunker, Glibble turned out to be a paedophile, who has returned with several Arab boys from a trip to Morocco to buy sand for the bunkers. 'Young lads running around stark naked – that's the game of golf for me,' he burbled.

Peter Cook Talks Golf Balls did not, sadly, bear comparison with *Clive Anderson Talks Back*. Peter looked uncomfortable, sweaty and out of shape, and the production values were poor. It was a joyless performance, which is hardly surprising considering the circumstances. In contrast to his newfound confidence regarding his acting abilities of the previous year, he told the *Daily Mail* that 'I don't think I'm a very good actor.'[26] Ciara handled the video's PR once more, but journalists were more interested in Peter's condition than in sketches about golf. Somehow he slogged through the round of promotional appearances. Excuses needed to be made: *London Tonight*'s Ken Andrew told viewers that his interviewee was 'suffering from a heavy cold' as Peter, bloated, blurred and heartbroken, mumbled something about popping into the 19th hole.

He made a number of writing trips to *Private Eye*, which he described as 'The only thing I do that I'm interested in.' John Wells remembers the intense expression in his eyes as he fought to hurl off the blanket of drunkenness: 'He was clearly being assailed by wave after wave of wildly comic ideas he was at that moment unable to express. He'd been reading a piece in the paper about the Frederick West murder story; the police were removing bodies from West's back garden, and his lawyer was complaining that 'this kind of publicity might well damage his client's case'. Peter had read out the quote, and we'd laughed, then he sat there thinking about it. He crooked his cigarette up to his mouth, rocking forward, shaking with laughter, half turning away, but when he looked back the expression was still there. It was intense, affectionate, full to overflowing with a kind of glittering amusement. You could regret he'd got himself into that state, but when he looked at you like that you could only love him.'[27] Peter continued to visit the *Eye* up until Christmas 1994, when he composed a trendy church service with the refrain 'Ooh ah, Cantona'.

Some days were better than others. There was the day when Peter decided to invite Jurgen Klinsmann to tea, and the Tottenham centre forward politely accepted the invitation. There was a lads' night out with David Baddiel, Frank Skinner and Jonathan Ross, at which they discussed the idea of setting up a company to abuse young women under the pretext of giving them a start in TV; the evening was great fun, although Ross recalls that Peter knocked back 'a serious number of Margaritas'. There was also the annual celebrity Perudo tournament at Commonwealth House, which Peter attended for the second year running: over 300 guests gathered to play the South American game of liar's dice, including Stephen Fry, Keith Allen, Sting, Mariella Frostrup and the equally ever-present Lady Carla Powell. Peter and Sting's team made it through to the semi-finals.

There were, also, more melancholy days. Visiting the supermarket with George, Peter saw an extremely pretty young blonde girl of about eighteen in one of the aisles. There was no suggestion of lust, explains George, just misty regret that she looked exactly like Ciara had done when Peter had first met her (Peter once famously commented that 'I might have some regrets . . . but I can't remember what they are'). There was also a *Literary Review* prize-giving, at which Peter had promised to present an award to the winner of the magazine's poetry competition. Drunk and depressed, he made a slurred and incoherent speech that no-one really understood about an enormous bee, which thoroughly confused the respectable middle-aged lady who'd won. As if in anticipation of further depression to come, Peter phoned Clive Bull at LBC and warned him to expect more nocturnal calls, this time from a new alter ego named Jurgen the German.

In September, Peter enjoyed one of his happiest days, at the wedding of his daughter Daisy to Simon Hardy. Lucy had already married in May 1990, a hurried registry office wedding to an American psychotherapist called John Shadley, followed by a blessing and honeymoon with Wendy in Majorca; Peter had been annoyed that the event had made the *Daily Mail*, so keen was he to protect his daughters from the public glare. Daisy's wedding was a grander, more traditional, but also more discreet affair, in the Sussex village where she had spent the latter part of her childhood. Peter came alone; Lin, he said, had the flu. The night before the wedding, Simon Hardy found Peter sitting alone in the hotel bar with a bottle of champagne. 'He had a piece of paper and was jotting down things to say about Daisy in his speech. He looked so vulnerable you wanted to hug him.

'On the day, he walked Daisy up the aisle and gave her away, then he made a speech which was moving in its simplicity. There were no absurdist voices, just the sentiments of a very proud father of both his daughters –

something I think he'd rather denied himself in the past. Later I remember seeing him and Wendy sitting at the back of the marquee talking in a way I don't suppose they had done for a very long time.' Peter and his first wife had, indeed, been reconciled for the first time in a quarter of a century. 'It was very nice – I'm so happy I saw him,'[28] she says. Daisy herself remembers the occasion as 'a great day – really good fun. Dad was very proud, and so good. I was worried about how it would all work out with him and Mum, but it was lovely'. Peter spent much of the afternoon dancing to a jazz band with a tiny child. Taking a breather from his exertions, he and Sarah sat in companionable silence on a tree stump in the Sussex drizzle. 'He remarked that he was looking forward to dancing continuously until January,'[29] she recalls. Then he returned alone to his hotel room, where he watched *Midnight Cowboy* on television, and depression stole over him once again.

In November, Lin organised a party for Peter's fifty-seventh birthday; the guests included Michael Palin and Stephen Fry, who gave Peter a green trilby hat that he described as 'one of the nicest birthday presents I've ever had.' It was to be Peter's last birthday. In December, he failed to turn up for the *Private Eye* Christmas lunch, because he had been compelled to return to hospital for further treatment. Barry Fantoni believes that 'He knew he was killing himself – although I think he thought that the end would come very much later. But he didn't want to become an old man – he wanted to die intact.' Sid Gottlieb, however, points out 'There are tomes about death wish and so forth, saying that "This man really wanted to die and so he behaved in a particular way." I say that's bollocks. If we were able to offer a person who's suffering from that sort of severity of intoxication a chemical therapy that would work, they'd grab it, of course they would. Peter was scared of dying – he was very scared. This was the case in his last days, and the last phase of his drinking was the worst, the longest-lasting and the most toxic.' Peter was allowed home for Christmas, and Lucy paid him a short visit. 'His voice was going, he'd obviously had a lot of tubes down his throat. He was on soft drinks and he was very scared. He was trying to put a brave face on it, but he was lost for words. And so was I.'

On the evening of 3 January 1995, a sobbing Lin came running to George's for help; Peter had collapsed, and she was trying to get him into her car. An ambulance was called, and Peter was lifted gently on to a stretcher. George came out into the street to see him go. Peter gripped his hand and breathed, 'Will I be OK, George? Will I be all right?' Without stopping to ponder his less than 100 per cent predictive record, George reassured him. 'You'll be fine Peter. Everything's going to be just fine,' he insisted. 'Oh fuck,' replied Peter, his fate sealed. It was his last joke. George watched the ambulance drive away. 'I love you,' he said, as it disappeared up the street.

CHAPTER 17

Zsa Zsa Man Dies

Death and Aftermath, 1995–97

Lin accompanied Peter to the Royal Free Hospital where he was admitted throwing up blood, his liver dying. Soon, he fell into a coma. By the time his sisters and his daughters arrived, they were too late to say goodbye to him. 'Things that happened in the hospital between Lin and Peter's family were unbelievably upsetting,' says Rainbow George. 'Things that I was there to witness.' Peter's sister Sarah explains that 'The staff made it clear that Lin had no right to forbid anyone to see him, but none of us were going to make anything more difficult given the dreadful circumstances.' The family stayed in the relatives' room; eventually, Lucy, Daisy, Sarah and Elizabeth were invited to sit with Peter's unconscious form for a few brief minutes. The outside world was still labouring under the misapprehension that Peter was no more than 'a bit poorly'. Ciara Parkes made him some special balloons, inscribed with secret satanic messages, and sent them to the ward. George told her, tactfully and untruthfully, that they had festooned Peter's bed in his last days. In fact he was far too ill to receive any presents.

Peter died on Monday 9 January 1995, after a week in Intensive Care. An official statement gave the cause of death as 'gastro-intestinal haemorrhage', a diplomatic attribution in that the haemorrhage was the direct result of severe liver damage. Elsewhere in North London, Spurs had just beaten Arsenal; Rory McGrath sat waiting for the gleeful telephone call that never came. 'Of course,' says McGrath, 'he was dead, and so I can't ever . . . Arsenal v. Spurs has a completely different meaning to me now.' In Majorca, Wendy sensed something terrible had happened, when her watch inexplicably stopped. The man that she later confessed she still 'loved very much' was dead. At the Royal Free, Peter's various distraught relatives thanked the medical staff and returned disconsolately to their homes. 'I was beside myself,' says Lin. 'I couldn't even speak normally. I kept talking in this very strange, high-pitched voice and I couldn't stop. Then suddenly Michael Palin's wife Helen was at my door. She found out where I was and she just turned up – she'd said "Lin mustn't be on her own."'[1] Judy, who found out about Peter's death only through the media, was equally devastated: 'I always half-expected it, that something horrible would happen; and yet when it happened it was such a shock, I felt so sick, shivering and awful. There was a gaping hole that nothing would make right. And I hadn't been there, I hadn't been able to help him. I knew his fear of dying, I'd seen it so clearly, I knew the fear he would have died with.'

The entertainment world greeted the sudden and unexpected news with something approaching horror. At *Private Eye*, Ian Hislop remembers that 'It was Monday morning, it was press day, and Michael Heath came in and said "Cook's dead." And someone said, "Fuck." I mean it was *absolute* disbelief. I don't know why – no reason Cookie should have been immortal, you just assumed he was really.' Richard Ingrams was in tears. Andrew Osmond recalls that 'Everybody was truly grief-stricken, slightly to their own surprise I think – because obviously he wasn't going to make old bones, you know. In a way people had expected him to conk out much sooner, but when he did everybody was shocked and horrified and utterly dismayed.' That week's edition of the magazine was hastily transformed into a special tribute issue.

The early sixties generation of Cambridge comedians found itself equally taken aback. 'I just felt that a big chunk of myself had been taken out,' says John Bird. 'I hadn't rung up Peter and said "What do you think about this?" for ten years, but the feeling of no longer being able to do so really affected me.' Bill Wallis felt numb at first, then suffered delayed shock: 'Two weeks after he died I became very emotional, and felt a great sense of loss, because of what he represented in my life.' According to John Cleese, 'It was the most painful death I've had, worse than Graham Chapman.'[2] Even the Rolling Stones, in their idiosyncratic manner, found Peter's death extremely difficult to come to terms with. Keith Richards tried to explain: 'Peter? You never miss people like Peter, because they're always around. See, he's just not . . . you can't call him up any more, but Peter's always around. He saved our lives on the road many times by cracking us up when we really needed cracking up. Er . . . I'll be seein' ya Pete . . . one dark day.'[3]

Of all Peter's friends and former colleagues, Dudley – naturally – was hit hardest. 'Oh God, the fucker's dead. There's a hole in the universe,'[4] he howled when he heard the news. His first act was to pick up the phone and ring the answering machine in Peter's empty house, thousands of miles away in the middle of the night, just to hear his partner's laconic drawl once more. 'Every now and again I sit up in bed at night, and I think, "God, he's not here, he's not here, he's not here . . ." Then I tell myself, "It's okay, it's okay . . ." and then I go back to sleep. It's been very difficult for me, to adjust to the whole thing.' Alone in his restaurant, his fourth marriage to Nicole Rothschild crumbling, Dudley spoke at length about Peter to the press. He was not entirely complimentary, likening his ex-colleague to a 'beached whale' and referring to the 'law of diminishing returns' that had regulated their work; he lamented his own fading memory and spoke of a time when he would one day forget that he had ever worked with Peter Cook. But Peter had also been his best friend, he declared, a best friend whose absence he felt so desperately keenly in his American exile. 'Who would have thought I would end up going to die in Newport Beach?' he mused, miserably, to the *Daily Telegraph*.

The press apportioned column yards to Peter's death with a kind of horrified relish. Television and radio followed suit. There were celebrity tributes by the bushel-load, offered up to the memory of a performer who was universally acclaimed as the funniest of his generation. Everyone, it seemed, had been Peter's friend, or had awarded themselves that honour in retrospect out of a desperate desire not to be excluded from the general rush to honour his talent. Even Bernard Manning described him as 'a really funny fellow and a great drinking pal',[5] presumably the same Bernard Manning that Peter had once described as 'a fat heap of lard, extremely good at being nasty'.[6] Five days of media mourning were declared by unspoken consent, sincere enough, although as Alan Bennett remarked, 'In the press coverage of his death one could detect a certain satisfaction, the feeling being that he had paid some sort of price for his gifts, had died in the way the press prefer funny men to die, like Hancock and Peter Sellers.'[7] Come Sunday the inevitable backlash occurred, as a result of there being simply nothing left to write. Columnists such as Gilbert Adair confessed themselves 'bemused' by the extent of the coverage of Peter's death, while A. A. Gill wrote obtusely in *The Sunday Times* that 'He was just a bloke who told jokes', arguing that 'being able to make people laugh is a minor gift' (quite where on the gift ladder this put journalists who compose self-consciously controversial newspaper columns was not made entirely clear).

The funeral took place the day before, on Saturday 14 January. Peter had asked to be buried in his parking space, but instead he wound up in St-John-at-Hampstead Parish Churchyard, where he had once joyously taken his daughters skateboarding. The service was an old-fashioned Christian ceremony, based around the Lord's Prayer and *Jerusalem*; a small choir sang Fauré's *Requiem*. Peter's blood relatives joined Lin at the church. Wendy and Judy were not invited, and made no defiant attempts to turn up.

On 1 May 1995, the same church was the venue for a huge memorial service in Peter's honour. Lin, who meticulously and devotedly organised the occasion, had originally wanted to hold it at Westminster Abbey, but finally settled for the cavernous spaces of his local church. A battery of celebrities was invited: Dudley of course, John Cleese, Barry Humphries, Michael Palin, David Frost, Spike Milligan, Willie Rushton, Ian Hislop, Paul Merton, Clive Anderson, Harry Enfield, Ben Elton, Hugh Laurie, Michael Winner, Henry Cooper, Melvyn Bragg, Dave Allen, Richard Ingrams, John Wells, Eleanor Bron, Barry Cryer, Barry Took, Frankie Vaughan, Terry Wogan, Bobby Charlton, Robert Powell, Richard Wilson, David Baddiel, Mel Smith, Griff Rhys Jones, Alan Bennett, Tim Brooke-Taylor, Pierce Brosnan, Jonathan Ross, Auberon Waugh, Ned Sherrin, Terry Jones, Terry Gilliam, Kenny Lynch and many, many others. There were also tickets for the readers of *Private Eye*, and for various school and university acquaintances, their names taken from old programmes and handbills. Peter's daughters Lucy and Daisy, his sisters Sarah and Elizabeth, and his two ex-wives were all pointedly not invited.

Gradually it dawned upon Peter's family, with a sense of mounting dismay, that their names had not been included on the guest list. Daisy approached Sid Gottlieb to see if he could intercede on their behalf, and long and tortuous negotiations followed. Harriet Garland, whose daughter was still close to Peter's daughters, separately contacted Michael Palin to see if he could put in a word. Lin wrote to Sarah to say that 'I am in no mood to give and take, be loving or charitable, or do anything other than as I wish.' Eventually, however, she relented, and invited Lucy, Daisy, Sarah and Elizabeth; the invitations were not extended to Judy or Wendy. Nor were any of the family invitations extended beyond the memorial service itself; there was also a lunch for some sixty people at the Everyman Café afterwards, to which none of them was invited. They lunched instead at La Sorpresa, with Sid Gottlieb.

The memorial service was a huge success, blessed with sunshine. There were readings by Auberon Waugh and Eleanor Bron, and from *The Tibetan Book of Life and Death* by John Cleese. There were personal tributes from Alan Bennett, Richard Ingrams and Sid Gottlieb. The Radley Clerkes, pupils from Peter's old school, sung Elvis Presley's *Love Me Tender*, and

Goodbyee, the latter with Dudley Moore at the piano. The hymns were
To Be a Pilgrim and *Lord of the Dance*, and a recording of E. L. Wisty
was played into the church. The order of service reproduced a tribute
written by Stephen Fry (sadly unable to attend as he had just pulled off
his famous vanishing act), and a potted biography of Peter. His marriages
were summed up with the words: 'Married 1964, 2 daughters. Married
1973. Married Lin, 18 Nov. 1989 (met 1982), 1 step daughter'. Both the
dates given for his first two marriages were incorrect.

All present agreed that the service had been a fitting tribute, although
some scepticism was expressed as to whether Peter would have been able
to take the extravagance seriously. 'He'd have gone off halfway through
this if he were here,'[8] said Spike Milligan. 'He would have left for the
bookmakers,' added Dave Allen. Dudley, who with some degree of irony
was surrounded by a film star's swarm of press and TV crews wherever
he went, was asked what Peter would make of it all if he were looking
down on Hampstead. 'Or looking up,' he snapped. 'Actually, I think he
would have been mildly embarrassed.'[9] David Frost, dissenting, expressed
the opinion that it was all 'wonderful'.[10] The tributes, especially Bennett's,
raised a number of laughs. Only Cleese's Tibetan contribution came in
for any specific criticism: Willie Rushton said that Cleese 'seemed lost,
and proved conclusively that this Care in the Community simply is
not working'.[11] Later, in the book *Something Like Fire*, Cleese described
addressing the service as 'emotionally speaking, a bit like going over the
top at the Somme', and quoted Elizabeth Kubler-Ross's statement that
'there is no need to be afraid of death.'[12] Peter's sister Sarah, reviewing
his efforts for the *Guardian*, responded by quoting E. L. Wisty: 'Isn't it
funny how all the people who say death is nothing to worry about are
all very much alive?'[13] One person hurt by the memorial service was
Rainbow George, who had hoped in vain to be asked to say a few words.
He had only discovered the existence of the post-service lunch when he
had strolled down to the Everyman Café to enquire about booking it for
a similar event. 'I felt such an idiot when they told me, and I realised I
hadn't been invited,' he says. He resolved instead that when he finally
made enough money to stage his Wembley Stadium concert, he would
call it *Liver Aid* in Peter's memory. 'All sorts of people at the service
claimed to have known Peter,' he added. 'I don't think anybody knew
him. I don't think he knew himself.'

Peter's estate was valued at £908,229 net, £1,095,900 gross. Most of
this was tied up in his London and Majorca properties; there was an
overdraft of £130,000 on his current account. His will, dated 10 October
1991 and posted to the executors on 12 January 1995, left the bulk of

his estate to Lin, with one or two significant exceptions. His Majorcan property interests went to Lucy and Daisy; his Lichtenstein-based company Aspera was divided between Judy, his daughters and his sisters; his majority shares in *Private Eye* were left not in the sole care of Lin, but divided three ways between Lin, Sarah and Elizabeth, giving no one overall control of the magazine; and his precious Tiffany lamp was bequeathed to Dudley. He had also taken the decision to appoint two executors, rather than one: Lin and Sarah were jointly named. Lin seemed to Sarah to be upset at one or two items in the will: the Tiffany lamp, she maintained, would have been better bequeathed to John Cleese, who 'hadn't stopped crying for a week since Peter's death.'

Lin requested that Sarah maintain a seemly discretion about the division of Peter's *Eye* shares, as she said she did not wish any publicity. She also asked her brother, Yin Chong, to talk to the magazine's Managing Director. Despite its cheap appearance and £10 prizes to readers, the magazine was swimming with money. According to the most recent accounts at Companies House, the *Eye* had made a pre-tax profit in 1992 of £600,000. It also had £1.5 million on bank deposit, a £1.7 million surplus in the pension fund and a cash mountain in excess of £2.2 million. Peter's original cash injection of £1,500 (about £16,000 in today's money) had exploded in value. Lin and Yin were determined that she should continue to receive an income from the magazine. The *Eye* staff, knowing nothing of the three-way share split, assumed that Lin was their new owner, and proceeded to talk to her on that basis. She made no attempt to inform them of the actual distribution of the shares.

Erroneously believing themselves to be at the beck and call of a new regime, the *Eye* staff acted defiantly. Ian Hislop threatened to resign if the new 'owner' tried to interfere: 'She can try if she likes, but *Private Eye* will continue as before. There may be a change of ownership but it's going to be run from here by the people who run it anyway. We won't be under her.'[14] David Cash added that 'If anyone started messing around with the *Eye*, it could all sort of crumble. It's one of the few totally independent publications around.'[15] Richard Ingrams affixed a sign to the front door of the Carlisle Street offices bearing the words *Private Eye* in Chinese. It was only by sheer coincidence that the *Eye* staff discovered the truth. After Peter's memorial service his sister Sarah was leaving the La Sorpresa restaurant when she spotted Ian Hislop and Paul Merton on the steps of the Everyman Café, on their way out of Lin's post-service lunch. She went across and introduced herself to Hislop as one of *Private Eye*'s new major shareholders. He was both dumbfounded and delighted, and rushed off to phone David Cash with the 'wonderful news'. He later informed the *Daily Mail* that 'No one has control. Peter made sure there was no largest single shareholder, which was presumably deliberate since he wasn't a fool by anyone's imagination.'[16]

For Sarah herself, though, there were one or two unpleasant surprises. She had written to the solicitors requesting information about her *Eye* shareholding on 18 March, and had received no reply; subsequently, on 29 March, Yin Chong had attended the magazine's AGM and had put forward his sister's point of view. Neither Lin, nor Yin, nor the solicitor had informed Sarah or her sister that the meeting was taking place. Worse still, Hislop and Cash had the unpleasant task of explaining to Sarah and Elizabeth that they did not in fact own a third of their brother's shares. Although his will had stipulated that 'all his shares' be divided three ways, the manner in which the document had been drawn up did not take into account a number of *Eye* shares transferred to Peter Cook Productions Ltd on 9 January 1992. This company, worth over a third of a million according to Companies House, was not mentioned in the will and therefore passed entirely to Lin as the major beneficiary. After Peter's death, Lin had produced more documents transferring further *Eye* shares into the company, which were dated September 1994, but which were signed not by him but by herself on his behalf. Neither the 1992 nor 1994 transfer documents had been presented for registration by Peter. The combined effect of these transfers was to leave Lin with over 40 per cent of the shares, and Elizabeth and Sarah just 12 per cent each. Sarah took independent legal advice about the matter; but although she wished to contest the transfer that had not been signed or registered by Peter, neither she nor her sister felt that they had the funds to undergo a protracted legal battle, and so reluctantly bowed to the inevitable. *Private Eye*, at least, remained mathematically independent. 'I would want to continue Peter's policy,' said Sarah, 'which was hands off.'[17] Relations between *Private Eye* and the Chong family remain watchful. Early in 1996 the journalist Tim Satchell founded *The Insider*, a rival to the *Eye*, with financial backing supplied in part by Yin Chong. When *Private Eye* parodied the Bruce Grobbelaar football bungs trial, the Malaysian businessman concerned was renamed 'Yin Cock'.

Further ructions occurred over the valuable Tiffany lamp, once Peter's gift to Wendy, which had become the Maltese Falcon of his life. Sarah became worried about whether or not Dudley had received his bequest, and telephoned him in May 1995, four months after she and Lin had received copies of the will, to ask if it was in his possession; he said that it was not. In Autumn 1995 she wrote to the solicitor to enquire as to when, if ever, Dudley would receive the lamp; a reply came back saying that he would get it in due course 'if it had not been gifted prior to Peter's death'. Sarah replied that as far as she was aware, it had not been gifted in such a manner. This prompted a letter from Lin to her sister-in-law:

> Dear Sarah
> You are the most unpleasant person I have come across in a long time. Currently, you are full of self-importance. You were not particularly close to Peter, however you might like to deceive yourself on this score. You do injustice to his memory: being petty, mean-minded and thinking you are carrying out his wishes whilst doing the reverse by going through them with a toothcomb. He would have been thoroughly ashamed of your actions since his death . . . Please act with dignity. You might further find that people might begin to be drawn to you and you will have more friends in your life than you seem to have at the moment. I had always felt sorry for you because you were a lonely person but you are apparently more wretched than I had suspected . . . Whilst you should be grieving over a person, you are more concerned about things like the Tiffany lamp. Eat your heart out, Dudley gave it to me.
> Yours sincerely
> Lin.

Lin subsequently spoke at length to Dudley Moore's biographer, Barbra Paskin, about her husband's decision to leave the lamp to his former partner:

> 'If Dudley ever doubted Peter loved or cared for him, all his doubts evaporated when he learned this. He was immensely moved, and in a mild state of shock.' Lin expected Dudley to take the lamp back with him to Los Angeles, but a few days later he told her he wanted her to have it. 'In my mind,' she says softly, 'that was his way of showing how much he cared about Peter. Dudley realised how much Peter and I meant to each other, and it was his way of comforting me. There's a wonderful, special continuity about it. The fact that Peter left this most treasured item to Dudley was beautiful. The fact that Dudley gave it back to Peter, through me, was doubly beautiful.'[18]

Lin proved adept at putting her side of the story in public. A number of positive profiles appeared in the newspapers. Lynda Lee-Potter wrote in the *Daily Mail* that:

Fifteen years ago, Peter Cook had a huge stroke of luck when wise, gentle, resolute Lin Chong came into his life . . . Sadly, Lin no longer speaks to her two sisters-in-law. She was bitterly hurt because they took legal advice about the will and the allocation of the *Private Eye* shares which Peter had left to them and Lin. 'They knew that I loved their brother and looked after him and that he loved me very much,' she says, 'so I would have thought they would be caring towards me. I tried to comfort them and then it suddenly went wrong. I thought: "You've got no compassion, no consideration for me, you're just thinking of yourselves".'[19]

The antagonistic division of Peter's estate continued to drag on for well over two years. Sarah wrote to Lin asking for the return of her father's CMG; Lin did not reply. Lin wrote to Margaret Cook's solicitors requesting the return of one of Peter's books that he had left in his mother's house, a signed autobiography of David Frost; this was returned with humorous alacrity, for Peter had only left it there in the first place because he did not actually want it. It was not until May 1997 that Elizabeth and Sarah received their *Private Eye* shares. They, Judy, Lucy and Daisy, never saw anything of Aspera, Peter's Lichtenstein-based company; it has been explained to them that there is no money in it and no accounts to inspect either. Lucy and Daisy decided to sell their Majorcan property, which had fallen into a state of dilapidation; 'Peter had let it crumble over the years,' explains Wendy, 'but he wouldn't ever sell it, as it was a rather nostalgic symbol. Peter wouldn't admit feelings such as nostalgia easily, even to himself, but they were there.' To admit nostalgia, of course, was to admit vulnerability; to disguise it under layers of performance was Peter's normal way. His gesture, though, had unquestionably been a sentimental one.

Adding to the confusion surrounding Peter's legacy, shortly after his death his friend Lawrence Levy claimed to have discussed with him the contents of a later will, less beneficial to Lin than the first, which he personally had witnessed. Unfortunately Levy died of cancer in April 1995, without providing any further details. The person identified by Levy as the other witness, a chartered accountant named Neil Benson, refuses to confirm or deny the story. If the later will existed, it seems that Peter had changed his mind and thrown it away.

A further row subsequently developed between George and Lin over George's cassette collection. He saw his hours of taped conversations with Peter as a means to raise the magic £30,000 that would enable him to launch the Rainbow Party as a national force, and interested BBC Radio 4 in the tapes via a company called Soundbite Productions Ltd. Lin, however, insisted that he had no right to exploit them commercially. A legal letter from Moorhead James, solicitors, landed on George's doormat, insisting that the recordings had been made in 'arrangements of confidence', and threatening him with legal action if he did not give an undertaking to halt publication, and to deliver up the cassettes to Lin or Moorhead James forthwith. 'It's ironic what she's doing,' said George, 'because Peter hated lawyers' (Peter, in fact, kept a framed cheque on his wall because it was the only one he'd ever received *from* a lawyer). Questioned by journalists, George insisted that 'Anyone who walked into my house was made aware the tapes were running. We'd joke about it and say they'd be worth a fortune one day. But it's not good to get on the wrong side of Lin. She was very angry, and told me that Peter found me terribly boring.'[20] George's solicitor David Price wrote back to refute as 'extraordinary' the allegation that any obligations of confidence were involved, and to question Lin's motives. The tennis rally of legal letters cost George £1,419.40, money that he simply did not possess. His telephone was cut off, and he had to resort to phoning LBC from call boxes. He was down to his last £100: optimistic to the last, he put the lot on himself at 500–1 to replace Kevin Keegan as the next manager of Newcastle United.

Lin frequently used the law to defend her corner. She took action against the *Daily Telegraph* and *The Sunday Times* over inaccuracies in articles about her. She also raised the spectre of legal action against the impoverished obsessives who had unilaterally founded the Peter Cook Appreciation Society, shortly after her husband's death. The PCAS had been born when a fan, John Wallis, had written to *Private Eye* enquiring if such a society existed; Ian Hislop had published the enquiry on the *Eye*'s letters page, and five people had written to Wallis asking to join. Feeling bound by this unexpected obligation, Wallis – under the name 'Reg Futtock-Armitage' – set himself the task of publishing a quarterly fanzine dedicated to Peter's humour, for the benefit of all his fellow 'Peterphiles' (geddit). Wallis would undoubtedly have appealed to Peter as the perfect person to administer his fan club. A boisterous Bristolian punk with scarlet hair and a pair of huge pink plasters invariably criss-crossing some drunken wound on the bridge of his nose, he had been fired from his job as a BBC security guard for hurling his hat at his boss in a disrespectful moment. He fronted a rock band called the Pop Stars, so that he could truthfully inform women that he was a Pop Star. He adored every aspect of Peter's humour, especially *Not Only . . . But Also*. His fanzine, *Publish and Bedazzled*, with a circulation of fifty copies, was a collection of photocopied sheets stapled together that jubilantly reflected the spirit of its author.

Relations between Lin and the PCAS were relatively cordial to begin with. Wallis wrote to seek her approval, and after a few months she replied in the affirmative, the caveat being that there should be no personal financial gain involved for him. His fanzine, she thought, could perhaps be made less smutty. He subsequently organised the first annual meeting of the society at the Everyman Cinema, and hired Elvis Chan ('The original Chinese Elvis') as the star turn. Some eighty people attended, including Rainbow George and Peter's sister Sarah, who drew the winning tickets in the society's raffle. A huge number of famous people were invited, along the lines of the glut of celebrities that had attended Peter's memorial service, but not one of them turned up.

Following that event, relations between Lin and Wallis deteriorated. She telephoned him to point out that he was photocopying jokes, scripts and photographs without permission from the copyright holders, and that if any of them became aware of these infringements and chose to pursue the matter in court, it could cost him a fortune. Even the name Peter Cook, she pointed out, was copyright in certain circumstances. Wallis conceived the futile plan of drawing a wig and false breasts on every photograph in the magazine, and renaming his creation 'The Rita Cook Appreciation Society'.

On 16 July 1996 the brief blaze of John Wallis's life came to an end, when he was found dead after seriously overindulging at a party the night before. He was just twenty-six years and two days old, and had departed life like his idol. Lin telephoned his colleague Paul Hamilton to suggest that it was an appropriate moment to close down the society. Hamilton, a central London postman, chose instead to keep the PCAS going in Wallis's memory. At the time of writing an uneasy truce exists between Peter's widow and the society. Lin briefly attended the 1997 meeting of the PCAS, a pleasantly ragged variety event at the ICA starring John Cooper Clarke and The Bastard Son of Tommy Cooper.

Lin herself attempted to mount a more substantial memorial show, and asked Belinda Harley, Ned Sherrin and Neil Shand to help her out. The event was originally planned for the Royal Festival Hall in April 1996, on a date which was later found to coincide with that of the BAFTA awards; it was then rescheduled to take place in September 1996. Bizarrely, the show was advertised in the press without any information about how to purchase tickets. The proceeds were intended to go to the Cambridge Footlights, which body decided to name a room after Peter in return. Even more bizarrely, the Footlights committee telephoned Ian Hislop to ask him which room they should name; 'The bar, of course,' he replied. When she heard of the society's alcoholic intentions Lin decided that the money should not go to them after all, and the project collapsed. America saw rather slicker memorial events: Dudley hosted *Bedazzling!*, a Hollywood tribute evening featuring a screening of *Bedazzled*, while the MetroStage Theater outside Washington, DC mounted a revival of *Good Evening* with a substitute cast. In the UK there was a further attempt to raise money in Peter's name: Pembroke, his old Cambridge college, appointed Tim Harrold to try to collect £250,000 for a variety of charitable causes, and announced that Peter's old room would be officially named after him.

Perhaps Lin's most successful commemorative achievement was *Something Like Fire*, a collection of mainly celebrity reminiscences about Peter edited by herself. It was packed with entertaining memories, although there was hardly any mention of Peter's parents, his family, his first two marriages, his children or *Private Eye* magazine. Following Lin's difficulties with the *Eye*, Richard Ingrams's name was retrospectively edited out of the list of speakers at the memorial service printed in the book. In many respects *Something Like Fire* served as a manifesto for Peter's third marriage, an affirmation of the strength of the bonds that tied him to Lin. As editor, Lin was proud rather than embarrassed to include unstinting praise of herself: 'She was gentle but also resolute and strong. Lucky old Peter – but men like him merit the fortune and the fair following wind that carries a Lin to them' (Nicholas Luard); 'Lin did as much as any loving human being could have done' (John Wells); 'He was lucky enough to earn the love of a good, kind woman' (Stephen Fry); 'She was his wife and chief supporter' (Adrian Slade); 'When Peter introduced Lin to me, I was bowled over' (Lewis Morley).

Lin publicised the book proudly, defending her corner as ever, talking freely about Wendy ('Peter told me that he didn't love his first wife') and Judy. 'After Peter died,' she informed the *Daily Mail*, 'one of the wives said I was his nurse, another said I was his housekeeper. I was so hurt by that.' In fact this was a double misunderstanding: Wendy had said that Lin had 'nursed' Peter through his illness, and Peter himself had lied to Judy that Lin was no more than his housekeeper. 'If being a good wife and loving Peter means being a nursemaid and a housekeeper, then I'm proud of that,' Lin continued. 'I loved the guy. If his wives couldn't cope with him then it's to their discredit. They failed him as wives but were happy to take the alimony.'[21] She noted that 'The divorce judge awarded Judy £480,000 for leaving him four years before I even met him.'[22] In fact, Judy had moved to Exmoor just one year before he had first encountered Lin at Stocks, and the judge had awarded her less than half that sum.

By this time, Lin had sadly fallen out with most of those whom Peter had lived with throughout his life: her understandable emotional possessiveness, where it took the form of commercial possessiveness, had aroused a great many suspicions. There is no question, however, that her devotion to her late husband was fierce and unquestioning; this was no cunning plot to accumulate a large sum of money. Laboriously, she sprayed every piece of graffito on the living-room wall of Perrin's Walk with fixative, in order to preserve it for posterity. A squashed fly, for instance, marked with the legend 'Fly'; and the word 'Virgin', accompanied by a trail of arrows leading round the corner to the scrawled remark: 'Not much chance here, mate. Try no. 23'. On one occasion, George emerged from his house to find Lin weeping in Perrin's Walk. Peter's favourite goldfish had died, and she was gripped by paroxysms of guilt and sorrow. 'I managed to convince her, I think, that the goldfish had wanted to be with Peter,' says George somewhat shamefacedly.

Whenever she spoke to journalists about her late husband, Lin referred to Peter in the present tense, as if he was still alive. It was extremely important to her, in all her dealings, to prove that she was the wife whose company Peter had needed the most, that she was the one who could fathom him best. When she wrote in *Something Like Fire* that 'Tottenham Hotspurs' was 'a team Peter was reputed to support', it was out of a desperate desire to be included, to show that she understood his life. She alone, she felt, had been able to make him truly happy. She wrote also of 'the private Peter Cook, my husband, calm, contented and happy in his home and especially his garden, whom no one, no journalist, no friend, no family member really knew. Only me, because I was his wife.' Happiness, explained Lynda Lee-Potter of the *Mail* in her profile of Lin, had finally arrived on Peter's doorstep in his last few years; his last Christmas on earth had been a happy one. 'Peter was a contented person', insisted Lin to the *Hampstead and Highgate Express*. Nicholas Luard, who had become one of Lin's greatest allies, wrote in *Something Like Fire* that 'Peter looked deep, deep and far and often sideways, and he saw and chuckled . . . Peter poured himself another vodka and laughed. The man died happy'. This was, by any stretch of the imagination, a quite extraordinary assertion. Peter may not have enjoyed discussing his personal happiness (one journalist wrote that 'To talk to him about it is to see the feelers of a giant shellfish withdraw to the safety of their protective crust'), but the idea that his reticence concealed a boundless supply of the stuff is hard to swallow. Peter's happiness level had its ups and downs like anyone else's, but he found the downs desperately difficult to cope with, especially the one that held him in its vice-like grip in the last months of his life.

Lin pointed defiantly to Peter's work-in-progress list: his stage show with Eleanor Bron, the possibility of him writing his autobiography, or of doing another *Clive Anderson Talks Back*. 'If you look at the Clive

Anderson show Peter looked very slim, he was wearing jeans and looked very handsome,'[23] she stressed. 'What made Peter's death so sad,' claimed Eleanor Bron, 'was that he was in such a creative period.'[24] But with the exception of the autobiography, first mooted many years previously but never pursued, these were all projects from 1993. Peter died in 1995. His last creative wave had subsided in the year before his death, just as its predecessors in 1979–81 and 1987 had faded away. Peter's whole life was littered with such unfinished ideas and projects, each studded with tantalising details. In *The Sunday Times*, John Lloyd listed some of the half-finished notions in his possession:

> There are limitations to the human mind . . . as this series will prove.
> Tragically, I was an only twin.
> Pulsars are small and immensely heavy and remind me strangely of my first wife.
> I'm sorry, M'lud, but I am unable to continue without an injection of nerve gas.

Not to mention sabre-tooth giraffes, the Burberry apes, the False Passport Office, clay stag-hunting, and living in Sherwood Forest with a band of in-laws; the last one, of course, being an old joke from *Goodbye Again*.

The debate over Peter's future potential was however utterly eclipsed in the newspapers and on radio and television by an exhaustive debate about his past potential, and whether or not he had managed to fulfil it. Some, like Christopher Booker, spoke of 'that lack of a master thread to his career which left such a sense of unfulfilled promise.'[25] Stephen Fry retorted on *The Late Show* by attacking such 'silly, ignorant nonsense . . . What does that mean? That his potential would have been realised by appearing in more Hollywood films or in having a regular prime-time TV show? Why commentators have to write and talk about extraordinary people as if they are composing school reports is beyond me.' Booker, of course, was not referring to a conventional career progression of the kind that Peter had unsuccessfully attempted to follow from the late 1960s until the early 1980s. He and others like him were reaching out for something they could not describe, because they did not know themselves what it comprised: something new, original and ground-breaking that a sober Peter might have come up with in later life, like the best of his early work. Barry Humphries felt that 'If Peter had managed to stop drinking he would have been a thousand times funnier, and right now he would have been absolutely at the height of his powers.' Richard Ingrams agreed that 'He never really did the things that he was capable of, in my view. Although you could say that what he did do was very brilliant, it was only a part of what he might have done.' It is not appropriate, though, to separate Peter's talent from his propensity to self-destruction in this manner: the two were inextricably bound by circumstance, if not by genetic make-up. Michael Parkinson compares Peter to George Best: 'For that brief moment in their careers they burned so brightly, didn't they. You wonder – is that what they were born to do?' Peter was always on target to hit his own personal ceiling far too fast for his own good, leaving him nowhere to go but downwards in mood. 'If I start feeling tremendously gloomy, I may look back and say yes, it was because I was successful too early,'[26] he once confessed.

Perhaps the most concisely accurate contribution to the debate was that made by Jonathan Ross: 'It's such a shame that Peter didn't get around to writing his own tributes – if he had, then we wouldn't have had to suffer halfwits and dunderheads prattling on about how he never fulfilled his youthful potential. Of course he fulfilled it, he fulfilled it when he was still young.'[27] (The author of this book, incidentally, was among those halfwits and dunderheads who spoke without thinking that week.) Although Peter couldn't indeed write his own tributes, he had offered his own opinion on this very subject just before his death, when Alan Titchmarsh had suggested on BBC 1's *Pebble Mill* that his potential remained unfulfilled. 'I'd certainly agree with you on that,' Peter had replied. 'I've never attempted to achieve my potential. What could be worse than achieving your potential so early in life?'

Most of the tributes published on Peter's death painted him either as the last great amateur (a description he had found flattering in life), restrained solely by his Olympian lack of drive who could easily have conquered the world again, whenever he liked, if only he'd set his lazy mind to it; or as a forlorn, hopeless drunk, no longer capable of focusing on a career direction. There was precious little room for complexities. Dudley, who was given space to reflect, remained as confused by his former partner as ever. 'Peter went to his grave as mysteriously as he came out of it,' he told the BBC's *Omnibus* programme. Perhaps the most ingenious summing-up of his life came from Alan Bennett in the *London Review of Books*:

> One thinks of one of the stock characters in an old-fashioned Western ... the doctor who's always to be found in the saloon and whose allegiance is never quite plain. Seldom sober, he is cleverer than most of the people he associates with, spending his time playing cards with the baddies but taking no sides. Still, when

the chips are down, and slightly to his own surprise, he does the right thing. But there is never any suggestion that, having risen to the occasion, he is going to mend his ways in any permanent fashion. He goes on much as ever down the path to self-destruction, knowing that redemption is not for him – and it is this that redeems him. As for us, his audience, we are comforted by the assurance that there is a truer morality than the demands of convention, that this is a figure from the parables, a publican, a sinner but never a pharisee. In him morality is discovered far from its official haunts, the message of a character like Peter's being that a life of complete self-indulgence, if led with the whole heart, may also bring wisdom.[28]

One might, perhaps, quibble with the last line: the message of a character like Peter's being that too much wisdom (too much awareness of one's own talent and one's own limitations) may also bring a life of complete self-indulgence.

Most of the obituarists, of course, mentioned Peter's colossal influence on British comedy, from Monty Python through Smith and Jones right up to Harry Enfield, whose Self-Righteous Brothers enjoy superior and imaginary altercations with celebrities in the manner of the first ever Pete and Dud sketch. Peter would probably have enjoyed the journalist Ed Porter's assertion that he was 'the Elvis of modern British comedy: he did much to invent it, grew bloated on hedonism, he made some dreadful films presumably for good money, and he died too young. But he won't be forgotten.' Peter himself always decried the power of comedy, and especially satire, to influence anything except the work of other comedians; but as John Bird pointed out, 'The funny thing is that, despite himself, he actually did change the world.'[29] Which, let's face it, is more than he could ever have achieved at the Foreign Office.

Postscript

In 1997, Rainbow George finally inherited £30,000 from his mother and decided to spend the entire sum on securing a party political broadcast, which would alert millions of potential voters and sweep the Rainbow Party to victory at the polls. To qualify for a broadcast, his party was required to field fifty candidates; he advertised for kindred spirits, and gave the fifty successful applicants £500 each to use as their deposit. Nineteen of them absconded with the money and were never seen again. The broadcast was cancelled by the BBC as a result.

At about the same time, Dudley Moore returned to England to find work. He finally secured the role of Buttons, in *Cinderella* at the Mayflower Theatre in Southampton.

David Frost remains hugely successful on both sides of the Atlantic.

Notes

All sources are given as accurately as possible. Where information is missing (specifically unidentified or undated newspaper cuttings), that information could not be provided by the library which supplied the cuttings.

Chapter 1 Raised by Goats: Early Life, 1937–51

1. *The Malay Mail*, 12 May 1914.
2. John Hind, *Comic Inquisition*.
3. *Radio Times*, 23 December 1978.
4. *Sunday People*, 4 January 1968.
5. *Person to Person*, BBC TV, 1979.
6. John Hind, *Comic Inquisition*.
7. *Daily Mail*, 14 November 1992.
8. *News of the World*, 29 May 1966.
9. John Hind, *Comic Inquisition*.
10. Ibid.
11. *A Life In Pieces*, TalkBack for BBC 2, 1990.

Chapter 2 I'm Much Bigger Than You Are, Sir: Radley and Abroad, 1951–57

1. Jonathan Harlow, 'Peter Cook's Schooldays', in *Something Like Fire*, ed. Lin Cook.
2. *Harpers & Queen*, December 1989; *Person to Person*, BBC TV, 1979; John Hind, *Comic Inquisition*.
3. *Parkinson*, BBC 1, 1977.
4. Ibid.

5. Ibid.; Decca promotional material, July 1965.
6. John Hind, *Comic Inquisition*; Roger Wilmut, *From Fringe to Flying Circus*.
7. Jonathan Harlow 'Peter Cook's Schooldays', in *Something Like Fire*, ed. Lin Cook.
8. *Cook's Tour*, BBC Radio 4, 1995; *Person to Person*, BBC TV, 1979.
9. *The Radleian*, 1995.
10. Jonathan Harlow, 'Peter Cook's Schooldays', in *Something Like Fire*, ed. Lin Cook.
11. Michael Bawtree, 'Black & White Blues', in *Something Like Fire*, ed. Lin Cook.
12. *Harpers & Queen*, December 1989.
13. *Person to Person*, BBC TV, 1979.
14. *Daily Mail*, 5 September 1977.
15. Unidentified press cutting, 1966 or 1967.
16. *Russell Harty*, LWT, 9 October 1975.
17. *Daily Mail*, 5 September 1977.
18. *The Radleian*, 1995.
19. Roger Wilmut, *From Fringe to Flying Circus*.
20. John Hind, *Comic Inquisition*.
21. *Person to Person*, BBC TV, 1979.
22. John Hind, *Comic Inquisition*.
23. *A Life in Pieces*, TalkBack for BBC 2, 1990.
24. *The Radleian*, 1995.
25. John Stow, *In Africa and the Caribbean*.
26. *Parkinson*, BBC 1, 1975.
27. Decca promotional material, July 1965.
28. *The Times*, 27 February 1987; The *Sun*, 28 October 1989.
29. Roger Wilmut, *From Fringe to Flying Circus*.
30. John Hind, *Comic Inquisition*.

Chapter 3 I Could Have Been a Judge: Cambridge, 1957–60

1. Roger Wilmut, *From Fringe to Flying Circus*.
2. *Daily Mail*, 12 November 1994; *Independent*, 14 December 1993.
3. *Sunday People*, 4 February 1968.
4. *News of the World*, 29 May 1966.
5. Adrian Slade, 'Thirty-Seven Years a Very Rare Friend', in *Something Like Fire*, ed. Lin Cook.
6. Ibid.
7. Ibid.
8. *Radio Times*, 1 June 1976.
9. *Cook's Tour*, BBC Radio 4, 1995.
10. Alan Bennett, 'Thoughts and Afterthoughts', in *Something Like Fire*, ed. Lin Cook.
11. Eleanor Bron, 'Peter', in *Something Like Fire*, ed. Lin Cook.
12. Unidentified press cutting, January 1959.

13. Unidentified press cutting, March 1959.
14. Ronald Bergan, *Beyond the Fringe . . . And Beyond.*
15. *Friday Night Saturday Morning*, BBC TV, 16 November 1979.
16. Roger Law, *A Nasty Piece of Work.*
17. *Harpers & Queen*, December 1989; *Sun* 29 September 1965.
18. *Cook's Tour*, BBC Radio 4, 1995.
19. *Manchester Guardian*, 10 June 1959.
20. *Daily Mail*, 12 November 1994.
21. Roger Wilmut, *From Fringe to Flying Circus.*
22. Ibid.
23. Ronald Bergan, *Beyond the Fringe . . . And Beyond.*
24. Peter Bellwood, 'The Seven Wild Strawberries are Flying', in *Something Like Fire*, ed. Lin Cook.
25. *Guardian*, 10 January 1995.
26. *Person to Person*, BBC TV, 1979.
27. *Beyond the Fringe*, Introduction by Michael Frayn.
28. Ronald Bergan, *Beyond The Fringe . . . And Beyond.*
29. *Daily Mail*, 28 September 1996.
30. *Junkin's Jokers*, BBC Radio 2, 19 October 1993.
31. Paul Donovan, *Dudley Moore.*
32. *QED*, BBC TV, 1990.
33. Ibid.
34. Ibid.
35. *The Late Clive James*, ITV, 22 June 1985.
36. In part from the *Daily Mail*, 10 January 1995.
37. *Person to Person*, BBC TV, 1979.

Chapter 4 So That's the Way You Like It: Beyond the Fringe, 1960–62

1. Roger Wilmut, *From Fringe to Flying Circus.*
2. *Sun*, 28 October 1989.
3. Roger Wilmut, *From Fringe to Flying Circus.*
4. Christopher Hitchens and Dudley Moore, 'The Other Half of the Sketch', in *Something Like Fire*, ed. Lin Cook.
5. Ronald Bergan, *Beyond the Fringe . . . And Beyond.*
6. Ibid.
7. *Guardian*, 10 January 1995.
8. Ronald Bergan, *Beyond the Fringe . . . And Beyond.*
9. Ibid.
10. *Harpers & Queen*, December 1989.
11. *Independent*, 10 January 1995.
12. Barbra Paskin, *Dudley Moore.*
13. Unmarked press cutting, January 1995.
14. Ronald Bergan, *Beyond the Fringe . . . And Beyond*; unidentified press cutting 1967; *Independent*, 14 December 1993.
15. *Junkin's Jokers*, BBC Radio 2, 19 October 1993.

16. Roger Wilmut, *From Fringe to Flying Circus*.
17. *Edinburgh Evening News*, 25 August 1960.
18. John Wells, 'The Mystic Spube', in *Something Like Fire*, ed. Lin Cook.
19. *Spectator*, 2 November 1996.
20. *London Review of Books*, 25 June 1995.
21. Alan Bennett, 'Postscript', in *The Complete Beyond the Fringe*, ed. Roger Wilmut.
22. Graham Chapman, *A Liar's Autobiography*.
23. *Granta*, 15 October 1960.
24. *The New Yorker*, 23 January 1995.
25. Eric Idle, 'The Funniest Man in the World', in *Something Like Fire*, ed. Lin Cook.
26. *Pembroke College Annual Gazette*, 1995.
27. Roger Wilmut, *From Fringe to Flying Circus*.
28. Paul Donovan, *Dudley*.
29. Ronald Bergan, *Beyond the Fringe . . . And Beyond*.
30. *Vanity Fair*, December 1995.
31. Michael Palin, 'I Had That Peter Cook in the Back of My Car', in *Something Like Fire*, ed. Lin Cook.
32. *Daily Mail*, 6 April 1961.
33. *Observer*, 1 October 1961.
34. Roger Wilmut, *From Fringe to Flying Circus*.
35. Ibid.
36. Ibid.
37. *The New Yorker*, 23 January 1995.
38. Ibid.
39. Roger Wilmut, *From Fringe to Flying Circus*.
40. *Observer*, 14 May 1961.
41. *Sunday Times*, 14 May 1961.
43. *Newsnight*, BBC 2 9 January 1995.
44. *Sunday Pictorial*, 18 February 1962.
45. Roger Wilmut, *From Fringe to Flying Circus*.
46. *Daily Mail*, 1 March 1962.
47. *Mavis Catches up with Peter Cook and Dudley Moore*, ITV, 22 November 1989.
48. *Sunday Express*, 15 January 1995.
49. *Daily Mail*, 24 November 1977.
50. *London Review of Books*, 25 May 1995.
51. Christopher Hitchens and Dudley Moore, 'The Other Half of the Sketch', in *Something Like Fire*, ed. Lin Cook.
52. *London Review of Books*, 25 May 1995.

Chapter 5 Sorry, Sir, There Is a £5 Waiting List: The Establishment Club, 1961–62

1. *Person to Person*, BBC TV, 1979.

2. *Observer*, 23 July 1961.
3. In part from *Evening Standard*, 10 January 1995.
4. *Friday Night Saturday Morning*, BBC TV 16 November 1979.
5. John Bird, 'Impresario', in *Something Like Fire*, ed. Lin Cook.
6. Promotional material, December 1961.
7. *Daily Express*, 5 October 1961.
8. *Observer*, 1 October 1961.
9. Roger Wilmut, *From Fringe to Flying Circus*.
10. *Daily Express*, 5 October 1961.
11. John Bird, 'Impresario', in *Something Like Fire*, ed. Lin Cook.
12. Barry Humphries, *More Please*.
    N.B. Humphries' autobiography places this evening subsequent to Peter offering him a slot at the club, but this cannot be the case. Peter and the regular cast had gone to America when the offer was made, and the cast did not return until Peter had left the club, after Humphries' engagement was finished.
13. Nicholas Luard, 'The Man Who Lit a Bonfire', in *Something Like Fire*, ed. Lin Cook.
14. Roger Wilmut, *From Fringe to Flying Circus*.
15. *Observer*, 14 January 1962.
16. Ronald Bergan, *Beyond The Fringe . . . And Beyond*.
17. *Person to Person*, BBC TV, 1979.
18. *Friday Night Saturday Morning*, BBC TV 16 November 1979.
19. *Cook's Tour*, BBC Radio 4, 2 January 1996.
20. Ibid.
21. Elisabeth Luard, 'To Pin A Butterfly', in *Something Like Fire*, ed. Lin Cook.
22. *Daily Mail*, 2 March 1962.
23. Roger Wilmut, *From Fringe to Flying Circus*.

Chapter 6 Heaving Thighs Across Manhattan: America 1962–64

1. *Manchester Guardian*, 30 October 1962.
2. Roger Wilmut, *From Fringe to Flying Circus*.
3. Alan Bennett, 'Thoughts and Afterthoughts', in *Something Like Fire*, ed. Lin Cook.
4. Ibid.
5. Ibid.
6. Barry Humphries, 'A Recollection', in *Something Like Fire*, ed. Lin Cook.
7. Gavin Young, *Observer*, 27 January 1963.
8. Christopher Hitchens and Joseph Heller, 'Heller's Version', in *Something Like Fire*, ed. Lin Cook.
9. *Daily Mail*, 10 January 1995.
10. *Vanity Fair*, December 1995.
11. *Sunday Times*, 19 July 1964.
12. *Varsity*, 12 October 1963.
13. John Bird, 'Impresario', in *Something Like Fire*, ed. Lin Cook.
14. *Varsity*, 12 October 1963.

15. Nicholas Luard, 'The Man Who Lit a bonfire', in *Something Like Fire*, ed. Lin Cook.
16. *Sunday Times*, 6 July 1969.
17. *Daily Mail*, 24 September 1963.
18. John Bird, 'Impresario', in *Something Like Fire*, ed. Lin Cook.
19. *Person to Person*, BBC TV, 1979.
20. *The Times*, 3 November 1973.
21. *Parkinson*, BBC TV, 1972.
22. Ronald Bergan, *Beyond The Fringe . . . And Beyond*.
23. Patrick Marnham, *The Private Eye Story*.
24. *Evening Standard*, 9 May 1968.
25. *Evening News*, 16 April 1964.
26. *Varsity*, 12 October 1963.
27. *Parkinson*, BBC TV, 1977.
28. *Sunday Mirror*, 22 August 1965.
29. *Daily Mail*, 20 April 1964.
30. *Sunday Times*, 31 October 1965.
31. Decca promotional material, July 1965.
32. Roger Wilmut, *From Fringe to Flying Circus*.

Chapter 7 The Seductive Brethren: Private Eye, 1964–70

1. John Wells, 'The Mystic Spube', in *Something Like Fire*, ed. Lin Cook.
2. Victor Lownes, 'Waiting in Line', in *Something Like Fire*, ed. Lin Cook.
3. In part from the *Guardian*, 10 January 1995.
4. Nicholas Luard, 'The Man Who Lit a Bonfire', in *Something Like Fire*, ed. Lin Cook.
5. *Evening Standard*, 9 May 1968.
6. *Daily Mail*, 12 November 1994.
7. *Person to Person*, BBC TV, 1979.
8. Auberon Waugh, *Will This Do?*
9. Richard Ingrams, *The Life and Times of Private Eye*.
10. *Woman's Own*, 1967.
11. *Evening Standard*, 9 May 1968.
12. John Wells, 'The Mystic Spube', in *Something Like Fire*, ed. Lin Cook.
13. Ibid.
14. *Evening News*, 6 February 1969.
15. *Observer*, 21 March 1965.
16. John Wells, 'The Mystic Spube', in *Something Like Fire*, ed. Lin Cook.
17. *The New Yorker*, 23 January 1995.
18. *Evening Standard*, 9 May 1968.

Chapter 8 We're Always Ready to be Jolted Out: Pete and Dud, 1964–67

1. *Daily Express*, 7 February 1967; *Radio Times*, 1977.
2. *Daily Express*, 7 February 1967.

3. Ibid.
4. *Sun*, 1 March 1965.
5. Roger Wilmut, *From Fringe to Flying Circus*.
6. *Daily Mail*, 6 April 1965.
7. *Time Out*, 30 January 1991.
8. Channel 4 News, 9 January 1995.
9. Christopher Hitchens and Dudley Moore, 'The Other Half of the Sketch', in *Something Like Fire*, ed. Lin Cook.
10. Roger Wilmut, *From Fringe to Flying Circus*.
11. *Daily Express*, 10 January 95.
12. Joseph McGrath, 'Not only Dudley Moore but also Peter Cook', in *Something Like Fire*, ed. Lin Cook.
13. *Daily Mail*, 6 April 1965.
14. Ronald Bergan, *Beyond the Fringe . . . And Beyond*.
15. *Wogan*, BBC TV 29 October 1990.
16. *Sunday Times*, 31 October 1965.
17. *Funny Business*, BBC TV, 6 December 1992.
18. *Daily Express*, 10 January 1995.
19. John Hind, *Comic Inquisition*; *Radio Times*, 1977.
20. Ronald Bergan, *Beyond the Fringe . . . And Beyond*.
21. *TV Times*, February 1967.
22. *Evening Standard*, 10 January 1995.
23. *Junkin's Jokers*, BBC Radio 2, 19 October 1993.
24. *Daily Mail*, 12 November 1994.
25. *TV Times*, 18 November 1989.
26. *Daily Mail*, 6 April 1965.
27. *The Times*, 13 March 1965.
28. *Sun*, 1 March 1965.
29. *Daily Mail*, 28 February 1966.
30. *Sunday Times*, 31 October 1965.
31. *Daily Mirror*, 14 December 1970.
32. *News of the World*, 10 September 1967.
33. *Sun*, 1 March 1965.
34. *Sunday Times*, 31 October 1965.
35. Paul Donovan, *Dudley Moore*.
36. Ibid.
37. *Sunday Times*, 31 October 1965.
38. *Sun*, 29 September 1965.
39. Paul Donovan, *Dudley Moore*.
40. *Daily Express*, 10 January 1995.
41. *News of the World*, 29 May 1966.
42. *Daily Mail*, 12 November 1994.
43. *Daily Express*, 25 November 1967.
44. *Daily Mail*, 12 July 1966.
45. *Funny Business*, BBC TV, 6 December 1992.
46. *Daily Mail*, 21 December 1967.

47. Christopher Hitchens and Dudley Moore, 'The Other Half of the Sketch' in *Something Like Fire*, ed. Lin Cook.
48. Roger Wilmut, *From Fringe to Flying Circus*.
49. Eleanor Bron, 'Peter', in *Something like Fire*, ed. Lin Cook.
50. *Funny Business*, BBC TV, 6 December 1992.
51. *Blitz*, March 1987.

Chapter 9 Nice Though This Be I Seek Yet Further Kicks: Family Life, 1964–71

1. Unidentified press cutting, 1993.
2. *Evening News*, 2 February 1967.
3. *Evening Standard*, 9 May 1968.
4. Nicholas Luard, 'The Man Who Lit A Bonfire', in *Something Like Fire*, ed. Lin Cook.
5. Jay Landesman, *Jaywalking*.
6. Elisabeth Luard, 'To Pin A Butterfly', in *Something Like Fire*, ed. Lin Cook.
7. *The New Yorker*, 23 January 1995.
8. *Sun*, 29 September 1965.
9. In part from Jay Landesman, *Jaywalking*.
10. *Daily Mail*, 12 November 1994.
11. Eleanor Bron, 'Peter', in *Something Like Fire*, ed. Lin Cook.
12. *Daily Mail*, 28 September 1996.
13. Graham Lord, *Just The One – The Wives and Times of Jeffrey Bernard*.
14. *Sunday Express*, 14 January 1968.
15. *Daily Mail*, 24 November 1977.
16. Ibid.
17. Ibid.
18. Ibid.
19. Ibid.
20. Ibid.
21. *Daily Mail*, 28 September 1996.
22. *Daily Mail*, 12 November 1994.
23. *News of the World*, 13 November 1970.
24. *Evening Standard*, 31 October 1970.

Chapter 10 Learning to Fly Underwater: Pete and Dud, 1968–71

1. *Evening Standard*, 9 May 1968.
2. *News of the World*, 10 September 1967.
3. *Daily Express*, 25 November 1967.
4. Roger Wilmut, *From Fringe to Flying Circus*.
5. *Daily Mirror*, 22 August 1980.
6. Douglas Thompson, *Dudley Moore*.
7. *Success Story*, BBC TV, 27 May 1974.
8. *Daily Mail*, 26 August 1968.

9. *Daily Sketch*, 19 August 1968.
10. *Evening Standard*, 31 October 1970.
11. Ronald Bergan, *Beyond the Fringe . . . And Beyond*.
12. Unidentified press cutting, 1970.
13. Roger Wilmut, *From Fringe to Flying Circus*.
14. Douglas Thompson, *Dudley Moore*.
15. Christopher Hitchens and Dudley Moore, 'The Other Half of the Sketch', in *Something Like Fire*, ed. Lin Cook.
16. *The Times*, 3 November 1973.
17. *Daily Mail*, 19 February 1970.
18. *The Times*, 18 November 1972.
19. *The New Yorker*, 23 January 1995.
20. Ibid.
21. Ronald Bergan, *Beyond the Fringe . . . And Beyond*.
22. *Daily Mail*, 10 November 1970.
23. *Liverpool Echo*, 14 November 1970.
24. *Evening Standard*, 9 May 1968.
25. *Radio Times*, 13 February 1971.
26. *Russell Harty*, LWT, 9 October 1975.
27. Ronald Bergan, *Beyond the Fringe . . . And Beyond*.
28. *Evening Standard*, 31 October 1970.
29. *Publish and Bedazzled*, No. 6.
30. *The Times*, 20 February 1971.
31. *Daily Telegraph*, 14 March 1971.
32. *Daily Mail*, 8 March 1971.
33. *Daily Telegraph*, 14 March 1971.
34. *Russell Harty*, 9 October 1975.
35. *Friday Night Saturday Morning*, BBC TV, 16 November 1979.
36. *Illustrated London News*, 1988.
37. *Publish and Bedazzled*, No. 6.
38. Douglas Thompson, *Dudley Moore*.

Chapter 11 3-D Lobster: The Humour of Peter Cook

1. *The New Yorker*, 23 January 1995.
2. *Sun*, 4 April 1970.
3. *Evening Standard*, 9 May 1968.
4. John Wells, 'The Mystic Spube', in *Something Like Fire*, ed. Lin Cook.
5. *Daily Mail*, 10 January 1995.
6. Christopher Hitchens and Dudley Moore, 'The Other Half of the Sketch', in *Something Like Fire*, ed. Lin Cook.
7. *Daily Mail*, 12 November 1994.
8. *Omnibus*, BBC TV, 19 December 1995.
9. *Cook's Tour*, BBC Radio 4, 26 December 1995.
10. *Harpers & Queen*, December 1989.
11. *Independent*, 2 October 1995.

12. *Publish and Bedazzled*, No. 8.
13. Nicholas Luard, 'The Man Who Lit A Bonfire', in *Something Like Fire*, ed. Lin Cook.
14. John Hind, *Comic Inquisition*.
15. Adrian Slade, 'Peter Cook: Thirty Seven Years a Very Rare Friend', in *Something Like Fire*, ed. Lin Cook.
16. In part from the *Guardian*, 10 January 1995.
17. *London Review of Books*, 25 May 1995.
18. *Morning Star*, 4 June 1966.
19. *Independent*, 10 January 1995.
20. *Guardian*, 10 January 1995.
21. Alan Bennett, 'Thoughts and Afterthoughts' in *Something Like Fire*, ed. Lin Cook.
22. *Illustrated London News*, December 1988.
23. *Sun*, 29 September 1965.
24. *Sun*, 4 April 1970.
25. Douglas Thompson, *Dudley Moore*.
26. Ronald Bergan, *Beyond the Fringe . . . And Beyond*.
27. *Person to Person*, BBC TV, 1979.
28. *Friday Night Saturday Morning*, BBC TV 16 December 1979.
29. Kay Redfield Jamison, *An Unquiet Mind*.
30. Oliver Sacks, *Excesses*.

Chapter 12 I Can't Talk Now, 'Cos He's Here: Behind the Fringe, 1971–75

1. *The Times*, 18 November 1972.
2. Shane Maloney, 'Hanging out at Hanging Rock', in *Something Like Fire*, ed. Lin Cook.
3. Barbra Paskin, *Dudley Moore*.
4. Lewis Morley, 'The Wings of Change', in *Something Like Fire*, ed. Lin Cook.
5. *Sun*, 7 July 1988.
8. Evening Standard, 25 February 1972.
9. Barbra Paskin, *Dudley Moore*.
10. *Sunday Express*, 15 January 1995.
11. Douglas Thompson, *Dudley Moore*.
12. *The Times*, 18 November 1972.
13. Ibid.
14. *Sunday Times*, 8 October 1972.
15. In part from Barbra Paskin, *Dudley Moore*.
16. Ibid.
17. *Daily Mail*, 20 November 1973.
18. Christopher Hitchens and Joseph Heller, 'Heller's Version', in *Something Like Fire*, ed. Lin Cook.
19. Ibid.
20. Barbra Paskin, *Dudley Moore*.

21. Ibid.
22. *New York Times*, 1973.
23. *Russell Harty*, LWT, 9 October 1975.
24. *The Radleian*, 1995.
25. Barbra Paskin, *Dudley Moore*.
26. *Penthouse*, Vol. 11, No. 9.
27. *Parkinson*, BBC 1, 1975.
28. *Penthouse*, Vol. 11, No. 9.
29. *The New Yorker*, 23 January 1995.
30. *Sunday Express*, 17 August 1975.
31. *Mavis Catches Up With . . . Peter Cook and Dudley Moore*, ITV, 22 November 1989.
32. *Daily Mail*, 15 March 1976.
33. John Hind, *Comic Inquisition*.
34. *The New Yorker*, 23 January 1995.
35. *Daily Mail*, 28 September 1996.

Chapter 13 *I Don't Want to See Plays About Rape: Derek and Clive, 1973–79*

1. Christopher Hitchens and Dudley Moore, 'The Other Half of the Sketch', in *Something Like Fire*, ed. Lin Cook.
2. *Penthouse*, Vol. 11, No. 9.
3. *Guardian*, 20 August 1976.
4. Ibid.
5. *Penthouse*, Vol. 11, No. 9.
6. *Evening Standard*, 9 January 1995.
7. *Time Out*, 1987.
8. *Daily Mail*, 11 April 1977.
9. *The South Bank Show*, LWT, 8 April 1978.
10. Ibid.
11. *Daily Mail*, 27 June 1977.
12. Roger Wilmut, *From Fringe to Flying Circus*.
13. Ronald Bergan, *Beyond The Fringe . . . And Beyond*.
14. *Sunday Express*, 15 January 1995.
15. Ibid.
16. *Daily Mail*, 24 November 1977.
17. Ibid.
18. *Evening Standard*, 2 December 1977.
19. *Sun*, 24 June 1978.
20. *Daily Express*, 20 May 1978.
21. *Sunday Times*, October 1978.
22. *Time Out*, 30 January 1991.
23. In part from *Cook's Tour*, BBC Radio 4, 9 January 1996.
24. *Today*, 1993.
25. Barbra Paskin, *Dudley Moore*.

26. *Melody Maker*, 2 December 1978.
27. Ibid.
28. *You Magazine*, 30 March 1997.
29. *The New Yorker*, 23 January 1995.
30. Barry Humphries, 'A Recollection', in *Something Like Fire*, ed. Lin Cook.
31. *Melody Maker*, 2 October 1993.
32. *Cook's Tour*, BBC Radio 4, 2 January 1996.
33. In part from *Sunday Express*, 15 January 1995.

Chapter 14 You Are to Be a Stud, Dud: Dudley's Hollywood Success, 1979–83

1. *News of the World*, 2 December 1979.
2. *Daily Mirror*, 29 June 1979.
3. Michael Palin, 'I Had That Peter Cook in the Back of My Car', in *Something Like Fire*, ed. Lin Cook.
4. *Sun*, 8 December 1979.
5. *Sunday Telegraph*, 12 June 1983.
6. *Observer*, 22 December 1996.
7. *Daily Express*, 13 September 1980.
8. Unidentified press cutting, February 1979.
9. Ronald Bergan, *Beyond the Fringe . . . And Beyond*.
10. Stephen Fry, 'Peter Cook', In *Something Like Fire*, ed. Lin Cook.
11. *The New Yorker*, 23 January 1995.
12. Barbra Paskin, *Dudley Moore*.
13. Ibid.
14. *Daily Mail*, 28 February 1980.
15. *Daily Express*, 10 March 1981.
16. Barbra Paskin, *Dudley Moore*.
17. Unidentified press cutting quoted in Ronald Bergan, *Beyond the Fringe . . . And Beyond*.
18. *Daily Mirror*, 22 August 1980.
19. *Guardian*, 22 August 1980.
20. *TV Times*, 11 September 1980.
21. *Daily Express*, 2 September 1980.
22. *Daily Mail*, 13 September 1980 & 9 December 1981.
23. *Daily Mirror*, 26 October 1981.
24. *Daily Mail*, 11 March 1982.
25. *Sun*, 17 March 1982.
26. *Sunday Express*, 12 September 1982.
27. *Sunday Telegraph*, 15 March 1987.
28. *Sunday Express*, 12 September 1982.
29. Ronald Bergan, *Beyond the Fringe . . . And Beyond*.
30. *Sunday Express*, 12 September 1982.
31. *Sun*, 17 March 1982.
32. Ibid.

32. *Sun*, 20 November 1984.
33. Douglas Thompson, *Dudley Moore*.
34. Channel Four News, 9 January 1995.
35. *Sunday Express*, 12 September 1982.
36. *Daily Mail*, 12 November 1994.
37. Eric Idle, 'The Funniest Man in the World', in *Something Like Fire*, ed. Lin Cook.
38. *Blitz*, March 1987.
39. *Evening Standard*, 9 January 1995.

Chapter 15 Whereupon I Immediately Did Nothing: The Single Life, 1983–89

1. *Independent on Sunday*, 30 July 1995.
2. *Daily Mail*, 17 February 1996.
3. *Independent on Sunday*, 30 July 1995.
4. *Independent*, 10 January 1995.
5. *Independent on Sunday*, 30 July 1995.
6. *Today*, 1993.
7. *Saturday Live*, LWT 15 March 1986.
8. *Time Out*, March 1987.
9. *Daily Mail*, 17 September 1979.
10. John Wells, 'The Mystic Spube', in *Something Like Fire*, ed. Lin Cook.
11. *Sunday Times*, 5 August 1984.
12. *After Midnight*, 19 November 1983, *Melody Maker*, 2 October 1993.
13. *The New Yorker*, 23 January 1995.
14. John Wells, 'The Mystic Spube', in *Something Like Fire*, ed. Lin Cook.
15. *Melody Maker*, 2 October 1993.
16. *Independent*, 14 December 1993.
17. *Independent*, 10 January 1995.
18. Stephen Fry, 'Peter Cook', in *Something Like Fire*, ed Lin Cook.
19. *Independent on Sunday*, 30 July 1995.
20. *Newsnight*, 9 January 1995.
21. BBC 6 O'Clock News, 9 January 1995.
22. *Pembroke College Annual Gazette*, 1995.
23. *Sunday Telegraph*, 15 March 1987.
24. *Sunday Times*, 25 September 1983.
25. *Daily Mail*, 14 November 1992.
26. *Sunday Times*, 5 August 1984.
27. John Wells, 'The Mystic Spube', in *Something Like Fire*, ed. Lin Cook.
28. *News of the World*, 3 February 1985.
29. *Sunday Times*, 10 February 1985.
30. *Publish and Bedazzled*, No. 7.
31. *The Times*, 27 February 1987.
32. Ibid.
33. *Illustrated London News*, December 1988.

34. Shane Maloney, 'Hanging Out at Hanging Rock', in *Something Like Fire*, ed. Lin Cook.
35. Ronald Bergan, *Beyond The Fringe . . . And Beyond*.
36. Unidentified press cutting, October 1993.
37. *Sunday Times*, March 1986.
38. Peter McKay, *Inside Private Eye*.
39. *South Bank Show*, LWT 15 September 1991.
40. *Sunday Telegraph*, 15 March 1987.
41. LWT, 1986; *The Listener*, November 1982.
42. *Independent*, 10 January 1995.
43. *Sun* 26 May 1989.
44. *Publish and Bedazzled*, No. 6.
45. *Daily Telegraph*, 14 October 1996.
46. *The Times*, 11 July 1992.
47. *Daily Telegraph*, 14 October 1996.
48. Ibid.
49. Ibid.
50. *Daily Star*, 22 September 1987.
51. *Daily Mail*, 28 September 1996.
52. *Daily Mail*, 10 January 1995.
53. *Daily Telegraph*, 14 October 1996.
54. *Daily Mail*, 17 February 1996.
55. Ibid.
56. *Daily Telegraph*, 14 October 1996.
57. *Sun*, 20 November 1984.
58. Barbra Paskin, *Dudley Moore*.
59. *TV Times*, 18 November 1989.
60. *Daily Express*, 4 December 1986.
61. Unidentified press cutting, 10 January 1995.
62. *Daily Telegraph*, 14 October 1996.
63. *Illustrated London News*, December 1988.
64. Douglas Thompson, *Dudley Moore*.
65. Barbra Paskin, *Dudley Moore*.
66. *Pembroke College Annual Gazette*, 1995.
67. *Independent on Sunday*, 30 July 1995.
68. Barbra Paskin, *Dudley Moore*.
69. *Daily Telegraph*, 14 October 1996.
70. *Daily Mail*, 12 November 1994.
71. *Daily Telegraph*, 14 October 1996.
72. *Sunday Express*, 15 January 1995.
73. *Daily Telegraph*, 14 October 1996.

Chapter 16 Now That the World Is In My Grasp:
The Final Years, 1989–95

1. Eleanor Bron, 'Peter', in *Something Like Fire*, ed. Lin Cook.

2. Lin Cook, 'Paradise in Perrin's Walk', in *Something Like Fire*, ed. Lin Cook.
3. *Cook's Tour*, BBC Radio 4, 9 January 1996.
4. Ronald Bergan, *Beyond the Fringe . . . And Beyond.*
5. *The New Yorker*, 23 January 1995.
6. *Radio Times*, 1990.
7. *Independent*, 12 June 1996.
8. *Time Out*, 30 January 1991.
9. *The New Yorker*, 23 January 1995.
10. John Lloyd, 'The Worst Job I Ever Had', in *Something Like Fire*, ed. Lin Cook.
11. *Cook's Tour*, BBC Radio 4, 9 January 1996.
12. *Evening Standard*, 23 August 1993.
13. *Evening Standard*, 8 September 1993.
14. *New Musical Express*, 25 September 1993.
15. *Daily Mail*, 14 November 1992.
16. *Daily Express*, 10 January 1995.
17. *Independent on Sunday*, 30 July 1995.
18. John Bird, 'The Last Pieces', in *Something Like Fire*, ed. Lin Cook.
19. John Cleese, 'Peter Amadeus Cook', in *Something Like Fire*, ed. Lin Cook.
20. *Independent*, 14 December 1993.
21. *Aspel & Co.*, LWT, 9 January 1988.
22. Michael Palin, 'I Had That Peter Cook in the Back of My Car', in *Something Like Fire*, ed. Lin Cook.
23. *Daily Mail*, 10 January 1995 & 12 December 1994.
24. *Hampstead and Highgate Express*, 20 December 1996.
25. Alan Bennett, 'Thoughts and Afterthoughts', in *Something Like Fire*, ed. Lin Cook.
26. *Daily Mail*, 12 November 1994.
27. John Wells, 'The Mystic Spube', in *Something Like Fire*, ed. Lin Cook.
28. *Daily Mail*, 10 January 1995.
29. *Guardian*, 15 October 1996.

Chapter 17 Zsa Zsa Man Dies: Death and Aftermath, 1995–97

1. *Daily Mail*, 15 March 1997.
2. *Daily Mail*, 17 December 1995.
3. *Cook's Tour*, BBC Radio 4, 9 January 1996.
4. *New Yorker*, 23 January 1995.
5. *Sun*, 10 January 1995.
6. *Daily Mail*, 23 May 1977.
7. Alan Bennett, 'Thoughts and Afterthoughts', in *Something Like Fire*, ed. Lin Cook.
8. *Guardian*, 2 May 1995.
9. *The Times*, 2 May 1995.
10. *Daily Telegraph*, 2 May 1995.
11. Unidentified press cutting.

12. John Cleese, 'Peter Amadeus Cook', in *Something Like Fire*, ed. Lin Cook.
13. *Guardian*, 15 October 1996.
14. *The Sunday Times*, 4 June 1995.
15. *Daily Mail*, 17 February 1996.
16. *Daily Telegraph*, 1996.
17. Barbra Paskin, *Dudley Moore*.
18. *Daily Mail*, 15 March 1997.
19. *Daily Mail*, 17 February 1996; *Sunday Times*, 4 June 1996.
20. *Daily Mail*, 15 March 1997.
21. *Evening Standard*, 14 October 1996.
22. *Daily Mail*, 15 March 1997.
23. *Hampstead and Highgate Express*, 20 December 1996.
24. *Cook's Tour*, BBC Radio 4, 9 January 1996.
25. *Daily Mail*, 10 January 1995.
26. *Person to Person*, BBC TV, 1979.
27. *The Sunday Times*, 15 January 1995.
28. *London Review of Books*, 25 May 1995.
29. *Cook's Tour*, BBC Radio 4, 26 December 1995.

Index

Abbott and Costello 303
Aboyade, Ogea 47, 50
Adams, Douglas 366
Adler, Jerry 232
Adventures of Barry McKenzie 164–65, 310
Aftermyth of War 106–7, 114
Alan A'Dale song 186, 257, 258
Albery, Donald 104, 108, 138
Alchemist, The (Ben Jonson) 27, 58, 63
Alcoholics Anonymous 369, 460
Alice in Wonderland (Lewis Carroll) 8, 211, 218–19
Allen, Woody 260, 323
Allibone, Geoffrey 55
Allsop, Kenneth 108
Almost the End 115
Altman, Jack 50, 57, 79
Altrincham, Lord 46
Amin, Idi 314, 320
Amnesiacs, The 381
Amnesty International 343, 345, 370, 436
Anderson, Clive: on PC 298; co-writes *Black Cinderella 2 Goes East* 366 *see also Clive Anderson Talks Back*
Anderson, Lindsay 322
Anderton, James 364
Andress, Ursula 276, 353
Andrews, Eamonn 315
Andrews, Julie 375
Anglia TV 78
Anne, Princess 345
Anti-Nazi League 296
Anton, Susan 376
Antrobus, John 284

Apple a Day, An (John Antrobus) 284
Argyle, Judge Michael 168, 284
Ark Royal, HMS 271
Arrowsmith, Pat 128
Art Gallery sketch 188–90
Arthur 387–88
Arthur 2 388–89
Asher, Jane 163
Aspel & Company 446
Aspera 356, 471, 474
Associated-Rediffusion 150
Astor, David 115
Astor, Lord 136
Astounding Facts 61
Athalie (Jean Racine) 52
Atkinson, Geoff 412
Atkinson, Rowan 374, 380, 381
ATV 175, 253
Aylen, 24

Babar the Elephant 8–9
Bacall, Lauren 141
Back of the Cab 355
Baddiel, David 364, 463
Balding, David 154, 158
Ballad of Spotty Muldoon, The 199, 381
Bancroft, Ann 259
Barber, John 317
Barclay, Humphrey 374, 379, 381, 417
Barclays Bank commercials 382
Bardot, Brigitte 222
Barker, Felix 109
Barnes, Clive 322
Barry Mackenzie Holds His Own 311

Bart, Lionel 99, 121
Bassett, John 89, 90, 126
Bastard Son of Tommy Cooper 476
Baws, Howard 399, 410, 453
Bawtree, Michael 18–19, 25, 29, 30, 33, 38, 39, 72, 245
BBC Duty Office 403
Bedazzled: origin of Dudley Moore's character's name 116; Dudley edged out of writing 212–13; plot 213–17; limited budget 218; assessment 218, 220–21, 222; filming of 220; reception 221, 222
Bedazzling! 477
Bedford, Duke of 66
Bedsitting Room, The 251–52
Beeside, The 199
Behind the Fridge: writing 285; in Australia 306–10; London run 313–20see also Good Evening
Bell, Colin 103, 121, 134
Bellwood, Peter 76, 103, 154, 155, 221
Benn, Tony 169
Bennett, Alan: sermon sketch 83, 94–95; career as historian 90, 91, 146; on PC 91, 111–12; PC enjoys shocking 92; and satire in Beyond the Fringe 93, 94, 111–12; summing-up of PC's life 480–81 see also Beyond the Fringe
Bennett, Lennie 407
Benson, Neil 474
Bentine, Michael 178
Beresford, Bruce 310
Berlin, Sir Isaiah 121
Bernard, Jeffrey 237
Bessell, Peter 370, 371
Best, George 480
Best of the Bard 61
Betjeman, John 171
Bewes, Rodney 257
Beyond the Fringe: origins of Perkins's name 3; changes British Comedy 89; origins 89; cast assembled 90; cast's initial impressions of each other 90–91; PC writes script 93; satire in 93; costumes 96; economy in production style 96; parts broadcast 96; cast nervousness followed by triumph 97; PC's family support 97; cast agree to West End run 99; rehearsals for London production 104; pre-West End provincial tour 105–8; cast argument about alienating audience 107; poor provincial reception 107–8; London opening 108; London success 109; satire label irritates cast 111–12; left-wing perspective 112; Establishment response to 113–14; project with the Goons 115–16; dissension among cast 117–18, 155–56; Broadway offer 119; arrival in America 140; pre-New York tour 140; celebrities going backstage 141; changes made for America

141, 142; Englishness of 141; decline in 156; new version after Jonathan Miller's resignation 156; BBC broadcast 159; cast's abortive film project 159; cast unable to work together any more 160 see also under names of sketches in
Billington, Kevin 260, 262
Billington, Michael 316
Bird, John: meets PC 56–57; scorns idea that PC was influenced by Ionescu 59–60; at Uplyme 60–61; becomes Assistant Director at Royal Court 60; directs The Last Laugh 67–9; roles played 99; on PC and satire 111; on satire 112, 113; and Establishment Club 123, 126, 129, 135; asked to appear in TW3 138; on PC and Frost 148–49; and Private Eye 169; in Thirty is a Dangerous Age, Cynthia 213; on PC changing the world 481
Birdsall, Timothy 59, 66, 69, 99, 136, 148
Bird Watching 100
Bishop, Mike 435
Bit of a Chat, A 205–6
Black, Cilla 205
Blackadder 418
Black and White Blues, The 33–36, 38
Black Beauty 452–53
Black Cinderella 2 Goes East 366
Black Equals White 106
Blower, Terence 33
Bob Monkhouse's Comedy Showcase 420
Bo Dudley 211
Bogarde, Dirk 163
Bollard 94
Bolt, Robert 271
Bonnassin, Madame 43, 44
Booker, Christopher 54, 64, 77–78, 87, 135, 148, 430, 479
Booker, Hylan 232
Booth, Mark 459
Boothby, Lord 168
Bore of the Year Awards xii, 452
Bosley, Deborah 439
Botham, Ian 407
Boyd, Hugo 96, 108, 119
Boylett, Mr 24–25, 50, 53, 56, 61–62, 63 see also Grole, A.; Wisty, E. L.
BP 172
Braden, Bernard 66, 67, 163, 175, 200
Brady, Terence 138
Bragg, Melvyn 346
Branson, Richard 360, 363
Brett, Peter 75
Bridge Over the River Wye 115–6
Bridge Over Troubled Waters 278
Brimacombe, Mrs 8
Brittan, Leon 46–47
Broadbent, Jim 451
Bron, Eleanor: in A Resounding Tinkle 56,

57, 59, 60; and John Bird 57; description 59; roles played by 59, 62, 86, 452, 453; at Uplyme 60; Footlights male-only rule scrapped for 67; PC uses her notes for Finals 87; and Establishment Club 123, 126, 128, 143–44, 158; on *TW3* 138; and *Private Eye* 169–70; in *Bedazzled* 213; on PC as actor 221; at *Secret Policeman's Ball* 370; on Lin's effect on PC 443; stage show with PC mooted 453, 462, 479
Brooke, Henry 151
Brooke-Taylor, Tim 200
Brooks, Mel 302
Brown, Gaye 117, 129, 239, 241, 243, 276, 323–24
Bruce, Lenny 131–32, 151
Bryan, Dora 249
Bull, Clive 400, 403, 464
Burge, Stuart 158
Burkim, Louise 61
Burton, Richard 272
Burton, Sybil 154, 155
Butcher, John 58
Butler, James 125
Butler, Rab 113, 114, 125
Butters, Paul ('Bill') 20, 25, 28

Cagney, James 387
Caine, Michael 127, 201, 284, 445
Calthrop, Bill 229
Cambridge: famous names produced by 45
    see also Footlights Club; Pembroke College; Pembroke Players
Camps, Tony 75
Cancer 336
Candy, John 339
Can English Satire Draw Blood? (Jonathan Miller) 110, 124–25
Cantley, Mr Justice 370–72
Can We Talk? 420–22
Carleton-Greene, Sir Hugh 157
Carmody, Jay 140
Carpendale, Captain and Mrs 4
Carroll, Diahann 178
Case, Brian 364
Cash, David 153, 167, 279, 312, 426, 429, 471
Cash, Johnny 278
Cassidy, Cynthia 158, 213
Cassidy, Denis 172
CBS 356, 384
CBS-TV 378, 379
Cedar Falls Health Centre 439
Chamberlain, Neville 122, 381
Chapman, Graham 101, 382, 392, 438; co-writes *The Rise and Rise of Michael Rimmer* 250, 259, 261
Chase, Chevy 343, 374

Chong, Lin see Cook, Lin
Chong, Yin 471, 472
Church, Colonel and Mrs 4
Church, Bob 2, 3, 12
Churchill, Randolph 127
Civil Defence (previously *Whose Finger on What Button?*) 118
Clare, Alan 410
Clarke, John Cooper 476
Clarke, Warren 451
Clary, Julian 438
Cleese, John: and Establishment Club 158; discovers Judy Huxtable in wardrobe 241; co-writes *The Rise and Rise of Michael Rimmer* 250, 259, 261; in *Goodbye Again* 257; on PC's speed of thought 288; at PC's memorial service 294, 470; at *Secret Policeman's Ball* 370; in *Peter Cook & Co.* 381; provokes Dudley into performing with PC 436; on PC and drink 444–45; treats friends to Nile cruise 452
Clement, Dick 204, 253, 254
Clive Anderson Talks Back 295, 456–57, 462, 463, 479
Clive James 423
Closer to Home 285–86
CND 49, 67, 82, 86, 296
Cockburn, Claud 164, 173, 278, 333–34
Cocker, Joe 263, 267
Codron, Michael 54, 70, 71, 74, 93, 101
Coghlan, Tim 117
Cohen, Alexander H. 140, 149, 310, 320, 324–25, 326, 327, 434
Cohn, Sidney 153
Coltrane, Robbie 424
Columbia 200, 201
Columbia-Warner 259
Combe, Dr 52, 66
Connery, Sean 316, 317
Connolly, Billy 371
Connolly, Ray 278
Consequences 349–52
Conway, Tom 374
Cook & Luard Productions Ltd 104, 134, 151, 152
Cook, Alec (father): becomes Assistant District Officer in Nigeria 2; and his father 2; falls in love 3; nature of duties 3; character 4; marriage 4; promoted to District Officer 5; introduced to son 6; cine enthusiast 7; becomes Assistant Secretary 9; loneliness after wife leaves Nigeria, 1944 9; return to England and posting to Gibraltar 10; thoughts about Nigerian independence 10; cautious gambling 12; integrity 12; posted back to Nigeria 21; decorated with CMG 23; sails to England and never returns to Nigeria 23–24; serves on Caribbean Federal

Capital Commission 40; posted to Libya
72; at *Pieces of Eight* 75; return from Libya
102; sees *Beyond the Fringe* 114; lectures
on America 155; falls ill with Parkinson's
disease 390–91; death 393, 407, 418
Cook, Daisy (daughter): born 203; asthma
237, 239, 311; enrolled in Spanish school
239; transferred to school in London 243;
in America with PC 323; cookery school
and art college 393; becomes ELT teacher
414; PC's help during nervous illness 414;
reconciliation with PC leads to row with Lin
438; career as artist 451; wedding 464–65;
bequests to 471
Cook, Edward (grandfather) 1
Cook, Elizabeth (sister): on her father 3;
accompanies parents to Libya 72; on PC as
rescuer 414; and *Eye* shares 471, 472, 474
Cook, Judy (second wife): mesmerised by
PC 117; Lenny Bruce falls for 132; meets
PC again after a few years 239; career 240;
character 240; falls in love with PC 240;
good looks 240; becomes pregnant and
has abortion 241; good with Daisy and
Lucy 244; moves into Kenwood Cottage
with PC 245; ill 284, 323; on PC 303; on
Australian trip 306; as dresser, monitors
PC's drinking 317; on relationship between
PC and Dudley 325; wedding to PC 326;
infection makes her unable to have children
334; quarrelling with PC 354; distrusts
PC's visits to Lownes' house 359; hides in
house to discover Peter's affair 366; begins
divorce proceeding but stops 367, 368;
obtains injunction against PC 367; lives in
separate part of house from PC 368, 369;
PC presents with Mitchell Leys Farm 383;
mother dies 386; moves to Exmoor 386;
determined not to return to London, and
lives alone 389; as love of PC's life 433; the
divorce from PC 439–40; finds out about
PC's death through media 467; not invited
to PC's funeral 469; bequests to 471
Cook, Lin (third wife): belief that PC had been
neglected by others 431, 434; first meeting
with PC 431; as nerveless gambler 431;
relationship with PC 433–34; first reactions
to and of PC's family 436–37; PC's friends
and 437; wants PC to marry her 438;
marries PC 440; and *Private Eye* 441, 445;
makes devoted couple with PC 442; and
PC's drinking 443–44; Lloyd's losses 445;
punches tourist 452; cancels PC's invitation
to Aletta Seymour to a launch party 455;
on effect of PC's mother's death 462; and
PC collapse 465; at hospital as PC lay dying
466; and Peter's death 467; allows PC's close
family to attend memorial service 469; asks
Sarah for discretion about PC's *Eye* shares
471; bequests to 471; and the Tiffany lamp
473; adept at public relations 474; asked
for return to PC's family of Alec's CMG
474; asks for return from PC's family of
signed autobiography of David Frost 474;
row with Rainbow George over his tapes
474–75; recourse to law 475; tries to mount
memorial show 476–77; and the Peter
Cook Appreciation Society 476; criticism of
PC's other wives 477–78; praise of her in
Something Like Fire 477; her devotion to PC
unquestionable 478; insists that PC was a
contented person 478
Cook, Lucy (daughter): birth 191; screen
debut 191; enrolled in Spanish school 239;
transferred to school in London 243; in
America with PC 331; becomes chef 393;
on her father's distressed state 413; becomes
aromatherapist 414; PC helping over eczema
414; marriage 464; bequests to 471
Cook, Margaret (mother): meets Alec Cook
3; character 4; marriage 4; sails for Nigeria,
becomes pregnant and returns to England 4;
letter to husband about Peter's development
5–6; dislike of Nigeria 6; has to leave Peter
to return to Nigeria 6; returns to England,
1944 9; goes to Gibraltar 10; regular
writing to her children 11; finds house in
Uplyme 22; returns to England for good
22; accompanies husband to Libya 72; at
Pieces of Eight 75; sees *Beyond the Fringe* 114;
illness 459; still alert in her eighties 459;
death 461
Cook, Minnie (grandmother) 2
Cook, Peter: autobiography ix, 459, 479;
author's first meeting with xi; pleads with
BBC about *Not Only . . . But Also* tapes
xi–xii; autobiographical element in his
comedy 1; family background 1–5; home in
Torquay 4–5; birth 5; introduced to father
6; lack of friends as toddler 6; fascinated
by creepie-crawles 7, 12; and the gardener
7; wartime separation from parents 7;
childhood 8–15; childhood fanaticism
about football 8; childhood reading 8–9,
12–13; mother rejoins towards end of war
9; adoration of parents 10; at St Bede's
prep. school 10–15; lack of intimacy with
parents 10; taken to Gibraltar 10; academic
brilliance 11; childhood loneliness 11;
entertains to avoid being bullied 11; school
report accuses of cynicism 11; stoicism
11; unhappiness at school 11; becomes
fascinated by bees 12; humour around as
a child 12–13; atmosphere in household
13–14; childhood comic favourites 13;
avoidance of being boring 14; career plan

for 14; disinclination to share problems 14;
final term's report from St Bede's 14; arrives
at Radley school 16; bullied at Radley 18;
and Ted Dexter 18–19; uses humour as
self-defence 18; avoidance of unwelcome
attentions from some older boys 19; and
authority 20, 29, 53, 294; character at
Radley 20; brief concern over 'withdrawn'
nature 20; and rugby 20, 30; effect of
parents' return to Gibraltar 21; applies
to Pembroke College, Cambridge 21;
holidays in Gibraltar 21; effect on of
mother's return to England 22;
develops ability to entertain 24, 30–31;
mimickry 24, 25–26; football at Radley
25–26, 32; politics at Radley 26; first
acting forays 27; mounts his first
revues 27–28; academic success at Radley
29, 31–32; emotional distance from
schoolfellows 29; as prefect 29–30; shyness
29, 85; popularity 30, 31; an early
work published in *Punch* 31; enthusiasm
for the Goons 31; accepted at Pembroke
32; attractiveness 33; bathing episode
with matron 33; early sexual experiences
33; in theatricals at Radley 33–36;
organisational talents 34; avoiding National
Service 36–37; desire to be an entertainer
36; final report at Radley 36; and Foreign
Office 36, 52, 54, 72, 78, 87, 95, 163, 327,
481; first proper girlfriend 37; in France
studying, 1956 37–38; oil painting 37;
on holiday with schoolfriend, 39;
and Henley Regatta 39, 44; tastes in pop
music 40–41, 56; works as waiter 40;
arrested in East Germany 41–42; studying
in Germany, 1956–57 41–42; conceives
idea for political cabaret club 42; in France
studying, 1957 42–44; success as beachfront
photographer 44; goes up to Cambridge
45; attitude to politicians 46–47;
entertains fellow undergraduates 46, 52;
early friendships at Cambridge 47;
football at Cambridge 47–48; and
Cambridge authority 48; character at
Cambridge 49; BBC rejects material
submitted 51; holiday on *Maid Marguerita*
51–52; noting successful lines 51;
academic work at Cambridge 52, 66; first
screen role 54; first year grades 54; plays
Launcelot Gobbo 55; clothes at Cambridge
56; cigarette smoking 58; girlfriends
at Cambridge 58–59; legacy enriches
58; parties at Cambridge 58; delights in
Eleanor Bron 59; pays for abortion 59; lyric
writing 62; acquires Donald Langdon as
agent 63; and David Frost 64–65, 101–2,
126, 137, 139, 148-49; political views 68,

295–97; admirer of Kenneth Williams 71;
commissioned to write *Pieces of Eight* 71;
meets first wife 72; parents abroad again
72; President of Footlights Club 72, 75;
income while still at Cambridge 75, 76;
liking for tarty girls 80; as landlord of
East Anglian Arts 81; attends college less
and less 83; always under pressure to
perform 84; friends all going places
84–85; friendship as performance 84;
contracts jaundice with effects on liver and
ability to drink 85; visits family in Libya
85; Finals 86, 87–88; fashionable dress 90;
newspapers devoured by 90, 162; and
satire 93–94, 111, 113, 128, 297; career
uncertainties 95; degree results 95;
Equity requires him to change his name
97; proposes to Wendy Snowden following
success of *Beyond the Fringe* 98; hopelessness
with money 99; moves into flat with
Wendy 101; gambling 102, 407, 419; leaves
Cambridge 102; ambition to open satirical
nightclub 103; gives dinner parties 103;
moves to flat in Battersea 103; starts up
umbrella company 103–4; moral perspective
of 113; wealth after *Beyond the Fringe* 114;
co-writes satire page in *Observer* 115; meets
Judy Huxtable 117; varies his performance
during *Beyond the Fringe* 118; attitude to
parking tickets 124; attacks smoking 128;
relationship with Wendy becomes strained
129; tries to find heroin for Lenny Bruce
131; desire to found satirical magazine
baulked as *Private Eye* starts 133; believes he
has bought *Private Eye* 134; establishes *Scene*
134; desire to merge *Private Eye* crowd with
Establishment Club crowd 135; approaches
BBC about satire show, but idea dropped
136; offer to tour America 137; refuses to
have Frost deputise for him in Establishment
Club 137; fury at Frost fronting *TW3* 139;
declines to take show to White House
141–42; uses David Merrick's name for
review quotes 142; seduces bunny girl
144–45; relationship with Wendy improves
146; annoyed about *TW3* and David Frost
147, 148–49; saves Frost's life 149, 299;
described as tightly coiled spring unwinding
150; appears on US television 150;
discovers that he's not co-owner of *Private
Eye* 153; fury at Luard 153; upset by
Establishment Club closing 153; announces
construction of Establishment Theatre (New
York) 154; Wendy's pregnancy and their
wedding 154–55; writes new Establishment
revue 158; takes up smoking again 160;
the saving of *Private Eye* 161–74; belief that
the human race cannot be improved 169;

desire to be a pop star 181–82; compulsion to entertain 187; constantly improvising with Dudley 191; daughter Lucy born 191; mastery of wordplay 191; uses background as source for comedy 193–94, 294–95; as a difficult performing partner 194; relationship with Dudley 194–95, 196–97; capacity for cruelty 195, 298; inability to reveal himself emotionally 196, 300; on Royal Variety Performance 197–98; on Sunday Night at the London Palladium 197; inability to sing 198; forms Peter Cook Productions Ltd. 200; wants to move into films 200, 212; attacks on actors 202–3, 274; daughter Daisy born 203; inability to play the piano mocked 210; decides to write Bedazzled alone 212; failure to show vulnerability or attract sympathy on screen 221; his mistaken assessment that the need to be funny and Dudley were holding him back 222; idea of becoming a romantic light comedy lead 223; buys house in Church Row 224; protective of family against publicity 224; gives celebrity dinner parties 226–28; as sixties icon 226, 229; goes to Spurs matches 230–32; attacked at Old Trafford 232; gives Wendy funds to start business 232; never seen to read a book 232, 406; terrified of being drunk 233; has little in common with Wendy 234; women a mystery to him 235; addictive personality 236, 240; drug taking 236–37, 311, 400, 412–13, 447; loneliness 236, 341; quest for reassurance 236; marriage to Wendy deteriorating 239, 241; runs into Judy Huxtable again 239; falls in love with Judy Huxtable 240; as solver of others' problems 242–43; tells Wendy about Judy 242; theory that others are features of his personal world 242; demands that Wendy return from Majorca 243; seeing psychiatrist 244–45; turns to drink and drugs on losing daughters 244; formal separation from Wendy 245; moves into Kenwood Cottage with Judy 245; way of life quieter 245; desperately unhappy at breakup of family 246; drink and drug use getting out of hand 246–47; takes up golf 246; working on book of children's verse 246; banned for drunk driving 247, 400; divorce from Wendy 247, 283, 350; rude to Zsa Zsa Gabor 249; becomes regular chat show guest 249; cigarette smoking worsens 251; in balloon accident-loses cartilege from knee 252; uses personal life in Goodbye Again 255; rewriting The Rise and Rise of Michael Rimmer 260; a sense of pointlessness settles over him 268;

disinclination to do more television 274; not comfortable with emotions 275; as actor 221–22, 253, 275; presents his own chat show 277–83; on drink and drugs during Where Do I Sit? 279, 280; devastation at failure of Where Do I Sit? 282; his reason for failing as chat show host 282; as solo performer at heart 282; edits Private Eye 284; offer to tour Australia 284; feted in Australia 284; sells Church Row house 285; analysis of his humour 287–305; writes his last substantial piece of work 287; rapidity of thought 287; improvisations repeated 288; degree of spontaneity 288; continually performing 290; did write things down 290; intimacy with is difficult 290; need for audience 290; desire to shock 291; preoccupation with boredom 292–93, 294, 319; types of character invented 293–94; accepts invitation to South Africa 295; voting record 296; personal morality 297; absence of malice in humour 298–99; kindness 298; humour as defence and barrier 299–300, 368; no illusions about powerlessness of humour to hurt its targets 299; comedic devices 300–3; uses comedy as coping mechanism 300; and clichés 301–2; influence of other comedians 302–3; alternating moods 303; loss of momentum in career 303; professional confidence combined with personal un-confidence 303; depression seen in light of suicide of grandfather 304; as manic depressive 304, 367; in Australia 306–9; Dudley identifies start of becoming an alcoholic 307; receives cable telling him of Daisy's asthma attack 307; starts drinking again 308; drinking in New Zealand 309; mutual dependence with Dudley 309; in New Zealand 309–10; drunk 310, 312, 315, 321, 386, 407, 419; buys house in Notting Hill Gate 311; changes writing methods 313; opinion on 'crickets' 313; affected by critics 315; an agreement limiting his drinking 317; interviewed by Mavis Nicholson 318–119, 436; tries to make life difficult for Dudley on stage 318; sells Denbigh Terrace House and buys Perrin's Walk house 320; in America with Good Evening 321–33; children visit in America for holiday 323; dislike of being alone 324; drink and drugs tighten grip 324; stage performance affected by drink 324–25; friction with Dudley 325; increasing desire for solo writing credit 325; remains in love with Judy 326; wedding to Judy 326; flies home to be with children

327–28; obsession with Dudley 328; touring in America 328, 330–31; differing attitudes to women 329; *Penthouse* interview 329–30; alarming robbery 330; flies to England to watch football 330; working on film script about Queen Victoria's gynaecologist 330; attempts to make pop record 331; drinking worsened 331; bereft when Dudley tells him partnership is over 332–33; returns to Perrin's Walk 332; acquires another agent 333; criminal occupies Kenwood Cottage 333; goes to Ireland to see Claud Cockburn 333–34; Judy suspects he had a breakdown 334; and rock stars 337, 358; orders parents not to listen to *Derek and Clive* 338; tops drinking 339; therapeutic effect of Dudley's return 339, 343; income from chat shows 340; visits massage parlours 341; goes to see James Goldsmith 342–43; contributes column to *Daily Mail* 344–45, 354; back on drink and drugs 348; makes public jokes at Dudley's expense again 348; daughters old enough to appreciate PC's mood swings 352; with his daughters 352–53; constant need for adulation 353; ebullience 353; takes daughters on holiday to Cornwall 353–54; quarrelling with Judy 354; sabotages relationship with Judy 354; sets up Aspera company in Lichtenstein 356; and punk bands 357; becoming more savage 359; malice shows 359; fear of women 361–62; blames Dudley for *Derek and Clive* excesses 363; attempts to stop drinking 365–66, 407; affair with pretty Australian girl with comic consequences 366; Judy obtains injunction against him 367; lives in separate part of house from Judy 367, 369; rages 367; and the press 368–69; doesn't stop taking drugs 369; gives up drinking and agrees to go to Alcoholics Anonymous 369; helps other alcoholics 369; plays showbiz golf 372; pet goldfish called Abe Ginsberg 372; reaction to Dudley's film success 375–77, 388; short girlfriends after breakup with Dudley 376; in Hollywood to look for work 378; Barclays Bank commercials 382; wins American awards 382; presents Judy with Mitchell Leys farm 383; writes letters to the press 383; reunited with Dudley for interview with *Daily Mail* 385; attacks Hollywood 386–87; dependent on drink again 386; appears in tribute to Dudley's success 387; tries to move to Exmoor with Judy 389; difficulty in coping with emotional setbacks 390; father falls ill

with Parkinson's disease 390–91; still loves Judy 390; gives up alcohol while making *Yellowbeard* 391; father's death 393, 407, 418; now alone 393; attachment to Ciara Parkes 394–95; friendship with Rainbow George 396; helps Rainbow George devise policies 398; spends much time with Rainbow George 399; phones LBC 400–3, 432, 464; phoning friends at length 403–4; devours broadcast information 404–5; collection of videos 405; top ten pleasures 406; alcoholism 408; and Antabuse 408–9; drunk driving ban 408; house dishevelled 409; financial disorganisation 410; ashamed to let his daughters see his state 413; goes to Majorca 414–15; helping others in crisis 414; meets Wendy in Majorca 414–15; still in regular contact with mother 414; mood swings becoming even more extreme 415; still not without ideas 415; inability to match past achievements 416; lack of confidence 416; writes new E. L. Wisty sketch 417; young comedians appreciate 417, 422, 424; attempts practical joke at Nether Wallop Arts Festival 419; flies out to Tahoe to meet Joan Rivers 420–21; uses cuttings service 420; reconciled with Dudley 421–22; opens Melbourne Comedy Festival 423–24; generosity to younger comedians 424; and Ian Hislop becoming editor of *Private Eye* 425–26; obtaining dummy of *Not Private Eye* 427; drinking and work for *Private Eye* 429–30; some 'spontaneity' prepared 430–31; love for Lin develops 431–32; *Daily Star* 'kiss and tell' about 432–33; relationship with Lin 433–34; another reconciliation with Dudley 434, 435, 436; emotional relationship with family 438; the divorce from Judy 439–40; in love with Lin 439; marries Lin 440; honeymoon with Lin 441; affectionate step-father to Lin's daughter 442–43; makes devoted couple with Lin 442; decision to live apart from Lin 443; depression caused by losing Judy 444; changes solicitors 445; requests a salary from *Private Eye* 445; attempted fund-raising speech in Sydney 446–47; preparing video of *Not Only . . . But Also* 447–48; financial problems 448–49, 451; relations with Dudley much improved 448; Lin tries to help combat alcoholism 451; hoax article in *Evening Standard* 453; devoted to his mother 459, 460; liver deteriorates 461; mother's death 461–62; at wedding of daughter Daisy 464; talks to Wendy at Daisy's wedding 464–65; 57th

birthday 465; collapses 465; death
466; reactions to his death 467–68;
funeral 468–69; media reaction to his death
468; memorial service 469–70; some of
close family not at first invited to memorial
service 469; estate 470–71; bequests 471;
antagonism over his estate 472–75; changes
his mind over later will 474; Pembroke
College room named after him 477;
debate about his potential 479–80; colossal
influence on British comedy 481 see also
under names of revues, programmes, films etc
which he appeared in, and under ventures (e.g.,
Establishment Club)
Cook, Sarah (sister): birth 9; Peter's holiday
companion 11–12; misery at prep. school
19; buys Elvis record 40–41; at Pieces of
Eight 75; and Beyond the Fringe 98; and
Establishment Club 126; too embarrassed to
join in song at Rustle of Spring 171; married
to Mike Seymour, has daughter Aletta 246;
and mother's death 462; and Eye shares 471,
472, 474; named as executor 471; bequests
to 472; tells Ian Hislop about distribution
of PC's Eye shares 472; and the Tiffany
lamp 472–73; asks Lin for return of father's
CMG 474
Cook, Wendy (first wife): on Peter's schooldays
18; meets PC 72; background 79–80; on
meeting PC when a waitress 79; beauty
80; remodels PC's appearance 80; sexuality
80; as good cook and entertainer 81; PC
confides childhood unhappiness to 85; PC
proposes to 98; moves into flat with PC
101; gets on well with PC's family 103;
moves to flat in Battersea 103; relationship
with PC strained 129; in New York
146–47; relationship with PC improves
146; pregnancy and wedding 154–55;
daughter Lucy born 191; daughter Daisy
born 203; finds house in Church Row 224;
longing for more conventional marriage
224; creates dream home 225–26; gives
celebrity dinner parties 226–28; growing
resentment at PC 230; given funds to start
business 232; interest in alternative
beliefs 234; putting PC down 235;
unhappiness 235; drinking 237; restlessness
237; seduced by Jeffrey Bernard 237; buys
house in Majorca 238; moves to Majorca
238; renovates Majorca house 239; wants
divorce 242; PC demands that she return
from Majorca 243; upset that most of their
friends stay loyal to Peter on separation 243;
sees psychiatrist 244; formal separation from
PC 245; moves into Kenwood Cottage 286;
and Eleanor Bron's balloon pregnancy 295;
writing letters when PC in Australia 308;

interest in macrobiotics 311; takes children
to Sussex 333; meets PC after years apart
414–15; talks to PC at Daisy's wedding
464–65; not invited to PC's funeral 469
Cooke, Alistair 70, 141, 220
Cooper, George A. 261
Cooper, Henry 204
Cotton, Billy 280, 281
Cotton, Jeremy 47, 120, 121
Cottrell, Richard 25, 82, 85, 108
Courtenay, Tom 227, 250
Coutt-Sykes, Anthony 153
Coward, Noel 141, 147
Crabbe, John 47, 51
Craig Ferguson Story, The 446
Creme, Lol 349, 350, 351
Cribbins, Bernard 108, 114
Critics' Choice 100
Croft, Annabel 410
Cryer, Barry 421
Curtis, Tony 253

Daddy, The 76
Damski, Mel 392
Dandy in Aspic, A 250–51
Daniels, Stanley 99
Dave Allen Show 306
David Wilkinson Associates 333
Davies, Russell 113
Davis, Carl 99
Dead Sea Tapes, The 336
de Groot, Myra 72, 75
Dempster, Nigel 425
de Paul, Lynsey 313
Derek, Bo 375
Derek and Clive: origin of Jayne Mansfield
and crustacea sketch 162–63; origins
335–36 bootlegged version 337; success
of 338; synthetic outrage about 338;
different opinions on 363–4 see also
following entries
Derek and Clive Ad Nauseam 360–64, 373
Derek and Clive Come Again 354
Derek and Clive Get the Horn 360, 364–65,
377, 453–54
Derek and Clive (Live) 337–39, 463
Dexter, Ted 18–19, 372
'Diarrhoea Expert' 314
Diet Coke advertisement 435
Dietrich, Marlene 314
Dimbleby, David 300, 303, 373, 374
Dixon, Stephen 24
Donaldson, Willie 70–71, 98–99, 104, 137,
138, 412, 416
Donen, Stanley 217–218, 220, 223
Donleavy, J. P. 125
Donovan 256
Donovan, Terry 158, 255

Don't Ask Me 69–70
Douglas-Home, Sir Alec 157, 163
Douglas, Kirk 279
Downes, Terry 204, 227
Drabble, Margaret 197
Driberg, Tom 127
Dr Jekyll and Mrs Hyde 330
Duchess of York 429
Dudley Moore Show 177
Duff, Sir James 157
Dunkley, Chris 279
Dunn, Nell 238
Dunwoody, Gwyneth 345
Dwyer, John 72, 83

Eamonn Andrews Show 249, 277
East Anglian Arts 81, 82
Easy Does It 275
Edmondson, Adrian 363, 424
Ed Sullivan Show 150
Edwards, Blake 375, 383
Edwards, Percy 262
Ege, Julie 280
Eichelberger, Alyce-Faye 452
Elizabeth II, Queen 52, 114, 198
Ellis, Chris 33–34
Ellison, Jane 425
Emery, Dick 339
End of the World, The 94, 370
Enfield, Harry 303, 403–4, 411, 437–38, 481
Entirely a Matter for You 371–72
Entitytainment 9
Epstein, Jerry 275
Eric Sykes Show 349
Establishment Club: finding premises for
    120–21; name 121; studios above 122;
    sketch writers 123; and the Establishment
    124–25, 126; opening night 125–26; PC's
    performances 127–28; PC's parents at 128;
    audience 129; success of 129; and gangsters
    130, 151–52; serious drama introduced
    130, 154, 158; replacement cast 137; to
    America 137, 138; finds permanent New
    York premises 142; New York reviews 143;
    losing money fast 151; voluntary liquidation
    of British club 152–53; subsequent owners
    153; acquires second US cast 154; closure of
    US club 158; TV parody of 220
Evening at Court, An 417
Everett, Kenny 283

Fairlie, Henry 121
Fantasy Football League 460
Fantoni, Barry: and *Private Eye* 161, 170; and
    PC 166, 429; on PC's phone calls 404; PC
    copes with his suicidal wishes 443
Faringdon, Lord 163
Farmer, Hugh 172

Farrow, Mia 250
Fazan, Eleanor 104, 123
Felker, Clay 150
Fellini, Federico 222
Fielding, Fenella 72, 74, 75, 99
Field, Shirley Anne 175
Fight of the Century, The 205
Fincham, Peter 438, 448, 449, 450, 451, 458
Find the Lady 339
Fish Called Wanda, A 452
Fleming, Nick 58
Footlights Club: PC's initial shyness about 45,
    53; PC joins 53; PC performs at smokers
    54, 56; Revues 54, 60, 66, 67–71, 86, 102;
    committee discusses David Frost 65; PC
    performs at/writes for revues 66, 67–71; and
    memorial show for PC 476–77
Foot, Paul 165, 166, 172, 296, 297, 299,
    312, 411
Forbes, Bryan 163, 201, 202, 203, 271
Forsyth, Bruce 410
Fortune, John 123, 126, 129, 135, 143–44
Foul Play 374
Fraser, Simon (1) 342
Fraser, Simon (2) 342
Frayn, Michael 77, 115
Freedom from Hunger Campaign
    307
Friday Night Saturday Morning 424
Frobe, Gert 253
Frog and Peach 208, 320, 420, 436
Frost, David: imitator of PC 63–64, 102;
    charged with riding a bicycle without
    lights 64–65; and PC 64–65, 101–2,
    149, 170, 437; accusations of plagiarism
    64, 102, 147–48; unpopularity 64, 127;
    telephone manner 81–82; mocked 100; and
    Establishment Club 126, 127; on *TW3* 138;
    life saved by PC 149; oleaginous eulogy to
    JFK 149; fronts *Not So Much a Programme
    . . .* 159; PC does imitation of 170; and *The
    Rise and Rise of Michael Rimmer* 250, 260;
    King of the TV chat show 277; referred
    to as 'Bubonic plagiarist' 298; as regular
    Private Eye target 299; PC puts down 437;
    maintains success 482
Frost, Jeffrey 31
Fry, Stephen 301, 405, 411, 424, 437,
    470, 479
Fuest, Bob 178, 181, 191

Gabor, Zsa Zsa 249, 292
Gaines, John 386
G*A*L*A*X*Y 82
Galbraith, Bob 204
Gappy, Sir Arthur 112
Garland, Harriet 130, 133, 141, 147, 226–27,
    243, 255

Garland, Nicholas 130, 142, 147, 164, 243, 276
Garrett, Anthony 50, 54, 75
Garwood, Colonel and Mrs 4
Gascoigne, Bamber 54, 75, 82
Gaskill, William 56
Gatty, Mrs Jean 8
Geidt, Jeremy 123, 128
Getting It Right 446
Gielgud, John 116, 147, 201
Gilbert, Jimmy 204, 262, 263, 264, 265, 271, 273, 274, 327
Gill, A. A. 468
Gilliam, Terry 269
Gilliat, Ivor 24, 36
Glatt, Max 369
Glidd of Glood, The 267, 448
Godfrey, Bob 185
Godley, Kevin 349, 350, 351, 352
Gold Mine Revue 28
Goldsmith, James 299, 342–43
Goldstone, John 348, 349
Gone to Seed 451–52
Goodbye Again 253–59
Goodbyee 182, 256, 365
Good Evening 321–33: title changed 320; celebrities queuing to go backstage 322; success of 322, 326–27; things start going wrong 323; regional tour of 327, 328, 330–31, 332
Goons: project with *Beyond the Fringe* (*Bridge over the River Wye*) 115–16
Gospel Truth 285, 306
Gottlieb, Dr Sid: on Peter's schooldays 18, 19; watching football with PC 230–31, 232, 330; on PC and happiness 235; PC and Wendy turn to for advice and therapy 235; on Peter's addiction to alcohol 340–41, 408; on holiday in Cornwall with PC and daughters 353–54; on PC's need for reassurance 353; puts PC on Antabuse 408; on PC and Lin Cook's relationship 433–34; and PC's drinking 444; intercedes to get PC's close family to memorial service 469
Gough, Michael 219
Gourmets, The 191
Gowers, Patrick 70, 86
Grade, Lew 253
Granta 102, 139
Great Balls of Fire 445–46
Great Train Robbery 302
Greene, Graham 121
Greenwood, Joan 346
Greta Garbo sketch 265
Griffith, Kenneth 284
Grizzle, Sandy 398, 432–33
Grole, A. 63, 69, 73, 98 *see also* Boylett, Mr; Wisty, E. L.

Guilty Party 69
Guinness ad campaign 339
Gussett, Sir Herbert 160

Hagman, Larry 387, 388
Hall, Reverend 227
Halliwell, Leslie 371
Hamilton, Alexander 27
Hamilton, Paul 476
Hammond, Celia 127, 144, 158, 213, 255
Hancock, Nick 462
Hancock, Sheila 71, 99
Hancock, Tony 201, 203
Hand up Your Sticks 100
Hanratty, James 128
Hardy, Patrick 50, 55
Hardy, Simon 414–15, 454, 456, 464
Harley, Belinda 476
Harlow, Jonathan 18, 24, 30, 36, 39, 65
Harris, Max 311
Harrold, Tim 47, 50, 51, 55, 84, 477
Harty, Russell 340, 344
Harvey, Lawrence 250
Harz, Claude 325, 340, 437
Hastings, Lysie 321, 340
Hatch, David 366
Hathaway, Terry 28
Have I Got News for You xii, 451, 452
Having a Wank 355
Hawn, Goldie 374
Heath, Edward 172, 314, 320, 429, 449
Hefner, Hugh 164
Heller, Joseph 147, 151, 324
Hello 286
Hemion, Dwight 259
Hendra, Tony 109
Here is the News 71
Hetherington, Sir Anthony 370
Hill, Chris 357
Hillier, Bevis 98
Hind, John 35, 364
Hippisley, Johnny 132
Hirst, David 170
Hislop, Ian: on PC and boredom 292; on Derek and Clive 363–64; becomes editor of *Private Eye* 425–26; first meeting with PC 425; on obtaining dummy of *Not Private Eye* 427–28; on PC's *Eye* contribution 429–30; determined against proprietorial interference 471; learns about distribution of PC's *Eye* shares 472
Hoare, Kenneth 99
Hobbs, Lyndall 306
Hobson, Harold 112
Hoffman, Dustin 158, 324
Hogg, Derek 108
Holiday Startime 275
Holmes, Peter 347

Holy Bee of Ephesus routine 65, 66, 101,
   135, 288
Home, Earl of 114
Honan, Corinna 461
Hound of the Baskervilles 339, 343–44, 345–49,
   351, 356–57, 360, 365
Howard, Trevor 125
Howerd, Frankie 132–33, 147
Hudson, Eleanor 14, 23
Humphries, Barry: and Establishment Club
   126, 137, 138, 151; and *Private Eye* 164,
   169, 429; critical of PC 173; in *Not Only . . .
   But Also* 185, 191; on PC as actor 221–22;
   on PC as drinker 310, 480; Edna ennobled
   311; and *Derek and Clive* 364
Hunter, Professor John 53
Hunter, Professor Martin 88
Hussey, Marmaduke 447
Huxtable, Judy *see* Cook, Judy

I Can't Draw Either 344
Idle, Eric 102–3, 244, 391, 438
If Only 73
Imison, Richard 50, 55
Imperial Service College 2
Inalienable Rights 417–18
Incidents in the Life of My Uncle Arly 191
In the Cubicles 355
Ingrams, Richard: first meets PC 134; at
   Establishment Club 137; and *Private Eye*
   161, 164, 165, 168, 169, 170; puritan
   streak 165, 167; relationship with PC
   166–67; on PC's politics 295; grandfather
   was Queen Victoria's gynaecologist 330;
   on PC's reaction to Dudley's film success
   376–77; on PC's phone calls 404; on PC's
   'muddiness' 416; on PC's *Eye* contribution
   429; on PC's potential 480
Interesting Facts 61–62, 86, 93, 370
In the Lav 336
Investigator (Reuben Ship) 82
Ionescu, Eugene 59, 71
Ismay, Lady 92, 95
Isn't She a Sweetie? 199, 208
I Thought I Saw It Move 102
It's a Square World 178
It Sucks! 340
Ivanov, Vladimir 136

Jackson, Glenda 296
Jacobi, Derek 82
Jacobs, David 108
Jagger, Mick 252
James, Clive 103, 438
Jamison, Kay Redfield 304
Jim's Inn 105, 147
John, Bronco 399
Johnson, Halfdan 47–48, 87

Johnson-Smith, Geoffrey 125
Jolly Good Show involving . . . 61
Jones, Brian 407–8
Jones, Diana Llewellyn 34
Jones, Griff Rhys 222, 299, 373, 449
Jones, Terry 269, 380
Julius Caesar 72
Junkin's Jokers 453

Karan, Chris 119, 252
Keeler, Christine 127, 136
Keen, Geoffrey 28
Kelly, Chris 82
Kendall, Suzy 200, 213, 234, 252, 284
Kennedy, President John F. 140, 141,
   145, 157
Kennedy, Jackie 145, 321
Kennedy, Ludovic 38, 449, 450
Kennedy, Mimi 384, 385
Kenny Everett's Christmas Carol 420
Kenny, Sean 71, 108, 117, 121, 122, 126,
   130, 133, 239, 240, 241, 242
Kingsley, Ben 445
Kinsey, Tony 123
Klinsmann, Jurgen 463
Knack, The 158
Kray Brothers 168
Kretzmer, Herbert 317
Krimsky, John 142
Kubler-Ross, Elizabeth 470

Lahr, John 449
Laine, Cleo 71
Landesman, Fran 228
Landesman, Jay 123, 200, 228, 424
Lane, Brogan 435, 436
Langdon, Donald 63, 70, 91, 98, 140, 142,
   310, 314
Last Laugh, The 67–71, 75, 104
Last Resort, The 423, 442
Last to Go, The 73–74
Late Clive James, The 386, 420
Late Show, The 479
Laughing Grains, The 73
Laurie, Hugh 424
Law, Roger: on PC's voices 63, 81; as 'Tiger
   from the Fens' 80; on meeting PC 81;
   co-writes satire page in *Observer* 115; and
   Establishment Club 123, 127, 131–32, 152;
   on PC's morality 297
Lawson, Wilfred 219
LBC 400–3, 464
Led Zeppelin 337
Lee-Potter, Lynda 474, 478
Leigh, Christopher 29, 34
Lemming, Steven 440
Lengths 270
Lennon, Cynthia 227

Lennon, John 178, 182, 185, 199, 220, 227, 228–29
Leroy, Anna 116
Lester, Richard 251–52
Levin, Bernard 109, 139, 147
Levine, Joseph E. 154
Levy, Lawrence 399, 410, 453, 474
Lewis, Jerry 303
Life in Pieces, A 294–95, 449–51, 459
Llewellyn, Dai 372
Llewellyn, Desmond 28
Lloyd, John 295, 371, 376, 386, 419, 420, 449, 450–51, 479
Lloyd, Sir Peter 46, 47, 55, 84
Logue, Christopher 123, 227, 228
Lollobrigida, Gina 386
London Tonight 463
London Weekend Television 379, 381
Longmore, Elisabeth *see* Luard, Elisabeth
Lownes, Victor 164, 359, 372–73, 383, 441
L. S. Bumblebee, The 198–99
Luard, Elisabeth 135, 152
Luard, Nick: starts umbrella company with PC 103–4; and Establishment Club 120–21, 124, 131, 138, 153; and *Scene* 134; marriage 135; Nicholas Luard Associates 152; on dinner party at Church Row 227–28
Lubowski, Mr 121
Lurie, Jerry 142
Lynch, Kenny 410

McCartney, Paul 227, 228
McCulloch, Joseph 248
McDermott, Louise 213
MacDonald, Hugh 62, 65
McEwan, Geraldine 312
MacFarlane, A. J. 31
McGrath, Joe: origins of *Not Only . . . But Also* 178, 181; writing scripts 178, 181, 184, 191; method of shooting 183–84; title sequences designed by 184; filming methods 186; on PC and Dudley's relationship 195; leaves BBC 204; co-scripting and directing of *Thirty Is a Dangerous Age, Cynthia* 213; comparison with Shaun O'Riordan 253; director of *Behind the Fridge* 314, 315, 316, 317, 318, 320, 323
McGrath, Rory 366, 373, 447, 449, 450
McGurk, Pete 119, 252
MacInnes, Colin 123
McKay, Peter 341, 425, 426
McKenna, Bernard 379, 381
McKenna, Siobhan 132
McLaren, Malcolm 358, 366, 367, 373
McLennan, Colin 314
Macleod, Iain 113
Macmillan, Harold: parodies of 61, 77–78, 93, 95, 125, 126, 145; ('*TVPM*') attends

Beyond the Fringe 113–14; pin-up of 121; government totters 136; resignation 157; PC's antagonism 296
MacNaughton, Ian 277, 278, 281
Maguire, Sir Alexander and Lady 4
Maloney, Shane 307, 423–24
Man Bites God 106
Mann, Anthony 250
Manning, Bernard 421, 468
Mansfield, Jayne 162–63
Marley, Bob 366
Marnham, Patrick 426
Marx, Groucho 303, 322
Mason, James 392
Matthews, Ron 356
Mattock, Professor John 49, 58
Maudling, Reginald 172
Maugham, W. Somerset 121
Maxwell, Robert 296, 299, 426–27, 452
Mayo, Caroline (grandmother) 4, 6, 8
Mayo, Charles (grandfather) 3–4, 85
Mayo, Joan (aunt) 4, 38, 78
Melia, Joe 137, 138, 186
Melly, George 138
Menuhin, Yehudi 121
Merchant of Venice 55, 63
Merrick, David 140, 142, 260
Merton, Paul 472
Miller, Jonathan: contributions to Footlights 54; writer of *So That's the Way You Like It* 56; sees PC for first time 76–77; recommends PC for *Beyond the Fringe* 77, 88; on *One Leg Too Few* 82; double act with PC 88; medical career 89, 91, 146; on PC's brilliance 91; and satire in *Beyond the Fringe* 93, 113; on PC's right-wing attitudes 106; on satire 110, 111, 124–25, 157; and Establishment Club 122, 124, 125; approaches Bill Wallis about appearing at Establishment Club 137–38; and *Ed Sullivan Show* 150; *Beyond the Fringe* cast as Beatles of comedy 151; anger at PC 155, 156; resigns from *Beyond the Fringe* 156; at helm of *Monitor* 159; attacks *Private Eye* 173; on PC and Dudley's partnership 196; film of *Alice in Wonderland* 211, 218–19
Miller, Rachel 155
Mill Hill 312
Milligan, Spike: meets PC 31; influence on PC 79, 302; writes *Bridge Over the River Wye* meets *The Goons* project 115, 116; *The Bedsitting Room* 251; on *Not Only . . . But Also* 264; on *Where Do I Sit?* 279; in *An Apple a Day* 284; in *Hound of the Baskervilles* 347; *Q9* 382; on PC's memorial service 470
Milligan, Warden 26
Mills, Don 11
Mills, John 201

Mills, Michael 276, 277
Mini Drama 285
Monitor 159, 178
Monte Carlo or Bust 252–53
Monty Python 269, 382, 481
Moon, Keith 331, 360, 381
Moore, Dudley: first impressions of *Beyond the Fringe* cast 91; lack of confidence 91, 92; background 92–93; solo spot in *Beyond the Fringe* 95; upset by conflict 104; jazz trio 108, 159, 178; jazz show on TV 114–15; collapses with exhaustion 116; love affairs 116, 144, 200, 325; professionalism 118, 186; and Establishment Club 122, 127; plays piano at PC's first wedding 155; first visit to psychiatrist 158; as only *Fringe* cast member left in USA 158; given his own TV music series by BBC 158; and *Private Eye* 169; as TV star 175; asks PC to be on his show 177; 'funny' catchphrase 180, 202; develops greater role in writing with PC 183; constantly improvising with PC 191; autobiographical aspects of his comedy 192–93; parents 193; relationship with PC 194, 196–97; the importance of his contribution 195–96; musical ability belittled 195, 208; and psychiatry 195; on Royal Variety Performance 197–98; on *Sunday Night at the London Palladium* 197; marries Suzy Kendall 200; friendship with Joe McGrath 204; edged out of writing *Bedazzled* 212–13; on PC as actor 222, 253; marriage to Suzy Kendall 252; anger at being considered PC's glove puppet 265; father dies 284; first marriage in trouble 284; offer to tour Australia 284; in Australia 306–9; wishes to end the partnership 308; accusation of manipulativeness 309; mutual dependence with PC 309; in New Zealand 309–10; divorce from Suzy Kendall 313; on continued use of psychiatry 313; no longer a subservient acoylte 314, 448; interviewed by Mavis Nicholson 318–19; affected by ennui 319; gives Suzy their Hampstead home 320; in America with *Good Evening* 321–32; begins affair with Tuesday Weld 325; friction with PC 325; not asked to be PC's best man and doesn't go to wedding 326; obsession with PC 328; *Penthouse* interview 329–30; marries Tuesday Weld 332; tells PC partnership is over 332; wants to be film star 332; father's death of cancer 355; splits up with Tuesday 357; tells PC he definitely won't work with him again 364; film career 374–76, 379, 387–89; after breakup with PC favours tall girlfriends 376; reunited with PC for interview with *Daily Mail* 385; belief that PC wasn't as good after their breakup 389; discusses the isolation felt by comedians 404; on *Can We Talk?* 421–22; reconciled with PC 421–22; relations with PC much improved in later life 448; reaction to PC's death 467–68; at PC's memorial service 470; still confused by PC 480; secures role of Buttons in Christmas pantomime 482 *see also under names of reviews, programmes, films etc which he appeared in*
Morley, Lewis 108, 121, 127, 308
Morley, Sheridan 317
Morris, Chris 111, 458
Morrisey, Paul 345, 348, 349
Mortimer, John 99, 100, 312
Morton, J. B. 302
Most, Mickie 357
Mower, Patrick 407
Mr Boylett Speaks 54
Mr Jolly Lives Next Door 424
Mr Moses 69, 70, 72
Mrs Wilson's Diary 169
Muggeridge, Malcolm 129, 173
Mulcahy, Russell 360
Muldoon, Spotty 176
Muller, Robert 110
Murphy, Brian 257
Myers, Stanley 123
My Mum Song 353
My Old Man's a Dustman 355

Nanette 262–63, 265
Napier, Ian 34
Nash, Raymond 153, 154
Nat West advertisements 449
Neasden FC 166
Neather, Ted 47
Nether Wallop Arts Festival 419
Newsnight 111
News Quiz, The xii, 416
Newton, Andrew 370, 371
Nichols, Mike 158, 242
Nicholson, Mavis 318–19, 436
Night of a Hundred Stars, The 386
Nightlife (John Mortimer) 100
19th Hole, The 418–19
Nisty, Kitty 144, 164
Not the Nine O'Clock News 416
Not Only . . . But Also: tapes copied xii; videotapes destroyed xi; and influence of PC's childhood reading 8–9; agreement to avoid satire 178; name 178, 181; original one-off programme 178–81; origins of name 178; working methods 182–84; no punchlines 183; first series 184–93; sets minimal 184; surviving materials from first series 184, 191; title sequences 184; PC and Dudley taken over by their characters 186;

first big row 187; PC's increasing laziness
190; teleprompter used 190; at first seen
as Dudley's achievement 197; PC and
Dudley voted Comedians of the Year 197;
press reactions to first series 197;
Christmas Special 1966: 199, 218, 219–20;
surviving material from second series 204;
second series 204–12; PC's power over
Dudley 205; show moves to ATV as *Goodbye
Again* 253; third TV series 262–74; surviving
material from third series 263; writing
third series 263; Dudley developing more
dominant role in writing 264; title sequences
from third series 264; Australian special
283–84; Jimmy Gilbert discovers that most
programmes have been wiped 327; video
447 *see also* Pete and Dud; *Goodbye Again;
and under names of sketches*
Not Only Lulu But Also Dudley Moore 310
Not Private Eye 427–28
Not So Much a Programme . . . 159, 170
Novel Reactions 64
Now! 199
Nunn, Trevor 65, 102

Oddie, Bill 244
Offbeat 158, 175
Old J. J. 51, 94, 105, 191
One Foot in the Algarve 452
One Leg Too Few 82–83, 86, 93, 100, 156,
198, 320, 347, 349, 435, 436
One over the Eight 99, 104, 109, 110
Ono, Yoko 448
On the Braden Beat 175, 200
Onu Beeby Frisky 74
Orion Films 382
O'Riordan, Shaun 253–54, 257
Orton, Joe 252
Osmond, Andrew: admires *Beyond the Fringe*
133; on Establishment Club 135; and *Private
Eye* 134, 168; on PC 289, 298, 430–1
Ostrander, Gilman 408
O'Toole, Peter 227, 272
Oxfam Charity concert 229

Packer, Clyde 306
Packer, Sir Frank 306
Palin, Helen 467
Palin, Michael 109–10, 199, 460,
467
Panama cigars advertisements 449
Parkes, Ciara 394, 395, 398, 409, 410, 432,
454, 460, 461, 463, 466
Parkinson, Michael: and Establishment Club
126; replaces PC as chat show host 282;
sees PC performing drunk in Australia 308,
446–47; PC on show 340, 365; and Barnsley
344–45; Dudley on show 365; playing golf

with PC 410–11; compares PC to George
Best 480
Parkin, Sue 232–33, 238
Paskin, Barbra 94, 324, 362, 473
Passing Wind 425
Pattie, Geoffrey 59, 65
Paxton, Geoff 50, 65
Payola scandal 172
Peace 86, 93, 100
Peacock, Michael 180, 181
Pembroke College: Alec Cook at 2; Peter's first
year room 45–46; dinners at 46, 50–51;
first friendships at 47; football at 47–48;
PC's popularity at 48; drama facilities at 49;
Smoking Concerts 50; PC's work at 52–53;
revues 61–63, 76, 82; PC cuts links with
83–84; PC's room named after him 477
Pembroke Players: membership of 49–50;
PC appears with 50, 58, 76; on tour in
Germany 55, 72; record made by 63
Penfold, Anthony 30
Penthouse magazine 329–30
Percival, Lance 71, 100
Perelman, S. J. 278, 279
Perkins, 3, 4
Person to Person 373–74 *see also* Dimbleby,
David
Pete and Dud in New York 327
Peter Cook & Co. 379–82, 384
Peter Cook Appreciation Society 475, 476
Peter Cook Productions Ltd. 200, 472
Peter Cook's London 420
Peter Cook's Monday Morning Feeling 344
Peter Cook Talks Golf Balls 462–63
Pieces of Eight 72–75, 93, 99, 453
Pile, Stephen 364, 381, 419
Pinter, Harold 73–74, 314
Playboy 164
Play It Again Sam 260
Poets Cornered 264, 274
Polar Bores 69, 79
Ponsonby, Robert 89, 91, 97
Pop Goes Mrs Jessop 86–87
Porter, Ed 294
Poulson scandal 172
Powell, Lady Carla 452
Powell, Sir Charles 452, 456
Powell, Enoch 261
Pregnancy Test 370
Price, David 475
Priestley, J. B. 121
Princess Bride, The 424
Private Eye: attacks PC 133–34; first issue 133;
bought by Cook & Luard Productions 134;
moved into Establishment Club 134–35;
dislike of Establishment Club 135; fortunes
improve 135, 136; moved to Greek Street
135; elements poached by *TW3* 148;

circulation crashes 157; cartoonists 164; advertising 167; PC refused to take money from 167, 426; PC never interfered with editorial decisions 167; attacks on Labour alienate some of readership 168; attacks on Wilson 168–69; giveaway records 169–70; bills for damages 171, 172, 427; courts unsympathetic to 171; fund-raising concert for 171; circulation climbs again 172; investigative journalism 172; PC's joke writing sessions in 172, 429–31, 463; PC's defence of 173; PC's love of 173; puritanical morality of 297; most of staff advised to give up drinking 341; Goldsmith sues 342–43; Maxwell sues 426–27; twenty-fifth anniversary 430; share distribution after PC's death 471–72; staff not informed about distribution of shared on PC's death 471; financial reserves of 471

Private Eye's Blue Record 170
Pro-Celebrity Golf 372
Profumo scandal 135–36
Publish and Bedazzled 476
Punch 171
Purser, Philip 358

Q9 382
Quant, Mary 227

Raby, Peter 27, 39, 51, 52, 65
racial prejudice sketch 267–68
Radio Night 453
Radleian magazine 26, 38
Radley school: nature of life at 16–18; bullying at 18–19; sporting life at 20, 26–27; PC's academic work at 20, 21, 22, 29, 31–2; PC's popularity at 24; PC's imitations of staff 24–6; PC accepts system 26; PC's theatrical achievements at 27–9; PC as prefect at 29–31; PC's visits to sanatorium 31, 33; marionette theatre 33–36; termly dance against girls' school 33; PC leaves 36
Radziwill, Lee 321, 325
Rainbow George *see* Weiss, George
Ramsbotham, Sir Peter 326
Raphael, Frederic 54
Ray, Robin 116, 138
Ready, Steady Go! 199
Real Class 106
Red Cross 122
Redhead, Brian 138
Reeves, Peter 75
Reid, Beryl 380, 381
Reiner, Rob 424
Renwick, David 422
Resounding Tinkle, A 56–57, 59–60
Revill, Clive 312
Revolver 357–58

Rhodesia 172
Richard III (William Shakespeare) 76
Richards, Keith 408, 456, 460, 467
Richardson, Ralph 201
Rise and Rise of Michael Rimmer, The 250, 253, 259–62, 274–75, 276
Rivers, Joan 420, 421, 458
Rix, Brian 121
Robertson, Ian 32
Roger Mellie 451
Rolling Stones, the 229, 337, 407, 448, 455, 467
Ronan Point 172
Room 101 462
Rooney, Mickey 339
Rose, J. A. 152
Ross, Annie 123
Ross, Jonathan 423, 441–42, 451, 463, 464, 480
Ross, Les 357
Rossington, Norman 178
Rothschild, Nicole 448, 468
Rotten, Johnny 358, 366
Routledge, Patricia 213
Roy, Uncle 38
Royal Box 94, 118
Royal Gala Show 198
Royal Variety Performance 197–98
Rubinstein, Anthony 445
Rushton, Willie: in *Beyond the Fringe* 102; and Establishment Club 122, 135; and *Private Eye* 133, 135, 148, 160, 169, 430; on *TW3* 139, 148; on *Not Only . . . But Also* 274; on *Where Do I Sit?* 279
Russell Harty 343
Russell Harty and Friends 418
Russell, Jane 387
Russell of Liverpool, Lord 121, 170–71
Rustle of Spring 171, 228
Rutherford, Margaret 202

Sacks, Oliver 304
Sadder and Wiser Beaver, The 105
Sadowitz, Gerry 364
Sahl, Mort 50, 136
St Peter's College *see* Radley school
Salaman, Nick 17, 27
Sale, Bob 186
Saturday Night Live 343, 422
Savalas, Telly 337
Sayle, Alexei 405
Scales, Prunella 347
Scarfe, Gerald 169
Scene magazine 134, 152
Science – Fact or Fiction? 76–77, 102
Scoop 159, 200
Scott, Brough 95
Scott, Norman 370, 371

Scott-Fox, Judy 121–22, 130, 131, 146, 200
Sebag-Montefiore, Dr Stephen 244
Secombe, Harry 115
Secret Policeman's Ball 370, 374
Secret Policeman's Biggest Ball 436
Segal, George 158
Sellers, Peter 31, 66, 67, 115, 116, 160, 163, 181, 191, 198, 201, 202, 302
Serjeant Musgrave's Dance 158
Seventh Deadly Seal, The 57–58
Seward, Ingrid 372, 373
Sex Pistols 358, 373
Seymour, Aletta 246, 454
Seymour, Sarah *see* Cook, Sarah
Shakespeare, William, parodies of 55–56, 61, 272
Shand, Neil 420–21, 476
Share My Lettuce 71, 104
Sharpling, Paul 46, 47, 49, 52
Shaw, Robert Carter 30
Shelley, Pete 357
Sherlock Holmes Investigates 256
Sherrin, Ned 136, 277, 476
Shower sketch 191–92, 208, 314
Shulman, Milton 109
Simeon, Clive 47, 50, 51
Simpson, Carole 123
Simpson, N. F. 56, 59, 71
Sitting on the Bench 77, 94, 320
Six of the Best 320
Skinner, Frank 460, 463
Slade, Adrian 53–54, 61, 65, 69, 296, 417
Sloan, Tom 180–81, 266
Slocock, Noel 29, 32, 36, 39, 51, 52
Smith, Chris 47, 49, 52, 59, 76
Smith, Garry 259
Smith, Maggie 54
Smith, Mel 222, 407, 419, 424, 428, 442, 446
Smith, Paul 379
Smoke Rings 62
Snowden, Wendy *see* Cook, Wendy
Something Borrowed 82
Something Like Fire 442, 477
Soskice, Sir Frank 225
So That's the Way You Like It 55–56, 94
Soundbite Productions Ltd. 475
South Bank Show 346, 347
Speight, Johnny 266, 279, 280
Spitting Image 80, 297
Sporting Life 427
Squatter and the Ant 336
Stamp, Terence 127
Steadman, Alison 452
Steadman, Ralph 164, 168
Steafel, Sheila 178
Stevens, Jocelyn 125
Stewart, Dave 455
Stick Yer Finger up Yer Bum 171

Stitty, Lady Pamela 128, 159
Stoppard, Tom 134
Stow, John 40
Streeb-Greebling, Sir Arthur 1, 37–38, 112, 179, 185, 267, 269, 283, 294, 420, 449 *see also* Streeve-Greevlings, Sir Arthur

Street-Porter, Janet 366
Strollers Theatre 142, 154, 155, 158
Sturgis, Norman and Laura 123
Sunday Night at the London Palladium 197
Supergirl 418
Superthunderstingcar 211
Suspense Is Killing Me, The 106
Sutcliffe, Sonia 428–29
Sykes, Eric 191

Tales from the Crypt 373
Tales of the Much As We Expected 379–80
Tales of the Seductive Brethren 161
TalkBack 449
Tarbuck, Jimmy 410
Taylor, Elizabeth 387
Tell the Truth 420
Tempo 114
10cc 349
10 364, 375–76
Ten Pipers Piping 450
Terry-Thomas 69, 229, 253, 347
Thant, U 141
Thatcher, Margaret xi, 295, 296
That Was the Week That Was (TW3) 138, 148, 157, 276
Theile, Herr 41
Thirty is a Dangerous Age, Cynthia 213
This Bloke Came Up to Me 336
This Is the End 94
This Is England 248
This Is Your Life 315, 435
Thompson, Emma 424
Thompson, J.V.P. (Rutch) 17–18, 25, 36
Thorneycroft, Peter 46
Thorpe, Jeremy 370–71, 423
3-D Lobster xi
Thunderbirds parody 211
Tiffany lamp 146, 226, 243, 311, 321, 471, 472–73
Tinker, Jack 317
Titchmarsh, Alan 480
Titheridge, Peter 31
Tomkinson, Martin 341, 342, 358, 359–60
Tonight 96, 108, 138, 163
Topes, Spiggy 166
Top Rank 336
Tormé, Mel 259
Torquay United 8, 11
Torvill and Dean 429
Town and Gown 78

Travers, Ben 121
Trewin, J. C. 74
Trotter, John 405–6
True Blue Love Song 73
Turner, Ike and Tina 254, 256, 259
Turner-Samuels, David 170
TVPM see Macmillan, Harold
TV Times 381
Twelve Days of Christmas, The 449–51
Twentieth Century Fox 212
Twenty Years On 420
Two of Us, The 378–79, 381, 384, 385–86
Two's Company 378
Tynan, Kathleen 169
Tynan, Kenneth 109, 111, 128–29, 173

Under Canvas 105
Unforgettable Alberts, The 123
Usborne, Peter 157, 169
US (Peter Hall/Peter Brook) 229
Ustinov, Peter 27, 147, 276, 302

Vaccaro, Brenda 378, 438
Vallance, Sir Iain 409
Vandenheuvel, Jay 150
Verity, Tony 50
Vinaver, Stephen 99
Virgin Records 356, 363
Voelcker, Robin 48, 49, 75

Waite, Michael 36
Wall, Max 347
Wallis, Bill: roles played by 59; on Frost 64;
    at Establishment Club 137–38, 154; in *Not
    Only . . . But Also* 186
Wallis, John 475, 476
Walrus and the Carpenter, The 211
Walsh, David 123
Walton, Tony 323
Ward, Stephen 136
Wardle, Irving 317
Waugh, Auberon: and *Private Eye* 167, 430; on
    Where Do I Sit ? 278; on PC's reviewing 407;
    and Ian Hislop 425, 426
Weiss, George (Rainbow George): introduction
    to 321; PC visits in Dublin 334; a fantasist
    386, 387; forms political party 396; stands
    against Portillo 396; Camden Palace party
    397; continues to fight elections 397–99;
    continual failures 398–99; recordings
    399–400, 440; on PC's sharpness 411;
    on *Daily Star* scoop 433; on Judy and Lin
    comparison 433; on Lin Cook 434; drugs
    bust 440; imprisoned 440; Lin tells him
    that PC doesn't enjoy his company any more
    460; Lin seeks his help when PC collapses
    465; and PC's funeral service 470; row with
    Lin Cook over his tapes 474–75; robbed of
    inheritance 481–82
Welch, Raquel 215, 220, 353
Weld, Tuesday: Dudley seduces 144; affair
    with PC 321, 325; affair with Dudley
    325, 331–32; PC's embarrassing question
    327; has abortion 328; pregnant again
    331; married Dudley 332; splits up with
    Dudley 357
Welensky, Sir Roy 113
Welles, Orson 276
Wells, John: on *Beyond the Fringe* 97–98;
    and Establishment Club 122, 126, 137;
    schoolmastership at Eton 122; on *TW3* 139,
    148; and *Private Eye* 148, 160, 169, 170,
    172; acting in and co-scripting *Thirty is a
    Dangerous Age, Cynthia* 213; on *Bedazzled*
    222; on *Goodbye Again* 257
Wentworth, Mr and Mrs 280–81
West, Frederick 463
West, Richard 426
What? Party 394, 399, 418
What's Going on Here? 150
Wheen, Francis 430
Where Do I Sit? 277–83, 287
Whitehead, Paxton 156
Whitehouse, Mary 279, 285
Whitlam, Gough 311
Who Dares Wins 420
Wholly Moses 379
Whoops Apocalypse 422–23, 427
Whose Finger on What Button? 86, 93, 118
W. H. Smith 427
Why Bother? 458–59
Why Vote, It Only Encourages Them 373
Wigg, George 136, 169
Wilcox, Paula 381
Wild, Michael 47, 75, 87, 88
Wilkinson, David 374, 410
Williams, Esther 202
Williams, Kenneth: and *Share My Lettuce* 54;
    and *Pieces of Eight* 71, 72, 73, 74, 75; and
    Fenella Fielding 74; and *One over the Eight*
    101; PC defers to 233, 302; and *Hound of
    the Baskervilles* 346, 347–48, 348, 349, 365;
    on *Can We Talk?* 422
Wilmut, Roger 35
Wilson, Cecil 74, 275
Wilson, Dennis Main 339
Wilson, Harold 52, 157, 168–69, 261, 342
Wilson, Richard 452
Wilson, Sandy 72
Wilson, Teddy 144
Windsor, Barbara 139
Winky Wanky Woo 336
Winner, Michael 429
Winterton, Mike 47, 95
Wispa advertisement 428